# Core HTML5 Canvas

# Core HTML5 Canvas

## Graphics, Animation, and Game Development

**David Geary**

PRENTICE
HALL

Upper Saddle River, NJ • Boston • Indianapolis • San Francisco
New York • Toronto • Montreal • London • Munich • Paris • Madrid
Capetown • Sydney • Tokyo • Singapore • Mexico City

Many of the designations used by manufacturers and sellers to distinguish their products are claimed as trademarks. Where those designations appear in this book, and the publisher was aware of a trademark claim, the designations have been printed with initial capital letters or in all capitals.

The author and publisher have taken care in the preparation of this book, but make no expressed or implied warranty of any kind and assume no responsibility for errors or omissions. No liability is assumed for incidental or consequential damages in connection with or arising out of the use of the information or programs contained herein.

The publisher offers excellent discounts on this book when ordered in quantity for bulk purchases or special sales, which may include electronic versions and/or custom covers and content particular to your business, training goals, marketing focus, and branding interests. For more information, please contact:

U.S. Corporate and Government Sales
(800) 382–3419
corpsales@pearsontechgroup.com

For sales outside the United States, please contact:

International Sales
international@pearson.com

Visit us on the Web: informit.com/ph

*Library of Congress Cataloging-in-Publication Data*

Geary, David M.
  Core HTML5 canvas : graphics, animation, and game development / David
Geary.
     p.  cm.
  Includes index.
  ISBN 978-0-13-276161-1 (pbk. : alk. paper)
  1.  HTML (Document markup language) 2.  Computer games—Programming. 3.
Computer animation.  I. Title.
  QA76.76.H94C66 2012
  006.6'6—dc23

                                                                    2012006871

ISBN-13: 978-0-13-276161-1
ISBN-10:    0-13-276161-0
Text printed in the United States on recycled paper at RR Donnelley in Crawfordsville, Indiana.
First printing, May 2012

# Contents

Preface .................................................................................. *xv*

Acknowledgments .................................................................. *xxiii*

About the Author .................................................................. *xxv*

**Chapter 1: Essentials** .......................................................... 1

1.1 The canvas Element .......................................................... 1

    1.1.1 Canvas Element Size vs. Drawing Surface Size .......................... 5

    1.1.2 The Canvas API ....................................................... 7

1.2 Canvas Contexts ............................................................. 8

    1.2.1 The 2d Context ....................................................... 9

        1.2.1.1 The WebGL 3d Context ......................................... 11

    1.2.2 Saving and Restoring Canvas State .................................... 11

1.3 Canonical Examples in This Book ............................................ 12

1.4 Getting Started ............................................................ 14

    1.4.1 Specifications ....................................................... 14

    1.4.2 Browsers ............................................................. 15

    1.4.3 Consoles and Debuggers .............................................. 16

    1.4.4 Performance .......................................................... 18

        1.4.4.1 Profiles and Timelines ....................................... 19

        1.4.4.2 jsPerf ....................................................... 20

1.5 Fundamental Drawing Operations ............................................. 22

1.6 Event Handling ............................................................. 26

    1.6.1 Mouse Events ......................................................... 26

        1.6.1.1 Translating Mouse Coordinates to Canvas Coordinates ......... 26

    1.6.2 Keyboard Events ...................................................... 31

    1.6.3 Touch Events ......................................................... 33

1.7 Saving and Restoring the Drawing Surface ................................... 33

1.8 Using HTML Elements in a Canvas ............................................ 36

    1.8.1 Invisible HTML Elements .............................................. 41

1.9    Printing a Canvas ................................................................ 46

1.10   Offscreen Canvases ............................................................. 51

1.11   A Brief Math Primer ........................................................... 53

       1.11.1  Solving Algebraic Equations ..................................... 54

       1.11.2  Trigonometry ......................................................... 54

               1.11.2.1  Angles: Degrees and Radians ..................... 54

               1.11.2.2  Sine, Cosine, and Tangent ........................ 55

       1.11.3  Vectors .................................................................. 56

               1.11.3.1  Vector Magnitude ................................... 57

               1.11.3.2  Unit Vectors .......................................... 58

               1.11.3.3  Adding and Subtracting Vectors ................ 59

               1.11.3.4  The Dot Product of Two Vectors ................ 60

       1.11.4  Deriving Equations from Units of Measure .............. 62

1.12   Conclusion ........................................................................ 64

**Chapter 2: Drawing** .................................................................. **65**

2.1    The Coordinate System ....................................................... 67

2.2    The Drawing Model ............................................................ 68

2.3    Drawing Rectangles ............................................................ 70

2.4    Colors and Transparency ..................................................... 72

2.5    Gradients and Patterns ....................................................... 76

       2.5.1  Gradients ................................................................ 76

              2.5.1.1   Linear Gradients .................................... 76

              2.5.1.2   Radial Gradients .................................... 78

       2.5.2  Patterns .................................................................. 79

2.6    Shadows ........................................................................... 83

       2.6.1  Inset Shadows .......................................................... 85

2.7    Paths, Stroking, and Filling ................................................. 88

       2.7.1  Paths and Subpaths .................................................. 93

              2.7.1.1   The Nonzero Winding Rule for Filling Paths .............. 94

       2.7.2  Cutouts ................................................................... 95

              2.7.2.1   Cutout Shapes ...................................... 98

2.8    Lines ............................................................................... 103

       2.8.1  Lines and Pixel Boundaries ...................................... 104

       2.8.2  Drawing a Grid ...................................................... 105

2.8.3 Drawing Axes ................................................................ 107

2.8.4 Rubberband Lines ......................................................... 110

2.8.5 Drawing Dashed Lines .................................................. 117

2.8.6 Drawing Dashed Lines by Extending
`CanvasRenderingContext2D` .................................... 118

2.8.7 Line Caps and Joins ..................................................... 121

2.9 Arcs and Circles ........................................................................ 124

2.9.1 The `arc()` Method ...................................................... 124

2.9.2 Rubberband Circles ..................................................... 126

2.9.3 The `arcTo()` Method ................................................. 127

2.9.4 Dials and Gauges ........................................................ 130

2.10 Bézier Curves ........................................................................... 137

2.10.1 Quadratic Curves ...................................................... 137

2.10.2 Cubic Curves ............................................................. 141

2.11 Polygons .................................................................................... 144

2.11.1 Polygon Objects ........................................................ 147

2.12 Advanced Path Manipulation ................................................. 150

2.12.1 Dragging Polygons ..................................................... 151

2.12.2 Editing Bézier Curves ................................................ 158

2.12.3 Scrolling Paths into View .......................................... 169

2.13 Transformations ....................................................................... 170

2.13.1 Translating, Scaling, and Rotating ............................ 171

2.13.1.1 Mirroring ................................................... 173

2.13.2 Custom Transformations ........................................... 174

2.13.2.1 Algebraic Equations for Transformations ........... 175

2.13.2.2 Using `transform()` and `setTransform()` ........... 176

2.13.2.3 Translating, Rotating, and Scaling with `transform()`
and `setTransform()` ...................................... 177

2.13.2.4 Shear ......................................................... 179

2.14 Compositing .............................................................................. 181

2.14.1 The Compositing Controversy .................................. 186

2.15 The Clipping Region .................................................................. 187

2.15.1 Erasing with the Clipping Region .............................. 187

2.15.2 Telescoping with the Clipping Region ....................... 194

2.16 Conclusion ................................................................................ 198

**Chapter 3: Text** ............................................................................ **201**

3.1    Stroking and Filling Text ........................................................ 202

3.2    Setting Font Properties ............................................................ 207

3.3    Positioning Text ...................................................................... 210

    3.3.1    Horizontal and Vertical Positioning ............................. 210

    3.3.2    Centering Text .............................................................. 214

    3.3.3    Measuring Text ............................................................. 215

    3.3.4    Labeling Axes ............................................................... 217

    3.3.5    Labeling Dials ............................................................... 221

    3.3.6    Drawing Text around an Arc ........................................ 223

3.4    Implementing Text Controls ................................................... 225

    3.4.1    A Text Cursor ............................................................... 225

        3.4.1.1    Erasing ........................................................ 228

        3.4.1.2    Blinking ...................................................... 230

    3.4.2    Editing a Line of Text in a Canvas ............................... 232

    3.4.3    Paragraphs .................................................................... 238

        3.4.3.1    Creating and Initializing a Paragraph ...... 242

        3.4.3.2    Positioning the Text Cursor in Response to Mouse Clicks ...................................................... 242

        3.4.3.3    Inserting Text ............................................. 243

        3.4.3.4    New Lines .................................................... 244

        3.4.3.5    Backspace .................................................... 245

3.5    Conclusion .............................................................................. 252

**Chapter 4: Images and Video** ..................................................... **253**

4.1    Drawing Images ...................................................................... 254

    4.1.1    Drawing an Image into a Canvas ................................. 255

    4.1.2    The drawImage() Method .............................................. 257

4.2    Scaling Images ........................................................................ 259

    4.2.1    Drawing Images outside Canvas Boundaries ............... 260

4.3    Drawing a Canvas into a Canvas ............................................ 266

4.4    Offscreen Canvases ................................................................. 270

4.5    Manipulating Images .............................................................. 274

    4.5.1    Accessing Image Data ................................................... 274

        4.5.1.1    ImageData Objects ....................................... 279

|   |   | 4.5.1.2 | Image Data Partial Rendering: `putImageData`'s Dirty Rectangle | 280 |
|   | 4.5.2 | Modifying Image Data | | 283 |
|   |   | 4.5.2.1 | Creating `ImageData` Objects with `createImageData()` | 285 |
|   |   |   | 4.5.2.1.1 The Image Data Array | 286 |
|   |   | 4.5.2.2 | Image Data Looping Strategies | 292 |
|   |   | 4.5.2.3 | Filtering Images | 293 |
|   |   | 4.5.2.4 | Device Pixels vs. CSS Pixels, Redux | 295 |
|   |   | 4.5.2.5 | Image Processing Web Workers | 299 |
| 4.6 | Clipping Images | | | 302 |
| 4.7 | Animating Images | | | 306 |
|   | 4.7.1 | Animating with an Offscreen Canvas | | 309 |
| 4.8 | Security | | | 312 |
| 4.9 | Performance | | | 313 |
|   | 4.9.1 | `drawImage(HTMLImage)` vs. `drawImage(HTMLCanvas)` vs. `putImageData()` | | 314 |
|   | 4.9.2 | Drawing a Canvas vs. Drawing an Image, into a Canvas; Scaled vs. Unscaled | | 316 |
|   | 4.9.3 | Looping over Image Data | | 317 |
|   |   | 4.9.3.1 | Avoid Accessing Object Properties in the Loop: Store Properties in Local Variables Instead | 317 |
|   |   | 4.9.3.2 | Loop over Every Pixel, Not over Every Pixel Value | 320 |
|   |   | 4.9.3.3 | Looping Backwards and Bit-Shifting Are Crap Shoots | 320 |
|   |   | 4.9.3.4 | Don't Call `getImageData()` Repeatedly for Small Amounts of Data | 321 |
| 4.10 | A Magnifying Glass | | | 321 |
|   | 4.10.1 | Using an Offscreen Canvas | | 325 |
|   | 4.10.2 | Accepting Dropped Images from the File System | | 326 |
| 4.11 | Video Processing | | | 328 |
|   | 4.11.1 | Video Formats | | 329 |
|   |   | 4.11.1.1 | Converting Formats | 330 |
|   | 4.11.2 | Playing Video in a Canvas | | 331 |
|   | 4.11.3 | Processing Videos | | 333 |
| 4.12 | Conclusion | | | 337 |

**Chapter 5: Animation** ................................................................. **339**

5.1    The Animation Loop ...................................................... 340

       5.1.1    The `requestAnimationFrame()` Method: Letting the Browser
               Set the Frame Rate ........................................... 343

             5.1.1.1    Firefox ............................................ 345

             5.1.1.2    Chrome .......................................... 346

       5.1.2    Internet Explorer ................................................ 348

       5.1.3    A Portable Animation Loop .................................. 348

5.2    Calculating Frame Rates ............................................... 358

5.3    Scheduling Tasks at Alternate Frame Rates ..................... 359

5.4    Restoring the Background .............................................. 360

       5.4.1    Clipping ............................................................ 361

       5.4.2    Blitting ............................................................. 363

5.5    Double Buffering ........................................................ 364

5.6    Time-Based Motion ..................................................... 367

5.7    Scrolling the Background .............................................. 370

5.8    Parallax ..................................................................... 377

5.9    User Gestures ............................................................. 383

5.10   Timed Animations ...................................................... 385

       5.10.1 Stopwatches ...................................................... 385

       5.10.2 Animation Timers ............................................... 389

5.11   Animation Best Practices ............................................. 390

5.12   Conclusion ............................................................... 391

**Chapter 6: Sprites** ...................................................................... **393**

6.1    Sprites Overview ........................................................ 394

6.2    Painters .................................................................... 398

       6.2.1    Stroke and Fill Painters ...................................... 398

       6.2.2    Image Painters ................................................... 404

       6.2.3    Sprite Sheet Painters .......................................... 406

6.3    Sprite Behaviors ........................................................ 411

       6.3.1    Combining Behaviors .......................................... 412

       6.3.2    Timed Behaviors ................................................ 416

6.4    Sprite Animators ........................................................ 417

6.5    A Sprite-Based Animation Loop ..................................... 424

6.6    Conclusion ................................................................ 425

**Chapter 7: Physics** ............................................................ **427**

7.1 Gravity ...................................................................... 428

    7.1.1 Falling ............................................................ 428

    7.1.2 Projectile Trajectories ..................................... 432

    7.1.3 Pendulums ..................................................... 445

7.2 Warping Time ............................................................ 450

7.3 Time-Warp Functions ................................................. 456

7.4 Warping Motion ........................................................ 458

    7.4.1 Linear Motion: No Acceleration ...................... 461

    7.4.2 Ease In: Gradually Accelerate ......................... 463

    7.4.3 Ease Out: Gradually Decelerate ...................... 465

    7.4.4 Ease In, Then Ease Out .................................. 468

    7.4.5 Elasticity and Bouncing .................................. 469

7.5 Warping Animation .................................................... 473

7.6 Conclusion ................................................................ 482

**Chapter 8: Collision Detection** ........................................ **483**

8.1 Bounding Areas ......................................................... 483

    8.1.1 Rectangular Bounding Areas .......................... 484

    8.1.2 Circular Bounding Areas ................................ 485

8.2 Bouncing Off Walls .................................................... 488

8.3 Ray Casting ............................................................... 490

    8.3.1 Fine-Tuning ................................................... 494

8.4 The Separating Axis Theorem (SAT) and Minimum Translation Vector (MTV) ..................................................................... 495

    8.4.1 Detecting Collisions with the SAT .................... 495

        8.4.1.1 Projection Axes ................................... 500

        8.4.1.2 Projections ......................................... 503

        8.4.1.3 Shapes and Polygons .......................... 504

        8.4.1.4 Collisions between Polygons ................. 511

        8.4.1.5 Circles ............................................... 516

        8.4.1.6 Images and Sprites ............................. 521

    8.4.2 Reacting to Collisions with the Minimum Translation Vector ....................................................................... 526

        8.4.2.1 The MTV ........................................... 526

        8.4.2.2 Sticking ............................................. 531

8.4.2.3   Bouncing ........................................................ 537

8.5   Conclusion ................................................................. 541

**Chapter 9: Game Development** ..................................... **543**

9.1   A Game Engine ........................................................ 544

9.1.1   The Game Loop ........................................... 545

9.1.1.1   Pause .............................................. 551

9.1.1.2   Time-Based Motion ...................... 553

9.1.2   Loading Images ........................................... 554

9.1.3   Multitrack Sound ........................................ 557

9.1.4   Keyboard Events ......................................... 558

9.1.5   High Scores ................................................. 560

9.1.6   The Game Engine Listing ........................... 561

9.2   The Ungame ............................................................ 572

9.2.1   The Ungame's HTML .................................. 573

9.2.2   The Ungame's Game Loop .......................... 576

9.2.3   Loading the Ungame ................................... 579

9.2.4   Pausing ....................................................... 581

9.2.4.1   Auto-Pause .................................... 583

9.2.5   Key Listeners .............................................. 584

9.2.6   Game Over and High Scores ....................... 585

9.3   A Pinball Game ...................................................... 589

9.3.1   The Game Loop ........................................... 590

9.3.2   The Ball ...................................................... 593

9.3.3   Gravity and Friction .................................... 594

9.3.4   Flipper Motion ............................................ 595

9.3.5   Handling Keyboard Events ......................... 597

9.3.6   Collision Detection ..................................... 601

9.3.6.1   SAT Collision Detection ............... 601

9.3.6.2   The Dome ...................................... 609

9.3.6.3   Flipper Collision Detection ........... 611

9.4   Conclusion ............................................................. 614

**Chapter 10: Custom Controls** ...................................... **615**

10.1   Rounded Rectangles ............................................. 617

10.2   Progress Bars ....................................................... 625

10.3 Sliders ....................................................................................... 631

10.4 An Image Panner ...................................................................... 643

10.5 Conclusion ................................................................................ 655

**Chapter 11: Mobile** ........................................................................ 657

11.1 The Mobile Viewport ............................................................... 659

    11.1.1 The `viewport` Metatag ................................................... 661

11.2 Media Queries .......................................................................... 666

    11.2.1 Media Queries and CSS ................................................. 666

    11.2.2 Reacting to Media Changes with JavaScript ........................... 668

11.3 Touch Events ............................................................................ 671

    11.3.1 Touch Event Objects ...................................................... 672

    11.3.2 Touch Lists .................................................................... 672

    11.3.3 Touch Objects ............................................................... 673

    11.3.4 Supporting Both Touch and Mouse Events ...................... 674

    11.3.5 Pinch and Zoom ........................................................... 675

11.4 iOS5 .......................................................................................... 677

    11.4.1 Application Icons and Startup Images ............................ 678

    11.4.2 Media Queries for iOS5 Application Icons and Startup Images ................................................................................ 679

    11.4.3 Fullscreen with No Browser Chrome ............................. 680

    11.4.4 Application Status Bar ................................................... 681

11.5 A Virtual Keyboard ................................................................. 682

    11.5.1 A Canvas-Based Keyboard Implementation ................... 683

        11.5.1.1 The Keys ......................................................... 689

        11.5.1.2 The Keyboard ................................................. 693

11.6 Conclusion ................................................................................ 701

*Index* ................................................................................................ 703

# Preface

In the summer of 2001, after 15 years of developing graphical user interfaces and graphics-intensive applications, I read a best-selling book about implementing web applications by someone I did not know—Jason Hunter—but whom, unbeknownst to me, would soon become a good friend on the No Fluff Just Stuff (NFJS) tour.

When I finished Jason's Servlets book,[1] I put it in my lap and stared out the window. After years of Smalltalk, C++, and Java, and after writing a passionate 1622 pages for *Graphic Java 2: Swing*,[2] I thought to myself, *am I really going to implement user interfaces with print statements that generate HTML?* Unfortunately, I was.

From then on, I soldiered on through what I consider the Dark Ages of software development. I was the second Apache Struts committer and I invented the Struts Template Library, which ultimately became the popular Tiles project. I spent more than six years on the JavaServer Faces (JSF) Expert Group, spoke about server-side Java at more than 120 NFJS symposiums and many other conferences, and coauthored a book on JSF.[3] I got excited about Google Web Toolkit and Ruby on Rails for a while, but in the end the Dark Ages was mostly concerned with the dull business of presenting forms to users on the client and processing them on the server, and I was never again able to capture that passion that I had for graphics and graphical user interfaces.

In the summer of 2010, with HTML5 beginning its inexorable rise in popularity, I came across an article about Canvas, and I knew salvation was nigh. I immediately dropped everything in my professional life and devoted myself fulltime to write the best Canvas book that I could. From then on, until the book was finalized in March 2012, I was entirely immersed in Canvas and in this book. It's by far the most fun I've ever had writing a book.

Canvas gives you all the graphics horsepower you need to implement everything from word processors to video games. And, although performance varies on specific platforms, in general, Canvas is fast, most notably on iOS5, which

---

1. *Java Servlet Programming*, 2001, by Jason Hunter with William Crawford, published by O'Reilly.
2. *Graphic Java 2, Volume 2, Swing*, 1999, by David Geary, published by Prentice Hall.
3. *Core JavaServer™ Faces, Third Edition*, 2010, by David Geary and Cay Horstmann, published by Prentice Hall.

hardware accelerates Canvas in Mobile Safari. Browser vendors have also done a great job adhering to the specification so that well-written Canvas applications run unmodified in any HTML5-compliant browser with only minor incompatibilities.

HTML5 is the Renaissance that comes after the Dark Ages of software development, and Canvas is arguably the most exciting aspect of HTML5. In this book I dive deeply into Canvas and related aspects of HTML5, such as the Animation Timing specification, to implement real-world applications that run across desktop browsers and mobile devices.

## Reading This Book

I wrote this book so that in the Zen tradition you can read it without reading.

I write each chapter over the course of months, constantly iterating over material without ever writing a word. During that time I work on outlines, code listings, screenshots, tables, diagrams, itemized lists, notes, tips, and cautions. Those things, which I refer to as scaffolding, are the most important aspects of this book. The words, which I write only at the last possible moment after the scaffolding is complete, are meant to provide context and illustrate highlights of the surrounding scaffolding. Then I iterate over the words, eliminating as many of them as I can.

By focusing on scaffolding and being frugal with words, this book is easy to read without reading. You can skim the material, concentrating on the screenshots, code listings, diagrams, tables, and other scaffolding to learn a great deal of what you need to know on any given topic. Feel free to consider the words as second-class citizens, and, if you wish, consult them only as necessary.

## An Overview of This Book

This book has two parts. The first part, which spans the first four chapters of the book and is nearly one half of the book, covers the Canvas API, showing you how to draw shapes and text into a canvas, and draw and manipulate images. The last seven chapters of the book show you how to use that API to implement animations and animated sprites, create physics simulations, detect collisions, and develop video games. The book ends with a chapter on implementing custom controls, such as progress bars, sliders, and image panners, and a chapter that shows you how to create Canvas-based mobile applications.

The first chapter—*Essentials*—introduces the canvas element and shows you how to use it in web applications. The chapter contains a short section on getting started with HTML5 development in general, briefly covering browsers, consoles, debuggers, profilers, and timelines. The chapter then shows you how to implement Canvas essentials: drawing into a canvas, saving and restoring Canvas parameters and the drawing surface itself, printing a canvas, and an introduction to offscreen canvases. The chapter concludes with a brief math primer covering basic algebra, trigonometry, vector mathematics, and deriving equations from units of measure.

The second chapter—*Drawing*—which is the longest chapter in the book, provides an in-depth examination of drawing with the Canvas API, showing you how to draw lines, arcs, curves, circles, rectangles, and arbitrary polygons in a canvas, and how to fill them with solid colors, gradients, and patterns. The chapter goes beyond the mere mechanics of drawing, however, by showing you how to implement useful, real-world examples of drawing with the Canvas API, such as drawing temporary rubber bands to dynamically create shapes, dragging shapes within a canvas, implementing a simple retained-mode graphics subsystem that keeps track of polygons in a canvas so users users can edit them, and using the clipping region to erase shapes without disturbing the Canvas background underneath.

The third chapter—*Text*—shows you how to draw and manipulate text in a canvas. You will see how to stroke and fill text, set font properties, and position text within a canvas. The chapter also shows you how to implement your own text controls in a canvas, complete with blinking text cursors and editable paragraphs.

The fourth chapter—*Images and Video*—focuses on images, image manipulation, and video processing. You'll see how to draw and scale images in a canvas, and you'll learn how to manipulate images by accessing the color components of each pixel. You will also see more uses for the clipping region and how to animate images. The chapter then addresses security and performance considerations, before ending with a section on video processing.

The fifth chapter—*Animation*—shows you how to implement smooth animations with a method named `requestAnimationFrame()` that's defined in a W3C specification titled *Timing control for script-based animations*. You will see how to calculate an animation's frame rate and how to schedule other activities, such as updating an animation's user interface at alternate frame rates. The chapter shows you how to restore the background during an animation with three different strategies and discusses the performance implications of each. The chapter also illustrates how to implement time-based motion, scroll an animation's background, use parallax to create the illusion of 3D, and detect and react to user gestures during an animation. The chapter concludes with a look at timed animations and the implementation of a simple animation timer, followed by a discussion of animation best practices.

The sixth chapter—*Sprites*—shows you how to implement sprites (animated objects) in JavaScript. Sprites have a visual representation, often an image, and you can move them around in a canvas and cycle through a set of images to animate them. Sprites are the fundamental building block upon which games are built.

The seventh chapter—*Physics*—shows you how to simulate physics in your animations, from modeling falling objects and projectile trajectories to swinging pendulums. The chapter also shows you how to warp both time and motion in your animations to simulate real-world movement, such as the acceleration experienced by a sprinter out of the blocks (ease-in effect) or the deceleration of a braking automobile (ease-out).

Another essential aspect of most games is collision detection, so the eighth chapter in the book—*Collision Detection*—is devoted to the science of detecting collisions between sprites. The chapter begins with simple collision detection using bounding boxes and circles, which is easy to implement but not very reliable. Because simple collision detection is not reliable under many circumstances, much of this chapter is devoted to the Separating Axis Theorem, which is one of the best ways to detect collisions between arbitrary polygons in both 2D and 3D; however, the theorem is not for the mathematically faint of heart, so this chapter goes to great lengths to present the theorem in layman terms.

The ninth chapter—*Game Development*—begins with the implementation of a simple but effective game engine that provides support for everything from drawing sprites and maintaining high scores to time-based motion and multitrack sound. The chapter then discusses two games. The first game is a simple Hello World type of game that illustrates how to use the game engine and provides a convenient starting point for a game. It also shows you how to implement common aspects of most games such as asset management, heads-up displays, and a user interface for high scores. The second game is an industrial-strength pinball game that draws on much of the previous material in the book and illustrates complex collision detection in a real-world game.

Many Canvas-based applications require custom controls, so the tenth chapter—*Custom Controls*—teaches you how to implement them. The chapter discusses implementing custom controls in general and then illustrates those techniques with four custom controls: a rounded rectangle, a progress bar, a slider, and an image panner.

The final chapter of this book—*Mobile*—focuses on implementing Canvas-based mobile applications. You'll see how to control the size of your application's viewport so that your application displays properly on mobile devices, and how to account for different screen sizes and orientations with CSS3 media queries.

You'll also see how to make your Canvas-based applications indistinguishable from native applications on iOS5 by making them run fullscreen and fitting them with desktop icons and startup screens. The chapter concludes with the implementation of a keyboard for iOS5 applications that do not receive text through a text field.

## Prerequisites

To make effective use of this book you must have more than a passing familiarity with JavaScript, HTML, and CSS. I assume, for example, that you already know how to implement objects with JavaScript's prototypal inheritance, and that you are well versed in web application development in general.

This book also utilizes some mathematics that you may have learned a long time ago and forgotten, such as basic algebra and trigonometry, vector math, and deriving equations from units of measure. At the end of the first chapter you will find a short primer that covers all those topics.

## The Book's Code

All the code in this book is copyrighted by the author and is available for use under the license distributed with the code. That license is a modified MIT license that lets you do anything you want with the code, including using it in software that you sell; however, you may not use the code to create educational material, such as books, instructional videos, or presentations. See the license that comes with the code for more details.

When implementing the examples, I made a conscious decision to keep comments in code listings to a bare minimum. Instead, I made the code itself as readable as possible; methods average about five lines of code so they are easy to understand.

I also adhered closely to Douglas Crawford's recommendations in his excellent book *JavaScript, The Good Parts*.[4] For example, all function-scoped variables are always declared at the top of the function, variables are declared on a line of their own, and I always use === and its ilk for equality testing.

Finally, all the code listings in this book are color coded. Function calls are displayed in `blue`, so they stand out from the rest of the listing. As you scan listings, pay particular attention to the `blue` function calls; after all, function calls are the verbs of JavaScript, and those verbs alone reveal most of what you need to know about the inner workings of any particular example.

---

4. *JavaScript, The Good Parts*, 2008, by Douglas Crawford, published by O'Reilly.

## The Future of Canvas and This Book

The HTML5 APIs are constantly evolving, and much of that evolution consists of new features. The Canvas specification is no exception; in fact, this book was just days from going to the printer when the WHATWG Canvas specification was updated to include several new features:

- An `ellipse()` method that creates elliptical paths
- Two methods, `getLineDash()` and `setLineDash()`, and an attribute `lineDashOffset` used for drawing dashed lines
- An expanded `TextMetrics` object that lets you determine the exact bounding box for text
- A `Path` object
- A `CanvasDrawingStyles` object
- Extensive support for hit regions

At that time, no browsers supported the new features, so it was not yet possible to write code to test them.

Prior the March 26, 2012 update to the specification, you could draw arcs and circles with Canvas, but there was no explicit provision for drawing ellipses. Now, in addition to arcs and circles, you can draw ellipses with the new `ellipse()` method of the Canvas 2d context. Likewise, the context now explicitly supports drawing dashed lines.

The `TextMetrics` object initially only reported one metric: the width of a string. However, with the March 26, 2012 update to the specification, you can now determine both the width and height of the rectangle taken up by a string in a canvas. That augmentation of the `TextMetrics` object will make it much easier, and more efficient, to implement Canvas-based text controls.

In addition to ellipses and an improved `TextMetrics` object, the updated specification has also added `Path` and `CanvasDrawingStyles` methods. Prior to the updated specification, there was no explicit mechanism for storing paths or drawing styles. Now, not only are there objects that represent those abstractions, but many of the Canvas 2d context methods have been duplicated to also take a `Path` object. For example, you stroke a context's path by invoking `context.stroke()`, which strokes the *current* path; however, the context now has a method `stroke(Path)` and that method strokes the path you send to the method instead of the context's current path. When you modify a path with `Path` methods such as `addText()`, you can specify a `CanvasDrawingStyle` object, which is used by the path, in this case to add text to the path.

The updated specification contains extensive support for hit regions. A hit region is defined by a path, and you can associate an optional mouse cursor and accessibility parameters, such as an Accessible Rich Internet Application (ARIA) role and a label, with a hit region. A single canvas can have multiple hit regions. Among other things, hit regions will make it easier and more efficient to implement collision detection and improve accessiblity.

Finally, both the WHATWG and W3C specifications have included two Canvas context methods for accessibility, so that applications can draw focus rings around the current path, letting users navigate with the keyboard in a Canvas. That functionality was not part of the March 26, 2012 update to the specification, and in fact, has been in the specification for some time; however, while the book was being written, no browser vendors supported the feature, so it is not covered in this book.

As the Canvas specification evolves and browser vendors implement new features, this book will be updated on a regular basis. In the meantime, you can read about new Canvas features and preview the coverage of those features in the next edition of this book, at corehtml5canvas.com.

## The Companion Website

This book's companion website is http://corehtml5canvas.com, where you can download the book's code, run featured examples from the book, and find other HTML5 and Canvas resources.

# Acknowledgments

Writing books is a team sport, and I was lucky to have great teammates for this book.

I'd like to start by thanking my longtime editor and good friend Greg Doench, who believed wholeheartedly in this book from the moment I proposed it and who gave me the latitude to write the book exactly as I wanted. Greg also oversaw the book from the moment of conception until, and after, it went to print. I couldn't ask for more.

I'm also fortunate that Greg comes with a great team of his own. Julie Nahil did a wonderful job of managing production and keeping everything on track, and Alina Kirsanova took my raw docbook XML and turned it into the beautiful color book you hold in your hands. Alina also did a superb job proofreading, weeding out small errors and inconsistencies.

Once again I was thrilled to have Mary Lou Nohr copy edit this book. Mary Lou is the only copy editor I've had in 15 years of writing books, and she not only makes each book better than I possibly could, but she continues to teach me the craft of writing.

Technical reviewers are vital to the success of any technical book, so I actively recruit reviewers who I think have an appropriate skill set to make significant contributions. For this book I was fortunate to land an excellent group of reviewers who helped me mold, shape, and polish the book's material. First, I'd like to thank Philip Taylor for being one of the most knowledgeable and thorough reviewers that I've ever had. Philip, who has implemented nearly 800 Canvas test cases—see http://philip.html5.org/tests/canvas/suite/tests—sent me pages of insightful comments for each chapter that only someone who knows the most intimate Canvas nuances could provide. Philip went way beyond the call of duty and single-handedly made this a much better book.

Next, I'd like to thank Scott Davis at thirstyhead.com, one of the foremost experts in HTML5 and mobile web application development. Scott has spoken at many conferences on HTML5 and mobile development, cofounded the HTML5 Denver Users Group, and taught mobile development to Yahoo! developers. Like Philip, Scott went way beyond the call of duty by offering excellent suggestions in many different areas of the book. I'm deeply indebted to Scott for delaying the publishing of this book for a full three months, while I entirely rewrote nearly a quarter of the book as the result of his scathing review. That rewrite took this book to the next level.

Ilmari Heikkinen, of Runfield fame (http://fhtr.org/runfield/runfield), provided some great insights for the Animation, Sprites, Physics, and Collision Detection chapters. Ted Neward, Dion Almaer, Ben Galbraith, Pratik Pratel, Doris Chen, Nate Schutta, and Brian Sam-Bodden also provided great review comments.

I'd also like to thank Mathias Bynens, the creator of jsperf.com, for giving me permission to use screenshots from that website.

I would like to acknowledge MJKRZAK for the sprite sheet used in the Physics chapter. That sprite sheet was downloaded from the public domain section of the People's Sprites website. I would also like to thank Ilmari Heikkinen for giving me permission to use his sky image for the parallax example in the Animation chapter. Some images in Sprites chapter are from the popular open source Replica Island game.

Finally, I'd like to thank Hiroko, Gaspé, and Tonka for enduring over the past year and a half while this book utterly consumed my life.

# About the Author

**David Geary** is a prominent author, speaker, and consultant, who began implementing graphics-based applications and interfaces with C and Smalltalk in the 1980s. David taught C++ and Object-Oriented Software Development for eight years at Boeing, and was a software engineer at Sun Microsystems from 1994–1997. He is the author of eight Java books, including two best-selling books on the Java component frameworks, Swing and JavaServer Faces (JSF). David's *Graphic Java 2: Swing* is the all-time best-selling Swing book, and *Core JavaServer™ Faces*, which David wrote with Cay Horstmann, is the best-selling book on JSF.

David is a passionate and prolific public speaker who has spoken at hundreds of conferences world-wide. He spoke on the No Fluff Just Stuff tour for six years, speaking at over 120 symposiums, and he is a three-time JavaOne Rock Star.

In 2011, David and Scott Davis co-founded the HTML5 Denver Meetup group—www.meetup.com/HTML5-Denver-Users-Group—which had grown to over 500 members when this book was published in 2012.

David can be found on Twitter (@davidgeary) and at the companion website for this book, http://corehtml5canvas.com.

# CHAPTER 1

# Essentials

In 1939, Metro-Goldwyn-Mayer Studios released a film that, according to the American Library of Congress, was destined to become the most watched film in history. *The Wizard of Oz* is the story of a young girl named Dorothy and her dog Toto, who are transported by a violent tornado from Kansas in the central United States to the magical land of Oz.

The film begins in Kansas and is shot in a bland and dreary black-and-white. When Dorothy and Toto arrive in the land of Oz however, the film bursts into vibrant color, and the adventure begins.

For more than a decade, software developers have been implementing bland and dreary web applications that do little more than present bored-to-death users with a seemingly unending sequence of banal forms. Finally, HTML5 lets developers implement exciting desktop-like applications that run in the browser.

In this HTML5 land of Oz, we will use the magical canvas element to do amazing things in a browser. We will implement image panning, as shown in Figure 1.1; an interactive magnifying glass; a paint application that runs in any self-respecting browser and that also runs on an iPad; several animations and games, including an industrial-strength pinball game; image filters; and many other web applications that in another era were almost entirely the realm of Flash.

Let's get started.

## 1.1 The canvas Element

The canvas element is arguably the single most powerful HTML5 element, although, as you'll see shortly, its real power lies in the Canvas context, which

Figure 1.1  Canvas offers a powerful graphics API

you obtain from the canvas element itself. Figure 1.2 shows a simple use of the canvas element and its associated context.

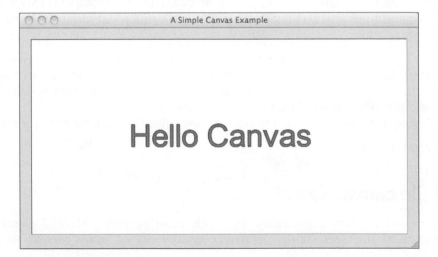

Figure 1.2  Hello canvas

The application shown in Figure 1.2 simply displays a string, approximately centered in the canvas itself. The HTML for that application is shown in Example 1.1.

The HTML in Example 1.1 uses a canvas element and specifies an identifier for the element and the element's width and height. Notice the text in the body of the canvas element. That text is known as the *fallback content*, which the browser displays only if it does not support the canvas element.

Besides those two elements, the HTML in Example 1.1 uses CSS to set the application's background color and some attributes for the canvas element itself. By default, a canvas element's background color matches the background color of its parent element, so the CSS sets the canvas element's background color to opaque white to set it apart from the application's light gray background.

The HTML is straightforward and not very interesting. As is typically the case for Canvas-based applications, the interesting part of the application is its JavaScript. The JavaScript code for the application shown in Figure 1.2 is listed in Example 1.2.

**Example 1.1** `example.html`

```html
<!DOCTYPE html>
<html>
   <head>
     <title>A Simple Canvas Example</title>

     <style>
        body {
           background: #dddddd;
        }
        #canvas {
           margin: 10px;
           padding: 10px;
           background: #ffffff;
           border: thin inset #aaaaaa;
        }
     </style>
   </head>

  <body>
    <canvas id='canvas' width='600' height='300'>
     Canvas not supported
    </canvas>

    <script src='example.js'></script>
  </body>
</html>
```

**Example 1.2** `example.js`

```js
var canvas = document.getElementById('canvas'),
    context = canvas.getContext('2d');

context.font = '38pt Arial';
context.fillStyle = 'cornflowerblue';
context.strokeStyle = 'blue';

context.fillText('Hello Canvas', canvas.width/2 - 150,
                                 canvas.height/2 + 15);

context.strokeText('Hello Canvas', canvas.width/2 - 150,
                                   canvas.height/2 + 15 );
```

The JavaScript in Example 1.2 employs a recipe that you will use in your Canvas-based applications:

1.  Use `document.getElementById()` to get a reference to a canvas.

2.  Call `getContext('2d')` on the canvas to get the graphics context (note: the 'd' in '2d' *must* be lowercase).

3.  Use the context to draw in the canvas.

After obtaining a reference to the canvas's context, the JavaScript sets the context's `font`, `fillStyle`, and `strokeStyle` attributes and fills and strokes the text that you see in Figure 1.2. The `fillText()` method fills the characters of the text using `fillStyle`, and `strokeText()` strokes the outline of the characters with `strokeStyle`. The `fillStyle` and `strokeStyle` attributes can be a CSS color, a gradient, or a pattern. We briefly discuss those attributes in Section 1.2.1, "The 2d Context," on p. 9 and take a more in-depth look at both the attributes and methods in Chapter 2.

The `fillText()` and `strokeText()` methods both take three arguments: the text and an (x, y) location within the canvas to display the text. The JavaScript shown in Example 1.2 approximately centers the text with constant values, which is not a good general solution for centering text in a canvas. In Chapter 3, we will look at a better way to center text.

 **CAUTION: The suffix px is not valid for canvas width and height**

Although it's widely permitted by browsers that support Canvas, the px suffix for the canvas `width` and `height` attributes is not technically allowed by the Canvas specification. The values for those attributes, according to the specification, can only be non-negative integers.

**NOTE: The default canvas size is 300 × 150 screen pixels**

By default, the browser creates canvas elements with a width of 300 pixels and a height of 150 pixels. You can change the size of a canvas element by specifying the width and height attributes.

You can also change the size of a canvas element with CSS attributes; however, as you will see in the next section, changing the width and height of a canvas element may have unwanted consequences.

### 1.1.1  Canvas Element Size vs. Drawing Surface Size

The application in the preceding section sets the size of the canvas element by setting the element's width and height attributes. You can also use CSS to set the size of a canvas element, as shown in Example 1.3; however, using CSS to size a canvas element is not the same as setting the element's width and height attributes.

**Example 1.3** Setting element size and drawing surface size to different values

```
<!DOCTYPE html>
   <head>
     <title>Canvas element size: 600 x 300,
            Canvas drawing surface size: 300 x 150</title>
     <style>
        body {
           background: #dddddd;
        }
        #canvas {
           margin: 20px;
           padding: 20px;
           background: #ffffff;
           border: thin inset #aaaaaa;
           width: 600px;
           height: 300px;
        }
     </style>
   </head>

   <body>
     <canvas id='canvas'>
       Canvas not supported
     </canvas>

     <script src='example.js'></script>
   </body>
</html>
```

The difference between using CSS and setting canvas element attributes lies in the fact that *a canvas actually has two sizes*: the size of the element itself and the size of the element's drawing surface.

When you set the element's width and height attributes, you set *both* the element's size and the size of the element's drawing surface; however, when you use CSS to size a canvas element, you set *only* the element's size and not the drawing surface.

By default, both the canvas element's size and the size of its drawing surface is 300 screen pixels wide and 150 screen pixels high. In the listing shown in Example 1.3, which uses CSS to set the canvas element's size, the size of the element is 600 pixels wide and 300 pixels high, but *the size of the drawing surface remains unchanged* at the default value of 300 pixels × 150 pixels.

And here is where things get interesting because when a canvas element's size does not match the size of its drawing surface, *the browser scales the drawing surface to fit the element.* That effect is illustrated in Figure 1.3.

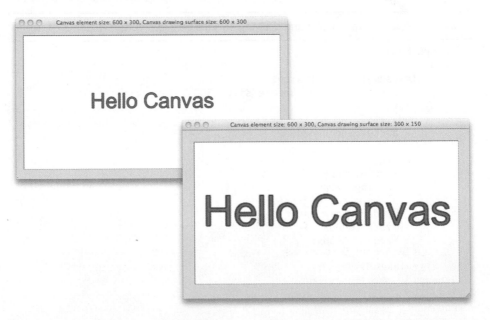

Figure 1.3  *Top*: element and coordinate system = 600 × 300; *bottom*: element = 600 × 300, coordinate system = 300 × 150

The application shown at the top of Figure 1.3 is the application that we discussed in the preceding section. It sets the canvas element's size with the element's width and height attributes, setting both the element's size and the size of the drawing surface to 600 pixels × 300 pixels.

The application shown at the bottom of Figure 1.3 is the application whose HTML is shown in Example 1.3. That application is identical to the application in the preceding section, except that it uses CSS to size the canvas element (and has a different title in the window's title bar).

Because the application shown in the bottom screenshot in Figure 1.3 uses CSS to size the canvas element and does not set the element's width or height attributes, the browser scales the drawing surface from 300 pixels × 150 pixels to 600 pixels × 300 pixels.

**CAUTION: The browser may automatically scale your canvas**

It's a good idea to use the canvas element's width and height attributes to size the element, instead of using CSS. If you use CSS to size the element without also specifying the width and height attributes of the canvas element, the element size will not match the canvas's drawing surface size, and the browser will scale the latter to fit the former, most likely resulting in surprising and unwanted effects.

## 1.1.2 The Canvas API

The canvas element does not provide much of an API; in fact, that API offers only two attributes and three methods that are summarized in Table 1.1 and Table 1.2.

**Table 1.1** canvas attributes

| Attribute | Description | Type | Allowed Values | Default |
|-----------|-------------|------|----------------|---------|
| width | The width of the canvas's *drawing surface*. By default, the browser makes the canvas element the same size as its drawing surface; however, if you override the element size with CSS, then the browser will *scale* the drawing surface to fit the element. | non-negative integer | Any valid non-negative integer. You may add a plus sign or whitespace at the beginning, but technically, you cannot add a px suffix. | 300 |

*(Continues)*

**Table 1.1** *(Continued)*

| Attribute | Description | Type | Allowed Values | Default |
|---|---|---|---|---|
| height | The height of the canvas's drawing surface. The browser may scale the drawing surface to fit the `canvas` element size. See the `width` attribute for more information. | non-negative integer | Any valid non-negative integer. You may add a plus sign or whitespace at the beginning, but technically, you cannot add a `px` suffix. | 150 |

**Table 1.2** canvas methods

| Method | Description |
|---|---|
| getContext() | Returns the graphics context associated with the canvas. Each canvas has one context, and each context is associated with one canvas. |
| toDataURL(type, quality) | Returns a data URL that you can assign to the `src` property of an `img` element. The first argument specifies the type of image, such as `image/jpeg`, or `image/png`; the latter is the default if you don't specify the first argument. The second argument, which must be a `double` value from 0 to 1.0, specifies a quality level for JPEG images. |
| toBlob(callback, type, args...) | Creates a `Blob` that represents a file containing the canvas's image. The first argument to the method is a function that the browser invokes with a reference to the blob. The second argument specifies the type of image, such as `image/png`, which is the default value. The final arguments represent a quality level from 0.0 to 1.0 inclusive, for JPEG images. Other arguments will most likely be added to this method in the future to more carefully control image characteristics. |

## 1.2  Canvas Contexts

The canvas element merely serves as a container for a context. The context provides all the graphics horsepower. Although this book focuses exclusively on the 2d context, the Canvas specification embraces other types of contexts as well; for example, a 3d context specification is already well underway. This section looks at the attributes of the 2d context, with a brief nod to the 3d context.

## 1.2.1 The 2d Context

In your JavaScript code, you will find little use for the canvas element itself, other than occasionally using it to obtain the canvas width or height or a data URL, as discussed in the preceding section. Additionally, you will use the canvas element to obtain a reference to the canvas's context, which provides a capable API for drawing shapes and text, displaying and manipulating images, etc. Indeed, for the rest of this book our focus will mainly be on the 2d context.

Table 1.3 lists all of the 2d context attributes. Other than the canvas attribute, which gives you a reference to the canvas itself, all of the 2d context attributes pertain to drawing operations.

**Table 1.3** CanvasRenderingContext2D attributes

| Attribute | Brief Description |
|---|---|
| canvas | Refers to the context's canvas. The most common use of the canvas attribute is to access the width and height of the canvas: context.canvas.width and context.canvas.height, respectively. |
| fillStyle | Specifies a color, gradient, or pattern that the context subsequently uses to fill shapes. |
| font | Specifies the font that the context uses when you call fillText() or strokeText(). |
| globalAlpha | Is the global alpha setting, which must be a number between 0 (fully transparent), and 1.0 (fully opaque). The browser multiplies the alpha value of every pixel you draw by the globalAlpha property, including when you draw images. |
| globalComposite-Operation | Determines how the browser draws one thing over another. See Section 2.14 for valid values. |
| lineCap | Specifies how the browser draws the endpoints of a line. You can specify one of the following three values: butt, round, and square. The default value is butt. |
| lineWidth | Determines the width, in screen pixels, of lines that you draw in a canvas. The value must be a non-negative, non-infinite double value. The default is 1.0. |
| lineJoin | Specifies how lines are joined when their endpoints meet. Valid values are: bevel, round, and miter. The default value is miter. |

*(Continues)*

**Table 1.3** *(Continued)*

| Attribute | Brief Description |
| --- | --- |
| miterLimit | Specifies how to draw a miter line join. See Section 2.8.7 for details about this property. |
| shadowBlur | Determines how the browser spreads out shadow; the higher the number, the more spread out the shadows. The shadowBlur value is not a pixel value, but a value used in a Gaussian blur equation. The value must be a positive, non-infinite double value. The default value is 0. |
| shadowColor | Specifies the color the browser uses to draw shadows. The value for this property is often specified as partially transparent to let the background show through. |
| shadowOffsetX | Specifies the horizontal offset, in screen pixels, for shadows. |
| shadowOffsetY | Specifies the vertical offset, in screen pixels, for shadows. |
| strokeStyle | Specifies the style used to stroke paths. This value can be a color, gradient, or pattern. |
| textAlign | Determines horizontal placement of text that you draw with fillText() or strokeText(). |
| textBaseline | Determines vertical placement of text that you draw with fillText() or strokeText(). |

The table gives you an overview of all the 2d context attributes. In Chapter 2, we examine all those attributes on a case-by-case basis.

 **NOTE: You can extend the 2d context's capabilities**

The context associated with each canvas is a powerful graphics engine that supports features such as gradients, image compositing, and animation, but it does have limitations; for example, the context does not provide a method for drawing dashed lines. Because JavaScript is a dynamic language, however, you can add new methods or augment existing methods of the context. See Section 2.8.6, "Drawing Dashed Lines by Extending CanvasRenderingContext2D," on p. 118 for more information.

### 1.2.1.1 The WebGL 3d Context

The Canvas 2d context has a 3d counterpart, known as WebGL, that closely conforms to the OpenGL ES 2.0 API. You can find the WebGL specification, which is maintained by the Khronos Group, at http://www.khronos.org/registry/webgl/specs/latest/.

At the time this book was written, browser vendors were just beginning to provide support for WebGL, and there are still some notable platforms, such as iOS4 and IE10, that do not provide support. Nonetheless, a 3d Canvas context is an exciting development that will open the door to all sorts of bleeding edge applications.

## 1.2.2 Saving and Restoring Canvas State

In Section 1.2.1, "The 2d Context," on p. 9 we discussed all of the attributes of the Canvas context. You will often set those attributes for drawing operations. Much of the time you will want to *temporarily* set those attributes; for example, you may draw a grid with thin lines in the background and subsequently draw on top of the grid with thicker lines. In that case you would temporarily set the lineWidth attribute while you draw the grid.

The Canvas API provides two methods, named save() and restore(), for saving and restoring all the canvas context's attributes. You use those methods like this:

```
function drawGrid(strokeStyle, fillStyle) {
   controlContext.save(); // Save the context on a stack

   controlContext.fillStyle = fillStyle;
   controlContext.strokeStyle = strokeStyle;

   // Draw the grid...

   controlContext.restore(); // Restore the context from the stack
}
```

The save() and restore() methods may not seem like a big deal, but after using Canvas for any length of time you will find them indispensable. Those two methods are summarized in Table 1.4.

---

 **NOTE: You can nest calls to save() and restore()**

The context's save() method places the current state of the context onto a stack. The corresponding call to restore() pops the state from the stack and restores the context's state accordingly. That means you can nest calls to save()/restore().

---

**Table 1.4** CanvasRenderingContext2D state methods

| Method | Description |
|--------|-------------|
| save() | Pushes the current state of the canvas onto a stack of canvas states. Canvas state includes the current transformation and clipping region and all attributes of the canvas's context, including strokeStyle, fillStyle, globalCompositeOperation, etc. |
| | The canvas state does not include the current path or bitmap. You can only reset the path by calling beginPath(), and the bitmap is a property of the canvas, not the context. |
| | Note that although the bitmap is a property of the canvas, you access the bitmap through the context (via the context's getImageData() method). |
| restore() | Pops the top entry off the stack of canvas states. The state that resides at the top of the stack, after the pop occurs, becomes the current state, and the browser must set the canvas state accordingly. Therefore, any changes that you make to the canvas state between save() and restore() method calls persist only until you invoke the restore() method. |

**NOTE: Saving and restoring the drawing surface**

This section shows you how to save and restore context state. It's also beneficial to be able to save and restore the drawing surface itself, which we discuss in Section 1.7, "Saving and Restoring the Drawing Surface," on p. 33.

## 1.3 Canonical Examples in This Book

Many of the examples in this book use the following canonical form:

```
<!-- example.html -->

<!DOCTYPE html>
<html>
   <head>
      <title>Canonical Canvas used in this book</title>

      <style>
         ...
         #canvas {
            ...
         }
      </style>
   </head>
```

```
<body>
   <canvas id='canvas' width='600' height='300'>
      Canvas not supported
   </canvas>

   <script src='example.js'></script>
</body>
</html>

// example.js

var canvas = document.getElementById('canvas'),
    context = canvas.getContext('2d');

// Use the context...
```

The preceding example has one canvas whose ID is canvas, and it uses one JavaScript file named example.js. That JavaScript file has two variables, one for the canvas and another for the canvas's context. The preceding example uses document.getElementById() to obtain a reference to the canvas and gets a reference to the canvas's context.

Most applications in this book that adhere to the preceding canonical form omit the HTML listings in the interests of brevity. Likewise, for inline code listings, meaning listings like the preceding listing that do not have an Example heading, you will often see the variables canvas and context with no code showing their initialization.

Finally, again in the interests of brevity, not every example in the book is fully listed. Often examples in the book build upon one other, and when they do, you will often see the full listing for the last example and partial listings for the other related examples.

---

**NOTE: A word about User Agents**

The Canvas specification refers to the implementor of the canvas element as a *User Agent*, which is often abbreviated to UA. The specification uses that term instead of the word *browser* because canvas elements can be implemented by any piece of software, not just browsers.

This book refers to the implementor of the canvas element as a browser because the term User Agent, or worse, the abbreviation UA, can be foreign and confusing to readers.

---

**NOTE: URLs referenced in this book**

In this book you will occasionally find references to URLs for further reading. Sometimes, if they are readable and not too long, those URLs will be the actual URLs. For unwieldy URLs, this book refers to shortened URLs that may be difficult to remember but are easy to type.

## 1.4 Getting Started

This section gives you a brief overview of your development environment, from the browsers in which your application will run to the development tools, such as profilers and timelines, that you will use during development. Feel free to skim this section and use it as a reference as necessary.

### 1.4.1 Specifications

Three specifications are pertinent to this book:

- HTML5 Canvas
- Timing control for script-based animations
- HTML5 video and audio

For historical reasons, there are actually two Canvas specifications that are nearly identical. One of those specifications is maintained by the W3C and can be found at http://dev.w3.org/html5/spec; the other specification is maintained by the WHATWG and can be found at http://bit.ly/qXWjOl. Furthermore, whereas the Canvas context is included in the WHATWG's specification, the WC3 has a separate specification for the context, at http://dev.w3.org/html5/2dcontext.

For a long time, people used `window.setInterval()` or `window.setTimeout()` for web-based animations; however, as you will see in Chapter 5, those methods are not suitable for performance-critical animations. Instead, you should use `window.requestAnimationFrame()`, which is defined in a specification of its own named *Timing control for script-based animations*. You can find that specification at http://www.w3.org/TR/animation-timing.

Finally, this book shows you how to incorporate HTML5 video and audio into your Canvas-based applications. HTML5 video and audio are covered in the same specification, which you can find at http://www.w3.org/TR/html5/video.html.

## 1.4.2 Browsers

At the time this book went to press in early 2012, all five major browsers—Chrome, Internet Explorer, Firefox, Opera, and Safari—provided extensive support for HTML5 Canvas. Although there are some minor incompatibilities that mostly stem from different interpretations of the Canvas specification—for example, see Section 2.14.1, "The Compositing Controversy," on p. 186, which explains incompatibilities for compositing—browser vendors have done an admirable job of both adhering to the specification and providing implementations that perform well.

Chrome, Firefox, Opera, and Safari have all had HTML5 support for some time. Microsoft's Internet Explorer was a bit late to the game and did not provide extensive support for HTML5 until IE9. However, Microsoft has done a phenomenal job with Canvas in IE9 and IE10; in fact, as this book went to press, those two browsers had the fastest Canvas implementation from among the five major browsers.

If you are implementing a Canvas-based application and you must support IE6, IE7, or IE8, you have two choices, depicted in Figure 1.4: explorercanvas, which

Figure 1.4 explorercanvas and Google Chrome Frame for IE6/7/8, from Google

adds Canvas support to those older versions of Internet Explorer, and Google Chrome Frame, which replaces the IE engine with the Google Chrome engine. Both explorercanvas and Google Chrome Frame are from Google.

### 1.4.3 Consoles and Debuggers

All the major browsers that support HTML5 give you access to a console and a debugger. In fact, because browser vendors often borrow ideas from each other, the consoles and debuggers provided by WebKit-based browsers—Firefox, Opera, and IE—are all pretty similar.

Figure 1.5 shows the console and debugger for Safari.

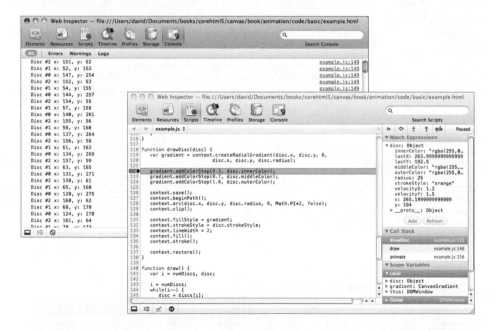

Figure 1.5  The Safari console and debugger

You can write to the console with the `console.log()` method. Just pass that method a string, and it will appear in the console. The debugger is standard debugger fare; you can set breakpoints, watch expressions, examine variables and the call stack, and so on.

A full treatment of the developer tools for various browsers is beyond the scope of this book. For more information about developer tools for Chrome, take a look at the Chrome Developer Tools documentation, shown in Figure 1.6. Similar documentation is available for other browsers.

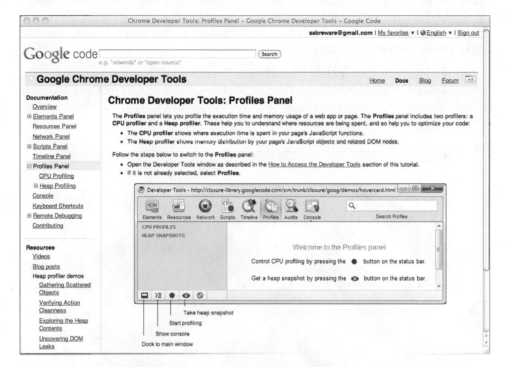

Figure 1.6  The Chrome Developer Tools documentation

---

 **TIP: Start and stop the profiler programmatically**

As you can see from Figure 1.6, you can start profiling in WebKit-based browsers by clicking the filled circle at the bottom of the profiler window.

Controlling the profiler by clicking buttons, however, is often insufficient; for example, you may want to start and stop profiling at specific lines of code. In WebKit-based browsers, you can do that with two methods: `console.profile()` and `console.profileEnd()`. You use them like this:

```
console.profile('Core HTML5 Animation,
                erasing the background');
//...

console.profileEnd();
```

### 1.4.4 Performance

Most of the time the applications that you implement with Canvas will perform admirably; however, if you are implementing animations or games or if you are implementing Canvas-based applications for mobile devices, you may need to make performance optimizations.

In this section we briefly look at the tools you have at your disposal for discovering performance bottlenecks in your code. To illustrate the use of those tools, we refer to the application shown in Figure 1.7. That animation, which is discussed in Chapter 5, simultaneously animates three filled circles.

Figure 1.7  An animation from Chapter 5

We discuss three tools:

- Profilers
- Timelines
- jsPerf

The first two tools in the preceding list are provided by browsers directly or are offered as add-ons. jsPerf, on the other hand, is a website that lets you create performance tests and make them public. In the sections that follow we will look at profiling and timeline tools available in Chrome and Safari, and then we will take a look at jsPerf.

### 1.4.4.1 Profiles and Timelines

Profiles and timelines are indispensable for discovering performance bottlenecks in your code. Figures 1.8 and 1.9 show a timeline and a profile, respectively, for the animation shown in Figure 1.7.

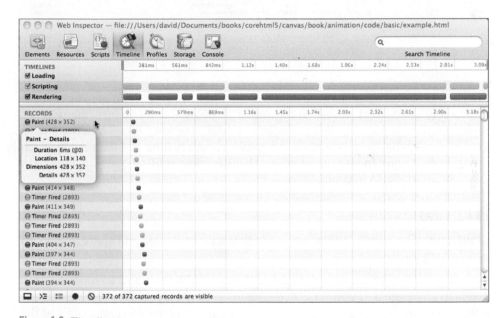

Figure 1.8  Timelines

Timelines give you a record of significant events that occur in your application, along with details of those events such as their duration and the area of the window they affect. In WebKit-based browsers, such as Chrome and Safari, you can hover the mouse over those events to obtain their associated details, as illustrated in Figure 1.8.

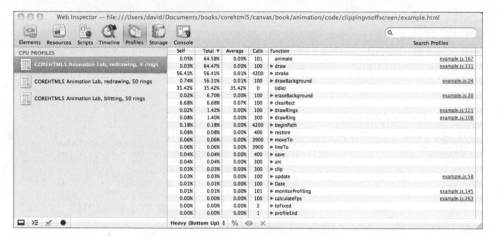

Figure 1.9  Profiles

Profilers give you a much more detailed view of how your code performs at the function level. As you can see in Figure 1.9, profiles show you how many times each function in your application is called, and how long those functions take. You can see what percentage of the total execution time is taken up by each function, and you can also discover exactly how many milliseconds each function takes, on average, to execute.

### 1.4.4.2  jsPerf

jsPerf, shown in Figure 1.10, is a website that lets you create and share JavaScript benchmarks.

You may wonder, for example, what's the most efficient way to loop through pixels in an image that you are processing in a canvas. If you click the "test cases" link, shown at the top of the screenshot in Figure 1.10, jsPerf displays all of the publicly available test cases, as shown in Figure 1.11.

In fact, not only are there many Canvas-related tests at jsperf.com, there is a test case that matches the description in the preceding paragraph, which is highlighted in Figure 1.11. If you click the link for that test case, jsPerf shows you the code for the test case, as shown in Figure 1.12. You can run the test case yourself, and your results will be added to the test case. You can also look at the results for all the different browsers that users have used to run the test case (not shown in Figure 1.12).

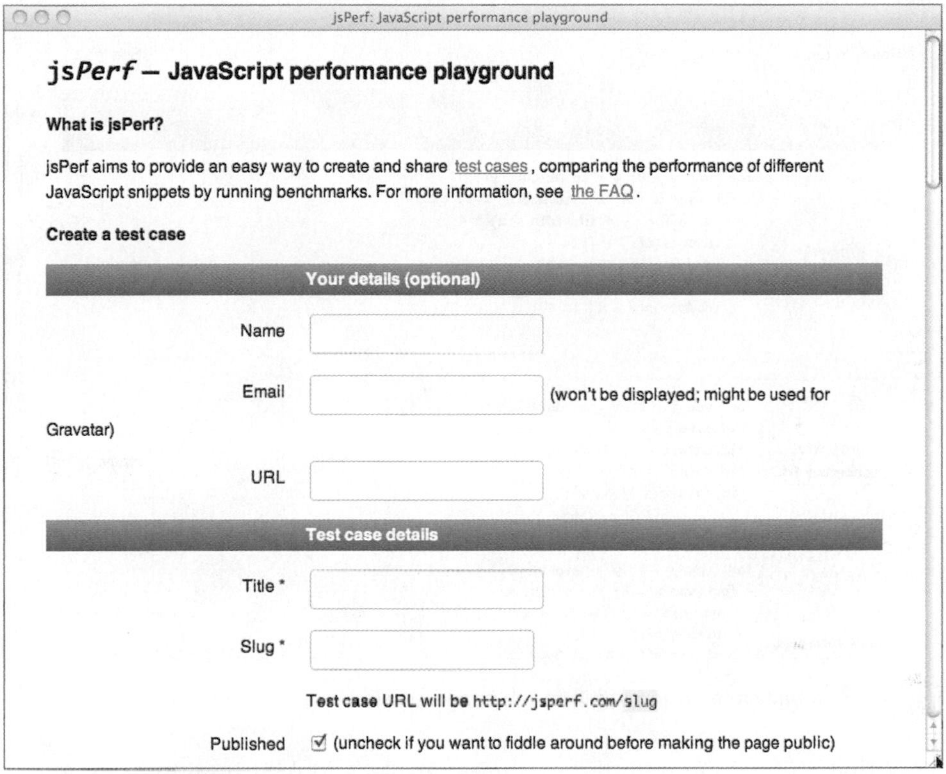

Figure 1.10  jsperf.com homepage

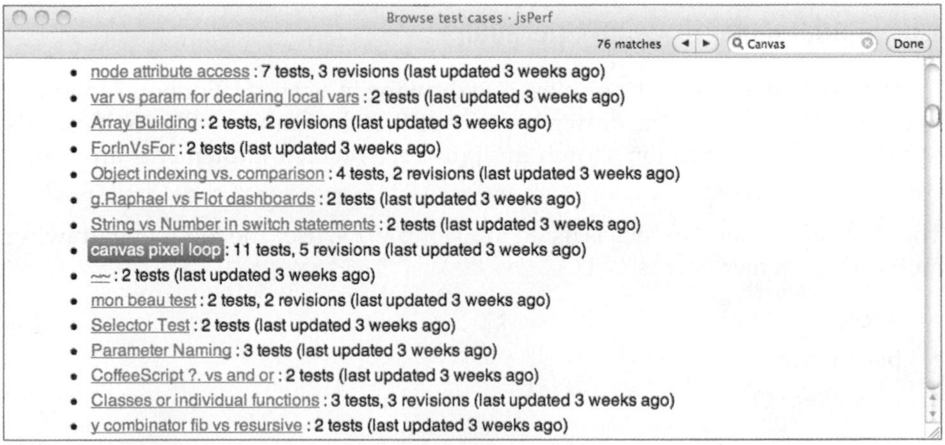

Figure 1.11  Code for a Canvas test case at jsfperf.com

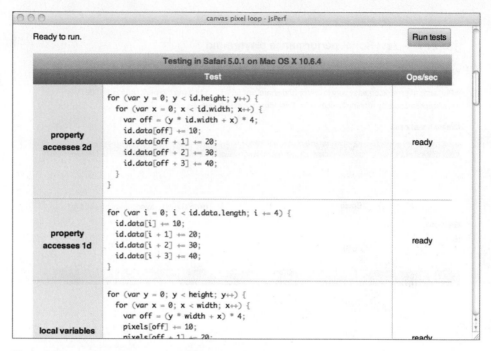

Figure 1.12  A test case for looping through image pixels

Now that we're done with the preliminaries, let's look at how to draw into a canvas.

## 1.5  Fundamental Drawing Operations

In the next chapter we will look closely at drawing in a canvas. For now, however, to familiarize you with the drawing methods that the Canvas API provides, let's begin with the application shown in Figure 1.13, which implements an analog clock.

The clock application, which is listed in Example 1.4, uses the following drawing methods from the Canvas API:

- `arc()`
- `beginPath()`
- `clearRect()`

- fill()
- fillText()
- lineTo()
- moveTo()
- stroke()

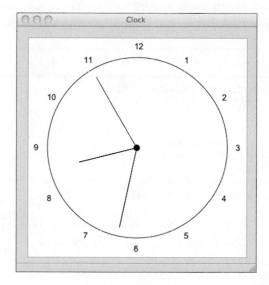

Figure 1.13 A clock

Like Adobe Illustrator and Apple's Cocoa, Canvas lets you draw shapes by creating invisible paths that you subsequently make visible with calls to stroke(), which strokes the outline of the path, or fill(), which fills the inside of the path. You begin a path with the beginPath() method.

The clock application's drawCircle() method draws the circle representing the clock face by invoking beginPath() to begin a path, and subsequently invokes arc() to create a circular path. That path is invisible until the application invokes stroke(). Likewise, the application's drawCenter() method draws the small filled circle at the center of the clock with a combination of beginPath(), arc(), and fill().

The application's drawNumerals() method draws the numbers around the face of the clock with the fillText() method, which draws filled text in the canvas. Unlike the arc() method, fillText() does not create a path; instead, fillText() immediately renders text in the canvas.

The clock hands are drawn by the application's drawHand() method, which uses three methods to draw the lines that represent the clock hands: moveTo(), lineTo(), and stroke(). The moveTo() method moves the graphics pen to a specific location in the canvas, lineTo() draws an invisible path to the location that you specify, and stroke() makes the current path visible.

The application animates the clock with setInterval(), which invokes the application's drawClock() function once every second. The drawClock() function uses clearRect() to erase the canvas, and then it redraws the clock.

**Example 1.4** A basic clock

```
var canvas = document.getElementById('canvas'),
    context = canvas.getContext('2d'),
    FONT_HEIGHT = 15,
    MARGIN = 35,
    HAND_TRUNCATION = canvas.width/25,
    HOUR_HAND_TRUNCATION = canvas.width/10,
    NUMERAL_SPACING = 20,
    RADIUS = canvas.width/2 - MARGIN,
    HAND_RADIUS = RADIUS + NUMERAL_SPACING;

// Functions.......................................................

function drawCircle() {
   context.beginPath();
   context.arc(canvas.width/2, canvas.height/2,
               RADIUS, 0, Math.PI*2, true);
   context.stroke();
}

function drawNumerals() {
   var numerals = [ 1, 2, 3, 4, 5, 6, 7, 8, 9, 10, 11, 12 ],
       angle = 0,
       numeralWidth = 0;

   numerals.forEach(function(numeral) {
      angle = Math.PI/6 * (numeral-3);
      numeralWidth = context.measureText(numeral).width;
      context.fillText(numeral,
         canvas.width/2  + Math.cos(angle)*(HAND_RADIUS) -
            numeralWidth/2,
         canvas.height/2 + Math.sin(angle)*(HAND_RADIUS) +
            FONT_HEIGHT/3);
   });
}
```

```
function drawCenter() {
    context.beginPath();
    context.arc(canvas.width/2, canvas.height/2, 5, 0, Math.PI*2, true);
    context.fill();
}

function drawHand(loc, isHour) {
    var angle = (Math.PI*2) * (loc/60) - Math.PI/2,
        handRadius = isHour ? RADIUS - HAND_TRUNCATION-HOUR_HAND_TRUNCATION
                            : RADIUS - HAND_TRUNCATION;

    context.moveTo(canvas.width/2, canvas.height/2);
    context.lineTo(canvas.width/2  + Math.cos(angle)*handRadius,
                    canvas.height/2 + Math.sin(angle)*handRadius);
    context.stroke();
}

function drawHands() {
    var date = new Date,
        hour = date.getHours();

    hour = hour > 12 ? hour - 12 : hour;

    drawHand(hour*5 + (date.getMinutes()/60)*5, true, 0.5);
    drawHand(date.getMinutes(), false, 0.5);
    drawHand(date.getSeconds(), false, 0.2);
}

function drawClock() {
    context.clearRect(0,0,canvas.width,canvas.height);

    drawCircle();
    drawCenter();
    drawHands();
    drawNumerals();
}

// Initialization.............................................

context.font = FONT_HEIGHT + 'px Arial';
loop = setInterval(drawClock, 1000);
```

---

**NOTE: A closer look at paths, stroking, and filling**

The clock example in this section gives you an overview of what it's like to draw into a canvas. In Chapter 2, we will take a closer look at drawing and manipulating shapes in a canvas.

## 1.6 Event Handling

HTML5 applications are event driven. You register event listeners with HTML elements and implement code that responds to those events. Nearly all Canvas-based applications handle either mouse or touch events—or both—and many applications also handle various events such as keystrokes and drag and drop.

### 1.6.1 Mouse Events

Detecting mouse events in a canvas is simple enough: You add an event listener to the canvas, and the browser invokes that listener when the event occurs. For example, you can listen to mouse down events, like this:

```
canvas.onmousedown = function (e) {
   // React to the mouse down event
};
```

Alternatively, you can use the more generic addEventListener() method:

```
canvas.addEventListener('mousedown', function (e) {
   // React to the mouse down event
});
```

In addition to onmousedown, you can also assign functions to onmousemove, onmouseup, onmouseover, and onmouseout.

Assigning a function to onmousedown, onmousemove, etc., is a little simpler than using addEventListener(); however, addEventListener() is necessary when you need to attach multiple listeners to a single mouse event.

#### 1.6.1.1 Translating Mouse Coordinates to Canvas Coordinates

The mouse coordinates in the event object that the browser passes to your event listener are *window* coordinates, instead of being relative to the canvas itself.

Most of the time you need to know where mouse events occur relative to the canvas, not the window, so you must convert the coordinates. For example, Figure 1.14 shows a canvas that displays an image known as a sprite sheet. Sprite sheets are a single image that contains several images for an animation. As an animation progresses, you display one image at a time from the sprite sheet, which means that you must know the exact coordinates of each image in the sprite sheet.

The application shown in Figure 1.14 lets you determine the location of each image in a sprite sheet by tracking and displaying mouse coordinates. As the user moves

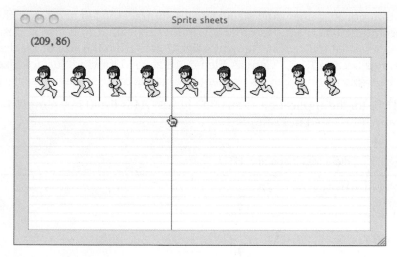

Figure 1.14  Sprite sheet inspector

the mouse, the application continuously updates the mouse coordinates above the sprite sheet and the guidelines.

The application adds a mousemove listener to the canvas, and subsequently, when the browser invokes that listener, the application converts the mouse coordinates from the window to the canvas, with a windowToCanvas() method, like this:

```
function windowToCanvas(canvas, x, y) {
    var bbox = canvas.getBoundingClientRect();

    return { x: x - bbox.left * (canvas.width  / bbox.width),
             y: y - bbox.top  * (canvas.height / bbox.height)
           };
}

canvas.onmousemove = function (e) {
    var loc = windowToCanvas(canvas, e.clientX, e.clientY);

    drawBackground();
    drawSpritesheet();
    drawGuidelines(loc.x, loc.y);
    updateReadout(loc.x, loc.y);
};
...
```

The windowToCanvas() method shown above invokes the canvas's getBoundingClientRect() method to obtain the canvas's bounding box relative to the window. The windowToCanvas() method then returns an object with x and y properties that correspond to the mouse location in the canvas.

Notice that not only does windowToCanvas() subtract the left and top of the canvas's bounding box from the x and y window coordinates, it also scales those coordinates when the canvas element's size differs from the size of the drawing surface. See Section 1.1.1, "Canvas Element Size vs. Drawing Surface Size," on p. 5 for an explanation of canvas element size versus canvas drawing surface size.

The HTML for the application shown in Figure 1.14 is listed in Example 1.5, and the JavaScript is listed in Example 1.6.

---

Example 1.5  A sprite sheet inspector: HTML

```html
<!DOCTYPE html>
  <head>
    <title>Sprite sheets</title>

    <style>
        body {
            background: #dddddd;
        }

        #canvas {
            position: absolute;
            left: 0px;
            top: 20px;
            margin: 20px;
            background: #ffffff;
            border: thin inset rgba(100,150,230,0.5);
            cursor: pointer;
        }

        #readout {
            margin-top: 10px;
            margin-left: 15px;
            color: blue;
        }
    </style>
  </head>

  <body>
    <div id='readout'></div>

    <canvas id='canvas' width='500' height='250'>
      Canvas not supported
    </canvas>

    <script src='example.js'></script>
  </body>
</html>
```

---

**Example 1.6** A sprite sheet inspector: JavaScript

```javascript
var canvas = document.getElementById('canvas'),
    readout = document.getElementById('readout'),
    context = canvas.getContext('2d'),
    spritesheet = new Image();

// Functions.......................................................

function windowToCanvas(canvas, x, y) {
   var bbox = canvas.getBoundingClientRect();
   return { x: x - bbox.left * (canvas.width  / bbox.width),
            y: y - bbox.top  * (canvas.height / bbox.height)
          };
}

function drawBackground() {
   var VERTICAL_LINE_SPACING = 12,
       i = context.canvas.height;

   context.clearRect(0,0,canvas.width,canvas.height);
   context.strokeStyle = 'lightgray';
   context.lineWidth = 0.5;

   while(i > VERTICAL_LINE_SPACING*4) {
      context.beginPath();
      context.moveTo(0, i);
      context.lineTo(context.canvas.width, i);
      context.stroke();
      i -= VERTICAL_LINE_SPACING;
   }
}

function drawSpritesheet() {
   context.drawImage(spritesheet, 0, 0);
}

function drawGuidelines(x, y) {
   context.strokeStyle = 'rgba(0,0,230,0.8)';
   context.lineWidth = 0.5;
   drawVerticalLine(x);
   drawHorizontalLine(y);
}

function updateReadout(x, y) {
   readout.innerText = '(' + x.toFixed(0) + ', ' + y.toFixed(0) + ')';
}
```

*(Continues)*

**Example 1.6** *(Continued)*

```javascript
function drawHorizontalLine (y) {
   context.beginPath();
   context.moveTo(0,y + 0.5);
   context.lineTo(context.canvas.width, y + 0.5);
   context.stroke();
}

function drawVerticalLine (x) {
   context.beginPath();
   context.moveTo(x + 0.5, 0);
   context.lineTo(x + 0.5, context.canvas.height);
   context.stroke();
}

// Event handlers.....................................................

canvas.onmousemove = function (e) {
   var loc = windowToCanvas(canvas, e.clientX, e.clientY);

   drawBackground();
   drawSpritesheet();
   drawGuidelines(loc.x, loc.y);
   updateReadout(loc.x, loc.y);
};

// Initialization....................................................

spritesheet.src = 'running-sprite-sheet.png';
spritesheet.onload = function(e) {
   drawSpritesheet();
};

drawBackground();
```

**TIP: x and y vs. clientX and clientY**

In pre-HTML5 days, obtaining window coordinates for mouse events from the event object that the browser passes to your event listeners was a mess. Some browsers stored those coordinates in x and y, and others stored them in clientX and clientY. Fortunately, modern browsers that support HTML5 have finally come to agreement, and they all support clientX and clientY. You can read more about those event properties at http://www.quirksmode.org/js/events_mouse.html.

**TIP: Tell the browser to butt out . . .**

When you listen to mouse events, the browser invokes your listener when the associated event occurs. After you handle the event, the browser also reacts to the event. Much of the time when you handle mouse events in a canvas, you don't want the browser to handle the event after you're done with it because you will end up with unwanted effects, such as the browser selecting other HTML elements or changing the cursor.

Fortunately, the event object comes with a preventDefault() method that, as its name suggests, prevents the browser from carrying out its default reaction to the event. Just invoke that method from your event handler, and the browser will no longer interfere with your event handling.

**NOTE: The Canvas context's drawImage() method**

The example shown in Figure 1.14 uses the 2d context's drawImage() method to draw the sprite sheet. That single method lets you copy all or part of an image stored in one place to another place, and if you wish, you can scale the image along the way.

The sprite sheet application uses drawImage() in the simplest possible way: The application draws all of an image, unscaled, that is stored in an Image object, into the application's canvas. In the Chapter 4 and throughout the rest of this book, you will see more advanced uses for drawImage().

## 1.6.2 Keyboard Events

When you press a key in a browser window, the browser generates key events. Those events are targeted at the HTML element that currently has focus. If no element has focus, key events bubble up to the window and document objects.

The canvas element is not a focusable element, and therefore in light of the preceding paragraph, adding key listeners to a canvas is an exercise in futility. Instead, you will add key listeners to either the document or window objects to detect key events.

There are three types of key events:

- keydown
- keypress
- keyup

The keydown and keyup events are low-level events that the browser fires for nearly every keystroke. Note that some keystrokes, such as command sequences, may be *swallowed* by the browser or the operating system; however, most keystrokes make it through to your keydown and keyup event handlers, including keys such as Alt, Esc, and so on.

When a keydown event generates a printable character, the browser fires a keypress event before the inevitable keyup event. If you hold a key that generates a printable character down for an extended period of time, the browser will fire a sequence of keypress events between the keydown and keyup events.

Implementing key listeners is similar to implementing mouse listeners. You can assign a function to the document or window object's onkeydown, onkeyup, or onkeypress variables, or you can call addEventListener(), with keydown, keyup, or keypress for the first argument, and a reference to a function for the second argument.

Determining which key was pressed can be complicated, for two reasons. First, there is a huge variety of characters among all the languages of the world. When you must take into consideration the Latin alphabet, Asian ideographic characters, and the many languages of India, just to mention a few, supporting them all is mind boggling.

Second, although browsers and keyboards have been around for a long time, key codes have never been standardized until DOM Level 3, which few browsers currently support. In a word, detecting exactly what key or combination of keys has been pressed is a mess.

However, under most circumstances you can get by with the following two simple strategies:

- For keydown and keyup events, look at the keyCode property of the event object that the browser passes to your event listener. In general, for printable characters, those values will be ASCII codes. Notice the *in general* caveat, however. Here is a good website that you can consult for interpreting key codes among different browsers: http://bit.ly/o3b1L2. Event objects for key events also contain the following boolean properties:

  - altKey
  - ctrlKey
  - metaKey
  - shiftKey

- For keypress events—which browsers fire only for printable characters—you can reliably get that character like this:

```
var key = String.fromCharCode(event.which);
```

In general, unless you are implementing a text control in a canvas, you will handle mouse events much more often than you handle key events. One other common use case for key events, however, is handling keystrokes in games. We discuss that topic in Chapter 9.

### 1.6.3 Touch Events

With the advent of smart phones and tablet computers, the HTML specification has added support for touch events. See Chapter 11 for more information about handling touch events.

## 1.7 Saving and Restoring the Drawing Surface

In Section 1.2.2, "Saving and Restoring Canvas State," on p. 11, you saw how to save and restore a context's state. Saving and restoring context state lets you make temporary state changes, which is something you will do frequently.

Another essential feature of the Canvas context is the ability to save and restore the drawing surface itself. Saving and restoring the drawing surface lets you draw on the drawing surface temporarily, which is useful for many things, such as rubber bands, guidewires, or annotations. For example, the application shown in Figure 1.15 and discussed in Section 2.13.1, "Translating, Scaling, and Rotating," on p. 171, lets users interactively create polygons by dragging the mouse.

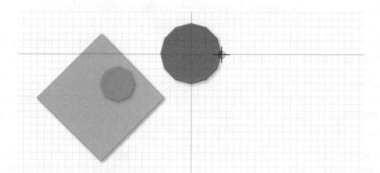

Figure 1.15 Drawing guidewires

On a mouse down event, the application saves the drawing surface. As the user subsequently drags the mouse, the application continuously restores the drawing surface to what it was when the mouse went down and then draws the polygon and the associated guidewires. When the user releases the mouse, the application restores the drawing surface one last time and draws a final representation of the polygon, without guidewires.

The JavaScript from the application shown in Figure 1.15 that pertains to drawing the guidewires is listed in Example 1.7. See Section 2.11.1, "Polygon Objects," on p. 147 for a more complete listing of the application.

**NOTE: Image manipulation with `getImageData()` and `putImageData()`**

The application shown in Figure 1.15 saves and restores the drawing surface with the context's `getImageData()` and `putImageData()` methods. Like `drawImage()`, `getImageData()` and `putImageData()` can be used in a number of different ways; one common use is implementing image filters that get an image's data, manipulate it, and put it back into a canvas. You will see how to implement image filters in Section 4.5.2.3, "Filtering Images," on p. 293, among other uses for `getImageData()` and `putImageData()`.

**NOTE: Immediate-mode graphics**

Canvas implements what's known as *immediate-mode graphics*, meaning that it immediately draws whatever you specify in the canvas. Then it immediately forgets what you have just drawn, meaning that canvases do not retain a list of objects to draw. Some graphics systems, such as SVG, do maintain a list of objects to draw. Those graphics systems are referred to as retained-mode graphics.

Immediate-mode graphics, because it does not maintain a list of objects to draw, is more low-level than retained-mode graphics. Immediate-mode graphics is also more flexible because you draw straight to the screen instead of adjusting objects that the graphics system draws for you.

Immediate-mode graphics is more suited to applications, such as paint applications, that do not keep track of what the user has drawn, whereas retained-mode graphics is more suited to applications, such as drawing applications, that let you manipulate graphical objects that you create.

In Section 2.11.1, "Polygon Objects," on p. 147 you will see how to implement a simple retained-mode graphics system that maintains an array of polygons in a drawing application, which lets users drag those polygons to reposition them.

**Example 1.7** Drawing guidewires by saving and restoring the drawing surface

```javascript
var canvas = document.getElementById('canvas'),
    context = canvas.getContext('2d'),
    ...

// Save and restore drawing surface................................

function saveDrawingSurface() {
   drawingSurfaceImageData = context.getImageData(0, 0,
                                    canvas.width,
                                    canvas.height);
}

function restoreDrawingSurface() {
   context.putImageData(drawingSurfaceImageData, 0, 0);
}

// Event handlers.................................................

canvas.onmousedown = function (e) {
   ...
   saveDrawingSurface();
   ...
};

canvas.onmousemove = function (e) {
   var loc = windowToCanvas(e);

   if (dragging) {
      restoreDrawingSurface();
      ...

      if (guidewires) {
        drawGuidewires(mousedown.x, mousedown.y);
      }
   }
};

canvas.onmouseup = function (e) {
   ...
   restoreDrawingSurface();
};
```

## 1.8  Using HTML Elements in a Canvas

Canvas is arguably the coolest feature of HTML5, but when you use it to implement web applications, you will rarely use it alone. Most of the time you will combine one or more canvases with other HTML controls so that your users can provide input or otherwise control the application.

To combine other HTML controls with your canvases, you may first be inclined to embed those controls inside your canvas elements, but that won't work, because anything you put in the body of a canvas element is displayed by the browser only if the browser does not support the canvas element.

Because browsers will display either a canvas element or HTML controls that you put inside that element, but not both, you must place your controls outside of your canvas elements.

To make it appear as though HTML controls are inside a canvas, you can use CSS to place the controls above the canvas. The application shown in Figure 1.16 illustrates that effect.

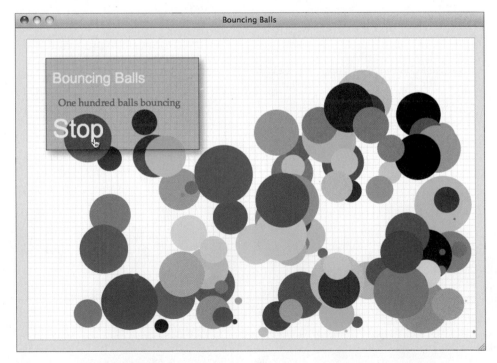

Figure 1.16  HTML elements above a canvas

The application shown in Figure 1.16 animates 100 balls and provides a link to start and stop the animation. That link resides in a DIV element that is partially transparent and floats above the canvas. We refer to that DIV as a *glass pane* because it appears to be a pane of glass floating above the canvas.

The HTML for the application shown in Figure 1.16 is listed in Example 1.8.

**Example 1.8** HTML controls in a canvas: HTML

```html
<!DOCTYPE html>
<html>
   <head>
      <title>Bouncing Balls</title>

      <style>
         body {
            background: #dddddd;
         }

         #canvas {
            margin-left: 10px;
            margin-top: 10px;
            background: #ffffff;
            border: thin solid #aaaaaa;
         }

         #glasspane {
            position: absolute;
            left: 50px;
            top: 50px;
            padding: 0px 20px 10px 10px;
            background: rgba(0, 0, 0, 0.3);
            border: thin solid rgba(0, 0, 0, 0.6);
            color: #eeeeee;
            font-family: Droid Sans, Arial, Helvetica, sans-serif;
            font-size: 12px;
            cursor: pointer;
            -webkit-box-shadow: rgba(0,0,0,0.5) 5px 5px 20px;
            -moz-box-shadow: rgba(0,0,0,0.5) 5px 5px 20px;
            box-shadow: rgba(0,0,0,0.5) 5px 5px 20px;
         }

         #glasspane h2 {
            font-weight: normal;
         }
```

*(Continues)*

**Example 1.8** *(Continued)*

```css
        #glasspane .title {
            font-size: 2em;
            color: rgba(255, 255, 0, 0.8);
        }

        #glasspane a:hover {
            color: yellow;
        }

        #glasspane a {
            text-decoration: none;
            color: #cccccc;
            font-size: 3.5em;
        }

        #glasspane p {
            margin: 10px;
            color: rgba(65, 65, 220, 1.0);
            font-size: 12pt;
            font-family: Palatino, Arial, Helvetica, sans-serif;
        }
    </style>
</head>

<body>
    <div id='glasspane'>
        <h2 class='title'>Bouncing Balls</h2>

        <p>One hundred balls bouncing</p>

        <a id='startButton'>Start</a>
    </div>

    <canvas id='canvas' width='750' height='500'>
        Canvas not supported
    </canvas>

    <script src='example.js'></script>
</body>
</html>
```

The HTML shown in Example 1.8 uses CSS absolute positioning to make the glass pane appear above the canvas, like this:

```
#canvas {
    margin-left: 10px;
    margin-top: 10px;
    background: #ffffff;
    border: thin solid #aaaaaa;
}

#glasspane {
    position: absolute;
    left: 50px;
    top: 50px;
    ...
}
```

The preceding CSS uses *relative* positioning for the canvas, which is the default for the position CSS property, whereas it specifies *absolute* positioning for the glass pane. The CSS specification states that elements with absolute positioning are drawn on top of elements with relative positioning, which is why the glass pane appears above the canvas in Figure 1.16.

If you also change the canvas's positioning to absolute, then the canvas will appear on top of the glass pane, and you won't see the glass pane because the canvas's background is not transparent. In that case, the glass pane is underneath the canvas because the canvas element comes after the glass pane's DIV element. If you switch the order of those elements, then the glass pane will once again appear above the canvas.

So, you have two options to position the glass pane above the canvas: Use relative positioning for the canvas and absolute positioning for the glass pane; or use either relative or absolute positioning for both elements and declare the glass pane's DIV after the canvas element.

A third option is to use either relative or absolute positioning for both elements and manipulate their z-index CSS property. The browser draws elements with a higher z-index above elements with a lower z-index.

In addition to placing HTML controls where you want them to appear, you also need to obtain references to those elements in your JavaScript so that you can access and manipulate their values.

The application shown in Figure 1.16 obtains references to the glass pane and the button that controls the animation and adds event handlers to them, like this:

```
var context = document.getElementById('canvas').getContext('2d'),
    startButton = document.getElementById('startButton'),
    glasspane = document.getElementById('glasspane'),
    paused = false,
    ...

startButton.onclick = function(e) {
   e.preventDefault();
   paused = ! paused;
   startButton.innerText = paused ? 'Start' : 'Stop';
};
...

glasspane.onmousedown = function(e) {
   e.preventDefault();
};
```

The preceding JavaScript adds an onclick handler to the button that starts or pauses the animation based on the current state of the application, and adds an onmousedown event handler to the glass pane to prevent the browser from its default reaction to that mouse click. The onmousedown handler prevents the browser from reacting to the event to avoid inadvertent selections.

---

 **NOTE: You can implement your own Canvas-based controls**

The Canvas specification states that you should prefer built-in HTML controls rather than implementing controls from scratch with the Canvas API, which in general is good advice. Implementing controls from scratch with the Canvas API generally involves a good deal of work, and most of the time it's wise to avoid a good deal of work when there's an easier alternative.

However, in some circumstances it makes sense to implement Canvas-based controls. In Chapter 10, will see both motivations for implementing your own Canvas-based controls and ways to do so.

---

 **NOTE: Drawing a grid**

The application discussed in this section draws a grid underneath the bouncing balls to emphasize that the floating DIV is indeed floating above the canvas.

In Chapter 2, we discuss how to draw a grid, but for now you can safely forge ahead without knowing grid drawing details.

---

## 1.8.1 Invisible HTML Elements

In the preceding section you saw how to combine static HTML controls with a canvas. In this section we explore a more advanced use of HTML controls that involves dynamically modifying the size of a DIV as the user drags the mouse.

Figure 1.17 shows an application that uses a technique known as rubberbanding to select a region of a canvas. That canvas initially displays an image, and when you select a region of that image, the application reacts by zooming into the region that you selected.

Figure 1.17  Implementing rubber bands with a DIV

First, let's take a look at the HTML for the application, which is listed in Example 1.9.

**Example 1.9** Rubber band with a floating DIV

```html
<!DOCTYPE html>
<html>
   <head>
      <title>Rubber bands with layered elements</title>

      <style>
         body {
            background: rgba(100, 145, 250, 0.3);
         }

         #canvas {
            margin-left: 20px;
            margin-right: 0;
            margin-bottom: 20px;
            border: thin solid #aaaaaa;
            cursor: crosshair;
            padding: 0;
         }

         #controls {
            margin: 20px 0px 20px 20px;
         }

         #rubberbandDiv {
            position: absolute;
            border: 3px solid blue;
            cursor: crosshair;
            display: none;
         }

      </style>
   </head>

  <body>
      <div id='controls'>
         <input type='button' id='resetButton' value='Reset'/>
      </div>

      <div id='rubberbandDiv'></div>

      <canvas id='canvas' width='800' height='520'>
         Canvas not supported
      </canvas>

    <script src='example.js'></script>
  </body>
</html>
```

The HTML uses a DIV that contains a button. If you click that button, the application draws the entire image as it is displayed when the application starts.

The application uses a second DIV for the rubber band. That DIV is empty, and its CSS display attribute is set to none, which makes it initially invisible. When you start dragging the mouse, the application makes that second DIV visible, which shows the DIV's border. As you continue dragging the mouse, the application continuously resizes the DIV to produce the illusion of a rubber band, as shown in Figure 1.17.

The JavaScript for the application shown in Figure 1.17 is listed in Example 1.10.

**Example 1.10** Rubber bands with a DIV

```javascript
var canvas = document.getElementById('canvas'),
    context = canvas.getContext('2d'),
    rubberbandDiv = document.getElementById('rubberbandDiv'),
    resetButton = document.getElementById('resetButton'),
    image = new Image(),
    mousedown = {},
    rubberbandRectangle = {},
    dragging = false;

// Functions.................................................

function rubberbandStart(x, y) {
    mousedown.x = x;
    mousedown.y = y;

    rubberbandRectangle.left = mousedown.x;
    rubberbandRectangle.top = mousedown.y;

    moveRubberbandDiv();
    showRubberbandDiv();

    dragging = true;
}

function rubberbandStretch(x, y) {
    rubberbandRectangle.left = x < mousedown.x ? x : mousedown.x;
    rubberbandRectangle.top  = y < mousedown.y ? y : mousedown.y;

    rubberbandRectangle.width  = Math.abs(x - mousedown.x),
    rubberbandRectangle.height = Math.abs(y - mousedown.y);

    moveRubberbandDiv();
    resizeRubberbandDiv();
}
```

*(Continues)*

**Example 1.10** *(Continued)*

```
function rubberbandEnd() {
   var bbox = canvas.getBoundingClientRect();

   try {
      context.drawImage(canvas,
                        rubberbandRectangle.left - bbox.left,
                        rubberbandRectangle.top - bbox.top,
                        rubberbandRectangle.width,
                        rubberbandRectangle.height,
                        0, 0, canvas.width, canvas.height);
   }
   catch (e) {
      // Suppress error message when mouse is released
      // outside the canvas
   }

   resetRubberbandRectangle();

   rubberbandDiv.style.width = 0;
   rubberbandDiv.style.height = 0;

   hideRubberbandDiv();

   dragging = false;
}

function moveRubberbandDiv() {
   rubberbandDiv.style.top  = rubberbandRectangle.top  + 'px';
   rubberbandDiv.style.left = rubberbandRectangle.left + 'px';
}

function resizeRubberbandDiv() {
   rubberbandDiv.style.width  = rubberbandRectangle.width  + 'px';
   rubberbandDiv.style.height = rubberbandRectangle.height + 'px';
}

function showRubberbandDiv() {
   rubberbandDiv.style.display = 'inline';
}

function hideRubberbandDiv() {
   rubberbandDiv.style.display = 'none';
}

function resetRubberbandRectangle() {
   rubberbandRectangle = { top: 0, left: 0, width: 0, height: 0 };
}
```

```
// Event handlers.................................................

canvas.onmousedown = function (e) {
   var x = e.clientX,
       y = e.clientY;

   e.preventDefault();
   rubberbandStart(x, y);
};

window.onmousemove = function (e) {
   var x = e.clientX,
       y = e.clientY;

   e.preventDefault();
   if (dragging) {
      rubberbandStretch(x, y);
   }
};

window.onmouseup = function (e) {
   e.preventDefault();
   rubberbandEnd();
};

image.onload = function () {
   context.drawImage(image, 0, 0, canvas.width, canvas.height);
};

resetButton.onclick = function(e) {
   context.clearRect(0, 0, context.canvas.width,
                          context.canvas.height);
   context.drawImage(image, 0, 0, canvas.width, canvas.height);
};

// Initialization..................................................

image.src = 'curved-road.png';
```

Again, we're getting ahead of ourselves a little bit by using the drawImage() method to both draw and zoom in on the image. In Section 4.1, "Drawing Images," on p. 254, we will look closely at that method, and we will also see an alternative way to implement rubber bands that involves manipulating the image's pixels to draw the rubber band itself.

For now, however, our focus is on the rubberband DIV and how the code manipulates that DIV as the user drags the mouse.

The onmousedown event handler for the canvas invokes the rubberbandStart() method, which moves the DIV's upper left-hand corner to the mouse down location and makes the DIV visible. Because the rubberband DIV's CSS position attribute is absolute, the coordinates for the DIV's upper left-hand corner must be specified in window coordinates, and not as coordinates relative to the canvas.

If the user is dragging the mouse, the onmousemove event handler invokes rubberbandStretch(), which moves and resizes the rubberband DIV.

When the user releases the mouse, the onmouseup event handler invokes rubberbandEnd(), which draws the scaled image and shrinks and hides the rubberband DIV.

Finally, notice that all three mouse event handlers invoke preventDefault() on the event object they are passed. As discussed in Section 1.6.1.1, "Translating Mouse Coordinates to Canvas Coordinates," on p. 26, that call prevents the browser from reacting to the mouse events. If you remove those calls to preventDefault(), the browser will try to select elements on the page, which produces undesired effects if the user drags the mouse outside of the canvas.

## 1.9  Printing a Canvas

It's often convenient to let users of your application access a canvas as an image. For example, if you implement a paint application, such as the one discussed in Chapter 2, users will expect to be able to print their paintings.

By default, although every canvas is a bitmap, it is not an HTML img element, and therefore users cannot, for example, right-click a canvas and save it to disk, nor can they drag a canvas to their desktop to print later on. The fact that a canvas is not an image is illustrated by the popup menu shown in Figure 1.18.

Fortunately, the Canvas API provides a method—toDataURL()—that returns a reference to a data URL for a given canvas. You can subsequently set the src attribute of an img element equal to that data URL to create an image of your canvas.

In Section 1.5, "Fundamental Drawing Operations," on p. 22, you saw how to implement an analog clock with the Canvas API. Figure 1.19 shows a modified version of that application that lets you take a snapshot of the clock and display it as an image, as described above. As you can see from Figure 1.19, when you right-click on the ensuing image, you can save the image to disk, and because the clock image shown in the bottom screenshot is an img element, you can also drag the image to your desktop.

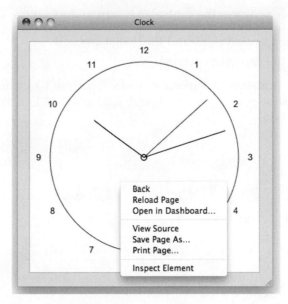

Figure 1.18 The right-click menu for a canvas

The application shown in **Figure 1.19** implements a common use case for printing a canvas: It provides a control—in this case, the Take snapshot button—that lets users take a snapshot of the canvas. The application displays that snapshot as an image, so users can right-click the image and save it to disk. Subsequently, when the user clicks the Return to Canvas button, the application replaces the image with the original canvas. Here's a recipe for that use case:

In your HTML page:

• Add an invisible image to the page, and give the image an id, but no src.
• Use CSS to position and size the image to exactly overlap your canvas.
• Add a control to the page for taking a snapshot.

In your JavaScript:

• Get a reference to the invisible image.
• Get a reference to the snapshot control.
• When the user activates the control to take a snapshot:

    1. Invoke toDataURL() to get a data URL.
    2. Assign the data URL to the invisible image's src attribute.
    3. Make the image visible and the canvas invisible.

- When the user activates the control to return to the Canvas:

    1.  Make the canvas visible and the image invisible.
    2.  Redraw the canvas as needed.

Let's see how to translate that recipe to code. Example 1.11 lists the HTML for the application shown in Figure 1.19, and Example 1.12 lists the application's JavaScript.

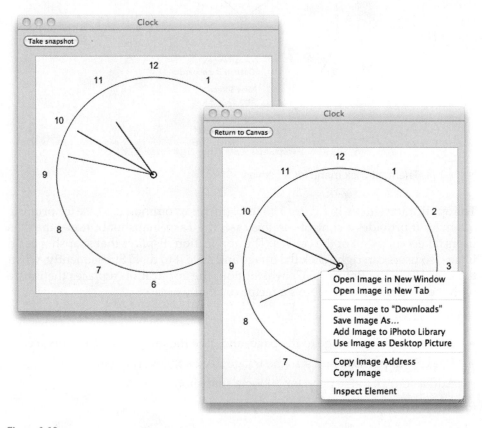

Figure 1.19 Using toDataURL()

**Example 1.11** Using `toDataURL()` to print a canvas: HTML

```html
<!DOCTYPE html>
  <head>
    <title>Clock</title>

    <style>
      body {
        background: #dddddd;
      }

      #canvas {
        position: absolute;
        left: 10px;
        top: 1.5em;
        margin: 20px;
        border: thin solid #aaaaaa;
      }

      #snapshotImageElement {
        position: absolute;
        left: 10px;
        top: 1.5em;
        margin: 20px;
        border: thin solid #aaaaaa;
      }
    </style>
  </head>

<body>
  <div id='controls'>
    <input id='snapshotButton' type='button' value='Take snapshot'/>
  </div>

  <img id='snapshotImageElement'/>

  <canvas id='canvas' width='400' height='400'>
    Canvas not supported
  </canvas>

  <script src='example.js'></script>
</body>
</html>
```

**Example 1.12** Using `toDataURL()` to print a canvas: JavaScript

```javascript
var canvas = document.getElementById('canvas'),
    context = canvas.getContext('2d'),
    snapshotButton = document.getElementById('snapshotButton'),
    snapshotImageElement =
        document.getElementById('snapshotImageElement'),
    loop;

// Clock drawing functions are omitted from this listing
// in the interests of brevity. See Example 1.4 on p. 24
// for a complete listing of those methods.

// Event handlers...................................................

snapshotButton.onclick = function (e) {
   var dataUrl;

   if (snapshotButton.value === 'Take snapshot') {
      dataUrl = canvas.toDataURL();
      clearInterval(loop);
      snapshotImageElement.src = dataUrl;
      snapshotImageElement.style.display = 'inline';
      canvas.style.display = 'none';
      snapshotButton.value = 'Return to Canvas';
   }
   else {
      canvas.style.display = 'inline';
      snapshotImageElement.style.display = 'none';
      loop = setInterval(drawClock, 1000);
      snapshotButton.value = 'Take snapshot';
   }
};

// Initialization...............................................

context.font = FONT_HEIGHT + 'px Arial';
loop = setInterval(drawClock, 1000);
```

The application accesses the `canvas` and `img` elements and uses CSS absolute positioning to overlap the two elements. When the user clicks the Take snapshot button, the application obtains a data URL from the canvas and assigns it to the `src` attribute of the image. Then it shows the image, hides the canvas, and sets the text of the button to Return to Canvas.

When the user clicks the Return to Canvas button, the application hides the image, displays the canvas, and returns the text of the button to Take snapshot.

**NOTE: Canvas blobs**

As this book was being written, the Canvas specification added a `toBlob()` method, so you can, among other things, save a canvas as a file. When the book went to press, no browsers supported that method.

## 1.10  Offscreen Canvases

Another essential Canvas feature is the ability to create and manipulate offscreen canvases. For example, you can, in most cases, considerably boost your performance by storing backgrounds in one or more offscreen canvases and copying parts of those offscreen canvases onscreen.

Another use case for offscreen canvases is the clock that we discussed in the preceding section. Although that application shows you how to implement a general solution that requires user interaction to switch from canvas to image, a clock is a better candidate for an application that does that switching behind the scenes without user intervention.

An updated version of the clock application is shown in Figure 1.20. Once a second, the application draws the clock into the offscreen canvas and assigns the

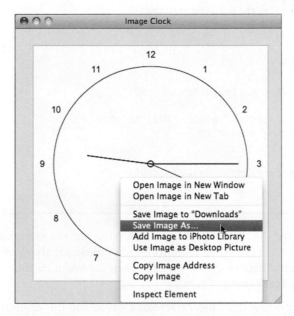

Figure 1.20  Using an offscreen canvas for an image clock

canvas's data URL to the `src` attribute of an image. The result is an animated image that reflects the offscreen canvas. See Section 1.9, "Printing a Canvas," on p. 46 for more information on canvas data URLs.

The HTML for the application shown in Figure 1.20 is listed in Example 1.13.

---

**Example 1.13** An image clock: HTML

---

```html
<!DOCTYPE html>
   <head>
      <title>Image Clock</title>

      <style>
         body {
            background: #dddddd;
         }

         #canvas {
            display: none;
         }

         #snapshotImageElement {
            position: absolute;
            left: 10px;
            margin: 20px;
            border: thin solid #aaaaaa;
         }
      </style>
   </head>

   <body>
      <img id='snapshotImageElement'/>

      <canvas id='canvas' width='400' height='400'>
         Canvas not supported
      </canvas>

      <script src='example.js'></script>
   </body>
</html>
```

---

Notice the CSS for the canvas in the HTML—the canvas is invisible because its `display` attribute is set to none. That invisibility makes it an *offscreen* canvas. You can also programmatically create an offscreen canvas, like this: `var offscreen = document.createElement('canvas');`.

The JavaScript pertinent to the offscreen canvas for the application shown in Figure 1.20 is listed in Example 1.14.

---

**Example 1.14** The image clock: JavaScript (excerpt)

---

```
// Some declarations and functions omitted for brevity.
// See Section 1.9 on p. 46 for a complete listing of
// the clock.

var canvas = document.getElementById('canvas'),
    context = canvas.getContext('2d'),
    ...

// Functions.......................................................

function updateClockImage() {
    snapshotImageElement.src = canvas.toDataURL();
}

function drawClock() {
    context.clearRect(0, 0, canvas.width, canvas.height);

    context.save();

    context.fillStyle = 'rgba(255,255,255,0.8)';
    context.fillRect(0, 0, canvas.width, canvas.height);

    drawCircle();
    drawCenter();
    drawHands();

    context.restore();

    drawNumerals();

    updateClockImage();
}
...
```

---

## 1.11  A Brief Math Primer

To do anything interesting with Canvas, you need a good understanding of basic mathematics, especially working with algebraic equations, trigonometry, and vectors. It also helps, for more complex applications like video games, to be able to derive equations, given units of measure.

Feel free to skim this section if you're comfortable with basic algebra and trigonometry and you can make your way to pixels/frame given pixels/second and milliseconds/frame. Otherwise, spending time in this section will prove fruitful throughout the rest of this book.

Let's get started with solving algebraic equations and trigonometry, and then we'll look at vectors and deriving equations from units of measure.

## 1.11.1  Solving Algebraic Equations

For any algebraic equation, such as $(10x + 5) \times 2 = 110$, you can do the following, and the equation will still be true:

- Add any real number to both sides
- Subtract any real number from both sides
- Multiply any real number by both sides
- Divide both sides by any real number
- Multiply or divide one or both sides by 1

For example, for $(10x + 5) \times 2 = 110$, you can solve the equation by dividing both sides by 2, to get: $10x + 5 = 55$; then you can subtract 5 from both sides to get: $10x = 50$; and finally, you can solve for $x$ by dividing both sides by 10: $x = 5$.

The last rule above may seem rather odd. Why would you want to multiply or divide one or both sides of an equation by 1? In Section 1.11.4, "Deriving Equations from Units of Measure," on p. 62, where we derive equations from units of measure, we will find a good use for that simple rule.

## 1.11.2  Trigonometry

Even the simplest uses of Canvas require a rudimentary understanding of trigonometry; for example, in the next chapter you will see how to draw polygons, which requires an understanding of sine and cosine. Let's begin with a short discussion of angles, followed by a look at right triangles.

### 1.11.2.1  Angles: Degrees and Radians

All the functions in the Canvas API that deal with angles require you to specify angles in radians. The same is true for the JavaScript functions `Math.sin()`, `Math.cos()`, and `Math.tan()`. Most people think of angles in terms of degrees, so you need to know how to convert from degrees to radians.

180 degrees is equal to $\pi$ radians. To convert from degrees to radians, you can create an algebraic equation for that relationship, as shown in Equation 1.1.

$$180 \text{ degrees} = \pi \text{ radians}$$

Equation 1.1  Degrees and radians

Solving Equation 1.1 for radians, and then degrees, results in Equations 1.2 and 1.3.

$$radians = (\pi \ / \ 180) \times degrees$$

Equation 1.2  Degrees to radians

$$degrees = (180 \ / \ \pi) \times radians$$

Equation 1.3  Radians to degrees

$\pi$ is roughly equal to 3.14, so, for example, 45 degrees is equal to (3.14 / 180) × 45 radians, which works out to 0.7853.

### 1.11.2.2  Sine, Cosine, and Tangent

To make effective use of Canvas, you must have a basic understanding of sin, cos, and tan, so if you're not already familiar with Figure 1.21, you should commit it to memory.

$$cos(\theta) = adjacent \ / \ hypotenuse$$
$$sin(\theta) = opposite \ / \ hypotenuse$$
$$tan(\theta) = opposite \ / \ adjacent$$

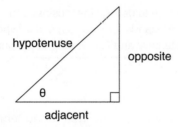

Figure 1.21  Sine, cosine, and tangent

You can also think of sine and cosine in terms of the X and Y coordinates of a circle, as illustrated in Figure 1.22.

Given the radius of a circle and a counterclockwise angle from 0 degrees, you can calculate the corresponding X and Y coordinates on the circumference of the circle by multiplying the radius times the cosine of the angle, and multiplying the radius by the sine of the angle, respectively.

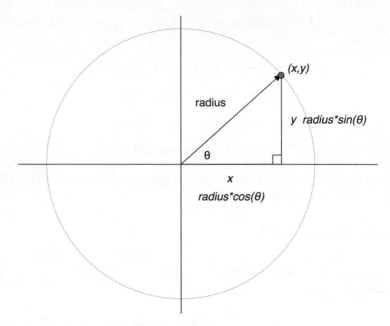

Figure 1.22  Radius, x, and y

 **NOTE: Soak a toe, ah!**
One of many ways to remember how to derive sine, cosine, and tangent from a
right triangle: SOHCAHTOA. SOH stands for sine, opposite, hypotenuse; CAH
stands for cosine, adjacent, hypotenuse; and TOA is tangent, opposite, adjacent.

## 1.11.3  Vectors

The two-dimensional vectors that we use in this book encapsulate two
values: direction and magnitude; they are used to express all sorts of physical
characteristics, such as forces and motion.

In Chapter 8, "Collision Detection," we make extensive use of vectors, so in this
section we discuss the fundamentals of vector mathematics. If you're not interested
in implementing collision detection, you can safely skip this section.

Near the end of Chapter 8 we explore how to react to a collision between two
polygons by bouncing one polygon off another, as illustrated in Figure 1.23.

In Figure 1.23, the top polygon is moving toward the bottom polygon, and the
two polygons are about to collide. The top polygon's incoming velocity and
outgoing velocity are both modeled with vectors. The edge of the bottom

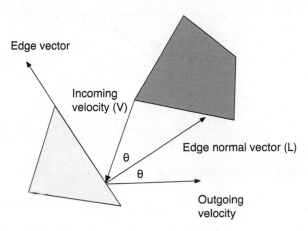

**Figure 1.23** Using vectors to bounce one polygon off another

polygon with which the top polygon is about to collide is also modeled as a vector, known as a edge vector.

Feel free to skip ahead to Chapter 8 if you can't wait to find out how to calculate the outgoing velocity, given the incoming velocity and two points on the edge of the bottom polygon. If you're not familiar with basic vector math, however, you might want to read through this section before moving to Chapter 8.

### 1.11.3.1 Vector Magnitude

Although two-dimensional vectors model two quantities—magnitude and direction—it's often useful to calculate one or the other, given a vector. You can use the Pythagorean theorem, which you may recall from math class in school (or alternatively, from the movie the Wizard of Oz), to calculate a vector's magnitude, as illustrated in Figure 1.24.

The Pythagorean theorem states that the hypotenuse of any right triangle is equal to the square root of the squares of the other two sides, which is a lot easier to understand if you look at Figure 1.24. The corresponding JavaScript looks like this:

```
var vectorMagnitude = Math.sqrt(Math.pow(vector.x, 2) +
                                Math.pow(vector.y, 2));
```

The preceding snippet of JavaScript shows how to calculate the magnitude of a vector referenced by a variable named vector.

Now that you know how to calculate a vector's magnitude, let's look at how you can calculate a vector's other quantity, direction.

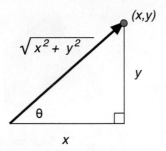

Figure 1.24  Calculating a vector's magnitude

### 1.11.3.2  Unit Vectors

Vector math often requires what's known as a unit vector. Unit vectors, which indicate direction only, are illustrated in Figure 1.25.

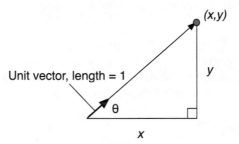

Figure 1.25  A unit vector

Unit vectors are so named because their magnitude is always 1 unit. To calculate a unit vector given a vector with an arbitrary magnitude, you need to strip away the magnitude, leaving behind only the direction. Here's how you do that in JavaScript:

```
var vectorMagnitude = Math.sqrt(Math.pow(vector.x, 2) +
                              Math.pow(vector.y, 2)),
    unitVector = new Vector();

    unitVector.x = vector.x / vectorMagnitude;
    unitVector.y = vector.y / vectorMagnitude;
```

The preceding code listing, given a vector named `vector`, first calculates the magnitude of the vector as you saw in the preceding section. The code then creates a new vector—see Chapter 8 for a listing of a `Vector` object—and sets that unit vector's X and Y values to the corresponding values of the original vector, divided by the vector's magnitude.

Now that you've seen how to calculate the two components of any two-dimensional vector, let's see how you combine vectors.

### 1.11.3.3  Adding and Subtracting Vectors

It's often useful to add or subtract vectors. For example, if you have two forces acting on a body, you can sum two vectors representing those forces together to calculate a single force. Likewise, subtracting one positional vector from another yields the edge between the two vectors.

Figure 1.26 shows how to add vectors, given two vectors named A and B.

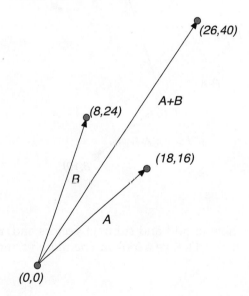

Figure 1.26  Adding vectors

Adding vectors is simple: You just add the components of the vector together, as shown in the following code listing:

```
var vectorSum = new Vector();

vectorSum.x = vectorOne.x + vectorTwo.x;
vectorSum.y = vectorOne.y + vectorTwo.y;
```

Subtracting vectors is also simple: you subtract the components of the vector, as shown in the following code listing:

```
var vectorSubtraction = new Vector();

vectorSubtraction.x = vectorOne.x - vectorTwo.x;
vectorSubtraction.y = vectorOne.y - vectorTwo.y;
```

Figure 1.27 shows how subtracting one vector from another yields a third vector whose direction is coincident with the edge between the two vectors. In Figure 1.27, the vectors A-B and B-A are parallel to each other and are also parallel to the edge vector between vectors A and B.

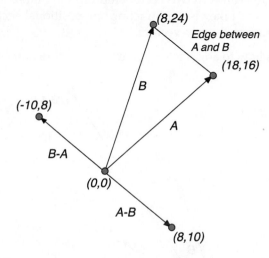

Figure 1.27 Subtracting vectors

Now that you know how to add and subtract vectors and, more importantly, what it means to do that, let's take a look at one more vector quantity: the dot product.

### 1.11.3.4 The Dot Product of Two Vectors

To calculate the dot product of two vectors you multiply the components of each vector by each other, and sum the values. Here is how you calculate the dot product for two two-dimensional vectors:

```
var dotProduct = vectorOne.x * vectorTwo.x + vectorOne.y * vectorTwo.y;
```

Calculating the dot product between two vectors is easy; however, understanding what a dot product means is not so intuitive. First, notice that unlike the result of adding or subtracting two vectors, the dot product is not a vector—it's what engineers refer to as a *scalar*, which means that it's simply a number. To understand what that number means, study Figure 1.28.

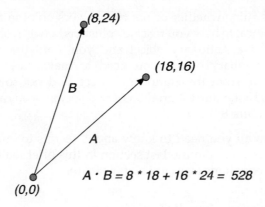

Figure 1.28 A positive dot product

The dot product of the two vectors in Figure 1.28 is 528. The significance of that number, however, is not so much its magnitude but the fact that it's greater than zero. That means that the two vectors point in roughly the same direction.

Now look at Figure 1.29, where the dot product of the two vectors is –528. Because that value is less than zero, we can surmise that the two vectors point in roughly different directions.

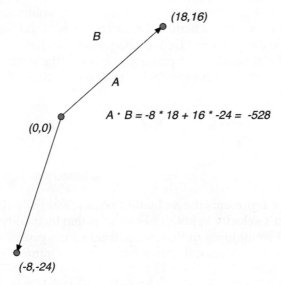

Figure 1.29 A negative dot product

The ability to determine whether or not two vectors point in roughly the same direction can be critical to how you react to collisions between objects. If a moving object collides with a stationary object and you want the moving object to bounce off the stationary object, you need to make sure that the moving object bounces *away* from the stationary object, and not toward the stationary object's center. Using the dot product of two vectors, you can do exactly that, as you'll see in Chapter 8.

That's pretty much all you need to know about vectors to implement collision detection, so let's move on to the last section in this brief math primer and see how to derive the equations from units of measure.

## 1.11.4  Deriving Equations from Units of Measure

As you will see in Chapter 5, motion in an animation should be time based, because the rate at which an object moves should not change with an animation's frame rate. Time-based motion is especially important for multiplayer games; after all, you don't want a game to progress more quickly for players with more powerful computers.

To implement time-based motion, we specify velocity in this book in terms of pixels per second. To calculate how many pixels to move an object for the current animation frame, therefore, we have two pieces of information: the object's velocity in *pixels per second*, and the current frame rate of the animation in *milliseconds per frame*. What we need to calculate is the number of *pixels per frame* to move any given object. To do that, we must derive an equation that has pixels per frame on the left side of the equation, and pixels per second (the object's velocity) and milliseconds per frame (the current frame rate) on the right of the equation, as shown in Equation 1.4.

$$\frac{\text{pixels}}{\text{frame}} \neq \frac{X\ \text{ms}}{\text{frame}} \times \frac{Y\ \text{pixels}}{\text{second}}$$

Equation 1.4  Deriving an equation for time-based motion, part I

In this *inequality*, X represents the animation's frame rate in milliseconds/frame, and Y is the object's velocity in pixels/second. As that inequality suggests, however, you cannot just multiply milliseconds/frame times pixels/second, because you end up with a nonsensical milliseconds-pixels/frame-seconds. So what do you do?

Recall the last rule we discussed in Section 1.11.1, "Solving Algebraic Equations," on p. 54 for solving algebraic equations: You can multiply or divide one or both sides of an equation by 1. Because of that rule, and because one second is equal to 1000 ms, and therefore 1 second / 1000 ms is equal to 1, we can multiply the right side of the equation by that fraction, as shown in Equation 1.5.

$$\frac{pixels}{frame} = \frac{X \text{ ms}}{frame} \times \frac{1 \text{ second}}{1000 \text{ ms}} \times \frac{Y \text{ pixels}}{second}$$

Equation 1.5  Deriving an equation for time-based motion, part 2

And now we are ready to move in for the kill because when you multiply two fractions together, *a unit of measure in the numerator of one fraction cancels out the same unit of measure in the denominator of the other fraction.* In our case, we cancel units of measure as shown in Equation 1.6.

$$\frac{pixels}{frame} = \frac{X \text{ m}\!\!\!/\text{s}}{frame} \times \frac{1 \text{ sec}\!\!\!/\text{ond}}{1000 \text{ m}\!\!\!/\text{s}} \times \frac{Y \text{ pixels}}{sec\!\!\!/\text{ond}}$$

Equation 1.6  Deriving an equation for time-based motion, part 3

Canceling those units of measure results in Equation 1.7.

$$\frac{pixels}{frame} = \frac{X}{frame} \times \frac{Y \text{ pixels}}{1000}$$

Equation 1.7  Deriving an equation for time-based motion, part 4

Carrying out the multiplication results in the simplified equation, shown in Equation 1.8.

$$\frac{pixels}{frame} = \frac{X \times Y}{1000}$$

$$X = \text{frame rate in ms/frame}$$

$$Y = \text{velocity in pixels/second}$$

Equation 1.8  Deriving an equation for time-based motion, part 5

Whenever you derive an equation, you should plug some simple numbers into your equation to see if the equation makes sense. In this case, if an object is moving at 100 pixels per second, and the frame rate is 500 ms per frame, you can easily figure out, without any equations at all, that the object should move 50 pixels in that 1/2 second.

Plugging those numbers into Equation 1.8 results in 500 × 100 / 1000, which equals 50, so it appears that we have a valid equation for any velocity and any frame rate.

In general, to derive an equation from variables with known units of measure, follow these steps:

1. Start with an inequality, where the result is on the left, and the other variables are on the right.
2. Given the units of measure on both sides of the equation, multiply the right side of the equation by one or more fractions, each equal to 1, whose units of measure cancel out the units of measure on the right side of the equation to yield the units of measure on the left side of the equation.
3. Cancel out the units of measure on the right side of the equation.
4. Multiply the fractions on the right side of the equation.
5. Plug simple values whose result you can easily verify into the equation to make sure the equation yields the expected value.

## 1.12  Conclusion

This chapter introduced you to the canvas element and its associated 2d context, and illustrated some essential features of that context, such as the difference between canvas element size and the size of the canvas's drawing surface.

From there we had a quick overview of your development environment, including browsers, consoles and debuggers, and performance tools.

Then we looked at the essentials of using a canvas, including fundamental drawing operations, event handling, saving and restoring the drawing surface, using HTML elements with a canvas, printing canvases, and using offscreen canvases. You will see the use of those essential features many times throughout this book, and you will use them yourself as you write Canvas-based applications.

Finally, we ended this chapter with a brief math primer, which you can consult as needed as you read the rest of the book.

In the next chapter we take a deep-dive into drawing in a canvas. In that chapter you will learn about the Canvas drawing API, and you'll see how to put that API to good use by implementing most of the features of a capable paint application.

# CHAPTER 2

# Drawing

The HTML5 Canvas 2d context provides a powerful graphics API for implementing sophisticated and compelling graphics applications that run in a browser.

Figure 2.1 shows a paint application that lets you draw text, lines, rectangles, circles, bézier curves, and arbitrary paths—both open and closed—that you trace with the mouse. You erase by selecting the bottom icon and subsequently dragging the eraser in the drawing area (see Section 2.15.1, "Erasing with the Clipping Region," on p. 187). You change drawing attributes with the HTML controls at the top of the page, and you can take a snapshot of the application so users can save their painting as an image.

The paint application uses rubber bands for interactive drawing; as the user drags the mouse to create a new shape, such as a circle or rectangle, the application continuously draws an outline of the shape. When the user releases the mouse, the application finalizes the shape by drawing and possibly filling the shape. The application fills shapes when the user has clicked in the lower-right corner of the icon representing that shape.

This chapter shows you how to use the Canvas APIs to do everything in the paint application and more. Here are some of the things you will learn how to do:

- Stroke and fill lines, arcs, circles, curves, and polygons
- Use context attributes to affect the appearance of shapes
- Draw rounded rectangles
- Draw and edit bézier curves
- Extend the 2d context to draw dashed lines
- Stroke and fill shapes with colors, gradients, and patterns
- Give shapes depth with shadows

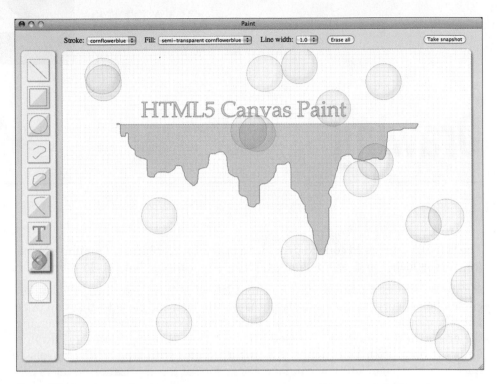

Figure 2.1  A paint application

- Use the clipping region to erase shapes and text, leaving the background intact
- Implement rubber bands so users can interactively draw shapes
- Drag objects in a canvas
- Transform the coordinate system

 **NOTE: The paint application**

The paint application shown in Figure 2.1 is implemented with approximately 1100 lines of JavaScript. That makes it prohibitively long for listing in this book; however, you can download the application from corehtml5canvas.com.

Although the paint application itself is not listed in this book, much of its functionality is illustrated with smaller applications in this chapter, starting with Section 2.8.4, "Rubberband Lines," on p. 110, which shows you how to let users interactively draw lines with rubber bands, and culminating in Section 2.15.1, "Erasing with the Clipping Region," on p. 187, which shows you how to use the clipping region to let users erase what they have drawn.

**NOTE: A mobile paint application**

This chapter shows you how to implement the paint application's features for devices equipped with a mouse. In Chapter 11, you will see how to modify the paint application for devices such as cell phones and tablet computers with touch events instead of mouse events. You will also see how to make other modifications to the application to make it more suitable for mobile devices.

# 2.1 The Coordinate System

By default, the Canvas coordinate system, depicted in Figure 2.2, places the origin at the upper-left corner of the canvas, with X coordinates increasing to the right and Y coordinates increasing toward the bottom of the canvas. Figure 2.2 shows the coordinate system for a canvas with a default size of 300 x 150 pixels.

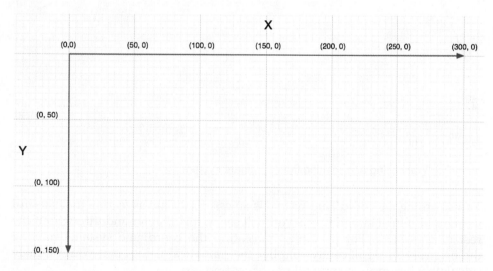

Figure 2.2  The Canvas coordinate system (default size)

The Canvas coordinate system is not fixed, however, as illustrated by Figure 2.3, which translates and rotates the coordinate system. In fact, you can transform the coordinate system in the following ways:

- Translate
- Rotate

- Scale
- Create custom transformations, such as shear

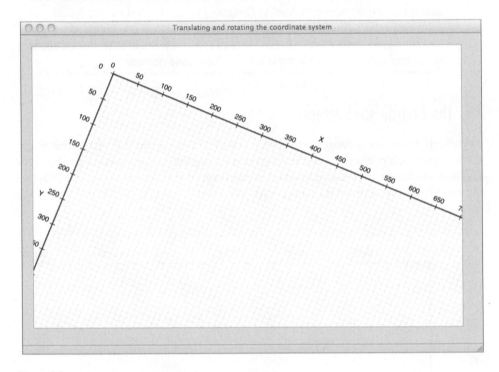

Figure 2.3 Translating and rotating the coordinate system

Transforming the coordinate system is an essential Canvas feature that's useful in many different situations, as you will see in this chapter and throughout the rest of this book. For example, translating the coordinate system—moving the origin—can significantly simplify the numerical values that you routinely calculate when drawing and filling shapes and text.

In Section 2.13, "Transformations," on p. 170 we will look closely at transforming the coordinate system. For now, let's take a look at the Canvas drawing model and how you can use it to draw simple shapes and text.

## 2.2  The Drawing Model

At some point when you're using Canvas, you will need to have a good understanding of exactly how Canvas draws shapes, images, and text, which in turn requires an understanding of shadows, alpha channels, the clipping region, and compositing; indeed, by the end of this chapter you will have a good grasp of all of those things. Right now, you don't need to understand any of them, so feel free to skip this section on first reading and use it as a reference later on.

When you draw shapes or images into a canvas, the browser does the following:

1. Draws the shape or image into an infinite, transparent bitmap, honoring the current fill, stroke, and line styles
2. Draws the shadow from the shape or image into a second bitmap, using the current context shadow settings
3. Multiplies every shadow pixel's alpha component by the `globalAlpha` property of the context
4. Composites the shadow bitmap into the canvas clipped to the clipping region, using the current composition
5. Multiplies every pixel for the shape or image by the `globalAlpha` property of the context
6. Composites the shape or image bitmap into the clipping region over the current canvas bitmap, using the current composition operator

Note: Steps 2–4 apply only when shadows are enabled.

The browser initially draws your shape or image into an infinite, transparent bitmap, using properties of the Canvas context that relate to filling and stroking shapes. Of course, there is no such thing as an infinite bitmap, but the browser behaves as if it has one.

Next, the browser deals with shadows in steps 2 through 4 above. If you've enabled shadows, as discussed in Section 2.6, "Shadows," on p. 83, the browser renders the shadows into another bitmap, multiplies every pixel within the shadow by the `globalAlpha` property, which sets the transparency of the shadow, and composites the shadow into the canvas element, using the current composition settings and clipped to the current clipping region.

Finally, the browser composites the shape or image into the canvas element according to the current composition settings and the clipping region.

If you are new to Canvas and you just read the preceding paragraphs without understanding much, don't despair. At sometime in the future, when you have a good understanding of shadows, alpha channels, clipping regions, and compositing, come back to this section, and it will all make sense.

Now that we're done with coordinate system and drawing model preliminaries, let's get down to business and start using Canvas to draw simple shapes and text.

## 2.3  Drawing Rectangles

The Canvas API provides three methods for clearing, drawing, and filling rectangles, respectively:

- `clearRect(double x, double y, double w, double h)`
- `strokeRect(double x, double y, double w, double h)`
- `fillRect(double x, double y, double w, double h)`

Figure 2.4 shows a simple application that uses all three of the preceding methods.

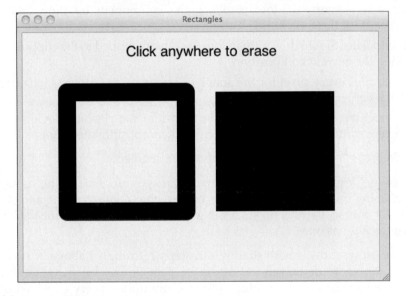

Figure 2.4  Drawing simple rectangles

The application uses `strokeRect()` to draw the rectangle on the left, and uses `fillRect()` to fill the rectangle on the right. If you click anywhere in the canvas, the application uses `clearRect()` to clear the entire canvas.

The application shown in Figure 2.4 is listed in Example 2.1.

Normally, as you will often see throughout this book, the `strokeRect()` method draws rectangles with square corners; however, the application sets the context's `lineJoin` property to round, and therefore, as you can see in Figure 2.4, the rectangle on the left has rounded corners. See Section 2.8.7, "Line Caps and Joins," on p. 121 for more information about how you can use the lineJoin property to control the appearance of corners when two lines meet.

---
**Example 2.1** Drawing simple rectangles
---

```
var canvas = document.getElementById('canvas'),
    context = canvas.getContext('2d');

context.lineJoin = 'round';
context.lineWidth = 30;

context.font = '24px Helvetica';
context.fillText('Click anywhere to erase', 175, 40);

context.strokeRect(75, 100, 200, 200);
context.fillRect(325, 100, 200, 200);

context.canvas.onmousedown = function (e) {
   context.clearRect(0, 0, canvas.width, canvas.height);
};
```

In addition to honoring the lineJoin property, strokeRect() also takes into account the lineWidth property, which specifies line width in pixels. The clearRect(), strokeRect(), and fillRect() methods are summarized in Table 2.1.

**Table 2.1** Clearing, stroking, and filling rectangles

| Method | Description |
| --- | --- |
| clearRect(double x, double y, double w, double h) | Clears all pixels in the intersection of the specified rectangle and the current clipping region. |
| | By default, the clipping region is the size of the canvas, so if you don't change the clipping region, the pixels cleared are exactly the pixels specified by the arguments to the method. |
| | Clearing pixels means turning their color to fully transparent black. That effectively erases, or clears, the pixel, allowing the canvas's background to show through. |

*(Continues)*

**Table 2.1**  *(Continued)*

| Method | Description |
|---|---|
| strokeRect(double x, double y, double w, double h) | Strokes the specified rectangle, using the following attributes:<br><br>• strokeStyle<br>• lineWidth<br>• lineJoin<br>• miterLimit<br><br>If you specify zero for either the width or the height, the method will draw a vertical or horizontal line, respectively. The method does nothing if you specify zero for both width and height. |
| fillRect(double x, double y, double w, double h) | Fills the specified rectangle with the fillStyle attribute. If you specify zero for either the width or the height, this method thinks you're an idiot, and therefore does nothing. |

**TIP: Rounded rectangles**

The example in this section used the lineJoin property to draw a rounded rectangle. The Canvas specification describes a detailed procedure for drawing those rounded corners, which leaves no room for improvisation. To control properties of the rounded corners, such as the radius of the rounded corner, you must draw those corners yourself. In Section 2.9.3, "The arcTo() Method," on p. 127 you will see how to do that.

## 2.4  Colors and Transparency

The application in the preceding section (see Figure 2.4) uses the default color—opaque black—to stroke and fill rectangles. In practice, you will undoubtedly want to use other colors, which you can do by setting the strokeStyle and fillStyle properties of the context. Figure 2.5 shows an application similar to the application shown in Figure 2.4 that uses colors other than opaque black for the two rectangles.

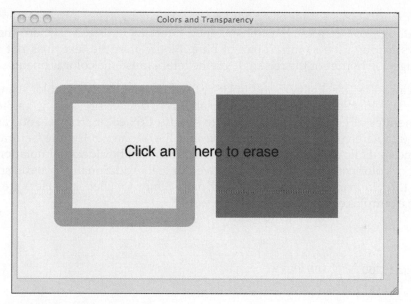

Figure 2.5 Colors and transparency

The application shown in **Figure 2.5** is listed in **Example 2.2**.

Example 2.2 Colors and transparency

```
var canvas = document.getElementById('canvas'),
    context = canvas.getContext('2d');

context.lineJoin = 'round';
context.lineWidth = 30;

context.font = '24px Helvetica';
context.fillText('Click anywhere to erase', 175, 200);

context.strokeStyle = 'goldenrod';
context.fillStyle = 'rgba(0,0,255,0.5)';

context.strokeRect(75, 100, 200, 200);
context.fillRect(325, 100, 200, 200);

context.canvas.onmousedown = function (e) {
   context.clearRect(0, 0, canvas.width, canvas.height);
};
```

The application uses two colors: goldenrod for stroking and semitransparent blue for filling. You can see the transparency effect in Figure 2.5, where the text shows through the semitransparent blue. Notice that the text does not show through the border of the rectangle on the left because the color is opaque.

The values for `strokeStyle` and `fillStyle` can be any valid CSS color string. An entire specification, which you can read at http://dev.w3.org/csswg/css3-color, enumerates all of the different ways to specify CSS color strings. You can use RGB (red/green/blue), RGBA (red/green/blue/alpha), HSL (hue/saturation/lightness), HSLA (hue/saturation/lightness/alpha), hexadecimal notations for RGB, or color names such as yellow, silver, or teal. Additionally, you can specify SVG 1.0 color names such as goldenrod, darksalmon, or chocolate. Here are some more examples of color strings:

- `#ffffff`
- `#642`
- `rgba(100,100,100,0.8)`
- `rgb(255,255,0)`
- `hsl(20,62%,28%)`
- `hsla(40,82%,33%,0.6)`
- `antiquewhite`
- `burlywood`
- `cadetblue`

---

 **TIP: Your browser may not support all SVG 1.0 color names**

The CSS3 color specification states:

*The Working Group doesn't expect that all implementations of CSS3 will implement all properties or values.*

Having read that statement, don't be surprised if some browsers do not support all the colors in the CSS3 color specification.

---

**NOTE: HSL color values**

The CSS3 color specification states that HSL was added to CSS3 because RGB has two main drawbacks: It is hardware oriented, based on cathode ray tubes (CRTs); and it's nonintuitive.

Like RGB, HSL values have three components, but whereas RGB represents red, green, and blue, HSL values represent hue, saturation, and lightness. HSL colors are selected from a color wheel, where red is at angle 0 degrees (and 360 degrees) on the color wheel, green is at 120 degrees, blue is at 240 degrees, and so forth.

The first value that you specify for HSL colors represents the angle on the color wheel. The second and third values represent percents for saturation and lightness. For saturation, 100% is full saturation, and 0% is a shade of gray. For lightness, 100% is white and 50% is normal. (Note: The CSS3 color specification puts the word normal in quotes and does not elaborate on what it means.)

HSL color values are easily converted to RGB, and vice versa. You can decide for yourself which is more intuitive and which you'd rather use.

**NOTE: The globalAlpha property**

In addition to specifying semitransparent colors with the alpha component of rgba() or hsla(), you can also use the globalAlpha property, which the browser applies to all shapes and images that you draw. The value for that property must be between 0.0, which is fully transparent, and 1.0, which is fully opaque. The default value for the globalAlpha property is 1.0.

**NOTE: Why strokeStyle and fillStyle instead of strokeColor and fillColor?**

You may wonder why the strokeStyle and fillStyle properties are not named strokeColor and fillColor, respectively. Although you can indeed specify CSS3 color strings for the strokeStyle and fillStyle attributes, you can also specify gradients or patterns for those properties. We explore gradients and patterns in the next section.

## 2.5  Gradients and Patterns

In addition to colors, you can specify gradients and patterns for the `strokeStyle` and `fillStyle` attributes. Let's see how to do that next.

### 2.5.1  Gradients

The Canvas element supports both linear and radial gradients. Let's start by looking at the former.

#### 2.5.1.1  Linear Gradients

Example 2.3 shows several ways to create linear gradients.

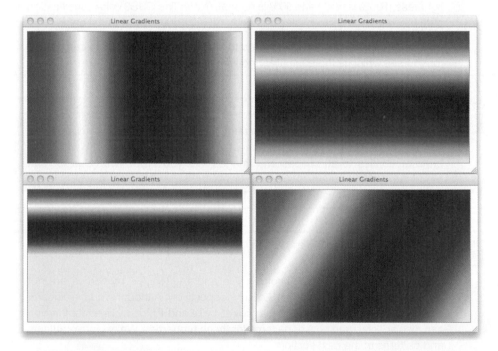

Figure 2.6  Linear gradients

The application shown in the Figure 2.6 is listed in Example 2.3.

The code creates a linear gradient with the `createLinearGradient()` method. You pass that method the X and Y coordinates of two points, which represent a line along which the canvas creates a color gradient, and `createLinearGradient()`

returns an instance of `CanvasGradient`. Ultimately, the application sets the fill style to the gradient, and subsequent calls to the `fill()` method will use the gradient to fill until you set the fill style to something else.

After creating the gradient, the code adds five color stops by invoking `CanvasGradient`'s lone method: `addColorStop()`. That method takes two parameters: a `double` value that must be between 0 and 1.0, representing the position of the color stop along the gradient line; and a `DOMString` value, which is a CSS3 color string.

---

**Example 2.3** Linear gradients

```
var canvas = document.getElementById('canvas'),
    context = canvas.getContext('2d'),
    gradient = context.createLinearGradient(0, 0, canvas.width, 0);

gradient.addColorStop(0,    'blue');
gradient.addColorStop(0.25, 'white');
gradient.addColorStop(0.5,  'purple');
gradient.addColorStop(0.75, 'red');
gradient.addColorStop(1,    'yellow');

context.fillStyle = gradient;
context.rect(0, 0, canvas.width, canvas.height);
```

---

The code creates the gradient shown in the upper-left corner in Figure 2.6. All the screenshots in Figure 2.6 were created by this application; the only difference is how the application creates the gradient. Starting with the screenshot in the upper-right corner and moving clockwise, the screenshots were created with the following gradients, respectively:

```
gradient = context.createLinearGradient(0, 0, 0, canvas.height);
```

The preceding gradient is created with a vertical line, resulting at the screenshot shown at the upper right in Figure 2.6.

```
gradient =
    context.createLinearGradient(0, 0, canvas.width, canvas.height);
```

The screenshot at the lower right in Figure 2.6 is created by the preceding gradient, whose gradient line is slanted at an angle.

```
gradient = context.createLinearGradient(0, 0, 0, canvas.height/2);
```

Finally, the screenshot at the lower left was created with the preceding gradient. Notice that the gradient line for the preceding gradient is a vertical line from the top of the canvas to the middle of the canvas. The application fills the entire canvas, and the Canvas element fills the bottom half of the canvas with the last color used in the gradient.

### 2.5.1.2 Radial Gradients

As you saw in the preceding section, you create linear gradients by specifying a gradient line. To create radial gradients, you specify two circles, which represent the ends of a cone. The radial gradient effect is shown in Figure 2.7.

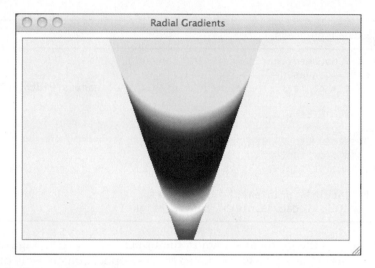

Figure 2.7 Radial gradients

The application shown in Figure 2.7 is listed in Example 2.4.

The code creates a radial gradient with a small circle (10 pixel radius) at the bottom of the canvas and a larger circle (100 pixel radius) at the top of the canvas. Both circles are centered horizontally within the canvas.

Like `createLinearGradient()`, `createRadialGradient()` returns an instance of `CanvasGradient`. The code adds four color stops to the gradient and sets the fill style to the gradient.

Notice that the code fills the entire canvas with the radial gradient; however, unlike linear gradients, which fill the area outside the gradient line with the last gradient color, radial gradients are restricted to the cone described by the two circles that you pass to the `createRadialGradient()` method.

---

Example 2.4 Radial gradients

---

```
var canvas = document.getElementById('canvas'),
    context = canvas.getContext('2d'),
    gradient = context.createRadialGradient(
                  canvas.width/2, canvas.height, 10,
                  canvas.width/2, 0, 100);

gradient.addColorStop(0, 'blue');
gradient.addColorStop(0.25, 'white');
gradient.addColorStop(0.5, 'purple');
gradient.addColorStop(0.75, 'red');
gradient.addColorStop(1, 'yellow');

context.fillStyle = gradient;
context.rect(0, 0, canvas.width, canvas.height);
context.fill();
```

---

The createLinearGradient() and createRadialGradient() methods are summarized in Table 2.2.

**Table 2.2** Gradients

| Method | Description |
| --- | --- |
| CanvasGradient createLinearGradient(double x0, double y0, double x1, double y1) | Creates a linear gradient. The parameters you pass to the method represent two points which specify the gradient line. The method returns an instance of CanvasGradient, to which you can add color stops with the CanvasGradient.addColorStop() method. |
| CanvasGradient createRadialGradient(double x0, double y0, double r0, double x1, double y1, double r1) | Creates a radial gradient. The parameters to the method represent two circles at the opposite ends of a cone. Like createLinearGradient(), this method returns an instance of CanvasGradient. |

## 2.5.2 Patterns

Besides colors and gradients, the Canvas element also lets you stroke and fill both shapes and text with a pattern. That pattern can be one of three things: an image, a canvas, or a video element.

You create patterns with the createPattern() method, which takes two arguments: the pattern itself and a string that specifies how the browser repeats the pattern. You can specify one of the following values for that second argument: repeat, repeat-x, repeat-y, or no-repeat. You can see the effects of those values in the application shown in Figure 2.8, which creates a pattern with an image, sets the fill style to that pattern, and subsequently fills the entire canvas with the pattern.

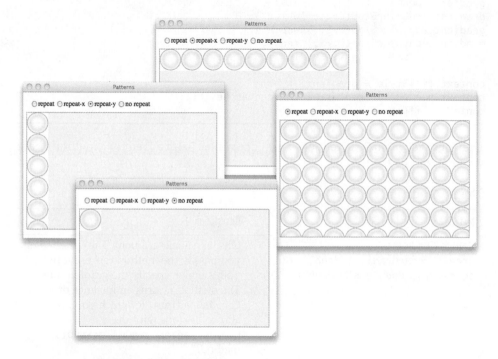

Figure 2.8 Controlling how patterns repeat

The HTML for the application shown in Figure 2.8 is listed in Example 2.5.

The HTML creates the radio buttons, the canvas, and includes the JavaScript for the example. That JavaScript is listed in Example 2.6.

The JavaScript creates an image, and subsequently creates a pattern with that image and the repetition argument that you specify when you select the radio button. The application then uses that pattern to fill the entire canvas.

---

Example 2.5 Using patterns: HTML

---

```html
<!DOCTYPE html>
    <head>
        <title>Patterns</title>

        <style>
            #canvas {
                background: #eeeeee;
                border: thin solid cornflowerblue;
            }

            #radios {
                padding: 10px;
            }
        </style>
    </head>

    <body>
        <div id='radios'>
            <input type='radio'
                   id='repeatRadio' name='patternRadio' checked/>repeat
            <input type='radio'
                   id='repeatXRadio' name='patternRadio'/>repeat-x
            <input type='radio'
                   id='repeatYRadio' name='patternRadio'/>repeat-y
            <input type='radio'
                   id='noRepeatRadio' name='patternRadio'/>no repeat
        </div>

        <canvas id='canvas' width='450' height='275'>
         Canvas not supported
        </canvas>

        <script src='example.js'></script>
    </body>
</html>
```

---

Notice that the code creates a new CanvasPattern object with createPattern()
every time you click a radio button. Creating a new pattern is necessary because
the CanvasPattern is what's known as an opaque JavaScript object, meaning it
provides no properties or methods for you to manipulate. If CanvasPattern objects provided a setPattern() method, you could create a single CanvasPattern
object and simply change the pattern; however, you cannot do that because
CanvasPattern objects are opaque.

**Example 2.6** Using Patterns: The JavaScript

```javascript
var canvas = document.getElementById('canvas'),
    context = canvas.getContext('2d'),
    repeatRadio   = document.getElementById('repeatRadio'),
    noRepeatRadio = document.getElementById('noRepeatRadio'),
    repeatXRadio  = document.getElementById('repeatXRadio'),
    repeatYRadio  = document.getElementById('repeatYRadio'),
    image = new Image();

// Functions.........................................................

function fillCanvasWithPattern(repeatString) {
    var pattern = context.createPattern(image, repeatString);
    context.clearRect(0, 0, canvas.width, canvas.height);
    context.fillStyle = pattern;
    context.fillRect(0, 0, canvas.width, canvas.height);
    context.fill();
}

// Event handlers...................................................

repeatRadio.onclick = function (e) {
  fillCanvasWithPattern('repeat');
};

repeatXRadio.onclick = function (e) {
  fillCanvasWithPattern('repeat-x');
};

repeatYRadio.onclick = function (e) {
  fillCanvasWithPattern('repeat-y');
};

noRepeatRadio.onclick = function (e) {
  fillCanvasWithPattern('no-repeat');
};

// Initialization...................................................

image.src = 'redball.png';
image.onload = function (e) {
    fillCanvasWithPattern('repeat');
};
```

The createPattern() method is described in **Table 2.3**.

**Table 2.3** `createPattern()` method

| Method | Description |
|---|---|
| `CanvasPattern`<br>`createPattern(HTMLImageElement \|`<br>`HTMLCanvasElement \|`<br>`HTMLVideoElement image, DOMString`<br>`repetition)` | Creates a pattern that you can use to stroke or fill shapes or text in the canvas. The image used in the pattern, specified with the first argument to the method, can be an image, a canvas, or a video element. The second argument specifies how the browser repeats the pattern when you use it to stroke or fill a shape. Valid values for the second argument are `repeat`, `repeat-x`, `repeat-y`, and `no-repeat`. |

## 2.6 Shadows

Whenever you draw into a canvas, whether you are drawing shapes, text, or images, you can also specify a shadow with four context attributes:

- `shadowColor`: a CSS3 color
- `shadowOffsetX`: the horizontal offset in pixels, from the shape or text, to the shadow
- `shadowOffsetY`: the vertical offset in pixels, from the shape or text, to the shadow
- `shadowBlur`: a value, that has nothing to do with pixels, used in a Gaussian blur equation to smear the shadow

The Canvas context will draw shadows if you

1. Specify a `shadowColor` that is not fully transparent
2. Specify a nonzero value for one of the other shadow attributes

Figure 2.9 shows some of the icons from the paint application shown in Figure 2.1 on p. 66.

The paint application applies shadows to all its icons to make it appear as though they're floating above the page. The application specifies a different shadow for the selected icon, however. That shadow has higher values for the shadow's offsets and blur, which makes it appear to float higher than the other icons, as you can see from the Text icon in Figure 2.9.

Figure 2.9  Shadows give the illusion of depth

The paint application sets the icon shadows with the methods shown in Example 2.7.

---

Example 2.7  Using shadows to portray depth

---

```
var SHADOW_COLOR = 'rgba(0,0,0,0.7)';
...

function setIconShadow() {
   iconContext.shadowColor = SHADOW_COLOR;
   iconContext.shadowOffsetX = 1;
   iconContext.shadowOffsetY = 1;
   iconContext.shadowBlur = 2;
}

function setSelectedIconShadow() {
   iconContext.shadowColor = SHADOW_COLOR;
   iconContext.shadowOffsetX = 4;
   iconContext.shadowOffsetY = 4;
   iconContext.shadowBlur = 5;
}
```

---

The icons shown in Figure 2.9 are filled rectangles with shadows, but the Canvas context also draws shadows when you stroke text or a path. Figure 2.10 illustrates the difference between shadows applied to a stroke and shadows applied to a fill.

Figure 2.10  Shadows for stroking (left) vs. filling (right)

**TIP: Use partially transparent colors for shadows**

In general, it's a good idea to use partially transparent colors for shadows so that the background shows through the shadows.

**NOTE: Turning shadows on and off**

According to the Canvas specification, the browser should draw shadows only if you a) specify a color with the `shadowColor` property, which is not fully transparent, and b) you specify a nonzero value for one of the other three shadow properties: `shadowBlur`, `shadowOffsetX`, or `shadowOffsetY`. An easy way to turn off shadows, therefore, is to set the `shadowColor` to `undefined`. However, at the time this book was written, setting the `shadowColor` to `undefined` works with WebKit browsers but does not work with Firefox or Opera. To ensure that you turn shadows on or off with all browsers, you should set all the shadow-related properties, which you can do by hand or by using the context `save()` and `restore()` methods.

At the time this book was written, the browser draws shadows regardless of the current composition setting, which determines how the browser draws one thing on top of another. Some browser vendors, however, would like to change that rule so that the browser draws shadows only when the composition setting is `source-over`. See Section 2.14, "Compositing," on p. 181 for more information about the composition setting.

## 2.6.1  Inset Shadows

If you specify nonzero, positive values for `shadowOffsetX` and `shadowOffsetY`, then whatever you draw will appear to float above the canvas. Larger numbers for those properties make it appear as though objects are floating higher above the canvas.

You can also use negative values for those properties, as illustrated in Figure 2.11.

Figure 2.11  Shadows with negative offsets: Stroking on the left, filling on the right

Shadows with negative offsets can be used to implement inset shadows, as illustrated in Figure 2.12, which shows the eraser for the paint application. The eraser has a faint inset shadow, that makes the eraser surface appear concave.

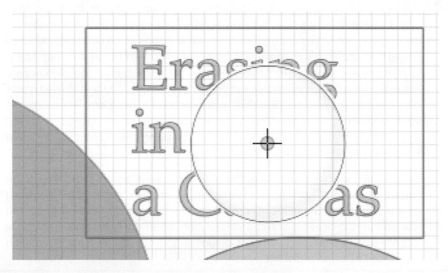

Figure 2.12  Inset shadows: the paint application's eraser

Example 2.8 shows the pertinent code from the paint application that draws the eraser and its inset shadow. The application specifies the inset shadow with X and Y shadow offsets of –5 pixels, which results in a shadow similar to the ones depicted in Figure 2.11.

Notice the call to the context's clip() method. That call restricts, to only the area within the circle, the subsequent call to stroke() and the shadow it generates. That means that, unlike the inset shadow for the stroked rectangle in Figure 2.12, the browser does not draw any shadows outside the circle. We discuss the clipping region and the clip() method in more detail in Section 2.15, "The Clipping Region," on p. 187.

---

**Example 2.8** Drawing inset shadows

```javascript
var drawingContext =
        document.getElementById('drawingCanvas').getContext('2d'),

    ERASER_LINE_WIDTH    = 1,
    ERASER_SHADOW_STYLE  = 'blue',
    ERASER_STROKE_STYLE  = 'rgba(0,0,255,0.6)',
    ERASER_SHADOW_OFFSET = -5,
    ERASER_SHADOW_BLUR   = 20,
    ERASER_RADIUS        = 60;


// Eraser......................................................

function setEraserAttributes() {
  drawingContext.lineWidth    = ERASER_LINE_WIDTH;
  drawingContext.shadowColor   = ERASER_SHADOW_STYLE;
  drawingContext.shadowOffsetX = ERASER_SHADOW_OFFSET;
  drawingContext.shadowOffsetY = ERASER_SHADOW_OFFSET;
  drawingContext.shadowBlur    = ERASER_SHADOW_BLUR;
  drawingContext.strokeStyle   = ERASER_STROKE_STYLE;
}

function drawEraser(loc) {
   drawingContext.save();
   setEraserAttributes();

   drawingContext.beginPath();
   drawingContext.arc(loc.x, loc.y, ERASER_RADIUS,
                      0, Math.PI*2, false);
   drawingContext.clip();
   drawingContext.stroke();

   drawingContext.restore();
}
```

---

The four attributes that control how shadows are drawn are summarized in Table 2.4.

**Table 2.4** CanvasRenderingContext2D shadow attributes

| Attribute | Description |
| --- | --- |
| shadowBlur | A double value that determines how spread out a shadow appears. This property's value is used when the browser performs a Gaussian blur on the shadow. The value is used in a Gaussian blur equation and has nothing to do with pixels. The default value is 0. |
| shadowColor | A CSS3 color string. The default value is rgba(0,0,0,0), which equates to fully transparent black. |
| shadowOffsetX | The offset, in pixels, in the X direction for the shadow. The default value is 0. |
| shadowOffsetY | The offset, in pixels, in the Y direction for the shadow. The default value is 0. |

**TIP: Shadows can be expensive to draw**

As discussed in Section 2.2, "The Drawing Model," on p. 68, drawing shadows requires the browser to use a secondary bitmap to render the shadows, which it ultimately composites into the onscreen canvas. As a result of that secondary bitmap, drawing shadows can be an expensive operation.

If you are drawing simple shapes, text, or images, drawing shadows is probably not much of a performance consideration. However, if you are using shadows for objects that you animate in a canvas, you'll almost certainly get better performance from your animation if you omit the shadows. See Section 5.11, "Animation Best Practices," on p. 390 for more information about animation and shadows.

## 2.7  Paths, Stroking, and Filling

So far in this chapter the only shapes we've drawn are rectangles with the Canvas context strokeRect() method. We also filled rectangles with fillRect(). Both of those methods take immediate effect; in fact, those are the only methods implemented by the Canvas context that immediately draw shapes (strokeText() and fillText() draw immediately, but text is not a shape). Other context methods that draw more complex shapes such as bézier curves are *path based*.

Most drawing systems, such as Scalable Vector Graphics (SVG), Apple's Cocoa, and Adobe's Illustrator are path based. With those drawing systems you define a *path* that you can subsequently stroke (draw the outline of the path), fill, or both, as shown in Figure 2.13.

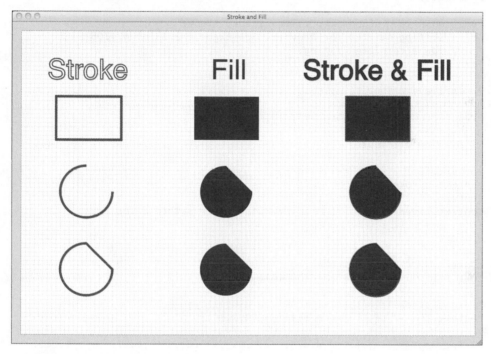

Figure 2.13 Stroking and filling shapes

The application creates nine separate paths, strokes the paths in the left-hand column, fills the paths in the middle column, and strokes and fills the paths in the right-hand column.

The rectangular paths in the first row and the arc paths in the bottom row are *closed paths*. The arc paths in the middle row are *open paths*. Notice you can fill a path whether it's open or closed. When you fill an open path, as illustrated by the arc path in the middle row of the right-hand column, the browser fills the path as if it were closed.

The application shown in Figure 2.13 is listed in Example 2.9.

**Example 2.9**  Stroking and filling text, rectangles, and arcs

```
var context = document.getElementById('drawingCanvas').getContext('2d');

// Functions...................................................

function drawGrid(context, color, stepx, stepy) {
   // Listing omitted for brevity. See Example 2.13 on p. 106
   // for a complete listing.
}

// Initialization...............................................

drawGrid(context, 'lightgray', 10, 10);

// Drawing attributes...........................................

context.font = '48pt Helvetica';
context.strokeStyle = 'blue';
context.fillStyle = 'red';
context.lineWidth = '2';        // Line width set to 2 for text

// Text.........................................................

context.strokeText('Stroke', 60, 110);
context.fillText('Fill', 440, 110);

context.strokeText('Stroke & Fill', 650, 110);
context.fillText('Stroke & Fill', 650, 110);

// Rectangles...................................................

context.lineWidth = '5';        // Line width set to 5 for shapes
context.beginPath();
context.rect(80, 150, 150, 100);
context.stroke();

context.beginPath();
context.rect(400, 150, 150, 100);
context.fill();

context.beginPath();
context.rect(750, 150, 150, 100);
context.stroke();
context.fill();
```

```
// Open arcs.........................................................

context.beginPath();
context.arc(150, 370, 60, 0, Math.PI*3/2);
context.stroke();

context.beginPath();
context.arc(475, 370, 60, 0, Math.PI*3/2);
context.fill();

context.beginPath();
context.arc(820, 370, 60, 0, Math.PI*3/2);
context.stroke();
context.fill();

// Closed arcs.......................................................

context.beginPath();
context.arc(150, 550, 60, 0, Math.PI*3/2);
context.closePath();
context.stroke();

context.beginPath();
context.arc(475, 550, 60, 0, Math.PI*3/2);
context.closePath();
context.fill();

context.beginPath();
context.arc(820, 550, 60, 0, Math.PI*3/2);
context.closePath();
context.stroke();
context.fill();
```

You begin a new path with the beginPath() method. The rect() and arc() methods both create paths for rectangles and arcs, respectively. Subsequently, the application strokes or fills those paths with the stroke() and fill() context methods.

Stroking and filling are governed by the current drawing attributes, such as lineWidth, strokeStyle, fillStyle, shadow attributes, etc. The application shown in Example 2.9, for example, sets the lineWidth to 2 for stroking the text and resets it to 5 for stroking the paths.

The path created by rect() is closed; however, paths created by arc() are not closed unless you use arc() to create a circular path. To close an arc path, you must call the closePath() method, as illustrated by Example 2.9.

The methods used by this application that pertain to paths are summarized in Table 2.5.

**Table 2.5** `CanvasRenderingContext2D` path-related methods

| Method | Description |
|---|---|
| `arc()` | Adds a subpath, representing an arc or a circle, to the current path. You can control the direction of the subpath (unlike the case with `rect()`) with a boolean variable. If that variable is `true`, `arc()` creates the subpath clockwise; otherwise, it creates the subpath counterclockwise. If a subpath already exists when you call this method, `arc()` draws a line from the last point in the existing subpath to the first point along the arc's path. |
| `beginPath()` | Resets the current path by clearing all subpaths from the current path. See Section 2.7.1 for more information about subpaths. Call this method when you want to begin a new path. |
| `closePath()` | Explicitly closes an open path. This method is for open arc paths and paths created with curves or lines. |
| `fill()` | Fills the inside of the current path with `fillStyle`. |
| `rect(double x, double y, double width, double height)` | Creates a rectangular subpath at (`x`, `y`) with the specified `width` and `height`. The subpath is implicitly closed and is always clockwise. |
| `stroke()` | Strokes the outline of the current path with `strokeStyle`. |

 **NOTE: Paths and invisible ink**

A good analogy for creating a path and subsequently stroking or filling that path is drawing with invisible ink.

Whatever you draw with invisible ink is not immediately visible; you must subsequently do something—for example, apply heat, chemicals, or infrared light—to make whatever you've drawn visible. You can read all about invisible ink, if you're so inclined, at http://en.wikipedia.org/wiki/Invisible_ink.

Using methods such as `rect()` or `arc()` is analogous to drawing with invisible ink. Those methods create an invisible path that you subsequently make visible with calls to `stroke()` or `fill()`.

## 2.7.1 Paths and Subpaths

At any given time there is only one path for a particular canvas, which the Canvas specification refers to as the *current path*. That path, however, can consist of multiple *subpaths*. A subpath, in turn, consists of two or more points. For example, you can draw two rectangles, like this:

```
context.beginPath();              // Clear all subpaths from
                                  // the current path
context.rect(10, 10, 100, 100);   // Add a subpath with four points
context.stroke();                 // Stroke the subpath containing
                                  // four points

context.beginPath();              // Clear all subpaths from the
                                  // current path
context.rect(50, 50, 100, 100);   // Add a subpath with four points
context.stroke();                 // Stroke the subpath containing
                                  // four points
```

The preceding code begins by calling beginPath(), which clears all subpaths from the current path. The code then invokes rect(), which adds a subpath containing four points to the current path. Finally, the code calls stroke(), which draws an outline of the current path, making the rectangle appear in the canvas.

Next, the code once again invokes beginPath(), which clears the subpath created by the previous call to rect(), and then calls rect() a second time, which once again adds a subpath with four points to the current path. Finally, the code strokes the current path, which makes the second rectangle appear in the canvas.

Now consider what happens if you remove the second call to beginPath(), like this:

```
context.beginPath();              // Clear all subpaths from the
                                  // current path
context.rect(10, 10, 100, 100);   // Add a subpath with four points
context.stroke();                 // Stroke the subpath containing
                                  // four points

context.rect(50, 50, 100, 100);   // Add a second subpath with
                                  // four points
context.stroke();                 // Stroke both subpaths
```

The preceding code starts off exactly as the previous code listing: It calls beginPath() to clear any subpaths from the current path, calls rect() to create a single subpath containing the rectangle's four points, and invokes stroke() to make the rectangle appear in the canvas.

Next, the code calls rect() again, but this time, because the code did not invoke beginPath() to clear out the previous subpath, the second call to rect() *adds a subpath* to the current path. Finally, when the code invokes stroke() for the second time, that call to stroke() strokes *both* of the subpaths in the current path, meaning it *redraws the first rectangle*.

### 2.7.1.1 The Nonzero Winding Rule for Filling Paths

If the current path loops back over itself or if you have multiple subpaths in the current path that intersect, the Canvas context must figure out how to fill the current path when the fill() method is invoked. Canvas uses what's known as the nonzero winding rule for filling a path that intersects with itself. Figure 2.14 illustrates the use of that rule.

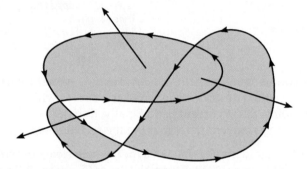

Figure 2.14  The nonzero winding rule for filling paths

Here's how the nonzero winding rule works for self-intersecting paths: For any particular area in the path, draw a straight line from inside the area until the line is long enough so the second point on the line lies completely outside the path. That step is depicted in Figure 2.14 with three arrows.

The next step is to initialize a counter to zero, and every time the line crosses a line or curve on the path itself, add one to the counter for clockwise segments of the path and subtract one from the counter for counterclockwise path segments. If the final count is nonzero, then the area lies within the path, and the browser fills it when you invoke fill(). If the final count is zero, the area does not lie within the path, and the browser does not fill it.

You can see how the nonzero winding rule works by looking at Figure 2.14. The arrow on the left first crosses a counterclockwise segment of the path and subsequently crosses a clockwise segment of the path. That means its counter is zero, so that area does not lie within the path, and the browser does not fill it when you invoke fill(). The counters for the other two arrows, however, are nonzero, so the areas from which they originate are filled by the browser.

## 2.7.2 Cutouts

Let's use our knowledge of paths, shadows, and the nonzero winding rule to implement cutouts, as shown in Figure 2.15.

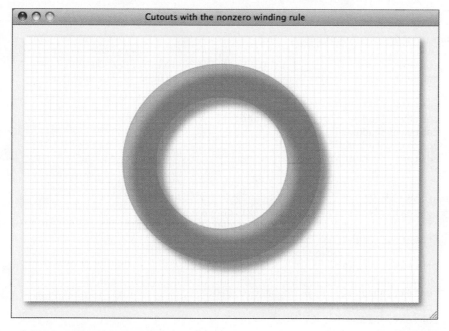

Figure 2.15   A cutout with two circles

The JavaScript for the application shown in Figure 2.15 is listed in Example 2.10.

This JavaScript creates a single path that consists of two circles, one inside the other. Using the last argument of the arc() method, the application draws the inner circle clockwise and draws the outer circle counterclockwise, as shown in the top screenshot in Figure 2.16.

After creating the path, the application shown in Figure 2.15 fills it. By applying the nonzero winding rule, the browser fills the interior of the outer circle but does not fill the inside of the inner circle. The result is a cutout, and you can cut out any shapes you like.

**Example 2.10** JavaScript for the application shown in **Figure 2.14**

```javascript
var context = document.getElementById('canvas').getContext('2d');

// Functions................................................

function drawGrid(color, stepx, stepy) {
   // Listing omitted for brevity. See Example 2.13 on p. 106
   // for a complete listing.
}

function drawTwoArcs() {
   context.beginPath();
   context.arc(300, 190, 150, 0, Math.PI*2, false); // Outer: CCW
   context.arc(300, 190, 100, 0, Math.PI*2, true);  // Inner: CW

   context.fill();
   context.shadowColor = undefined;
   context.shadowOffsetX = 0;
   context.shadowOffsetY = 0;
   context.stroke();
}

function draw() {
   context.clearRect(0, 0, context.canvas.width,
                           context.canvas.height);
   drawGrid('lightgray', 10, 10);

   context.save();

   context.shadowColor = 'rgba(0,0,0,0.8)';
   context.shadowOffsetX = 12;
   context.shadowOffsetY = 12;
   context.shadowBlur = 15;

   drawTwoArcs();

   context.restore();
}

// Initialization...........................................

context.fillStyle = 'rgba(100,140,230,0.5)';
context.strokeStyle = context.fillStyle;
draw();
```

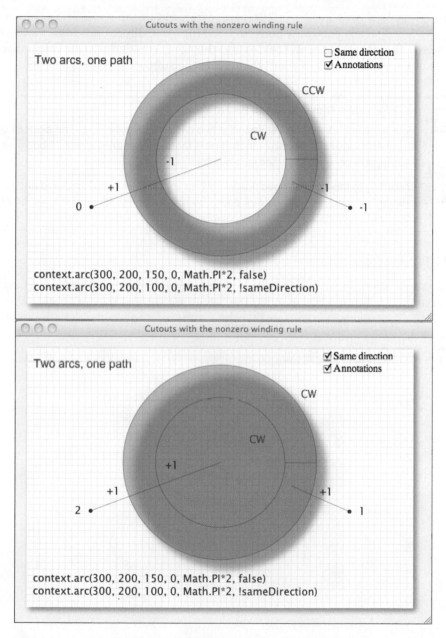

Figure 2.16  Implementing cutouts with the nonzero winding rule

The example shown in Figure 2.16 is an extension of the application shown in Figure 2.15 that lets you draw both circles in the same direction, adds annotations showing the directions of the circles and the nonzero winding rule calculations, and shows you the calls to arc() that create the subpaths for the circles.

 **NOTE: What's that horizontal line in Figure 2.16?**

Notice the horizontal line between the two circles in Figure 2.16. The same line is drawn in Figure 2.15; however, the line is more distinct in Figure 2.16 because that application uses a darker stroke color.

According to the Canvas specification, when you call the arc() method and an existing subpath is in the current path, the method must connect the last point in the existing subpath to the first point on the arc.

### 2.7.2.1 Cutout Shapes

The application shown in Figure 2.17 cuts three shapes out of a rectangle. Unlike the application discussed in the preceding section, the application shown in Figure 2.17 uses a fully opaque fill color for the rectangle containing the cutouts.

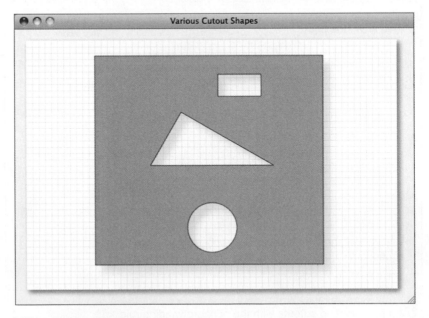

Figure 2.17  Various cutout shapes

The application has two interesting aspects. First, notice that the shape surrounding the cutouts is a rectangle, not a circle. That rectangle illustrates that you can use any shape, including arbitrary paths, to enclose cutouts. Here's how the application creates the cutouts:

```
function drawCutouts() {
   context.beginPath();

   addOuterRectanglePath(); // Clockwise (CW)

   addCirclePath();        // Counter-clockwise (CCW)
   addRectanglePath();     // CCW
   addTrianglePath();      // CCW

   context.fill(); // Cut out shapes
}
```

The methods addOuterRectanglePath(), addCirclePath(), addRectanglePath(), and addTrianglePath() add subpaths to the current path representing the cutouts.

The second interesting thing about the application shown in Figure 2.17 is the rectangle cutout. Whereas arc() lets you control the direction of the arc, the rect() method is not so accommodating: rect() always creates a clockwise path. However, in this case we need a counterclockwise rectangular path, so we create one with a rect() method of our own that, like arc(), lets us control the rectangular path's direction:

```
function rect(x, y, w, h, direction) {
   if (direction) { // CCW
       context.moveTo(x, y);
       context.lineTo(x, y + h);
       context.lineTo(x + w, y + h);
       context.lineTo(x + w, y);
   }
   else {
       context.moveTo(x, y);
       context.lineTo(x + w, y);
       context.lineTo(x + w, y + h);
       context.lineTo(x, y + h);
   }
   context.closePath();
}
```

The preceding code uses the moveTo() and lineTo() methods to create a rectangular path either clockwise or counterclockwise. We look more closely at those methods in Section 2.8, "Lines," on p. 103.

The application creates the outer rectangle and the cutout rectangle's paths differently:

```
function addOuterRectanglePath() {
   context.rect(110, 25, 370, 335);
}

function addRectanglePath() {
   rect(310, 55, 70, 35, true);
}
```

The addOuterRectanglePath() method uses the context's rect() method, which always draws clockwise rectangles, with no option to do otherwise; addRectanglePath(), which creates the rectangle cutout's path, uses the rect() method listed above to draw a counterclockwise rectangle.

The JavaScript for the application shown in Figure 2.17 is listed in Example 2.11.

---

**TIP: Direction matters**

The last argument to arc() is a boolean variable that controls the direction of the arc. If the value is true, which is the default, the browser draws the arc clockwise; otherwise, the browser draws the arc counterclockwise (or, as it's referred to in the Canvas specification, anti-clockwise).

---

**NOTE: arc() lets you control direction—rect() does not**

Both context methods arc() and rect() add subpaths to the current path, but only arc() lets you control the direction in which it draws the path. Fortunately, you can easily implement a function that creates a rectangular path with a specific direction, as illustrated by the rect() method in Example 2.11.

---

**TIP: Get rid of the arc() method's unsightly connecting line**

If you call arc() with an existing subpath in the current path, arc() will connect the last point in the existing subpath to the first point in the arc. Usually, you don't want that line to be seen.

You can hide that connection line by invoking beginPath() before stroking the arc with arc(). The call to beginPath() clears all subpaths from the current path, so arc() doesn't stroke the connection line.

---

---

Example 2.11  Refining cutout shapes

---

```
var context = document.getElementById('canvas').getContext('2d');

// Functions.......................................................

function drawGrid(color, stepx, stepy) {
   // Listing omitted for brevity. See Example 2.13 on p. 106
   // for a complete listing.
}

function draw() {
   context.clearRect(0, 0, context.canvas.width,
                           context.canvas.height);
   drawGrid('lightgray', 10, 10);

   context.save();

   context.shadowColor = 'rgba(200,200,0,0.5)';
   context.shadowOffsetX = 12;
   context.shadowOffsetY = 12;
   context.shadowBlur = 15;

   drawCutouts();
   strokeCutoutShapes();
   context.restore();
}

function drawCutouts() {
   context.beginPath();
   addOuterRectanglePath(); // CW

   addCirclePath();     // CCW
   addRectanglePath();  // CCW
   addTrianglePath();   // CCW

   context.fill(); // Cut out shapes
}

function strokeCutoutShapes() {
   context.save();

   context.strokeStyle = 'rgba(0,0,0,0.7)';

   context.beginPath();
   addOuterRectanglePath(); // CW
   context.stroke();

   context.beginPath();
```

---

(Continues)

**Example 2.11**  *(Continued)*

```
    addCirclePath();
    addRectanglePath();
    addTrianglePath();
    context.stroke();

    context.restore();
}

function rect(x, y, w, h, direction) {
  if (direction) { // CCW
      context.moveTo(x, y);
      context.lineTo(x, y + h);
      context.lineTo(x + w, y + h);
      context.lineTo(x + w, y);
      context.closePath();
  }
  else {
      context.moveTo(x, y);
      context.lineTo(x + w, y);
      context.lineTo(x + w, y + h);
      context.lineTo(x, y + h);
      context.closePath();
  }
}

function addOuterRectanglePath() {
   context.rect(110, 25, 370, 335);
}

function addCirclePath() {
   context.arc(300, 300, 40, 0, Math.PI*2, true);
}

function addRectanglePath() {
   rect(310, 55, 70, 35, true);
}

function addTrianglePath() {
   context.moveTo(400, 200);
   context.lineTo(250, 115);
   context.lineTo(200, 200);
   context.closePath();
}

// Initialization.................................................

context.fillStyle = 'goldenrod';
draw();
```

## 2.8 Lines

The Canvas context provides two methods with which you can create linear paths: moveTo() and lineTo(). To make a linear path, more commonly referred to as a line, appear in the canvas, you subsequently call stroke(), as illustrated in the application shown in Figure 2.18, which draws two lines in a canvas.

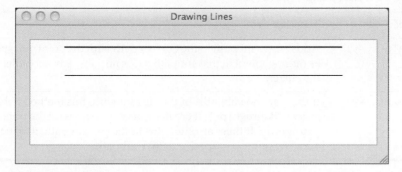

Figure 2.18  Drawing lines

The application shown in Figure 2.18 is listed in Example 2.12.

Example 2.12  Drawing two lines in a canvas

```
var context = document.getElementById('canvas').getContext('2d');

context.lineWidth = 1;
context.beginPath();
context.moveTo(50, 10);
context.lineTo(450, 10);
context.stroke();
context.beginPath();
context.moveTo(50.5, 50.5);
context.lineTo(450.5, 50.5);
context.stroke();
```

After setting the lineWidth property to 1 pixel, the code moves to (50, 10) and draws a horizontal line to (450, 10). That combination of moveTo()/lineTo() creates a linear path, which the code strokes to make the horizontal line appear in the canvas.

Next, the application invokes beginPath(), which removes the linear subpath from the current path. The code then draws another horizontal line beneath the first line.

The code shown in Example 2.12 is simple, but if you look carefully at Figure 2.18, you will see something strange. The top line is two pixels wide, even though the code set the lineWidth property to one pixel before drawing the line. The following section explains why that happens.

Table 2.6 summarizes the moveTo() and lineTo() methods.

**Table 2.6** moveTo() and lineTo()

| Method | Description |
|---|---|
| moveTo(x, y) | Adds a new subpath to the current path with the point you specify as the only point in that subpath. Does not clear any subpaths from the current path. |
| lineTo(x, y) | If there are no subpaths in the current path, this method behaves exactly like moveTo(): It creates a new subpath with the point that you specify. If there are subpaths in the current path, this method adds the point you specify to that subpath. |

### 2.8.1 Lines and Pixel Boundaries

If you draw a one-pixel-wide line on a pixel boundary, the line will actually be two pixels wide, as illustrated in Figure 2.19.

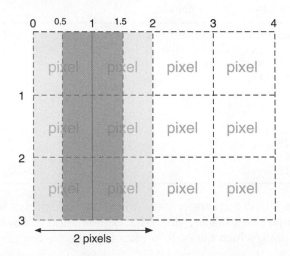

Figure 2.19 Drawing on pixel boundaries

When you draw a one-pixel-wide vertical line on a pixel boundary, the canvas context tries to draw one half of the pixel on the right side of the middle of the line and one half of the pixel on the left side of the middle of the line. However, it's not possible to draw one half of a pixel, so that line extends to one pixel in each direction. In Figure 2.19, the dark gray is what you intend to draw, but the light gray is what the browser actually draws.

On the other hand, consider what happens when you draw between pixels, as illustrated by Figure 2.20.

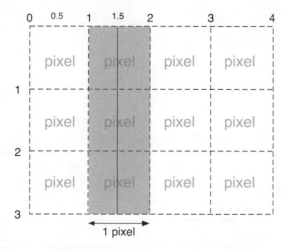

Figure 2.20  Drawing between pixels

In Figure 2.20, the vertical line is drawn between pixels, so drawing one half of the pixel on either side fills exactly one pixel. To draw a true one-pixel line, therefore, you must draw the line between pixels, and not on a pixel boundary. Notice that in Figure 2.18, the two-pixel-wide line is drawn on pixel boundaries, whereas the one-pixel-wide line is drawn between pixels.

Now that you understand how to draw true one-pixel-wide lines, let's put that knowledge to use and draw a grid.

## 2.8.2  Drawing a Grid

Figure 2.21 shows a grid drawn by an application.

The JavaScript for the application shown in Figure 2.21 is listed in Example 2.13.

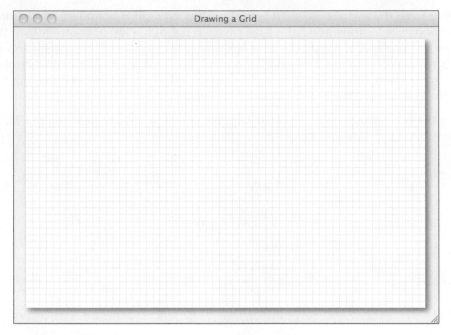

Figure 2.21  Drawing a grid

Example 2.13  Drawing a grid

```
var context = document.getElementById('canvas').getContext('2d');

// Functions................................................

function drawGrid(context, color, stepx, stepy) {
   context.strokeStyle = color;
   context.lineWidth = 0.5;

   for (var i = stepx + 0.5; i < context.canvas.width; i += stepx) {
      context.beginPath();
      context.moveTo(i, 0);
      context.lineTo(i, context.canvas.height);
      context.stroke();
   }

   for (var i = stepy + 0.5; i < context.canvas.height; i += stepy) {
      context.beginPath();
      context.moveTo(0, i);
      context.lineTo(context.canvas.width, i);
      context.stroke();
   }
}
```

```
// Initialization.................................................

drawGrid(context, 'lightgray', 10, 10);
```

Not only does the JavaScript draw lines between pixels as discussed in the preceding section, but it also draws lines that are only 0.5 pixels wide. Although not explicitly required by the Canvas specification, all browser Canvas implementations use anti-aliasing, which can create the illusion of subpixel lines.

## 2.8.3 Drawing Axes

Figure 2.22 shows an application that draws graph axes. The JavaScript for that application is listed in Example 2.14.

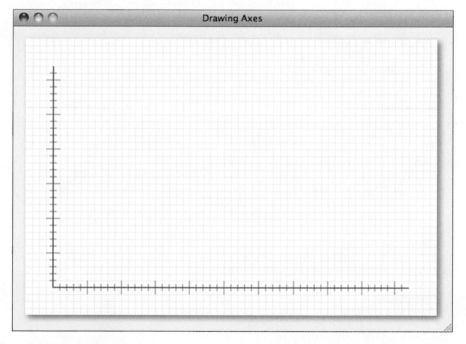

Figure 2.22 Drawing axes

**Example 2.14** Drawing axes

```
var canvas = document.getElementById('canvas'),
    context = canvas.getContext('2d'),

    AXIS_MARGIN = 40,
    AXIS_ORIGIN = { x: AXIS_MARGIN, y: canvas.height-AXIS_MARGIN },

    AXIS_TOP   = AXIS_MARGIN,
    AXIS_RIGHT = canvas.width-AXIS_MARGIN,

    HORIZONTAL_TICK_SPACING = 10,
    VERTICAL_TICK_SPACING = 10,

    AXIS_WIDTH  = AXIS_RIGHT - AXIS_ORIGIN.x,
    AXIS_HEIGHT = AXIS_ORIGIN.y - AXIS_TOP,

    NUM_VERTICAL_TICKS   = AXIS_HEIGHT / VERTICAL_TICK_SPACING,
    NUM_HORIZONTAL_TICKS = AXIS_WIDTH  / HORIZONTAL_TICK_SPACING,

    TICK_WIDTH = 10,
    TICKS_LINEWIDTH = 0.5,
    TICKS_COLOR = 'navy',

    AXIS_LINEWIDTH = 1.0,
    AXIS_COLOR = 'blue';

// Functions.......................................................

function drawGrid(color, stepx, stepy) {
    // Listing omitted for brevity. See Example 2.13 on p. 106
    // for a complete listing.
}

function drawAxes() {
    context.save();
    context.strokeStyle = AXIS_COLOR;
    context.lineWidth = AXIS_LINEWIDTH;

    drawHorizontalAxis();
    drawVerticalAxis();

    context.lineWidth = 0.5;
    context.lineWidth = TICKS_LINEWIDTH;
    context.strokeStyle = TICKS_COLOR;

    drawVerticalAxisTicks();
    drawHorizontalAxisTicks();

    context.restore();
}
```

```
function drawHorizontalAxis() {
   context.beginPath();
   context.moveTo(AXIS_ORIGIN.x, AXIS_ORIGIN.y);
   context.lineTo(AXIS_RIGHT,    AXIS_ORIGIN.y);
   context.stroke();
}

function drawVerticalAxis() {
   context.beginPath();
   context.moveTo(AXIS_ORIGIN.x, AXIS_ORIGIN.y);
   context.lineTo(AXIS_ORIGIN.x, AXIS_TOP);
   context.stroke();
}

function drawVerticalAxisTicks() {
   var deltaY;

   for (var i=1; i < NUM_VERTICAL_TICKS; ++i) {
      context.beginPath();
      if (i % 5 === 0) deltaX = TICK_WIDTH;
      else             deltaX = TICK_WIDTH/2;

      context.moveTo(AXIS_ORIGIN.x - deltaX,
                     AXIS_ORIGIN.y - i * VERTICAL_TICK_SPACING);
      context.lineTo(AXIS_ORIGIN.x + deltaX,
                     AXIS_ORIGIN.y - i * VERTICAL_TICK_SPACING);
      context.stroke();
   }
}

function drawHorizontalAxisTicks() {
   var deltaY;

   for (var i=1; i < NUM_HORIZONTAL_TICKS; ++i) {
      context.beginPath();
      if (i % 5 === 0) deltaY = TICK_WIDTH;
      else             deltaY = TICK_WIDTH/2;

      context.moveTo(AXIS_ORIGIN.x + i * HORIZONTAL_TICK_SPACING,
                     AXIS_ORIGIN.y - deltaY);
      context.lineTo(AXIS_ORIGIN.x + i * HORIZONTAL_TICK_SPACING,
                     AXIS_ORIGIN.y + deltaY);
      context.stroke();
   }
}
// Initialization..............................................

drawGrid('lightgray', 10, 10);
drawAxes();
```

The JavaScript uses constants to calculate characteristics of the axes, such as axis width and height, spacing between tick marks, etc. The rest of the code is mostly concerned with invoking the following sequence of context methods: beginPath(), moveTo(), lineTo(), and stroke() for both the axes and their tick marks.

Now that you know how to draw lines, let's take a look at how you can let users interactively draw them.

### 2.8.4  Rubberband Lines

The paint application discussed at the beginning of this chapter lets users draw lines by interactively drawing a line over the background as the user drags the mouse. The application shown in Figure 2.23 does likewise.

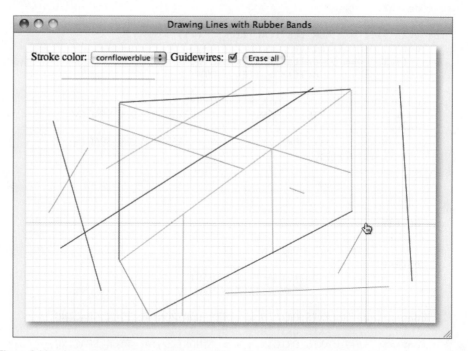

Figure 2.23  Drawing lines with rubber bands

The HTML and JavaScript for the application shown in Figure 2.23 are listed in Examples 2.15 and 2.16, respectively. Notice the methods in the Rubber bands section of the code, and the mouse event handlers.

In the onmousedown event handler, the application converts window coordinates to canvas coordinates, and invokes the event's preventDefault() method to inhibit the browser's default reaction to the event.

The onmousedown event handler then saves the drawing surface, records the location of the mouse down event, and sets a boolean flag named dragging to true.

---

**Example 2.15** Rubberband lines: HTML

---

```html
<!DOCTYPE html>
<html>
    <head>
        <title>Drawing Lines with Rubber Bands</title>

        <style>
            body {
                background: #eeeeee;
            }

            #controls {
                position: absolute;
                left: 25px;
                top: 25px;
            }

            #canvas {
                background: #ffffff;
                cursor: pointer;
                margin-left: 10px;
                margin-top: 10px;
                -webkit-box-shadow: 4px 4px 8px rgba(0,0,0,0.5);
                -moz-box-shadow: 4px 4px 8px rgba(0,0,0,0.5);
                -box-shadow: 4px 4px 8px rgba(0,0,0,0.5);
            }
        </style>
    </head>

    <body>
        <canvas id='canvas' width='600' height='400'>
            Canvas not supported
        </canvas>
```

---

*(Continues)*

**Example 2.15**  *(Continued)*

```
    <div id='controls'>
        Stroke color: <select id='strokeStyleSelect'>
        <option value='red'>red</option>
        <option value='green'>green</option>
        <option value='blue'>blue</option>
        <option value='orange'>orange</option>
        <option value='cornflowerblue' selected>cornflowerblue</option>
        <option value='goldenrod'>goldenrod</option>
        <option value='navy'>navy</option>
        <option value='purple'>purple</option>
        </select>

        Guidewires:
        <input id='guidewireCheckbox' type='checkbox' checked/>
        <input id='eraseAllButton' type='button' value='Erase all'/>
    </div>

    <script src = 'example.js'></script>
  </body>
</html>
```

**Example 2.16**  Rubberband lines: JavaScript

```
var canvas = document.getElementById('canvas'),
    context = canvas.getContext('2d'),
    eraseAllButton = document.getElementById('eraseAllButton'),
    strokeStyleSelect = document.getElementById('strokeStyleSelect'),
    guidewireCheckbox = document.getElementById('guidewireCheckbox'),
    drawingSurfaceImageData,
    mousedown = {},
    rubberbandRect = {},
    dragging = false,
    guidewires = guidewireCheckbox.checked;

// Functions.......................................................

function drawGrid(color, stepx, stepy) {
    // Listing omitted for brevity. See Example 2.13 on p. 106
    // for a complete listing.
}

function windowToCanvas(x, y) {
    var bbox = canvas.getBoundingClientRect();
    return { x: x - bbox.left * (canvas.width  / bbox.width),
             y: y - bbox.top  * (canvas.height / bbox.height) };
}
```

```
// Save and restore drawing surface...................................

function saveDrawingSurface() {
   drawingSurfaceImageData = context.getImageData(0, 0,
                                          canvas.width,
                                          canvas.height);
}

function restoreDrawingSurface() {
   context.putImageData(drawingSurfaceImageData, 0, 0);
}

// Rubber bands.....................................................

function updateRubberbandRectangle(loc) {
   rubberbandRect.width  = Math.abs(loc.x - mousedown.x);
   rubberbandRect.height = Math.abs(loc.y - mousedown.y);

   if (loc.x > mousedown.x) rubberbandRect.left = mousedown.x;
   else                     rubberbandRect.left = loc.x;

   if (loc.y > mousedown.y) rubberbandRect.top = mousedown.y;
   else                     rubberbandRect.top = loc.y;
}

function drawRubberbandShape(loc) {
   context.beginPath();
   context.moveTo(mousedown.x, mousedown.y);
   context.lineTo(loc.x, loc.y);
   context.stroke();
}

function updateRubberband(loc) {
   updateRubberbandRectangle(loc);
   drawRubberbandShape(loc);
}

// Guidewires.......................................................

function drawHorizontalLine (y) {
   context.beginPath();
   context.moveTo(0,y+0.5);
   context.lineTo(context.canvas.width, y+0.5);
   context.stroke();
}
```

*(Continues)*

**Example 2.16** *(Continued)*

```
function drawVerticalLine (x) {
   context.beginPath();
   context.moveTo(x+0.5,0);
   context.lineTo(x+0.5, context.canvas.height);
   context.stroke();
}

function drawGuidewires(x, y) {
   context.save();
   context.strokeStyle = 'rgba(0,0,230,0.4)';
   context.lineWidth = 0.5;
   drawVerticalLine(x);
   drawHorizontalLine(y);
   context.restore();
}

// Canvas event handlers...........................................

canvas.onmousedown = function (e) {
   var loc = windowToCanvas(e.clientX, e.clientY);

   e.preventDefault(); // Prevent cursor change
   saveDrawingSurface();
   mousedown.x = loc.x;
   mousedown.y = loc.y;
   dragging = true;
};

canvas.onmousemove = function (e) {
   var loc;

   if (dragging) {
      e.preventDefault(); // Prevent selections

      loc = windowToCanvas(e.clientX, e.clientY);
      restoreDrawingSurface();
      updateRubberband(loc);

      if(guidewires) {
         drawGuidewires(loc.x, loc.y);
      }
   }
};
```

```
canvas.onmouseup = function (e) {
   loc = windowToCanvas(e.clientX, e.clientY);
   restoreDrawingSurface();
   updateRubberband(loc);
   dragging = false;
};

// Controls event handlers......................................

eraseAllButton.onclick = function (e) {
   context.clearRect(0, 0, canvas.width, canvas.height);
   drawGrid('lightgray', 10, 10);
   saveDrawingSurface();
};

strokeStyleSelect.onchange = function (e) {
   context.strokeStyle = strokeStyleSelect.value;
};

guidewireCheckbox.onchange = function (e) {
   guidewires = guidewireCheckbox.checked;
};

// Initialization..............................................

context.strokeStyle = strokeStyleSelect.value;
drawGrid('lightgray', 10, 10);
```

Subsequently, as the user drags the mouse, the application maintains a rectangle it calls `rubberbandRect`. That rectangle, which is illustrated in Figure 2.24, is defined by two corners: the location of the mouse down event and the mouse's current location.

For every mouse move event that occurs while the user is dragging the mouse, the application does three things:

1.   Restores the drawing surface
2.   Updates `rubberbandRect`
3.   Draws a line from the mouse down location to the current mouse location

The application's `onmousedown` event handler saves the drawing surface, so restoring the drawing surface in the `onmousemove` event handler effectively erases the rubberband line.

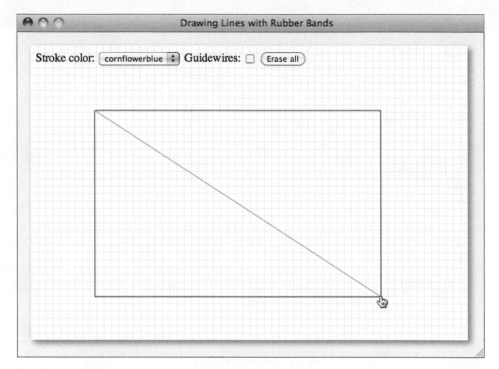

Figure 2.24  The rubberband rectangle

---

 **NOTE: Future uses for the rubberband rectangle**

The application in Example 2.16 maintains a rubberband rectangle while the user is dragging the mouse. Notice that the function that draws the rubberband line is named drawRubberbandShape(). Because the application maintains a rubberband rectangle, we can modify drawRubberbandShape() to support any shape, such as circles or arbitrary polygons, that fits inside a rectangle.

In fact, we reimplement drawRubberbandShape() to do just that in the pages that follow.

---

## 2.8.5 Drawing Dashed Lines

As this book was written, the Canvas context did not provide methods to draw dashed or dotted lines; however, it's easy to implement that functionality yourself. Figure 2.25 shows an application that draws dashed lines.

Figure 2.25  Dashed lines

The application shown in Figure 2.25 is listed in Example 2.17.

The code calculates the length of the line and, based on the length of each dash, figures out how many dashes the line will contain. Based on the number of dashes, the code draws a dashed line by repeatedly drawing short line segments.

**Example 2.17** Dashed lines

```
var context = document.getElementById('canvas').getContext('2d');

function drawDashedLine(context, x1, y1, x2, y2, dashLength) {
   dashLength = dashLength === undefined ? 5 : dashLength;

   var deltaX = x2 - x1;
   var deltaY = y2 - y1;
   var numDashes = Math.floor(
      Math.sqrt(deltaX * deltaX + deltaY * deltaY) / dashLength);

   for (var i=0; i < numDashes; ++i) {
      context[ i % 2 === 0 ? 'moveTo' : 'lineTo' ]
         (x1 + (deltaX / numDashes) * i, y1 + (deltaY / numDashes) * i);
   }

   context.stroke();
};

context.lineWidth = 3;
context.strokeStyle = 'blue';
drawDashedLine(context, 20, 20, context.canvas.width-20, 20);
drawDashedLine(context, context.canvas.width-20, 20,
   context.canvas.width-20, context.canvas.height-20, 10);
drawDashedLine(context, context.canvas.width-20,
   context.canvas.height-20, 20, context.canvas.height-20, 15);
drawDashedLine(context, 20, context.canvas.height-20, 20, 20, 2);
```

## 2.8.6 Drawing Dashed Lines by Extending CanvasRenderingContext2D

The drawDashedLine() function in the preceding section draws a dashed line in a specified context, but what if you want to add a dashedLineTo() method to the Canvas context that works like lineTo()?

The fundamental roadblock to adding a dashedLineTo() method to the Canvas context is that there's no way to get the position that you last passed to moveTo(). That position is where the line starts, so a CanvasRenderingContext2D. dashedLineTo() method must have access to that position.

Although the Canvas context does not give you explicit access to the position you specified the last time you called moveTo(), you can add that functionality to the context as follows:

1. Obtain a reference to the context's moveTo() method.
2. Add a property named lastMoveToLocation to the Canvas context.
3. Redefine the context's moveTo() method to store the point that you pass to the method in the lastMoveToLocation property.

Once you have access to the last position that you passed to the moveTo() method, implementing a dashedLineTo() method that you add to the CanvasRenderingContext2D's prototype object is easy. Example 2.18 shows the code described above.

**Example 2.18** Extending CanvasRenderingContext2D

```
var context = document.getElementById('canvas').getContext('2d'),
    moveToFunction = CanvasRenderingContext2D.prototype.moveTo;

CanvasRenderingContext2D.prototype.lastMoveToLocation = {};

CanvasRenderingContext2D.prototype.moveTo = function (x, y) {
   moveToFunction.apply(context, [x,y]);
   this.lastMoveToLocation.x = x;
   this.lastMoveToLocation.y = y;
};

CanvasRenderingContext2D.prototype.dashedLineTo =
      function (x, y, dashLength) {
   dashLength = dashLength === undefined ? 5 : dashLength;

   var startX = this.lastMoveToLocation.x;
   var startY = this.lastMoveToLocation.y;

   var deltaX = x - startX;
   var deltaY = y - startY;
   var numDashes = Math.floor(Math.sqrt(deltaX * deltaX
                         + deltaY * deltaY) / dashLength);

   for (var i=0; i < numDashes; ++i) {
      this[ i % 2 === 0 ? 'moveTo' : 'lineTo' ]
         (startX + (deltaX / numDashes) * i,
             startY + (deltaY / numDashes) * i);
   }

   this.moveTo(x, y);
};
```

With this modification to CanvasRenderingContext2D, you can draw dashed lines like this:

```
context.lineWidth = 3;
context.strokeStyle = 'blue';

context.moveTo(20, 20);
context.dashedLineTo(context.canvas.width-20, 20);
context.dashedLineTo(context.canvas.width-20,
                     context.canvas.height-20);
context.dashedLineTo(20, context.canvas.height-20);
context.dashedLineTo(20, 20);
context.dashedLineTo(context.canvas.width-20,
                     context.canvas.height-20);
context.stroke();
```

Figure 2.26 shows the result of the preceding code.

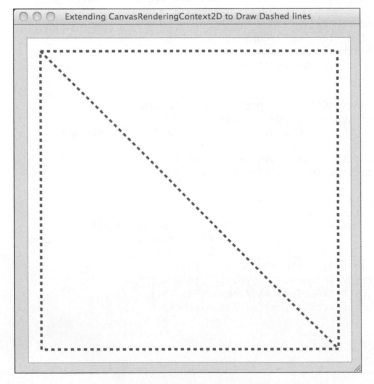

Figure 2.26   Implementing dashed lines by extending the 2d context

**CAUTION: Be careful when extending CanvasRenderingContext2D**

Although some developers regard JavaScript as a toy language, it's actually quite powerful, as the code in this section illustrates. The technique used in this section goes by many names, such as *metaprogramming*, *monkey patching*, and *clobbering* methods, meaning you obtain a reference to an object's method, redefine that method, and then optionally use the original method in the redefined method.

However, you should be judicious when it comes to extending the context's capabilities. If you extend the context as shown in this section with a drawDashedLineTo() method and you are unlucky enough that CanvasRenderingContext2D adds a dashedLineTo() method or a lastMoveToLocation property in the future, then your addition to the context could wreak havoc with the new, official capabilities in CanvasRenderingContext2D.

**NOTE: The HTML5 Canvas specification is constantly evolving**

As this book went to press, support for dashed lines was added to the Canvas specification. It's important to keep in mind that HTML5 specifications are constantly evolving. Because of that evolution, it's a good idea to check the specifications once in a while for changes.

## 2.8.7 Line Caps and Joins

When you draw lines in a canvas you can control what the endpoints—known as line caps—of those lines look like, as illustrated by Figure 2.27. Line caps are controlled by the aptly named lineCap property of the Canvas context.

Figure 2.27  Line caps

The default line cap is butt, which leaves the end of the line untouched. Both round and square add a cap to the end of the line; round adds a semicircle to the end of the line with a diameter equal to one half the width of the line; square adds a rectangle to the end of the line whose length is equal to the line width and whose width is half of the line width.

When you draw lines or rectangles, you can control what the corners look like where the lines meet, known as the line join, as shown in Figure 2.28. Line joins are controlled by the `lineJoin` property.

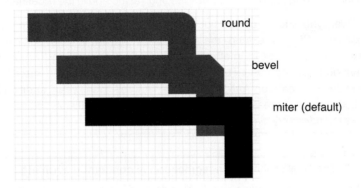

**Figure 2.28** Line joins

A bevel value for the `lineJoin` property results in a triangle connecting the opposite corners of the two lines with a straight line. `miter`, which is the default value for the `lineJoin` property, is the same as bevel, except that `miter` adds an extra triangle to square the corner. Finally, a round value for `lineJoin` results in a filled arc connecting the two corners. Line joins are further illustrated in Figure 2.29.

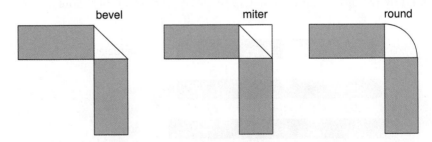

**Figure 2.29** Constructing line joins

When you use `miter` for line joins, you can also specify a `miterLimit` property, which is a ratio of *miter length* divided by *one-half of the line width*. Miter length is illustrated in Figure 2.30.

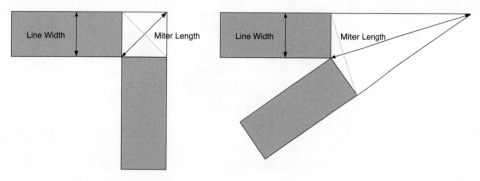

Figure 2.30  Miter length

As Figure 2.30 illustrates, the miter length can get pretty long if the angle between two lines is small enough. If the miter length is long enough that the ratio of (miter length / ½ of the line width) is greater than the value you specify for the miterLimit property, the browser treats the line join as if it were a bevel, as illustrated in Figure 2.31.

Table 2.7 summarizes Canvas context properties that pertain to lines.

Table 2.7  CanvasRenderingContext2D line attributes

| Attribute | Description | Type | Allowed Values | Default |
|---|---|---|---|---|
| lineWidth | Line width, in pixels. | double | A positive, nonzero number | 1.0 |
| lineCap | Determines how the browser draws the ends of lines. | DOMString | butt, round, square | butt |
| lineJoin | Determines how the browser joins lines that meet. | DOMString | round, bevel, miter | bevel |
| miterLimit | A ratio of the miter length divided by one-half of the line width. If the miter limit is exceeded for a miter line join, the browser treats the line join as a bevel. | double | A positive, nonzero number | 10.0 |

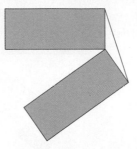

Figure 2.31  Miter limit exceeded, so browser joins the lines with a bevel

## 2.9  Arcs and Circles

The Canvas context provides two methods for drawing arcs and circles: `arc()` and `arcTo()`. In this section we look at both of those methods.

### 2.9.1  The `arc()` Method

The `arc()` method takes six parameters: `arc(x, y, radius, startAngle, endAngle, counterClockwise)`. The first two parameters represent a point at the center of a circle; the third argument represents the radius of the circle; and the fourth and fifth arguments represent the starting angle and end angle, respectively, of the arc that the browser draws around the circumference of the circle. The last argument to `arc()` is optional and represents the direction in which the browser draws the arc. If that value is `false`, which is the default, the browser draws the arc clockwise; if the value is `true`, the browser draws the arc counterclockwise. The `arc()` method is illustrated in **Figure 2.32**.

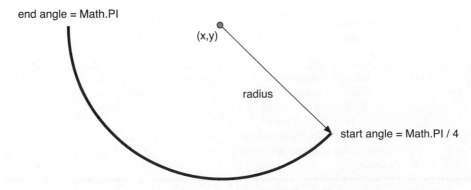

Figure 2.32  Drawing an arc with `arc(x, y, radius, Math.PI/4, Math.PI, false)`

The arc() method may draw more than an arc, however. If there are any subpaths in the current path, the browser will connect the last point in the subpath to the first point on the arc, as shown in Figure 2.33.

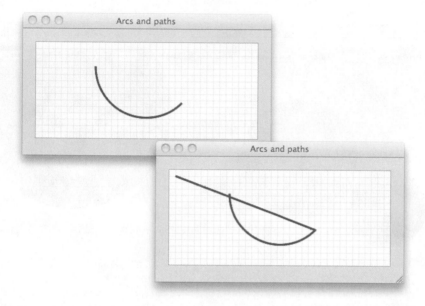

Figure 2.33 Drawing arcs after clearing subpaths (*top*) and without clearing subpaths (*bottom*)

The arc in the top screenshot was created like this:

```
context.beginPath();
context.arc(canvas.width/2, canvas.height/4, 80, Math.PI/4,
        Math.PI, false);
```

Before invoking arc(), the preceding code calls beginPath(), which as you know from Section 2.8, "Lines," on p. 103, clears any subpaths from the current path.

The bottom screenshot in Figure 2.33 was created like this:

```
context.beginPath();
context.moveTo(10, 10);
context.arc(canvas.width/2, canvas.height/4, 80, Math.PI/4,
        Math.PI, false);
```

The preceding code invokes moveTo() before it calls the arc() method. As you also know from Section 2.8, moveTo() adds a new subpath to the current path with a single point. In this case, the point is (10, 10), and before drawing the arc, the browser connects that point to the first point in the arc with a straight line.

## 2.9.2 Rubberband Circles

The application shown in Figure 2.34 lets users draw circles by dragging the mouse. As the user drags the mouse, the application continuously draws the circle.

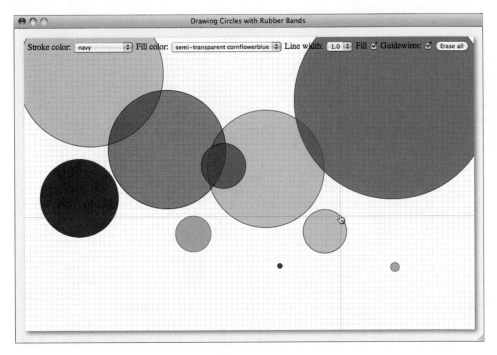

Figure 2.34  Drawing circles with rubber bands

In Example 2.16 on p. 112, you saw how to draw rubberband lines. Recall that the application in that section could support other shapes besides lines by reimplementing the drawRubberbandShape() function. That's exactly how the application shown in Figure 2.34 was implemented. The drawRubberbandShape() function is listed in Example 2.19.

The loc object passed to drawRubberbandShape() contains the current X and Y mouse coordinates. The location where the mouse down event occurred is stored in a variable named mousedown, which, like the loc object, stores X and Y coordinates.

The application calculates the distance between the mouse down location and the current mouse location, accounting for horizontal lines. The application subsequently uses that distance for the circle's radius.

---

Example 2.19 Drawing circles with rubber bands

---

```
function drawRubberbandShape(loc) {
    var angle,
        radius;

    if (mousedown.y === loc.y) { // Horizontal line
        // Horizontal lines are a special case. See the else
        // block for an explanation

        radius = Math.abs(loc.x - mousedown.x);
    }
    else {
        // For horizontal lines, the angle is 0, and Math.sin(0)
        // is 0, which means we would be dividing by 0 here to get NaN
        // for radius. The if block above catches horizontal lines.

        angle = Math.atan(rubberbandRect.height/rubberbandRect.width),
        radius = rubberbandRect.height / Math.sin(angle);
    }

    context.beginPath();
    context.arc(mousedown.x, mousedown.y, radius, 0, Math.PI*2, false);
    context.stroke();

    if (fillCheckbox.checked)
        context.fill();
}
```

---

**CAUTION: Optional arguments are not always optional**

The Canvas specification clearly states that the last argument to the arc() method—a boolean that determines whether to draw the arc clockwise or counterclockwise—is optional. That means you don't need to specify that boolean value, except for the Opera browser. Opera, at the time this book was written, requires the optional argument, and to add insult to injury, it *fails silently* if you don't specify the optional argument.

## 2.9.3 The arcTo() Method

In addition to arc(), the Canvas context provides another method for creating arc paths: arcTo(), which takes five arguments: arcTo(x1, y1, x2, y2, radius).

The arguments to arcTo() represent two points and the radius of the circle. The method draws an arc from the first point to the second, with the specified radius. The arc is tangent to the line from the current point to (x1, y1), and is tangent to the line from the current point to (x2, y2). Those qualities make arcTo() well suited for drawing rounded corners, as illustrated in Figure 2.35.

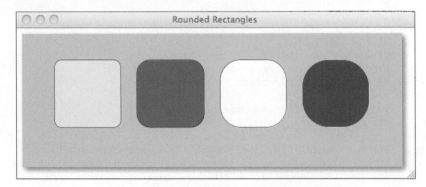

Figure 2.35  Rounded rectangles: Corner radii in pixels, from left to right: 10, 20, 30, 40

The application shown in Figure 2.35 is listed in Example 2.20.

**Example 2.20** Using arcTo()

```
var context = document.getElementById('canvas').getContext('2d');

// Functions......................................................

function roundedRect(cornerX, cornerY,
                     width, height, cornerRadius) {
   if (width > 0) context.moveTo(cornerX + cornerRadius, cornerY);
   else           context.moveTo(cornerX - cornerRadius, cornerY);

   context.arcTo(cornerX + width, cornerY,
             cornerX + width, cornerY + height,
             cornerRadius);

   context.arcTo(cornerX + width, cornerY + height,
             cornerX, cornerY + height,
             cornerRadius);

   context.arcTo(cornerX, cornerY + height,
             cornerX, cornerY,
             cornerRadius);
```

```
    if (width > 0) {
        context.arcTo(cornerX, cornerY,
                      cornerX + cornerRadius, cornerY,
                      cornerRadius);
    }
    else {
        context.arcTo(cornerX, cornerY,
                      cornerX - cornerRadius, cornerY,
                      cornerRadius);
    }
}

function drawRoundedRect(strokeStyle, fillStyle, cornerX, cornerY,
                         width, height, cornerRadius) {
    context.beginPath();

    roundedRect(cornerX, cornerY, width, height, cornerRadius);

    context.strokeStyle = strokeStyle;
    context.fillStyle = fillStyle;

    context.stroke();
    context.fill();
}

// Initialization.............................................

drawRoundedRect('blue',   'yellow',  50,  40,  100,  100, 10);
drawRoundedRect('purple', 'green',  275,  40, -100,  100, 20);
drawRoundedRect('red',    'white',  300, 140,  100, -100, 30);
drawRoundedRect('white',  'blue',   525, 140, -100, -100, 40);
```

Like arc(), arcTo() draws a straight line from the last point in the most recent subpath that you added to the current path to the point specified with the first two arguments to arcTo(). That line is why the roundedRect() method listed in Example 2.20 does not explicitly draw any lines.

The arc() and arcTo() methods are summarized in Table 2.8.

**NOTE: Adding a roundedRect() method to CanvasRenderingContext2D**

You can easily add a roundedRect() method to the Canvas context; if you do, however, you should be aware that there is some risk. See Section 2.8.6, "Drawing Dashed Lines by Extending CanvasRenderingContext2D," on p. 118 for more information about adding methods to the Canvas context and the associated risks.

**Table 2.8** CanvasRenderingContext2D methods for drawing arcs and circles

| Method | Description |
|---|---|
| arc(double x, double y, double radius, double startAngle, double endAngle, boolean counter-clockwise) | Creates an arc path at (x, y) with the specified radius, from startAngle to endAngle. You specify angles in radians, not degrees. (180 degrees = π radians). The last argument is optional; if true, the arc is drawn counterclockwise, if the argument is false (which is the default), the arc is drawn clockwise. |
| | If there are any subpaths in the current path when you call this method, the browser will connect the starting point of the arc to the last point in the subpath with a line. |
| arcTo(double x1, double y1, double x2, double y2, double radius) | Creates an arc path from (x1, x2) to (x2, y2) with the specified radius. The arc is tangent to the line from the last point in current path to (x1, y1), and is tangent to the line from the current point to (x2, y2). |
| | As is the case for arc(), if there are any subpaths in the current path when you call this method, the browser will connect the starting point of the arc to the last point in the subpath with a line. |

## 2.9.4  Dials and Gauges

Arcs, and especially circles, are often used to portray physical objects; for example, in Section 1.5, "Fundamental Drawing Operations," on p. 22, you saw how to implement a clock with a circular face. Figure 2.36 shows an application that implements a dial with five circles. That dial represents the degrees of a circle and is used in Section 2.13.1, "Translating, Scaling, and Rotating," on p. 171 for interactively rotating polygon objects.

The application shown in Figure 2.36 uses much of what you learned so far in this chapter. To draw the dial, the application draws circles and lines, uses colors and transparency, strokes and fills circular paths, and uses shadows to give the dial some depth. It also implements a cutout—similar to those discussed in Section 2.7.2.1, "Cutout Shapes," on p. 98—that gives the ring around the outside of the dial its semitransparent color.

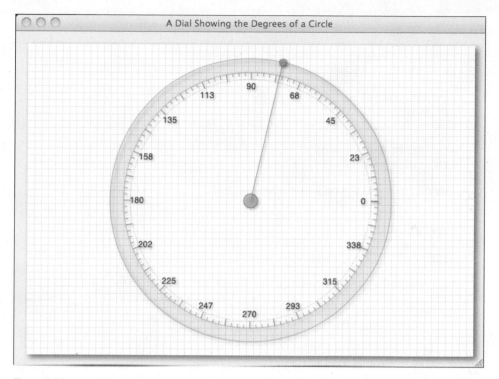

**Figure 2.36** Drawing a dial

An excerpt of the JavaScript for the application shown in **Figure** 2.36 is listed in **Example** 2.21. The application's drawDial() function invokes other functions to draw pieces of the dial:

```
function drawDial() {
    var loc = {x: circle.x, y: circle.y};

    drawCentroid();
    drawCentroidGuidewire(loc);

    drawRing();
    drawTickInnerCircle();
    drawTicks();
    drawAnnotations();
}
```

As you look through the JavaScript in **Example** 2.21, notice the functions invoked by drawDial().

Example 2.21 Drawing a dial

```javascript
var canvas = document.getElementById('canvas'),
    context = canvas.getContext('2d'),

    CENTROID_RADIUS = 10,
    CENTROID_STROKE_STYLE = 'rgba(0,0,0,0.5)',
    CENTROID_FILL_STYLE   = 'rgba(80,190,240,0.6)',

    RING_INNER_RADIUS = 35,
    RING_OUTER_RADIUS = 55,

    ANNOTATIONS_FILL_STYLE = 'rgba(0,0,230,0.9)',
    ANNOTATIONS_TEXT_SIZE = 12,

    TICK_WIDTH = 10,
    TICK_LONG_STROKE_STYLE = 'rgba(100,140,230,0.9)',
    TICK_SHORT_STROKE_STYLE = 'rgba(100,140,230,0.7)',

    TRACKING_DIAL_STROKING_STYLE = 'rgba(100,140,230,0.5)',

    GUIDEWIRE_STROKE_STYLE = 'goldenrod',
    GUIDEWIRE_FILL_STYLE = 'rgba(250,250,0,0.6)',

    circle = { x: canvas.width/2,
               y: canvas.height/2,
               radius: 150
             };

// Functions.....................................................

function drawGrid(color, stepx, stepy) {
   context.save()
   context.shadowColor = undefined;
   context.shadowOffsetX = 0;
   context.shadowOffsetY = 0;
   context.strokeStyle = color;
   context.fillStyle = '#ffffff';
   context.lineWidth = 0.5;
   context.fillRect(0, 0, context.canvas.width,
                          context.canvas.height);

   for (var i = stepx + 0.5;
           i < context.canvas.width; i += stepx) {
     context.beginPath();
     context.moveTo(i, 0);
     context.lineTo(i, context.canvas.height);
     context.stroke();
   }
```

```
   for (var i = stepy + 0.5;
            i < context.canvas.height; i += stepy) {
      context.beginPath();
      context.moveTo(0, i);
      context.lineTo(context.canvas.width, i);
      context.stroke();
   }
   context.restore();
}

function drawDial() {
   var loc = {x: circle.x, y: circle.y};

   drawCentroid();
   drawCentroidGuidewire(loc);
   drawRing();
   drawTickInnerCircle();
   drawTicks();
   drawAnnotations();
}

function drawCentroid() {
   context.beginPath();
   context.save();
   context.strokeStyle = CENTROID_STROKE_STYLE;
   context.fillStyle = CENTROID_FILL_STYLE;
   context.arc(circle.x, circle.y,
               CENTROID_RADIUS, 0, Math.PI*2, false);
   context.stroke();
   context.fill();
   context.restore();
}

function drawCentroidGuidewire(loc) {
   var angle = -Math.PI/4,
       radius, endpt;

  radius = circle.radius + RING_OUTER_RADIUS;

  if (loc.x >= circle.x) {
     endpt = { x: circle.x + radius * Math.cos(angle),
               y: circle.y + radius * Math.sin(angle)
     };
  }
  else {
     endpt = { x: circle.x - radius * Math.cos(angle),
               y: circle.y - radius * Math.sin(angle)
     };
  }
```

*(Continues)*

**Example 2.21** *(Continued)*

```
   context.save();

   context.strokeStyle = GUIDEWIRE_STROKE_STYLE;
   context.fillStyle = GUIDEWIRE_FILL_STYLE;

   context.beginPath();
   context.moveTo(circle.x, circle.y);
   context.lineTo(endpt.x, endpt.y);
   context.stroke();

   context.beginPath();
   context.strokeStyle = TICK_LONG_STROKE_STYLE;
   context.arc(endpt.x, endpt.y, 5, 0, Math.PI*2, false);
   context.fill();
   context.stroke();

   context.restore();
}

function drawRing() {
   drawRingOuterCircle();

   context.strokeStyle = 'rgba(0,0,0,0.1)';
   context.arc(circle.x, circle.y,
               circle.radius + RING_INNER_RADIUS,
               0, Math.PI*2, false);

   context.fillStyle = 'rgba(100,140,230,0.1)';
   context.fill();
   context.stroke();
}

function drawRingOuterCircle() {
   context.shadowColor = 'rgba(0,0,0,0.7)';
   context.shadowOffsetX = 3,
   context.shadowOffsetY = 3,
   context.shadowBlur = 6,
   context.strokeStyle = TRACKING_DIAL_STROKING_STYLE;
   context.beginPath();
   context.arc(circle.x, circle.y, circle.radius +
               RING_OUTER_RADIUS, 0, Math.PI*2, true);
   context.stroke();
}
```

```
function drawTickInnerCircle() {
   context.save();
   context.beginPath();
   context.strokeStyle = 'rgba(0,0,0,0.1)';
   context.arc(circle.x, circle.y,
               circle.radius + RING_INNER_RADIUS - TICK_WIDTH,
               0, Math.PI*2, false);
   context.stroke();
   context.restore();
}

function drawTick(angle, radius, cnt) {
   var tickWidth = cnt % 4 === 0 ? TICK_WIDTH : TICK_WIDTH/2;

   context.beginPath();
   context.moveTo(circle.x + Math.cos(angle) * (radius - tickWidth),
               circle.y + Math.sin(angle) * (radius - tickWidth));

   context.lineTo(circle.x + Math.cos(angle) * (radius),
               circle.y + Math.sin(angle) * (radius));
   context.strokeStyle = TICK_SHORT_STROKE_STYLE;
   context.stroke();
}

function drawTicks() {
   var radius = circle.radius + RING_INNER_RADIUS,
       ANGLE_MAX = 2*Math.PI,
       ANGLE_DELTA = Math.PI/64,
       tickWidth;

   context.save();

   for (var angle = 0, cnt = 0; angle < ANGLE_MAX;
                           angle += ANGLE_DELTA, cnt++) {
      drawTick(angle, radius, cnt++);
   }

   context.restore();
}

function drawAnnotations() {
   var radius = circle.radius + RING_INNER_RADIUS;

   context.save();
   context.fillStyle = ANNOTATIONS_FILL_STYLE;
   context.font = ANNOTATIONS_TEXT_SIZE + 'px Helvetica';
```

*(Continues)*

---

Example 2.21  *(Continued)*

---

```
    for (var angle=0; angle < 2*Math.PI; angle += Math.PI/8) {
        context.beginPath();
        context.fillText((angle * 180 / Math.PI).toFixed(0),
            circle.x + Math.cos(angle) * (radius - TICK_WIDTH*2),
            circle.y - Math.sin(angle) * (radius - TICK_WIDTH*2));
    }
    context.restore();
}

// Initialization.................................................

context.shadowColor = 'rgba(0,0,0,0.4)';
context.shadowOffsetX = 2;
context.shadowOffsetY = 2;
context.shadowBlur = 4;

context.textAlign = 'center';
context.textBaseline = 'middle';

drawGrid('lightgray', 10, 10);
drawDial();
```

---

There are some things to note in general about the JavaScript listed in Example 2.21. First, as is often the case, the application calls beginPath() before (nearly) each call to arc() to begin a new path before creating the arc's path. Recall that the arc() method connects the first point in the arc to the last point in the last subpath added to the current path. The calls to beginPath() clear out all subpaths from the current path, so arc() does not draw unsightly lines.

The application uses the cutout technique to give the ring a translucent background by using arc() to draw the outer circle of the ring clockwise, and the inner circle counter-clockwise. In this case, the application does *not* invoke beginPath() before the second call to arc() for the cutout.

Second, notice that temporary modifications to context attributes such as strokeStyle and fillStyle are placed between calls to save() and restore(). The Canvas context's save() and restore() methods let you implement drawing functions that stand on their own, without side effects.

Finally, notice how the application draws the text around the dial. By initially setting the context's textAlign and textBaseline to center and middle, the application is able to easily calculate positions for the text. We discuss that technique in Section 3.3.5, "Labeling Dials," on p. 221.

## 2.10 Bézier Curves

Originally developed by a French physicist and mathematician named Paul de Casteljau, bézier curves were popularized by a French engineer named Pierre Bézier.

Bézier curves were originally used to design automobile bodies and today are used in most computer graphics systems such as Adobe Illustrator, Apple's Cocoa, and HTML5 Canvas.

There are two types of bézier curves: quadratic and cubic. Quadratic curves are second degree curves, meaning they are defined by three points: two anchor points and one control point. Cubic bézier curves are third-degree curves so they are defined with four points: two anchor points and two control points.

Canvas supports both quadratic and cubic bézier curves. The sections that follow explore generating those curves with Canvas.

### 2.10.1 Quadratic Curves

Quadratic bézier curves are simple curves that curve in one direction. Figure 2.37 shows the use of three quadratic bézier curves that together constitute a checkbox.

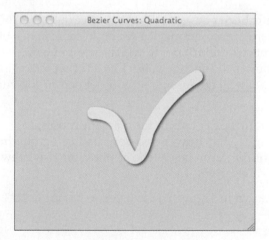

Figure 2.37  Using quadratic curves to draw a checkbox

The JavaScript for the application shown in Figure 2.37 is listed in Example 2.22.

**Example 2.22** Drawing quadratic curves

```
var context = document.getElementById('canvas').getContext('2d');

context.fillStyle      = 'cornflowerblue';
context.strokeStyle    = 'yellow';

context.shadowColor    = 'rgba(50,50,50,1.0)';
context.shadowOffsetX = 2;
context.shadowOffsetY = 2;
context.shadowBlur     = 4;

context.lineWidth = 20;
context.lineCap = 'round';

context.beginPath();
context.moveTo(120.5, 130);
context.quadraticCurveTo(150.8, 130, 160.6, 150.5);
context.quadraticCurveTo(190, 250.0, 210.5, 160.5);
context.quadraticCurveTo(240, 100.5, 290, 70.5);

context.stroke();
```

You draw quadratic bézier curves with the quadraticCurveTo() method, which takes four arguments representing the X and Y coordinates of two points. The first point is the curve's control point, which determines the shape of the curve, and the second point is the anchor point. The quadraticCurveTo() method connects the anchor point to the last point you defined in the current path with a bézier curve.

You can use quadratic bézier curves for many purposes; for example, the application shown in Figure 2.38 draws an arrowhead using quadratic bézier curves for the three tips of the arrowhead. The application also draws the control and anchor points for each curve.

The application shown in Figure 2.38 is listed in Example 2.23.

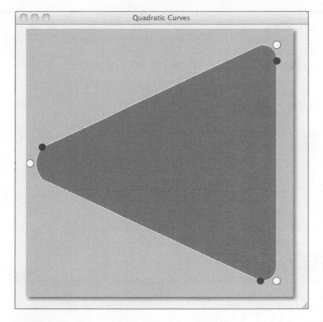

**Figure 2.38** Drawing rounded corners with bézier curves: White dots are control points, blue dots are the anchor points

---

**Example 2.23** An arrow with rounded corners

---

```
var canvas = document.getElementById('canvas'),
    context = canvas.getContext('2d'),
    ARROW_MARGIN = 30,
    POINT_RADIUS = 7,
    points = [
       { x: canvas.width - ARROW_MARGIN,
         y: canvas.height - ARROW_MARGIN },

       { x: canvas.width - ARROW_MARGIN*2,
         y: canvas.height - ARROW_MARGIN },

       { x: POINT_RADIUS,
         y: canvas.height/2 },
```

---

*(Continues)*

---

**Example 2.23** *(Continued)*

---

```
            { x: ARROW_MARGIN,
              y: canvas.height/2 - ARROW_MARGIN },

            { x: canvas.width - ARROW_MARGIN,
              y: ARROW_MARGIN },

            { x: canvas.width - ARROW_MARGIN,
              y: ARROW_MARGIN*2 },
         ];

// Functions........................................................

function drawPoint(x, y, strokeStyle, fillStyle) {
   context.beginPath();
   context.fillStyle = fillStyle;
   context.strokeStyle = strokeStyle;
   context.lineWidth = 0.5;
   context.arc(x, y, POINT_RADIUS, 0, Math.PI*2, false);
   context.fill();
   context.stroke();
}

function drawBezierPoints() {
   var i,
       strokeStyle,
       fillStyle;
   for (i=0; i < points.length; ++i) {
      fillStyle   = i % 2 === 0 ? 'white' : 'blue',
      strokeStyle = i % 2 === 0 ? 'blue' : 'white';
      drawPoint(points[i].x, points[i].y,
                strokeStyle, fillStyle);
   }
}

function drawArrow() {
   context.strokeStyle = 'white';
   context.fillStyle = 'cornflowerblue';

   context.moveTo(canvas.width - ARROW_MARGIN, ARROW_MARGIN*2);

   context.lineTo(canvas.width - ARROW_MARGIN,
                  canvas.height - ARROW_MARGIN*2);

   context.quadraticCurveTo(points[0].x, points[0].y,
                            points[1].x, points[1].y);
```

```
    context.lineTo(ARROW_MARGIN, canvas.height/2 + ARROW_MARGIN);

    context.quadraticCurveTo(points[2].x, points[2].y,
                             points[3].x, points[3].y);

    context.lineTo(canvas.width - ARROW_MARGIN*2, ARROW_MARGIN);

    context.quadraticCurveTo(points[4].x, points[4].y,
                             points[5].x, points[5].y);
    context.fill();
    context.stroke();
}

// Initialization.........................................................

context.clearRect(0, 0, canvas.width, canvas.height);
drawArrow();
drawBezierPoints();
```

The quadraticCurve() method is summarized in Table 2.9.

**Table 2.9** quadraticCurveTo()

| Method | Description |
| --- | --- |
| quadraticCurveTo(double cpx, double cpy, double x, double y) | Creates a path for a quadratic bézier curve. You pass two points to this method; the first point is a control point for the curve; the second point is the anchor point. |

## 2.10.2 Cubic Curves

In the previous section you saw how to create quadratic bézier curves. Those curves are two-dimensional, which means they curve in a single direction. If you want a curve that curves in two directions, such as the curve shown in Figure 2.39, you need a third-order curve, which is referred to as a cubic bézier curve.

The application shown in Figure 2.39 uses the bezierCurveTo() method to create a path for a cubic bézier curve. The code for that application is listed in Example 2.24.

In addition to drawing the curve itself, the code also draws filled circles for the curve's control and anchor points.

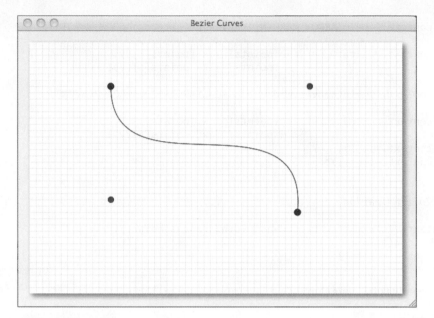

Figure 2.39  Cubic curves

---

**Example 2.24**  Drawing cubic bézier curves

```
var canvas = document.getElementById('canvas'),
    context = canvas.getContext('2d'),
    endPoints    = [ { x: 130, y: 70 },  { x: 430, y: 270 }, ],
    controlPoints = [ { x: 130, y: 250 }, { x: 450, y: 70 }, ];

// Functions.......................................................

function drawGrid(color, stepx, stepy) {
   // Listing omitted for brevity. See Example 2.13 on p. 106
   // for a complete listing.
}

function drawBezierCurve() {
   context.strokeStyle = 'blue';

   context.beginPath();
   context.moveTo(endPoints[0].x, endPoints[0].y);
   context.bezierCurveTo(controlPoints[0].x, controlPoints[0].y,
                         controlPoints[1].x, controlPoints[1].y,
                         endPoints[1].x, endPoints[1].y);
   context.stroke();
}
```

```
function drawEndPoints() {
   context.strokeStyle = 'blue';
   context.fillStyle = 'red';

   endPoints.forEach( function (point) {
      context.beginPath();
      context.arc(point.x, point.y, 5, 0, Math.PI*2, false);
      context.stroke();
      context.fill();
   });
}

function drawControlPoints() {
   context.strokeStyle = 'yellow';
   context.fillStyle = 'blue';

   controlPoints.forEach( function (point) {
      context.beginPath();
      context.arc(point.x, point.y, 5, 0, Math.PI*2, false);
      context.stroke();
      context.fill();
   });
}

// Initialization.................................................

drawGrid('lightgray', 10, 10);

drawControlPoints();
drawEndPoints();
drawBezierCurve();
```

The bezierCurveTo() method is summarized in Table 2.10.

**Table 2.10** bezierCurveTo()

| Method | Description |
|---|---|
| bezierCurveTo(double cpx, double cpy, double cp2x, double cp2y, double x, double y) | Creates a path for a cubic bézier curve. You pass three points to this method; the first two points are control points for the curve; and the last point is the anchor point. |

## 2.11  Polygons

At this point we have run the gamut for all the primitive shapes supported by the Canvas context: lines, rectangles, arcs, circles, and bézier curves. However, you will no doubt want to draw other types of shapes in a canvas; for example, triangles, hexagons, and octagons. In this section you will see how to stroke and fill arbitrary polygons, with the application shown in Figure 2.40.

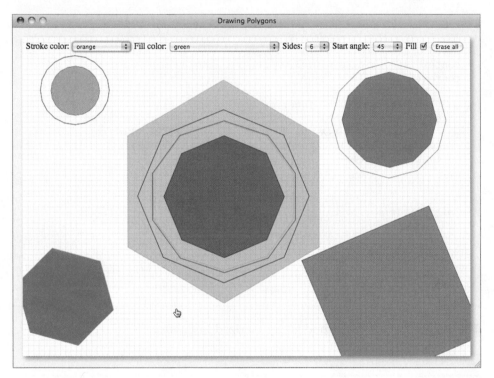

Figure 2.40  ■  Polygons

You can use moveTo() and lineTo() combined with some simple trigonometry to draw polygons with any number of sides. Figure 2.41 illustrates the simple trigonometry part.

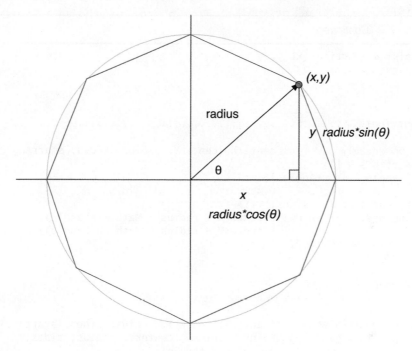

Figure 2.41 Calculating polygon vertices

Figure 2.41 shows how to calculate a single polygon vertex, given the middle of the smallest circle that encloses the polygon, and the radius of that circle. Example 2.25 is an excerpt of the JavaScript for the application shown in Figure 2.40. It shows how to use those vertices to draw arbitrary polygons.

Example 2.25 Drawing polygons (excerpt)

```
var canvas = document.getElementById('canvas'),
    context = canvas.getContext('2d'),

    sidesSelect = document.getElementById('sidesSelect'),
    startAngleSelect = document.getElementById('startAngleSelect'),

    fillCheckbox = document.getElementById('fillCheckbox'),

    mousedown = {},
    rubberbandRect = {},
```

*(Continues)*

Example 2.25 *(Continued)*

```
   Point = function (x, y) {
      this.x = x;
      this.y = y;
   },

// Functions.........................................................

function getPolygonPoints(centerX, centerY, radius, sides, startAngle) {
   var points = [],
       angle = startAngle || 0;

   for (var i=0; i < sides; ++i) {
      points.push(new Point(centerX + radius * Math.sin(angle),
                            centerY - radius * Math.cos(angle)));
      angle += 2*Math.PI/sides;
   }

   return points;
}

function createPolygonPath(centerX, centerY, radius, sides, startAngle) {
   var points = getPolygonPoints(centerX, centerY, radius, sides,
                                 startAngle);
   context.beginPath();
   context.moveTo(points[0].x, points[0].y);

   for (var i=1; i < sides; ++i) {
      context.lineTo(points[i].x, points[i].y);
   }
   context.closePath();
}

function drawRubberbandShape(loc, sides, startAngle) {
   createPolygonPath(mousedown.x, mousedown.y,
                     rubberbandRect.width,
                     parseInt(sidesSelect.value),
                     (Math.PI / 180) * parseInt(startAngleSelect.value));
   context.stroke();

   if (fillCheckbox.checked) {
      context.fill();
   }
}
```

The code listed in Example 2.25 begins by obtaining a reference to the Canvas context and defining a Point object.

The getPolygonPoints() function creates and returns an array of points for a polygon defined by the five parameters you pass to the function. That function uses the equations for polygon vertices depicted in Figure 2.41 to create that array of points.

The createPolygonPath() function calls getPolygonPoints() to obtain the array of points for the specified polygon, moves to the first point, and then creates a path encompassing all the polygon's vertices.

Finally, it's the drawRubberbandShape() function that actually draws the polygon. That function is a modification of the drawRubberbandShape() function introduced in Section 2.8.4, "Rubberband Lines," on p. 110, and is used by the application in Figure 2.40 to interactively draw polygons as the user drags the mouse. See Section 2.8.4 for more information about drawing rubberband shapes in general.

## 2.11.1 Polygon Objects

Recall that HTML5 Canvas is an immediate-mode graphics system. When you draw into a canvas, the browser draws immediately and then immediately forgets. Immediate-mode graphics is fine if you want to implement a paint application for example, but if you want to implement a drawing application that lets you create graphical objects that you can manipulate, it would be better to have a list of objects that you can edit and draw.

In this section, we modify the application in the preceding section to maintain a list of polygon objects. An excerpt of the modified application is listed in Example 2.26.

---

Example 2.26  Using polygon objects

---

```
var canvas = document.getElementById('canvas'),
    context = canvas.getContext('2d'),
    startAngleSelect = document.getElementById('startAngleSelect'),
    sidesSelect = document.getElementById('sidesSelect'),
    ...

    mousedown = {},
    rubberbandRect = {};
```

---

*(Continues)*

Example 2.26   *(Continued)*

```
function drawRubberbandShape(loc, sides, startAngle) {
    var polygon = new Polygon(mousedown.x, mousedown.y,
                     rubberbandRect.width,
                     parseInt(sidesSelect.value),
                     (Math.PI / 180) * parseInt(startAngleSelect.value),
                     context.strokeStyle,
                     context.fillStyle,
                     fillCheckbox.checked);

    context.beginPath();
    polygon.createPath(context);
    polygon.stroke(context);

    if (fillCheckbox.checked) {
        polygon.fill(context);
    }
    else {
        polygons.push(polygon);
    }
}
```

The application calls the `drawRubberbandShape()` function as the user drags the mouse to create a polygon. That function creates a polygon object, calls the polygon's `createPath()` method, and then strokes and possibly fills that path.

If the user has finished dragging the mouse, the `drawRubberbandShape()` function adds the polygon to the list of polygons the application maintains.

The polygon objects implemented in this section have the following methods:

- `points[] getPoints()`
- `void createPath(context)`
- `void stroke(context)`
- `void fill(context)`
- `void move(x, y)`

Example 2.27 shows the implementation of the `Polygon` object.

---

Example 2.27 A polygon object

---

```
// Point constructor...............................................

var Point = function (x, y) {
   this.x = x;
   this.y = y;
};

// Polygon constructor............................................

var Polygon = function (centerX, centerY, radius,
              sides, startAngle, strokeStyle, fillStyle, filled) {
   this.x = centerX;
   this.y = centerY;
   this.radius = radius;
   this.sides = sides;
   this.startAngle = startAngle;
   this.strokeStyle = strokeStyle;
   this.fillStyle = fillStyle;
   this.filled = filled;
};

// Polygon prototype..............................................

Polygon.prototype = {
   getPoints: function () {
      var points = [],
          angle = this.startAngle || 0;

      for (var i=0; i < this.sides; ++i) {
         points.push(new Point(this.x + this.radius * Math.sin(angle),
                         this.y - this.radius * Math.cos(angle)));
         angle += 2*Math.PI/this.sides;
      }
      return points;
   },

   createPath: function (context) {
      var points = this.getPoints();

      context.beginPath();
      context.moveTo(points[0].x, points[0].y);

      for (var i=1; i < this.sides; ++i) {
         context.lineTo(points[i].x, points[i].y);
      }
      context.closePath();
   },
```

*(Continues)*

Example 2.27  *(Continued)*

```
stroke: function (context) {
   context.save();
   this.createPath(context);
   context.strokeStyle = this.strokeStyle;
   context.stroke();
   context.restore();
},

fill: function (context) {
   context.save();
   this.createPath(context);
   context.fillStyle = this.fillStyle;
   context.fill();
   context.restore();
},

move: function (x, y) {
   this.x = x;
   this.y = y;
}
};
```

When you create a polygon, you specify the polygon's location, which corresponds to the center of the smallest circle that can enclose the polygon. You also specify the radius of the circle, the number of sides for the polygon, the starting angle for the first point in the polygon, the polygon's stroke and fill styles, and whether the polygon is filled.

Polygons can generate an array of points that represent their vertices, and they can create a path from those points. They can also stroke that path or fill that path, and you can move them by invoking their move() method.

## 2.12  Advanced Path Manipulation

To keep track of what they draw, many applications, such as drawing applications, computer-aided design systems, and games, maintain a list of display objects. Often, such applications let users edit their display objects; for example, CAD applications let users select, move, and resize elements of the design.

Users typically select display objects with either mouse clicks or finger touches. To facilitate selection, among other things, the Canvas API provides a pointInPath() method that returns true if a specified point lies within the current path. In this section, we make use of that method through an extension of the polygon application discussed in Section 2.11.1, "Polygon Objects," on p. 147 that lets users drag polygons.

We also explore, in Section 2.12.2, "Editing Bézier Curves," on p. 158, an application that lets users create and edit bézier curves.

## 2.12.1  Dragging Polygons

In this section you will see how to maintain a list of polygon objects as the user creates them. That list of polygons lets you implement lots of interesting things; for example, dragging polygons, as shown in Figure 2.42, or as you will see in Section 2.13, "Transformations," on p. 170, rotating polygons.

The application in Figure 2.42 has two modes: draw and edit. Initially, the application is in draw mode, so you can create polygons by dragging the mouse. Subsequently, if you click the Edit checkbox, the application switches to edit mode, and you can drag polygons around.

The application maintains an array of Polygon objects. When a mouse down event occurs in edit mode, the application iterates over that array, creates a path for each polygon, and checks to see whether the mouse down location was in the path. If so, the application stores a reference to the associated polygon and saves the X and Y offsets from the upper-left corner of the polygon to the mouse down location.

From then on, the application's mouse move event handler moves the selected polygon in accordance with mouse movement. When you uncheck the Edit checkbox, the application reverts to draw mode.

The JavaScript that pertains to dragging polygons for the application shown in Figure 2.42 is listed in Example 2.28. In the interest of brevity, the HTML for the application is not listed.

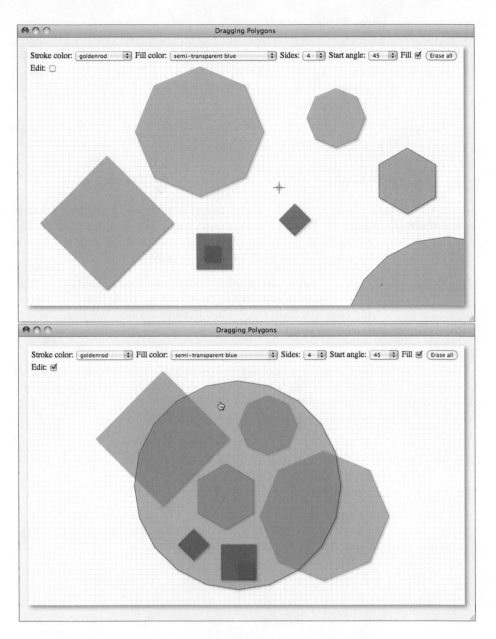

Figure 2.42  Dragging polygons

---

**Example 2.28** Dragging polygons

---

```javascript
var canvas = document.getElementById('canvas'),
    context = canvas.getContext('2d'),
    eraseAllButton = document.getElementById('eraseAllButton'),
    strokeStyleSelect = document.getElementById('strokeStyleSelect'),
    fillStyleSelect = document.getElementById('fillStyleSelect'),
    fillCheckbox = document.getElementById('fillCheckbox'),
    editCheckbox = document.getElementById('editCheckbox'),
    sidesSelect = document.getElementById('sidesSelect'),

    drawingSurfaceImageData,

    mousedown = {},
    rubberbandRect = {},

    dragging = false,
    draggingOffsetX,
    draggingOffsetY,

    sides = 8,
    startAngle = 0,

    guidewires = true,
    editing = false,
    polygons = [];

// Functions......................................................

function drawGrid(color, stepx, stepy) {
    // Listing omitted for brevity. See Example 2.13 on p. 106
    // for a complete listing.
}

function windowToCanvas(x, y) {
    var bbox = canvas.getBoundingClientRect();
    return { x: x - bbox.left * (canvas.width  / bbox.width),
             y: y - bbox.top  * (canvas.height / bbox.height)
           };
}

// Save and restore drawing surface.................................

function saveDrawingSurface() {
    drawingSurfaceImageData = context.getImageData(0, 0,
                              canvas.width,
                              canvas.height);
}
```

*(Continues)*

**Example 2.28**  *(Continued)*

```
function restoreDrawingSurface() {
   context.putImageData(drawingSurfaceImageData, 0, 0);
}

// Draw a polygon...............................................

function drawPolygon(polygon) {
   context.beginPath();
   polygon.createPath(context);
   polygon.stroke(context);

   if (fillCheckbox.checked) {
      polygon.fill(context);
   }
}

// Rubber bands.................................................

function updateRubberbandRectangle(loc) {
   rubberbandRect.width = Math.abs(loc.x - mousedown.x);
   rubberbandRect.height = Math.abs(loc.y - mousedown.y);

   if (loc.x > mousedown.x) rubberbandRect.left = mousedown.x;
   else                     rubberbandRect.left = loc.x;

   if (loc.y > mousedown.y) rubberbandRect.top = mousedown.y;
   else                     rubberbandRect.top = loc.y;
}

function drawRubberbandShape(loc, sides, startAngle) {
   var polygon = new Polygon(mousedown.x, mousedown.y,
                     rubberbandRect.width,
                     parseInt(sidesSelect.value),
                     (Math.PI / 180) * parseInt(startAngleSelect.value),
                     context.strokeStyle,
                     context.fillStyle,
                     fillCheckbox.checked);
   drawPolygon(polygon);

   if (!dragging) {
      polygons.push(polygon);
   }
}

function updateRubberband(loc, sides, startAngle) {
   updateRubberbandRectangle(loc);
   drawRubberbandShape(loc, sides, startAngle);
}
```

```
// Guidewires...................................................

function drawHorizontalLine (y) {
   context.beginPath();
   context.moveTo(0,y+0.5);
   context.lineTo(context.canvas.width,y+0.5);
   context.stroke();
}

function drawVerticalLine (x) {
   context.beginPath();
   context.moveTo(x+0.5,0);
   context.lineTo(x+0.5,context.canvas.height);
   context.stroke();
}

function drawGuidewires(x, y) {
   context.save();
   context.strokeStyle = 'rgba(0,0,230,0.4)';
   context.lineWidth = 0.5;
   drawVerticalLine(x);
   drawHorizontalLine(y);
   context.restore();
}

function drawPolygons() {
   polygons.forEach( function (polygon) {
      drawPolygon(polygon);
   });
}

// Dragging......................................................

function startDragging(loc) {
  saveDrawingSurface();
  mousedown.x = loc.x;
  mousedown.y = loc.y;
}

function startEditing() {
   canvas.style.cursor = 'pointer';
   editing = true;
}

function stopEditing() {
   canvas.style.cursor = 'crosshair';
   editing = false;
}
```

*(Continues)*

Example 2.28 *(Continued)*

```javascript
// Event handlers...................................................

canvas.onmousedown = function (e) {
   var loc = windowToCanvas(e.clientX, e.clientY);

   e.preventDefault(); // Prevent cursor change

   if (editing) {
     polygons.forEach( function (polygon) {
        polygon.createPath(context);
        if (context.isPointInPath(loc.x, loc.y)) {
           startDragging(loc);
           dragging = polygon;
           draggingOffsetX = loc.x - polygon.x;
           draggingOffsetY = loc.y - polygon.y;
           return;
        }
     });
   }
   else {
     startDragging(loc);
     dragging = true;
   }
};

canvas.onmousemove = function (e) {
   var loc = windowToCanvas(e.clientX, e.clientY);

   e.preventDefault(); // Prevent selections

   if (editing && dragging) {
     dragging.x = loc.x - draggingOffsetX;
     dragging.y = loc.y - draggingOffsetY;
     context.clearRect(0, 0, canvas.width, canvas.height);
     drawGrid('lightgray', 10, 10);
     drawPolygons();
   }
   else {
     if (dragging) {
        restoreDrawingSurface();
        updateRubberband(loc, sides, startAngle);

        if (guidewires) {
           drawGuidewires(mousedown.x, mousedown.y);
        }
     }
   }
};
```

```
canvas.onmouseup = function (e) {
   var loc = windowToCanvas(e.clientX, e.clientY);

   dragging = false;

   if (editing) {
   }
   else {
      restoreDrawingSurface();
      updateRubberband(loc);
   }
};

eraseAllButton.onclick = function (e) {
   context.clearRect(0, 0, canvas.width, canvas.height);
   drawGrid('lightgray', 10, 10);
   saveDrawingSurface();
};

strokeStyleSelect.onchange = function (e) {
   context.strokeStyle = strokeStyleSelect.value;
};

fillStyleSelect.onchange = function (e) {
   context.fillStyle = fillStyleSelect.value;
};

editCheckbox.onchange = function (e) {
   if (editCheckbox.checked) {
      startEditing();
   }
   else {
      stopEditing();
   }
};

// Initialization.................................................

context.strokeStyle = strokeStyleSelect.value;
context.fillStyle = fillStyleSelect.value;

context.shadowColor = 'rgba(0,0,0,0.4)';
context.shadowOffsetX = 2;
context.shadowOffsetY = 2;
context.shadowBlur = 4;

drawGrid('lightgray', 10, 10);
```

## 2.12.2 Editing Bézier Curves

The ability to drag shapes in a canvas—as we did in Section 2.12.1, "Dragging Polygons," on p. 151—opens the doors to many possibilities. For example, the application shown in Figure 2.43 lets you draw bézier curves and subsequently edit them by dragging their end- and control points.

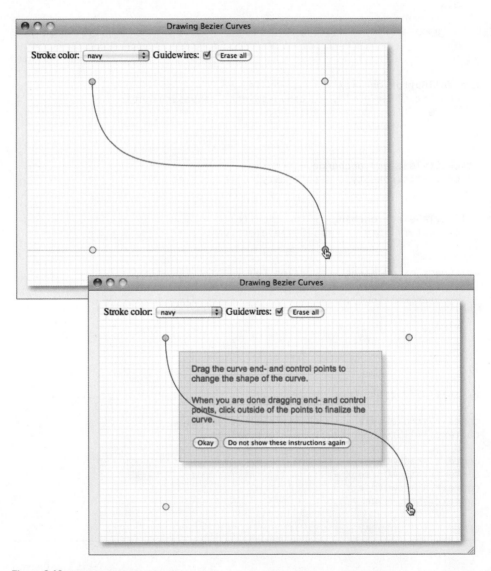

Figure 2.43  Editing bézier curves

The top screenshot in Figure 2.43 shows how you draw a curve by dragging the mouse. The bottom screenshot shows the instructions the application displays when the user stops dragging the mouse. After dismissing the instructions, you can adjust the curve by dragging its end- or control point, which is illustrated in the top screenshot in Figure 2.44.

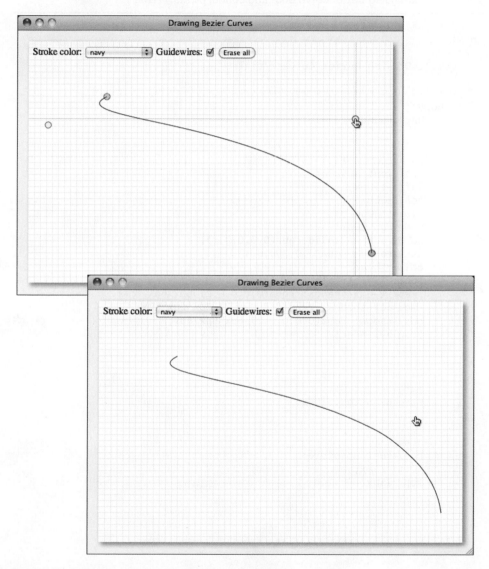

Figure 2.44  Dragging bézier end- and control points

Finally, if you click outside the end- or control points, the application finalizes the curve, as shown in the bottom screenshot in Figure 2.44.

The HTML for the application shown in Figure 2.43 is listed in Example 2.29.

---

Example 2.29  Dragging bézier curve end- and control points: HTML

---

```html
<!DOCTYPE html>
<html>
  <head>
    <title>Drawing Bezier Curves</title>

    <style>
      body {
        background: #eeeeee;
      }

      .floatingControls {
        position: absolute;
        left: 150px;
        top: 100px;
        width: 300px;
        padding: 20px;
        border: thin solid rgba(0,0,0,0.3);
        background: rgba(0,0,200,0.1);
        color: blue;
        font: 14px Arial;
        -webkit-box-shadow: rgba(0,0,0,0.2) 6px 6px 8px;
        -moz-box-shadow: rgba(0,0,0,0.2) 6px 6px 8px;
        box-shadow: rgba(0,0,0,0.2) 6px 6px 8px;
        display: none;
      }

      .floatingControls p {
        margin-top: 0px;
        margin-bottom: 20px;
      }

      #controls {
        position: absolute;
        left: 25px;
        top: 25px;
      }
```

```
    #canvas {
        background: #ffffff;
        cursor: pointer;
        margin-left: 10px;
        margin-top: 10px;
        -webkit-box-shadow: 4px 4px 8px rgba(0,0,0,0.5);
        -moz-box-shadow: 4px 4px 8px rgba(0,0,0,0.5);
        -box-shadow: 4px 4px 8px rgba(0,0,0,0.5);
    }
  </style>
</head>

<body>
    <canvas id='canvas' width='605' height='400'>
        Canvas not supported
    </canvas>

  <div id='controls'>
     Stroke color: <select id='strokeStyleSelect'>
        <option value='red'>red</option>
        <option value='green'>green</option>
        <option value='blue'>blue</option>
        <option value='orange'>orange</option>
        <option value='cornflowerblue'>cornflowerblue</option>
        <option value='goldenrod'>goldenrod</option>
        <option value='navy' selected>navy</option>
        <option value='purple'>purple</option>
        </select>
     Guidewires:
     <input id='guidewireCheckbox' type='checkbox' checked/>
     <input id='eraseAllButton' type='button' value='Erase all'/>
  </div>

  <div id='instructions' class='floatingControls'>
     <p>Drag the curve end- and control points to
        change the shape of the curve.</p>

     <p>When you are done dragging end- and control points,
        click outside of the points to finalize the curve.</p>

     <input id='instructionsOkayButton' type='button'
            value='Okay' autofocus/>
     <input id='instructionsNoMoreButton' type='button'
            value='Do not show these instructions again'/>
  </div>

  <script src = 'example.js'></script>
</body>
</html>
```

For the instructions, the application employs the strategy discussed in Section 1.8, "Using HTML Elements in a Canvas," on p. 36 to implement a glass pane that floats above the canvas. The class for the DIV containing the instructions is floatingControls, which sets the background and positions the DIV over the canvas.

The HTML also creates the elements for selecting stroke color, turning guidewires on and off, and erasing all curves.

The JavaScript for the application shown in Figure 2.43 is listed in Example 2.30.

As you look through the code, notice the cursorInEndPoint() and cursorInControlPoint() functions, about two thirds of the way through the listing. Those functions determine whether you clicked the mouse inside an end- or control point.

Also notice the mouse move event handler. Either you are dragging the mouse to draw a curve or you are dragging a point, either an endpoint or a control point, of an existing curve. If you are doing either of those things, the event handler restores the drawing surface and temporarily draws guidewires if they are enabled.

If you are drawing the curve, the mouse move event handler subsequently redraws the curve and its end- and control points. If you are dragging a point, the application updates the location of the point and then redraws the curve's end- and control points and the curve itself.

---

**Example 2.30** Dragging bézier curve end- and control points: JavaScript

```javascript
var canvas = document.getElementById('canvas'),
    context = canvas.getContext('2d'),
    eraseAllButton = document.getElementById('eraseAllButton'),
    strokeStyleSelect = document.getElementById('strokeStyleSelect'),
    guidewireCheckbox = document.getElementById('guidewireCheckbox'),
    instructions = document.getElementById('instructions'),
    instructionsOkayButton =
        document.getElementById('instructionsOkayButton'),
    instructionsNoMoreButton =
        document.getElementById('instructionsNoMoreButton'),

    showInstructions = true,

    AXIS_MARGIN = 40,
    HORIZONTAL_TICK_SPACING = 10,
    VERTICAL_TICK_SPACING = 10,
    TICK_SIZE = 10,

    AXIS_ORIGIN = { x: AXIS_MARGIN, y: canvas.height-AXIS_MARGIN },
    AXIS_TOP    = AXIS_MARGIN,
```

```
      AXIS_RIGHT = canvas.width - AXIS_MARGIN,
      AXIS_WIDTH  = AXIS_RIGHT    - AXIS_ORIGIN.x,
      AXIS_HEIGHT = AXIS_ORIGIN.y - AXIS_TOP,

      NUM_VERTICAL_TICKS   = AXIS_HEIGHT / VERTICAL_TICK_SPACING,
      NUM_HORIZONTAL_TICKS = AXIS_WIDTH  / HORIZONTAL_TICK_SPACING,

      GRID_STROKE_STYLE = 'lightblue',
      GRID_SPACING = 10,

      CONTROL_POINT_RADIUS = 5,
      CONTROL_POINT_STROKE_STYLE = 'blue',
      CONTROL_POINT_FILL_STYLE = 'rgba(255,255,0,0.5)',

      END_POINT_STROKE_STYLE = 'navy',
      END_POINT_FILL_STYLE   = 'rgba(0,255,0,0.5)',

      GUIDEWIRE_STROKE_STYLE = 'rgba(0,0,230,0.4)',

      drawingImageData,       // Image data stored on mouse down events

      mousedown = {},         // Cursor location for last mouse down event
      rubberbandRect = {},    // Constantly updated for mouse move events

      dragging = false,       // If true, user is dragging the cursor
      draggingPoint = false,  // End- or control point user is dragging

      endPoints     = [ {}, {} ],  // Endpoint locations (x, y)
      controlPoints = [ {}, {} ],  // Control point locations (x, y)
      editing  = false,            // If true, user is editing the curve

      guidewires = guidewireCheckbox.checked;

// Functions.......................................................

function drawGrid(color, stepx, stepy) {
   // Listing omitted for brevity. See Example 2.13 on p. 106
   // for a complete listing.
}

function windowToCanvas(x, y) {
   var bbox = canvas.getBoundingClientRect();

   return { x: x - bbox.left * (canvas.width  / bbox.width),
            y: y - bbox.top  * (canvas.height / bbox.height)
          };
}

// Save and restore drawing surface.................................
```

*(Continues)*

Example 2.30   *(Continued)*

```javascript
function saveDrawingSurface() {
   drawingImageData = context.getImageData(0, 0,
                      canvas.width, canvas.height);
}

function restoreDrawingSurface() {
   context.putImageData(drawingImageData, 0, 0);
}

// Rubber bands......................................................

function updateRubberbandRectangle(loc) {
   rubberbandRect.width  = Math.abs(loc.x - mousedown.x);
   rubberbandRect.height = Math.abs(loc.y - mousedown.y);

   if (loc.x > mousedown.x) rubberbandRect.left = mousedown.x;
   else                     rubberbandRect.left = loc.x;

   if (loc.y > mousedown.y) rubberbandRect.top = mousedown.y;
   else                     rubberbandRect.top = loc.y;
}

function drawBezierCurve() {
   context.beginPath();
   context.moveTo(endPoints[0].x, endPoints[0].y);
   context.bezierCurveTo(controlPoints[0].x, controlPoints[0].y,
                    controlPoints[1].x, controlPoints[1].y,
                    endPoints[1].x, endPoints[1].y);
   context.stroke();
}

function updateEndAndControlPoints() {
   endPoints[0].x = rubberbandRect.left;
   endPoints[0].y = rubberbandRect.top;

   endPoints[1].x = rubberbandRect.left + rubberbandRect.width;
   endPoints[1].y = rubberbandRect.top  + rubberbandRect.height;

   controlPoints[0].x = rubberbandRect.left;
   controlPoints[0].y = rubberbandRect.top  + rubberbandRect.height;

   controlPoints[1].x = rubberbandRect.left + rubberbandRect.width;
   controlPoints[1].y = rubberbandRect.top;
}

function drawRubberbandShape(loc) {
   updateEndAndControlPoints();
   drawBezierCurve();
}
```

```
function updateRubberband(loc) {
   updateRubberbandRectangle(loc);
   drawRubberbandShape(loc);
}

// Guidewires.......................................................

function drawHorizontalGuidewire (y) {
   context.beginPath();
   context.moveTo(0, y + 0.5);
   context.lineTo(context.canvas.width, y + 0.5);
   context.stroke();
}

function drawVerticalGuidewire (x) {
   context.beginPath();
   context.moveTo(x + 0.5, 0);
   context.lineTo(x + 0.5, context.canvas.height);
   context.stroke();
}

function drawGuidewires(x, y) {
   context.save();
   context.strokeStyle = GUIDEWIRE_STROKE_STYLE;
   context.lineWidth = 0.5;
   drawVerticalGuidewire(x);
   drawHorizontalGuidewire(y);
   context.restore();
}

// Endpoints and control points....................................

function drawControlPoint(index) {
   context.beginPath();
   context.arc(controlPoints[index].x, controlPoints[index].y,
               CONTROL_POINT_RADIUS, 0, Math.PI*2, false);
   context.stroke();
   context.fill();
}
function drawControlPoints() {
   context.save();
   context.strokeStyle = CONTROL_POINT_STROKE_STYLE;
   context.fillStyle  = CONTROL_POINT_FILL_STYLE;
   drawControlPoint(0);
   drawControlPoint(1);
   context.stroke();
   context.fill();
   context.restore();
}
```

*(Continues)*

**Example 2.30** *(Continued)*

```javascript
function drawEndPoint(index) {
   context.beginPath();
   context.arc(endPoints[index].x, endPoints[index].y,
               CONTROL_POINT_RADIUS, 0, Math.PI*2, false);
   context.stroke();
   context.fill();
}

function drawEndPoints() {
   context.save();
   context.strokeStyle = END_POINT_STROKE_STYLE;
   context.fillStyle   = END_POINT_FILL_STYLE;

   drawEndPoint(0);
   drawEndPoint(1);

   context.stroke();
   context.fill();
   context.restore();
}

function drawControlAndEndPoints() {
   drawControlPoints();
   drawEndPoints();
}

function cursorInEndPoint(loc) {
   var pt;

   endPoints.forEach( function(point) {
      context.beginPath();
      context.arc(point.x, point.y,
                  CONTROL_POINT_RADIUS, 0, Math.PI*2, false);

      if (context.isPointInPath(loc.x, loc.y)) {
         pt = point;
      }
   });

   return pt;
}
```

```
function cursorInControlPoint(loc) {
   var pt;

   controlPoints.forEach( function(point) {
      context.beginPath();
      context.arc(point.x, point.y,
                  CONTROL_POINT_RADIUS, 0, Math.PI*2, false);

      if (context.isPointInPath(loc.x, loc.y)) {
         pt = point;
      }
   });

   return pt;
}

function updateDraggingPoint(loc) {
   draggingPoint.x = loc.x;
   draggingPoint.y = loc.y;
}

// Canvas event handlers...........................................

canvas.onmousedown = function (e) {
   var loc = windowToCanvas(e.clientX, e.clientY);

   e.preventDefault(); // Prevent cursor change

   if (!editing) {
      saveDrawingSurface();
      mousedown.x = loc.x;
      mousedown.y = loc.y;
      updateRubberbandRectangle(loc);
      dragging = true;
   }
   else {
      draggingPoint = cursorInControlPoint(loc);

      if (!draggingPoint) {
         draggingPoint = cursorInEndPoint(loc);
      }
   }
};
```

*(Continues)*

**Example 2.30** *(Continued)*

```
canvas.onmousemove = function (e) {
   var loc = windowToCanvas(e.clientX, e.clientY);

   if (dragging || draggingPoint) {
      e.preventDefault(); // Prevent selections
      restoreDrawingSurface();

      if(guidewires) {
         drawGuidewires(loc.x, loc.y);
      }
   }

   if (dragging) {
      updateRubberband(loc);
      drawControlAndEndPoints();
   }
   else if (draggingPoint) {
      updateDraggingPoint(loc);
      drawControlAndEndPoints();
      drawBezierCurve();
   }
};

canvas.onmouseup = function (e) {
   loc = windowToCanvas(e.clientX, e.clientY);

   restoreDrawingSurface();

   if (!editing) {
      updateRubberband(loc);
      drawControlAndEndPoints();
      dragging = false;
      editing = true;
      if (showInstructions) {
         instructions.style.display = 'inline';
      }
   }
   else {
      if (draggingPoint) drawControlAndEndPoints();
      else              editing = false;

      drawBezierCurve();
      draggingPoint = undefined;
   }
};
```

```
// Control event handlers..........................................

eraseAllButton.onclick = function (e) {
   context.clearRect(0, 0, canvas.width, canvas.height);
   drawGrid(GRID_STROKE_STYLE, GRID_SPACING, GRID_SPACING);

   saveDrawingSurface();

   editing = false;
   dragging = false;
   draggingPoint = undefined;
};

strokeStyleSelect.onchange = function (e) {
   context.strokeStyle = strokeStyleSelect.value;
};

guidewireCheckbox.onchange = function (e) {
   guidewires = guidewireCheckbox.checked;
};

// Instructions event handlers.....................................

instructionsOkayButton.onclick = function (e) {
   instructions.style.display = 'none';
};

instructionsNoMoreButton.onclick = function (e) {
   instructions.style.display = 'none';
   showInstructions = false;
};

// Initialization..................................................

context.strokeStyle = strokeStyleSelect.value;
drawGrid(GRID_STROKE_STYLE, GRID_SPACING, GRID_SPACING);
```

## 2.12.3 Scrolling Paths into View

As this book was being written, the Canvas specification added a scrollPathIntoView() method to the Canvas context. The method, which scrolls the current path into view, was not implemented by any browsers when the book went to press, so this book does not contain a working example that uses that method. When browsers implement that feature, you can find a working example at the book's companion site at http://corehtml5canvas.com.

**NOTE: `scrollPathIntoView()` is primarily for mobile applications**

The `scrollPathIntoView()` method was added to the Canvas specification primarily for mobile devices that have small screens. With that method, developers can support scrolling part of the canvas that is offscreen into view.

## 2.13 Transformations

As mentioned in Section 2.1, "The Coordinate System," on p. 67, you can translate, rotate, and scale the Canvas coordinate system, and there are plenty of good reasons to do one or all of those things.

It's often useful to translate the origin to someplace other than the upper-left corner of the canvas, which is its default location. Fundamentally, translating the origin simplifies the calculations you need to make to position shapes and text within the canvas. For example, you can draw a rectangle centered in the canvas, like this:

```
var canvas = document.getElementById('canvas'),
    context = canvas.getContext('2d'),
    RECTANGLE_WIDTH = 100,
    RECTANGLE_HEIGHT = 100;

context.strokeRect(canvas.width/2 - RECTANGLE_WIDTH/2,
                   canvas.height/2 - RECTANGLE_HEIGHT/2,
                   RECTANGLE_WIDTH, RECTANGLE_HEIGHT);
```

The preceding code calculates the X and Y coordinates for the upper left-hand corner of the rectangle by subtracting half of the rectangle's width and half of the rectangle's height, respectively, from the center of the canvas.

By translating the origin to that point, you simplify the call to `strokeRect()`:

```
var canvas = document.getElementById('canvas'),
    context = canvas.getContext('2d'),
    RECTANGLE_WIDTH = 100,
    RECTANGLE_HEIGHT = 100;

context.translate(canvas.width/2 - RECTANGLE_WIDTH/2,
                  canvas.height/2 - RECTANGLE_HEIGHT/2);

context.strokeRect(0, 0, RECTANGLE_WIDTH, RECTANGLE_HEIGHT);
```

You may argue that translating the origin simplifies nothing in this case because the preceding code still has to calculate the same location. The only difference is that the preceding code passes that location to `translate()` instead of to `strokeRect()`. And you would be correct. However, imagine that you are drawing several shapes at the center of the canvas. In that case, translating the origin could significantly simplify the ensuing calculations for drawing the other shapes.

## 2.13.1 Translating, Scaling, and Rotating

The application shown in Figure 2.45 illustrates translating and rotating the coordinate system, by letting you interactively rotate polygons.

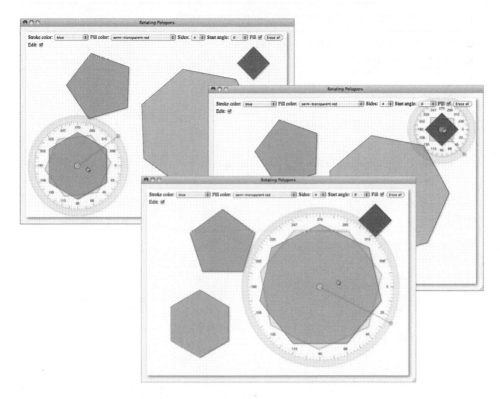

Figure 2.45 Translating and rotating the coordinate system

If you check the Edit checkbox and subsequently click a polygon, the application shown in Figure 2.45 annotates the polygon with a dial representing degrees and adds a guidewire showing the current rotation angle. You can read more about the implementation of the dial and guidewire in Section 2.9.4, "Dials and Gauges," on p. 130.

After you select a polygon to rotate, you can change the rotation angle by moving the mouse. The guidewire follows the mouse, and the application draws a second representation of the polygon, rotated at the current rotation angle. When you subsequently click the mouse, the application removes the rotation annotations and rotates the polygon to the selected rotation angle.

In the interest of brevity, the application shown in **Figure 2.45** is not entirely listed in this book; however, you can try the example and download the code at http://corehtml5canvas.com. **Example 2.31** lists the function that the application uses to draw a polygon at a given rotation angle.

---

**Example 2.31** Translating and rotating the coordinate system

```javascript
function drawPolygon(polygon, angle) {
   var tx = polygon.x,
       ty = polygon.y;

   context.save();

   context.translate(tx, ty);

   if (angle) {
     context.rotate(angle);
   }

   polygon.x = 0;
   polygon.y = 0;

   polygon.createPath(context);
   context.stroke();

   if (fillCheckbox.checked) {
      context.fill();
   }

   context.restore();

   polygon.x = tx;
   polygon.y = ty;
}
```

---

Polygons, as implemented in the application shown in **Figure 2.45**, maintain their location, which is at the center of the polygon. To draw a rotated polygon, the function listed in **Example 2.31** temporarily translates the coordinate system to the polygon's center and rotates the coordinate system by the specified angle. The application then invokes the polygon's createPath() method and strokes and possibly fills that path. When the function is finished stroking and then filling the polygon, it restores the context and the X and Y coordinates of the polygon.

The rotate(), scale(), and translate() methods are summarized in **Table 2.11**.

Table 2.11 `CanvasRenderingContext2D` translation and rotation methods

| Method | Description |
|--------|-------------|
| `rotate(double angleInRadians)` | Rotates the coordinate system, by the specified number of radians. (Note: $\pi$ radians is equal to 180 degrees.) |
| `scale(double x, double y)` | Scales the coordinate system in the X and Y directions. |
| `translate(double x, double y)` | Translates the coordinate system in the X and Y directions. |

**TIP: Sometimes it's useful to scale the context during developing**

If you are doing some intricate drawing in a canvas—perhaps you are implementing a custom control, such as the slider discussed in Chapter 10—it's a good idea to scale the canvas so that you can get a better look at exactly what you are drawing. The statement `context.scale(2.5, 2.5)`, for example, gives you a close-up view of your work, and when you are done developing, simply remove the statement from your code.

If you do scale the context during development, you may find that things slide out of view because you've zoomed in on the context as a whole. If that's the case, you can use `context.translate()` to temporarily translate the context and bring your desired part of the magnified canvas into view.

## 2.13.1.1 Mirroring

Coordinate system transformations are useful for many different things. For example, you can draw a shape and subsequently mirror that shape horizontally by invoking `scale(-1, 1)` (or vertically by calling `scale(1, -1)`), as illustrated by the application shown in Figure 2.46.

The application mirrors the arrow like this:

```
drawArrow(context);

context.translate(canvas.width, 0);
context.scale(-1, 1);

drawArrow(context);
```

The preceding code invokes a method named `drawArrow()`, that draws the arrow on the left in Figure 2.46. To mirror the arrow about the vertical center of the

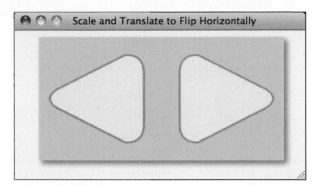

Figure 2.46  Mirroring with scale()

canvas, the application translates the origin to the right edge of the canvas, invokes scale(-1, 1), and redraws the arrow exactly as it did before. You can see the implementation of the drawArrow() method in Section 2.10.1, "Quadratic Curves," on p. 137.

## 2.13.2  Custom Transformations

In the previous sections you saw how to use scale(), rotate(), and translate() to transform the coordinate system. Those three methods are convenience methods that manipulate the context's *transformation matrix*. Whenever you draw anything into a canvas, whether it's a shape, text, or an image, the browser applies the transformation matrix to the object you are drawing. By default, the transformation matrix is what's known as an *identity matrix*, which does nothing to the object that you are drawing. When you invoke scale(), rotate(), or translate(), you are modifying the transformation matrix, thereby affecting all future drawing operations.

Most of the time those three methods will suffice; however, sometimes you may need to manipulate the transformation matrix directly. For example, applying shear to objects that you draw is not possible with any combination of those three methods, so in that case you would need to manipulate the transformation matrix yourself.

The Canvas context provides two methods that directly manipulate the transformation matrix: transform(), which applies a transformation to the current transformation matrix, and setTransform(), which resets the matrix to its original value—the identity matrix—and then applies the transformation to that identity matrix. The upshot is that successive calls to transform() are cumulative, whereas successive calls to setTransform() wipe the transformation matrix slate clean each time.

Because `translate()`, `rotate()`, and `scale()` all manipulate the transformation matrix, you can also translate, rotate, and scale with `transform()` and `setTransform()`. There are two advantages to manipulating the transformation matrix directly with `transform()` and `setTransform()`:

1.  You can achieve effects, such as shear, that are not possible with `scale()`, `rotate()`, and `translate()` alone.
2.  You can combine effects, such as scaling, rotating, translating, and shear, in one call to `transform()` or `setTransform()`.

The major drawback to using `transform()` and `setTransform()` is that those methods are not as intuitive as `scale()`, `rotate()`, and `translate()`.

Both `transform()` and `setTransform()` take six arguments. In this section you will learn what those arguments are for and how to specify them for any type of transformation including translating, scaling, rotating, and shearing objects that you draw in a canvas.

### 2.13.2.1 Algebraic Equations for Transformations

Let's begin with some simple algebraic equations for translating, scaling, and rotating. First, Equation 2.1 shows the equations for translating $(x, y)$ to $(x', y')$.

$$x' = x + dx$$
$$y' = y + dy$$

Equation 2.1  Equation for translating

The equations add a delta $x$, signified as $dx$, to the $x$ coordinate, and a delta $y$, signified as $dy$, to the $y$ coordinate. For example, if you translate $(5, 10)$ to $(10, 20)$, delta $x$ would be 5 and delta $y$ would be 10, and you have Equation 2.2.

$$x' = 5 + 5$$
$$y' = 10 + 10$$

Equation 2.2  Translating (5, 10) to (10, 20)

The equations for scaling are shown in Equation 2.3.

$$x' = x \times sx$$
$$y' = y \times sy$$

Equation 2.3  Equation for scaling

The equations multiply a scale $x$, signified as $sx$, by the $x$ coordinate, and a scale $y$, signified as $sy$, by the $y$ coordinate. For example, if you scale (5, 10) to (40, 60), scale $x$ would be 8 and scale $y$ would be 6, and you have Equation 2.4.

$$x' = 5 \times 8$$
$$y' = 10 \times 6$$

Equation 2.4  Scaling (5, 5) to (10, 20)

The equations for rotating use some trigonometry, as shown in Equation 2.5.

$$x' = x \times \cos(\text{angle}) - (y \times \sin(\text{angle}))$$
$$y' = y \times \cos(\text{angle}) + (x \times \sin(\text{angle}))$$

Equation 2.5  Equations for rotating

If you rotate (5, 10) 45 degrees about (0, 0), you end up at (3.5, 10.6), as shown in Equation 2.6.

$$x' = 5 \times \cos(\pi / 4) - (10 \times \sin(\pi / 4))$$
$$y' = 10 \times \cos(\pi / 4) + (5 \times \sin(\pi / 4))$$

Equation 2.6  Rotating (5, 5) 45 degrees about (0, 0)

## 2.13.2.2  Using `transform()` and `setTransform()`

Now that you have a good grasp of the fundamental equations for rotating, scaling, and translating, let's go back to the six arguments for `transform()` and `setTransform()`. Those two methods look like this:

```
transform(a, b, c, d, e, f)
setTransform(a, b, c, d, e, f)
```

Those six arguments are used in equations that encompass all the equations that we've seen for translating, scaling, and rotating. Those equations are shown in Equation 2.7.

$$x' = ax + cy + e$$
$$y' = bx + dy + f$$

Equation 2.7  Equations for general transformations

In Equation 2.7, the letters a . . . f represent the six arguments to `transform()` and `setTransform()`. The arguments e and f, when combined with a = 1, b = 0, c = 0, and d = 1, represent a pure translation. In that case, the equation for $x'$ becomes $x' = 1 \times x + 0x +$ e, and the equation for $y'$ becomes $y' = 1 \times x + 0x +$ f. Those equations simplify as shown in Equation 2.8.

$$x' = x + e$$
$$y' = y + f$$

Equation 2.8   A pure translation with the arguments for transform() and setTransform()

So, if you want to use transform() or setTransform() to translate the coordinate system, use the fifth argument (e) to translate in the X direction, the sixth argument (f) to translate in the Y direction, and set a and d to 1 and b and c to 0.

To scale the coordinate system using transform() or setTransform(), you use the arguments a and d, with all the other arguments set to 0, to scale in the X and Y directions, respectively. In that case, the equations become $x' = a \times x + 0x + 0y + 0$ and $y' = 0 \times x + dy + 0$. Those equations simplify to the equations shown in Equation 2.9.

$$x' = ax$$
$$y' = dy$$

Equation 2.9   Scaling with the arguments for transform() and setTransform()

To rotate about the origin through an angle (specified in radians), use the following arguments to transform() and setTransform(): a = cos(angle), b = sin(angle), c = sin(angle), d = cos(angle), and 0 for e and f, as shown in Equation 2.10.

$$x' = \cos(angle) \times x - \sin(angle) \times y + 0$$
$$y' = \sin(angle) \times x + \cos(angle) \times y + 0$$

Equation 2.10   Rotating with the arguments for transform() and setTransform()

## 2.13.2.3  Translating, Rotating, and Scaling with transform() and setTransform()

The application shown in Figure 2.47 rotates and scales text like this:

```
context.clearRect(-origin.x, -origin.y, canvas.width, canvas.height);
context.rotate(clockwise ? angle : -angle);
context.scale(scale, scale);
drawText();
```

You can achieve the same effect with transform(), like this:

```
var sin = clockwise ? Math.sin(angle) : Math.sin(-angle),
    cos = clockwise ? Math.cos(angle) : Math.cos(-angle);

if (!paused) {
    context.clearRect(-origin.x, -origin.y,
                      canvas.width, canvas.height);
    context.transform(cos, sin, -sin, cos, 0, 0);
    context.transform(scale, 0, 0, scale, 0, 0);
    drawText();
}
```

In the preceding code, the first call to `transform()` rotates the coordinate system; the second call scales it.

You can also combine the two calls to `transform()`, like this:

```
context.transform(scale*cos, sin, -sin, scale*cos, 0, 0);
```

Figure 2.47  Spinning text

This section showed you how to use `transform()` and `setTransform()` to translate, scale, and rotate, which you can also achieve with `translate()`, `scale()`, and `rotate()`, respectively. Now let's use `transform()` and `setTransform()` to do something that you cannot achieve with `translate()`, `scale()`, and `rotate()`.

### 2.13.2.4 Shear

From Section 2.13.2.2, "Using `transform()` and `setTransform()`," on p. 176, recall the equations for general transformations, shown in Equation 2.11.

$$x' = ax + cy + e$$
$$y' = bx + dy + f$$

Equation 2.11 Equations for general transformations, redux

Also recall that in Equation 2.11, the letters a...f correspond to the arguments that you pass to `transform()` and `setTransform()`:

```
transform(a, b, c, d, e, f)
setTransform(a, b, c, d, e, f)
```

Now take a look at the variables c and b in Equation 2.11. Notice that c is multiplied by $y$ to generate $x'$, and b is multiplied by $x$ to generate $y'$. That means that the value of $x$ influences the value of $y$, and vice versa, which means that c and b can be used to implement shear, as shown in Figure 2.48.

The application shown in Figure 2.48, which is a simple paint program, uses a separate canvas for the icons. Before drawing those icons, the application transforms the context for that canvas, like this:

```
controlsContext.transform(1, 0, 0.75, 1, 0, 0);
```

If you plug those six arguments into Equation 2.11, you end up with $x' = 1 \times x + 0.75 \times y + 0$ and $y' = 0 \times x + 1 \times y + 0$, which simplifies to

$$x' = x + 0.75y$$
$$y' = y$$

Equation 2.12 Equations for shear in the horizontal direction

The equations shear each $x$ coordinate of every point drawn in the icons, leaving the $y$ coordinates untouched, as depicted in Figure 2.48. The `transform()` and `setTransform()` methods are summarized in Table 2.12.

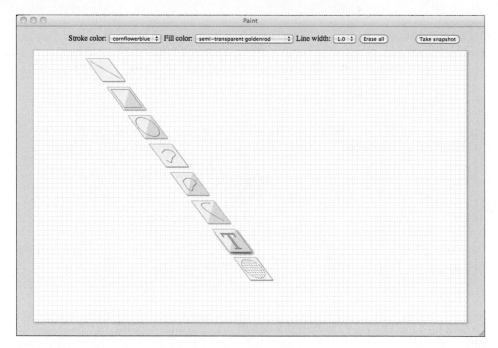

Figure 2.48  Using shear to implement 3D floating icons

Table 2.12  CanvasRenderingContext2D transformation methods

| Method | Description |
| --- | --- |
| transform(double a, double b, double c, double d, double e, double f) | Applies the transformation specified by the six arguments |
| setTransform(double a, double b, double c, double d, double e, double f) | Resets the current transformation to the identity matrix and applies the transformation specified by the six arguments |

**NOTE: Floating Icons**
In Figure 2.48, the icons appear to float above the drawing surface. See Section 1.8, "Using HTML Elements in a Canvas," on p. 36 for a discussion on how to create floating controls.

## 2.14 Compositing

By default, when you draw one object (the source) on top of another (the destination) in a canvas, the browser simply draws the source over the destination. That *compositing* behavior should not be surprising; after all, that's exactly what happens if you draw one thing on top of another on a piece of paper.

However, by setting a Canvas context's globalCompositeOperation property, you can change that default compositing behavior to any of the values that you see in Table 2.13. Those values are known as *Porter-Duff* operators, which are described by Thomas Porter and Tom Duff from LucasFilm Ltd., in an article published in *Computer Graphics* magazine in July 1984. You can read that article at http://keithp.com/~keithp/porterduff/p253-porter.pdf.

In addition to listing all the different values for globalCompositeOperation, Table 2.13 also shows how a source object, depicted by the circle, is composited with a destination object, shown as a square. The default value, which is source-over, is emphasized in the table.

To illustrate the use of the globalCompositeOperation, the application shown in Figure 2.49 draws an orange circle that follows the mouse.

As Figure 2.49 illustrates, the globalCompositeOperation is useful for all sorts of special effects. The rightmost screenshot uses the lighter composite operation, making the orange circle look like a spotlight as it moves over the text.

The HTML for the application shown in Figure 2.49 is listed in Example 2.32.

The HTML creates a select element for the globalCompositeOperation values and also creates the canvas. Using CSS, the HTML positions the canvas to the right of the select element.

**Table 2.13** CanvasRenderingContext2D composite operations

| Operation | Sample | Operation | Sample |
|---|---|---|---|
| source-atop | | source-in | |
| source-out | | *source-over* | |
| destination-atop | | destination-in | |
| destination-out | | destination-over | |
| lighter | | copy | |
| xor | | | |

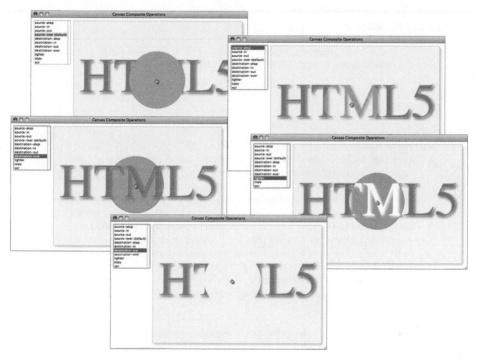

**Figure 2.49** Composition modes. Clockwise from top: source-over, source-atop, lighter, destination-out, and destination-over

**Example 2.32** Compositing: HTML

```
<!DOCTYPE html>
<html>
   <head>
      <title>Canvas Composite Operations</title>

      <style>
         #canvas {
            border: 1px solid cornflowerblue;
            position: absolute;
            left: 150px;
            top: 10px;
            background: #eeeeee;
            border: thin solid #aaaaaa;
            cursor: pointer;
            -webkit-box-shadow: rgba(200,200,255,0.9) 5px 5px 10px;
```

*(Continues)*

**Example 2.32** *(Continued)*

```
            -moz-box-shadow: rgba(200,200,255,0.9) 5px 5px 10px;
            box-shadow: rgba(200,200,255,0.9) 5px 5px 10px;
         }
      </style>
   </head>

   <body>
      <select id='compositingSelect' size='11'>
         <option value='source-atop'>source-atop</option>
         <option value='source-in'>source-in</option>
         <option value='source-out'>source-out</option>
         <option value='source-over'>source-over (default)</option>
         <option value='destination-atop'>destination-atop</option>
         <option value='destination-in'>destination-in</option>
         <option value='destination-out'>destination-out</option>
         <option value='destination-over'>destination-over</option>
         <option value='lighter'>lighter</option>
         <option value='copy'>copy</option>
         <option value='xor'>xor</option>
      </select>

      <canvas id='canvas' width='600' height='420'>
         Canvas not supported
      </canvas>

      <script src='example.js'></script>
   </body>
</html>
```

The JavaScript for the application shown in Figure 2.49 is listed in Example 2.33.

**Example 2.33** Compositing: JavaScript

```
var context = document.getElementById('canvas').getContext('2d'),
    selectElement = document.getElementById('compositingSelect');

// Functions..................................................

function drawText() {
   context.save();

   context.shadowColor   = 'rgba(100, 100, 150, 0.8)';
   context.shadowOffsetX = 5;
   context.shadowOffsetY = 5;
   context.shadowBlur    = 10;
   context.fillStyle = 'cornflowerblue';
```

```
   context.fillText('HTML5', 20, 250);

   context.strokeStyle = 'yellow';
   context.strokeText('HTML5', 20, 250);

   context.restore();
}

// Event handlers............................................
function windowToCanvas(canvas, x, y) {
   var bbox = canvas.getBoundingClientRect();
   return { x: x - bbox.left * (canvas.width  / bbox.width),
            y: y - bbox.top  * (canvas.height / bbox.height)
          };
}

context.canvas.onmousemove = function(e) {
   var loc = windowToCanvas(context.canvas, e.clientX, e.clientY);
   context.clearRect(0, 0, context.canvas.width,
                     context.canvas.height);
   drawText();

   context.save();
   context.globalCompositeOperation = selectElement.value;
   context.beginPath();
   context.arc(loc.x, loc.y, 100, 0, Math.PI*2, false);
   context.fillStyle = 'orange';
   context.stroke();
   context.fill();

   context.restore();
}

// Initialization.............................................

selectElement.selectedIndex = 3;
context.lineWidth = 0.5;
context.font = '128pt Comic-sans';
drawText();
```

The JavaScript implements a mouse move event handler that continuously draws an orange circle that follows the mouse. That event handler sets the Canvas context's globalCompositeOperation to the compositingSelect element's value.

As an aside, notice that the drawText() method temporarily enables shadows when drawing the text by enclosing the code that draws text in between calls to save() and restore(). Those calls ensure that the text will be drawn with shadows but the orange circle will not.

### 2.14.1 The Compositing Controversy

At the time this book was written, browser vendors disagreed on how to implement five of the values for globalCompositeOperation. Those five values, and how they are implemented by Safari and Chrome versus Firefox and Opera, are shown in Table 2.14.

Table 2.14 Nonportable composite operations

| Composition Mode | Chrome and Safari | Firefox and Opera |
| --- | --- | --- |
| source-in | | |
| source-out | | |
| destination-in | | |
| destination-atop | | |
| copy | | |

The bottom line concerning the disagreement about how to implement compositing is that you cannot portably use the compositing modes shown in Table 2.14. If you are not interested in the technical details about the two different implementations, feel free to skip ahead to the next section.

Chrome and Safari implement *local* compositing, which means they perform compositing only on the pixels that make up the source. Firefox and Opera, on the other hand, implement *global* compositing, which means they perform compositing on all pixels in a canvas, restricted to the canvas's clipping region.

The difference between local compositing implemented by Chrome and Safari versus the global compositing implemented by Firefox and Opera is evident in Table 2.14: Local compositing leaves the destination untouched, whereas global compositing erases the destination outside the area encompassed by the source.

At the time this book was written, the Canvas specification specified global compositing, as implemented by Firefox and Opera. However, there's a good chance that in the future the specification will be changed to local compositing, as implemented by Chrome and Safari.

## 2.15 The Clipping Region

This section discusses what is arguably the single most powerful Canvas feature: the clipping region. The clipping region is an area of the canvas, defined by a path, to which the browser restricts all drawing operations. By default, the clipping region is the same size as the canvas. Until you explicitly set the clipping region—by creating a path and subsequently invoking the Canvas context's clip() method—the clipping region has no effect on what you draw in the canvas. However, once you set the clipping region, anything you draw in the canvas will be restricted to that region, meaning that anything you draw outside of the clipping region has no effect.

In this section we look at two examples that use the clipping region. The first example implements an eraser and the second implements a telescoping animation.

 **NOTE: Canvas's Swiss Army knife**

The clipping region is Canvas's Swiss Army knife because the effects you can create with it are endless. Throughout the rest of this book you will see many uses for the clipping region, including the implementation of a magnifying glass discussed in Section 4.10, "A Magnifying Glass," on p. 321. You will also see how to use the clipping region to pan a large image inside the canvas in Chapter 10.

### 2.15.1 Erasing with the Clipping Region

Figure 2.50 shows an application that uses the clipping region to implement an eraser.

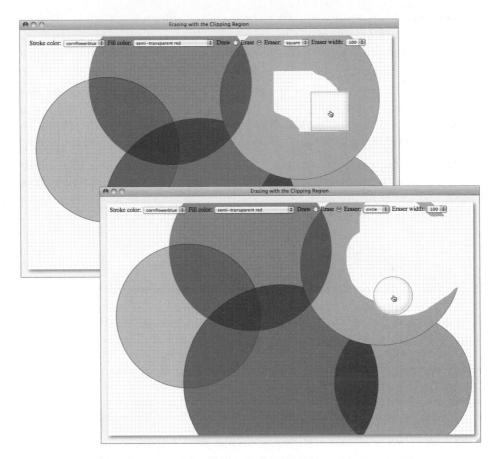

Figure 2.50  Erasing with the clipping region

Using the eraser is simple: As you drag the mouse in the canvas, the application erases either a circular or rectangular area—depending upon the value the user selected from the Eraser pulldown—surrounding the mouse cursor.

Implementing the eraser is also simple: As you drag the mouse when the eraser is rectangular, the application sets the clipping region to the rectangular area surrounding the mouse cursor and invokes clearRect(0, 0, canvas.width, canvas.height). As you've seen several times in this chapter, and as you will see many times throughout this book, that call to clearRect() erases the entire canvas *unless you've set the clipping region*. If you set the clipping region and make that call to clearRect(), the erasure will be limited to the clipping region only, and you have an eraser.

The entire JavaScript code for the application shown in Figure 2.50 is listed in
Example 2.34.

---

**Example 2.34** Erasing with the clipping region

---

```javascript
var canvas = document.getElementById('canvas'),
    context = canvas.getContext('2d'),
    strokeStyleSelect = document.getElementById('strokeStyleSelect'),
    fillStyleSelect = document.getElementById('fillStyleSelect'),
    drawRadio = document.getElementById('drawRadio'),
    eraserRadio = document.getElementById('eraserRadio'),
    eraserShapeSelect = document.getElementById('eraserShapeSelect'),
    eraserWidthSelect = document.getElementById('eraserWidthSelect'),

    ERASER_LINE_WIDTH = 1,
    ERASER_SHADOW_COLOR  = 'rgb(0,0,0)',


    ERASER_SHADOW_STYLE  = 'blue',
    ERASER_STROKE_STYLE  = 'rgb(0,0,255)',
    ERASER_SHADOW_OFFSET = -5,
    ERASER_SHADOW_BLUR   = 20,

    GRID_HORIZONTAL_SPACING = 10,
    GRID_VERTICAL_SPACING = 10,
    GRID_LINE_COLOR = 'lightblue',
    drawingSurfaceImageData,

    lastX,
    lastY,
    mousedown = {},
    rubberbandRect = {},
    dragging = false,
    guidewires = true;

// Functions........................................................

function drawGrid(color, stepx, stepy) {
   // Listing omitted for brevity. See Example 2.13 on p. 106
   // for a complete listing.
}

function windowToCanvas(x, y) {
   var bbox = canvas.getBoundingClientRect();
   return { x: x - bbox.left * (canvas.width  / bbox.width),
            y: y - bbox.top  * (canvas.height / bbox.height)
}
```

---

*(Continues)*

**Example 2.34**   *(Continued)*

```
// Save and restore drawing surface..................................

function saveDrawingSurface() {
   drawingSurfaceImageData = context.getImageData(0, 0,
                                   canvas.width,
                                   canvas.height);
}

function restoreDrawingSurface() {
   context.putImageData(drawingSurfaceImageData, 0, 0);
}

// Rubber bands.....................................................

function updateRubberbandRectangle(loc) {
   // Listing omitted for brevity. See Example 2.16 on p. 112
   // for a complete listing.
}

function drawRubberbandShape(loc) {
   var angle = Math.atan(rubberbandRect.height/rubberbandRect.width),
       radius = rubberbandRect.height / Math.sin(angle);

   if (mousedown.y === loc.y) {
      radius = Math.abs(loc.x - mousedown.x);
   }

   context.beginPath();
   context.arc(mousedown.x, mousedown.y, radius, 0, Math.PI*2, false);
   context.stroke();
   context.fill();
}

function updateRubberband(loc) {
   updateRubberbandRectangle(loc);
   drawRubberbandShape(loc);
}

// Guidewires.......................................................

function drawGuidewires(x, y) {
   // Listing omitted for brevity. See Example 2.16 on p. 112
   // for a complete listing.
}
```

```
// Eraser..........................................................

function setDrawPathForEraser(loc) {
   var eraserWidth = parseFloat(eraserWidthSelect.value);

   context.beginPath();

   if (eraserShapeSelect.value === 'circle') {
      context.arc(loc.x, loc.y,
                  eraserWidth/2,
                  0, Math.PI*2, false);
   }
   else {
      context.rect(loc.x - eraserWidth/2,
                   loc.y - eraserWidth/2,
                   eraserWidth, eraserWidth);
   }
   context.clip();
}

function setErasePathForEraser() {
   var eraserWidth = parseFloat(eraserWidthSelect.value);

   context.beginPath();

   if (eraserShapeSelect.value === 'circle') {
      context.arc(lastX, lastY,
                  eraserWidth/2 + ERASER_LINE_WIDTH,
                  0, Math.PI*2, false);
   }
   else {
      context.rect(lastX - eraserWidth/2 - ERASER_LINE_WIDTH,
                   lastY - eraserWidth/2 - ERASER_LINE_WIDTH,
                   eraserWidth + ERASER_LINE_WIDTH*2,
                   eraserWidth + ERASER_LINE_WIDTH*2);
   }
   context.clip();
}

function setEraserAttributes() {
  context.lineWidth     = ERASER_LINE_WIDTH;
  context.shadowColor   = ERASER_SHADOW_STYLE;
  context.shadowOffsetX = ERASER_SHADOW_OFFSET;
  context.shadowOffsetY = ERASER_SHADOW_OFFSET;
  context.shadowBlur    = ERASER_SHADOW_BLUR;
  context.strokeStyle   = ERASER_STROKE_STYLE;
}
```

*(Continues)*

**Example 2.34**  *(Continued)*

```javascript
function eraseLast() {
   context.save();

   setErasePathForEraser();
   drawGrid(GRID_LINE_COLOR,
            GRID_HORIZONTAL_SPACING,
            GRID_VERTICAL_SPACING);

   context.restore();
}

function drawEraser(loc) {
   context.save();

   setEraserAttributes();
   setDrawPathForEraser(loc);
   context.stroke();

   context.restore();
}

// Canvas event handlers.......................................

canvas.onmousedown = function (e) {
   var loc = windowToCanvas(e.clientX, e.clientY);

   e.preventDefault(); // Prevent cursor change

   if (drawRadio.checked) {
      saveDrawingSurface();
   }

   mousedown.x = loc.x;
   mousedown.y = loc.y;

   lastX = loc.x;
   lastY = loc.y;

   dragging = true;
};
```

```
canvas.onmousemove = function (e) {
   var loc;

   if (dragging) {
      e.preventDefault(); // Prevent selections

      loc = windowToCanvas(e.clientX, e.clientY);

      if (drawRadio.checked) {
         restoreDrawingSurface();
         updateRubberband(loc);

         if(guidewires) {
            drawGuidewires(loc.x, loc.y);
         }
      }
      else {
         eraseLast();
         drawEraser(loc);
      }
      lastX = loc.x;
      lastY = loc.y;
   }
};

canvas.onmouseup = function (e) {
   loc = windowToCanvas(e.clientX, e.clientY);

   if (drawRadio.checked) {
      restoreDrawingSurface();
      updateRubberband(loc);
   }

   if (eraserRadio.checked) {
      eraseLast();
   }

   dragging = false;
};

// Controls event handlers....................................

strokeStyleSelect.onchange = function (e) {
   context.strokeStyle = strokeStyleSelect.value;
};
```

*(Continues)*

---

**Example 2.34**  *(Continued)*

---

```
fillStyleSelect.onchange = function (e) {
   context.fillStyle = fillStyleSelect.value;
};

// Initialization.............................................

context.strokeStyle = strokeStyleSelect.value;
context.fillStyle = fillStyleSelect.value;
drawGrid(GRID_LINE_COLOR,
         GRID_HORIZONTAL_SPACING,
         GRID_VERTICAL_SPACING);
```

---

Take a look at the mouse move event handler in the code listing. When the user is dragging the mouse, that event handler erases the area that the eraser last occupied, and draws the eraser at the new location. The application erases by drawing the entire background, clipped to the eraser's path.

It's important to understand that *calls to* `clip()` *set the clipping region to the intersection of the current clipping region and the current path*. For a rectangular eraser, if you comment out the calls to `save()` and `restore()` in Example 2.34, all you will ever erase is one rectangle that's 60 pixels wide and 40 pixels high, regardless of how long or how vigorously you drag the mouse within the canvas. That's because the first call to `clip()` sets the clipping region to the initial rectangle and successive calls to `clip()` are restricted to that initial rectangle.

Because calls to `clip()` operate on the clipping region itself as discussed in the preceding paragraphs, you will hardly, if ever, see calls to `clip()` that are not embedded between calls to `save()` and `restore()`.

Now that you have a good grasp on the clipping region, let's look at one more example that uses the clipping region to implement an animation.

## 2.15.2  Telescoping with the Clipping Region

The application shown in Figure 2.51 implements a telescoping animation. The top screenshot shows the application as it appears initially. The other screenshots, going clockwise from the top, show how the application swallows up the text by manipulating the clipping region.

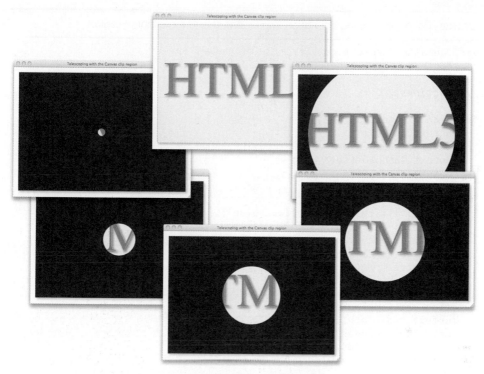

Figure 2.51 Telescoping with the clipping region

After the canvas goes completely dark, the application restores the canvas to its original state, as shown in the upper screenshot.

The JavaScript for the application shown in Figure 2.51 is listed in Example 2.35. The animate() function is where all the action happens.

The animate() function, which is called by the onmousedown event handler, loops 100 times at 60 frames per second. Every time through the loop, the animate() function fills the entire canvas with charcoal and draws the animation frame. Each frame of the animation fills the canvas with light gray and draws the HTML5 text, all of which is clipped to the telescope.

**Example 2.35** A telescoping animation implemented with the clipping region

```
var canvas = document.getElementById('canvas'),
    context = canvas.getContext('2d');

// Functions.................................................

function drawText() {
   context.save();
   context.shadowColor = 'rgba(100,100,150,0.8)';
   context.shadowOffsetX = 5;
   context.shadowOffsetY = 5;
   context.shadowBlur = 10;

   context.fillStyle = 'cornflowerblue';
   context.fillText('HTML5', 20, 250);
   context.strokeStyle = 'yellow';
   context.strokeText('HTML5', 20, 250);
   context.restore();
}

function setClippingRegion(radius) {
   context.beginPath();
   context.arc(canvas.width/2, canvas.height/2,
               radius, 0, Math.PI*2, false);
   context.clip();
}

function fillCanvas(color) {
   context.fillStyle = color;
   context.fillRect(0, 0, canvas.width, canvas.height);
}

function endAnimation(loop) {
   clearInterval(loop);

   setTimeout( function (e) {
      context.clearRect(0, 0, canvas.width, canvas.height);
      drawText();
   }, 1000);
}

function drawAnimationFrame(radius) {
   setClippingRegion(radius);
   fillCanvas('lightgray');
   drawText();
}
```

```
function animate() {
    var radius = canvas.width/2,
        loop;

    loop = window.setInterval(function() {
        radius -= canvas.width/100;

        fillCanvas('charcoal');

        if (radius > 0) {
            context.save();
            drawAnimationFrame(radius);
            context.restore();
        }
        else {
            endAnimation(loop);
        }
    }, 16);
};


// Event handlers.....................................................

canvas.onmousedown = function (e) {
    animate();
};

// Initialization....................................................

context.lineWidth = 0.5;
context.font = '128pt Comic-sans';
drawText();
```

The clip() method is described in Table 2.15.

**Table 2.15** The clip() method

| Method | Description |
|--------|-------------|
| clip() | Sets the clipping region to the intersection of the current clipping region and the current path. Initially, the clipping region is equal to the entire canvas until you invoke clip() for the first time. |
|        | Because calls to clip() set the clipping region to the intersection of the current clipping region and the current path, calls to clip() are almost always contained within calls to save() and restore(); otherwise, the clipping region becomes successively smaller, which is typically not what you want. |

## 2.16 Conclusion

This chapter took an in-depth look at drawing in a canvas. We began by discussing the coordinate system and the Canvas drawing model, and then we looked at drawing simple rectangles, specifying colors and transparencies, using gradients and patterns, and applying shadows.

Then we took a look at paths and subpaths, and stroking and filling. We also looked at the nonzero winding rule that Canvas uses when filling intersecting subpaths, and you saw how to put that knowledge to practical use by implementing cutouts.

Then we focused on drawing lines, and you learned how to draw true one-pixel-wide lines and how to draw lines that appear to be less than one pixel wide. You saw how to use lines to draw grids and axes, and you learned how to let users interactively draw lines with rubber bands. You also saw how to draw dashed lines, which are not explicitly supported by the Canvas context, and then you saw how to extend the Canvas context so that dashed lines are explicitly supported. Finally, we wrapped up the section on lines by looking at line caps and joins, which determines how the Canvas context draws line endpoints.

From there we moved on to arcs and circles, and you saw how to let users interactively create circles by dragging the mouse. You also learned how to draw a rounded rectangles with the `arcTo()` method and how to implement dials and gauges.

From arcs and circles, we moved on to bézier curves, both quadratic and cubic, and you saw how to use those types of curves to implement a checkmark and an arrowhead. Then we looked at drawing polygons, implementing polygon objects and using the Canvas context's `isPointInPath()` method to drag polygons. You also saw how to use `isPointInPath()` to implement an interactive editor that creates bézier curves.

From there we moved on to transformations, where you saw how to translate, rotate, and scale the Canvas coordinate system. You also saw how to create custom transformations, such as shear.

Finally, we looked at compositing, which determines how Canvas draws shapes on top of each other. We wrapped up the chapter by looking at the Canvas's Swiss Army knife—the clipping region—and you saw how to erase and implement a telescoping animation with that knife.

At this point you know how to draw pretty much anything you can imagine in a canvas. In the chapters that follow we will put that knowledge to good use by exploring images, animation, sprites, physics, collision detection, game development, implementing custom controls, and manipulating video frames, as a video is running, inside the canvas. And we will also explore using Canvas to implement mobile applications that you can run on smart phones or tablet computers.

Canvas provides a powerful drawing API that's based on other, proven graphics system such as Adobe Illustrator and Apple's Cocoa. In the pages that follow, we will continue to explore that API.

# CHAPTER 3

# Text

Nearly every Canvas-based application deals with text. Some applications merely configure and display text, whereas other applications provide sophisticated text editing support.

The canvas element only minimally supports text; at the time this book was written, it does not offer many of the features that you will find in basic text editors, features such as text selection, copy and paste, and text scrolling. However, it does support basic necessities such as stroking and filling text, placing text within the canvas, and measuring the width, in pixels, of an arbitrary string. The Canvas context provides three methods pertaining to text:

- strokeText(text, x, y)
- fillText(text, x, y)
- measureText(text)

The measureText() method returns an object with a width property, which represents the width of the text you pass to the method. Three Canvas context properties are related to text:

- font
- textAlign
- textBaseline

The font property lets you set the font of text that you subsequently draw, and textAlign and textBaseline let you position text within the canvas. Let's take a closer look at those methods and properties.

## 3.1 Stroking and Filling Text

Figure 3.1 shows an application that strokes and fills text.

Figure 3.1  Stroking and filling text

This application provides checkboxes that let you control whether the text is stroked, filled, or drawn with shadows.

The HTML for the application shown in Figure 3.1, which is omitted from the book in the interests of brevity, creates the checkboxes and canvas and includes the application's JavaScript, which is listed in Example 3.1.

This JavaScript obtains references to the three checkboxes and adds an onchange handler to each that draws the background and text.

The application uses fillText() and strokeText() to fill and stroke the text, respectively. Each of those methods takes three arguments. The first argument is the text, and the remaining two arguments specify the text's location. Exactly where the text is drawn depends on the textAlign and textBaseline properties, which we discuss in Section 3.3, "Positioning Text," on p. 210.

---

Example 3.1 Stroking and filling text

---

```
var canvas = document.getElementById('canvas'),
    context = canvas.getContext('2d'),
    fillCheckbox   = document.getElementById('fillCheckbox'),
    strokeCheckbox = document.getElementById('strokeCheckbox'),
    shadowCheckbox = document.getElementById('shadowCheckbox'),
    text='HTML5';

// Functions.......................................................

function draw() {
    context.clearRect(0, 0, canvas.width, canvas.height);
    drawBackground();

    if (shadowCheckbox.checked) turnShadowsOn();
    else                        turnShadowsOff();

    drawText();
}

function drawBackground() {   // Ruled paper
    var STEP_Y = 12,
        TOP_MARGIN = STEP_Y * 4,
        LEFT_MARGIN = STEP_Y * 3,
        i = context.canvas.height;

    // Horizontal lines

    context.strokeStyle = 'lightgray';
    context.lineWidth = 0.5;

    while(i > TOP_MARGIN) {
        context.beginPath();
        context.moveTo(0, i);
        context.lineTo(context.canvas.width, i);
        context.stroke();
        i -= STEP_Y;
    }

    // Vertical line

    context.strokeStyle = 'rgba(100,0,0,0.3)';
    context.lineWidth = 1;
    context.beginPath();
    context.moveTo(LEFT_MARGIN,0);
    context.lineTo(LEFT_MARGIN,context.canvas.height);
    context.stroke();
}
```

---

*(Continues)*

**Example 3.1** *(Continued)*

```
function turnShadowsOn() {
   context.shadowColor = 'rgba(0,0,0,0.8)';
   context.shadowOffsetX = 5;
   context.shadowOffsetY = 5;
   context.shadowBlur    = 10;
}

function turnShadowsOff() {
   context.shadowColor = undefined;
   context.shadowOffsetX = 0;
   context.shadowOffsetY = 0;
   context.shadowBlur    = 0;
}

function drawText() {
   var TEXT_X = 65,
       TEXT_Y = canvas.height/2 + 35;

   context.strokeStyle = 'blue';

   if (fillCheckbox.checked)   context.fillText  (text, TEXT_X, TEXT_Y);
   if (strokeCheckbox.checked) context.strokeText(text, TEXT_X, TEXT_Y);
}

// Event handlers................................................

fillCheckbox.onchange   = draw;
strokeCheckbox.onchange = draw;
shadowCheckbox.onchange = draw;

// Initialization................................................

context.font = '128px Palatino';
context.lineWidth = 1.0;
context.fillStyle = 'cornflowerblue';

turnShadowsOn();
draw();
```

Both fillText() and strokeText() take an optional fourth argument that specifies the maximum width, in pixels, of the text. In Figure 3.2, the top screenshot shows the application in Figure 3.1 drawing text normally. The bottom screenshot shows the application restricting the width of the text with the optional fourth argument to strokeText() and fillText().

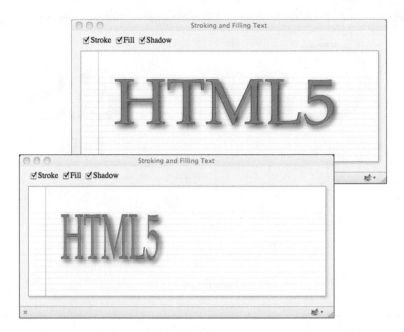

Figure 3.2 Setting the maximum width for text

If you use strokeText() or fillText() with the optional fourth argument that specifies the maximum width of the text, and the text exceeds that width, then the Canvas specification requires browsers to resize the text so that it fits in the specified width. Browsers can either change the size of the font or scale the text horizontally, but in either case the text must still be readable.

When this book was written, support for the maxWidth argument was spotty; neither Safari nor Chrome supported the argument. Firefox, however, has supported it since version 5.0, as the screenshots in Figure 3.2 attest to, and Internet Explorer has had support since IE9.

In addition to filling and stroking text with colors, you can also use patterns and gradients, just like you can with shapes, as illustrated in Figure 3.3.

The JavaScript for the application shown in Figure 3.3 is listed in Example 3.2.

Example 3.2 creates a linear gradient and a pattern, exactly as we did in Section 2.5.1.1, "Linear Gradients," on p. 76. Before drawing the text at the top of the page, the application sets the fill style to the gradient, and before drawing the text at the bottom of the page, the application sets the fill style to the pattern.

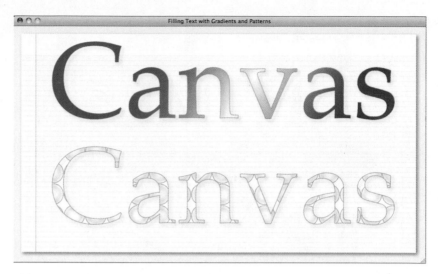

Figure 3.3 Filling text with patterns and gradients

Example 3.2 Filling text with color gradients and patterns

```
var canvas = document.getElementById('canvas'),
    context = canvas.getContext('2d'),
    image = new Image(),
    gradient = context.createLinearGradient(0, 0,
                   canvas.width, canvas.height),
    text = 'Canvas',
    pattern; // Create pattern after image loads

// Functions......................................................

function drawBackground() {
   // Listing omitted for brevity. See Example 3.1 on p. 203
   // for a complete listing.
}

function drawGradientText() {
   context.fillStyle = gradient;
   context.fillText(text, 65, 200);
   context.strokeText(text, 65, 200);
}

function drawPatternText() {
   context.fillStyle = pattern;
   context.fillText(text, 65, 450);
   context.strokeText(text, 65, 450);
}
```

```
// Event handlers.............................................

image.onload = function (e) {
   pattern = context.createPattern(image, 'repeat');
   drawPatternText();
};

// Initialization.............................................

image.src = 'redball.png';

context.font = '256px Palatino';
context.strokeStyle = 'cornflowerblue';

context.shadowColor   = 'rgba(100,100,150,0.8)';
context.shadowOffsetX = 5;
context.shadowOffsetY = 5;
context.shadowBlur    = 10;

gradient.addColorStop(0,    'blue');
gradient.addColorStop(0.25, 'blue');
gradient.addColorStop(0.5,  'white');
gradient.addColorStop(0.75, 'red');
gradient.addColorStop(1.0,  'yellow');

drawBackground();
drawGradientText();
```

Now that you've seen how to stroke and fill text, let's see how to set font properties.

## 3.2 Setting Font Properties

You can set the font of the text that you draw in a canvas with the context's font property, which is a CSS3 font string consisting of the components in Table 3.1. From top to bottom, the font components in the table are listed in the order you use them for the context's font property.

The default Canvas font is 10px sans-serif. The default values for font-style, font-variant, and font-weight are all normal.

Figure 3.4 shows an application that fills text with different fonts.

The strings in the application were generated by setting the context's font property and subsequently printing that property using the context's fillText() method.

**Table 3.1** Components of the font property

| Font Property | Valid Values |
|---|---|
| font-style | Three values are allowed: normal, italic, oblique. |
| font-variant | Two values are allowed: normal, small-caps. |
| font-weight | Determines the thickness of a font's characters: normal, bold, bolder (one font weight darker than base font), lighter (one font weight lighter than base font), 100, 200, 300, ... , 900. A weight of 400 is normal, 700 is bold. |
| font-size | Values for the size of the font: xx-small, x-small, medium, large, x-large, xx-large, smaller, larger, length, %. |
| line-height | The browser always forces this property to its default value, which is normal. If you set this property, the browser will ignore your setting. |
| font-family | Two types of font family names are allowed: family-name, such as helvetica, verdana, palatino, etc., and generic-family names: serif, sans-serif, monospace, cursive, and fantasy. You can use either family-name or generic-family, or both for the font-family component of the font. |

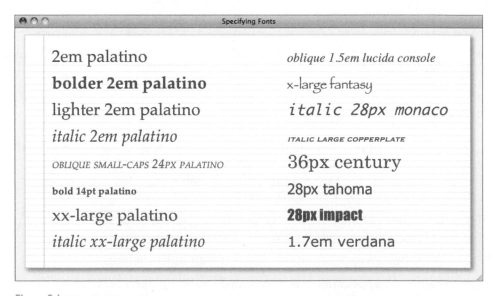

**Figure 3.4** Specifying fonts

The fonts used for the strings in the left-hand column are all variations of the Palatino font family. The right-hand column shows some other web-safe fonts.

All the fonts used in the application are web safe. There is nothing inherently dangerous about fonts; the web-safe moniker simply means that those fonts are widely available under Windows, Mac, and Linux. Because of their widespread availability, you can safely assume that those fonts will be properly rendered in nearly all browsers on the three major operating systems.

The application shown in Figure 3.4 is listed in Example 3.3.

Example 3.3 Setting the font property

```
var canvas = document.getElementById('canvas'),
    context = canvas.getContext('2d'),

    LEFT_COLUMN_FONTS = [
        '2em palatino',                        'bolder 2em palatino',
        'lighter 2em palatino',                'italic 2em palatino',
        'oblique small-caps 24px palatino', 'bold 14pt palatino',
        'xx-large palatino',                   'italic xx-large palatino'
    ],
    RIGHT_COLUMN_FONTS = [
        'oblique 1.5em lucida console',        'x-large fantasy',
        'italic 28px monaco',                  'italic large copperplate',
        '36px century',                        '28px tahoma',
        '28px impact',                         '1.7em verdana'
    ],

    LEFT_COLUMN_X = 25,
    RIGHT_COLUMN_X = 425,
    DELTA_Y = 50,
    TOP_Y = 50,
    y = 0;

context.fillStyle = 'blue';

LEFT_COLUMN_FONTS.forEach( function (font) {
    context.font = font;
    context.fillText(font, LEFT_COLUMN_X, y += DELTA_Y);
});

y = 0;

RIGHT_COLUMN_FONTS.forEach( function (font) {
    context.font = font;
    context.fillText(font, RIGHT_COLUMN_X, y += DELTA_Y);
});
```

Example 3.3 sets the font property and then prints it out. Notice that in every case what the application prints is exactly what it specified for the font property, which makes sense.

However, if you set the font property to an invalid value—for example, you specify the components of the property, such as font-style and font-family, in the wrong order or you specify an illegal value for the font-style—then the browser will not change the font and therefore will leave the font unchanged.

---

 **NOTE: Specifying fonts with CSS3 vs. Canvas**

The context's font property supports CSS3 font syntax, except for property-independent stylesheet syntax such as inherit or initial. If you are unfortunate enough to use inherit or initial, the browser will silently fail without throwing any exceptions and will not set the font.

There is one other difference between setting a font for Canvas and setting the font with CSS3: With Canvas, the browser will ignore any value that you set for line-height. Browsers are required to always set that value to normal.

---

 **NOTE: Lists of web-safe fonts**

Here are some links to sites that list web-safe fonts:

http://www.speaking-in-styles.com/web-typography/Web-Safe-Fonts

http://www.codestyle.org/css/font-family/sampler-CombinedResultsFull.shtml

http://www.apaddedcell.com/web-fonts

---

## 3.3 Positioning Text

Now that you've seen how to stroke and fill text, and set fonts, let's see how to position text within a canvas.

### 3.3.1 Horizontal and Vertical Positioning

When you draw text in a canvas with strokeText() or fillText(), you specify the X and Y coordinates of the text; however, exactly where the browser draws the text depends on two context properties: textAlign and textBaseline. Those properties are illustrated in the application shown in Figure 3.5.

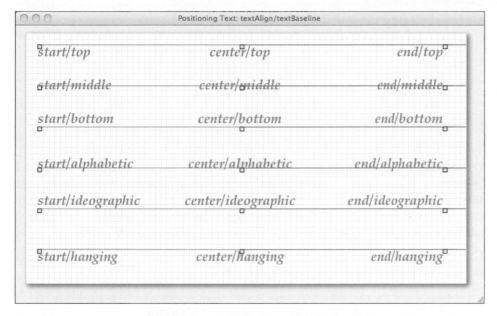

**Figure 3.5**  Text alignment/baseline: Defaults are `start` and `alphabetic`, respectively

The filled rectangles in Figure 3.5 depict the X and Y coordinates that the application passed to the `fillText()` method. Each string displayed by the application shows a combination of the `textAlign` and `textBaseline` properties.

Valid values for `textAlign` are as follows:

- `start`
- `center`
- `end`
- `left`
- `right`

The default value for `textAlign` is `start`, and when the browser displays text from left to right, meaning the `dir` attribute of the canvas element is `ltr`, `left` is the same as `start`, and `right` is the same as `end`. Likewise, when the browser displays text from right to left, meaning the `dir` attribute's value is `rtl`, `right` is the same as `start` and `left` is the same as `end`. The application shown in Figure 3.5 displays text from left to right.

Valid values for textBaseline are as follows:

- top
- bottom
- middle
- alphabetic
- ideographic
- hanging

The default value for textBaseline is alphabetic, which is used for Latin-based languages. ideographic is used for languages such as Japanese and Chinese, and hanging is used for many of the languages of India. The values top, bottom, and middle do not pertain to any languages; instead, they represent locations within a bounding box around the text, known as the *em square* of the font.

The application shown in Figure 3.5 is listed in Example 3.4. The textAlign and textBaseline context properties are described in Table 3.2.

**Example 3.4** Positioning text with textAlign and textBaseline

```
var canvas = document.getElementById('canvas'),
    context = canvas.getContext('2d'),
    fontHeight = 24,
    alignValues = ['start', 'center', 'end'],
    baselineValues = ['top', 'middle', 'bottom',
                      'alphabetic', 'ideographic', 'hanging'],
    x, y;

// Functions......................................................

function drawGrid(color, stepx, stepy) {
    // Listing omitted for brevity. See Example 2.13 on p. 106
    // for more information
}

function drawTextMarker() {
    context.fillStyle = 'yellow';
    context.fillRect  (x, y, 7, 7);
    context.strokeRect(x, y, 7, 7);
}
```

```
function drawText(text, textAlign, textBaseline) {
   if(textAlign) context.textAlign = textAlign;
   if(textBaseline) context.textBaseline = textBaseline;

   context.fillStyle = 'cornflowerblue';
   context.fillText(text, x, y);
}

function drawTextLine() {
   context.strokeStyle = 'gray';
   context.beginPath();
   context.moveTo(x, y);
   context.lineTo(x + 738, y);
   context.stroke();
}

// Initialization....................................................

context.font = 'oblique normal bold 24px palatino';

drawGrid('lightgray', 10, 10);

for (var align=0; align < alignValues.length; ++align) {
   for (var baseline=0; baseline < baselineValues.length; ++baseline) {
      x = 20 + align*fontHeight*15;
      y = 20 + baseline*fontHeight*3;

      drawText(alignValues[align] + '/' + baselineValues[baseline],
               alignValues[align], baselineValues[baseline]);

      drawTextMarker();
      drawTextLine();
   }
}
```

**Table 3.2** Text align and baseline properties

| Property | Description |
|---|---|
| textAlign | Specifies how text is aligned horizontally. Valid values are start, left, center, right, end. The default value is start. |
| textBaseline | Specifies how text is aligned vertically. Valid values are top, bottom, middle, alphabetic, ideographic, and hanging. The default value is alphabetic. |

---

 **NOTE: The em square**

Before the digital era, when characters were printed on printing presses, the point size of a font was defined to be the height of the plate from which the character arises. The plates looked like this:

The height of the plate is the point size, and the width of the letter M was traditionally known as the em square.

However, over time the meaning of em square has evolved to include languages that don't have an M character, and today the em square is generally regarded as the height of a particular font.

---

## 3.3.2 Centering Text

You can center text about a point with the `textAlign` and `textBaseline` attributes of the Canvas context discussed in the preceding section. Figure 3.6 shows an application that centers text in the middle of a canvas.

An excerpt of the application's JavaScript is listed in Example 3.5.

---

**Example 3.5** Centering text about a point

```javascript
function drawText() {
   context.fillStyle = 'blue';
   context.strokeStyle = 'yellow';

   context.fillText(text, canvas.width/2, canvas.height/2);
   context.strokeText(text, canvas.width/2, canvas.height/2);
}

context.textAlign = 'center';
context.textBaseline = 'middle';
```

---

The application sets `textAlign` and `textBaseline` to `center` and `middle`, respectively, and strokes and fills the text.

The application fills and then strokes the text, and the location it passes to `fillText()` and `strokeText()` is the center of the canvas. Because the application

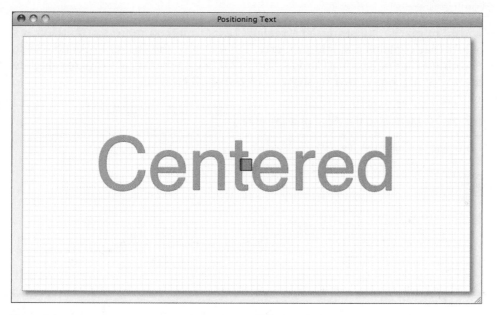

Figure 3.6  Centering text in the middle of a canvas

also sets `textAlign` and `textBaseline` to `center` and `middle`, respectively, the text is drawn in the middle of the canvas, as shown in Figure 3.6.

### 3.3.3  Measuring Text

To do anything interesting with text, you must be able to measure the width and height, in pixels, of a string. For example, Figure 3.7 shows a simple text editor with a text cursor. The editor must know where to place the cursor in the canvas, and therefore it needs to know the dimensions of the text.

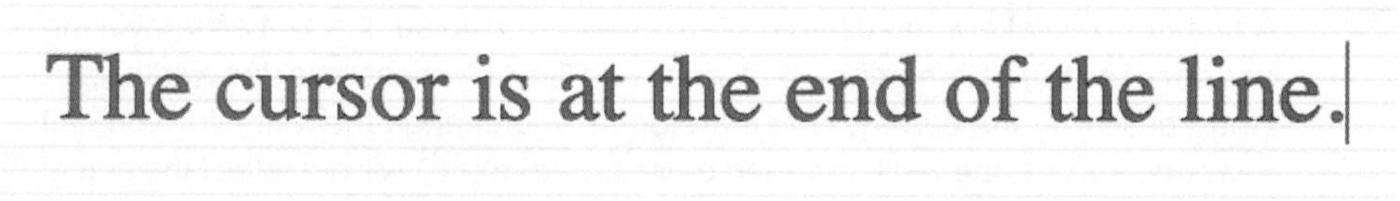

## The cursor is at the end of the line.

Figure 3.7  Placing a cursor at a pixel location

To place the cursor at the end of a line of text, you must calculate the width of that text.

The Canvas context provides a measureText() method that lets you measure the width, in pixels, of a string. The measureText() method returns a TextMetrics object that contains a single property: the width of the string. In Section 3.4.2, "Editing a Line of Text in a Canvas," on p. 232, we use measureText() to calculate the width of a line of text, as shown in Example 3.6.

**Example 3.6** Measuring the width of a line of text

```
TextLine = function (x, y) {
   this.text = '';
   ...
};

TextLine.prototype = {
   getWidth: function(context) {
      return context.measureText(this.text).width;
   },
   ...
};
```

The measureText() method is summarized in Table 3.3.

**Table 3.3** The measureText() method

| Method | Description |
| --- | --- |
| TextMetrics measureText(DOMString text) | Returns a TextMetrics object that contains a single property: the width of the text, in pixels, passed to the method. That width is based on the current font, and is the only metric you can get, at the time this book was written, from the TextMetrics object. |

 **CAUTION: Set the font before calling measureText()**

A common mistake when using measureText() is to set the font *after* invoking measureText(). Remember that measureText() measures the width of a string based on the current font; therefore, if you change the font after you call measureText(), the width returned by measureText() will not reflect the actual width of the text in the current font.

**CAUTION: Text measurement is inexact**

You can only obtain the width, in pixels, of an arbitrary string with the `width` property of the `TextMetrics` object returned from `measureText()`. That `TextMetrics` object does not (at least as of the time this book was published) have a corresponding `height` property. However, there's a twist to the text measurement story because as the Canvas specification states:

*Glyphs rendered using `fillText()` and `strokeText()` can spill out of the box given by the font size (the em square size) and the width returned by `measureText()` (the text width).*

That quote from the specification means that the width returned by `measureText()` is not exact. Often, it's not important if that value is inexact; however, sometimes it's crucial, as you will see in Section 3.4.2, "Editing a Line of Text in a Canvas," on p. 232.

## 3.3.4 Labeling Axes

In Section 2.8.3, "Drawing Axes," on p. 107 you saw how to draw graph axes. In this section we add text labels to those axes, as illustrated in Figure 3.8.

An excerpt of the JavaScript for the application shown in Figure 3.8 is listed in Example 3.7.

Drawing vertical and horizontal axis labels is straightforward. The application draws text at positions dependent on the location of the axes, the length of the tick marks on the axes, and the space between the axes and the labels.

**Example 3.7** Adding labels to axes

```
var canvas = document.getElementById('canvas'),
    context = canvas.getContext('2d'),

    HORIZONTAL_AXIS_MARGIN = 50,
    VERTICAL_AXIS_MARGIN = 50,

    AXIS_ORIGIN = { x: HORIZONTAL_AXIS_MARGIN,
                    y: canvas.height-VERTICAL_AXIS_MARGIN },

    AXIS_TOP   = VERTICAL_AXIS_MARGIN,
    AXIS_RIGHT = canvas.width-HORIZONTAL_AXIS_MARGIN,
```

*(Continues)*

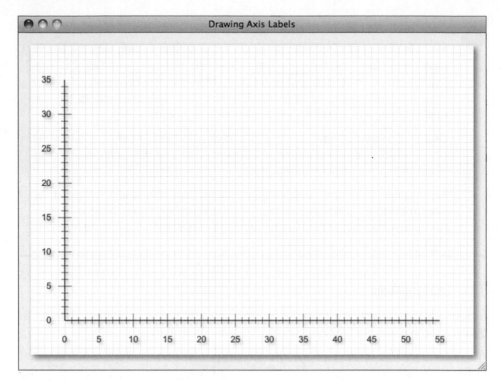

Figure 3.8  Axes

Example 3.7  *(Continued)*

```
HORIZONTAL_TICK_SPACING = 10,
VERTICAL_TICK_SPACING = 10,

AXIS_WIDTH  = AXIS_RIGHT - AXIS_ORIGIN.x,
AXIS_HEIGHT = AXIS_ORIGIN.y - AXIS_TOP,

NUM_VERTICAL_TICKS   = AXIS_HEIGHT / VERTICAL_TICK_SPACING,
NUM_HORIZONTAL_TICKS = AXIS_WIDTH  / HORIZONTAL_TICK_SPACING,

TICK_WIDTH = 10,

SPACE_BETWEEN_LABELS_AND_AXIS =  20;
```

```
// Functions.......................................................

function drawAxes() {
   context.save();
   context.lineWidth = 1.0;
   context.fillStyle = 'rgba(100,140,230,0.8)';
   context.strokeStyle = 'navy';

   drawHorizontalAxis();
   drawVerticalAxis();

   context.lineWidth = 0.5;
   context.strokeStyle = 'navy';

   context.strokeStyle = 'darkred';
   drawVerticalAxisTicks();
   drawHorizontalAxisTicks();

   context.restore();
}

// Axis drawing methods omitted for brevity. See Example 2.14 on p. 108
// for a complete listing
...

function drawAxisLabels() {
   context.fillStyle = 'blue';
   drawHorizontalAxisLabels();
   drawVerticalAxisLabels();
}

function drawHorizontalAxisLabels() {
   context.textAlign = 'center';
   context.textBaseline = 'top';

   for (var i=0; i <= NUM_HORIZONTAL_TICKS; ++i) {
      if (i % 5 === 0) {
         context.fillText(i,
            AXIS_ORIGIN.x + i * HORIZONTAL_TICK_SPACING,
            AXIS_ORIGIN.y + SPACE_BETWEEN_LABELS_AND_AXIS);
      }
   }
}
```

*(Continues)*

Example 3.7 *(Continued)*

```
function drawVerticalAxisLabels() {
   context.textAlign = 'right';
   context.textBaseline = 'middle';

   for (var i=0; i <= NUM_VERTICAL_TICKS; ++i) {
      if (i % 5 === 0) {
         context.fillText(i,
                     AXIS_ORIGIN.x - SPACE_BETWEEN_LABELS_AND_AXIS,
                     AXIS_ORIGIN.y - i * VERTICAL_TICK_SPACING);
      }
   }
}

function drawGrid(color, stepx, stepy) {
   // Listing omitted for brevity. See Example 2.13 on p. 106
   // for more information
}

// Initialization...................................................

context.font = '13px Arial';

drawGrid('lightgray', 10, 10);

context.shadowColor = 'rgba(100,140,230,0.8)';
context.shadowOffsetX = 3;
context.shadowOffsetY = 3;
context.shadowBlur = 5;

drawAxes();
drawAxisLabels();
```

Notice the application's settings for the `textAlign` and `textBaseLine`. For labels on the horizontal axis, the application sets those properties to `center` and `top`, and for the vertical axis, `right` and `middle`, respectively, as shown in **Figure 3.9**.

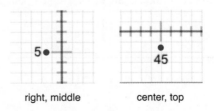

right, middle        center, top

Figure 3.9 Baseline and alignment for axis labels

### 3.3.5 Labeling Dials

As you saw in Section 3.3.4, "Labeling Axes," on p. 217, it's easy to draw text labels for horizontal and vertical axes. Labeling along arcs and circles is a little more challenging because we bring trigonometry into the mix.

Figure 3.10 shows an application that draws a dial representing the degrees of a circle.

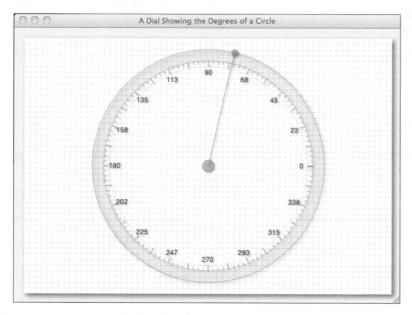

Figure 3.10  Labeling a dial

For each label, the application calculates the label's location, illustrated by the yellow dot in Figure 3.11. The application draws each label at their respective locations with textAlign set to center and textBaseline set to middle.

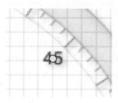

Figure 3.11  Positioning dial labels, textAlign = 'center' and textBaseline = 'middle'

An excerpt of the JavaScript for the application shown in Figure 3.10 is listed in Example 3.8.

---

**Example 3.8** Labeling a dial

---

```
var canvas = document.getElementById('canvas'),
    context = canvas.getContext('2d'),
    ...

    DEGREE_ANNOTATIONS_FILL_STYLE = 'rgba(0,0,230,0.9)',
    DEGREE_ANNOTATIONS_TEXT_SIZE = 12;

// Functions......................................................

function drawDegreeAnnotations() {
   var radius = circle.radius + DEGREE_DIAL_MARGIN;

   context.save();
   context.fillStyle = DEGREE_ANNOTATIONS_FILL_STYLE;
   context.font = DEGREE_ANNOTATIONS_TEXT_SIZE + 'px Helvetica';

   for (var angle=0; angle < 2*Math.PI; angle += Math.PI/8) {
      context.beginPath();

      context.fillText((angle * 180 / Math.PI).toFixed(0),
         circle.x + Math.cos(angle) * (radius - TICK_WIDTH*2),
         circle.y - Math.sin(angle) * (radius - TICK_WIDTH*2));
   }
   context.restore();
}

// Initialization.............................................
...

context.textAlign = 'center';
context.textBaseline = 'middle';

drawGrid('lightgray', 10, 10);
drawDial();
```

---

Notice the call to fillText() in Example 3.8. The last two parameters that the application passes to fillText() represent the X and Y coordinates of the text. An alternative implementation would be to translate the context to the text's location, and then fill the text at (0, 0), like this:

```
function drawDegreeAnnotations() {
    ...
    for (var angle=0; angle < 2*Math.PI; angle += Math.PI/8) {
        ...
      context.translate(
          circle.x + Math.cos(angle) * (radius - TICK_WIDTH*2),
          circle.y - Math.sin(angle) * (radius - TICK_WIDTH*2));
      context.fillText((angle * 180 / Math.PI).toFixed(0), 0, 0);
    }
}
```

In the next section we translate the context to draw text around an arc.

### 3.3.6  Drawing Text around an Arc

You can draw text around an arc, as illustrated in Figure 3.12 and listed in Example 3.9, with the following steps:

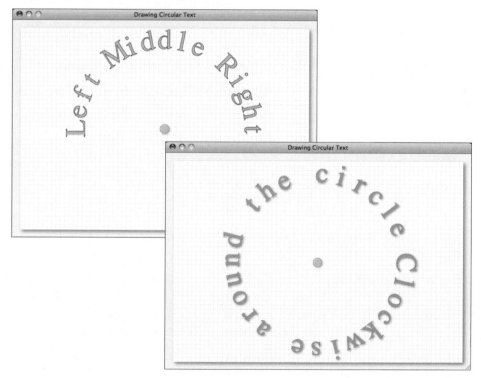

Figure 3.12  Drawing text, rotated, along an arc

1. Calculating each character's position along the arc
2. Translating the context to that position
3. Rotating the context by $\pi - \text{angle}$
4. Stroking or filling the character (or both)

---

**Example 3.9** Drawing circular text

---

```javascript
var canvas = document.getElementById('canvas'),
    context = canvas.getContext('2d'),
    ...
    TEXT_FILL_STYLE = 'rgba(100,130,240,0.5)',
    TEXT_STROKE_STYLE = 'rgba(200,0,0,0.7)',
    TEXT_SIZE = 64,

    circle = { x: canvas.width/2,
               y: canvas.height/2,
               radius: 200
             };

// Functions.......................................................

function drawCircularText(string, startAngle, endAngle) {
   var radius = circle.radius,
       angleDecrement = (startAngle - endAngle)/(string.length-1),
       angle = parseFloat(startAngle),
       index = 0,
       character;

   context.save();

   context.fillStyle = TEXT_FILL_STYLE;
   context.strokeStyle = TEXT_STROKE_STYLE;
   context.font = TEXT_SIZE + 'px Lucida Sans';

   while (index < string.length) {
      character = string.charAt(index);

      context.save();
      context.beginPath();

      context.translate(circle.x + Math.cos(angle) * radius,
                        circle.y - Math.sin(angle) * radius);

      context.rotate(Math.PI/2 - angle);

      context.fillText(character, 0, 0);
      context.strokeText(character, 0, 0);
```

```
        angle -= angleDecrement;
        index++;

        context.restore();
    }
    context.restore();
}

// Initialization..............................................

context.textAlign = 'center';
context.textBaseline = 'middle';
...

drawCircularText("Clockwise around the circle", Math.PI*2, Math.PI/8);
```

The `drawCircularText()` function implements the four steps listed above.
Note that the application must call `translate()` and `rotate()` in that order. If
you rotate about the context's default origin and then translate, you end up with
a wildly different (and unintelligible) result.

Now that you have a good grasp of drawing text in a canvas, let's put that
knowledge to use by implementing a simple text editor.

## 3.4  Implementing Text Controls

Although Canvas does not provide sophisticated text editing capabilities, such
as cursors, text selection, or cut, copy, and paste, it does provide substantial
graphics horsepower to implement that functionality. For the rest of this chapter,
we explore the implementation of a simple text editor with the Canvas APIs.

We begin with a simple text cursor and end with paragraphs that have their own
cursor and contain multiple lines of editable text.

### 3.4.1  A Text Cursor

Let's start with a simple text cursor that you can draw but cannot erase, as shown
in Figure 3.13.

The application in Figure 3.13 creates a single cursor and redraws it every time
you click the mouse. The original implementation of the TextCursor object—which
is listed in Example 3.10—lacks an `erase()` method, so although it may appear
that the application in Figure 3.13 has multiple cursors, it in fact has only one
cursor that's repeatedly reconfigured and redrawn, but never erased.

The application links the HTML controls at the top of the page to the `font` and `fillColor` attributes of the Canvas context, and the cursor uses those attributes. Cursors, therefore, take on the characteristics of the HTML controls at the top of the page.

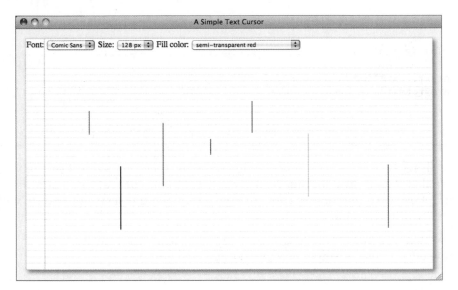

**Figure 3.13** Text cursors

**Example 3.10** Text cursors

```
TextCursor = function (width, fillStyle) {
   this.fillStyle = fillStyle || 'rgba(0,0,0,0.5)';
   this.width     = width || 2;
   this.left      = 0;
   this.top       = 0;
};

TextCursor.prototype = {
   getHeight: function (context) {
      var h = context.measureText('W').width;
      return h + h/6;
   },

   createPath: function (context) {
      context.beginPath();
      context.rect(this.left, this.top,
                   this.width, this.getHeight(context));
   },
```

```
draw: function (context, left, bottom) {
   context.save();

   this.left = left;
   this.top = bottom - this.getHeight(context);

   this.createPath(context);

   context.fillStyle = this.fillStyle;
   context.fill();

   context.restore();
   },
};
```

TextCursor is a simple filled rectangle that calculates its height in accordance with the context's current font. Recall that the only metric available in the TextMetric object returned from the context's measureText() method is the *width* of the string that you pass to that method. Text cursors calculate their *height* as 1 1/6 times the width of the character M.

The TextCursor object is implemented in a file of its own, named text.js. The application includes that file in its HTML, as shown in Example 3.11.

**Example 3.11** A simple text cursor: HTML

```
<!DOCTYPE html>
<html>
   <head>
      <title>A Simple Text Cursor</title>
      ...
   </head>

   <body>
      <canvas id='canvas' width='780' height='440'>
         Canvas not supported
      </canvas>
      ...

      <script src='text.js'></script>
      <script src='example.js'></script>
   </body>
</html>
```

An excerpt of the JavaScript for the application shown in Figure 3.13 is listed in Example 3.12. The application creates a TextCursor and draws that cursor when and where you click the mouse.

---

**Example 3.12** A simple text cursor: JavaScript

---

```
var canvas = document.getElementById('canvas'),
    context = canvas.getContext('2d'),
    ...

    cursor = new TextCursor();

function moveCursor(loc) {
    cursor.draw(context, loc.x, loc.y);
}

canvas.onmousedown = function (e) {
    var loc = windowToCanvas(e);
    moveCursor(loc);
};
...
```

---

Admittedly, the text cursor discussed above is nothing to write home about, so let's make it a little more interesting with an `erase()` method.

---

 **NOTE: Text height: a rule of thumb**

The `measureText()` method returns a `TextMetrics` object whose only metric is the width of the string that you specify. That means you're on your own if you need to calculate the height of a string. Fortunately, for most fonts, a little more than the width of the M character is a close approximation of the font's height.

---

### 3.4.1.1 Erasing

The text cursor in the preceding section sidestepped the most complicated aspect of implementing text cursors: erasing them. When you draw a cursor, you only want to draw it temporarily, so you need a way to erase it.

Canvas offers many ways to temporarily draw into a canvas; for example, in the Section 2.8.4, "Rubberband Lines," on p. 110, you saw how to draw rubberband lines as a user interactively creates a line. In that example, we simply saved the entire drawing surface before drawing a rubberband line and then restored the drawing surface to erase the line.

To erase cursors, we can take a similar approach. At some point before drawing cursors, we take a snapshot of the canvas with the context's `getImageData()` method. Then we draw cursors into the canvas, and subsequently erase by copying the cursor's rectangle from that image data to the canvas.

The TextCursor.erase() method takes an image data parameter, and the method copies the cursor's rectangle from that data into the canvas. Example 3.13 lists the TextCursor's implementation of the erase() method.

**Example 3.13** TextCursor with an erase() function

```
TextCursor.prototype = {
   ...

   erase: function (context, imageData) {
      context.putImageData(imageData, 0, 0,
                           this.left, this.top,
                           this.width, this.getHeight(context));
   }
};
```

The text cursor's erase() method assumes that the image data it receives represents the entire canvas. To erase the cursor, the method uses the context's putImageData() method. In Section 2.8.4, "Rubberband Lines," on p. 110, we used that same method with three arguments, representing the image data and the destination X and Y location in the canvas. Here, we are adding four arguments representing the rectangle, inside the image data, that we want to copy to the canvas.

The point here is to use putImageData() to erase cursors, not to learn about that method in detail: We will take a close look at getImageData() and putImageData() in Chapter 4. For now, it's enough to understand that the erase() method in Example 3.13 copies a specific rectangle from some image data into the canvas. That image data is created by the application with the getImageData() method, as shown in Example 3.14.

**Example 3.14** Erasing the cursor

```
var canvas = document.getElementById('canvas'),
    context = canvas.getContext('2d'),
    ...

    drawingSurfaceImageData,
    cursor = new TextCursor();

// Drawing surface.........................................
```

*(Continues)*

---

Example 3.14   *(Continued)*

```
function saveDrawingSurface() {
   drawingSurfaceImageData = context.getImageData(0, 0,
                                 canvas.width,
                                 canvas.height);
}

// Text.........................................................
...

function moveCursor(loc) {
   cursor.erase(context, drawingSurfaceImageData);
   cursor.draw(context, loc.x, loc.y);
}

// Event handlers...............................................
...

canvas.onmousedown = function (e) {
   var loc = windowToCanvas(e);
   moveCursor(loc);
};

// Initialization...............................................
...

drawGrid(GRID_STROKE_STYLE,
         GRID_HORIZONTAL_SPACING,
         GRID_VERTICAL_SPACING);

saveDrawingSurface();
```

---

The application listed in Example 3.14 starts by drawing a grid in the background and then saves the drawing surface with `getImageData()`. Subsequently, when the user clicks the mouse, the application erases the cursor at its previous location and redraws the cursor where the user clicked the mouse.

### 3.4.1.2  Blinking

Once you can erase a cursor, it's a simple matter to make it blink, as illustrated in Example 3.15.

The application listed in Example 3.15 creates a cursor and makes it blink with the `blinkCursor()` function. Every second, the application erases the cursor and, 300 ms later, draws it again. That means the cursor is visible for 700 ms out of every second.

---

**Example 3.15** A blinking cursor

---

```
var canvas = document.getElementById('canvas'),
    context = canvas.getContext('2d'),
    ...

    blinkingInterval,
    BLINK_ON = 500,
    BLINK_OFF = 500,

    cursor = new TextCursor();

// Functions........................................................

function blinkCursor(loc) {
   blinkingInterval = setInterval( function (e) {
      cursor.erase(context, drawingSurfaceImageData);

      setTimeout( function (e) {
         cursor.draw(context, cursor.left,
                      cursor.top + cursor.getHeight(context));
      }, BLINK_OFF);
   }, BLINK_ON + BLINK_OFF);
}

function moveCursor(loc) {
   cursor.erase(context, drawingSurfaceImageData);
   cursor.draw(context, loc.x, loc.y);

   if (!blinkingInterval)
      blinkCursor(loc);
}

// Event handlers...................................................

canvas.onmousedown = function (e) {
   var loc = windowToCanvas(e);
   moveCursor(loc);
};
...
```

---

The first time the user clicks the mouse, the application calls `blinkCursor()`, which sends the cursor into a never-ending blinking loop. You can stop the blinking, for example, if you need to hide the cursor completely, by invoking `clearInterval()`.

Now that we have a blinking cursor that we can move around, let's use it to insert some text into a canvas.

### 3.4.2 Editing a Line of Text in a Canvas

Figure 3.14 shows an application that lets you type lines of text into a canvas. The application adds the characters you type to the end of the current line and repositions the cursor so that it remains at the end of the line as you type.

You can erase the last character in the line by pressing the Backspace key. If you click anywhere in the canvas, the application ends the current line, moves the cursor to the mouse click location, and begins a new line.

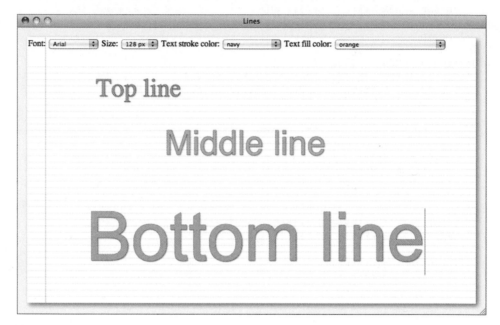

Figure 3.14  Single lines of text in a canvas

The application shown in Figure 3.14 implements a TextLine object as listed in Example 3.16.

Example 3.16  A TextLine Object

```
// Constructor.................................................

TextLine = function (x, y) {
    this.text = '';
    this.left = x;
    this.bottom = y;
    this.caret = 0;
};
```

```
// Prototype.................................................

TextLine.prototype = {
   insert: function (text) {
      this.text = this.text.substr(0, this.caret) + text +
                  this.text.substr(this.caret);
      this.caret += text.length;
   },

   removeCharacterBeforeCaret: function () {
      if (this.caret === 0)
         return;

      this.text = this.text.substring(0, this.caret-1) +
                  this.text.substring(this.caret);

      this.caret--;
   },

   getWidth: function(context) {
      return context.measureText(this.text).width;
   },

   getHeight: function (context) {
      var h = context.measureText('W').width;
      return h + h/6;
   },

   draw: function(context) {
      context.save();
      context.textAlign = 'start';
      context.textBaseline = 'bottom';

      context.strokeText(this.text, this.left, this.bottom);
      context.fillText(this.text, this.left, this.bottom);

      context.restore();
   },

   erase: function (context, imageData) {
      context.putImageData(imageData, 0, 0);
   }
};
```

Each TextLine object maintains a string, the string's position in the canvas, and
the insertion point for inserting text into that string, referred to as the caret. The
TextLine methods—insert(), draw(), erase(), getWidth(), and getHeight()—let
you insert text at the caret, draw and erase the text, and get the text line's width
and height, respectively.

The application shown in Figure 3.14 creates and manipulates a `TextLine` object entirely in the application's event handlers, which are listed in Example 3.17.

**Example 3.17** Drawing lines of text

```javascript
var canvas = document.getElementById('canvas'),
    context = canvas.getContext('2d'),

    fontSelect = document.getElementById('fontSelect'),
    sizeSelect = document.getElementById('sizeSelect'),
    strokeStyleSelect = document.getElementById('strokeStyleSelect'),
    fillStyleSelect = document.getElementById('fillStyleSelect'),

    GRID_STROKE_STYLE = 'lightgray',
    GRID_HORIZONTAL_SPACING = 10,
    GRID_VERTICAL_SPACING = 10,

    cursor = new TextCursor(),

    line,

    blinkingInterval,
    BLINK_TIME = 1000,
    BLINK_OFF = 300;

// General-purpose functions...................................

function drawBackground() { // Ruled paper
   // Listing omitted for brevity. See Example 3.2 on p. 206
   // for a complete listing.
}

function windowToCanvas(x, y) {
   var bbox = canvas.getBoundingClientRect();
   return { x: x - bbox.left * (canvas.width  / bbox.width),
            y: y - bbox.top  * (canvas.height / bbox.height)
          };
}

// Drawing surface.............................................

function saveDrawingSurface() {
   drawingSurfaceImageData = context.getImageData(0, 0,
                                              canvas.width,
                                              canvas.height);

}

// Text........................................................
```

```
function setFont() {
   context.font = sizeSelect.value + 'px ' + fontSelect.value;
}

function blinkCursor(x, y) {
   clearInterval(blinkingInterval);
   blinkingInterval = setInterval( function (e) {
      cursor.erase(context, drawingSurfaceImageData);

      setTimeout( function (e) {
         if (cursor.left == x &&
            cursor.top + cursor.getHeight(context) == y) {
            cursor.draw(context, x, y);
         }
      }, 300);
   }, 1000);
}

function moveCursor(x, y) {
   cursor.erase(context, drawingSurfaceImageData);
   saveDrawingSurface();
   context.putImageData(drawingSurfaceImageData, 0, 0);

   cursor.draw(context, x, y);
   blinkCursor(x, y);
}

// Event handlers...........................................

canvas.onmousedown = function (e) {
   var loc = windowToCanvas(e.clientX, e.clientY),
       fontHeight = context.measureText('W').width;

   fontHeight += fontHeight/6;
   line = new TextLine(loc.x, loc.y);
   moveCursor(loc.x, loc.y);
};

fillStyleSelect.onchange = function (e) {
   cursor.fillStyle = fillStyleSelect.value;
   context.fillStyle = fillStyleSelect.value;
}

strokeStyleSelect.onchange = function (e) {
   cursor.strokeStyle = strokeStyleSelect.value;
   context.strokeStyle = strokeStyleSelect.value;
}

// Key event handlers.......................................
```

*(Continues)*

**Example 3.17** *(Continued)*

```
document.onkeydown = function (e) {
    if (e.keyCode === 8 || e.keyCode === 13) {
        // The call to e.preventDefault() suppresses the browser's
        // subsequent call to document.onkeypress(), so
        // only suppress that call for Backspace and Enter.
        e.preventDefault();
    }

    if (e.keyCode === 8) {  // Backspace
        context.save();

        line.erase(context, drawingSurfaceImageData);
        line.removeCharacterBeforeCaret();

        moveCursor(line.left + line.getWidth(context), line.bottom);

        line.draw(context);
        context.restore();
    }
}

document.onkeypress = function (e) {
    var key = String.fromCharCode(e.which);

    if (e.keyCode !== 8 && !e.ctrlKey && !e.metaKey) {
        e.preventDefault(); // No further browser processing

        context.save();

        line.erase(context, drawingSurfaceImageData);
        line.insert(key);

        moveCursor(line.left + line.getWidth(context), line.bottom);

        context.shadowColor = 'rgba(0,0,0,0.5)';
        context.shadowOffsetX = 1;
        context.shadowOffsetY = 1;
        context.shadowBlur = 2;

        line.draw(context);
        context.restore();
    }
}

// Initialization.............................................

fontSelect.onchange = setFont;
sizeSelect.onchange = setFont;
```

```
cursor.fillStyle = fillStyleSelect.value;
cursor.strokeStyle = strokeStyleSelect.value;

context.fillStyle = fillStyleSelect.value;
context.strokeStyle = strokeStyleSelect.value;
context.lineWidth = 2.0;

setFont();
drawBackground();
saveDrawingSurface();
```

When the user clicks the mouse, the application creates a new TextLine object and moves that text line and the cursor to the mouse click location.

When the application detects a key down event, it checks to see if the key is a Backspace; if it is, the application erases the line of text, removes the character before the caret, repositions the cursor, and redraws the line of text. Subsequently, when the browser invokes the application's onkeypress() method, the application inserts the character into the line of text, provided that it was not a Backspace and the user was not holding down the Ctrl or Meta keys.

Now that you've seen how to implement a simple one-line text control, let's extend that one line to multiple lines and implement a paragraph.

---

 **CAUTION: You *must* replace the entire Canvas to erase text**

Section 3.3.3, "Measuring Text," on p. 215 discussed the following quote from the Canvas specification:

*Glyphs rendered using fillText() and strokeText() can spill out of the box given by the font size (the em square size) and the width returned by measureText() (the text width) . . .*

The specification goes on to say:

*. . . If the text is to be rendered and removed, care needs to be taken to replace the entire area of the canvas that the clipping region covers, not just the box given by the em square height and measured text width.*

That last sentence means that the TextLine object implemented in this section should implement its erase() method so that it replaces the entire canvas (clipped to the clipping region). That's in contrast to TextCursor, discussed in Section 3.4.1.1, "Erasing," on p. 228, which erased itself by only restoring its bounding box.

---

### 3.4.3 Paragraphs

In the preceding sections you saw how to implement blinking cursors and lines of text. In this section we implement a Paragraph object. Each paragraph contains an array of TextLine objects and maintains a reference to the line the user is editing. Paragraphs also keep a cursor in sync with a user's editing. Figure 3.15 shows an application that lets you create paragraphs.

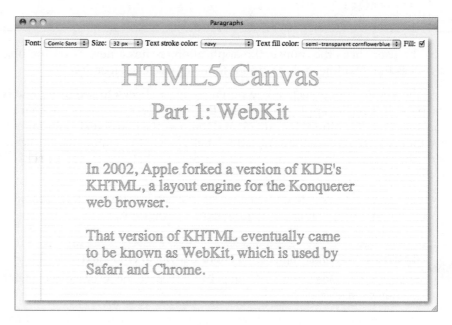

Figure 3.15  Paragraphs

Paragraphs logically connect the text lines they contain; for example, if you backspace when the cursor is at the far left edge of a line, the paragraph object moves the text in front of the cursor—and the cursor itself—up one line, as depicted in Figure 3.16. Likewise, if you press Enter while editing a line of text in a paragraph, the paragraph creates a new text line and inserts the line below the cursor.

Paragraph provides some key methods that are used by the application shown in Figures 3.15 and 3.16:

- isPointInside(): Returns true if the specified point is inside the paragraph.
- moveCursorCloseTo(): For X, Y coordinates, moves cursor to the closest cursor position.

- addLine(): Adds a TextLine to the paragraph.
- backspace(): Performs a backspace at the current caret.
- newline(): Performs a new line at the current caret.
- insert(): Inserts text at the current caret point.

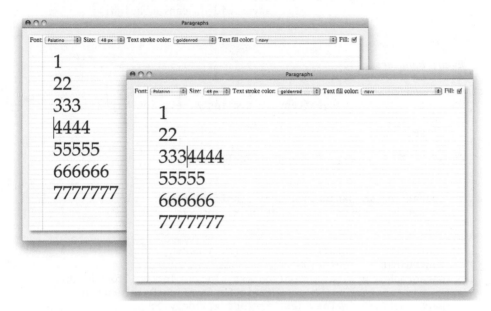

Figure 3.16 *Top:* just before the user hits Backspace; *bottom:* the result

The JavaScript for the application shown in Figure 3.15 is partially listed in Example 3.18. Notice how the application uses the preceding Paragraph methods.

Example 3.18 Working with paragraphs

```
var canvas = document.getElementById('canvas'),
    context = canvas.getContext('2d'),
    ...
    cursor = new TextCursor(),
    paragraph;
...

function drawBackground() {
    // Listing omitted for brevity, see Example 3.1 on p. 203
}
```

*(Continues)*

**Example 3.18**  *(Continued)*

```
// Drawing surface.................................................

function saveDrawingSurface() {
    drawingSurfaceImageData = context.getImageData(0, 0,
                              canvas.width, canvas.height);
}
...

// Event handlers.................................................

canvas.onmousedown = function (e) {
    var loc = windowToCanvas(canvas, e.clientX, e.clientY),
        fontHeight,
        line;

    cursor.erase(context, drawingSurfaceImageData);
    saveDrawingSurface();

    if (paragraph && paragraph.isPointInside(loc)) {
        paragraph.moveCursorCloseTo(loc.x, loc.y);
    }
    else {
        fontHeight = context.measureText('W').width,
        fontHeight += fontHeight/6;
        paragraph = new Paragraph(context, loc.x, loc.y - fontHeight,
                                  drawingSurfaceImageData, cursor);
        paragraph.addLine(new TextLine(loc.x, loc.y));
    }
};
...

// Key event handlers.................................................

document.onkeydown = function (e) {
    if (e.keyCode === 8 || e.keyCode === 13) {
        // The call to e.preventDefault() suppresses the browser's
        // subsequent call to document.onkeypress(), so
        // only suppress that call for Backspace and Enter.
        e.preventDefault();
    }
    if (e.keyCode === 8) {  // Backspace
        paragraph.backspace();
    }
    else if (e.keyCode === 13) { // Enter
        paragraph.newline();
    }
}
```

```
document.onkeypress = function (e) {
   var key = String.fromCharCode(e.which);

   // Only process if user is editing text and they aren't
   // holding down the Ctrl or Meta keys.

   if (e.keyCode !== 8 && !e.ctrlKey && !e.metaKey) {
      e.preventDefault(); // No further browser processing

      context.fillStyle = fillStyleSelect.value;
      context.strokeStyle = strokeStyleSelect.value;

      paragraph.insert(key);
   }
}

// Initialization...............................................
...

cursor.fillStyle = fillStyleSelect.value;
cursor.strokeStyle = strokeStyleSelect.value;

context.lineWidth = 2.0;
setFont();

drawBackground();
saveDrawingSurface();
```

If the user is editing a paragraph and clicks the mouse somewhere within that paragraph, the onmousedown() event handler invokes the paragraph's moveCursorCloseTo() method to place the cursor in a location that's closest to the mouse down location.

If the user is not yet editing a paragraph, or clicks outside the active paragraph, the application saves the drawing surface, creates a new paragraph, and adds a text line to the paragraph. The Paragraph's constructor function takes a reference to a context, the paragraph's location, the image data for the drawing surface, and a cursor.

The application handles the Backspace and Enter keys in the onkeydown() event handler, which merely invokes the paragraph's backspace() and newline() methods, respectively.

The application's onkeypress() event handler inserts characters into the paragraph with the paragraph's insert() method.

In Example 3.19 on p. 246 we look at the code for the Paragraph object, but before we do, let's see how Paragraph objects perform some common tasks.

### 3.4.3.1  Creating and Initializing a Paragraph

The application shown in Figure 3.15 on p. 238 creates a paragraph like this:

```
var cursor = new TextCursor(),
    paragraph = new Paragraph(context, loc.x, loc.y - fontHeight,
                                drawingSurfaceImageData, cursor);
```

Then the application adds a `TextLine` object to the paragraph:

```
paragraph.addLine(new TextLine(loc.x, loc.y));
```

The `Paragraph`'s constructor function looks like this:

```
Paragraph = function (context, left, top, imageData, cursor) {
   this.context = context;
   this.drawingSurface = imageData;
   this.left = left;
   this.top = top;
   this.lines =[]
   this.activeLine = undefined;
   this.cursor = cursor;
   this.blinkingInterval = undefined;
};
```

Paragraphs maintain references to a Canvas context, the image data for the canvas when the paragraph was created, an array of `TextLine` objects, and a cursor. Paragraphs also keep track of their location and the `TextLine` object that the user is currently editing.

The `Paragraph`'s `addLine()` method pushes the new line onto the `TextLine` object array, sets the paragraph's active line, and moves the cursor to the beginning of the new line:

```
Paragraph.prototype = {
   addLine: function (line) {
      this.lines.push(line);
      this.activeLine = line;
      this.moveCursor(line.left, line.bottom);
   },
   ...
}
```

Notice the `moveCursor()` method in the previous list. Let's look at that next.

### 3.4.3.2  Positioning the Text Cursor in Response to Mouse Clicks

Paragraphs provide a `moveCursor()` method that moves the cursor to a specific location in the canvas:

```
moveCursor: function (x, y) {
   this.cursor.erase(this.context, this.drawingSurface);
   this.cursor.draw(this.context, x, y);
   this.blinkCursor(x, y);
},
```

The moveCursor() method erases the cursor at its current location and draws the cursor at its new location. Then the moveCursor() method invokes blinkCursor().

Paragraphs place cursors between characters with Paragraph.moveCursor-CloseTo(). That method places the cursor at a space between two characters that is closest to the specified location in the canvas. The moveCursorCloseTo() method is implemented like this:

```
moveCursorCloseTo: function (x, y) {
   var line = this.getLine(y);

   if (line) {
      line.caret = this.getColumn(line, x);
      this.activeLine = line;
      this.moveCursor(line.getCaretX(context), line.bottom);
   }
},

getLine: function (y) {
   var line;

   for (i=0; i < this.lines.length; ++i) {
      line = this.lines[i];
      if (y > line.bottom - line.getHeight(context) &&
         y < line.bottom) {
         return line;
      }
   }
   return undefined;
},
```

### 3.4.3.3  Inserting Text

Paragraph objects provide an insert() method that inserts text into a paragraph:

```
insert: function (text) {
   var t = this.activeLine.text.substring(0, this.activeLine.caret),
       w = this.context.measureText(t).width;

   this.activeLine.erase(this.context, this.drawingSurface);
   this.activeLine.insert(text);
   this.moveCursor(this.activeLine.left + w, this.activeLine.bottom);
   this.activeLine.draw(this.context);
}
```

The `insert()` method erases the active line, inserts the text into that line, and then redraws the line. The method also moves the cursor to the caret location inside the line. Recall that a line's `erase()` method restores the entire canvas to what it was before the paragraph was created, effectively erasing the entire paragraph.

### 3.4.3.4 New Lines

When you type Enter in a paragraph in the application shown in Figure 3.15 on p. 238, the application invokes the paragraph's `newline()` method, which is implemented like this:

```
newline: function () {
   var textBeforeCursor =
         this.activeLine.text.substring(0, this.activeLine.caret),
       textAfterCursor =
         this.activeLine.text.substring(this.activeLine.caret),
       height = this.context.measureText('W').width +
                this.context.measureText('W').width/6,
       bottom = this.activeLine.bottom + height,
       activeIndex,
       line;

   // Erase paragraph and set active line's text

   this.erase(this.context, this.drawingSurface);
   this.activeLine.text = textBeforeCursor;

   // Create a new line that contains the text after the cursor

   line = new TextLine(this.activeLine.left, bottom);
   line.insert(textAfterCursor);

   // Splice in new line, set active line, and reset caret

   activeIndex = this.lines.indexOf(this.activeLine);
   this.lines.splice(activeIndex+1, 0, line);

   this.activeLine = line;
   this.activeLine.caret = 0;

   // Starting at the new line, loop over remaining lines

   activeIndex = this.lines.indexOf(this.activeLine);

   for(var i=activeIndex+1; i < this.lines.length; ++i) {
      line = this.lines[i];
      line.bottom += height; // Move line down one row
   }
```

```
    this.draw();
    this.cursor.draw(this.context, this.activeLine.left,
                    this.activeLine.bottom);
},
```

The newline() method erases the cursor and the paragraph itself, creates a new TextLine object, and inserts it into the array of TextLine maintained by the paragraph. The newline() method then iterates over all the lines below the newly created line and moves them each down one line. Finally, the newline() method draws the updated paragraph and the cursor.

### 3.4.3.5 Backspace

Paragraphs handle the Backspace key with a backspace() method, which is implemented like this:

```
backspace: function () {
    var lastActiveLine,
        activeIndex,
        t, w;

    this.context.save();

    if (this.activeLine.caret === 0) {
        if ( ! this.activeLineIsTopLine(); {
            this.erase();
            this.moveUpOneLine();
            this.draw();
        }
    }
    else {  // Active line has text
        this.context.fillStyle = fillStyleSelect.value;
        this.context.strokeStyle = strokeStyleSelect.value;

        this.activeLine.erase(this.context, drawingSurfaceImageData);
        this.activeLine.removeCharacterBeforeCaret();

        t = this.activeLine.text.slice(0, this.activeLine.caret);
        w = this.context.measureText(t).width;

        this.moveCursor(this.activeLine.left + w,
                        this.activeLine.bottom);
        this.activeLine.draw(this.context);
    }
    context.restore();
}
```

The backspace() method checks a) that the insertion caret the current line is at the left edge of the line and b) the line is not the first line in the paragraph; if so, the method erases the paragraph, moves all lines below the active line up one line, and redraws the modified paragraph. Otherwise, the `backspace()` method removes the character before the caret in the active line and redraws that line.

The `Paragraph` object is listed in its entirety in Example 3.19.

**Example 3.19** A paragraph object

```
// Constructor......................................................

Paragraph = function (context, left, top, imageData, cursor) {
   this.context = context;
   this.drawingSurface = imageData;
   this.left = left;
   this.top = top;
   this.lines = [];
   this.activeLine = undefined;
   this.cursor = cursor;
   this.blinkingInterval = undefined;
};

// Prototype.......................................................

Paragraph.prototype = {
   isPointInside: function (loc) {
      var c = this.context;

      c.beginPath();
      c.rect(this.left, this.top,
            this.getWidth(), this.getHeight());

      return c.isPointInPath(loc.x, loc.y);
   },

   getHeight: function () {
      var h = 0;

      this.lines.forEach( function (line) {
         h += line.getHeight(this.context);
      });

      return h;
   },
```

```
getWidth: function () {
   var w = 0,
       widest = 0;

   this.lines.forEach( function (line) {
      w = line.getWidth(this.context);
      if (w > widest) {
         widest = w;
      }
   });

   return widest;
},

draw: function () {
   this.lines.forEach( function (line) {
      line.draw(this.context);
   });
},

erase: function (context, imageData) {
   context.putImageData(imageData, 0, 0);
},

addLine: function (line) {
   this.lines.push(line);
   this.activeLine = line;
   this.moveCursor(line.left, line.bottom);
},

insert: function (text) {
  this.erase(this.context, this.drawingSurface);
  this.activeLine.insert(text);

  var t = this.activeLine.text.substring(0, this.activeLine.caret),
      w = this.context.measureText(t).width;

  this.moveCursor(this.activeLine.left + w,
                  this.activeLine.bottom);

  this.draw(this.context);
},
```

*(Continues)*

Example 3.19  *(Continued)*

```javascript
blinkCursor: function (x, y) {
    var self = this,
        BLINK_OUT = 200,
        BLINK_INTERVAL = 900;

    this.blinkingInterval = setInterval( function (e) {
        cursor.erase(context, self.drawingSurface);

        setTimeout( function (e) {
            cursor.draw(context, cursor.left,
                        cursor.top + cursor.getHeight(context));
        }, BLINK_OUT);
    }, BLINK_INTERVAL);
},

moveCursorCloseTo: function (x, y) {
    var line = this.getLine(y);

    if (line) {
        line.caret = this.getColumn(line, x);
        this.activeLine = line;
        this.moveCursor(line.getCaretX(context), line.bottom);
    }
},

moveCursor: function (x, y) {
    this.cursor.erase(this.context, this.drawingSurface);
    this.cursor.draw(this.context, x, y);

    if ( ! this.blinkingInterval)
        this.blinkCursor(x, y);
},

moveLinesDown: function (start) {
    for (var i=start; i < this.lines.length; ++i) {
        line = this.lines[i];
        line.bottom += line.getHeight(this.context);
    }
},

newline: function () {
    var textBeforeCursor =
            this.activeLine.text.substring(0, this.activeLine.caret),
        textAfterCursor =
            this.activeLine.text.substring(this.activeLine.caret),
        height = this.context.measureText('W').width +
                this.context.measureText('W').width/6,
```

```
            bottom = this.activeLine.bottom + height,
            activeIndex,
            line;

    // Erase paragraph and set active line's text

    this.erase(this.context, this.drawingSurface);
    this.activeLine.text = textBeforeCursor;

    // Create a new line that contains the text after the cursor

    line = new TextLine(this.activeLine.left, bottom);
    line.insert(textAfterCursor);

    // Splice in new line, set active line, and reset caret

    activeIndex = this.lines.indexOf(this.activeLine);
    this.lines.splice(activeIndex+1, 0, line);

    this.activeLine = line;
    this.activeLine.caret = 0;

    // Starting at the new line, loop over remaining lines

    activeIndex = this.lines.indexOf(this.activeLine);

    for(var i=activeIndex+1; i < this.lines.length; ++i) {
        line = this.lines[i];
        line.bottom += height; // Move line down one row
    }

    this.draw();
    this.cursor.draw(this.context, this.activeLine.left,
                    this.activeLine.bottom);
},

getLine: function (y) {
    var line;
    for (i=0; i < this.lines.length; ++i) {
        line = this.lines[i];
        if (y > line.bottom - line.getHeight(context) &&
            y < line.bottom) {
            return line;
        }
    }
    return undefined;
},
```

*(Continues)*

**Example 3.19** *(Continued)*

```
getColumn: function (line, x) {
    var found = false,
        before,
        after,
        closest,
        tmpLine,
        column;

    tmpLine = new TextLine(line.left, line.bottom);
    tmpLine.insert(line.text);

    while ( ! found && tmpLine.text.length > 0) {
        before = tmpLine.left + tmpLine.getWidth(context);
        tmpLine.removeLastCharacter();
        after = tmpLine.left + tmpLine.getWidth(context);

        if (after < x) {
            closest = x - after < before - x ? after : before;
            column = closest === before ?
                    tmpLine.text.length + 1 : tmpLine.text.length;
            found = true;
        }
    }
    return column;
},

activeLineIsOutOfText: function () {
    return this.activeLine.text.length === 0;
},

activeLineIsTopLine: function () {
    return this.lines[0] === this.activeLine;
},

moveUpOneLine: function () {
    var lastActiveText, line, before, after;

    lastActiveLine = this.activeLine;
    lastActiveText = '' + lastActiveLine.text;

    activeIndex = this.lines.indexOf(this.activeLine);
    this.activeLine = this.lines[activeIndex - 1];
    this.activeLine.caret = this.activeLine.text.length;

    this.lines.splice(activeIndex, 1);
```

```
      this.moveCursor(
          this.activeLine.left + this.activeLine.getWidth(this.context),
          this.activeLine.bottom);

      this.activeLine.text += lastActiveText;

      for (var i=activeIndex; i < this.lines.length; ++i) {
          line = this.lines[i];
          line.bottom -= line.getHeight(this.context);
      }
   },

   backspace: function () {
      var lastActiveLine,
          activeIndex,
          t, w;

      this.context.save();

      if (this.activeLine.caret === 0) {
          if ( ! this.activeLineIsTopLine()) {
              this.erase(this.context, this.drawingSurface);
              this.moveUpOneLine();
              this.draw();
          }
      }

      else {  // Active line has text
          this.context.fillStyle = fillStyleSelect.value;
          this.context.strokeStyle = strokeStyleSelect.value;

          this.erase(this.context, this.drawingSurface);
          this.activeLine.removeCharacterBeforeCaret();

          t = this.activeLine.text.slice(0, this.activeLine.caret),
          w = this.context.measureText(t).width;

          this.moveCursor(this.activeLine.left + w,
                          this.activeLine.bottom);

          this.draw(this.context);

          context.restore();
      }
   }
};
```

---

 **NOTE: WHATWG Canvas specification best practice: Don't implement text controls**

The WHATWG Canvas specification contains a short section on best practices. One of those best practices encourages you *not* to implement text editing controls with the Canvas element, but instead use the HTML input or textarea elements, in combination with the HTML5 contenteditable attribute. (The same note is absent from the W3C's Canvas 2d context specification)

Why? Because according to the WHATWG, it's too much work to implement text controls. To effectively implement a text editing control, you have to implement features such as copy and paste, drag and drop, text selection, and scrolling, none of which is built into the canvas element by default.

However, just because the WHATWG does not believe it's a good idea to implement text editing controls, doesn't mean you should blindly follow their advice. In fact, people have implemented text editing controls; the Bespin editor is one example. As with all best practices, take this one with a grain of salt and decide for yourself if it's worth the effort. Just be aware that the canvas element's support for text is minimal and that you may have to put in some extra work to implement text controls.

---

## 3.5 Conclusion

Canvas provides the fundamentals for manipulating text; however, it does not provide explicit support for sophisticated text handling, such as drawing text along an arc or enabling editing for a line of text.

In this chapter you learned how to apply the minimal text API that Canvas provides to implement sophisticated text handling, including drawing text along an arc. You also saw how to draw text labels for axes and dials and how to set text parameters such as alignment and fonts.

The last half of this chapter showed you how to implement text controls, starting with text cursors, followed by editable lines of text, and finally paragraphs. Those objects are a good starting point if you decide to implement your own text controls.

In the next chapter we explore displaying and manipulating images in a canvas.

# Images and Video

HTML5 Canvas provides extensive support for images. You can draw all or part of an image, scaled or unscaled, anywhere inside a canvas, and you can access and manipulate the color and transparency of each pixel. And by combining image manipulation with other aspects of the Canvas API such as clipping regions and offscreen canvases, you can create stunning effects, such as animations and multiplayer games, data visualization, or particle physics simulations.

Figure 4.1 shows a magnifying glass that demonstrates some of what's possible with Canvas image manipulation. As you drag the magnifying glass, the application scales the pixels underneath the magnifying glass, and draws them back into the canvas, clipped to the magnifying glass lens.

The Canvas context provides four methods for drawing and manipulating images:

- `drawImage()`
- `getImageData()`
- `putImageData()`
- `createImageData()`

As you might suspect, `drawImage()` lets you draw an image into a canvas. As you might not suspect, that method also lets you draw *another canvas* into a canvas, or a *video frame* into a canvas. That's a large can of whoopass.

The image data methods let you access, and manipulate, the individual pixels of an image. `getImageData()` gives you access to the underlying pixels of an image, and `putImageData()` lets you put pixels back into an image. In the meantime, so the thinking goes, you will manipulate those pixels in some manner, although that is not always the case, as you will see in Section 4.5.1, "Accessing Image Data," on p. 274.

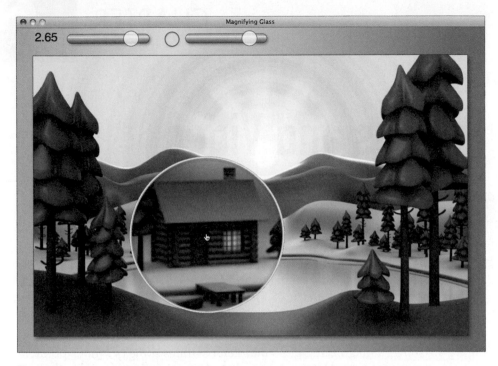

Figure 4.1  A magnifying glass that scales pixels and uses the clipping region

You can also create blank image data objects with `createImageData()`. You can pass that method either the width and height of the image data in CSS pixels, or you can pass the method an existing `ImageData` object, in which case the method returns a new blank `ImageData` object with the same width and height as the object you passed to the method.

## 4.1  Drawing Images

The `drawImage()` method lets you draw all or part of an image, anywhere inside a canvas, and it lets you scale the image along the way. You can also draw into an offscreen canvas, which lets you do clever things with images, such as panning an image, or fading an image into a canvas. We discuss several uses for offscreen canvases in this chapter.

## 4.1.1 Drawing an Image into a Canvas

Let's start by drawing an image into a canvas, as shown in Figure 4.2 and listed in Example 4.1.

Figure 4.2 Drawing an image into a canvas

---

**Example 4.1** Drawing an image

---

```
var canvas = document.getElementById('canvas'),
    context = canvas.getContext('2d'),
    image = new Image();

image.src = 'fence.png';
image.onload = function(e) {
   context.drawImage(image, 0, 0);
};
```

---

Example 4.1 creates an image, sets the source of the image, and, after waiting for the image to load, draws the image into the canvas's upper-left corner.

This is the simplest use of drawImage()—drawing an entire image, unscaled, into a canvas—and the only pitfall here is that you must wait for the image to load before you draw it into the canvas. If you draw the image before it's loaded, then according to the Canvas specification, drawImage() should fail silently.

**CAUTION: Images cannot be drawn before they are loaded**

The drawImage() method draws images into a canvas, but if the image hasn't been loaded, drawImage() is supposed to do nothing. When you use drawImage(), make sure the image has been loaded, typically by putting the call to drawImage() in an onload callback.

**CAUTION: According to the Canvas specification**

According to the Canvas specification, drawImage() should fail silently if you try to draw an image that hasn't been loaded; however, many browsers throw an exception instead. See http://bit.ly/ilW6ET for verification.

In general, it's important to remember that browsers do not always adhere exactly to the Canvas specification. That's why it's a good idea to have a test suite that tests a browser's adherence to the specification. See http://w3c-test.org for more information.

**TIP: Shadows, clipping, and composition are applied when you draw an image**

The drawImage() method draws images without respect to the current path, and takes into account the globalAlpha setting, shadow effects, the clipping region, and global composition operators.

**TIP: Loading images**

Before they begin, some applications need to load more than a few images. Games are the prototypical application. In Section 9.1.2, "Loading Images," on p. 554 you'll see how to load multiple images and display a progress bar while the images are loading.

Now that you know how to draw an image into a canvas, let's take a closer look at the drawImage() method.

## 4.1.2 The `drawImage()` Method

The `drawImage()` method is illustrated in Figure 4.3.

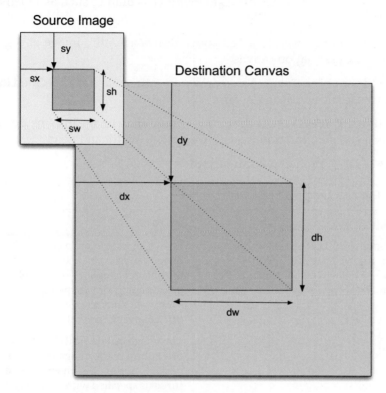

Figure 4.3 `drawImage()` lets you draw all or part of an image, scaled or unscaled, into a canvas

The `drawImage()` method draws an image, referred to as the source image, into a canvas, referred to as the destination canvas. In Figure 4.3, the variables beginning with 's' correspond to source, and variables beginning with 'd' correspond to destination. The `drawImage()` method can take three different argument sets:

- `drawImage(image, dx, dy)`
- `drawImage(image, dx, dy, dw, dh)`
- `drawImage(image, sx, sy, sw, sh, dx, dy, dw, dh)`

The first argument in all three cases is an image (HTMLImageElement), but that argument can also be another canvas (HTMLCanvasElement) or a video (HTMLVideoElement). So you can effectively treat a canvas or video as though it were an image, which opens doors to many possibilities, such as video-editing software.

The first use of drawImage() listed above draws an entire image at a specified location in the destination canvas.

The second use of drawImage() also draws an entire image at a specified location, scaled to a specific width and height.

The third use of drawImage() draws all or part of an image into the destination canvas at a specified location, scaled to a specific width and height.

The drawImage() method is summarized in Table 4.1.

**Table 4.1** The drawImage() method

| Method | Description |
|---|---|
| drawImage(HTMLImageElement image, double sx, double sy, double sw, double sh, double dx, double dy, double dw, double dh); | Draws an image into a canvas. That image can also be a video (HTMLVideoElement)—in which case drawImage() draws the video's current frame—or another canvas (HTMLCanvasElement). |
| | The image can be either an entire image or a subset of the image into a canvas, possibly scaling the image. The image's subset is specified with the sx, sy, sw, and sh parameters, and the browser scales the image to the dw and dh parameters. Only the first three arguments are required. |

**TIP: You can draw images, canvases, and videos into a canvas**

The drawImage() method is flexible: You can draw either part or all of one of the following into a canvas: an image, a canvas, or a video frame. You can place the image, canvas, or video anywhere you want in the canvas, at any scale you wish.

## 4.2 Scaling Images

We've seen how to use drawImage() to draw an image, unscaled, into a canvas. Now we'll see how to use that method to draw and scale an image, as shown in Figure 4.4.

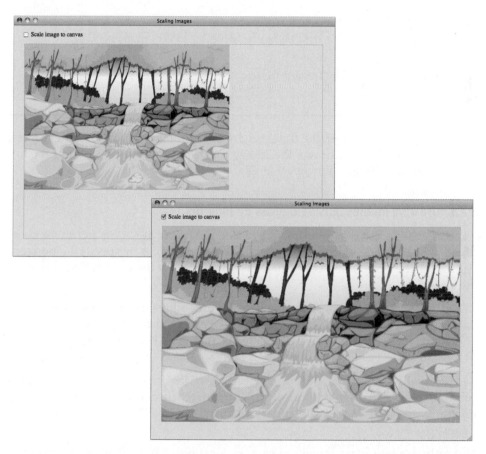

Figure 4.4 Scaling an image

The image shown in Figure 4.4 is initially smaller than the canvas in which it resides, as you can see from the top picture. However, when the user checks the checkbox, the application redraws the image, scaled to fit the canvas, as shown in the bottom picture.

The function that draws the image in Figure 4.4 is shown in Example 4.2.

---

**Example 4.2  Scaling an image**

```
function drawImage() {
   context.clearRect(0, 0, canvas.width, canvas.height);

   if (scaleCheckbox.checked) {
      context.drawImage(image, 0, 0, canvas.width, canvas.height);
   }
   else {
      context.drawImage(image, 0, 0);
   }
}
```

---

If the checkbox is checked, the function draws the image, scaled to fit the canvas; otherwise, the function draws the image unscaled. In both cases, the function draws the entire image at location (0, 0) in the canvas.

## 4.2.1  Drawing Images outside Canvas Boundaries

The application listed in Example 4.2 placed the image at (0, 0) in canvas coordinates, but you can place an image anywhere in a canvas by specifying nonzero values for the destination coordinate, as illustrated by the application shown in Figure 4.5.

The application contains a slider that lets the user adjust the image's scale. As the user moves the slider, the application clears the canvas and then repaints the image at the specified scale. Notice that the application also keeps the image centered in the canvas.

Besides scaling the image, the application shown in Figure 4.5 has another interesting aspect: The scale readout in the upper-left corner scales along with the image as the user moves the slider. You can see how that's implemented in Example 4.5.

Not only can you place images at specific locations *inside* a canvas, but you can also place images *outside* a canvas. That's what the application shown in Figure 4.5 does to keep the image centered, as illustrated in Figure 4.6.

Figure 4.5 Scaling and centering an image

Figure 4.6 shows how the application shown in Figure 4.5 draws the image at a specific scale, in this case, 2.0. To illustrate which parts of the image are displayed in the canvas and which parts are not, Figure 4.6 shows the part of the image displayed in the canvas as fully opaque, whereas the rest of the image, which lies outside the boundaries of the canvas, appears faded.

This application scales the image by multiplying the canvas width and height by the selected scale and calculates the upper-left corner of the image, as shown in Example 4.3.

Figure 4.6 The entire image shown in Figure 4.5; the darkened portion of the image is outside the canvas

Example 4.3 Scaling and centering an image

```
function drawImage() {
   var w = canvas.width,
       h = canvas.height,
       sw = w * scale,
       sh = h * scale;

   context.clearRect(0, 0, w, h);
   context.drawImage(image, -sw/2 + w/2, -sh/2 + h/2, sw, sh);
}
```

Example 4.4 shows the HTML for the application shown in Figure 4.5, and the JavaScript for the application is shown in Example 4.5.

Example 4.4  Scaling images: HTML

```html
<!DOCTYPE html>
<html>
  <head>
    <title>Scaling images</title>

    <style>
      body {
        background: rgba(100, 145, 250, 0.3);
      }

      #scaleSlider {
        vertical-align: 10px;
        width: 100px;
        margin-left: 90px;
      }

      #canvas {
        margin: 10px 20px 0px 20px;
        border: thin solid #aaaaaa;
        cursor: crosshair;
      }

      #controls {
        margin-left: 15px;
        padding: 0;
      }

      #scaleOutput {
        position: absolute;
        width: 60px;
        height: 30px;
        margin-left: 10px;
        vertical-align: center;
        text-align: center;
        color: blue;
        font: 18px Arial;
        text-shadow: 2px 2px 4px rgba(100, 140, 250, 0.8);
      }

    </style>
  </head>
```

*(Continues)*

**Example 4.4** *(Continued)*

```
<body>
    <div id='controls'>
        <output id='scaleOutput'>1.0</output>
        <input id='scaleSlider' type='range'
               min='1' max='3.0' step='0.01' value='1.0'/>
    </div>

    <canvas id='canvas' width='800' height='520'>
        Canvas not supported
    </canvas>

    <script src='example.js'></script>
</body>
</html>
```

**Example 4.5** Scaling images: JavaScript

```
var canvas = document.getElementById('canvas'),
    context = canvas.getContext('2d'),
    image = new Image(),

    scaleSlider = document.getElementById('scaleSlider'),
    scale = 1.0,
    MINIMUM_SCALE = 1.0,
    MAXIMUM_SCALE = 3.0;

// Functions.......................................................

function drawImage() {
    var w = canvas.width,
        h = canvas.height,
        sw = w * scale,
        sh = h * scale;

    context.clearRect(0, 0, canvas.width, canvas.height);
    context.drawImage(image, -sw/2 + w/2, -sh/2 + h/2, sw, sh);
}

function drawScaleText(value) {
    var text = parseFloat(value).toFixed(2);
    var percent = parseFloat(value - MINIMUM_SCALE) /
                  parseFloat(MAXIMUM_SCALE - MINIMUM_SCALE);

    scaleOutput.innerText = text;
    percent = percent < 0.35 ? 0.35 : percent;
    scaleOutput.style.fontSize = percent*MAXIMUM_SCALE/1.5 + 'em';
}
```

```
// Event handlers.............................................

scaleSlider.onchange = function(e) {
   scale = e.target.value;

   if (scale < MINIMUM_SCALE) scale = MINIMUM_SCALE;
   else if (scale > MAXIMUM_SCALE) scale = MAXIMUM_SCALE;

   drawScaleText(scale);
   drawImage();
};

// Initialization.............................................

context.fillStyle      = 'cornflowerblue';
context.strokeStyle    = 'yellow';
context.shadowColor    = 'rgba(50, 50, 50, 1.0)';
context.shadowOffsetX = 5;
context.shadowOffsetY = 5;
context.shadowBlur     = 10;

image.src = 'waterfall.png';

image.onload = function(e) {
   drawImage();
   drawScaleText(scaleSlider.value);
};
```

 **TIP: You can draw images outside of a canvas**

You can draw images inside or outside a canvas. For example, the application listed in Example 4.5 specifies a location in the canvas that lies outside of the canvas for all scales greater than 1.0.

When you draw an image into a canvas and part of that image lies outside the bounds of the canvas, the browser ignores the content outside of the canvas.

Being able to draw images outside the boundaries of the canvas is an important feature. For example, Section 5.7, "Scrolling the Background," on p. 370, discusses scrolling backgrounds that are implemented by drawing outside the boundaries of the canvas, and translating the canvas coordinate system to scroll that content into view.

**TIP: Render unto Canvas**

In Example 4.5, the application scales the readout in the upper-left corner as the user adjusts the scale slider. You might be tempted to implement that readout with a canvas that uses fillText() and scales the canvas to match the slider's scale. However, the Canvas specification states:

*Authors should not use the canvas element in a document when a more suitable element is available. For example, it is inappropriate to use a canvas element to render a page heading.*

For the application shown in Example 4.5, an output element is more appropriate than a canvas element and is considerably easier to implement.

## 4.3  Drawing a Canvas into a Canvas

The application shown in Figure 4.7 draws an image into a canvas, and then draws some text, known as a watermark, on top of the image.

When the user adjusts the scale with the slider in the upper-left corner, the application scales both the image and text. You could scale the image and text together by drawing them into an offscreen canvas at the specified scale and subsequently copying the offscreen canvas back into the onscreen canvas; in this case, however, an offscreen canvas is not strictly necessary because drawImage() can draw a canvas *back into itself*, like this:

```
var canvas = document.getElementById('canvas'),
    context = canvas.getContext('2d'),
    scaleWidth = ...,  // Calculate scales for width and height
    scaleHeight = ...;

...
context.drawImage(canvas, 0, 0, scaleWidth, scaleHeight);
...
```

The preceding code draws a canvas into itself, scaling the canvas along the way. When the user changes the scale, the application clears the canvas and draws the image, scaled to canvas width and height, into the canvas. Then it draws the watermark on top of the image.

Figure 4.7  A watermark

However, the user never sees the canvas in that state, because the application immediately draws the canvas back into itself, scaled at the scale specified by the user. That has the effect of scaling not only the image, but also the watermark along with it.

Although it's convenient in this case to draw the canvas back into itself, it's not very efficient. Every time the user modifies the scale, the application draws the image and the watermark, and then subsequently redraws the entire canvas, scaled. That means the application ends up drawing everything twice every time the scale changes, as you can see from the full listing of the application's JavaScript in Example 4.6.

---

**Example 4.6** Watermarks: JavaScript

---

```javascript
var canvas = document.getElementById('canvas'),
    context = canvas.getContext('2d'),
    image = new Image(),

    scaleOutput = document.getElementById('scaleOutput');
    scaleSlider = document.getElementById('scaleSlider'),
    scale = scaleSlider.value,
    scale = 1.0,

    MINIMUM_SCALE = 1.0,
    MAXIMUM_SCALE = 3.0;

// Functions.......................................................

function drawScaled() {
    var w = canvas.width,
        h = canvas.height,
        sw = w * scale,
        sh = h * scale;

    // Clear the canvas, and draw the image scaled to canvas size

    context.clearRect(0, 0, canvas.width, canvas.height);
    context.drawImage(image, 0, 0, canvas.width, canvas.height);

    // Draw the watermark on top of the image

    drawWatermark();

    // Finally, draw the canvas scaled according to the current
    // scale, back into itself. Note that the source and
    // destination canvases are the same canvas.

    context.drawImage(canvas, 0, 0, canvas.width, canvas.height,
                      -sw/2 + w/2, -sh/2 + h/2, sw, sh);
}

function drawScaleText(value) {
    var text = parseFloat(value).toFixed(2);
    var percent = parseFloat(value - MINIMUM_SCALE) /
                  parseFloat(MAXIMUM_SCALE - MINIMUM_SCALE);

    scaleOutput.innerText = text;
    percent = percent < 0.35 ? 0.35 : percent;
    scaleOutput.style.fontSize = percent*MAXIMUM_SCALE/1.5 + 'em';
}
```

```javascript
function drawWatermark() {
    var lineOne = 'Copyright',
        lineTwo = 'Acme Inc.',
        textMetrics,
        FONT_HEIGHT = 128;

    context.save();
    context.font = FONT_HEIGHT + 'px Arial';

    textMetrics = context.measureText(lineOne);

    context.globalAlpha = 0.6;
    context.translate(canvas.width/2,
                      canvas.height/2-FONT_HEIGHT/2);

    context.fillText(lineOne, -textMetrics.width/2, 0);
    context.strokeText(lineOne, -textMetrics.width/2, 0);

    textMetrics = context.measureText(lineTwo);
    context.fillText(lineTwo, -textMetrics.width/2, FONT_HEIGHT);
    context.strokeText(lineTwo, -textMetrics.width/2, FONT_HEIGHT);

    context.restore();
}

// Event handlers.....................................................

scaleSlider.onchange = function(e) {
    scale = e.target.value;

    if (scale < MINIMUM_SCALE) scale = MINIMUM_SCALE;
    else if (scale > MAXIMUM_SCALE) scale = MAXIMUM_SCALE;

    drawScaled();
    drawScaleText(scale);
}

// Initialization.....................................................

context.fillStyle     = 'cornflowerblue';
context.strokeStyle   = 'yellow';
context.shadowColor   = 'rgba(50, 50, 50, 1.0)';
context.shadowOffsetX = 5;
context.shadowOffsetY = 5;
context.shadowBlur    = 10;

var glassSize = 150;
var scale = 1.0;
```

*(Continues)*

---

Example 4.6  *(Continued)*

---

```
image.src = 'lonelybeach.png';
image.onload = function(e) {
    context.drawImage(image, 0, 0, canvas.width, canvas.height);
    drawWatermark();
    drawScaleText(scaleSlider.value);
};
```

---

Although an offscreen canvas requires a little more code, in this case it is worth the effort because it's much more efficient. Let's see how to implement the watermark example with an offscreen canvas.

---

 **TIP: You can draw a canvas into itself, but beware**

The drawImage() method can draw one canvas into another. You can also draw a canvas into itself. Although for some use cases, such as scaling a canvas as in Example 4.6, it's convenient to draw a canvas into itself, it's not very efficient because the browser creates an intermediate offscreen canvas to scale the canvas.

---

## 4.4 Offscreen Canvases

Offscreen canvases, which are often used as temporary holding places for images, are useful in many different scenarios. For example, the magnifying glass application shown in Figure 4.1 uses an offscreen canvas to scale part of the onscreen canvas, and then subsequently copies the contents of the offscreen canvas back to the onscreen canvas.

Figure 4.8 illustrates another use of an offscreen canvas. In this case, the offscreen canvas contains an unscaled version of an image and a watermark. As the user manipulates the scale slider, the application copies the offscreen canvas to the onscreen canvas, scaling the offscreen canvas in the process.

Using an offscreen canvas typically involves four steps:

1. Create the offscreen canvas element.
2. Set the offscreen canvas's width and height.
3. Draw into the offscreen canvas.
4. Copy all, or part of, the offscreen canvas onscreen.

The preceding steps are illustrated in the code listed in Example 4.7.

Offscreen canvas

Onscreen canvas

Figure 4.8  An offscreen canvas

Example 4.7  A recipe for offscreen canvases

```
var canvas = document.getElementById('canvas'),
    context = canvas.getContext('2d'),
    offscreenCanvas = document.createElement('canvas'),
    offscreenContext = offscreenCanvas.getContext('2d'),
...

// Set the offscreen canvas's size to match the onscreen canvas

offscreenCanvas.width = canvas.width;
offscreenCanvas.height = canvas.height;
...

// Draw into the offscreen context

offscreenContext.drawImage(anImage, 0, 0);
...
// Draw the offscreen context into the onscreen canvas

context.drawImage(offscreenCanvas, 0, 0,
                  offscreenCanvas.width, offscreenCanvas.height);
```

You create an offscreen canvas like this: var offscreenCanvas = document. createElement('canvas');. That line of code creates a new canvas that is not attached to any DOM element and therefore will not be visible; thus the term offscreen.

By default, the offscreen canvas's size will be the default size for canvases: 300 pixels wide by 150 pixels high. Usually those dimensions will not suffice for your particular use case, so you will need to resize the canvas.

After you have created an offscreen canvas and set its size, you typically draw into the offscreen canvas and subsequently draw some, or all, of the offscreen canvas onscreen.

The application shown in Figure 4.8 is listed in Example 4.8.

---

**Example 4.8** Using an offscreen canvas

---

```
var canvas = document.getElementById('canvas'),
    context = canvas.getContext('2d'),

    offscreenCanvas = document.createElement('canvas'),
    offscreenContext = offscreenCanvas.getContext('2d'),

    image = new Image(),

    scaleOutput = document.getElementById('scaleOutput'),
    canvasRadio = document.getElementById('canvasRadio'),
    imageRadio = document.getElementById('imageRadio'),

    scale = scaleSlider.value,
    scale = 1.0,

    MINIMUM_SCALE = 1.0,
    MAXIMUM_SCALE = 3.0;

// Functions.......................................................

function drawScaled() {
   var w = canvas.width,
       h = canvas.height,
       sw = w * scale,
       sh = h * scale;

   context.drawImage(offscreenCanvas, 0, 0,
                     offscreenCanvas.width, offscreenCanvas.height,
                     -sw/2 + w/2, -sh/2 + h/2, sw, sh);
}
```

```
function drawScaleText(value) {
   var text = parseFloat(value).toFixed(2);
   var percent = parseFloat(value - MINIMUM_SCALE) /
                 parseFloat(MAXIMUM_SCALE - MINIMUM_SCALE);

   scaleOutput.innerText = text;
   percent = percent < 0.35 ? 0.35 : percent;
   scaleOutput.style.fontSize = percent*MAXIMUM_SCALE/1.5 + 'em';
}

function drawWatermark(context) {
   var lineOne = 'Copyright',
       lineTwo = 'Acme, Inc.',
       textMetrics = null,
       FONT_HEIGHT = 128;

   context.save();
   context.fillStyle = 'rgba(100,140,230,0.5);';
   context.strokeStyle = 'yellow';
   context.shadowColor = 'rgba(50, 50, 50, 1.0)';
   context.shadowOffsetX = 5;
   context.shadowOffsetY = 5;
   context.shadowBlur = 10;

   context.font = FONT_HEIGHT + 'px Arial';
   textMetrics = context.measureText(lineOne);
   context.translate(canvas.width/2, canvas.height/2);
   context.fillText(lineOne, -textMetrics.width/2, 0);
   context.strokeText(lineOne, -textMetrics.width/2, 0);

   textMetrics = context.measureText(lineTwo);
   context.fillText(lineTwo, -textMetrics.width/2, FONT_HEIGHT);
   context.strokeText(lineTwo, -textMetrics.width/2, FONT_HEIGHT);
   context.restore();
}

// Event handlers....................................................

scaleSlider.onchange = function(e) {
   scale = e.target.value;

   if (scale < MINIMUM_SCALE) scale = MINIMUM_SCALE;
   else if (scale > MAXIMUM_SCALE) scale = MAXIMUM_SCALE;

   drawScaled();
   drawScaleText(scale);
}
```

*(Continues)*

---

Example 4.8  *(Continued)*

---

```
// Initialization.................................................

offscreenCanvas.width = canvas.width;
offscreenCanvas.height = canvas.height;

image.src = 'lonelybeach.png';
image.onload = function(e) {
   context.drawImage(image, 0, 0, canvas.width, canvas.height);
   offscreenContext.drawImage(image, 0, 0,
                              canvas.width, canvas.height);
   drawWatermark(context);
   drawWatermark(offscreenContext);
   drawScaleText(scaleSlider.value);
};
```

---

**TIP: Increase performance with offscreen canvases**

Offscreen canvases take up some memory, but they can greatly increase performance.

Notice how much more efficient the `drawScaled()` method is in Example 4.8 than in Example 4.6. The example listed in Example 4.8 draws from the offscreen canvas. The application listed in Example 4.6, on the other hand, had to clear the canvas, draw the image, draw the watermark, and finally, copy the canvas into itself.

---

Now that you've seen how to draw images, scale them, and draw them into an offscreen canvas, let's see how to access and manipulate the individual pixels of an image.

## 4.5  Manipulating Images

The `getImageData()` and `putImageData()` methods let you access the pixels of an image and insert pixels into an image, respectively. In the meantime, if you wish, you can modify those pixels, so those two methods let you perform just about any image manipulation you can imagine.

### 4.5.1  Accessing Image Data

Let's start with a common use case, selecting a region of a canvas with a rubber band, as shown in Figure 4.9.

Figure 4.9  Rubber bands

In Figure 4.9, the user selects an area of the canvas with a rubber band, and the application subsequently redraws the canvas and displays the selected area, scaled to the canvas width and height.

Every time the user drags the mouse, the application calculates the rubber band's bounding box, captures the pixels of the image within that bounding box, and then draws the rubber band. The next time the user drags the mouse, the application restores the pixels of the image that it captured the last time the user dragged the mouse, thereby erasing the rubber band, and the process begins anew.

The application shown in Figure 4.9 and listed in Example 4.9 does not manipulate the pixels of the image, rather it simply captures and restores the pixels as the user drags the rubber band.

Notice that the application's `rubberbandEnd()` method uses the nine-argument version of `drawImage()` to draw, and scale, the part of the image selected by the user.

Also realize that it's easy for users to size the rubberband rectangle so that either its width or height is zero. According to the Canvas specification, if you specify zero for either the width or height, `getImageData()` must throw an exception. When that happens in the application shown in Example 4.9, the image data for the current rubberband rectangle is not updated the next time the user moves the mouse, and so leaves remnants of the rubberband rectangle that the application does not erase.

In light of the possible exception that may be thrown by `getImageData()`, the `rubberbandStretch()` method checks to make sure that it doesn't call `getImageData()` when the width or height is zero. In fact, `rubberbandStretch()` doesn't restore captured pixels or update the rubberband rectangle unless the rectangle is large enough to accommodate the rubber band itself, taking the context's line width into account.

---

Example 4.9  Rubber bands implemented with `getImageData()` and `putImageData()`

---

```
var canvas = document.getElementById('canvas'),
    context = canvas.getContext('2d'),

    resetButton = document.getElementById('resetButton'),

    image = new Image(),
    imageData,

    mousedown = {},
    rubberbandRectangle = {},
    dragging = false;

// Functions.....................................................

function windowToCanvas(canvas, x, y) {
   var canvasRectangle = canvas.getBoundingClientRect();
   return { x: x - canvasRectangle.left,
            y: y - canvasRectangle.top };
}

function captureRubberbandPixels() {
   imageData = context.getImageData(rubberbandRectangle.left,
                                    rubberbandRectangle.top,
                                    rubberbandRectangle.width,
                                    rubberbandRectangle.height);
}
```

```
function restoreRubberbandPixels() {
   context.putImageData(imageData, rubberbandRectangle.left,
                                   rubberbandRectangle.top);
}

function drawRubberband() {
   context.strokeRect(rubberbandRectangle.left + context.lineWidth,
                      rubberbandRectangle.top + context.lineWidth,
                      rubberbandRectangle.width - 2*context.lineWidth,
                      rubberbandRectangle.height - 2*context.lineWidth);
}

function setRubberbandRectangle(x, y) {
   rubberbandRectangle.left   = Math.min(x, mousedown.x);
   rubberbandRectangle.top    = Math.min(y, mousedown.y);
   rubberbandRectangle.width  = Math.abs(x - mousedown.x),
   rubberbandRectangle.height = Math.abs(y - mousedown.y);
}

function updateRubberband() {
   captureRubberbandPixels();
   drawRubberband();
}

function rubberbandStart(x, y) {
   mousedown.x = x;
   mousedown.y = y;

   rubberbandRectangle.left = mousedown.x;
   rubberbandRectangle.top = mousedown.y;

   dragging = true;
}

function rubberbandStretch(x, y) {
   if (rubberbandRectangle.width > 2*context.lineWidth &&
       rubberbandRectangle.height > 2*context.lineWidth) {
      if (imageData !== undefined) {
         restoreRubberbandPixels();
      }
   }

   setRubberbandRectangle(x, y);

   if (rubberbandRectangle.width > 2*context.lineWidth &&
       rubberbandRectangle.height > 2*context.lineWidth) {
      updateRubberband();
   }
}
```

*(Continues)*

**Example 4.9** *(Continued)*

```
function rubberbandEnd() {
    // Draw and scale image to the onscreen canvas.
    context.drawImage(canvas,
                      rubberbandRectangle.left + context.lineWidth*2,
                      rubberbandRectangle.top + context.lineWidth*2,
                      rubberbandRectangle.width - 4*context.lineWidth,
                      rubberbandRectangle.height - 4*context.lineWidth,
                      0, 0, canvas.width, canvas.height);
    dragging = false;
    imageData = undefined;
}

// Event handlers.....................................................

canvas.onmousedown = function (e) {
    var loc = windowToCanvas(canvas, e.clientX, e.clientY);
    e.preventDefault();
    rubberbandStart(loc.x, loc.y);
};

canvas.onmousemove = function (e) {
    var loc;

    if (dragging) {
        loc = windowToCanvas(canvas, e.clientX, e.clientY);
        rubberbandStretch(loc.x, loc.y);
    }
};

canvas.onmouseup = function (e) {
    rubberbandEnd();
};

// Initialization....................................................

image.src = 'arch.png';
image.onload = function () {
    context.drawImage(image, 0, 0, canvas.width, canvas.height);
};

resetButton.onclick = function(e) {
    context.clearRect(0, 0, canvas.width, canvas.height);
    context.drawImage(image, 0, 0, canvas.width, canvas.height);
};

context.strokeStyle = 'navy';
context.lineWidth = 1.0;
```

**TIP: Rubberband alternatives**

Section 1.8.1, "Invisible HTML Elements," on p. 41 discussed an application that implemented rubber bands by floating an empty span with a visible border on top of a canvas. As the user drags the mouse, that application resizes the span to produce the rubberband effect.

The rubberbanding implementation in this section is a little more complicated and a little less efficient than the span rubberbanding implementation. By implementing rubberbanding in the canvas itself, however, we can add other effects, such as modifying the transparency of the selected pixels, as illustrated in Figure 4.11 on p. 284.

## 4.5.1.1 `ImageData` Objects

The rubberband application discussed in Section 4.5.1, "Accessing Image Data," on p. 274 calls `getImageData()` to obtain a reference to an `ImageData` object. The application subsequently passes that object to `putImageData()` to erase the last rubber band.

`ImageData` objects returned from `getImageData()` have the following three properties:

- `width`: the width of the image data, in device pixels
- `height`: the height of the image data, also in device pixels
- `data`: an array of values representing device pixels

The `width` and `height` properties are both read-only unsigned `long`s. The `data` attribute is an array of 8-bit integer values representing color components for each device pixel in the image data. We look more closely at `ImageData` objects in Section 4.5.2, "Modifying Image Data," on p. 283.

**NOTE: Device pixels vs. CSS pixels**

For higher image fidelity, browsers may use multiple *device pixels* for each *CSS pixel*. For example, you may have a 200-pixel square canvas, for a total of 40,000 CSS pixels, but if the browser represents each CSS pixel with 2 device pixels, you would have 160,000 (400×400) device pixels. You can find out how many device pixels you have with the `ImageData` object's `width` and `height` properties.

### 4.5.1.2 Image Data Partial Rendering: `putImageData`'s Dirty Rectangle

For every mouse move event as the user drags the mouse, the rubberband application discussed in Section 4.5.1, "Accessing Image Data," on p. 274 calls `putImageData()` to erase the previous rubber band, and then, before the application draws the rubber band, it calls `getImageData()` to capture pixels at the new mouse location.

That's a valid implementation, but it has one drawback: `getImageData()` can be slow, and the rubberband application calls it every time the user moves the mouse. Under most circumstances the canvas will be fast enough that calling `getImageData()` repeatedly is inconsequential; however, if the application is running on a low-powered device, such as a cell phone or a tablet computer, the price that you pay for calling `getImageData()` could become a performance concern.

There is a more efficient implementation: Call `getImageData()` only once for each mouse down event and capture all the pixels in the canvas. Subsequently, invoke `putImageData()` for every mouse move event, copying only the pertinent rectangle from the image data to the canvas. That implementation results in a substantial reduction in the number of calls to `getImageData()`.

The more efficient implementation is made possible by four optional arguments to `putImageData()` that let you specify a *dirty rectangle*, meaning a rectangle, within the image data, that the browser copies to the canvas: `putImageData( HTMLImage, dx, dy, dirtyX, dirtyY, dirtyWidth, dirtyHeight)`.

Figure 4.10 shows how the seven-argument version of `putImageData()` copies a subset of an image's data into a canvas.

The `dx` and `dy` arguments to `putImageData()` represent the destination X and Y offsets, *in CSS pixels*, from the top-left corner of the canvas. The browser places the upper-left corner of the image data at those offsets, and from there it calculates the location in the canvas of the dirty rectangle within the image data.

The last four arguments to `putImageData()` represent the dirty rectangle in *device pixels*. When the browser copies the dirty rectangle into the canvas, it converts those device pixels into CSS pixels, as illustrated in Figure 4.10.

You can easily modify the rubberband application discussed in Section 4.5.1, "Accessing Image Data," on p. 274 to capture all the canvas's pixels for each mouse down event, and then subsequently copy only the rubberband rectangle from those pixels as the user drags the mouse. Example 4.10 shows the necessary modifications to `captureRubberbandPixels()` and `restoreRubberbandPixels()`.

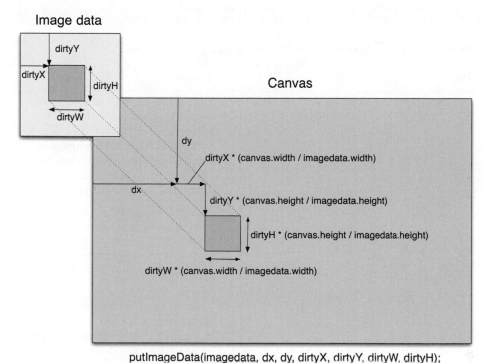

putImageData(imagedata, dx, dy, dirtyX, dirtyY, dirtyW, dirtyH);

**Figure 4.10** `putImageData()`'s dirty rectangle

**Example 4.10** Capturing a canvas's pixels

```
function captureRubberbandPixels() {
   // Capture the entire canvas
   imageData = context.getImageData(0, 0, canvas.width, canvas.height);
}

function restoreRubberbandPixels() {
   var deviceWidthOverCSSPixels = imageData.width / canvas.width,
       deviceHeightOverCSSPixels = imageData.height / canvas.height;

   // Put data for the rubberband rectangle, scaled to device pixels

   context.putImageData(imageData, 0, 0,
      rubberbandRectangle.left,
      rubberbandRectangle.top,
      rubberbandRectangle.width * deviceWidthOverCSSPixels,
      rubberbandRectangle.height * deviceHeightOverCSSPixels);
}
```

The getImageData() and putImageData() methods are summarized in Table 4.2.

**Table 4.2** CanvasRenderingContext2D image manipulation methods

| Method | Description |
|---|---|
| getImageData(in double sx, in double sy, in double sw, in double sh) | Returns an ImageData object that contains a data array of 4×*w*×*h* integers, where *w* and *h* are the width and height of the image *in device pixels*. You can find out the width and height with ImageData's width and height attributes. |
| | An ImageData object's data array contains four integers per pixel, one each for red, green, blue, and the transparency of each pixel, known as the alpha value. |
| | Realize that the width of the ImageData object returned from getImageData() is not necessarily the same as the width that you pass to getImageData(). That's because the former represents device pixels, whereas the latter represents CSS pixels. |
| putImageData(in ImageData imagedata, in double dx, in double dy, in optional double dirtyX, in double dirtyY, in double dirtyWidth, in double dirtyHeight); | Puts image data into a canvas at (dx,dy), where (dx,dy) are in *CSS pixels*. The dirty rectangle represents the region of the image data that the browser will copy to the onscreen canvas. You specify that rectangle in *device pixels*. |

**TIP: putImageData() is not affected by global settings**

When you put image data into a canvas with putImageData(), that image data is unaffected by global canvas settings, such as globalAlpha and globalCompositeOperation. The browser also does not perform compositing, alpha blending, or application of shadows. That's the opposite of drawImage(), which is affected by all those things.

**TIP: The `putImageData()` method's optional arguments**

The last four arguments to `putImageData()` represent a dirty rectangle within that image data. The idea is that the dirty rectangle has been modified in some manner and subsequently needs to be copied to a location inside a canvas.

Those arguments are optional, so they have defaults when you do not specify them. Here is a summary of those arguments, and their default values:

- The horizontal offset from the upper-left corner of the image data, in device pixels. *Default*: 0.

- The vertical offset from the upper-left corner of the image data, in device pixels. *Default*: 0.

- The width of the dirty rectangle, in device pixels. *Default*: Width of the image data.

- The height of the dirty rectangle, in device pixels. *Default*: Height of the image data.

**CAUTION: `putImageData()` requires both device and CSS pixels**

When you call `putImageData()` with all seven arguments, you specify both an offset into the canvas (with the second and third arguments), and a dirty rectangle inside the image data that you want to copy into the canvas (the final four arguments).

You specify the canvas offset in *CSS pixels*, whereas you specify the image data's dirty rectangle in *device pixels*. If you inadvertently use the same units for both, `putImageData()` may not work as you expect.

## 4.5.2 Modifying Image Data

You've seen how to use `getImageData()` and `putImageData()` to store and retrieve image data. Now let's look at how you can modify image data.

Figure 4.11 shows a rubberband implementation that modifies the transparency of every pixel in the rubberband rectangle.

To temporarily increase the transparency of pixels within the rubberband rectangle, the application shown in Figure 4.11 uses two `ImageData` objects, both of which are the same size as the canvas.

Figure 4.11  Rubber bands, with effects

One of the `ImageData` objects contains a snapshot of the canvas when the user last pressed the mouse. The other `ImageData` object contains a copy of that snapshot; however, the transparency of the copy is double the transparency of the original snapshot, as shown in Figure 4.12.

As the user drags the mouse, the application does three things:

1.  Restores the entire canvas from the background snapshot (Figure 4.12, top) to erase the previous rubber band
2.  Copies the rubberband rectangle from the more transparent copy (Figure 4.12, bottom) to the onscreen canvas
3.  Strokes the rubberband rectangle

Figure 4.12 Two image data objects. *Top:* the image used for the background; *bottom:* the image used for the rubberband rectangle

### 4.5.2.1 Creating `ImageData` Objects with `createImageData()`

When the application shown in Figure 4.11 starts, it calls `createImageData()` to create an `ImageData` object. Subsequently, when the user presses the mouse, the application initializes that image data in `captureCanvasPixels()` as shown in Example 4.11.

When it detects a mouse down event, the application calls `getImageData()` to grab all the pixels in the canvas. Then the `copyCanvasPixels()` function copies those pixels into the previously allocated `imageDataCopy`, doubling the transparency of each pixel along the way. So, after each mouse down event, the application has image data for the canvas and a more transparent copy of that data.

---

**Example 4.11** Creating and initializing an `ImageData` object

---

```
var canvas = document.getElementById('canvas'),
    context = canvas.getContext('2d'),

    image = new Image(),
    imageData,
    imageDataCopy = context.createImageData(canvas.width, canvas.height),
    ...

// Functions.......................................................
...

function copyCanvasPixels() {
   // Copy imageData into imageDataCopy, doubling the transparency
   // of each pixel in the array.
}

function captureCanvasPixels() {
   imageData = context.getImageData(0, 0, canvas.width, canvas.height);
   copyCanvasPixels();
}
...

function rubberbandStart(x, y) {
   ...
   captureCanvasPixels();
}

// Event handlers....................................................

canvas.onmousedown = function (e) {
   var loc = windowToCanvas(canvas, e.clientX, e.clientY);
   e.preventDefault();
   rubberbandStart(loc.x, loc.y);
};
...
```

---

In Example 4.11, it's the copyCanvasPixels() method that modifies image data to create a more transparent copy of the pixels in the canvas. In the next section, we look more closely at that method.

### 4.5.2.1.1 The Image Data Array

The data property of an `ImageData` object is a reference to an array of 8-bit integers, with values from 0 to 255, each representing the red, green, blue, and alpha values of a pixel, as shown in Figure 4.13.

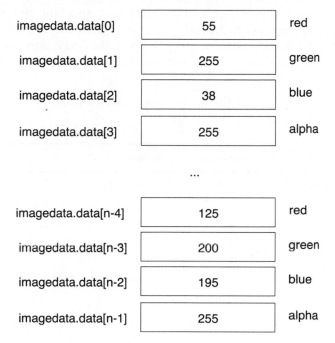

Figure 4.13 The image data array whose length is n

The application shown in Figure 4.11 on p. 284 copies image data representing the entire canvas to a separate ImageData object, with the following function:

```
function copyCanvasPixels() {
   var i=0;

   // Copy red, green, and blue components of the first pixel

   for (i=0; i < 3; i++) {
      imageDataCopy.data[i] = imageData.data[i];
   }

   // Starting with the alpha component of the first pixel,
   // copy imageData, but make the copy more transparent

   for (i=3; i < imageData.data.length - 4; i+=4) {
      imageDataCopy.data[i]   = imageData.data[i] / 2; // Alpha
      imageDataCopy.data[i+1] = imageData.data[i+1];   // Red
      imageDataCopy.data[i+2] = imageData.data[i+2];   // Green
      imageDataCopy.data[i+3] = imageData.data[i+3];   // Blue
   }
}
```

The preceding code copies each pixel's red, green, and blue components and doubles the transparency of each pixel. The code loops through the array, jumping over four integers every time through the loop. In the body of the loop, the code copies the next four values from the array, cutting the alpha value for each pixel in half.

The complete JavaScript for the application shown in Figure 4.11 on p. 284 is listed in Example 4.12.

**Example 4.12** A rubber band that modifies image data

```javascript
var canvas = document.getElementById('canvas'),
    context = canvas.getContext('2d'),

    resetButton = document.getElementById('resetButton'),

    image = new Image(),
    imageData,
    imageDataCopy = context.createImageData(canvas.width, canvas.height),

    mousedown = {},
    rubberbandRectangle = {},
    dragging = false;

// Functions.......................................................

function windowToCanvas(canvas, x, y) {
    var canvasRectangle = canvas.getBoundingClientRect();
    return { x: x - canvasRectangle.left,
             y: y - canvasRectangle.top };
}

function copyCanvasPixels() {
    var i=0;

    // Copy red, green, and blue components of the first pixel
    for (i=0; i < 3; i++) {
        imageDataCopy.data[i] = imageData.data[i];
    }

    // Starting with the alpha component of the first pixel,
    // copy imageData, and make the copy more transparent
    for (i=3; i < imageData.data.length - 4; i+=4) {
        imageDataCopy.data[i]   = imageData.data[i] / 2; // Alpha
        imageDataCopy.data[i+1] = imageData.data[i+1];   // Red
        imageDataCopy.data[i+2] = imageData.data[i+2];   // Green
        imageDataCopy.data[i+3] = imageData.data[i+3];   // Blue
    }
}
```

```
function captureCanvasPixels() {
   imageData = context.getImageData(0, 0, canvas.width, canvas.height);
   copyCanvasPixels();
}

function restoreRubberbandPixels() {
   var deviceWidthOverCSSPixels = imageData.width / canvas.width,
       deviceHeightOverCSSPixels = imageData.height / canvas.height;

   // Restore the canvas to what it looked like when the mouse went down

   context.putImageData(imageData, 0, 0);

   // Put the more transparent image data into the rubberband rectangle

   context.putImageData(imageDataCopy, 0, 0,

      rubberbandRectangle.left + context.lineWidth,
      rubberbandRectangle.top + context.lineWidth,

      (rubberbandRectangle.width - 2*context.lineWidth)
         * deviceWidthOverCSSPixels,
      (rubberbandRectangle.height - 2*context.lineWidth)
         * deviceHeightOverCSSPixels);
}

function setRubberbandRectangle(x, y) {
   rubberbandRectangle.left = Math.min(x, mousedown.x);
   rubberbandRectangle.top = Math.min(y, mousedown.y);
   rubberbandRectangle.width = Math.abs(x - mousedown.x),
   rubberbandRectangle.height = Math.abs(y - mousedown.y);
}

function drawRubberband() {
   context.strokeRect(rubberbandRectangle.left + context.lineWidth,
                      rubberbandRectangle.top + context.lineWidth,
                      rubberbandRectangle.width - 2*context.lineWidth,
                      rubberbandRectangle.height - 2*context.lineWidth);
}

function rubberbandStart(x, y) {
   mousedown.x = x;
   mousedown.y = y;

   rubberbandRectangle.left = mousedown.x;
   rubberbandRectangle.top = mousedown.y;
```

*(Continues)*

**Example 4.12**   *(Continued)*

```
    rubberbandRectangle.width = 0;
    rubberbandRectangle.height = 0;

    dragging = true;

    captureCanvasPixels();
}

function rubberbandStretch(x, y) {
    if (rubberbandRectangle.width > 2*context.lineWidth &&
        rubberbandRectangle.height > 2*context.lineWidth) {
        if (imageData !== undefined) {
            restoreRubberbandPixels();
        }
    }

    setRubberbandRectangle(x, y);

    if (rubberbandRectangle.width > 2*context.lineWidth &&
        rubberbandRectangle.height > 2*context.lineWidth) {
        drawRubberband();
    }
}

function rubberbandEnd() {
    context.putImageData(imageData, 0, 0);

    // Draw the canvas back into itself, scaling along the way
    context.drawImage(canvas,
                    rubberbandRectangle.left + context.lineWidth*2,
                    rubberbandRectangle.top + context.lineWidth*2,
                    rubberbandRectangle.width - 4*context.lineWidth,
                    rubberbandRectangle.height - 4*context.lineWidth,
                    0, 0, canvas.width, canvas.height);

    dragging = false;
    imageData = undefined;
}

// Event handlers.....................................................

canvas.onmousedown = function (e) {
    var loc = windowToCanvas(canvas, e.clientX, e.clientY);
    e.preventDefault();
    rubberbandStart(loc.x, loc.y);
};
```

```
canvas.onmousemove = function (e) {
   var loc;

   if (dragging) {
      loc = windowToCanvas(canvas, e.clientX, e.clientY);
      rubberbandStretch(loc.x, loc.y);
   }
};

canvas.onmouseup = function (e) {
   rubberbandEnd();
};

// Initialization......................................................

image.src = 'arch.png';
image.onload = function () {
   context.drawImage(image, 0, 0, canvas.width, canvas.height);
};

resetButton.onclick = function(e) {
   context.clearRect(0, 0, canvas.width, canvas.height);
   context.drawImage(image, 0, 0, canvas.width, canvas.height);
};

context.strokeStyle = 'navy';
context.lineWidth = 1.0;
```

---

 **NOTE: Canvas specification update: Image data is an ArrayBuffer**

In this section you saw how to access an array of eight-bit integers representing the red, green, blue, and alpha color components for pixels in an image. You reference that array through the data property of the ImageData object returned from getImageData().

As this book went to press, the W3C changed the type of that reference to a TypedArray. Typed arrays are data buffers that can be read by views. The idea is that one data buffer can be read in different formats.

Technically, the image data array must be an ArrayBuffer, and the reference to the array must be a Uint8ClampedArray. You can read more about typed arrays at https://developer.mozilla.org/en/JavaScript_typed_arrays.

In practice, the change to the Canvas specification will not cause you to rewrite your code, because you will continue to access the image data array as an array. But under the covers, the array will be more flexible and efficient.

### 4.5.2.2 Image Data Looping Strategies

Given the following:

```
var canvas = document.getElementById('canvas'),
    context = canvas.getContext('2d'),
    imagedata = context.getImageData(0,0,canvas.width,canvas.height),
    data = imagedata.data,
    length = imagedata.data.length,
    width = imagedata.width,
    index = 0,
    value;
```

Here are some ways to loop through image data:

Loop over every pixel:

```
for (var index=0; index < length; ++i) {
   value = data[index];
}
```

Loop backwards:

```
index = length-1;
while (index >= 0) {
   value = data[index];
   index--;
}
```

Only process alpha, not red, green, or blue:

```
for(index=3; index < length-4; index+=4) {
   data[index] = ...;   // Alpha
}
```

Process red, green, and blue, but not alpha:

```
for(index=0; index < length-4; index+=4) {
   data[index] = ...;     // Red
   data[index+1] = ...;   // Green
   data[index+2] = ...;   // Blue
}
```

See Section 4.9, "Performance," on p. 313 for more information about looping over image data and performance.

### 4.5.2.3 Filtering Images

Now that you know how to manipulate the individual pixels of an image, let's see how to implement image filters. Figure 4.14 shows two filters, a negative filter and black-and-white filter, which are listed in Examples 4.13 and 4.14, respectively.

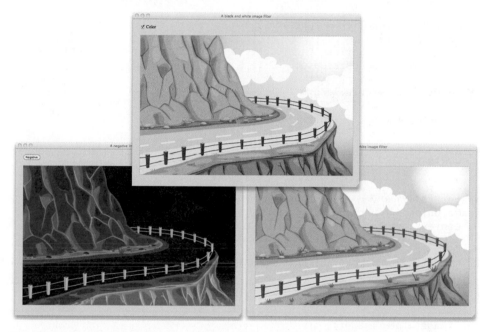

Figure 4.14 *Top:* original image; *bottom:* negative and black-and-white filters

Both the negative and black-and-white filters loop over the image data by leaping over four values at a time, which consistently lands on the red value of a particular pixel. Inside the loop, the filters change the red, green, and blue values of the pixel. That algorithm leaves the alpha values of all the pixels unchanged.

The negative filter sets the red, green, and blue values of each pixel to 255 minus the current value; that setting inverts the colors.

The black-and-white filter takes the average of the red, green, and blue values of each pixel, and assigns that average to each of the values; that process drains the color from the image.

**Example 4.13** A negative filter

```javascript
var image = new Image(),
    canvas = document.getElementById('canvas'),
    context = canvas.getContext('2d'),
    negativeButton = document.getElementById('negativeButton');

negativeButton.onclick = function() {
  var imagedata =
        context.getImageData(0, 0, canvas.width, canvas.height),
      data = imagedata.data;

  for(i=0; i <= data.length - 4; i+=4) {
     data[i]   = 255 - data[i]
     data[i+1] = 255 - data[i+1];
     data[i+2] = 255 - data[i+2];
  }
  context.putImageData(imagedata, 0, 0);
};

image.src = 'curved-road.png';
image.onload = function() {
  context.drawImage(image, 0, 0, image.width, image.height, 0, 0,
                    context.canvas.width, context.canvas.height);
};
```

**Example 4.14** A black-and-white filter

```javascript
var image = new Image(),
    canvas = document.getElementById('canvas'),
    context = canvas.getContext('2d'),
    drawInColorToggleCheckbox =
        document.getElementById('drawInColorToggleCheckbox');

function drawInBlackAndWhite() {
  var data = undefined,
      i = 0;

  imagedata = context.getImageData(0, 0, canvas.width, canvas.height);
  data = imagedata.data;

  for(i=0; i < data.length - 4; i+=4) {
     average = (data[i] + data[i+1] + data[i+2]) / 3;
     data[i]   = average;
     data[i+1] = average;
     data[i+2] = average;
  }
  context.putImageData(imagedata, 0, 0);
}
```

```
function drawInColor() {
   context.drawImage(image, 0, 0,
      image.width, image.height, 0, 0,
      context.canvas.width, context.canvas.height);
}

colorToggleCheckbox.onclick = function() {
   if (colorToggleCheckbox.checked) {
      drawInColor();
   }
   else {
      drawInBlackAndWhite();
   }
};

image.src = 'curved-road.png';
image.onload = function() {
   drawInColor();
};
```

### 4.5.2.4 Device Pixels vs. CSS Pixels, Redux

Some image filters, such as the embossing filter shown in Figure 4.15, take into account the width of the image data they filter. For example, the embossing filter

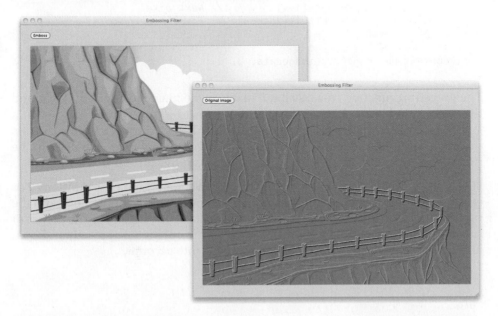

Figure 4.15 An embossing filter

calculates pixel colors with a simple equation that uses the color values of the current pixel, the pixel to the current pixel's immediate right, and the pixel in the next row underneath the current pixel. The width of the image data is needed to calculate the location, in the image data array, of that pixel in the next row.

The gist of the application shown in Figure 4.15 is this:

```
function emboss() {
    var imagedata, data, length, width;

    imagedata = context.getImageData(0, 0, canvas.width, canvas.height);
    data = imagedata.data;
    width = imagedata.width;
    length = data.length;

    for (i=0; i < length; i++) {
        if ((i+1) % 4 !== 0) {

            // Use imagedata.width instead of the width you pass
            // to getImageData(). Most of the time the two values
            // are the same, but if the browser uses multiple device
            // pixels per CSS pixel, only imagedata.width represents
            // the true width of the image data.

            data[i] = 255/2              // Average value
                    + 2*data[i]          // Current pixel
                    - data[i+4]          // Next pixel
                    - data[i+width*4];   // Pixel underneath
        }
    }
    context.putImageData(imagedata, 0, 0);
}
```

The preceding function smears all the pixels in the image to a muddy gray, and then uses a technique known as edge detection to intensify that gray when a sudden change in color—an edge—is detected. The algorithm that implements the edge detection calculates pixel colors with the current pixel, the pixel to the right of the current pixel, and the pixel underneath the current pixel.

However, the preceding function does not account for boundary conditions. For example, the last row of pixels does not have another row underneath it, and the rightmost pixel in a row does not have another pixel to the right of it. The emboss() function listed in Example 4.15, which is the JavaScript for the application shown in Figure 4.15, takes those boundary conditions into account.

---

Example 4.15  An embossing filter

---

```
var image = new Image(),
    canvas = document.getElementById('canvas'),
    context = canvas.getContext('2d'),
    embossButton = document.getElementById('embossButton'),
    embossed = false;

// Functions.......................................................

function emboss() {
    var imagedata, data, length, width, index=3;

    imagedata = context.getImageData(0, 0, canvas.width, canvas.height);
    data = imagedata.data;
    width = imagedata.width;
    length = data.length;

    for (i=0; i < length; i++) { // Loop through every pixel

        // If we won't overrun the bounds of the array

        if (i <= length-width*4) {

            // If it's not an alpha

            if ((i+1) % 4 !== 0) {

                // If it's the last pixel in the row, there is no pixel
                // to the right, so copy previous pixel's values.

                if ((i+4) % (width*4) == 0) {
                    data[i] = data[i-4];
                    data[i+1] = data[i-3];
                    data[i+2] = data[i-2];
                    data[i+3] = data[i-1];
                    i+=4;
                }
                else { // Not the last pixel in the row
                    data[i] = 255/2                // Average value
                            + 2*data[i]            // Current pixel
                            - data[i+4]            // Next pixel
                            - data[i+width*4]; // Pixel underneath
                }
            }
        }
    }
```

---

*(Continues)*

Example 4.15   *(Continued)*

```
      else { // Last row, no pixels underneath, so copy pixel above
         if ((i+1) % 4 !== 0) {
            data[i] = data[i-width*4];
         }
      }
   }
   context.putImageData(imagedata, 0, 0);
}

function drawOriginalImage() {
   context.drawImage(image, 0, 0,
                     image.width, image.height,
                     0, 0, canvas.width, canvas.height);
}

embossButton.onclick = function() {
   if (embossed) {
      embossButton.value = 'Emboss';
      drawOriginalImage();
      embossed = false;
   }
   else {
      embossButton.value = 'Original image';
      emboss();
      embossed = true;
   }
};

// Initialization.................................................

image.src = 'curved-road.png';
image.onload = function() {
   drawOriginalImage();
};
```

The image manipulation examples that we've looked at in this chapter use small, simple images, and therefore they have no performance issues. However, if you are using complicated algorithms on relatively large images, you don't want to lock up the browser while you are performing those algorithms. Let's see what we can do to fix that case.

### 4.5.2.5 Image Processing Web Workers

It's quite possible that you may run into performance issues when you process images; for example, you may be processing large images on an underpowered cell phone. If performance is an issue, you may want to consider offloading image processing to web workers.

Browsers execute JavaScript on the main thread, which means that long running scripts can make an application feel sluggish. Fortunately, HTML5 lets you use web workers to execute code on a different thread. The application shown in Figure 4.16 and listed in Example 4.16 applies a sunglass filter to its image, using a web worker to do the actual image manipulation.

Figure 4.16  A sunglass filter

The main thread creates the worker with the statement `sunglassFilter = new Worker('sunglassFilter.js')`. The filename passed to the `Worker` constructor specifies a file that contains the worker's JavaScript.

**Example 4.16** The main thread

```javascript
var image = new Image(),
    canvas = document.getElementById('canvas'),
    context = canvas.getContext('2d'),
    sunglassButton = document.getElementById('sunglassButton'),
    sunglassesOn = false,
    sunglassFilter = new Worker('sunglassFilter.js');

// Functions......................................................

function putSunglassesOn() {
    sunglassFilter.postMessage(
        context.getImageData(0, 0, canvas.width, canvas.height);

    sunglassFilter.onmessage = function (event) {
        context.putImageData(event.data, 0, 0);
    };
}

function drawOriginalImage() {
    context.drawImage(image, 0, 0,
                      image.width, image.height, 0, 0,
                      canvas.width, canvas.height);
}

// Event handlers..................................................

sunglassButton.onclick = function() {
    if (sunglassesOn) {
        sunglassButton.value = 'Sunglasses';
        drawOriginalImage();
        sunglassesOn = false;
    }
    else {
        sunglassButton.value = 'Original picture';
        putSunglassesOn();
        sunglassesOn = true;
    }
};

// Initialization..................................................

image.src = 'curved-road.png';
image.onload = function() {
    drawOriginalImage();
};
```

The main thread interacts with the worker in putSunglassesOn(), which posts a message to the worker, passing the worker the image data from the canvas, and then sets the worker's onmessage property. Subsequently, after the worker manipulates the pixels of the image and posts a message of its own, the browser invokes the worker's onmessage() method. In our case, that method puts the image data modified by the worker back into the canvas.

The worker is listed in Example 4.17. It implements an image filter that darkens color and sharpens contrast. After filtering the image data that it was passed, the web worker posts the modified image data, which is received by the main thread.

**Example 4.17** sunglassFilter.js: the web worker

```javascript
onmessage = function (event) {
    var imagedata = event.data,
        data = imagedata.data,
        length = data.length,
        width = imagedata.width;

    for (i=0; i < length; ++i) {
        if ((i+1) % 4 != 0) {
            if ((i+4) % (width*4) == 0) { // Last pixel in a row
                data[i] = data[i-4];
                data[i+1] = data[i-3];
                data[i+2] = data[i-2];
                data[i+3] = data[i-1];
                i+=4;
            }
            else {
                data[i] = 2*data[i] - data[i+4] - 0.5*data[i+4];
            }
        }
    }

    postMessage(imagedata);
};
```

Recall that workers are useful because you can put long-running code on another thread, which helps to keep the browser responsive. But image manipulation web workers are useful for another reason: They encapsulate an image manipulation algorithm, and therefore they are reusable. In fact, let's see how to reuse the web worker listed in Example 4.17.

## 4.6 Clipping Images

The application shown in Figure 4.17 takes the application shown in Figure 4.16 to its logical conclusion.

The sunglasses application, which is listed in Example 4.18, uses web workers, image manipulation, an offscreen canvas, clipping, and the Canvas drawing APIs. At a high level, here's how it works:

```
var sunglassFilter = new Worker('sunglassFilter.js');
...
imagedata = context.getImageData(0, 0, canvas.width, canvas.height);
sunglassFilter.postMessage(imagedata);

sunglassFilter.onmessage = function(event) {
   offscreenContext.putImageData(event.data, 0, 0);
   drawLenses(leftLensLocation, rightLensLocation);
   drawWire(center);
   drawConnectors(center);
};
...
```

The application gets the image data from the canvas and subsequently posts it to the sunglass web worker listed in Example 4.17.

The web worker filters the image data, making the image darker with higher contrast, and subsequently posts the modified image data. That post causes the browser to call the worker's onmessage() method. That method, as you can see in the preceding code snippet, copies the modified pixels into an offscreen canvas and then draws the lens, the wire, and the connectors.

The drawLenses() method saves the context and begins a path. Then it adds the two circles representing the lenses to the path, sets the clipping region to that path, and draws the offscreen canvas onscreen. Because clipping is set to the two circles, that's the only part of the canvas that's affected when the offscreen canvas is drawn on screen. The drawLenses() method ends by restoring the context, and that resets the clipping region to whatever it was before the call to context.clip().

The drawWire() and drawConnectors() methods in Example 4.18 use the Canvas drawing APIs to draw the wire and connectors, respectively.

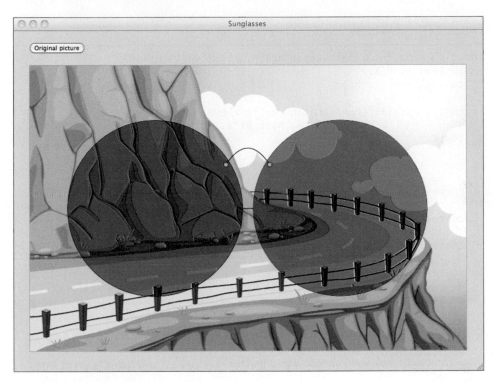

Figure 4.17 Sunglasses

Example 4.18 Sunglasses: image manipulation, an offscreen canvas, and clipping

```
var image = new Image(),
    canvas = document.getElementById('canvas'),
    context = canvas.getContext('2d'),

    offscreenCanvas = document.createElement('canvas'),
    offscreenContext = offscreenCanvas.getContext('2d'),

    sunglassButton = document.getElementById('sunglassButton'),
    sunglassesOn = false,
    sunglassFilter = new Worker('sunglassFilter.js'),

    LENS_RADIUS = canvas.width/5;

// Functions.......................................................
```

*(Continues)*

---

Example 4.18 *(Continued)*

---

```
function drawLenses(leftLensLocation, rightLensLocation) {
   context.save();
   context.beginPath();

   context.arc(leftLensLocation.x, leftLensLocation.y,
               LENS_RADIUS, 0, Math.PI*2, false);
   context.stroke();

   moveTo(rightLensLocation.x, rightLensLocation.y);

   context.arc(rightLensLocation.x, rightLensLocation.y,
               LENS_RADIUS, 0, Math.PI*2, false);
   context.stroke();

   context.clip();

   context.drawImage(offscreenCanvas, 0, 0,
                     canvas.width, canvas.height);
   context.restore();
}

function drawWire(center) {
   context.beginPath();
   context.moveTo(center.x - LENS_RADIUS/4, center.y - LENS_RADIUS/2);

   context.quadraticCurveTo(center.x, center.y - LENS_RADIUS+20,
                            center.x + LENS_RADIUS/4,
                            center.y - LENS_RADIUS/2);
   context.stroke();
}

function drawConnectors(center) {
   context.beginPath();

   context.fillStyle = 'silver';
   context.strokeStyle = 'rgba(0,0,0,0.4)';
   context.lineWidth = 2;

   context.arc(center.x - LENS_RADIUS/4, center.y - LENS_RADIUS/2,
               4, 0, Math.PI*2, false);
   context.fill();
   context.stroke();

   context.beginPath();
   context.arc(center.x + LENS_RADIUS/4, center.y - LENS_RADIUS/2,
               4, 0, Math.PI*2, false);
   context.fill();
   context.stroke();
}
```

```
function putSunglassesOn() {
   var imagedata,
       center = {
         x: canvas.width/2,
         y: canvas.height/2
       },
       leftLensLocation = {
         x: center.x - LENS_RADIUS - 10,
         y: center.y
       },
       rightLensLocation = {
         x: center.x + LENS_RADIUS + 10,
         y: center.y
       },

   imagedata = context.getImageData(0, 0,
                                    canvas.width, canvas.height);

   sunglassFilter.postMessage(imagedata);

   sunglassFilter.onmessage = function(event) {
      offscreenContext.putImageData(event.data, 0, 0);
      drawLenses(leftLensLocation, rightLensLocation);
      drawWire(center);
      drawConnectors(center);
   };
}

function drawOriginalImage() {
   context.drawImage(image, 0, 0, image.width, image.height,
                     0, 0, canvas.width, canvas.height);
}

// Event handlers.................................................

sunglassButton.onclick = function() {
   if (sunglassesOn) {
      sunglassButton.value = 'Sunglasses';
      drawOriginalImage();
      sunglassesOn = false;
   }
   else {
      sunglassButton.value = 'Original picture';
      putSunglassesOn();
      sunglassesOn = true;
   }
};
```

*(Continues)*

---

Example 4.18   *(Continued)*

---

```
offscreenCanvas.width = canvas.width;
offscreenCanvas.height = canvas.height;

// Initialization.................................................

image.src = 'curved-road.png';
image.onload = function() {
   drawOriginalImage();
};
```

---

Now that you know how to manipulate images with the Canvas API, let's see how we can put image manipulation into motion.

## 4.7  Animating Images

You can animate images by successively applying image filters over a period of time. For example, the application in Figure 4.18 fades an image.

The application uses `setInterval()` to repeatedly decrease the alpha channel of every pixel in the image until the image fades from view.

When the user clicks the Fade Out button, the application starts an animation that cycles 25 times. Each cycle runs at 60 frames per second, so the entire animation takes about 1/2 second.

The tricky part about the fadeout animation is that different pixels may have different alpha values to begin with, and therefore, for every step in the animation, the application must decrease the alpha value for different pixels differently, depending on their initial value. To facilitate this variable-alpha-channel reduction, the application takes a snapshot of all the image's original pixels with `getImageData()`, and subsequently consults those initial values when calculating how much to decrease a pixel's alpha for a given step in the animation.

The application shown in Figure 4.18 listed in Example 4.19.

Figure 4.18  Fading an image out of a canvas

Example 4.19  Fading an image out of a canvas

```
var image = new Image(),
    canvas = document.getElementById('canvas'),
    context = canvas.getContext('2d'),
    fadeButton = document.getElementById('fadeButton'),
    originalImageData = null,
    interval = null;

// Functions.........................................................
```

(Continues)

Example 4.19 *(Continued)*

```javascript
function increaseTransparency(imagedata, steps) {
   var alpha, currentAlpha, step, length = imagedata.data.length;

   for (var i=3; i < length; i+=4) { // For every alpha component
      alpha = originalImageData.data[i];

      if (alpha > 0 && imagedata.data[i] > 0) { // Not transparent yet
         currentAlpha = imagedata.data[i];
         step = Math.ceil(alpha/steps);

         if (currentAlpha - step > 0) { // Not too close to the end
            imagedata.data[i] -= step;  // Increase transparency
         }
         else {
            imagedata.data[i] = 0; // End: totally transparent
         }
      }
   }
}

function fadeOut(context, imagedata, x, y,
                 steps, millisecondsPerStep) {
   var frame = 0,
       length = imagedata.data.length;

   interval = setInterval(function () { // Once every millisecondsPerStep
      frame++;

      if (frame > steps) { // Animation is over
         clearInterval(interval); // End animation
         animationComplete();     // Put picture back in 1s
      }
      else {
         increaseTransparency(imagedata, steps);
         context.putImageData(imagedata, x, y);
      }
   }, millisecondsPerStep);
}

// Animation.....................................................

function animationComplete() {
   setTimeout(function() {
      context.drawImage(image, 0, 0, canvas.width, canvas.height);
   }, 1000);
}
```

```
// Event handlers.....................................................

fadeButton.onclick = function() {
   fadeOut(context,
      context.getImageData(0, 0, canvas.width, canvas.height),
      0, 0, 20, 1000/60);
};

// Initialization.....................................................

image.src = 'log-crossing.png';
image.onload = function() {
   context.drawImage(image, 0, 0, canvas.width, canvas.height);
   originalImageData = context.getImageData(0, 0,
                             canvas.width, canvas.height);
};
```

**TIP: There are easier ways to fade an image**

The application shown in **Figure 4.18** fades an image by manipulating the alpha values of each pixel in the image. As is typically the case, there are several ways to accomplish the same thing with canvas; for example, you could fade the image by setting the context's `globalAlpha` variable and simply drawing the image.

## 4.7.1 Animating with an Offscreen Canvas

The application shown in **Figure 4.18** faded an image from view by repeatedly increasing the transparency of every pixel in the image. An image's pixels may have varying levels of transparencies to begin with, however, so after initially drawing the image, the application calls `getImageData()` to capture the image's pixels. The application subsequently uses the pixel's original transparency value (the alpha value), stored in the image data, to calculate how much to decrease a pixel's transparency for each step of the animation.

It would be convenient to use the same algorithm for fading images *into* view, by initially taking a snapshot of the image's pixels and using those alpha values to determine how much to *increase* each pixel's transparency for each step of the animation. However, when fading an image into view, the image is not initially displayed, and therefore you cannot capture its pixels.

To capture the image's pixels before the image is displayed, the application shown in **Figure 4.19** draws the image into an offscreen canvas and captures the pixels from that canvas.

Figure 4.19  Fading an image into a canvas

Example 4.20 lists the application shown in Figure 4.19 in its entirety.

Example 4.20  Fading an image into a canvas

```
var image = new Image(),
    canvas = document.getElementById('canvas'),
    context = canvas.getContext('2d'),
    offscreenCanvas = document.createElement('canvas'),
    offscreenContext = offscreenCanvas.getContext('2d'),
    fadeButton = document.getElementById('fadeButton'),
    imagedata,
    imagedataOffscreen,
    interval = null;

// Functions.......................................................
```

```
function increaseTransparency(imagedata, steps) {
    var alpha,
        currentAlpha,
        step,
        length = imagedata.data.length;

    for (var i=3; i < length; i+=4) { // For every alpha component
        alpha = imagedataOffscreen.data[i];

        if (alpha > 0) {
            currentAlpha = imagedata.data[i];
            step = Math.ceil(alpha/steps);

            if (currentAlpha + step <= alpha) { // Not at original alpha yet
                imagedata.data[i] += step; // Increase transparency
            }
            else {
                imagedata.data[i] = alpha; // End: original transparency
            }
        }
    }
}

function fadeIn(context, imagedata, steps, millisecondsPerStep) {
    var frame = 0;

    for (var i=3; i < imagedata.data.length; i+=4) { // For every alpha
        imagedata.data[i] = 0;
    }

    interval = setInterval(function () { // Every millisecondsPerStep
        frame++;

        if (frame > steps) {
            clearInterval(interval);
        }
        else {
            increaseTransparency(imagedata, steps);
            context.putImageData(imagedata, 0, 0);
        }
    }, millisecondsPerStep);
}

// Animation.......................................................
```

*(Continues)*

---

**Example 4.20**  *(Continued)*

---

```
function animationComplete() {
   setTimeout(function() {
      context.clearRect(0, 0, canvas.width, canvas.height);
   }, 1000);
}

// Event handlers....................................................

fadeButton.onclick = function() {
   imagedataOffscreen = offscreenContext.getImageData(0, 0,
                          canvas.width, canvas.height);

   fadeIn(context,
          offscreenContext.getImageData(0, 0,
                          canvas.width, canvas.height),
          50,
          1000 / 60);
};

// Initialization...................................................

image.src = 'log-crossing.png';
image.onload = function() {
   offscreenCanvas.width = canvas.width;
   offscreenCanvas.height = canvas.height;
   offscreenContext.drawImage(image,0,0);
};
```

---

## 4.8 Security

Images are often security risks; for example, you may want to restrict access to pictures you post to a social network, or a corporation may wish to keep product prototype pictures under wraps. Or you may be a politician.

So, because of security concerns, the HTML5 Canvas specification lets you *draw* images that are not your own (meaning images from other domains), but you cannot *save* or *manipulate* cross-domain images with the Canvas API.

Here's how Canvas image security works:

Every canvas has a flag called `origin-clean` whose value is originally `true`. If you use `drawImage()` to draw a cross-domain image, the `origin-clean` flag is set to `false`. Likewise, if you use `drawImage()` to draw another canvas whose `origin-clean` flag is set to `false`, then the canvas that you are drawing into will also have its `origin-clean` flag set to `false`.

In and of itself, setting up a canvas's `origin-clean` flag to `false` does not result in any immediate action, such as throwing an exception. However, if you call `toDataURL()` or `getImageData()` for a canvas whose `origin-clean` flag is `false`, the browser will throw a SECURITY_ERR exception.

The browser considers your file system to be a different domain from the domain in which your application runs, so, by default, you cannot save or manipulate images from your own file system. That restriction is not practical during development, however, so most browsers provide a workaround. For example, Chrome lets you specify a command-line argument, `--allow-file-access-from-files`, when you start the browser. That argument circumvents that restriction and lets you save or manipulate cross-domain images. With Firefox, you can call the following function:

```
netscape.security.PrivilegeManager.enablePrivilege(
                                    "UniversalBrowserRead");
```

If you start Chrome from the command line with the `--allow-file-access-from-files` command-line argument, your entire application can save or manipulate cross-domain images. If, however, you call the `enablePrivilege()` method on Firefox's `PrivilegeManager`, requesting the `UniversalBrowserRead` privilege, you will only be able to save or manipulate cross-domain images *in the same method* in which you made the call to `enablePrivilege()`.

---

 **TIP: Running this book's examples**

You can download the code for all of the examples in this book from corehtml5canvas.com, or you can run many of the book's examples online from that website. If you choose to download the code and run the examples on your file system, be aware that you will have to take one of the steps mentioned in this section to relax the cross-domain restrictions to run any of the book's examples that use `toDataURL()` or `getImageData()` to create or manipulate images.

---

## 4.9 Performance

Performance can be an important consideration when you are manipulating images. This section discusses three benchmarks from jsperf.com that address the following performance concerns:

- Looping through image data
- Using `drawImage()` vs. `putImageData()`

- Drawing a canvas instead of an image with `drawImage()`
- Scaling when you draw images with `drawImage()`

As always, be aware that the results of any benchmark can change significantly over time and across different browsers. You should regard all the performance recommendations that follow as guidelines for your own code, not as fundamental principles. It's also a good idea to go to jsperf.com to look the current state of the benchmarks.

## 4.9.1 `drawImage(HTMLImage)` vs. `drawImage(HTMLCanvas)` vs. `putImageData()`

Both `drawImage()` and `putImageData()` can draw images into a canvas. At the time this book was written, `drawImage()` was considerably faster than `putImageData()`.

As an added bonus to its performance advantage, `drawImage()` can do something that `putImageData()` cannot: It can draw one canvas into another. The test discussed in this section illustrates that, on average, you do not pay too high of a performance penalty drawing a canvas versus drawing an image.

- *Prefer drawImage() to putImageData().*
- *On average, drawing a canvas is on par with drawing an image.*

Here's the setup code:

```
<canvas width=364 height=126 id="c1"></canvas>
<canvas width=364 height=126 id="c2"></canvas>
<img src='...'/>

<script>
   var c1 = document.getElementById('c1').getContext('2d');
   var c2 = document.getElementById('c2').getContext('2d');
   var c2_c = document.getElementById('c2');
   var img = document.getElementById('imgd');
   c1.drawImage(img, 0, 0);
   var imgData = c1.getImageData(0, 0, parseInt(img.width),
                                       parseInt(img.height));

   function execute(drawMethod) {
      for(var i=0; i< 100; i++) {
         drawMethod(i);
      }
   }
</script>
```

The test creates a couple of canvases and an image, draws the image in one of the canvases, and gets a reference to the corresponding image data. The setup code also implements a function that calls one of three test methods.

The test cases and results are shown in Figure 4.20.

| | Test | Ops/sec |
|---|---|---|
| **DrawImage** | ```function d(i) {    c1.drawImage(img, 0, 0); } execute(d)``` | ready |
| **PutPixel** | ```function p(i) {    c2.putImageData(imgData, 0, 0); } execute(p)``` | ready |
| **DrawImage(canvas)** | ```function p(i) {    c1.drawImage(c2_c, 0, 0); } execute(p)``` | ready |

**Compare results of other browsers**

# Browserscope

| UserAgent | DrawImage | DrawImage canvas | PutPixel | # Tests |
|---|---|---|---|---|
| Chrome 11.0.696 | 146 | 141 | 33 | 1 |
| Chrome 12.0.742 | 193 | 198 | 37 | 12 |
| Chrome 13.0.782 | 237 | 247 | 37 | 4 |
| Chrome 14.0.791 | 99 | 143 | 109 | 1 |
| *Chrome 14.0.814* | 92 | 141 | 104 | 2 |
| Firefox 5.0 | 533 | 537 | 16 | 8 |
| iPad 4.3 | 148 | 143 | 18 | 6 |
| iPad 4.3.3 | 22 | 16 | 18 | 2 |
| Opera 11.50 | 224 | 137 | 50 | 1 |
| Safari | 29 | 16 | 2 | 1 |

Browserscope thinks you are using **Chrome 14.0.814** No?

Figure 4.20 `drawImage(HTMLImage)` vs. `drawImage(HTMLCanvas)` vs. `putImageData()`; higher numbers indicate better performance

As you can see from the test cases, `putImageData()` is almost always slower than `drawImage()`, often in a big way. In general then, it's best to prefer the former over the latter, all other things being equal.

### 4.9.2 Drawing a Canvas vs. Drawing an Image, into a Canvas; Scaled vs. Unscaled

In Section 4.3, "Drawing a Canvas into a Canvas," on p. 266 you saw how to draw a canvas into itself, scaling the canvas's image along the way. As it turns out, drawing a canvas into itself is expensive, and scaling the canvas's image along the way is even more expensive.

- *Drawing a canvas into itself is expensive.*
- *Scaling a canvas can be expensive.*

Here's the setup for this simple test:

```
<script>
    var c = document.createElement('canvas');
    c.width = 256;
    c.height = 256;

    var ctx = c.getContext('2d');
    ctx.clearRect(0, 0, c.width, c.height);

    var img = new Image(),
        img.src = c.toDataURL();
</script>
```

| | Test | Ops/sec |
|---|---|---|
| **Copy, unscaled** | ctx.drawImage(ctx.canvas, 0, 0); | ready |
| **Copy, scaled** | ctx.drawImage(ctx.canvas, 0, 0, ctx.canvas.width*2, ctx.canvas.height*2); | ready |
| **Draw image** | ctx.drawImage(img, 0, 0); | ready |

You can edit these tests or add even more tests to this page by appending /edit to the URL.

Compare results of other browsers

♟ Browserscope

| UserAgent | Copy scaled | Copy unscaled | Draw image | # Tests |
|---|---|---|---|---|
| *Chrome 14.0.814* | 292 | 1,270 | 8,863 | 1 |
| Firefox 5.0.1 | 352 | 660 | 12,292 | 1 |
| iPad 4.3.2 | 180 | 639 | 1,427 | 1 |
| Safari 5.0.1 | 380 | 772 | 11,641 | 1 |

Browserscope thinks you are using **Chrome 14.0.814** No?

Figure 4.21 Drawing a canvas into itself; higher numbers translate to better performance

The setup code creates a canvas and clears part of it with clear black. Then the code creates an image and sets the image's source to the image from the canvas.

The test cases are shown in Figure 4.21.

### 4.9.3 Looping over Image Data

Image manipulation, by its very nature, is performance intensive. Looping through an array that can contain a huge amount of data is an expensive operation. Fortunately, there are some things you can do to increase performance when you manipulate image data in a canvas:

- *Avoid accessing object properties in the loop: Store properties in local variables instead.*
- *Loop over every pixel, not every pixel value.*
- *Looping backwards and bit-shifting are crap shoots.*
- *Don't call getImageData() repeatedly for small amounts of data.*

Let's take a look at a jsPerf test that benchmarks various ways to loop through image data. First, the setup code:

```
var canvas = document.createElement('canvas');
canvas.width = 256;
canvas.height = 256;

var ctx = canvas.getContext('2d');
ctx.fillRect(0, 0, 256, 256);

var id = ctx.getImageData(0, 0, 256, 256);
var pixels = id.data;
var length = pixels.length;
var width = id.width;
var height = id.height;
```

The preceding code creates a canvas element, sets the canvas's width and height, and fills the canvas with clear black. The code subsequently uses getImageData() to get a reference to the canvas's image data. Finally, the code stores image data parameters, such as the length and width of the image data array, into local variables.

Figure 4.22 and Figure 4.23 show the various test cases.

#### 4.9.3.1 Avoid Accessing Object Properties in the Loop: Store Properties in Local Variables Instead

The first four test cases in Figure 4.22 contrast repeatedly accessing image data properties, such as width and height, versus storing those values in local variables.

| Test | | Ops/sec |
|---|---|---|
| property accesses 2d | ```for (var y = 0; y < id.height; y++) {```<br>```  for (var x = 0; x < id.width; x++) {```<br>```    var off = (y * id.width + x) * 4;```<br>```    id.data[off] += 10;```<br>```    id.data[off + 1] += 20;```<br>```    id.data[off + 2] += 30;```<br>```    id.data[off + 3] += 40;```<br>```  }```<br>```}``` | ready |
| property accesses 1d | ```for (var i = 0; i < id.data.length; i += 4) {```<br>```  id.data[i] += 10;```<br>```  id.data[i + 1] += 20;```<br>```  id.data[i + 2] += 30;```<br>```  id.data[i + 3] += 40;```<br>```}``` | ready |
| local variables 2d | ```for (var y = 0; y < height; y++) {```<br>```  for (var x = 0; x < width; x++) {```<br>```    var off = (y * width + x) * 4;```<br>```    pixels[off] += 10;```<br>```    pixels[off + 1] += 20;```<br>```    pixels[off + 2] += 30;```<br>```    pixels[off + 3] += 40;```<br>```  }```<br>```}``` | ready |
| local variables 1d | ```for (var i = 0; i < length; i += 4) {```<br>```  pixels[i] += 10;```<br>```  pixels[i + 1] += 20;```<br>```  pixels[i + 2] += 30;```<br>```  pixels[i + 3] += 40;```<br>```}``` | ready |
| local variables 1d<br>hack one | ```for (var i = -1; i < length;) {```<br>```  pixels[++i] += 10;```<br>```  pixels[++i] += 20;```<br>```  pixels[++i] += 30;```<br>```  pixels[++i] += 40;```<br>```}``` | ready |
| local variables 1d<br>hack two | ```var i = -1;```<br>```while (i < length) {```<br>```  pixels[++i] += 10;```<br>```  pixels[++i] += 20;```<br>```  pixels[++i] += 30;```<br>```  pixels[++i] += 40;```<br>```}``` | ready |
| local variables 1d<br>hack three | ```var i = length;```<br>```while (i >= 0) {```<br>```  pixels[--i] += 40;```<br>```  pixels[--i] += 30;```<br>```  pixels[--i] += 20;```<br>```  pixels[--i] += 10;```<br>```}``` | ready |

Figure 4.22  Looping over image data (http://bit.ly/novcmK)

| | | |
|---|---|---|
| local variables 2d cache-unfriendly | ```for (var x = 0; x < width; x++) {
  for (var y = 0; y < height; y++) {
    var off = (y * width + x) * 4;
    pixels[off]     += 10;
    pixels[off + 1] += 20;
    pixels[off + 2] += 30;
    pixels[off + 3] += 40;
  }
}``` | ready |
| local variables 1d hack four | ```for (var i = 0; i < length;) {
  pixels[i++] += 10;
  pixels[i++] += 20;
  pixels[i++] += 30;
  pixels[i++] += 40;
}``` | ready |
| local variables 2d w/ bit-shifts | ```for (var y = 0; y < height; y++) {
  for (var x = 0; x < width; x++) {
    var off = (((y << 8) + x) << 2);
    pixels[off]     += 10;
    pixels[off + 1] += 20;
    pixels[off + 2] += 30;
    pixels[off + 3] += 40;
  }
}``` | ready |
| multiple getImageData calls | ```for (var y = 0; y < height; y++) {
  for (var x = 0; x < width; x++) {
    var pixel = ctx.getImageData(x, y, 1, 1).data;
    pixel[0] += 10;
    pixel[1] += 20;
    pixel[2] += 30;
    pixel[3] += 40;
  }
}``` | ready |

**Compare results of other browsers**

## ≗Browserscope

| UserAgent | local variables 1d | local variables 1d hack four | local variables 1d hack one | local variables 1d hack three | local variables 1d hack two | local variables 2d | local variables 2d cache unfriendly | local variables 2d w bit shifts | multiple getImageData calls | property accesses 1d | property accesses 2d | # Tests |
|---|---|---|---|---|---|---|---|---|---|---|---|---|
| Chrome 12.0.742 | 1,443 | 51 | 276 | 28 | 277 | 1,279 | 50 | 50 | 1 | 1,451 | 196 | |
| Chrome 13.0.782 | 1,968 | 500 | 55 | 27 | 55 | 1,687 | 467 | 485 | 2 | 1,962 | 205 | |
| *Chrome 14.0.814* | 1,452 | 840 | 45 | 44 | 44 | 1,311 | 677 | 860 | 2 | 1,501 | 201 | |
| Firefox 5.0 | 512 | 740 | 335 | 336 | 335 | 589 | 545 | 656 | | 568 | 565 | |
| iPad 4.3.3 | 13 | 12 | 14 | 19 | 13 | 18 | 17 | 18 | 1 | 17 | 14 | |
| Safari 5.0.5 | 86 | 84 | 83 | 122 | 84 | 116 | 112 | 117 | 10 | 111 | 93 | |

Browserscope thinks you are using **Chrome 14.0.814** No?

Figure 4.23  Looping over image data statistics; higher numbers indicate better performance

They also show the difference between looping over the image data with one loop versus two.

If you loop over the image data in one loop, it makes no difference whether you access properties or store them in local variables. If you loop over the data in two loops, however, local variables are much faster than properties. As a result, it appears that storing properties in local variables is a good strategy.

### 4.9.3.2  Loop over Every Pixel, Not over Every Pixel Value

Recall that image data for each pixel is represented by four 8-bit integer values, one each for the red, green, blue, and alpha components of the pixel, ranging from 0 to 255. Also recall that browsers may represent each pixel with multiple pixel values for higher image fidelity.

If you loop over every one of those values, you are looping four times more than you need to. It's better to loop over pixel boundaries, instead of the individual pixel components; that's why you see the number 4 in several of the test cases.

You might suspect that looping four times more than necessary will significantly degrade performance, and you would be correct. The results of the tests shown in Figure 4.23 validate that performance degradation, with the exception of iPad and Safari.

The test cases `local variables 1d` and `local variables 1d hack one` in Figure 4.22 contrast looping over every pixel (`local variables 1d`) vs. looping over every pixel component (`local variables 1d hack one`). Notice that looping over every pixel is, in general, faster, sometimes considerably so.

### 4.9.3.3  Looping Backwards and Bit-Shifting Are Crap Shoots

The prevailing conventional wisdom concerning looping through arrays in JavaScript is to loop backwards, and to use bit-shifting to calculate array offsets. The tests in Figure 4.23 indicate that bit-shifting makes no significant difference and that looping backwards can, in some cases significantly, degrade performance. Looping backwards (test case `local variables 1d hack three`) is astoundingly slow on Chrome, makes no difference on Firefox, and is a little faster than looping forward (test case `local variables 1d hack one`) on Safari and iPad. In other words, a crap shoot.

Before you loop backwards or use bit-shifting, it's a good idea to do some benchmarking of your own. Hopefully, you will always have better opportunities to increase performance other than restoring to looping backwards and using bit-shifting.

### 4.9.3.4 Don't Call `getImageData()` Repeatedly for Small Amounts of Data

Instead of calling `getImageData()` once to get all of the pixels in an image, the last test case in Figure 4.23 calls `getImageData()` repeatedly to access each pixel in the image data array.

Although it's risky to make dogmatic statements about performance, it's probably safe to assume that `getImageData()` is relatively expensive, and that calling it once for every pixel in an image data array is a strategy that you should avoid at all costs.

## 4.10 A Magnifying Glass

Figure 4.24 shows the magnifying glass application that was introduced at the beginning of this chapter. You can drag the magnifying glass to magnify different parts of the image, and you can change the size of the magnifying glass lens and the magnification scale with the sliders at the top of the application.

Figure 4.24 A magnifying glass

Here's how the magnifying glass works:

As the user drags the mouse, the application captures the pixels of the smallest rectangle that encloses the magnifying glass lens.

Then the application sets the clipping region to the magnifying glass lens and draws the canvas into itself, scaling the canvas pixels along the way with the nine-argument version of drawImage().

Besides drawing the magnified pixels in the magnifying glass, the application also erases the magnifying glass as the user drags it around the canvas. Every time the mouse moves while the user is dragging the magnifying glass, the application calls putImageData() to restore the background that the application saved with getImageData() the last time the user moved the mouse.

So every time the user moves the mouse while dragging the magnifying glass, the application performs the following steps:

1. Call putImageData() to restore the background at the previous magnifying glass location.
2. Call getImageData() to save pixels underneath the glass at its new location.
3. Set the clipping region to the magnifying glass lens.
4. Call drawImage() to draw the magnified pixels back into the canvas.
5. Draw the magnifying glass lens.

Here's the application's mouse move event handler:

```
canvas.onmousemove = function (e) {
   if (dragging) {
      eraseMagnifyingGlass();
      drawMagnifyingGlass(windowToCanvas(e.clientX, e.clientY));
   }
};
```

The eraseMagnifyingGlass() method performs the first step listed above.

```
function eraseMagnifyingGlass() { // Called when the mouse moves
   if (imageData != null) {
      context.putImageData(imageData,
         magnifyRectangle.x, magnifyRectangle.y);
   }
}
```

The first time the application calls eraseMagnifyingGlass(), there's nothing to erase; thus, the check for imageData != null; otherwise, the application calls putImageData() to erase the previous drawing of the magnifying glass.

After erasing the magnifying glass, the application's mouse move event handler invokes drawMagnifyingGlass(), which is implemented like this:

```
function drawMagnifyingGlass(mouse) {
   var scaledMagnifyRectangle = null;

   magnifyingGlassX = mouse.x;
   magnifyingGlassY = mouse.y;

   calculateMagnifyRectangle(mouse);

   imageData = context.getImageData(magnifyRectangle.x,
                                    magnifyRectangle.y,
                                    magnifyRectangle.width,
                                    magnifyRectangle.height);
   context.save();

   scaledMagnifyRectangle = {
      width:  magnifyRectangle.width  * magnificationScale,
      height: magnifyRectangle.height * magnificationScale
   };

   setClip();

   context.drawImage(canvas,
      magnifyRectangle.x, magnifyRectangle.y,
      magnifyRectangle.width, magnifyRectangle.height,

      magnifyRectangle.x + magnifyRectangle.width/2 -
         scaledMagnifyRectangle.width/2,

      magnifyRectangle.y + magnifyRectangle.height/2 -
         scaledMagnifyRectangle.height/2,

      scaledMagnifyRectangle.width,
      scaledMagnifyRectangle.height);

   context.restore();

   drawMagnifyingGlassCircle(mouse);
}

function setClip() {
   context.beginPath();
   context.arc(magnifyingGlassX, magnifyingGlassY,
               magnifyingGlassRadius, 0, Math.PI*2, false);

   context.clip();
}
```

The drawMagnifyingGlass() function calculates the smallest rectangle enclosing
the magnifying glass at its new location and captures the pixels for that rectangle
so that the application can erase the magnifying glass.

Then the application calculates the scaled width and height for the magnified pixels and sets the clipping region to the magnifying glass lens.

Finally, `drawMagnifyingGlass()` draws the canvas into itself, scaling pixels along the way. Figure 4.25 illustrates how the call to `drawImage()` works.

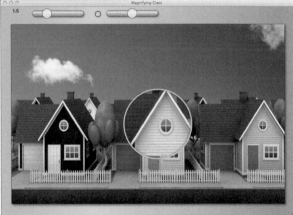

Figure 4.25   Copying magnified pixels to the magnifying glass lens. *Top:* unclipped; *bottom:* clipped

The top screenshot in Figure 4.25 was taken with the call to `setClip()` commented out. Without setting the clipping region, you can see all of the magnified pixels drawn by the call to `drawImage()` in `drawMagnifyingGlass()`.

The bottom screenshot shows the application with the call to setClip() restored. With clipping, the magnified pixels are restricted to the inside of the magnifying glass lens.

---

**NOTE: The magnifying glass application's sliders**

The magnifying glass application places sliders at the top of the page so that you can change the magnification scale and the size of the magnifying glass lens. Those sliders are custom controls, implemented in a canvas of their own, and they are discussed in Chapter 10.

---

## 4.10.1 Using an Offscreen Canvas

The magnifying glass implementation discussed in Section 4.10, "A Magnifying Glass," on p. 321 draws a canvas into itself, scaling along the way. Alternatively, you can use an offscreen canvas to scale the pixels, and subsequently draw from that offscreen canvas back into the onscreen canvas, as illustrated in Example 4.21.

---

**Example 4.21** Using offscreen canvases

```
var ...
    offscreenCanvas = document.createElement('canvas'),
    offscreenContext = offscreenCanvas.getContext('2d');
...

function drawMagnifyingGlass(mouse) {
   var scaledMagnifyRectangle = null;

   magnifyingGlassX = mouse.x;
   magnifyingGlassY = mouse.y;

   calculateMagnifyRectangle(mouse);

   imageData = context.getImageData(magnifyRectangle.x,
                                    magnifyRectangle.y,
                                    magnifyRectangle.width,
                                    magnifyRectangle.height);
   context.save();

   scaledMagnifyRectangle = {
      width:  magnifyRectangle.width  * magnificationScale,
      height: magnifyRectangle.height * magnificationScale
   };

   setClip();
```

---

*(Continues)*

---

**Example 4.21**  *(Continued)*

```
offscreenContext.drawImage(canvas,
   magnifyRectangle.x, magnifyRectangle.y,
   magnifyRectangle.width, magnifyRectangle.height,
   0, 0,
   scaledMagnifyRectangle.width,
   scaledMagnifyRectangle.height);

context.drawImage(offscreenCanvas, 0, 0,
   scaledMagnifyRectangle.width,
   scaledMagnifyRectangle.height,

   magnifyRectangle.x + magnifyRectangle.width/2 -
      scaledMagnifyRectangle.width/2,

   magnifyRectangle.y + magnifyRectangle.height/2 -
      scaledMagnifyRectangle.height/2,

   scaledMagnifyRectangle.width,
   scaledMagnifyRectangle.height);

context.restore();

drawMagnifyingGlassCircle(mouse);
}
```

---

For the magnifying glass application, drawing the canvas into itself rather than using an offscreen canvas resulted in slightly better performance.

## 4.10.2  Accepting Dropped Images from the File System

The magnifying glass application uses the HTML5 Drag and Drop and FileSystem APIs, so you can drag an image from your desktop and drop it onto the application. Figure 4.26 shows the application accepting an image that a user dragged from the desktop and dropped on the application. When the user drops the image, the application responds by displaying the image, as shown in the bottom screenshot in Figure 4.26.

At the time this book was written, Chrome was the only browser that supported the FileSystem API. Example 4.22 shows how the magnifying glass application uses that API.

The magnifying glass application implements drag enter and drag over event listeners to prevent the browser from its default reaction to dragging and to indicate that drops are allowed.

**Figure 4.26** *Top:* user drops image (note drag-and-drop icon in the upper-right corner); *bottom:* app displays dropped image

The application also has a drop listener that uses the FileSystem API to request 5 MB of disk space on the file system. The application then creates an image file and sets the image element's `src` attribute to a URL obtained from the file system.

**Example 4.22** Using the FileSystem API

```
canvas.addEventListener('dragenter', function (e) {
    e.preventDefault();
    e.dataTransfer.effectAllowed = 'copy';
}, false);

canvas.addEventListener('dragover', function (e) {
    e.preventDefault();
}, false);

window.requestFileSystem =
        window.requestFileSystem || window.webkitRequestFileSystem;
```

*(Continues)*

Example 4.22 *(Continued)*

```
canvas.addEventListener('drop', function (e) {
    var file = e.dataTransfer.files[0];

    window.requestFileSystem(window.TEMPORARY, 5*1024*1024,
        function (fs) {
            fs.root.getFile(file.name, {create: true},
                function (fileEntry) {
                    fileEntry.createWriter( function (writer) {
                        writer.write(file);
                    });
                    image.src = fileEntry.toURL();
                },

                function (e) {
                    alert(e.code);
                }
            );
        },

        function (e) {
            alert(e.code);
        }
    );
}, false);
```

## 4.11 Video Processing

Videos are big business. In 2006, Google acquired YouTube for $1.65 billion, and today according to Google, YouTube accounts for more than 20 percent of Internet traffic worldwide. Once almost exclusively the realm of Flash, the landscape of video on the web has tilted drastically toward HTML5.

HTML5 provides a video element that lets you play and control videos. And the Canvas API lets you process videos, frame by frame, as the video plays.

Recall from Section 4.1.2, "The drawImage() Method," on p. 257 that besides drawing images, drawImage() can draw a video frame into a canvas, like this:

```
var video = document.getElementById('video'); // A <video> element
...

context.drawImage(video, 0, 0); // Draw video frame
```

The video argument to drawImage() in the preceding code listing is an HTMLVideoElement. Once you can draw a video frame into a canvas, you can combine animation with the video and canvas elements to do video processing on the fly. Section 4.11.3, "Processing Videos," on p. 333 shows how to do that.

## 4.11.1 Video Formats

As this book went to press, three video formats were in widespread use, as shown in Table 4.3.

**Table 4.3** Browser support for video formats

| Format | First Supported in |
| --- | --- |
| H.264 (MPEG-4) | IE9.0, Chrome 3.0 (to be removed), Safari 3.1 |
| Ogg Theora | Firefox 3.5, Chrome 3.0, Opera 10.5 |
| VP8 (WebM) | Firefox 4.0, Chrome 6.0, Opera 10.6 |

Notice that none of the three formats are supported by all major browsers. Because of that restriction, you must specify multiple formats to ensure that your videos run on all platforms. You can do that by embedding source elements in video elements, like this:

```
<video>
    <source src='video.ogg'/>
    <source src='video.mp4'/>
</video>
```

**NOTE: A short history of video formats**

The HTML5 specification originally required the Ogg Theora format for video because it was freely available and open source and because the specification's authors believed it was better to specify a single format rather than many. Mozilla and Opera are big supporters of Ogg Theora.

However, some companies, such as Apple and Nokia, were concerned about patent issues (see the note below), and Apple didn't think it was a good idea to directly specify a video format in the specification.

As a result, the specification was rewritten, and the requirement for Ogg Theora removed.

Subsequently, in 2010, Google acquired On2's VP8 format and released the software under an irrevocable free patent, BSD-like license. In January 2011, Google announced that it would end native support for MPEG-4 in Chrome.

**NOTE: Submarine patents and patent ambushes**

Until 1995, US patent terms were measured from the date of issuance, instead of from the original filing date. Although it was somewhat expensive, one could file for a patent, and file a succession of continuation applications to delay the patent's issuance. Such patents are known as *submarine patents*.

Subsequently, when a wealthy corporation violates a submarine patent, whoever filed the patent originally stops filing continuations, the patent is issued, and the patent holder sues the unsuspecting corporation, presumably for a large payoff.

Submarine patents are just one aspect of the arcane world of software patents. Another strategy is a *patent ambush*, where someone who's company is about to file a patent joins a software standards body and influences the standard to violate the patent.

*Even though no known patents* violate the free and open source Ogg format, both Apple and Nokia objected to Ogg, partially because of concerns for submarine patents and patent ambushes.

## 4.11.1.1  Converting Formats

Because none of the three most widely used video formats are used by all major browsers, you must provide multiple formats of all your videos to ensure portability across all platforms. Because of that requirement, sooner or later you will need to convert videos from one format to another.

There are many ways to convert videos from one format to another. Figure 4.27 shows a Firefox extension that does just that.

Figure 4.27  Converting formats

## 4.11.2  Playing Video in a Canvas

Ultimately our goal in exploring Canvas's video support is to implement on-the-fly video processing. The first step is to simply play a video in a canvas. Figure 4.28 shows an application that draws frames from an *invisible* video element into a *visible* canvas element, scaling each video frame to fit the canvas.

Figure 4.28  Playing a video in a canvas

The HTML for the application shown in Figure 4.28 is listed in Example 4.23.

Notice the CSS for the video element in the listing. The video's display attribute makes it invisible.

The application plays the invisible video and in an animation loop—implemented with the requestNextAnimationFrame() polyfill function discussed in Section 5.1.3, "A Portable Animation Loop," on p. 348—continually draws the current video frame into the canvas. As a result, the video plays in the canvas. The application's JavaScript is listed in Example 4.24.

When the video loads, the code plays the video and initiates the animation loop by calling requestNextAnimationFrame(). When the browser is ready to draw the next animation frame, it invokes the `animate()` function, which—if the video is still playing—draws the current video frame into the canvas and perpetuates the animation by again invoking `requestNextAnimationFrame()`. If the video has ended, the `animate()` function does not invoke `requestNextAnimationFrame()`, and thus ends the animation.

**Example 4.23** Playing video: HTML

```
<!DOCTYPE html>
   <head>
     <title>Video</title>

      <style>
         body {
            background: #dddddd;
         }

         #canvas {
            background: #ffffff;
            border: thin solid darkgray;
         }

         #video {
            display: none;
         }
      </style>
   </head>

  <body>
    <video id='video' poster>
      <source src='dog-stealing.mp4'/>
      <source src='dog-stealing.ogg'/>
    </video>

    <canvas id='canvas' width='720' height='405'>
      Canvas not supported
    </canvas>

    <script src='requestNextAnimationFrame.js'></script>
    <script src='example.js'></script>
  </body>
</html>
```

Notice that the code uses the five-argument version of `drawImage()`, discussed in Section 4.1.2, "The `drawImage()` Method," on p. 257, to scale the video to fit the canvas.

---

Example 4.24  Playing video: The JavaScript

---

```
var canvas = document.getElementById('canvas'),
    context = canvas.getContext('2d'),
    video = document.getElementById('video');

function animate() {
   if (!video.ended) {
     context.drawImage(video, 0, 0, canvas.width, canvas.height);
     window.requestNextAnimationFrame(animate);
   }
}

video.onload = function (e) {
   video.play();
   window.requestNextAnimationFrame(animate);
};
```

---

Now that we can capture each frame of a video and display it in a canvas, let's see how we can process frames before displaying them.

## 4.11.3  Processing Videos

The application shown in Figure 4.29, like the application discussed in the preceding section, displays frames from an invisible video element in a visible canvas element. Additionally, the application shown in Figure 4.29 optionally processes each video frame before displaying it in the canvas.

The application provides two checkboxes to control the video's color and orientation and lets the user start the video with the Play button.

The HTML for the application shown in Figure 4.29 is listed in Example 4.25.

The application's JavaScript, which is listed in Example 4.26, implements the animation that continuously draws frames from the invisible video element into the visible canvas element.

The nextVideoFrame() function, which the browser invokes when it's ready to draw the next animation frame, is where all the action takes place. If the video has ended, that function simply replaces the text of the button to Play, and the method does not invoke requestNextAnimationFrame() to perpetuate the animation.

If the video has not ended, nextVideoFrame() draws the current video frame into an offscreen canvas, and optionally removes the color and flips the orientation of the frame before drawing the frame into the onscreen canvas.

---

Example 4.25 Video controls: HTML

---

```html
<!DOCTYPE html>
  <head>
    <title>Video</title>

    <style>
       body {
          background: #dddddd;
       }

       .floatingControls {
          position: absolute;
          left: 175px;
          top: 300px;
       }

       #canvas {
          background: #ffffff;
          border: thin solid #aaaaaa;
       }

       #video {
          display: none;
       }
    </style>
  </head>

  <body>
    <video id='video' controls src='dog-stealing.mp4'></video>

    <canvas id='canvas' width='480' height='270'>
      Canvas not supported
    </canvas>

    <div id='controls' class='floatingControls'>
       <input id='controlButton' type='button' value='Play'/>
       <input id='colorCheckbox' type='checkbox' checked> Color
       <input id='flipCheckbox' type='checkbox'> Flip
    </div>

    <script src='requestNextAnimationFrame.js'></script>
    <script src='example.js'></script>
  </body>
</html>
```

---

Figure 4.29  Processing video

Example 4.26  Video controls: JavaScript

```javascript
var canvas = document.getElementById('canvas'),
    offscreenCanvas = document.createElement('canvas'),
    offscreenContext = offscreenCanvas.getContext('2d'),
    context = canvas.getContext('2d'),
    video = document.getElementById('video'),
    controlButton = document.getElementById('controlButton'),
    flipCheckbox = document.getElementById('flipCheckbox'),
    colorCheckbox = document.getElementById('colorCheckbox'),
    imageData,
    poster = new Image();

// Functions.........................................................
```

(Continues)

---

**Example 4.26**  *(Continued)*

---

```javascript
function removeColor() {
   var data,
       width,
       average;

   imageData = offscreenContext.getImageData(0, 0,
                   offscreenCanvas.width, offscreenCanvas.height);
   data = imageData.data;
   width = data.width;

   for (i=0; i < data.length-4; i += 4) {
      average = (data[i] + data[i+1] + data[i+2]) / 3;
      data[i]   = average;
      data[i+1] = average;
      data[i+2] = average;
   }

   offscreenContext.putImageData(imageData, 0, 0);
}

function drawFlipped() {
   context.save();

   context.translate(canvas.width/2, canvas.height/2);
   context.rotate(Math.PI);
   context.translate(-canvas.width/2, -canvas.height/2);
   context.drawImage(offscreenCanvas, 0, 0);

   context.restore();
}

function nextVideoFrame() {
   if (video.ended) {
      controlButton.value = 'Play';
   }
   else {
      offscreenContext.drawImage(video, 0, 0);

      if (!colorCheckbox.checked)
         removeColor();

      if (flipCheckbox.checked)
         drawFlipped();
      else
         context.drawImage(offscreenCanvas, 0, 0);

      requestNextAnimationFrame(nextVideoFrame);
   }
}
```

```
function startPlaying() {
   requestNextAnimationFrame(nextVideoFrame);
   video.play();
}

function stopPlaying() {
   video.pause();
}

// Event handlers......................................................

controlButton.onclick = function(e) {
   if (controlButton.value === 'Play') {
      startPlaying();
      controlButton.value = 'Pause';
   }
   else {
      stopPlaying();
      controlButton.value = 'Play';
   }
};

poster.onload = function() {
   context.drawImage(poster, 0, 0);
};

// Initialization......................................................

poster.src = 'dog-stealing-poster.png';

offscreenCanvas.width = canvas.width;
offscreenCanvas.height = canvas.height;
```

## 4.12 Conclusion

The Canvas API packs a lot of functionality into four Canvas context methods: drawImage(), which lets you draw into a canvas other canvases or video frames in addition to images; getImageData(), which lets you grab a rectangle of pixels from a canvas; putImageData(), which lets you insert a rectangle of pixels into a canvas; and createImageData(), which lets you create a blank array of pixel color values.

With those four methods, you can implement sophisticated image manipulation such as image filters and magnifying glasses.

In this chapter you saw how to draw and scale images, implement image filters, and process images in offscreen canvases and with web workers. Additionally, you learned how to combine image manipulation with other aspects of HTML5 Canvas, such as clipping and the Canvas drawing API, and how to combine image manipulation with other aspects of HTML5 outside of Canvas, such as web workers. By encapsulating image filters in a web worker, you can offload work from the main browser UI thread, and you can reuse those web workers in multiple contexts. And you also learned some performance tips for drawing and manipulating images.

Then we looked at the implementation of a magnifying glass that used a great deal of what we covered in this chapter. The application also illustrated how you can use the Drag and Drop and FileSystem APIs to accept dropped images that the user dragged from the desktop.

Finally, we looked at processing videos by using `video` and `canvas` elements together, along with some animation and the `drawImage()` method.

In the next chapter we see how to put images and drawings into motion with an exploration of Canvas animation.

# Animation

Human beings are drawn to animation. Our visual apparatus continuously processes a never-ending animation that we call reality, so animations are a natural and intuitive communication medium.

Animations are also big business. From advertisements to video games, animations play a huge role in money-changing hands. Not only that, but implementing animations is about as much fun as you're going to have writing software.

Flash-based animations have dominated the web; however, that landscape is rapidly changing, and the new upstart that is unseating Flash is HTML5 Canvas. So it may surprise you to hear that Canvas has no explicit support for animation. Canvas provides the underlying graphics horsepower necessary to create animation frames, but the animation loop itself is specified in another W3C specification. In this chapter we look at how to incorporate that animation loop with the Canvas graphics API.

The first section of this chapter, "The Animation Loop," on p. 340, discusses the various options for implementing animation loops, from old-school `window.setTimeout()` to the newer and far more capable `window.request-AnimationFrame()`. That section culminates in Section 5.1.3, "A Portable Animation Loop," on p. 348, by implementing a portable solution that uses `window.requestAnimationFrame()`.

After discussing the animation loop, this chapter concentrates on implementing smooth animations. You'll see the different options for repairing damage to the background and the performance ramifications of those options. You'll also see how to implement time-based motion, how to scroll backgrounds, and how to simulate three dimensions with parallax.

## 5.1 The Animation Loop

Fundamentally, implementing animations with Canvas is simple: You continuously update and draw whatever you are animating. For example, the application shown in Figure 5.1 continuously animates three discs.

Figure 5.1  Basic animation

That continuous updating and redrawing is referred to as the animation loop, and it's central to every animation. Let's see how it works.

Animations are continuous loops, but it's not possible to implement a continuous loop, at least not in the traditional sense, in JavaScript running in a browser. For instance, Example 5.1 is valid JavaScript, but it will lock up any respectable browser.

The while loop in Example 5.1 is an endless loop. Because browsers run JavaScript on the main thread, that endless loop will lock up the browser, including the animation. Instead, you must let the browser breathe, by periodically giving it control for short amounts of time.

Example 5.1  Locking up the browser: Do not do this

```
function animate() {
    // Update and draw animation objects
}

while(true) { // Locks up the browser: don't do this
    animate();
}
```

One way to let the browser breathe is with either window.setInterval() or window.setTimeout() as shown in Examples 5.2 and 5.3, respectively.

Example 5.2  Using setInterval() in an animation loop

```
function animate() {
    // Update and draw animation objects
}
...

// Start the animation at 60 frames/second

setInterval(animate, 1000 / 60);
```

Example 5.3  Using setTimeout() in an animation loop

```
// Approximating setInterval() with setTimeout()

function animate() {
    var start = +new Date(),
        finish;

    // Update and draw animation objects

    finish = +new Date();

    setTimeout(animate, (1000 / 60) - (finish - start));
}
...

animate(); // Start the animation
```

The `setInterval()` method repeatedly invokes a method at a specific interval, whereas `setTimeout()` simply invokes a method once, at a specified time in the future. Because of that discrepancy between the two methods, you call `setInterval()` once, but you must call `setTimeout()` repeatedly. Notice that because `setTimeout()` forces you to explicitly tell the browser when to make the next call to your animation method, you must calculate the time of that call; on the other hand, for `setInterval()`, you simply specify the interval once.

The `setTimeout()` and `setInterval()` methods suffice for many purposes, but they were not made for animations. The preferred way to implement your animation loop is with a W3C standard method named `requestAnimationFrame()`, which we discuss next.

 **CAUTION: Do not use `window.setInterval()` or `window.setTimeout()` to implement animations**

It's important to understand that `window.setInterval()` and `window.setTimeout()` are not precise timing mechanisms for animation. Instead, they are general-purpose methods that let applications run some code at an approximate time in the future.

For example, according to the HTML5 specification, browsers can pad timeouts to optimize power usage. In browser lingo, it's known as *clamping* the timeout interval. And browsers do indeed clamp the interval. Firefox, for example, at the time this book was written, used a minimum of 10 ms for a single call to `setTimeout()` and a minimum of 5 ms for subsequent calls. So, for example, you can call `setTimeout()` with a timeout of 3 ms, but the browser may overrule that number, and make you wait 10 ms instead.

 **NOTE: You should not tell the browser when to draw the next animation frame: It should tell you**

When you call `setTimeout()` or `setInterval()` *you* specify the time, however imprecise it may be, that you want to draw the next animation frame.

However, you don't really know the best time to draw the next animation; most likely, you have no idea. The browser, on the other hand, can undoubtedly select the best time to draw the next animation frame better than you can.

So instead of telling the browser when you want to draw the next animation frame, as is the case with `setTimeout()` and `setInterval()`, it's much better to let the browser call you when it's ready to draw the next animation frame. You do that with `requestAnimationFrame()`.

### 5.1.1 The `requestAnimationFrame()` Method: Letting the Browser Set the Frame Rate

If you use `window.setInterval()` or `window.setTimeout()`, your animations may not be as smooth as you would like, and they may use more resources than necessary. That's because `setInterval()` and `setTimeout()`

- Are general-purpose methods; they were not meant for animations
- Are not millisecond-precise, despite your sending them millisecond values
- Do not optimize the manner in which they invoke your methods
- Blindly call your methods at approximate times, without regard to when it's best to animate

The fundamental problem with `window.setInterval()` and `window.setTimeout()` is that they are at the wrong level of abstraction. What we want from the browser is an *animation* API that takes care of mundane details such as optimal frame rates and choosing the best time to draw the next frame. Because `window.setInterval()` and `window.setTimeout()` know nothing about animation, those details are left to the developer.

Fortunately, the browser development community recognized the need for animation support and specified a method, `requestAnimationFrame()`, that you should use to drive your animations, as illustrated in Example 5.4.

---

**Example 5.4** Animating with `window.requestAnimationFrame()`

---

```
function animate(time) {
    // Update and draw animation objects

    requestAnimationFrame(animate); // Sustain the animation
}
...

requestAnimationFrame(animate); // Start the animation
```

---

To start an animation, you invoke `requestAnimationFrame()`, passing a reference to a function that the browser calls when it's time to draw the first animation frame. Typically, inside that function you will conditionally invoke `requestAnimationFrame()` again to keep the animation loop running.

Notice that unlike `window.setTimeout()` and `window.setInterval()`, `requestAnimationFrame()` does not let you specify a frame rate; instead, the browser selects the optimal frame rate.

The W3C also added a cancelRequestAnimationFrame() method that cancels a given callback. requestAnimationFrame() returns a long object that serves as a handle to the callback. Subsequently, you can pass that handle to cancelRequestAnimationFrame() to cancel the callback.

The requestAnimationFrame() and cancelRequestAnimationFrame() methods are summarized in Table 5.1.

---

 **CAUTION: Browser-specific implementations of requestAnimationFrame()**

The requestAnimationFrame() method is specified in a W3C specification named *Timing control for script-based animations*. See http://webstuff. nfshost.com/anim-timing/Overview.html.

At the time this book went to press, the specification was a relative newcomer in the fast moving world of HTML5 specifications, and so browsers supported only their own browser-specific implementations of requestAnimationFrame(), as shown in the following table.

| Browser | Method |
| --- | --- |
| Chrome 10 | window.webkitRequestAnimationFrame( FrameRequestCallback callback, Element element) |
| Firefox (Gecko) 4.0 (2.0) | window.mozkitRequestAnimationFrame( FrameRequestCallback callback) |
| Internet Explorer 10, Platform Preview 2 | window.msRequestAnimationFrame( FrameRequestCallback callback) |

Chrome and IE also provide methods to cancel the next animation frame—webkitCancelAnimationFrame() and msCancelAnimationFrame(), respectively. Firefox does not have a similar method.

Because support for the W3C's requestAnimationFrame() and cancel- RequestAnimationFrame() methods may not be universal when you use them, you should use a polyfill method instead of the standard methods directly. Section 5.1.3, "A Portable Animation Loop," on p. 348 discusses an implementation of that polyfill method.

---

**Table 5.1** The W3C's requestAnimationFrame() and cancelRequestAnimationFrame() methods

| Method | Description |
|---|---|
| `long window.requestAnimationFrame(FrameRequestCallback callback)` | Requests that the browser invoke the specified callback when it's time to draw the next animation frame. Returns a handle that you can pass to cancelRequestAnimationFrame(). |
| `void window.cancelRequestAnimationFrame(long handle)` | Lets you cancel a callback that you have previously registered with requestAnimationFrame(). You must call this method before the browser invokes your callback. |

**NOTE: requestAnimationFrame() and time**

Animations are typically time based, so requestAnimationFrame() passes the time—as the number of milliseconds since January 1, 1970—to your animation function.

**NOTE: Feel free to skip ahead**

If you're not interested in the history behind requestAnimationFrame() or details of the browser-specific implementations of that method, feel free to skip ahead to Section 5.1.3, "A Portable Animation Loop," on p. 348, where a polyfill method for requestAnimationFrame() is discussed.

### 5.1.1.1 Firefox

Firefox 4.0 had the first implementation of a browser-specific variant of requestAnimationFrame(): mozRequestAnimationFrame(). You use that method just like requestAnimationFrame(), as shown in Example 5.5.

**Example 5.5** Firefox callbacks

```
function animate(time) {
  // Update and draw animation objects

  window.mozRequestAnimationFrame(animate);
}

window.mozRequestAnimationFrame(animate);
```

Firefox's `mozRequestAnimationFrame()` method adheres to the following rules:

- Firefox calls the animation callback a maximum of 60 times per second.
- Firefox calls the animation callback once per second or less when the animation's tab is not visible.
- Firefox doesn't invoke callbacks faster than the page is rendering.

Like `requestAnimationFrame()`, Firefox passes to your animation callback method, the time at which your animation frame will be drawn.

**CAUTION: Firefox 4.0's `window.mozRequestAnimationFrame()` has a bug**

A bug in Firefox 4.0 restricts animation frame rates to around 30 or 40 frames per second for most animations, when you use `window.mozRequestAnimationFrame()`. That bug was addressed in Firefox 5.0. If you plan to support animations on Firefox 4.0, avoid using `mozRequestAnimationFrame()`.

The `mozRequestAnimationFrame()` method is described in Table 5.2.

**Table 5.2** Firefox's `mozRequestAnimationFrame()`

| Method | Description |
|---|---|
| `window.mozRequestAnimationFrame(FrameRequestCallback)` | Requests that the browser invoke the specified callback when it's time to draw the next animation frame. The callback argument is optional because Firefox gives you the option of specifying the callback by adding an event listener to the `window` object instead. |

### 5.1.1.2 Chrome

Chrome adopted the callback model invented by Firefox, naming its function `window.webkitRequestAnimationFrame()`. The use of that method is identical to Firefox's `window.mozRequestAnimationFrame()`, as shown by the code in Example 5.6.

The rules that Chrome follows for calling your animation callback are also nearly identical to Firefox:

- Chrome calls the animation callback a maximum of 60 times per second.

- Chrome does not invoke the callback unless the tab is visible.
- Chrome does not invoke callbacks faster than the page is rendering.

---

**Example 5.6** Chrome callbacks

```
function animate(time) {
    if (time == undefined)
        time = +new Date();

    // Update and draw animation objects

    window.webkitRequestAnimationFrame(animate);
}
...

window.webkitRequestAnimationFrame(animate);
```

---

The `webkitRequestAnimationFrame()` and `webkitCancelAnimationFrame()` methods are summarized in Table 5.3.

**Table 5.3** Chrome's `webkitRequestAnimationFrame()`

| Method | Description |
|--------|-------------|
| `long window.`<br>`webkitRequestAnimationFrame(`<br>`FrameRequestCallback callback,`<br>`optional Element element)` | Schedules a request to invoke the callback function when it's time to draw the next animation frame. Returns a handle that you can pass to `webkitCancelRequestAnimationFrame()` to cancel the next animation frame.<br><br>The optional `element` argument, which does not exist for the Firefox implementation, specifies the element performing the animation. If the element is not visible, Chrome will not invoke the callback. |
| `void window.`<br>`webkitCancelRequestAnimationFrame(`<br>`long handle)` | If you register a callback with `webkitRequestAnimationFrame()`, this method lets you subsequently cancel the callback, provided that you call this method before the browser invokes your callback. |

**NOTE: webkitRequestAnimationFrame() method's optional element argument**

The webkitRequestAnimationFrame() method takes an optional second argument that's a reference to an HTML element. When the element is not visible, webkitRequestAnimationFrame() will not invoke the animation callback. Typically, you pass a reference to the canvas in which your animation is running to webkitRequestAnimationFrame().

**CAUTION: Time bug in Chrome 10**

Like Firefox, Chrome also passes, to your animation callback method, the time at which your animation frame will be drawn. However, Chrome first provided support for webkitRequestAnimationFrame() in version 10, and that initial implementation did not pass the time to the animation callback method, so the time variable in your animation function will be undefined. In that case, you can assign the time yourself, as shown in Example 5.6.

## 5.1.2  Internet Explorer

Starting with Internet Explorer 10, Platform Preview 2, Microsoft provides msRequestAnimationFrame() and msCancelRequestAnimationFrame() methods that are similar to the W3C standard methods. You use msRequestAnimationFrame() as shown in Example 5.7.

**Example 5.7** Internet Explorer callbacks

```
function animate(time) {
    // Update and draw animation objects

    window.msRequestAnimationFrame(animate);
}
window.msRequestAnimationFrame(animate);
```

## 5.1.3  A Portable Animation Loop

As you saw in Section 5.1.1, "The requestAnimationFrame() Method: Letting the Browser Set the Frame Rate," on p. 343, the W3C defines a standard request-AnimationFrame() method that you can, and should, use to drive your animations.

However, until all the browsers that you support have implemented that method, you need a way to call the method as it exists but fall back to a default implementation when the method is not available.

Let's look at a portable solution that uses the W3C's implementation when it's available; otherwise, it falls back on a proprietary solution. And finally, if neither the W3C's implementation nor proprietary solutions are available, the portable solution falls back to an implementation that does its best to drive animations at 60 frames per second using setTimeout().

The portable solution is a method named window.requestNextAnimationFrame() (notice the addition of the word "Next" to the method name) that you use just like webkitRequestAnimationFrame(), mozRequestAnimationFrame(), and requestAnimationFrame():

```
function animate(time) {
    // Update and draw animation objects

    window.requestNextAnimationFrame(animate);
}

window.requestNextAnimationFrame(animate);
```

Here's a first attempt at implementing requestNextAnimationFrame():

```
window.requestNextAnimationFrame =
    (function () {
        return window.requestAnimationFrame      ||
            window.webkitRequestAnimationFrame ||
            window.mozRequestAnimationFrame    ||
            window.msRequestAnimationFrame     ||

        function (callback, element) { // Assume element is visible
            var self = this,
                start,
                finish;

            window.setTimeout( function () {
                start = +new Date();
                callback(start);
                finish = +new Date();

                self.timeout = 1000 / 60 - (finish - start);

            }, self.timeout);
        };
    }
)
();
```

The preceding code assigns a value to a requestNextAnimationFrame property of the window object. The value is a function that's returned from what's known in JavaScript as a self-executing function.

If the W3C standard methods or any of the proprietary implementations are available, the preceding code assigns `window.requestNextAnimationFrame()` to the standard or proprietary function.

If neither the W3C standard methods nor any of the proprietary implementations are supported, `code.requestNextAnimationFrame()` falls back to a function that uses `window.setTimeout()` to drive the animation at approximately 60 frames per second.

The preceding implementation of `window.requestNextAnimationFrame()` will work well under most conditions, but has two problems:

1. If your animation is running on Chrome 10, you will get an undefined object for the time in your `animate()` function. If you use time-based motion, discussed in Section 5.6, "Time-Based Motion," on p. 367, passing that undefined object to your `update()` will wreak havoc with your animation.

2. As mentioned previously in Section 5.1.1.1, "Firefox," on p. 345, Firefox 4.0's implementation of `window.mozRequestAnimationFrame()` has a bug that restricts frame rates for most animations to around 30 to 40 frames per second, which for most animations is unacceptably slow. If you're going to support Firefox 4.0, you will have to deal with that bug.

Example 5.8 shows a final version of `window.requestNextAnimationFrame()` that takes those two problems into account. If your animation is running on Chrome 10, the call to `window.webkitRequestAnimationFrame()` is wrapped in a function that makes sure that the callback function is passed a valid time. If your animation is running on Firefox 4.0, the code unplugs `window.mozRequestAnimationFrame()` and falls back to the `setTimeout()` implementation.

---

**NOTE: Polyfills**

The word polyfill is a portmanteau of *polymorphically backfill*. Like polymorphism in object-oriented languages, a polyfill conditionally executes code at runtime. Polyfills also backfill functionality into browsers that do not yet implement a particular specification. For example, the `requestNextAnimationFrame()` polyfill discussed in this section executes code at runtime that depends on the browser's support for `requestAnimationFrame()`, backfilling as needed with a `setTimeout()` implementation for browsers that do not support the *Timing control for script-based animations* specification.

Polyfills represent an important paradigm shift: Instead of programming to the lowest common denominator—a common strategy in the past for cross-platform software—polyfills let you access new advances when they are available, falling back to the lowest common denominator only when necessary.

---

Example 5.8 A requestAnimationFrame() polyfill

```
window.requestNextAnimationFrame =
    (function () {
        var originalWebkitMethod,
            wrapper = undefined,
            callback = undefined,
            geckoVersion = 0,
            userAgent = navigator.userAgent,
            index = 0,
            self = this;

        // Workaround for Chrome 10 bug where Chrome
        // does not pass the time to the animation function

        if (window.webkitRequestAnimationFrame) {
            // Define the wrapper

            wrapper = function (time) {
                if (time === undefined) {
                    time = +new Date();
                }
                self.callback(time);
            };

            // Make the switch

            originalWebkitMethod = window.webkitRequestAnimationFrame;

            window.webkitRequestAnimationFrame =
            function (callback, element) {
                self.callback = callback;

                // Browser calls wrapper; wrapper calls callback

                originalWebkitMethod(wrapper, element);
            }
        }

        // Workaround for Gecko 2.0, which has a bug in
        // mozRequestAnimationFrame() that restricts animations
        // to 30-40 fps.
```

*(Continues)*

Example 5.8   *(Continued)*

```
    if (window.mozRequestAnimationFrame) {
        // Check the Gecko version. Gecko is used by browsers
        // other than Firefox. Gecko 2.0 corresponds to
        // Firefox 4.0.

        index = userAgent.indexOf('rv:');

        if (userAgent.indexOf('Gecko') != -1) {
            geckoVersion = userAgent.substr(index + 3, 3);

            if (geckoVersion === '2.0') {
                // Forces the return statement to fall through
                // to the setTimeout() function.

                window.mozRequestAnimationFrame = undefined;
            }
        }
    }

    return window.requestAnimationFrame       ||
        window.webkitRequestAnimationFrame ||
        window.mozRequestAnimationFrame    ||
        window.oRequestAnimationFrame      ||
        window.msRequestAnimationFrame     ||

        function (callback, element) {
            var start,
                finish;

            window.setTimeout( function () {
                start = +new Date();
                callback(start);
                finish = +new Date();

                self.timeout = 1000 / 60 - (finish - start);

            }, self.timeout);
        };
    }
)
();
```

Figure 5.2 shows an application that uses the requestNextAnimationFrame() function discussed in Example 5.8.

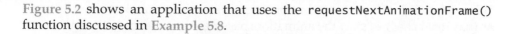

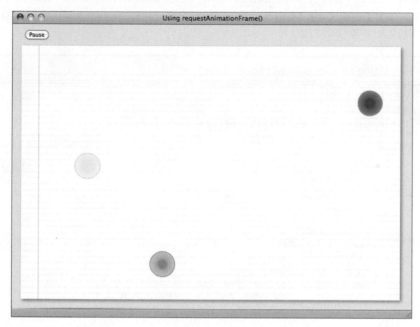

Figure 5.2 A requestAnimationFrame() polyfill

The application shown in Figure 5.2 animates three discs, similar to the application shown in Figure 5.1, except that the application shown in Figure 5.2 erases the background before drawing each animation frame.

The HTML and JavaScript for the application shown in Figure 5.2 are listed in Examples 5.9 and 5.10, respectively. Notice that the HTML page includes a JavaScript file named requestNextAnimationFrame.js. That file contains the implementation of the requestNextAnimationFrame() polyfill listed in Example 5.8.

Most of the application is concerned with defining and drawing the discs; all the animation code is encapsulated in the animate() method and the Animate button's onclick handler at the end of the listing.

When you click the Animate button, the click handler invokes requestNext-AnimationFrame() to start the animation, passing it a reference to the animate() function. The animate() function, in turn, erases the canvas, draws the next animation frame, and calls requestNextAnimationFrame() once again to keep the animation going.

**Example 5.9** Using requestAnimationFrame(): HTML

```html
<!DOCTYPE html>
  <head>
    <title>Using requestAnimationFrame()</title>

    <style>
      body {
        background: #dddddd;
      }

      #canvas {
        background: #ffffff;
        cursor: pointer;
        margin-left: 10px;
        margin-top: 10px;
        -webkit-box-shadow: 3px 3px 6px rgba(0,0,0,0.5);
        -moz-box-shadow: 3px 3px 6px rgba(0,0,0,0.5);
        box-shadow: 3px 3px 6px rgba(0,0,0,0.5);
      }

      #controls {
        margin-top: 10px;
        margin-left: 15px;
      }
    </style>
  </head>

  <body>
    <div id='controls'>
      <input id='animateButton' type='button' value='Animate'/>
    </div>

    <canvas id='canvas' width='750' height='500'>
      Canvas not supported
    </canvas>

    <script src='requestNextAnimationFrame.js'></script>
    <script src='example.js'></script>
  </body>
</html>
```

Example 5.10 Using `requestAnimationFrame()`: JavaScript

```javascript
var canvas = document.getElementById('canvas'),
    context = canvas.getContext('2d'),
    paused = true,
    discs = [
        {
            x: 150,
            y: 250,
            lastX: 150,
            lastY: 250,
            velocityX: -3.2,
            velocityY: 3.5,
            radius: 25,
            innerColor: 'rgba(255,255,0,1)',
            middleColor: 'rgba(255,255,0,0.7)',
            outerColor: 'rgba(255,255,0,0.5)',
            strokeStyle: 'gray',
        },

        {
            x: 50,
            y: 150,
            lastX: 50,
            lastY: 150,
            velocityX: 2.2,
            velocityY: 2.5,
            radius: 25,
            innerColor: 'rgba(100,145,230,1.0)',
            middleColor: 'rgba(100,145,230,0.7)',
            outerColor: 'rgba(100,145,230,0.5)',
            strokeStyle: 'blue'
        },

        {
            x: 150,
            y: 75,
            lastX: 150,
            lastY: 75,
            velocityX: 1.2,
            velocityY: 1.5,
            radius: 25,
            innerColor: 'rgba(255,0,0,1.0)',
            middleColor: 'rgba(255,0,0,0.7)',
            outerColor: 'rgba(255,0,0,0.5)',
            strokeStyle: 'orange'
        },
    ],
```

*(Continues)*

Example 5.10    *(Continued)*

```
    numDiscs = discs.length,
    animateButton = document.getElementById('animateButton');

// Functions.......................................................

function drawBackground() {
    // Listing omitted for brevity See Example 3.1 on p. 203
    // for a complete listing
}

function update() {
    var disc = null;

    for(var i=0; i < numDiscs; ++i) {
        disc = discs[i];

        if (disc.x + disc.velocityX + disc.radius >
                context.canvas.width ||
                disc.x + disc.velocityX - disc.radius < 0)
            disc.velocityX = -disc.velocityX;

        if (disc.y + disc.velocityY + disc.radius >
                context.canvas.height ||
                disc.y + disc.velocityY - disc.radius  < 0)
            disc.velocityY= -disc.velocityY;

        disc.x += disc.velocityX;
        disc.y += disc.velocityY;
    }
}

function draw() {
    var disc = discs[i];

    for(var i=0; i < numDiscs; ++i) {
        disc = discs[i];

        gradient = context.createRadialGradient(disc.x, disc.y, 0,
                        disc.x, disc.y, disc.radius);
        gradient.addColorStop(0.3, disc.innerColor);
        gradient.addColorStop(0.5, disc.middleColor);
        gradient.addColorStop(1.0, disc.outerColor);
```

```
            context.save();
            context.beginPath();
            context.arc(disc.x, disc.y, disc.radius, 0, Math.PI*2, false);
            context.fillStyle = gradient;
            context.strokeStyle = disc.strokeStyle;
            context.fill();
            context.stroke();
            context.restore();
        }
    }

    // Animation.......................................................

    function animate(time) {
        if (!paused) {
            context.clearRect(0,0,canvas.width,canvas.height);
            drawBackground();
            update();
            draw();

            window.requestNextAnimationFrame(animate);
        }
    }

    // Event handlers..................................................

    animateButton.onclick = function (e) {
        paused = paused ? false : true;
        if (paused) {
            animateButton.value = 'Animate';
        }
        else {
            window.requestNextAnimationFrame(animate);
            animateButton.value = 'Pause';
        }
    };

    // Initialization.................................................

    context.font = '48px Helvetica';
```

## 5.2  Calculating Frame Rates

Animations are a sequence of images, known as frames, that are displayed at a rate known as the frame rate. It's often necessary to calculate an animation's frame rate; for example, you may use an animation's frame rate to implement time-based motion, as discussed in Section 5.6, "Time-Based Motion," on p. 367, or you may simply want to ensure that your animation's frame rate is sufficient for smooth animation.

The application shown in Figure 5.3 calculates the animation's frame rate and displays it in the canvas.

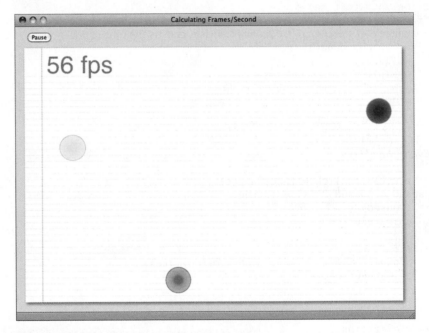

Figure 5.3  Calculating frames per second

The code that calculates the frame rate is listed in Example 5.11, along with the application's animation loop. Using a simple equation, the application calculates frames per second, given the elapsed time for the most recent animation frame.

The application subtracts the current time from the last time it drew an animation frame to get a time delta, in milliseconds. Then the application divides 1000 by the time delta to get the frame rate in frames per second.

**Example 5.11** Calculating frame rates

```
var lastTime = 0;

function calculateFps() {
   var now = (+new Date),
       fps = 1000 / (now - lastTime);

   lastTime = now;

   return fps;
}

function animate(time) {
   eraseBackground();
   drawBackground();
   update();
   draw();

   context.fillStyle = 'cornflowerblue';
   context.fillText(calculateFps().toFixed() + ' fps', 20, 60);

   window.requestNextAnimationFrame(animate);
}

window.requestNextAnimationFrame(animate);
```

 **NOTE: 3D Monster Maze: 6 frames per second**
The first 3D first-person shooter game for PCs was 3D Monster Maze released in 1981 for the Sinclair ZX81. It ran at approximately 6 frames per second.

## 5.3 Scheduling Tasks at Alternate Frame Rates

Many animations do other things besides animation. For example, an animation may display narrative text as the animation proceeds, play music, or update a game scoreboard. Most of those types of activities do not need to be carried out 60 times per second so it's important to be able to schedule tasks at alternate frame rates.

The code listed in Example 5.12 shows an animation loop for an application that updates a frames-per-second display once per second, by keeping track of the last time the display was updated.

---

Example 5.12 Scheduling tasks

```
var lastFpsUpdateTime = 0,
    lastFpsUpdate = 0;

function animate(time) {
   var fps = 0;

   if (time == undefined) {
      time = +new Date;
   }

   if (!paused) {
      eraseBackground();
      drawBackground();
      update(time);
      draw();

      fps = calculateFps();

      // Once per second, update the frame rate

      if (now - lastFpsUpdateTime > 1000) {
         lastFpsUpdateTime = now;
         lastFpsUpdate = fps;
      }

      context.fillStyle = 'cornflowerblue';
      context.fillText(lastFpsUpdate.toFixed() + ' fps', 50, 48);
   }
}
```

---

## 5.4  Restoring the Background

Most aspects of implementing animations are relatively easy. It's easy to period-ically call your animate() method with requestAnimationFrame(), and it's typi-cally easy to calculate a new location for whatever it is that you're animating and draw that object at the new location. The challenging aspect of animation is how you deal with the background. Fundamentally, you have three choices:

- Erase and redraw everything.
- Clip to damaged areas.
- Blit to damaged areas from offscreen buffers.

Erasing and redrawing everything is the most straightforward approach. Clipping to damaged areas also entails erasing and redrawing the entire background, but clipped to areas of the screen that have actually changed. Finally, copying from an offscreen buffer to damaged areas of the background (also known as blitting) is a third option.

We've seen how to erase and redraw everything in the preceding sections, so let's focus on clipping and blitting.

**TIP: Redraw everything for every frame?**

It may seem counterintuitive, but sometimes you get the best performance by redrawing everything, for every frame of your animation. Generally, if your background is simple and the objects that you are animating are also relatively simple, it may be a good idea to erase the background and redraw everything for every animation frame.

## 5.4.1 Clipping

Erasing the background and subsequently redrawing the next frame of an animation can work well for simple backgrounds. If, however, you have a complex background, the cost of redrawing the entire background for every frame could become prohibitively expensive. In that case, you might consider using the clipping region to restrict your drawing to a specific region of the canvas.

As you saw in Section 2.15, "The Clipping Region," on p. 187, you can restrict all your drawing operations to an arbitrary path, known as the clipping region. After you set the clipping region, subsequent drawing commands will affect only the inside of that region.

Figure 5.4 shows an animation that uses the clipping region to restore the background as the discs animate. Normally, you would initially draw the entire background and use clipping to repair the damaged areas as the discs animate. In this case, however, the application does not initially draw the background, so you can see how clipping fills in the background behind the discs.

The following is a recipe for using the clipping region to repair damage to the background during animation.

1. Save the state of the onscreen canvas with a call to `context.save()`.
2. Begin a path (by calling `beginPath()`).
3. Set the path with context methods (`arc()`, `rect()`, etc.).
4. Clip the onscreen canvas to the path (with `context.clip()`).
5. Erase the onscreen canvas (clipped to the clipping region).

6. Draw the background into the onscreen canvas (clipped to the clipping region).

7. Restore the state of the onscreen canvas, primarily to reset the clipping region.

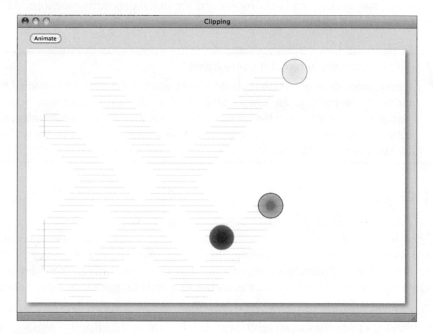

Figure 5.4 Clipping animations

The application shown in Figure 5.4 implements the preceding recipe, like this:

```
function draw() {
    var numDiscs,
        disc,
        i;

    for(i=0; i < numDiscs; ++i) {
        drawDiscBackground(discs[i]);
    }
    ...

    for(i=0; i < numDiscs; ++i) {
        drawDisc(discs[i]);
    }
    ...
}
```

```
function drawDiscBackground(disc) {
    context.save();

    context.beginPath();
    context.arc(disc.lastX, disc.lastY,
                disc.radius+1, 0, Math.PI*2, false);

    context.clip();

    eraseBackground();
    drawBackground();

    context.restore();
}
```

The draw() method erases all the discs at their previous locations and then draws them at their current locations.

When drawDiscBackground() draws the background over a disc at its previous location, it sets the clipping region to the path that the disk occupied at that location; it then erases and draws the background. Subsequently, the method restores the context, thereby resetting the clipping region. If the context were not restored then every call to context.clip() would set the clipping region to the union of the current clipping region and the current path, and that would quickly shrink the clipping region to nothing, rendering all graphics operations ineffective.

---

**TIP: Clipping can be fast, or not**

Drawing the entire background clipped to a small region of the screen can be considerably faster than drawing the entire background to the screen. Therefore, for a small number of objects, clipping may be preferable to redrawing the background. However, as you increase the number of objects that you animate, you increase the number of times you must draw the background per frame. Eventually, the cost of all that background drawing will catch up with you, and the performance advantage that clipping affords for a small number of objects will disappear.

---

## 5.4.2 Blitting

In the preceding section, you saw how to use the clipping region to avoid redrawing the entire background to the screen for every frame of an animation. Although using the clipping region restricts drawing to a region in a canvas, you still have to draw the entire background for every animation frame.

Another approach is to draw the background—once—into an offscreen canvas and subsequently to copy from the offscreen canvas to the onscreen display, as necessary to repair damage to the background.

Blitting the background from an offscreen canvas involves the same seven steps that we discussed in the preceding section, except that step 6—drawing the background, clipped to the clipping region—is replaced by copying the region from an offscreen canvas, like this:

```
function drawDiscBackground(context, disc) {
   var x = disc.lastX,
       y = disc.lastY,
       r = disc.radius,
       w = r*2,
       h = r*2;

   context.save();

   context.beginPath();
   context.arc(x, y, r+1, 0, Math.PI*2, false);
   context.clip();

   context.clearRect(0, 0, canvas.width, canvas.height);
   context.drawImage(offscreenCanvas,
                     x-r, y-r, w, h, x-r, y-r, w, h);

   context.restore();
}
```

**TIP: Clipping vs. Blitting**

Both clipping and blitting repair the damaged regions of the background instead of redrawing the entire thing. Clipping redraws the damaged regions, whereas blitting copies the damaged regions from an offscreen canvas. As a general rule, blitting is faster than clipping, but requires an offscreen canvas, which, in turn, requires more memory.

## 5.5 Double Buffering

So far in this chapter, we've used an animation loop that looks something like this:

```
var canvas = document.getElementById('canvas'),
    context = canvas.getContext('2d'),
    ...
```

```
function animate(time) {
   context.clearRect(0, 0, canvas.width, canvas.height);

   // Update and draw animation objects...

   requestNextAnimationFrame(time); // Keep the animation going
}

requestNextAnimationFrame(time); // Start the animation
```

The preceding animation loop first erases the canvas and then draws the next animation frame. If the animation were *single* buffered, meaning that it immediately drew directly into the onscreen canvas, then erasing the background would cause flicker if we perceive that momentary blanking of the canvas.

One way to eliminate flickering is to use *double* buffering. With double buffering, instead of drawing directly to the onscreen canvas, you draw everything into an offscreen canvas, then subsequently copy the offscreen canvas—all at once—into the onscreen canvas, as illustrated in Example 5.13.

---

**Example 5.13** Double buffering

---

```
// For illustration only. Do not do this.

var canvas = document.getElementById('canvas'),
    context = canvas.getContext('2d'),

    // Create an offscreen canvas

    offscreenCanvas = document.createElement('canvas'),
    offscreenContext = offscreenCanvas.getContext('2d'),
    ...

offscreenCanvas.width = canvas.width;
offscreenCanvas.height = canvas.height;

function animate(now) {
   offscreenContext.clearRect(
      0, 0, offscreenCanvas.width, offscreenCanvas.height);

   // Update and draw animation objects into the offscreen canvas...

   // Clear the onscreen canvas and draw the offscreen
   // into the onscreen canvas

   context.clearRect(0, 0, canvas.width, canvas.height);
   context.drawImage(offscreenCanvas, 0, 0);
}
```

---

Double buffering is so effective at eliminating flickering that *browsers automatically double buffer canvas elements, so you don't have to.* In fact, you will degrade your animation's performance by manually implementing double buffering as illustrated in Example 5.13. In that case, you are paying the cost of copying the offscreen buffer onscreen for every animation frame, with no benefit.

If you've ever stepped through Canvas code in a debugger, you may have doubts that the browser automatically double buffers canvas elements. After all, when you step through the code in the debugger, you immediately see the effect of each call to the Canvas API. However, the debugger runs in a different thread, so it appears that Canvas API calls take immediate effect, when in reality, they are double buffered.

You can verify that the browser double buffers canvas elements with some code that looks like this:

```
var canvas = document.getElementById('canvas'),
    context = canvas.getContext('2d'),
    sum = 0,
    ...

function animate(now) {
   eraseBackground(); // Erase the onscreen canvas

   // Erased background, starting busy work

   for (var i=0; i < 500000; ++i) {
      sum += i;
   }

   // Done with busy work

   drawBackground();  // Draw the background into onscreen canvas
   draw();            // Draw animation objects into onscreen canvas

   requestNextAnimationFrame(time); // Keep the animation going
}

requestNextAnimationFrame(time); // Start the animation
```

The preceding code erases the canvas background and then goes into a loop to complete some busy work.

If the canvas was not double buffered, meaning that each Canvas API command took immediate effect, most of the time the preceding code should produce a blank canvas because the code erases the canvas, does some busy work for a perceivable amount of time, draws the background and discs, and repeats the process. However, that's not what happens; in fact, you never see a blank canvas at all. The call to erase the canvas does not immediately take effect, because that call, like all Canvas API calls, is double buffered by the browser. Therefore, the browser does not actually erase the background before it performs its busy work. That erasing takes place at a *later time, when the browser copies its offscreen buffer onscreen.*

 **CAUTION: Canvas is automatically double buffered by the browser**

Browser vendors across the board implement double buffering for canvas elements, so it's counterproductive for you to do the same thing. Your manual double buffering will incur a performance penalty by copying your offscreen buffer onscreen, with no benefit because the browser is already double buffering for you.

That does not mean you should not use *multiple* buffers. Section 5.4.2, "Blitting," on p. 363 illustrated that copying from an offscreen background buffer can increase performance for complex backgrounds. However, traditional double buffering, where you draw everything into an offscreen canvas and then subsequently copy the offscreen canvas, is unnecessary and counterproductive for canvas elements.

## 5.6 Time–Based Motion

Imagine two players in a multiplayer shooter game traveling down intersecting corridors. At their current rate of travel, they will converge at the intersection of the corridors at the same time. If one player has a more powerful computer than the other, and therefore the game's animation runs faster on that player's computer, you don't want the player with a faster computer to arrive at the intersection early.

Animations should run at a steady speed, regardless of the underlying frame rate. And it's not too difficult to lower an animation's frame rate, as evidenced by Figures 5.5 and 5.6. Multiple animations running concurrently will almost undoubtedly slow them all.

The application shown in Figure 5.5 has two modes. If the checkbox at the top of the application is selected, the application uses time-based motion, meaning the disc's speed, measured in pixels/second, is constant. If the checkbox is not selected, the application does not use time-based motion, and the disc's speed fluctuates with the animation's frame rate.

With time-based motion, the discs all run at the same speed, but that doesn't mean that they look good. At approximately 30 frames per second, the animations will not be able to keep up with the monitor refresh rate, and therefore certain frames of the animation will not be drawn (a phenomenon known as

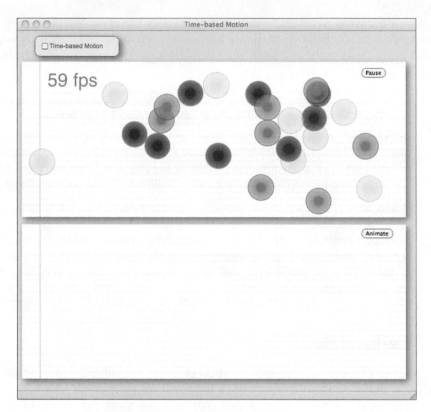

Figure 5.5 One animation running at 60 fps

dropping frames), and the discs will suddenly jump from one location to the next, making the animations choppy.

However, at 30 frames per second, regardless of whether they use time-based motion, animations are going to drop frames, and therefore they will be choppy. So all other things being equal, it's better to use time-based motion so that the animations run at the same speed.

To make an animation run at a steady rate regardless of the animation's frame rate, you calculate the number of pixels an object moves for a given frame from the frame rate itself, given the object's velocity, like this:

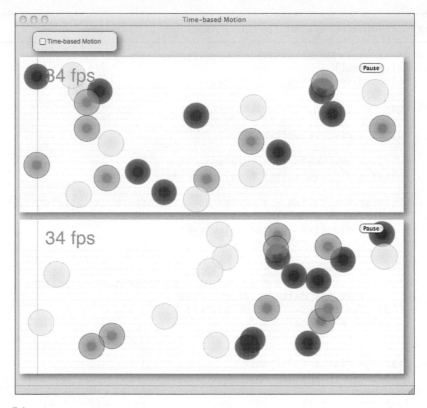

Figure 5.6 Multiple animations mean slower frame rates

$$\frac{\text{pixels}}{\text{frame}} = \frac{\text{pixels}}{\text{second}} \ / \ \frac{\text{frame}}{\text{second}}$$

Or . . .

$$\frac{\text{pixels}}{\text{frame}} = \frac{\text{pixels}}{\text{second}} \times \frac{\text{second}}{\text{frame}}$$

The preceding equation calculates *the number of pixels an object should move for a given frame*. When in time-based mode, the application shown in Figure 5.5 uses that equation to calculate the number of pixels to move each disc for every frame, as shown in Example 5.14.

Example 5.14 Animating at a constant speed, regardless of frame rate

```
function updateTimeBased(time) {
   var disc = null,
       elapsedTime = time - lastTime,

   for(var i=0; i < discs.length; ++i) {
      disc = discs[i];
      deltaX = disc.velocityX

      deltaX = disc.velocityX * (elapsedTime / 1000);
      deltaY = disc.velocityY * (elapsedTime / 1000);

      if (disc.x + deltaX + disc.radius > topContext.canvas.width ||
            disc.x + deltaX - disc.radius < 0) {
         disc.velocityX = -disc.velocityX;
         deltaX = -deltaX;
      }

      if (disc.y + deltaY + disc.radius > topContext.canvas.height ||
            disc.y + deltaY - disc.radius < 0) {
         disc.velocityY= -disc.velocityY;
         deltaY = -deltaY;
      }

      disc.x = disc.x + deltaX;
      disc.y = disc.y + deltaY;

      lastTime = time;
   }
}
```

The application multiplies the disc's velocity, measured in pixels per second, by the elapsed time of the last frame, measured in seconds, to come up with the number of pixels to move each disc per frame. The discs move the same number of pixels per second, regardless of frame rate.

## 5.7 Scrolling the Background

So far in this chapter, you've seen how to animate objects without disturbing the static background underneath. Many animations also animate the backgrounds themselves; for example, you might have drifting clouds, as shown in Figure 5.7, or you might implement an animated background for a side-scroller video game.

Figure 5.7 Simulating drifting clouds: From top to bottom, clouds move right to left

The application shown in Figure 5.7 scrolls the background by translating the canvas's context, like this:

```
var SKY_VELOCITY = 30, // 30 pixels/second
    skyOffset = 0;      // Translate by this offset
    ...

function draw() {
    skyOffset = skyOffset < canvas.width ?
                skyOffset + SKY_VELOCITY/fps : 0;

    context.save();
    context.translate(-skyOffset, 0);
    context.drawImage(sky, 0, 0);
    context.drawImage(sky, sky.width, 0);
    context.restore();
}
```

The application draws the sky image at the same location for each frame of the animation, but because the application also translates the context, it appears as though the clouds are moving from right to left, as illustrated in Figure 5.7.

The context is translated only while the application draws the background, because the application saves the context before translating and restores it afterwards.

The application draws the sky image twice: once at (0, 0) and again at (canvas.width, 0). Initially, that means that the entire background image drawn at (0, 0) is visible, whereas the image drawn at (sky.width, 0) is entirely invisible, as shown in the top picture in Figure 5.8.

As the application translates the context, the image that's initially offscreen scrolls into view, and the image that's initially displayed scrolls out of view, as illustrated from top to bottom in Figure 5.8.

It's not readily apparent, but the left and right edges of the sky image are identical. Figure 5.9 shows the right edge (on the left side), and the left edge (on the right side) next to each other, and now the effect is easily identifiable. Because the left and right edges of the background image are identical, there is no discontinuity as the image flows from offscreen to onscreen.

In this example, the background image that's initially offscreen and the background image that's initially onscreen are identical. However, that does not need to be the case; the only requirement is that the left and right edges of the two (or more) background images are identical. As long as those edges match up, the

Figure 5.8 Scrolling the background by translating the context

rest of the background image can vary as much as you like, and you will still have a smooth scrolling background.

The HTML for the application shown in Figure 5.7 is listed in Example 5.15, and the JavaScript is listed in Example 5.16.

**Example 5.15** Scrolling the background: HTML

```html
<!DOCTYPE html>
  <head>
    <title>Scrolling Backgrounds</title>

    <style>
        body {
            background: #dddddd;
        }

        #canvas {
            position: absolute;
            top: 30px;
            left: 10px;
            background: #ffffff;
            cursor: crosshair;
            margin-left: 10px;
            margin-top: 10px;
            -webkit-box-shadow: 4px 4px 8px rgba(0,0,0,0.5);
            -moz-box-shadow: 4px 4px 8px rgba(0,0,0,0.5);
            box-shadow: 4px 4px 8px rgba(0,0,0,0.5);
        }

        input {
            margin-left: 15px;
        }

    </style>
  </head>

  <body>
    <canvas id='canvas' width='1024' height='512'>
      Canvas not supported
    </canvas>

    <input id='animateButton' type='button' value='Animate'/>

    <script src='requestNextAnimationFrame.js'></script>
    <script src='example.js'></script>
  </body>
</html>
```

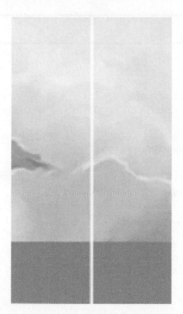

Figure 5.9 The left and right edges of the background image are identical

Example 5.16 Scrolling the background: JavaScript

```javascript
var canvas = document.getElementById('canvas'),
    context = canvas.getContext('2d'),
    controls = document.getElementById('controls'),
    animateButton = document.getElementById('animateButton'),
    sky = new Image(),

    paused = true,
    lastTime = 0,
    fps = 0,

    skyOffset = 0,
    SKY_VELOCITY = 30; // 30 pixels/second

// Functions........................................................

function erase() {
   context.clearRect(0, 0, canvas.width, canvas.height);
}
```

*(Continues)*

**Example 5.16** *(Continued)*

```
function draw() {
   context.save();

   skyOffset = skyOffset < canvas.width ?
               skyOffset + SKY_VELOCITY/fps : 0;

   context.save();
   context.translate(-skyOffset, 0);

   context.drawImage(sky, 0, 0);
   context.drawImage(sky, sky.width-2, 0);

   context.restore();
}

function calculateFps(now) {
   var fps = 1000 / (now - lastTime);
   lastTime = now;
   return fps;
}

function animate(now) {
   if (now === undefined) {
      now = +new Date;
   }

   fps = calculateFps(now);

   if (!paused) {
      erase();
      draw();
   }

   requestNextAnimationFrame(animate);
}

// Event handlers.................................................

animateButton.onclick = function (e) {
   paused = paused ? false : true;
   if (paused) {
      animateButton.value = 'Animate';
   }
   else {
      animateButton.value = 'Pause';
   }
};
```

```
// Initialization........................................

canvas.width = canvas.width;
canvas.height = canvas.height;

sky.src = 'sky.png';
sky.onload = function (e) {
  draw();
};

requestNextAnimationFrame(animate);
```

## 5.8 Parallax

Nobody knows why birds bob their heads up and down when they walk, but one popular theory is that it gives them stereo vision. The rapid vertical movement may give them two slightly different perspectives nearly simultaneously, producing something known as motion parallax, letting them perceive depth.

Luckily for us, our eyes have overlapping vision, so we get parallax, and depth perception, without looking ridiculous. Parallax is the perceived difference in position of an object, when that object is viewed from a different line of sight, and is the reason that things far away appear to move more slowly than things that are close by.

Animators implement parallax effects by scrolling multiple layers of an animation at different speeds. For example, the application shown in Figure 5.10 has four layers, as you can see in Figure 5.11. In that animation, the sky and clouds are much further away from the observer than anything else, so the sky scrolls very slowly from right to left. The next closest objects in the animation are the small trees in the background. Those trees move considerably faster than the sky, but not quite as fast as the larger trees, which are even closer to the observer. Finally, the grass in the forefront of the animation scrolls more rapidly than any other objects in the animation.

When combined, the four layers of the animation scrolling by at different speeds create an illusion of three dimensions that cannot be captured in a book. To access the example online, go to corehtml5canvas.com.

Figure 5.10  Using parallax to simulate three dimensions: From top to bottom, the bigger trees in front, moving right to left, overtake the smaller ones in back

Figure 5.11 The parallax layers

The JavaScript for the parallax example shown in Figure 5.10 is listed in Example 5.17. Pay attention to the draw() method, which calculates translation offsets for each of the four layers, and then subsequently saves the context, translates it, draws the objects in the layer, and restores the context. The save/translate/draw/restore cycle relieves us of any responsibility for calculating the positions of the objects that we're scrolling—we just draw the objects at the same coordinates every frame, and the translation of the context gives them apparent motion.

**Example 5.17** Parallax

```javascript
var canvas = document.getElementById('canvas'),
    context = canvas.getContext('2d'),
    controls = document.getElementById('controls'),
    animateButton = document.getElementById('animateButton'),

    tree = new Image(),
    nearTree = new Image(),
    grass = new Image(),
    grass2 = new Image(),
    sky = new Image(),

    paused = true,
    lastTime = 0,
    lastFpsUpdate = { time: 0, value: 0 },
    fps=60,

    skyOffset = 0,
    grassOffset = 0,
    treeOffset = 0,
    nearTreeOffset = 0,

    TREE_VELOCITY = 20,
    FAST_TREE_VELOCITY = 40,
    SKY_VELOCITY = 8,
    GRASS_VELOCITY = 75;

// Functions........................................................

function erase() {
    context.clearRect(0, 0, canvas.width, canvas.height);
}

function draw() {
    context.save();

    skyOffset = skyOffset < canvas.width ?
                skyOffset + SKY_VELOCITY/fps : 0;

    grassOffset = grassOffset < canvas.width ?
                  grassOffset +  GRASS_VELOCITY/fps : 0;

    treeOffset = treeOffset < canvas.width ?
                treeOffset + TREE_VELOCITY/fps : 0;

    nearTreeOffset = nearTreeOffset < canvas.width ?
                     nearTreeOffset + FAST_TREE_VELOCITY/fps : 0;
```

```
    context.save();
    context.translate(-skyOffset, 0);
    context.drawImage(sky, 0, 0);
    context.drawImage(sky, sky.width-2, 0);
    context.restore();

    context.save();
    context.translate(-treeOffset, 0);
    context.drawImage(tree, 100, 240);
    context.drawImage(tree, 1100, 240);
    context.drawImage(tree, 400, 240);
    context.drawImage(tree, 1400, 240);
    context.drawImage(tree, 700, 240);
    context.drawImage(tree, 1700, 240);
    context.restore();

    context.save();
    context.translate(-nearTreeOffset, 0);
    context.drawImage(nearTree, 250, 220);
    context.drawImage(nearTree, 1250, 220);
    context.drawImage(nearTree, 800, 220);
    context.drawImage(nearTree, 1800, 220);
    context.restore();

    context.save();
    context.translate(-grassOffset, 0);

    context.drawImage(grass, 0,
                      canvas.height-grass.height);

    context.drawImage(grass, grass.width-5,
                      canvas.height-grass.height);

    context.drawImage(grass2, 0,
                      canvas.height-grass2.height);

    context.drawImage(grass2, grass2.width,
                      canvas.height-grass2.height);

    context.restore();

}

function calculateFps(now) {
    var fps = 1000 / (now - lastTime);
    lastTime = now;
    return fps;
}
```

*(Continues)*

**Example 5.17** *(Continued)*

```javascript
function animate(now) {
   if (now === undefined) {
      now = +new Date;
   }

   fps = calculateFps(now);

   if (!paused) {
      erase();
      draw();
   }

   requestNextAnimationFrame(animate);
}

// Event handlers..................................................

animateButton.onclick = function (e) {
   paused = paused ? false : true;
   if (paused) {
      animateButton.value = 'Animate';
   }
   else {
      animateButton.value = 'Pause';
   }
};

// Initialization..................................................

context.font = '48px Helvetica';

tree.src = 'smalltree.png';
nearTree.src = 'tree-twotrunks.png';
grass.src = 'grass.png';
grass2.src = 'grass2.png';
sky.src = 'sky.png';
sky.onload = function (e) {
   draw();
};

requestNextAnimationFrame(animate);
```

## 5.9 User Gestures

Some animations run on their own, but others require some kind of user interaction. Users typically interact with animations by user gestures, usually with mouse or fingers, on the desktop or mobile devices, respectively.

The application shown in Figure 5.12 is the same magnifying glass application discussed in Section 4.10, "A Magnifying Glass," on p. 321. However, this version of the magnifying glass lets the user *throw* the magnifying glass by quickly dragging and releasing it. Once the user throws it, the magnifying glass continues to move in the direction of the throw, at a speed relative to the speed of the throw. When the magnifying glass reaches an edge of the canvas, it bounces off the edge and continues animating. Figure 5.12 shows the magnifying glass animating.

Figure 5.12 User gestures: an animated magnifying glass (moving from bottom-left to top-right)

Example 5.18 is a partial listing of the application shown in Figure 5.12. That listing shows how the application implements the throwing gesture.

When the user drags the mouse, the application records the time and location of both the mouse down and mouse up events. After the mouse up event ends the drag, the application's didThrow() method evaluates the user's gesture by using a simple equation that takes into account the cursor's velocity. If the velocity is sufficiently high enough, the application determines that the user threw the magnifying glass and subsequently starts the animation.

---

**Example 5.18** Implementing a user gesture to start an animation (partial listing)

```javascript
var canvas = document.getElementById('canvas'),
    context = canvas.getContext('2d'),
    ...

    animating = false,
    dragging = false,
    mousedown = null,
    mouseup = null;

// Functions.......................................................

function didThrow() {
    var elapsedTime = mouseup.time - mousedown.time;
    var elapsedMotion = Math.abs(mouseup.x - mousedown.x) +
                        Math.abs(mouseup.y - mousedown.y);
    return (elapsedMotion / elapsedTime * 10) > 3;
}

// Event handlers..................................................

canvas.onmousedown = function (e) {
    var mouse = windowToCanvas(e.clientX, e.clientY);
    mousedown = { x: mouse.x, y: mouse.y, time: (new Date).getTime() };
    e.preventDefault(e);

    if (animating) { // Stop the current animation
        animating = false;
        clearInterval(animationLoop);
        eraseMagnifyingGlass();
    }
    else { // Start dragging
        dragging = true;
        context.save();
    }
};
```

```
canvas.onmousemove = function (e) {
   if (dragging) {
      eraseMagnifyingGlass();
      drawMagnifyingGlass(
         windowToCanvas(e.clientX, e.clientY));
   }
};

canvas.onmouseup = function (e) {
   var mouse = windowToCanvas(canvas, e.clientX, e.clientY);
   mouseup = { x: mouse.x, y: mouse.y, time: (new Date).getTime() };

   if (dragging) {
      if (didThrow()) {
         velocityX = (mouseup.x-mousedown.x)/100;
         velocityY = (mouseup.y-mousedown.y)/100;
         animate(mouse, { vx: velocityX, vy: velocityY });
      }
      else {
         eraseMagnifyingGlass();
      }
   }
   dragging = false;
};
```

## 5.10 Timed Animations

All of the animations so far in this chapter run continuously; however, most animations run for a specific amount of time. In this section you'll see how to use stopwatches to run animations for various periods of time, and you'll also see how to encapsulate a stopwatch in a simple `Animation` object.

### 5.10.1 Stopwatches

Figure 5.13 shows an application that simulates a stopwatch. You set the duration of the stopwatch with the application's input field, and you start the stopwatch by clicking the Start button. As the stopwatch runs, the application smoothly winds the one hand of the stopwatch toward zero.

The application shown in Figure 5.13 uses a `Stopwatch` object, which has the following methods:

- `void start()`
- `void stop()`

- Number getElapsedTime()
- Boolean isRunning()
- void reset()

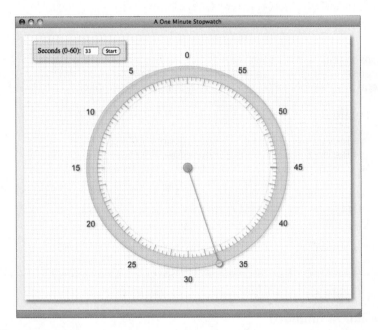

Figure 5.13  Stopwatches

You can start and stop a stopwatch, get its elapsed time, determine whether it's running, and reset its value to zero. The Stopwatch implementation is shown in Example 5.19.

An excerpt of the JavaScript for the application shown in Figure 5.13 is listed in Example 5.20.

The Start button serves two purposes: It both starts and stops the stopwatch. If you click the button when its text is Start, the application starts the stopwatch, sets the button's text to Stop, disables the seconds input, and requests the next animation frame to kick off the stopwatch animation.

If you click the button when its text is Stop, the application stops the stopwatch, resets the button's text to Start, and enables the seconds input. Notice that the application does not call requestNextAnimationFrame() when you stop the stopwatch, so clicking the Stop button stops the animation in addition to the stopwatch.

---

Example 5.19 A stopwatch implementation

---

```javascript
// Stopwatch.............................................
//
// Like the real thing, you can start and stop a stopwatch, and you
// can find out the elapsed time the stopwatch has been running.
// After you stop a stopwatch, its getElapsedTime() method returns
// the elapsed time between the start and stop.
//
// Stopwatches are used primarily for timing animations.

// Constructor..........................................

Stopwatch = function () { };

// Prototype............................................

Stopwatch.prototype = {
    startTime: 0,
    running: false,
    elapsed: undefined,

    start: function () {
        this.startTime = +new Date();
        this.elapsedTime = undefined;
        this.running = true;
    },

    stop: function () {
        this.elapsed = (+new Date()) - this.startTime;
        this.running = false;
    },

    getElapsedTime: function () {
        if (this.running) {
            return (+new Date()) - this.startTime;
        }
        else {
            return this.elapsed;
        }
    },

    isRunning: function() {
        return this.running;
    },

    reset: function() {
        this.elapsed = 0;
    }
};
```

**Example 5.20** Using a stopwatch

```javascript
var stopwatch = new Stopwatch(),
    secondsInput = document.getElementById('secondsInput'),
    startStopButton = document.getElementById('startStopButton');
...

startStopButton.onclick = function (e) {
   var value = startStopButton.value;
   if (value === 'Start') {
      stopwatch.start();
      startStopButton.value = 'Stop';
      requestNextAnimationFrame(animate);
      secondsInput.disabled = true;
   }
   else {
      stopwatch.stop();
      timerSetting = parseFloat(secondsInput.value);
      startStopButton.value = 'Start';
      secondsInput.disabled = false;
   }
   stopwatch.reset();
};

function animate() {
   if (stopwatch.isRunning() &&
       stopwatch.getElapsedTime() > timerSetting*1000) {

      // Animation is over

      stopwatch.stop();
      startStopButton.value = 'Start';
      secondsInput.disabled = false;
      secondsInput.value = 0;

   }
   else if (stopwatch.isRunning()) { // Animation is running
     redraw();
     requestNextAnimationFrame(animate);
   }
}
```

As long as the stopwatch's elapsed time is less than the timer setting, the animate() function redraws the stopwatch and recursively calls itself by invoking requestNextAnimationFrame(). When the stopwatch's elapsed time exceeds the timer setting, the application stops the stopwatch and shuts down the animation.

## 5.10.2 Animation Timers

In Example 5.20 you saw how to control the duration of an animation with a stopwatch. Although stopwatches are useful for controlling animations, it's more convenient to work at a higher level of abstraction so this section implements an AnimationTimer, as listed in Example 5.21.

**Example 5.21** Animation timer

```
// Constructor.....................................................

AnimationTimer = function (duration)  {
   this.duration = duration;
};

// Prototype......................................................

AnimationTimer.prototype = {
   duration: undefined,
   stopwatch: new Stopwatch(),

   start: function () {
      this.stopwatch.start();
   },

   stop: function () {
      this.stopwatch.stop();
   },

   getElapsedTime: function () {
      var elapsedTime = this.stopwatch.getElapsedTime();

      if (!this.stopwatch.running)
         return undefined;
      else
         return elapsedTime;
   },

   isRunning: function() {
      return this.stopwatch.isRunning();
   },

   isOver: function () {
      return this.stopwatch.getElapsedTime() > this.duration;
   },
};
```

The `AnimationTimer` object is a thin wrapper around the `Stopwatch` object discussed in the preceding section. `AnimationTimer` mostly delegates directly to a stopwatch, but adds one new method: `isOver()`. That method tells you whether the animation's elapsed time is greater than its duration. If you find that an animation is over, you typically will want to stop it—animations do not stop themselves.

You use `AnimationTimer`s just like you use stopwatches, except that you have the advantage of the `isOver()` method. Notice that `AnimationTimer` doesn't actually animate anything; it is simply a time construct. In Section 7.2, "Warping Time," on p. 450, we will exploit the fact that `Animation` deals with a single abstraction—time—by extending that object to incorporate time warping, which allows all sorts of nonlinear effects, including nonlinear motion such as easing and elasticity.

## 5.11 Animation Best Practices

As you create your own animations, here are some best practices to keep in mind:

- Use a `requestAnimationFrame()` polyfill method.
- Separate updating and drawing.
- Use time-based motion.
- Use clipping or blitting for restoring complex backgrounds.
- Keep one or more offscreen buffers for backgrounds.
- Don't implement traditional double buffering: the browser does it for you.
- Avoid CSS shadows and rounded corners.
- Avoid Canvas shadows.
- Do not allocate memory during animations.
- Use profiling and timelines to monitor and improve performance.

You should use a `requestAnimationFrame()` polyfill function for your animations. That polyfill function should take into account the bugs specific to Firefox 4.0 and Chrome 10, as discussed in this chapter. `requestAnimationFrame()` is preferable to `setTimeout()` or `setInterval()` because `requestAnimationFrame()` is implemented specifically for animations.

It's always a good idea to separate updating the objects that you animate from the actual drawing of those objects, because modifying one object can affect another.

You should also use time-based motion to make sure that all of your animations run at the same rate, regardless of the underlying animation's frame rate. For most animations, especially games, it's essential that the animations proceed at a steady rate, even if the application slows down. As you saw in this chapter, it's easy to implement time-based motion that's frame rate independent, at least for simple cases of motion.

Keep in mind that the browser automatically implements double buffering for you in Canvas elements. Because the browser double buffers the display, you don't need to implement double buffering yourself, but it's often useful to use one or more offscreen buffers, especially for complicated backgrounds. Remember that all other things being equal, you will generally get better performance by copying complicated backgrounds from offscreen buffers rather than redrawing those backgrounds for every animation frame.

Shadows, along with gradients, whether they are of the CSS Canvas variety, can be performance killers, especially on mobile devices. Be sure to test your applications both with and without shadows and gradients if your application is running slowly.

Finally, you should try to avoid allocating memory during your animations so the browser does not run the garbage collector, or at least that it collects garbage as infrequently as possible. You can also use profiling and timelines to locate performance bottlenecks.

## 5.12 Conclusion

In this chapter, you've seen how to implement Canvas animations. You saw that, although it's possible to implement animations with `setTimeout()` or `setInterval()`, you should prefer `requestAnimationFrame()`, or one of the browser-specific variants of that method, for your animations.

You saw how to implement time-based motion, to keep your animations running at a constant speed, regardless of the animation's underlying frame rate.

You learned how to scroll an animation's background and how to take advantage of parallax—the fact that things close to you appear to be moving faster than things far away—to simulate three dimensions.

Finally, you saw how to detect user gestures to control animations, and then we wrapped up the chapter by discussing some best practices for implementing Canvas-based animations. In the next chapter, we take a short detour to encapsulate some of what you learned in this chapter, so that implementing animations doesn't require you to start from scratch every time.

CHAPTER **6**

# Sprites

In the last chapter you learned how to implement animations in a canvas. You saw how to use `requestAnimationFrame()` to implement smooth animations, and you saw how to incorporate clipping and offscreen canvases into your animations. You also learned how to implement time-based motion and how to time animations with stopwatches and animation timers.

Now that you know the fundamentals of implementing Canvas-based animations, it's a good idea to encapsulate those fundamentals in some JavaScript objects so that you don't have to start from scratch every time you implement an animation. This chapter explores the implementation of *sprites*, which are graphical objects that you can incorporate into animations. You'll see how to move sprites without disturbing the background underneath and how to give them behaviors; for example, you could add a bouncing behavior to a ball or an exploding behavior to a bomb. You'll see how to implement behaviors that repeat indefinitely and behaviors that persist only for a specific amount of time.

Sprites can also change their appearance over time to simulate things like explosions. You'll see how to do that with sprite animators, which are objects that animate sprites by periodically changing a sprite's appearance.

---

 **NOTE: The history of sprites**

The word *sprite*, which originally meant Greek fairy, was coined by an implementer of the Texas Instruments 9918(A) video display processor. Sprites can be implemented in either software or hardware; for example, the Commodore Amiga in 1985 had support for eight hardware sprites. You can read more about the history of sprites on Wikipedia at http://en.wikipedia.org/wiki/Sprite_(computer_graphics).

---

**NOTE: Sprites are not part of the Canvas API**

The Canvas API does not explicitly support sprites; however, it does provide all the graphics capabilities that you need to implement your own sprites. All of the objects discussed in this chapter, such as sprites, painters, and animators, are not part of the Canvas API but are derived from it.

There are countless ways to implement the sprites, sprite behaviors, and sprite animations discussed in this chapter. You can use the implementations in this chapter directly, modify them to suit your tastes, or use the concepts for your own sprite implementation.

**NOTE: Design patterns, behaviors, and animators**

This chapter implements three design patterns: Strategy, Command, and Flyweight. The Strategy pattern is used to decouple sprites from their painters, the Command pattern is used to implement behaviors, and the Flyweight pattern is used to represent many sprites with a single instance.

This chapter also implements concepts from two open source projects. First, the idea for behaviors comes from Replica Island, which is a popular open source Android game. Second, the idea for sprite animators, and their final implementation discussed in Chapter 7, come from Animator.js, which is a popular low-level animation library.

You can read more about Replica Island and Animator.js at http://bit.ly/kNzDVc and http://bit.ly/krLlo6, respectively.

## 6.1 Sprites Overview

For sprites to be useful, you must be able to paint them, place them at specific locations in an animation, and move them from one place to another at a specified velocity. Sprites may also be called upon to perform certain activities such as falling, bouncing, flying, exploding, colliding with other sprites, etc. Table 6.1 lists Sprite properties.

The painter property refers to an object that paints sprites with a paint(sprite, context) method. The behaviors property refers to an array of objects, each of which manipulates a sprite in some manner with an execute(sprite, context, time) method. Example 6.1 shows the implementation of the Sprite object.

Sprites have two methods: paint() and update(). The update() method executes each of the sprite's behaviors—in the order they were added to the sprite,—and

**Table 6.1** `Sprite` properties

| Property | Description |
| --- | --- |
| `top` | The Y location of the sprite's upper left-hand corner (ulhc) |
| `left` | The X location of the sprite's ulhc |
| `width` | The sprite's width |
| `height` | The sprite's height |
| `velocityX` | The sprite's velocity in the X direction |
| `velocityY` | The sprite's velocity in the Y direction |
| `behaviors` | An array of behaviors that are invoked when a sprite is updated |
| `painter` | The object that paints the sprite |
| `visible` | A boolean that indicates whether the sprite is visible |
| `animating` | A boolean that indicates whether the sprite is animating |

`paint()` delegates painting to the sprite's painter, but only if the sprite actually has a painter and the sprite is visible.

The `Sprite` constructor takes three arguments: the sprite's name, its painter, and an array of behaviors.

**Example 6.1** Sprites

```
// Constructor..................................................

var Sprite = function (name, painter, behaviors) {
    if (name !== undefined)     this.name = name;
    if (painter !== undefined)  this.painter = painter;

    this.top = 0;
    this.left = 0;
    this.width = 10;
    this.height = 10;
    this.velocityX = 0;
    this.velocityY = 0;
    this.visible = true;
    this.animating = false;
    this.behaviors = behaviors || [];

    return this;
};
```

*(Continues)*

Example 6.1  *(Continued)*

```
// Prototype.................................................................

Sprite.prototype = {
   paint: function (context) {
      if (this.painter !== undefined && this.visible) {
         this.painter.paint(this, context);
      }
   },

   update: function (context, time) {
      for (var i = 0; i < this.behaviors.length; ++i) {
         this.behaviors[i].execute(this, context, time);
      }
   }
};
```

Now that we've seen how to implement sprites, let's see how to use them. **Figure 6.1** shows an application that displays a simple sprite.

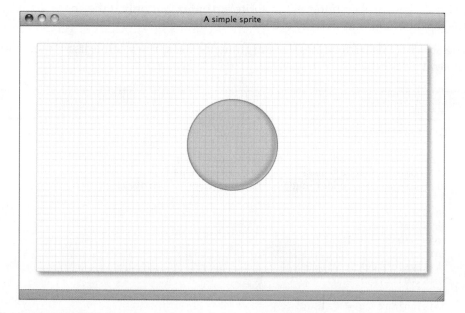

Figure 6.1  A simple sprite

The JavaScript for the application shown in **Figure 6.1** is listed in **Example 6.2**.

**Example 6.2** A simple sprite: JavaScript

```javascript
var context = document.getElementById('canvas').getContext('2d'),
    RADIUS = 75,
    ball = new Sprite('ball',
        {
            paint: function(sprite, context) {
                context.beginPath();
                context.arc(sprite.left + sprite.width/2,
                            sprite.top + sprite.height/2,
                            RADIUS, 0, Math.PI*2, false);
                context.clip();

                context.shadowColor = 'rgb(0,0,0)';
                context.shadowOffsetX = -4;
                context.shadowOffsetY = -4;
                context.shadowBlur = 8;

                context.lineWidth = 2;
                context.strokeStyle = 'rgb(100,100,195)';
                context.fillStyle = 'rgba(30,144,255,0.15)';
                context.fill();
                context.stroke();
            }
        }
    );

function drawGrid(color, stepx, stepy) {
    // Draws a grid. See Section 2.8.2 on p. 105
    // for a full listing
}

drawGrid('lightgray', 10, 10);

ball.left = 320;
ball.top = 160;
ball.paint(context);
```

Example 6.2 creates a sprite named `ball` with a painter that paints the ball. The `ball` sprite is easy to implement, but it's mostly uninteresting because it has no behaviors. In Section 6.3, "Sprite Behaviors," on p. 411, we see how to add behaviors to sprites.

## 6.2  Painters

Sprites are decoupled from the objects that paint them. That way, you can assign painters to a sprite at runtime, which gives you a great deal of flexibility. For example, you could implement a sprite animator that swaps out a sprite's painter at a specified time interval; in fact, you will see the implementation of just such an animator in Section 6.4, "Sprite Animators," on p. 417.

Painters are required to implement a single method: `void paint(sprite, context)`. Painters can be categorized into three types:

- Stroke and fill
- Image
- Sprite sheet

A stroke and fill painter uses the Canvas graphics API to paint a sprite, whereas an image painter paints an image. Finally, a sprite sheet painter paints individual sprites from a sprite sheet. Let's look at each type of painter.

---

**NOTE: Painters and strategies**

Sprites do not paint themselves; instead, they delegate painting to another object. Painters are essentially interchangeable painting algorithms that you can assign to sprites at runtime, which means that painters are an example of the Strategy design pattern. See http://bit.ly/k94Fro for more information about the Strategy pattern.

---

**NOTE: sprites.js**

The `Sprite` implementation, along with the implementation of other sprite-related classes, such as `ImagePainter`, reside in a file named `sprites.js`. All the examples in this chapter include that file in their HTML page.

---

### 6.2.1  Stroke and Fill Painters

Stroke and fill painters paint their sprites with Canvas graphics calls, including `stroke()` and `fill()`; for example, Figure 6.2 shows a clock that uses a sprite to paint the clock hands.

First, the application creates an object that paints the sprite and then passes that painter to the `Sprite` constructor:

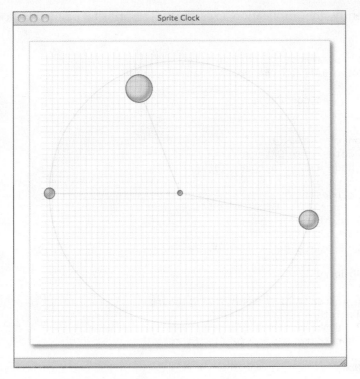

Figure 6.2 A sprite clock at 11:17:45

```
var ballPainter = {
    paint: function (sprite, context) {
        var x = sprite.left + sprite.width/2,
            y = sprite.top  + sprite.height/2,
            ...
            radius = sprite.width/2;

        context.save();
        context.beginPath();
        context.arc(x, y, radius, 0, Math.PI*2, false);
        context.clip();

        // Continue drawing the sprite...

        context.restore();
    }
},
...
ball = new Sprite('ball', ballPainter);
```

Subsequently, the application uses the `ball` sprite to paint the clock hands, like this:

```
function drawHand(loc, isHour) {
    // Move ball to the appropriate location
    ...
    ball.paint(context);
}

function drawHands() {
    var date = new Date(),
        hour = date.getHours();

    // Seconds

    ball.width = 20;
    ball.height = 20;
    drawHand(date.getSeconds(), false);

    // Minutes

    hour = hour > 12 ? hour - 12 : hour;
    ball.width = 35;
    ball.height = 35;
    drawHand(date.getMinutes(), false);

    // Hours

    ball.width = 50;
    ball.height = 50;
    drawHand(hour*5 + (date.getMinutes()/60)*5, true);

    // Centerpiece

    ball.width = 10;
    ball.height = 10;
    ball.left = canvas.width/2 - ball.width/2;
    ball.top = canvas.height/2 - ball.height/2;
    ballPainter.paint(ball, context);
}
```

The complete JavaScript for the application shown in Figure 6.2 is listed in Example 6.3.

---

**Example 6.3** A sprite clock: JavaScript

---

```javascript
var canvas = document.getElementById('canvas'),
    context = canvas.getContext('2d'),

    CLOCK_RADIUS = canvas.width/2 - 15,
    HOUR_HAND_TRUNCATION = 35,

    // Painter.......................................................

    ballPainter = {
      paint: function (sprite, context) {
          var x = sprite.left + sprite.width/2,
              y = sprite.top  + sprite.height/2,
              width = sprite.width,
              height = sprite.height,
              radius = sprite.width/2;

          context.save();
          context.beginPath();
          context.arc(x, y, radius, 0, Math.PI*2, false);
          context.clip();

          context.shadowColor = 'rgb(0,0,0)';
          context.shadowOffsetX = -4;
          context.shadowOffsetY = -4;
          context.shadowBlur = 8;

          context.fillStyle = 'rgba(218,165,32,0.1)';
          context.fill();

          context.lineWidth = 2;
          context.strokeStyle = 'rgb(100,100,195)';
          context.stroke();

          context.restore();
      }
    },

    // Sprite.......................................................

    ball = new Sprite('ball', ballPainter);

// Functions.......................................................
```

---

*(Continues)*

---

**Example 6.3**   *(Continued)*

---

```javascript
function drawGrid(color, stepx, stepy) {
   // Omitted for brevity. See Example 2.13 on p. 106
   // for a complete listing.
   ...
}

function drawHand(loc, isHour) {
   var angle = (Math.PI*2) * (loc/60) - Math.PI/2,
       handRadius = isHour ? CLOCK_RADIUS - HOUR_HAND_TRUNCATION
                           : CLOCK_RADIUS,
       lineEnd = {
          x: canvas.width/2 +
             Math.cos(angle)*(handRadius - ball.width/2),

          y: canvas.height/2 +
             Math.sin(angle)*(handRadius - ball.width/2)
       };

   context.beginPath();
   context.moveTo(canvas.width/2, canvas.height/2);
   context.lineTo(lineEnd.x, lineEnd.y);
   context.stroke();

   ball.left = canvas.width/2  +
               Math.cos(angle)*handRadius - ball.width/2;

   ball.top  = canvas.height/2 +
               Math.sin(angle)*handRadius - ball.height/2;

   ball.paint(context);
}

function drawClock() {
   drawClockFace();
   drawHands();
}

function drawHands() {
   var date = new Date(),
       hour = date.getHours();

   ball.width = 20;
   ball.height = 20;
   drawHand(date.getSeconds(), false);

   hour = hour > 12 ? hour - 12 : hour;
   ball.width = 35;
   ball.height = 35;
   drawHand(date.getMinutes(), false);
```

```
   ball.width = 50;
   ball.height = 50;
   drawHand(hour*5 + (date.getMinutes()/60)*5);

   ball.width = 10;
   ball.height = 10;
   ball.left = canvas.width/2 - ball.width/2;
   ball.top = canvas.height/2 - ball.height/2;
   ballPainter.paint(ball, context);
}

function drawClockFace() {
   context.beginPath();
   context.arc(canvas.width/2, canvas.height/2,
            CLOCK_RADIUS, 0, Math.PI*2, false);

   context.save();
   context.strokeStyle = 'rgba(0,0,0,0.2)';
   context.stroke();
   context.restore();
}

// Animation.........................................................

function animate() {
   context.clearRect(0, 0, canvas.width, canvas.height);

   drawGrid('lightgray', 10, 10);
   drawClock();

   window.requestNextAnimationFrame(animate);
}

// Initialization...................................................

context.lineWidth = 0.5;
context.strokeStyle = 'rgba(0,0,0,0.2)';
context.shadowColor = 'rgba(0,0,0,0.5)';
context.shadowOffsetX = 2;
context.shadowOffsetY = 2;
context.shadowBlur = 4;
context.stroke();

window.requestNextAnimationFrame(animate);

drawGrid('lightgray', 10, 10);
```

Now that you've seen how to use stroke and fill painters, let's see how to implement an image painter.

**TIP: Flyweight sprites**

Although it may look as though four sprites are in the application shown in Figure 6.2 on p. 399, there's actually only one. As you can see from Example 6.3, the application uses the same sprite to paint all three hands and the pivot in the center of the clock.

Using one object to represent several is known as the Flyweight design pattern. That pattern reduces the number of objects that you create, which reduces the amount of memory that you use. That reduction is important for performance in animations and video games.

**TIP: Controlling animations with `window.requestNextAnimationFrame()`**

The application shown in Figure 6.2 uses `window.requestNextAnimation-Frame()`, which is a polyfill method discussed in Section 5.1.3, "A Portable Animation Loop," on p. 348. That method is implemented in `request-NextAnimationFrame.js`, which is included by the application's HTML page.

## 6.2.2 Image Painters

Image painters maintain a reference to an image, and they use the context they receive in their `paint()` method to draw that image. The image painter's implementation is straightforward, as illustrated in Example 6.4.

Example 6.4 A sprite image painter

```
var ImagePainter = function (imageUrl) {
   this.image = new Image();
   this.image.src = imageUrl;
};

ImagePainter.prototype = {
   paint: function (sprite, context) {
      if (this.image.complete) {
         context.drawImage(this.image, sprite.left, sprite.top,
                           sprite.width, sprite.height);
      }
   }
};
```

When you create an image painter, you pass the `ImagePainter` constructor a reference to the image URL. Subsequently, the image painter's `paint()` method draws the image only if it's been loaded.

Figure 6.3 shows a sprite equipped with an image painter.

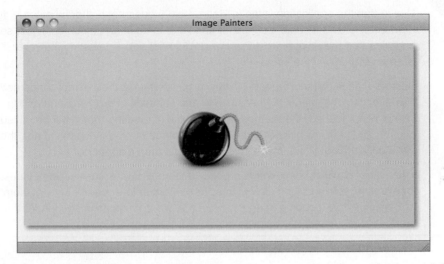

Figure 6.3 An image painter

The JavaScript for the application shown in Figure 6.3 is listed in Example 6.5. The application is a simple animation that repeatedly draws the bomb sprite.

Example 6.5 Using an image painter: JavaScript

```
var canvas = document.getElementById('canvas'),
    context = canvas.getContext('2d'),
    bomb = new Sprite('bomb', new ImagePainter('bomb.png')),
    BOMB_LEFT = 220,
    BOMB_TOP = 80,
    BOMB_WIDTH = 180,
    BOMB_HEIGHT = 130;

function animate() {
   context.clearRect(0, 0, canvas.width, canvas.height);
   bomb.paint(context);
   window.requestNextAnimationFrame(animate);
}

bomb.left = BOMB_LEFT;
bomb.top = BOMB_TOP;
bomb.width = BOMB_WIDTH;
bomb.height = BOMB_HEIGHT;

window.requestNextAnimationFrame(animate);
```

**CAUTION: Image loading**

Notice that the application listed in Example 6.5 does not just draw a sprite, it *repeatedly* draws a sprite, because it uses the sprite in an animation. It just so happens that the animation in Example 6.5 is not very interesting; however, it is an animation just the same.

Because image painters repeatedly draw a sprite's image, they are not concerned about loading the image. If you call an image painter's `draw()` method and the image is not loaded, the method does nothing, expecting that it will be called again in the next few milliseconds when the image has been loaded; if not, the cycle continues until the image is available, and then it appears.

That rather cavalier image loading policy does not always suffice. Sometimes, for example, you must load all your images up-front before you draw any of them. In Section 9.1.2, "Loading Images," on p. 554 we discuss an image loader that addresses that need.

## 6.2.3 Sprite Sheet Painters

To save space and reduce download times, animation frames for the small, animated objects known as sprites are stored in a single image, like the one shown in Figure 6.4. That single image, which contains all of the frames of an animation, is known as a sprite sheet.

Figure 6.4 A sprite sheet

When you draw an animation frame, you copy the appropriate rectangles from the sprite sheet to the display. Copying multiple rectangles from a single image is considerably faster than copying multiple images, and storing multiple images in a single file can significantly reduce the number of HTTP requests your application makes. So sprite sheets are a good idea all around.

Sprite sheet painters paint animation cells from sprite sheets. They also keep track of an index into the array of animation cells contained in the sprite sheet. You can advance that index with the advance() method, which is implemented in Example 6.6.

**Example 6.6** A sprite sheet painter

```javascript
SpriteSheetPainter = function (cells) {
    this.cells = cells || [];
    this.cellIndex = 0;
};

SpriteSheetPainter.prototype = {
    advance: function () {
        if (this.cellIndex == this.cells.length-1) {
            this.cellIndex = 0;
        }
        else {
            this.cellIndex++;
        }
    },

    paint: function (sprite, context) {
        var cell = this.cells[this.cellIndex];
        context.drawImage(spritesheet, cell.x, cell.y, cell.w, cell.h,
                          sprite.left, sprite.top, cell.w, cell.h);
    }
};
```

Figure 6.5 shows an application with a simple sprite sheet at the top of the page and an animation of that sprite underneath. The application uses a sprite sheet painter to paint the sprite sheet cells.

The JavaScript for the application shown in Figure 6.5 is listed in Example 6.7. The application sets the frame rate for the animation to 10 frames/second because at 60 frames/second, those nine images fly by pretty quickly. The application also uses the nine-argument version of the drawImage() method to draw the appropriate rectangle from the sprite sheet to the canvas. See Section 4.1.2, "The drawImage() Method," on p. 257 for more information about drawImage().

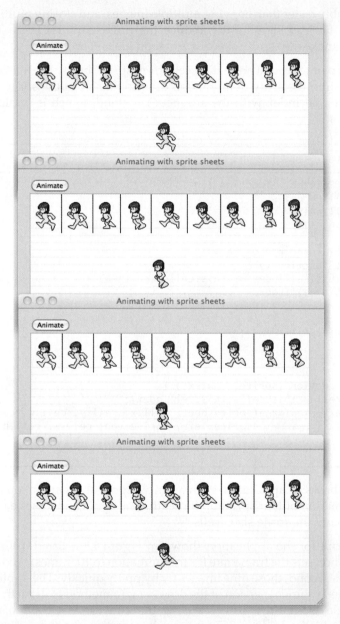

Figure 6.5  A sprite sheet animation

Example 6.7  Animation with a sprite sheet painter: JavaScript

```javascript
var canvas = document.getElementById('canvas'),
    context = canvas.getContext('2d'),
    animateButton = document.getElementById('animateButton'),
    spritesheet = new Image(),
    runnerCells = [
        { left: 0,   top: 0, width: 47, height: 64 },
        { left: 55,  top: 0, width: 44, height: 64 },
        { left: 107, top: 0, width: 39, height: 64 },
        { left: 150, top: 0, width: 46, height: 64 },
        { left: 208, top: 0, width: 49, height: 64 },
        { left: 265, top: 0, width: 46, height: 64 },
        { left: 320, top: 0, width: 42, height: 64 },
        { left: 380, top: 0, width: 35, height: 64 },
        { left: 425, top: 0, width: 35, height: 64 },
    ],
    sprite = new Sprite('runner', new SpriteSheetPainter(runnerCells)),
    interval,
    lastAdvance = 0,
    paused = false,
    PAGEFLIP_INTERVAL = 100;

// Functions.........................................................

function drawBackground() {
    var STEP_Y = 12,
        i = context.canvas.height;

    while(i < STEP_Y*4) {
        context.beginPath();
        context.moveTo(0, i);
        context.lineTo(context.canvas.width, i);
        context.stroke();
        i -= STEP_Y;
    }
}

function pauseAnimation() {
    animateButton.value = 'Animate';
    paused = true;
}

function startAnimation() {
    animateButton.value = 'Pause';
    paused = false;
    lastAdvance = +new Date();
    window.requestNextAnimationFrame(animate);
}
```

*(Continues)*

---

*Example 6.7 (Continued)*

```
// Event handlers...............................................

animateButton.onclick = function (e) {
    if (animateButton.value === 'Animate') startAnimation();
    else                                   pauseAnimation();
};

// Animation...................................................

function animate(time) {
    if ( ! paused) {
        context.clearRect(0, 0, canvas.width, canvas.height);
        drawBackground();
        context.drawImage(spritesheet, 0, 0);

        sprite.paint(context);

        if (time - lastAdvance > PAGEFLIP_INTERVAL) {
            sprite.painter.advance();
            lastAdvance = time;
        }
        window.requestNextAnimationFrame(animate);
    }
}

// Initialization...............................................

spritesheet.src = 'running-sprite-sheet.png';
spritesheet.onload = function(e) {
    context.drawImage(spritesheet, 0, 0);
};

sprite.left = 200;
sprite.top = 100;

context.strokeStyle = 'lightgray';
context.lineWidth = 0.5;

drawBackground();
```

---

The application's animate() method clears the canvas, draws the background, and then draws the sprite sheet at the top of the page. Then it paints the sprite.

After painting the sprite, the animate() method advances the sprite painter if the painter has not been advanced for PAGEFLIP_INTERVAL milliseconds. Finally, the application requests the next animation frame from the window, which ultimately results in a subsequent call to animate(), and the cycle starts again.

## 6.3  Sprite Behaviors

Now that we've seen how to paint sprites, let's see how give them some personality by assigning behaviors to them.

Behaviors are nothing more than objects that implement an execute(sprite, context, time) method. That method typically modifies the sprite in some manner, perhaps moving the sprite or changing its appearance.

Sprites maintain an array of behaviors. A sprite's update() method iterates over that array, giving each behavior a chance to execute. That lets you encapsulate behaviors as objects that you can assign, at runtime, to various sprites. The application listed in Example 6.8 illustrates implementing behaviors by encapsulating running in place, as shown in Figure 6.5.

**Example 6.8** Running in place

```
var canvas = document.getElementById('canvas'),
    context = canvas.getContext('2d'),
    ...

    runInPlace = {
       lastAdvance: 0,
       PAGEFLIP_INTERVAL: 1000,

       execute: function (sprite, context, now) {
          if (now - this.lastAdvance > this.PAGEFLIP_INTERVAL) {
             sprite.painter.advance();
             this.lastAdvance = now;
          }
       }
    },
    sprite = new Sprite('runner',
            new SpriteSheetPainter(runnerCells), [ runInPlace ]);
...

function animate(time) {
   context.clearRect(0, 0, canvas.width, canvas.height);
   drawBackground();

   context.drawImage(spritesheet, 0, 0);

   sprite.update(context, time);
   sprite.paint(context);

   window.requestNextAnimationFrame(animate);
}
...
```

Example 6.8 creates a `runInPlace` object that has an `execute()` method, which means that the object qualifies as a behavior. The application then creates a sprite and passes the `runInPlace` object as the lone member of the sprite's array of behaviors. Subsequently, the animation loop repeatedly calls the sprite's `update()` method, which invokes the `runInPlace` object's `execute()` method, and the sprite appears to run in place.

---

**NOTE: Behaviors are commands**

Behaviors, which encapsulate a command of some sort, are an example of the Command design pattern. Behaviors can be executed as well as stored in a queue, as is the case for a sprite's array of behaviors. You can read more about the Command pattern at Wikipedia at http://bit.ly/lhla5q.

---

### 6.3.1 Combining Behaviors

Sprites have an array of behaviors, so you can assign as many behaviors as you want to any particular sprite. The sprite's `update()` method invokes each behavior's `execute()` method, starting with the first behavior in the sprite's behavior array and ending with the last.

The application shown in Figure 6.6 combines the running-in-place behavior discussed in Section 6.3, "Sprite Behaviors," on p. 411 with a behavior that moves the sprite from right to left. The resulting effect is that the sprite appears to run from the right side of the page to the left.

The application creates the sprite like this:

```
sprite = new Sprite('runner',
                new SpriteSheetPainter(runnerCells),
                [ runInPlace, moveLeftToRight ]),
```

Sprites can have as many behaviors as you want, and you can add and remove behaviors at runtime by directly manipulating the sprite's `behaviors` array. It would be a simple matter, for example, to endow the sprite shown in Figure 6.6 with a jumping behavior that's triggered by user input.

The JavaScript for the application shown in Figure 6.6 is listed in Example 6.9.

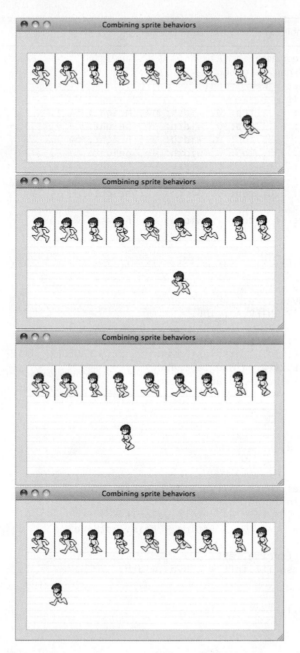

Figure 6.6  Combining sprite behaviors: run in place and move left to right

**Example 6.9** Combining behaviors: JavaScript

```javascript
var canvas = document.getElementById('canvas'),
    context = canvas.getContext('2d'),
    spritesheet = new Image(),
    runnerCells = [
        { left: 0,   top: 0, width: 47, height: 64 },
        { left: 55,  top: 0, width: 44, height: 64 },
        { left: 107, top: 0, width: 39, height: 64 },
        { left: 150, top: 0, width: 46, height: 64 },
        { left: 208, top: 0, width: 49, height: 64 },
        { left: 265, top: 0, width: 46, height: 64 },
        { left: 320, top: 0, width: 42, height: 64 },
        { left: 380, top: 0, width: 35, height: 64 },
        { left: 425, top: 0, width: 35, height: 64 },
    ];

    // Behaviors.............................................

    runInPlace = {
        lastAdvance: 0,
        PAGEFLIP_INTERVAL: 100,

        execute: function (sprite, context, time) {
            if (time - this.lastAdvance > this.PAGEFLIP_INTERVAL) {
                sprite.painter.advance();
                this.lastAdvance = time;
            }
        }
    },

    moveLeftToRight = {
        lastMove: 0,

        execute: function (sprite, context, time) {
            if (this.lastMove !== 0) {
                sprite.left -= sprite.velocityX *
                            ((time - this.lastMove) / 1000);

                if (sprite.left < 0) {
                    sprite.left = canvas.width;
                }
            }
            this.lastMove = time;
        }
    },

    // Sprite................................................
```

```
      sprite = new Sprite('runner', new SpriteSheetPainter(runnerCells),
                          [ runInPlace, moveLeftToRight ]);

// Functions.................................................

function drawBackground() {
   var STEP_Y = 12,
       i = context.canvas.height;

   while(i > STEP_Y*4) {
      context.beginPath();

      context.moveTo(0, i);
      context.lineTo(context.canvas.width, i);
      context.stroke();

      i -= STEP_Y;
   }
}

// Animation.................................................

function animate(time) {
   context.clearRect(0,0,canvas.width,canvas.height);
   drawBackground();

   context.drawImage(spritesheet, 0, 0);

   sprite.update(context, time);
   sprite.paint(context);

   window.requestNextAnimationFrame(animate);
}

// Initialization...........................................

spritesheet.src = 'running-sprite-sheet.png';

spritesheet.onload = function(e) {
   context.drawImage(spritesheet, 0, 0);
};

sprite.velocityX = 50;  // pixels/second
sprite.left = 200;
sprite.top = 100;

context.strokeStyle = 'lightgray';
context.lineWidth = 0.5;

window.requestNextAnimationFrame(animate);
```

### 6.3.2 Timed Behaviors

When you add a behavior to a sprite, that behavior is invoked by the sprite's update() method, which you typically call repeatedly from your animation loop. In effect, once you add a behavior to a sprite, the sprite exhibits that behavior until you remove it from the sprite's behavior array.

However, sometimes you want a behavior to last only for a specific period of time. For example, you may want to apply thrust to a moving object for a short period of time after some input from the user.

The application shown in Figure 6.7 uses a *timed* behavior that persists for a specific time. Each time you click either the left or right arrows, the application moves the ball in that direction for 200 ms.

Figure 6.7  Timed behaviors

The ball's motion is time-based, so the ball's velocity is specified in pixels per second—110 pixels/second to be exact. Therefore, 200 ms of movement equates to exactly 22 pixels (200 ms is 1/5 of a second, and 1/5 of 110 is 22).

The ledge upon which the ball rests is 44 pixels wide, so clicking on either arrow when the ball is in the middle puts the ball on the edge of the ledge, as shown in Figure 6.7. If the user pushes the ball off the edge, the application puts it back in the center.

When the user clicks on one of the arrows, the application starts an animation timer—see Section 5.10.2, "Animation Timers," on p. 389 for more about animation timers—and sets a flag that indicates direction. Subsequently, the ball's moveBall behavior moves the ball, like this:

```
var ANIMATION_DURATION = 200,
    pushAnimationTimer = new AnimationTimer(ANIMATION_DURATION),

    moveBall = {
       execute: function (sprite, context, time) {
          if (pushAnimationTimer.isRunning()) {
             if (arrow === LEFT) ball.left -= ball.velocityX / fps;
             else                ball.left += ball.velocityX / fps;

             if (isBallOnLedge()) {
                if (pushAnimationTimer.isOver()) {
                   pushAnimationTimer.stop();
                }
             }
             else {
                pushAnimationTimer.stop();
                ball.left = LEDGE_LEFT + LEDGE_WIDTH/2 - BALL_RADIUS;
                ball.top = LEDGE_TOP - BALL_RADIUS*2;
             }
          }
       }
    },

    ball = new Sprite('ball', painter, [ moveBall ]);
    ...
```

If the animation timer is running, the moveBall behavior moves the ball either left or right, depending on which arrow the user clicked last.

The application implements time-based motion by dividing the ball's velocity, which is measured in pixels per second, by the animation's frame rate, which is measured in frames per second. The result is the number of pixels the ball must travel for the current frame. See Section 5.6, "Time-Based Motion," on p. 367 for more information on time-based motion.

After adjusting the ball's position, the moveBall behavior checks to see if the ball is still on the ledge; if it is, and if the ball has been moving for more than 200 ms, the behavior stops the animation timer. Otherwise, if the ball has fallen off the ledge, the behavior stops the animation timer and places the ball in the middle of the ledge.

Now that you've seen how to implement timed behaviors, let's see how to generalize and encapsulate that concept with sprite animators.

## 6.4 Sprite Animators

Not only is it common to move sprites from one location to another, it's also common to animate sprite images, as shown in Figure 6.8.

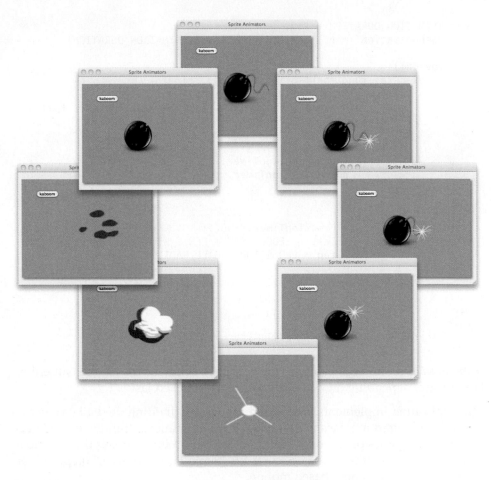

Figure 6.8  Two sprite animators, one for the fuse and another for the explosion. From top, clockwise: Fuse burns, bomb explodes, and reappears.

The application shown in **Figure 6.8** contains a button and a sprite. If you click the button, the application animates the sprite's image to make it look as though the fuse were burning.

After the fuse has burned all the way down, the application animates the sprite's image through a sequence of images that makes it appear as if the bomb were exploding.

Finally, the application restores the original sprite in two steps: drawing the bomb without the fuse and adding the fuse shortly thereafter.

Figure 6.9 and Figure 6.10 show the sequence of images for the fuse-burning and explosion animations.

Figure 6.9  Fuse animation cells (left to right, top row to bottom)

Figure 6.10  Explosion animation cells (left to right, top to bottom)

Sprite animator objects control a sprite's animations. The SpriteAnimator object is listed in Example 6.10.

The SpriteAnimator object maintains an array of sprite painters, which, as you saw in Section 6.2, "Painters," on p. 398, are simply objects that paint sprites with a paint(sprite, context) method. Every sprite has a single sprite painter that paints it.

Sprite animators cycle through an array of painters assigning each one in turn, for a specific period of time, to a single sprite.

When you create a SpriteAnimator, you pass the constructor function the animator's painters, and an optional callback that the animator will invoke when the animation is finished.

You start an animation with the SpriteAnimator.start() method. You pass to that method the sprite that you want to animate, and the animation's duration in milliseconds.

**Example 6.10** A sprite animator

```
// Constructor.......................................................

var SpriteAnimator = function (painters, elapsedCallback) {
    this.painters = painters || [];
    this.elapsedCallback = elapsedCallback;
    this.duration = 1000;
    this.startTime = 0;
    this.index = 0;
};

// Prototype.........................................................

SpriteAnimator.prototype = {
    end: function (sprite, originalPainter) {
        sprite.animating = false;

        if (this.elapsedCallback) this.elapsedCallback(sprite);
        else                      sprite.painter = originalPainter;
    },

    start: function (sprite, duration) {
        var endTime = +new Date() + duration,
            period = duration / (this.painters.length),
            animator = this,
            originalPainter = sprite.painter,
            lastUpdate = 0;

        this.index = 0;
        sprite.animating = true;
        sprite.painter = this.painters[this.index];

        requestNextAnimationFrame( function spriteAnimatorAnimate(time) {
            if (time < endTime) {
                if ((time - lastUpdate) > period) {
                    sprite.painter = animator.painters[++animator.index];
                    lastUpdate = time;
                }
                requestNextAnimationFrame(spriteAnimatorAnimate);
            }
            else {
                animator.end(sprite, originalPainter);
            }
        });
    },
};
```

To perform the animation, the animator's start() method calculates the animation's end time by adding the animation's duration to the current time. Then it calculates the animation's *period*, which is the amount of time allotted to each image in the animation.

Finally, the SpriteAnimator.start() method invokes window.requestNext-AnimationFame(), which is a polyfill method discussed in Section 5.1.3, "A Portable Animation Loop," on p. 348 for the standard requestAnimationFrame() function. The application passes requestNextAnimationFrame() a function that updates the sprite's painter. If you specify a callback function when you create a SpriteAnimator, the animator invokes the callback when the animation is complete. If you do not specify a callback, the animator restores the sprite's original painter.

The application shown in Figure 6.8 is listed in Example 6.11.

**Example 6.11** Using sprite animators

```
var canvas = document.getElementById('canvas'),
    context = canvas.getContext('2d'),
    explosionButton = document.getElementById('explosionButton'),

    BOMB_LEFT = 100,
    BOMB_TOP = 80,
    BOMB_WIDTH = 180,
    BOMB_HEIGHT = 130,

    NUM_EXPLOSION_PAINTERS = 9,
    NUM_FUSE_PAINTERS = 9,

    // Painters.....................................................

    bombPainter = new ImagePainter('bomb.png'),
    bombNoFusePainter = new ImagePainter('bomb-no-fuse.png'),
    fuseBurningPainters = [],
    explosionPainters = [],

    // Animators....................................................

    fuseBurningAnimator = new SpriteAnimator(
       fuseBurningPainters,
       function () { bomb.painter = bombNoFusePainter; });

    explosionAnimator = new SpriteAnimator(
       explosionPainters,
       function () { bomb.painter = bombNoFusePainter; });
```

*(Continues)*

**Example 6.11** *(Continued)*

```
    // Bomb...................................................

    bomb = new Sprite('bomb', bombPainter),

// Functions...................................................

function resetBombNoFuse() {
    bomb.painter = bombNoFusePainter;
}

// Event handlers...................................................

explosionButton.onclick = function (e) {
    if (bomb.animating) // Not now...
        return;

    // Burn fuse for 2 seconds

    fuseBurningAnimator.start(bomb, 2000);

    // Wait for 3 seconds, then explode for 1 second

    setTimeout(function () {
        explosionAnimator.start(bomb, 1000);

        // Wait for 2 seconds, then reset to the original bomb image

        setTimeout(function () {
            bomb.painter = bombPainter;
        }, 2000);
    }, 3000);
};

// Animation...................................................

function animate(now) {
    context.clearRect(0, 0, canvas.width, canvas.height);
    bomb.paint(context);
    window.requestNextAnimationFrame(animate);
}

// Initialization...................................................

bomb.left = BOMB_LEFT;
bomb.top = BOMB_TOP;
```

```
bomb.width = BOMB_WIDTH;
bomb.height = BOMB_HEIGHT;

for (var i=0; i < NUM_FUSE_PAINTERS; ++i) {
   fuseBurningPainters.push(
      new ImagePainter('fuse-0' + i + '.png'));
}

for (var i=0; i < NUM_EXPLOSION_PAINTERS; ++i) {
   explosionPainters.push(
      new ImagePainter('explosion-0' + i + '.png'));
}

window.requestNextAnimationFrame(animate);
```

The application creates two animators: `fuseBurningAnimator` and `explosion-Animator`. Each animator originally contains an empty array of sprite painters; the application later initializes those arrays with image painters.

The button's click handler is where most of the action in the application takes place. If the bomb sprite is already animating, that click handler simply returns; otherwise, it starts the fuse-burning animator, which runs for 2 seconds. When the fuse is done burning, the fuse-burning animator's elapsed callback sets the bomb sprite's painter to a painter that paints the bomb without the fuse.

Subsequently, after a delay of one second, the bomb explodes for one second. At the end of the explosion animation, the explosion animator sets the ball sprite's painter to the painter that paints the bomb without the fuse.

Finally, one second after the bomb finishes exploding, the application sets the bomb's painter to a painter that paints the bomb with the fuse.

---

 **NOTE: Support for nonlinear animations**

The `SpriteAnimator` listed in Example 6.10 on p. 420 divides the animation's duration by the number of painters to calculate the period of time that it displays each painter. For linear animations, meaning animations that progress at a steady rate, that's exactly what you want; however, many animations are nonlinear. For instance, in Figure 6.9 on p. 419 the fuse burns at a constant rate. But when fuses are short they appear to burn faster than when they are long, so you may want the fuse-burning animation to speed up as it progresses.

In Chapter 7, we explore moving and animating sprites in a nonlinear fashion.

---

## 6.5 A Sprite-Based Animation Loop

Occasionally, you may paint sprites directly, as we've done so far in this chapter; however, most of the time you will probably paint them from a reusable sprite-based animation loop, that looks something like this:

```
var sprites = [ new Sprite(...), ... ], // An array of sprites
    context = ...;
...
function animate(time) {
   var i;
   ...
   context.clearRect(0, 0, context.canvas.width,
                           context.canvas.height);
   drawBackground();

   for (i=0; i < sprites.length; ++i) {
      sprites.update(context, time);
   }

   for (i=0; i < sprites.length; ++i) {
      sprites.paint(context);
   }
   ...
   window.requestNextAnimationFrame(animate);
}
```

Given an array of sprites, the preceding animation loop iterates over the array twice, first to update all the sprites and subsequently to paint them.

The separation between updating and painting is deliberate. Updating one sprite may affect another; for example, if the sprite that you are updating collides with another sprite, then both sprites are likely to have their locations modified by the collision.

If you interleave updating and painting, it's possible to paint a sprite at one location, and subsequently have its location modified when a related sprite is updated, and therefore the original sprite would be out of position. So, because of possible dependencies between sprites, you must update all the sprites first, and then paint them.

## 6.6 Conclusion

Sprites are an essential ingredient for creating interesting animations. In this chapter, you have seen how to encapsulate sprites, sprite painters, sprite behaviors, and sprite animations in objects of their own that you can reuse. Those objects let you write code at a higher level of abstraction and therefore greatly simplify the code that you need to write.

In the next chapter we look at another essential animation ingredient: physics.

# 7

# Physics

Physics, or some approximation thereof, often plays a role in sprite-based animations, especially games. This chapter discusses fundamental physics used in a wide variety of animations:

- Gravity
- Nonlinear motion
- Nonlinear animation

From Sonic the Hedgehog to Cut the Rope, gravity is prevalent in video games, so we start with three of the most common applications of gravity: falling, projectile trajectories, and gravity applied to harmonic motion.

Harmonic motion provides the mathematical dropback for things such as springs and swinging pendulums. After an introduction to harmonic motion, we explore warping time to implement effects such as ease in, ease out, oscillations, and bouncing.

Let's begin by looking at the weakest force in the universe.

**NOTE: The weakest force**

Gravity is by far the weakest force in the universe. There are four fundamental forces that we currently know about (from strongest to weakest): strong nuclear, electromagnetic, weak nuclear, and gravity.

The strong nuclear force, which keeps the nuclei of atoms together, is by far the strongest force. The electromagnetic force, the tug on a magnet, is about 100 times weaker than strong nuclear force. The weak nuclear force, which is responsible for radioactive decay, is about 100 billion times weaker than the electromagnetic force. Finally, gravity is approximately 100,000,000,000,000,000,000,000,000,000,000,000,000 times weaker than the electromagnetic force.

## 7.1  Gravity

Like light (which, although neutrinos may prove otherwise, sets the cosmic speed limit and can behave either as a wave or a particle) and water (the elixir of life and one of the few known substances that expands when it freezes), gravity is one of the most fascinating things in the universe. Unfathomably weaker than the tiny tug that you feel on a small magnet close to metal, gravity is weak weak weak. But without gravity, nothing as we know it would exist.

In the real world, anything that falls close to the earth accelerates at a rate of 9.81 m/s/s, or if you prefer, 32 ft/s/s. To simulate gravity in software, you just need to make falling sprites accelerate at that rate. It sounds easy, and for the most part, it is.

### 7.1.1  Falling

Figure 7.1 shows an application that simulates falling. The ball starts out in the middle of the ledge, but if you click the arrow a couple of times in a row, you can push the ball off the ledge and make it fall out of sight. As the ball is falling, the application calculates its vertical velocity with the simple formula shown in Equation 7.1.[1]

$$v_y = gt$$

Equation 7.1  Vertical velocity of a falling body at time $t$, with gravitational constant $g$

---

1. Wikipedia: Equations for a Falling Body, http://bit.ly/jURRlf.

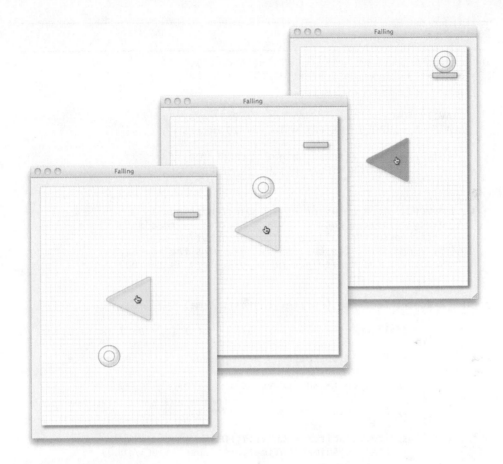

Figure 7.1 Falling off a platform

It's not difficult to translate Equation 7.1 to JavaScript. Because the gravitational constant is expressed in meters or feet, however, and not in pixels, the challenge when simulating gravity is simply to convert from meters to pixels. Example 7.1 shows how the application in Figure 7.1 does it.

The application creates a ball sprite with a single behavior that moves the ball. It also creates an animation timer that keeps track of the animation's elapsed time. See Section 5.10.2, "Animation Timers," on p. 389 for more information about animation timers.

**Example 7.1** Falling

```
var canvas = document.getElementById('canvas'),
    context = canvas.getContext('2d'),
    ...

    GRAVITY_FORCE = 9.81,              // 9.81 m/s/s
    PLATFORM_HEIGHT_IN_METERS = 10,   // 10 meters

    pixelsPerMeter = (canvas.height - LEDGE_TOP) /
                      PLATFORM_HEIGHT_IN_METERS,
    ...

    // moveBall is a behavior -- an object with an
    // execute(sprite, context, time)  method -- that's
    // attached to the ball. When the application calls
    // ball.update(), the ball sprite executes the moveBall
    // behavior. The sprite passed to execute() is the ball.

    moveBall = {
       execute: function (sprite, context, time) {
          ...
          if (fallingAnimationTimer.isRunning()) { // Ball is falling

             // Reposition the ball at a steady pixels/second rate

             sprite.top += sprite.velocityY / fps;

             // Recalculate the ball's velocity

             sprite.velocityY = GRAVITY_FORCE *
                 (fallingAnimationTimer.getElapsedTime()/1000) *
                 pixelsPerMeter;

             if (sprite.top > canvas.height) {
                stopFalling();
             }
          }
       }
    },

    function stopFalling() {
       fallingAnimationTimer.stop();
       ...

       ball.left = LEDGE_LEFT + LEDGE_WIDTH/2 - BALL_RADIUS;
       ball.top = LEDGE_TOP - BALL_RADIUS*2;

       ball.velocityY = 0;
    },
```

```
...

// Create the animation timer and the ball sprite.

fallingAnimationTimer = new AnimationTimer(),

ball = new Sprite(
    'ball', // Name
    { paint: function(sprite, context) { ... } }, // Painter
    [ moveBall ]), // Behaviors
...
}
```

The application arbitrarily sets the distance from the ledge to the bottom of the canvas to 10 meters. Given the height of the canvas in pixels, the application calculates a pixels/meter ratio that it subsequently uses to convert the ball's velocity from meters/second to pixels/second.

As the animation timer is running, meaning the ball is falling, the `moveBall` behavior's `execute()` method continuously updates the ball's position, like this:

```
ball.top += ball.velocityY / fps;
```

Dividing the velocity (pixels/second) by the animation rate (frames/second) yields the number of pixels the ball moves for the current animation frame (pixels/frame). The method then calculates the ball's vertical velocity, like this:

```
ball.velocityY = GRAVITY_FORCE *
                (fallingTimer.getElapsedTime()/1000) * pixelsPerMeter;
```

The preceding line of code multiplies the force of gravity (9.81 m/s/s) by the elapsed time, in seconds, that the ball has been falling. Because the seconds cancel out (see Section 1.11.4, "Deriving Equations from Units of Measure," on p. 62 for more about deriving equations from units of measure), we end up with a velocity specified in meters/second. However, the application specifies the ball's velocity in pixels/second, so it converts the velocity from meters/second to pixels/second by multiplying that velocity by `pixelsPerMeter`.

---

**NOTE: Sprites**

The examples in this chapter use the sprites implemented in Chapter 6, which lets us concentrate on the physics aspects of the examples, instead of animation details. As is the case for the application shown in **Figure 7.1**, the interesting code in this chapter's examples are in sprite behaviors, such as the `moveBall` behavior in **Example 7.1**.

---

**NOTE: Friction**

Assuming your proximity to the earth is constant, gravity is a constant force that pulls objects toward the center of the earth.

Assuming that an object is sliding on a homogeneous surface, friction is also a constant force. However, instead of always acting in one direction like gravity, friction always acts in the opposite direction of an object's motion.

In Example 7.1, you saw how to adjust a sprite's velocity to account for the acceleration due to gravity. Accounting for deceleration due to friction is very similar; see Section 9.3.3, "Gravity and Friction," on p. 594 for an example of incorporating friction into a pinball game.

## 7.1.2 Projectile Trajectories

In the previous section you saw how to adjust a falling object's vertical velocity to account for gravity. This section adds horizontal motion, thereby simulating projectile trajectories.

The application shown in Figure 7.2 is a simple game in which the player tries to shoot balls into a bucket. As the user moves the mouse, the application

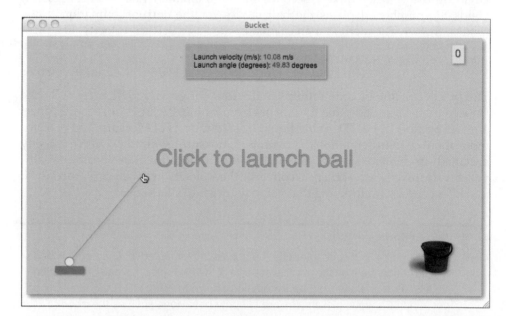

Figure 7.2 The bucket game

continuously draws a guidewire from the middle of the ball to the mouse cursor. That guidewire represents the angle and velocity at which the application shoots the ball—the longer the guidewire the greater the force applied when the application launches the ball.

Besides continuously updating the guidewire as the user moves the mouse, the application also constantly updates the launch velocity and angle that are displayed by the heads-up display.

The application shows the current score in the upper-right corner. You get two points for shots that go in the bucket but do not leave the canvas bounds, as depicted in the upper screenshot in Figure 7.3. You get three points for shots that escape the bounds of the canvas and ultimately return to go into the bucket, as shown in the bottom screenshot.

The application creates a ball sprite, like this:

```
ball = new Sprite('ball', ballPainter, [ lob ]),
```

The application defines the canvas width to be 10 meters and subsequently calculates the corresponding number of pixels per meter:

```
ARENA_LENGTH_IN_METERS = 10,
pixelsPerMeter = canvas.width / ARENA_LENGTH_IN_METERS,
```

The ball sprite has a single behavior—listed in Example 7.2—that lobs the ball through the air.

If the ball is in flight, the lob behavior calculates the elapsed time for the last animation frame and the elapsed flight time for the ball. Subsequently, it uses those values to update the ball's position and to apply gravity to the ball's velocity, respectively.

To update the ball position, the lob behavior multiplies the ball's velocity (m/s) by the number of seconds it took for the last animation frame to execute. That multiplication results in the ball's displacement, in meters, for the current animation frame. Finally, the lob behavior multiplies that displacement by pixelsPerMeter to obtain the displacement in pixels.

To apply gravity to the ball's vertical velocity, the lob behavior uses Equation 7.2.[2]

$$v_y = v_{y0} - gt$$

Equation 7.2 **Velocity of a projectile**

---

2. Wikipedia: Trajectory of a Projectile, http://bit.ly/lwNcox.

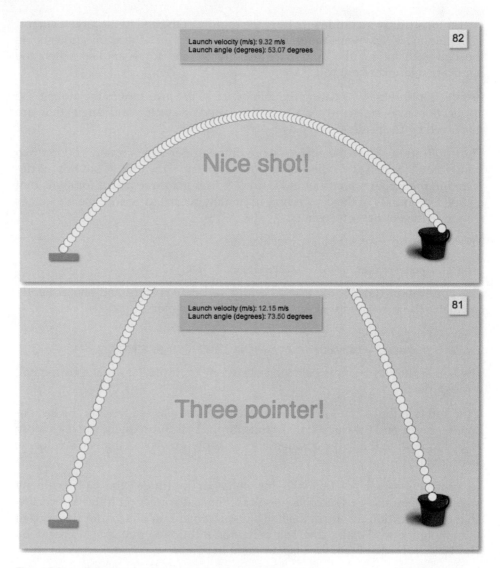

Figure 7.3  A two-pointer (*top*) and a three-pointer (*bottom*)

Example 7.2  Lobbing a ball

```
lob = {
   lastTime: 0,
   GRAVITY_FORCE: 9.81, // m/s/s

   applyGravity: function (elapsed) {
      ball.velocityY = (this.GRAVITY_FORCE * elapsed) -
                       (launchVelocity * Math.sin(launchAngle));
   },

   updateBallPosition: function (updateDelta) {
      ball.left += ball.velocityX * (updateDelta) * pixelsPerMeter;
      ball.top  += ball.velocityY * (updateDelta) * pixelsPerMeter;
   },

   checkForThreePointer: function () {
      if (ball.top < 0) {
         threePointer = true;
      }
   },

   checkBallBounds: function () {
      if (ball.top > canvas.height || ball.left > canvas.width)  {
         reset();
      }
   },

   execute: function (ball, context, time) {
      var updateDelta,
          elapsedFlightTime;

      if (ballInFlight) {
         elapsedFrameTime  = (time - this.lastTime)/1000;
         elapsedFlightTime = (time - launchTime)/1000;

         this.applyGravity(elapsedFlightTime);
         this.updateBallPosition(elapsedFrameTime);
         this.checkForThreePointer();
         this.checkBallBounds();
      }
      this.lastTime = time;
   }
},
```

Notice the similarities between Equation 7.1 on p. 428, which calculates the vertical velocity of a falling body, and Equation 7.2, which calculates the vertical velocity of a projectile. The difference between the two is that the latter takes into account the projectile's initial vertical velocity ($v_{y0}$).

The HTML for the application shown in Figure 7.2 is listed in Example 7.3 and the JavaScript is listed in Example 7.4. Besides illustrating how to implement projectile trajectories, the bucket application has many of the ingredients for a more industrial-strength game, including a scoreboard, a heads-up display, and feedback when the user scores.

**Example 7.3** Bucket game: HTML

```html
<!DOCTYPE html>
<html>
   <head>
      <title>Bucket</title>

      <style>
         output {
            color: blue;
         }

         .floatingControls {
            background: rgba(0,0,0,0.1);
            border: thin solid skyblue;
            -webkit-box-shadow: rgba(0,0,0,0.3) 2px 2px 4px;
            -moz-box-shadow: rgba(100,140,230,0.5) 2px 2px 6px;
            box-shadow: rgba(100,140,230,0.5) 2px 2px 6px;
            padding: 15px;
            font: 12px Arial;
         }

         #canvas {
            background: skyblue;
            -webkit-box-shadow: 4px 4px 8px rgba(0,0,0,0.5);
            -moz-box-shadow: 4px 4px 8px rgba(0,0,0,0.5);
            box-shadow: 4px 4px 8px rgba(0,0,0,0.5);
            cursor: pointer;
         }

         #scoreboard {
            background: rgba(255,255,255,0.5);
            position: absolute;
            left: 755px;
            top: 20px;
            color: blue;
            font-size: 18px;
            padding: 5px;
         }
```

```
        #controls {
            position: absolute;
            left: 285px;
            top: 20px;
        }
    </style>
</head>

<body>
    <canvas id='canvas' width='800' height='450'>
       Canvas not supported
    </canvas>

    <div id='scoreboard' class='floatingControls'>0</div>

    <div id='controls' class='floatingControls'>
       Launch velocity   (m/s):
       <output id='launchVelocityOutput'></output> m/s<br/>

       Launch angle (degrees):
       <output id='launchAngleOutput'></output> degrees<br/>
    </div>

    <script src = 'requestNextAnimationFrame.js'></script>
    <script src = 'sprites.js'></script>
    <script src = 'example.js'></script>
</body>
</html>
```

In addition to the canvas element, the bucket game's HTML creates two DIVs: scoreboard and controls. The application's CSS positions the scoreboard in the upper right of the canvas, and the controls in the upper middle.

The bucket game's HTML also includes three JavaScript files. The requestNextAnimationFrame.js file contains the implementation of the requestAnimationFrame() polyfill method discussed in Section 5.1.3, "A Portable Animation Loop," on p. 348; the sprites.js file contains the implementation of sprites as discussed in Chapter 6; and finally, the HTML includes the JavaScript for the application itself, which is listed in Example 7.4.

---

**NOTE: requestAnimationFrame() polyfill**

The examples in this chapter use the requestAnimationFrame() polyfill method discussed in Section 5.1.3, "A Portable Animation Loop," on p. 348. That polyfill method is named request*Next*AnimationFrame(); it behaves just like requestAnimationFrame() by invoking a callback method when it's time to draw the next animation frame.

---

---

Example 7.4 Bucket game: JavaScript

---

```javascript
var canvas = document.getElementById('canvas'),
    context = canvas.getContext('2d'),
    scoreboard = document.getElementById('scoreboard'),
    launchAngleOutput = document.getElementById('launchAngleOutput'),
    launchVelocityOutput =
        document.getElementById('launchVelocityOutput'),

    elapsedTime = undefined,
    launchTime = undefined,

    score = 0,
    lastScore = 0,
    lastMouse = { left: 0, top: 0 },

    threePointer = false,
    needInstructions = true,

    LAUNCHPAD_X = 50,
    LAUNCHPAD_Y = context.canvas.height-50,
    LAUNCHPAD_WIDTH = 50,
    LAUNCHPAD_HEIGHT = 12,
    BALL_RADIUS = 8,
    ARENA_LENGTH_IN_METERS = 10,
    INITIAL_LAUNCH_ANGLE = Math.PI/4,

    launchAngle = INITIAL_LAUNCH_ANGLE,
    pixelsPerMeter = canvas.width / ARENA_LENGTH_IN_METERS,

    // Launch pad....................................................

    launchPadPainter = {
       LAUNCHPAD_FILL_STYLE: 'rgb(100,140,230)',

       paint: function (ledge, context) {
          context.save();
          context.fillStyle = this.LAUNCHPAD_FILL_STYLE;
          context.fillRect(LAUNCHPAD_X, LAUNCHPAD_Y,
                           LAUNCHPAD_WIDTH, LAUNCHPAD_HEIGHT);
          context.restore();
       }
    },

    launchPad = new Sprite('launchPad', launchPadPainter),

    // Ball..........................................................
```

```
ballPainter = {
   BALL_FILL_STYLE: 'rgb(255,255,0)',
   BALL_STROKE_STYLE: 'rgb(0,0,0,0.4)',

   paint: function (ball, context) {
      context.save();
      context.shadowColor = undefined;
      context.lineWidth = 2;
      context.fillStyle = this.BALL_FILL_STYLE;
      context.strokeStyle = this.BALL_STROKE_STYLE;

      context.beginPath();
      context.arc(ball.left, ball.top,
                  ball.radius, 0, Math.PI*2, false);

      context.clip();
      context.fill();
      context.stroke();
      context.restore();
   }
},

// Lob behavior...............................................

lob = {
   lastTime: 0,
   GRAVITY_FORCE: 9.81, // m/s/s

   applyGravity: function (elapsed) {
      ball.velocityY = (this.GRAVITY_FORCE * elapsed) -
                       (launchVelocity * Math.sin(launchAngle));
   },

   updateBallPosition: function (updateDelta) {
      ball.left +=
         ball.velocityX * (updateDelta) * pixelsPerMeter;

      ball.top +=
         ball.velocityY * (updateDelta) * pixelsPerMeter;
   },

   checkForThreePointer: function () {
      if (ball.top < 0) {
         threePointer = true;
      }
   },
```

*(Continues)*

**Example 7.4** *(Continued)*

```
    checkBallBounds: function () {
        if (ball.top > canvas.height || ball.left > canvas.width)  {
            reset();
        }
    },

    execute: function (ball, context, time) {
        var updateDelta,
            elapsedFlightTime;

        if (ballInFlight) {
            elapsedFrameTime  = (time - this.lastTime)/1000;
            elapsedFlightTime = (time - launchTime)/1000;

            this.applyGravity(elapsedFlightTime);
            this.updateBallPosition(elapsedFrameTime);
            this.checkForThreePointer();
            this.checkBallBounds();
        }
        this.lastTime = time;
    }
},

ball = new Sprite('ball', ballPainter, [ lob ]),
ballInFlight = false,

// Bucket.......................................................

catchBall = {
    ballInBucket: function() {
        return ball.left > bucket.left + bucket.width/2 &&
               ball.left < bucket.left + bucket.width   &&
               ball.top > bucket.top && ball.top <
               bucket.top + bucket.height/3;
    },

    adjustScore: function() {
        if (threePointer) lastScore = 3;
        else              lastScore = 2;

        score += lastScore;
        scoreboard.innerText = score;
    },
```

```
        execute: function (bucket, context, time) {
            if (ballInFlight && this.ballInBucket()) {
                reset();
                this.adjustScore();
            }
        }
    },

    BUCKET_X = 668,
    BUCKET_Y = canvas.height - 100,
    bucketImage = new Image(),

    bucket = new Sprite('bucket',
        {
            paint: function (sprite, context) {
                context.drawImage(bucketImage, BUCKET_X, BUCKET_Y);
            }
        },

        [ catchBall ]
    );

// Functions.....................................................

function windowToCanvas(x, y) {
    var bbox = canvas.getBoundingClientRect();

    return { x: x - bbox.left * (canvas.width  / bbox.width),
             y: y - bbox.top  * (canvas.height / bbox.height)
           };
}

function reset() {
    ball.left = LAUNCHPAD_X + LAUNCHPAD_WIDTH/2;
    ball.top = LAUNCHPAD_Y - ball.height/2;
    ball.velocityX = 0;
    ball.velocityY = 0;
    ballInFlight = false;
    needInstructions = false;
    lastScore = 0;
}
```

*(Continues)*

**Example 7.4** *(Continued)*

```javascript
function showText(text) {
    var metrics;

    context.font = '42px Helvetica';
    metrics = context.measureText(text);

    context.save();
    context.shadowColor = undefined;
    context.strokeStyle = 'rgb(80,120,210)';
    context.fillStyle = 'rgba(100,140,230,0.5)';

    context.fillText(text,
                     canvas.width/2 - metrics.width/2,
                     canvas.height/2);

    context.strokeText(text,
                       canvas.width/2 - metrics.width/2,
                       canvas.height/2);
    context.restore();
}

function drawGuidewire() {
    context.moveTo(ball.left, ball.top);
    context.lineTo(lastMouse.left, lastMouse.top);
    context.stroke();
};

function updateBackgroundText() {
    if (lastScore == 3)          showText('Three pointer!');
    else if (lastScore == 2)     showText('Nice shot!');
    else if (needInstructions) showText('Click to launch ball');
};

function resetScoreLater() {
    setTimeout(function () {
        lastScore = 0;
    }, 1000);
};

function updateSprites(time) {
    bucket.update(context, time);
    launchPad.update(context, time);
    ball.update(context, time);
}
```

```
function paintSprites() {
   launchPad.paint(context);
   bucket.paint(context);
   ball.paint(context);
}

// Event handlers.................................................

canvas.onmousedown = function(e) {
   var rect;

   e.preventDefault();

   if ( ! ballInFlight) {
      ball.velocityX = launchVelocity * Math.cos(launchAngle);
      ball.velocityY = launchVelocity * Math.sin(launchAngle);
      ballInFlight = true;
      threePointer = false;
      launchTime = +new Date();
   }
};

canvas.onmousemove = function (e) {
   var rect;

   e.preventDefault();

   if ( ! ballInFlight) {
      loc = windowToCanvas(e.clientX, e.clientY);
      lastMouse.left = loc.x;
      lastMouse.top = loc.y;

      deltaX = Math.abs(lastMouse.left - ball.left);
      deltaY = Math.abs(lastMouse.top - ball.top);

      launchAngle =
         Math.atan(parseFloat(deltaY) / parseFloat(deltaX));

      launchVelocity =
         4 * deltaY / Math.sin (launchAngle) / pixelsPerMeter;

      launchVelocityOutput.innerText = launchVelocity.toFixed(2);
      launchAngleOutput.innerText =
         (launchAngle * 180/Math.PI).toFixed(2);
   }
};
```

*(Continues)*

---

Example 7.4 *(Continued)*

```javascript
// Animation loop.....................................................

function animate(time) {
    elapsedTime = (time - launchTime) / 1000;
    context.clearRect(0, 0, canvas.width, canvas.height);

    if (!ballInFlight) {
        drawGuidewire();
        updateBackgroundText();

        if (lastScore !== 0) { // Just scored
            resetScoreLater();
        }
    }

    updateSprites(time);
    paintSprites();

    window.requestNextAnimationFrame(animate);
}

// Initialization....................................................

ball.width = BALL_RADIUS*2;
ball.height = ball.width;
ball.left = LAUNCHPAD_X + LAUNCHPAD_WIDTH/2;
ball.top = LAUNCHPAD_Y - ball.height/2;
ball.radius = BALL_RADIUS;

context.lineWidth = 0.5;
context.strokeStyle = 'rgba(0,0,0,0.5)';
context.shadowColor = 'rgba(0,0,0,0.5)';
context.shadowOffsetX = 2;
context.shadowOffsetY = 2;
context.shadowBlur = 4;
context.stroke();

bucketImage.src = 'bucket.png';
bucketImage.onload = function (e) {
    bucket.left = BUCKET_X;
    bucket.top = BUCKET_Y;
    bucket.width = bucketImage.width;
    bucket.height = bucketImage.height;
};

window.requestNextAnimationFrame(animate);
```

---

### 7.1.3 Pendulums

To complete this section on gravity, let's see how to simulate gravity's effects on a pendulum.

The simple equations that we used in the preceding sections to calculate the velocity of a falling body or a projectile were linear, meaning that the velocity was directly proportional to the amount of time the object had been moving.

Pendulums, on the other hand are a nonlinear system, so we cannot simply multiply time by the gravitational constant, as we have previously. Instead, we use Equation 7.3 to calculate the pendulum's given the elapsed time of the animation.[3]

$$\theta = \theta_0 \times \cos(\sqrt{g \; / \; l} \times t)$$

Equation 7.3  Equation for simple pendulum motion

In Equation 7.3, $\theta$ represents the pendulum's angle, and $\theta_0$ is the pendulum's initial angle, $g$ is the force of gravity, $l$ is the length of the pendulum's rod, and $t$ is elapsed time. It's interesting to note that the mass of the weight at the end of the pendulum does not enter into the equation; it doesn't matter how much the weight weighs.

Figure 7.4 shows an application that simulates a pendulum.

The application creates a sprite for the pendulum:

```
pendulum = new Sprite('pendulum', pendulumPainter, [ swing ]),
```

The pendulum sprite has a single swing behavior. That behavior calculates the pendulum angle, with Equation 7.3, like this:

```
swing = {
   GRAVITY_FORCE: 32, // 32 ft/s/s,
   ROD_LENGTH: 0.8,   // 0.8 ft

   execute: function(pendulum, context, time) {
      pendulum.angle =
         pendulum.initialAngle * Math.cos(
            Math.sqrt(this.GRAVITY_FORCE/this.ROD_LENGTH) *
            elapsedTime);
```

---

3. Wikipedia: Motion Equations for a Pendulum, http://bit.ly/mvpGu7.

```
      pendulum.weightX =
          pendulum.x + Math.sin(pendulum.angle) * pendulum.rodLength;

      pendulum.weightY =
          pendulum.y + Math.cos(pendulum.angle) * pendulum.rodLength;
   }
};
```

From the pendulum's angle, the swing behavior calculates the location of the pendulum's weight.

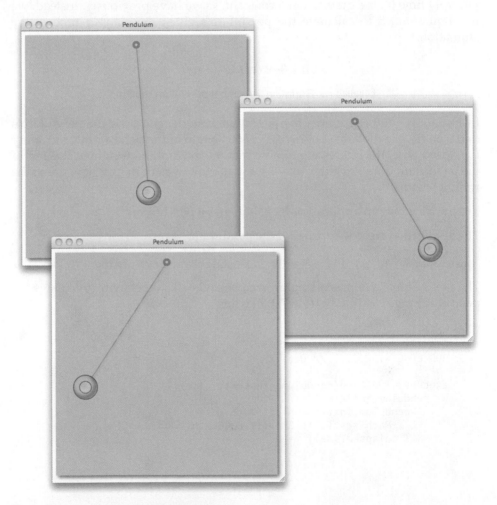

Figure 7.4  A pendulum: nonlinear motion

The JavaScript for the application shown in Figure 7.4 is listed in Example 7.5.

---

**Example 7.5** A pendulum

---

```javascript
var canvas = document.getElementById('canvas'),
    context = canvas.getContext('2d'),

    elapsedTime = undefined,
    startTime = undefined,

    PIVOT_Y = 20,
    PIVOT_RADIUS = 7,
    WEIGHT_RADIUS = 25,
    INITIAL_ANGLE = Math.PI/5,
    ROD_LENGTH_IN_PIXELS = 300,

    // Pendulum painter.............................................

    pendulumPainter = {
        PIVOT_FILL_STYLE:     'rgba(0,0,0,0.2)',
        WEIGHT_SHADOW_COLOR:  'rgb(0,0,0)',
        PIVOT_SHADOW_COLOR:   'rgb(255,255,0)',
        STROKE_COLOR:         'rgb(100,100,195)',

        paint: function (pendulum, context) {
            this.drawPivot(pendulum);
            this.drawRod(pendulum);
            this.drawWeight(pendulum, context);
        },

        drawWeight: function (pendulum, context) {
            context.save();
            context.beginPath();
            context.arc(pendulum.weightX, pendulum.weightY,
                        pendulum.weightRadius, 0, Math.PI*2, false);
            context.clip();

            context.shadowColor = this.WEIGHT_SHADOW_COLOR;
            context.shadowOffsetX = -4;
            context.shadowOffsetY = -4;
            context.shadowBlur = 8;

            context.lineWidth = 2;
            context.strokeStyle = this.STROKE_COLOR;
            context.stroke();
```

*(Continues)*

---

**Example 7.5** *(Continued)*

---

```
        context.beginPath();
        context.arc(pendulum.weightX, pendulum.weightY,
                    pendulum.weightRadius/2, 0, Math.PI*2, false);

        context.clip();

        context.shadowColor = this.PIVOT_SHADOW_COLOR;
        context.shadowOffsetX = -4;
        context.shadowOffsetY = -4;
        context.shadowBlur = 8;
        context.stroke();

        context.restore();
    },

    drawPivot: function (pendulum) {
        context.save();
        context.beginPath();
        context.shadowColor = undefined;
        context.fillStyle = 'white';
        context.arc(pendulum.x + pendulum.pivotRadius,
                    pendulum.y, pendulum.pivotRadius/2,
                    0, Math.PI*2, false);
        context.fill();
        context.stroke();

        context.beginPath();
        context.fillStyle = this.PIVOT_FILL_STYLE;
        context.arc(pendulum.x + pendulum.pivotRadius,
                    pendulum.y, pendulum.pivotRadius,
                    0, Math.PI*2, false);
        context.fill();
        context.stroke();
        context.restore();
    },

    drawRod: function (pendulum) {
        context.beginPath();

        context.moveTo(
            pendulum.x + pendulum.pivotRadius +
            pendulum.pivotRadius*Math.sin(pendulum.angle),

            pendulum.y + pendulum.pivotRadius *
                Math.cos(pendulum.angle)
        );
```

```
        context.lineTo(
            pendulum.weightX -
                pendulum.weightRadius*Math.sin(pendulum.angle),

            pendulum.weightY -
                pendulum.weightRadius*Math.cos(pendulum.angle)
        );

        context.stroke();
        }
    },

    // Swing behavior...............................................

    swing = {
        // For a gravity force of 32 ft/s/s, and a rod
        // length of 0.8 ft (about 10 inches), the time period
        // for the pendulum is about one second. Make the rod
        // longer for a longer time period.

        GRAVITY_FORCE: 32, // 32 ft/s/s,
        ROD_LENGTH: 0.8,   // 0.8 ft

        execute: function(pendulum, context, time) {
            pendulum.angle = pendulum.initialAngle * Math.cos(
                Math.sqrt(this.GRAVITY_FORCE/this.ROD_LENGTH) *
                elapsedTime);

            pendulum.weightX = pendulum.x +
                Math.sin(pendulum.angle) * pendulum.rodLength;

            pendulum.weightY = pendulum.y +
                Math.cos(pendulum.angle) * pendulum.rodLength;
        }
    };

    // Pendulum....................................................

    pendulum = new Sprite('pendulum', pendulumPainter, [ swing ]);

// Animation loop.................................................

function animate(time) {
    elapsedTime = (time - startTime) / 1000;
    context.clearRect(0, 0, canvas.width, canvas.height);
    pendulum.update(context, time);
    pendulum.paint(context);
    window.requestNextAnimationFrame(animate);
}
```

*(Continues)*

---

**Example 7.5**  *(Continued)*

---

```
// Initialization.................................................

pendulum.x = canvas.width/2;
pendulum.y = PIVOT_Y;
pendulum.weightRadius = WEIGHT_RADIUS;
pendulum.pivotRadius  = PIVOT_RADIUS;
pendulum.initialAngle = INITIAL_ANGLE;
pendulum.angle        = INITIAL_ANGLE;
pendulum.rodLength    = ROD_LENGTH_IN_PIXELS;

context.lineWidth = 0.5;
context.strokeStyle = 'rgba(0,0,0,0.5)';
context.shadowColor = 'rgba(0,0,0,0.5)';
context.shadowOffsetX = 2;
context.shadowOffsetY = 2;
context.shadowBlur = 4;
context.stroke();

startTime = + new Date();
animate(startTime);
```

---

## 7.2  Warping Time

Section 7.1.3, "Pendulums," on p. 445 used a nonlinear equation to calculate a pendulum's angle. As it turns out, nonlinear systems are quite common, from springs and pendulums to bouncing balls, so it's important to be able to simulate nonlinear systems in your animations.

The pendulum's *motion* in Section 7.1.3 is nonlinear, but you might want to animate other aspects of your animations besides motion in a nonlinear fashion. For example, if you were simulating someone blushing, you would show an initial rush of red that slowly fades away. In that case, it is the change in color, not the change in location, that is nonlinear.

Fundamentally, we want to depict changes to any property over time—whether that property is location, color, or some other property—in a nonlinear manner, so it's time, and not those individual properties, that we want to manipulate.

Section 5.10.2, "Animation Timers," on p. 389 discussed the implementation of a simple AnimationTimer that you can use to control animations. You use AnimationTimers like this:

```
var ANIMATION_DURATION = 1000, // One second

    // Create an animation timer
    animationTimer = new AnimationTimer(ANIMATION_DURATION);
    ...

function animate() {
   var elapsed;
   ...
   if ( ! animationTimer.isOver()) {

      // Update the animation, based on the
      // animation timer's elapsed time

      updateAnimation(animationTimer.getElapsedTime());
      ...
   }

   // Keep the animation going

   requestNextAnimationFrame(animate);
}
...
animationTimer.start();                 // Start the animation timer
requestNextAnimationFrame(animate);     // Start the animation
```

You create an animation timer, start it, and until the animation is over, you periodically get the animation's elapsed time and update the animation correspondingly.

Animation timers are nothing special; they are just timers that maintain an animation's duration, and therefore they can tell you whether an animation is over.

The real utility of animation timers lies in the fact that *you can implement* AnimationTimer.getElapsedTime() *to return something other than the actual elapsed time*; by doing so, you can effectively warp time.

For example, you could implement getElapsedTime() so that it initially returns an elapsed time that is much less than the actual elapsed time. Over the duration of the animation, you could steadily decrease the gap between the actual elapsed time and the value that you return from getElapsedTime(); as a result, time would initially move very slowly and steadily speed up throughout the animation.

That algorithm—starting slowly, and gradually accelerating—is known as an ease-in effect; it is illustrated in Figure 7.5.

The application shown in Figure 7.5 animates a sprite through a sequence of images that make it look like the sprite is running. The application also moves the sprite from right to left; otherwise, the sprite would appear to run in place.

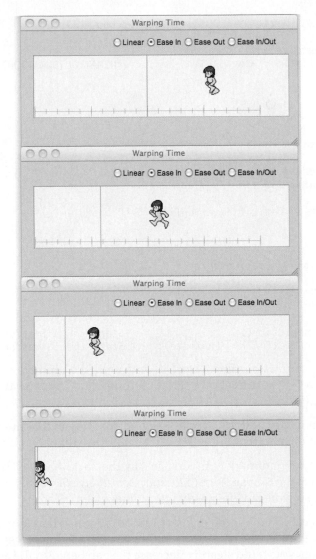

Figure 7.5  The ease-in effect

The application uses the animation's *real elapsed time* to place the vertical line; however, it uses the *warped elapsed time* that AnimationTimer.getElapsedTime() returns to position the sprite.

For the ease-in effect shown in Figure 7.5, the sprite initially lags behind the timeline, but the application slowly closes the gap between the two until the end of the animation, when they finally align.

Contrast the ease-in motion shown in Figure 7.5 to the linear motion shown in Figure 7.6. With linear motion, the sprite moves at a constant velocity, in concert with the timeline.

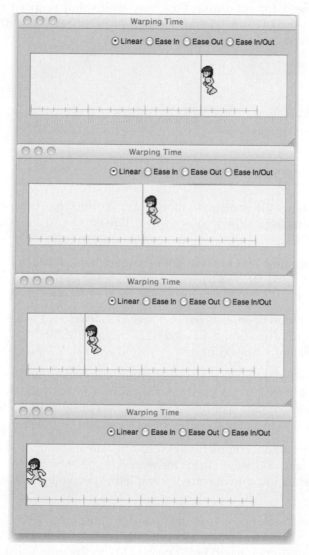

Figure 7.6  The linear effect

The ease-in effect shown in Figure 7.5 is one of many time-warping effects that you can create. Other common time-warping effects are ease out, ease in/out, elastic, and bounce. Section 7.4, "Warping Motion," on p. 458 discusses the application shown in Figure 7.5 so you can see how to implement those effects.

To implement time-warping, we need to modify the behavior of AnimationTimer.getElapsedTime() for each case. One way to do that is to let the developer provide a time-warping function that AnimationTimer.getElapsedTime() applies to the actual elapsed time, as shown in Figure 7.7.

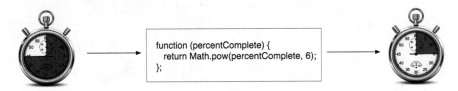

```
function (percentComplete) {
    return Math.pow(percentComplete, 6);
};
```

Figure 7.7  Warping time with a function

Example 7.6 shows an implementation of AnimationTimer that lets you specify a time-warp function. When you call getElapsedTime(), the animation timer passes the real elapsed time through your time-warp function.

The most interesting line of code is in the getElapsedTime() method: return elapsedTime * (this.timeWarp(percentComplete) / percentComplete). Let's see what it means.

The implementation of AnimationTimer.getElapsedTime() gets the animation's elapsed time and divides the elapsed time by the duration to determine what percent of the animation is complete.

The getElapsedTime() method passes the animation's completion percentage—a number from 0.0 to 1.0—to the time-warp function that you supply when you create an AnimationTimer. The time-warp function presumably returns a different value between 0.0 to 1.0 that represents the warped completion percentage.

Armed with the actual completion percentage and the warped completion percentage, getElapsedTime() returns the warped time, which is the actual elapsed time multiplied by the ratio of warped completion percentage / actual completion percentage.

Here's an example: Suppose that an animation's duration is 100 seconds and the elapsed time is 17 seconds. In real time, the anima- tion is 17% complete, so AnimationTimer.getElapsedTime() passes 0.17 to the time-warp function. Let's say the time-warp function squares the percent, so it returns a warped percent of 0.034, meaning only 3.4% complete instead of 17%. That means the warped percent (3.4%) is one-fifth (0.034 / 0.17 = 0.2) of the actual percent (17%). So `AnimationTimer.getElapsedTime()` returns 3.4, which is one-fifth of the actual time, by multiplying the actual time by (warped percent / actual percent).

---

**Example 7.6** `AnimationTimer`, refactored to support time-warping

---

```
// Constructor.................................................

AnimationTimer = function (duration, timeWarp)  {
    if (timeWarp !== undefined) this.timeWarp = timeWarp;
    if (duration !== undefined) this.duration = duration;
    this.stopwatch = new Stopwatch();

};

// Prototype...................................................

AnimationTimer.prototype = {
    start: function () {
        this.stopwatch.start();
    },

    stop: function () {
        this.stopwatch.stop();
    },

    getElapsedTime: function () {
        var elapsedTime = this.stopwatch.getElapsedTime(),
            percentComplete = elapsedTime / this.duration;

        if (!this.stopwatch.running)     return undefined;
        if (this.timeWarp == undefined) return elapsedTime;

        return elapsedTime *
            (this.timeWarp(percentComplete) / percentComplete);
    },

    isRunning: function() {
        return this.stopwatch.running;
    },

    isOver: function () {
        return this.stopwatch.getElapsedTime() > this.duration;
    },
};
```

---

Here's how you use a time-warp function with an animation timer:

```
var ANIMATION_DURATION = 1000, // One second
    animation = new AnimationTimer(ANIMATION_DURATION,
        function (percentComplete) {
            return Math.pow(percentComplete, 2);
        });
    ...

    function animate() {  // Repeatedly called from animation loop
        ...
        if ( ! animation.isOver()) {
            elapsed = animation.getElapsedTime();

            // Update the animation, based on the elapsed time
            update(elapsed);
        }
        ...
    }
    ...
```

In the preceding code listing, the time-warping function squares the actual elapsed time. As it turns out, squaring the value results in an implementation of the ease-in effect discussed previously. When the value is small—for example, 0.2—the squared value is much smaller—0.2 squared is 0.04, whereas larger values, such as 0.9, when squared, are very close to the original value—0.9 squared is 0.81. As a result of the time-warp function, time initially flows slowly and gradually speeds up.

## 7.3 Time–Warp Functions

The AnimationTimer object listed in Example 7.6 also has some built-in time-warp functions, as shown in Example 7.7.

You can use the methods listed in Example 7.7 to implement a time-warp. For example, to implement the ease-in effect, you could do the following:

```
var ANIMATION_DURATION = 1000, // One second
    animation = new AnimationTimer(ANIMATION_DURATION,
                                   AnimationTimer.makeEaseIn(1));
    ...
```

The value that the preceding listing passes to AnimationTimer.makeEaseIn() controls the strength of the effect. In the next section, we show how that strength variable works, and we take a look at each of the effects implemented in Example 7.7.

---

**Example 7.7** Time-warping functions

```javascript
var DEFAULT_ELASTIC_PASSES = 3;

AnimationTimer.makeEaseIn = function (strength) {
    return function (percentComplete) {
        return Math.pow(percentComplete, strength*2);
    };
};

AnimationTimer.makeEaseOut = function (strength) {
    return function (percentComplete) {
        return 1 - Math.pow(1 - percentComplete, strength*2);
    };
};

AnimationTimer.makeEaseInOut = function () {
    return function (percentComplete) {
        return percentComplete - Math.sin(percentComplete*2*Math.PI) /
                (2*Math.PI);
    };
};

AnimationTimer.makeElastic = function (passes) {
    passes = passes || DEFAULT_ELASTIC_PASSES;
    return function (percentComplete) {
        return ((1-Math.cos(percentComplete * Math.PI * passes)) *
                (1 - percentComplete)) + percentComplete;
    };
};

AnimationTimer.makeBounce = function (bounces) {
    var fn = AnimationTimer.makeElastic(bounces);
    return function (percentComplete) {
        percentComplete = fn(percentComplete);
        return percentComplete <= 1 ? percentComplete : 2-percentComplete;
    };
};

AnimationTimer.makeLinear = function () {
    return function (percentComplete) {
        return percentComplete;
    };
};
```

---

 **NOTE: Tweening**

You may recognize the time-warping discussed in this chapter as tweening in Flash or CSS3. You define keyframes in an animation, and either Flash or CSS3 generates the frames in be*tween*, using a time-warping (tweening) function that you specify.

Canvas does not provide any native tweening functionality that you find in higher-level abstractions such as CSS3 and Flash, so in this section we've implemented it ourselves.

---

## 7.4  Warping Motion

Now that you've seen how to use animation timers with time-warp functions to manipulate the flow of time through your animations, let's look at some classic examples of motion tweening with an application, shown in **Figure 7.8**, that lets you apply those time-warp functions to the movement of a ball.

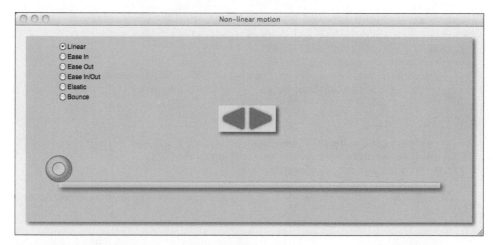

Figure 7.8  Various motion tweening algorithms

The following time-warp functions are supported by the application:

- Linear: Move at constant velocity
- Ease In: Start slowly, gradually accelerate
- Ease Out: Start quickly, gradually decelerate
- Ease In/Out: Start slowly; accelerate; decelerate

- Elastic: Oscillate about a point
- Bounce: Bounce off a point

If you select a function and click one of the arrows, the application animates the ball with the selected function. Example 7.8 illustrates how the application moves the ball.

Using the time-warp functions listed in Example 7.7, the application creates six functions, one for each radio button. The application sets the animation duration to 3.6 seconds and creates an animation timer with that duration. Because the application does not specify a time-warp function when it creates the animation timer, the animation timer uses the default time-warp function, which is linear.

The application creates a sprite named `ball` with a single `moveBall` behavior. If the animation timer is running, that behavior's `execute()` method moves the ball according to the animation timer's elapsed time.

---

Example 7.8  Animating a ball

```
var linear    = AnimationTimer.makeLinear(),
    easeIn     = AnimationTimer.makeEaseIn(1),
    easeOut    = AnimationTimer.makeEaseOut(1),
    easeInOut  = AnimationTimer.makeEaseInOut(1),
    elastic    = AnimationTimer.makeElastic(5),
    bounce     = AnimationTimer.makeBounce(5),

    PUSH_ANIMATION_DURATION = 3600,

    pushAnimationTimer = new AnimationTimer(PUSH_ANIMATION_DURATION),
    ...

// Move ball behavior.........................................

moveBall = {
    lastTime: undefined,

    resetBall: function () {
        ball.left = LEDGE_LEFT - BALL_RADIUS;
        ball.top  = LEDGE_TOP - BALL_RADIUS*2;
    },

    updateBallPosition: function (elapsed) {
        if (arrow === LEFT)
            ball.left -= ball.velocityX * (elapsed/1000);
        else
            ball.left += ball.velocityX * (elapsed/1000);
    },
```

*(Continues)*

---

Example 7.8 *(Continued)*

```
    execute: function (ball, context, time) {
        if (pushAnimationTimer.isRunning()) {
            var animationElapsed = pushAnimationTimer.getElapsedTime(),
                elapsed;

            if (this.lastTime !== undefined) {
                elapsed = animationElapsed - this.lastTime;

                this.updateBallPosition(elapsed);

                if (isBallOnLedge()) {
                    if (pushAnimationTimer.isOver()) {
                        pushAnimationTimer.stop();
                    }
                }
                else { // Ball fell off the ledge
                    pushAnimationTimer.stop();
                    this.resetBall();
                }
            }
        }
        this.lastTime = animationElapsed;
    }
},

// Ball sprite................................................

ball = new Sprite('ball', ..., [ moveBall ]);
```

---

Notice that the behavior's execute() method knows nothing about any possible time-warping that takes place in the animation timer; the method just obtains the elapsed time from the timer and uses that time to position the ball.

When you select a radio button, the application assigns the appropriate time-warp function to the animation timer like this:

```
var
linearRadioButton    = document.getElementById('linearRadioButton'),
easeInRadioButton    = document.getElementById('easeInRadioButton'),
easeOutRadioButton   = document.getElementById('easeOutRadioButton'),
easeInOutRadioButton = document.getElementById('easeInOutRadioButton'),
elasticRadioButton   = document.getElementById('elasticRadioButton'),
bounceRadioButton    = document.getElementById('bounceRadioButton');
```

```
linearRadioButton.onchange = function (e) {
    pushAnimationTimer.timeWarp = linear;
};

easeInRadioButton.onchange = function (e) {
    pushAnimationTimer.timeWarp = easeIn;
};

easeOutRadioButton.onchange = function (e) {
    pushAnimationTimer.timeWarp = easeOut;
};

easeInOutRadioButton.onchange = function (e) {
    pushAnimationTimer.timeWarp = easeInOut;
};

elasticRadioButton.onchange = function (e) {
    pushAnimationTimer.timeWarp = elastic;
};

bounceRadioButton.onchange = function (e) {
    pushAnimationTimer.timeWarp = bounce;
};

linearRadioButton.onchange = function (e) {
    pushAnimationTimer.timeWarp = linear;
};
```

As the preceding event handlers illustrate, to warp time you just need to assign the appropriate time-warp function to an animation timer and subsequently use that timer to drive the animation.

The sections that follow briefly discuss the different algorithms for warping time that AnimationTimer supports.

## 7.4.1 Linear Motion: No Acceleration

Newtonian mechanics states that a moving body will continue moving at its current velocity and direction in the absence of air resistance, friction, or collisions with other bodies. That movement, which has no acceleration, is known as linear motion; it is depicted in Figure 7.9.

In Figure 7.9, the ball moves at a constant velocity from left to right. Mathematically, the function that describes linear motion is simple: Given the actual elapsed time of the animation, you return that elapsed time, as shown in Equation 7.4.

$$f(x) = x$$

Equation 7.4  Linear motion

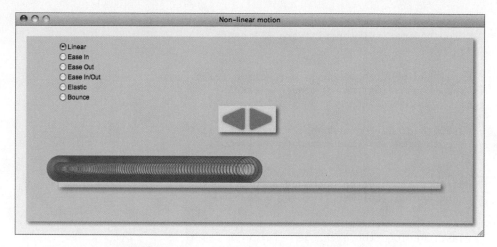

Figure 7.9  Linear motion (each ball represents one frame of the animation)

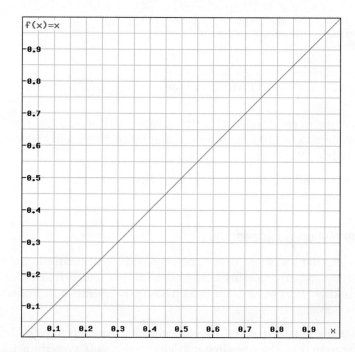

Figure 7.10  Linear motion graph

The function that implements Equation 7.4 is equally simple:

```
function (percentComplete) {
    return percentComplete;
};
```

If you plot a graph of actual elapsed percent on the horizontal axis versus the warped percent on the vertical axis, you will get a straight line at a 45 degree angle, as shown in Figure 7.10.

## 7.4.2 Ease In: Gradually Accelerate

In the real world, most things don't move indefinitely at a constant velocity. Many times, things start slowly and accelerate, from a sprinter who starts out at 0 mph and accelerates out of the blocks, or a diver who starts with no vertical velocity, but acquires a good deal of it as she plunges toward the water.

In animation terms, gradual acceleration is referred to as easing in, as depicted in Figure 7.11.

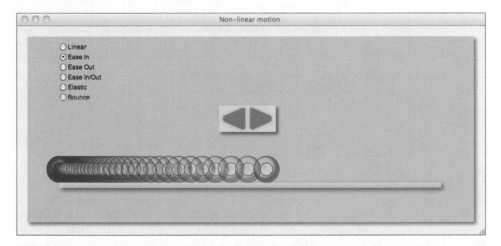

Figure 7.11 Ease in

The equation for easing in is a power function. In Equation 7.5, that power is two, but you are not restricted to that number; for example, you could raise that exponent to the fourth or fifth power to exaggerate the ease-in effect.

$$f(x) = x^2$$

Equation 7.5 Ease in

Here's the JavaScript that implements Equation 7.5:

```
function (percentComplete) {
    return Math.pow(percentComplete, 2);
};
```

The power curve implemented with the preceding JavaScript is depicted graphically in Figure 7.12.

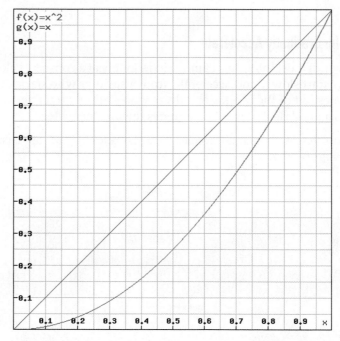

Figure 7.12  Ease-in graph

In Figure 7.12 the horizontal axis represents the percent of the animation that has elapsed in real time. The vertical axis represents the warped time that an animation system uses to advance an animation's properties; in our case, it's the value returned by `AnimationTimer.getElapsedTime()`.

The line representing linear motion is shown as a reference in Figure 7.12. It's the curve that shows the squared power curve. That curve shows the warped elapsed time (vertical axis) versus the actual elapsed time (horizontal axis). For example, 0.5 on the horizontal axis, which represents halfway through the animation in real time, equates to a warped elapsed time of 0.25, so the corresponding animation would appear as if it were only one-fourth of the way through the animation.

Both axes in the graph in Figure 7.12 represent time, and the slopes of the line and the curve represent the *movement* of time. The slope of the line in Figure 7.12 is constant, so time moves along at a steady pace; however, the slope of the curve changes continuously—that's what makes it a curve. Initially, the slope of the curve is very small, so time moves very slowly. As you move further along the curve from left to right, the curve's slope steadily increases, which means time moves faster as you move along the curve.

Power curves like the one shown in Figure 7.12 are prevalent in all kinds of systems, from springs to economics, and of course, animations.

Figure 7.13 shows two other power curves in addition to $x^2$: $x^3$ and $x^4$. Notice the slopes of those curves. The higher the exponent, the more exaggerated the ease-in effect. The $x^4$ curve is initially much flatter than the $x^2$ curve, and its slope is much steeper in the second half of the animation.

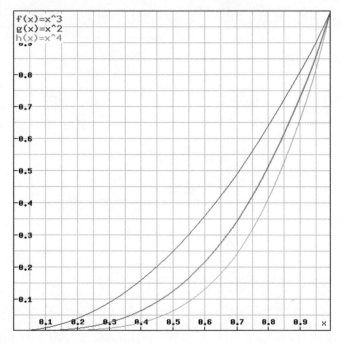

Figure 7.13 Ease-in power curves

## 7.4.3 Ease Out: Gradually Decelerate

The preceding section discussed the ease-in effect, where time initially moves slowly and then gradually accelerates. The opposite effect is known as ease out, where time initially moves quickly and gradually decelerates, as shown in Figure 7.14.

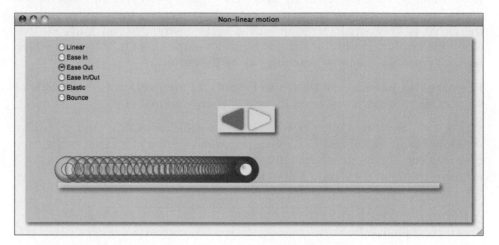

Figure 7.14  Ease out

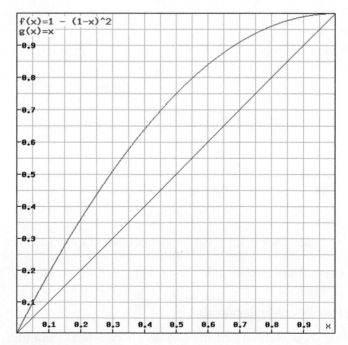

Figure 7.15  Ease-out graph

An equation for the ease-out effect is shown in Equation 7.6, and the corresponding graph is shown in Figure 7.15. The slope of the curve is initially steep, and the slope gradually decreases until it is nearly 0; therefore, time will initially move quickly and gradually decelerate.

$$f(x) = 1 - (1 - x)^2$$

Equation 7.6 Ease out

Here's the JavaScript implementation of Equation 7.6:

```javascript
function (percentComplete) {
    return 1 - Math.pow(1 - percentComplete, 2);
}
```

As for ease-in power curves, Figure 7.16 illustrates third- and fourth-order power curves for the ease-out effect. As was the case for ease-in, the higher the order, the more pronounced the effect.

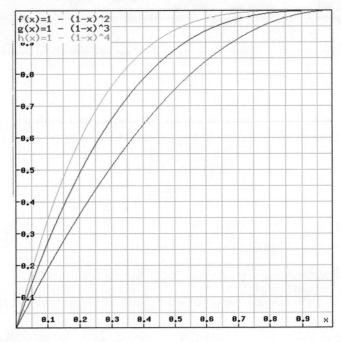

Figure 7.16 Ease-out power curves

### 7.4.4  Ease In, Then Ease Out

Once again, imagine a sprinter accelerating out of the blocks. The sprinter accelerates, reaches maximum velocity, and at some point thereafter, gradually slows down until he comes to a stop. That type of motion is a combination of ease in and ease out, and is depicted in Figure 7.17.

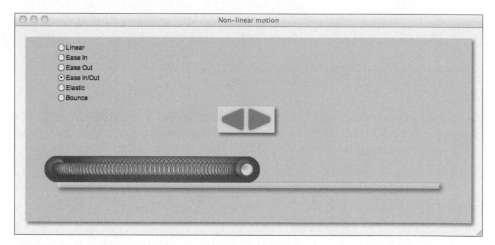

Figure 7.17  Ease in, then out

Ease in/out is periodic in nature, so we can represent it with a sine wave, as shown in Equation 7.7 and depicted in Figure 7.18.

$$f(x) = x - \sin(x \times 2\pi) / (2\pi)$$

Equation 7.7  Ease in/out

The graph for Equation 7.7 is shown in Figure 7.18.

Here's the JavaScript implementation of Equation 7.7:

```
function (percentComplete) {
    return percentComplete
        - Math.sin(percentComplete*2*Math.PI) / (2*Math.PI);
};
```

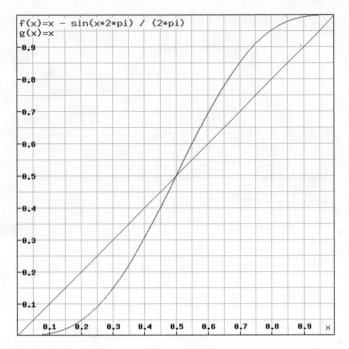

Figure 7.18  Ease in/out graph

## 7.4.5  Elasticity and Bouncing

Two other common effects are elasticity and bouncing, which are illustrated in Figures 7.19 and 7.21.

The equation for elasticity is shown in Equation 7.8.

$$f(x) = (1 - \cos(x \times N_{passes} \times \pi) \times (1 - x)) + x$$

Equation 7.8  Elastic motion

Unlike the previous equations in this section, Equation 7.8 contains a variable besides $x$ ($x$ represents the animation completion percentage). In terms of motion, that variable represents the number of passes the object makes about a central pivot. For example, $N_{passes}$ is 3 for the motion shown in Figure 7.19.

Figure 7.20 shows the graph for Equation 7.8.

Figure 7.19  Elastic motion (from top to bottom)

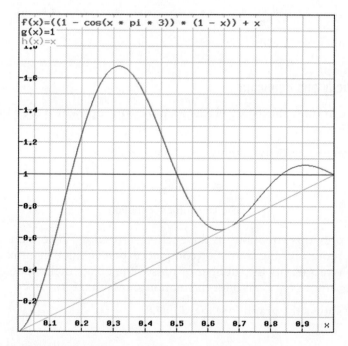

Figure 7.20  Elastic motion graph

Like the equation, the corresponding graph is different from the graphs we have seen so far because the vertical axis goes up to 2.0 instead of 1.0, and the curve extends beyond 1.0.

In practical terms, if you are using the time on the vertical axis to drive motion, the object will go past where it normally would be at the end of the animation, and then, as the curve goes down, the object goes in the opposite direction, once again past the endpoint, and the cycle repeats. In Figure 7.20 the curve crosses 1.0 three times because the number of passes ($N_{\text{passes}}$) is 3.

Bouncing, which is similar to elasticity, is depicted in Figure 7.21. Initially, the ball is in the center of the ledge and moving left, and it bounces once it reaches the left edge of the ledge.

Figure 7.21  Bouncing motion

For bouncing, we employ two equations. The first, listed in Equation 7.9, is the same as the elasticity equation shown in Equation 7.8. The value produced by that equation is used by the bounce algorithm if the value is less than or equal to 1.0; otherwise, the bounce algorithm uses Equation 7.10.

$$f(x) = (1 - \cos(x \times N_{bounces} \times \pi) \times (1 - x)) + x$$

**Equation 7.9** Bounce equation #1, for $x \leq 1$

$$f(x) = 2 - (((1 - \cos(x \times \pi \times N_{bounces})) \times (1 - x)) + x)$$

**Equation 7.10** Bounce equation #2, for $x > 1$

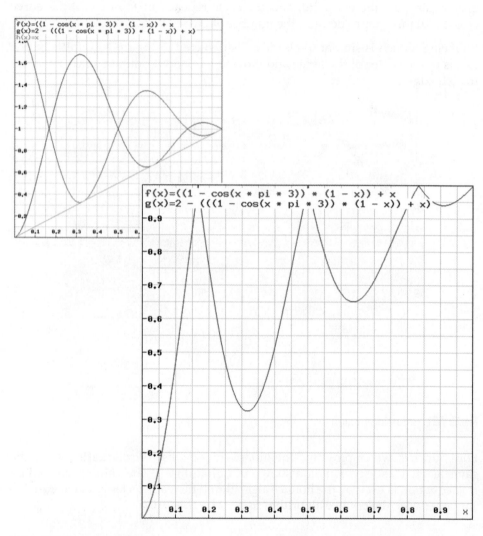

**Figure 7.22** Bouncing graphs

Figure 7.22 shows the graphs for Equations 7.9 and 7.10. The smaller graph in the back shows both equations, as does the larger graph in front; however, the larger graph only shows the portions of the curves that are used by the bounce algorithm.

In this section you saw how to warp time, and how to use that warped time to drive motion. But you can use warped time to drive other properties of objects besides movement. For example, you may want to apply effects such as ease in, ease out, etc. to an animation's cells, so that the animation speeds up or slows down. We will see how to do that in the next section.

## 7.5  Warping Animation

Now that you've seen how to warp time and subsequently motion, let's see how to warp other properties based on time.

The application shown in Figure 7.23 warps time according to the algorithm that you select with the radio buttons at the top of the page. Figure 7.23 shows the ease-out effect, where the warped time, which is represented by the sprite's movement, steadily outruns real time, which is represented by the vertical timeline for the first three-quarters of the animation, and then, in the last quarter, warped time slows dramatically until real time and warped time align at the end of the animation.

Real time and warped time in Figure 7.23 are illustrated by the timeline and sprite, respectively. Something that's not illustrated by Figure 7.23 is the *rate at which the sprite animates in accordance with its motion*. When the effect is ease out, the sprite quickly animates through its cells for the first three-quarters of the animation, running frenetically as it bursts ahead of the timeline. In the last quarter of the animation, however, the sprite's speed *and its animation rate* drop quickly, and the timeline catches up at the end.

The application creates a sprite with two behaviors: moveRightToLeft and runInPlace:

```
sprite = new Sprite('runner',
                    new SpriteSheetPainter(runnerCells),
                    [ moveRightToLeft, runInPlace ]);
```

If the elapsed time since the last time the sprite's painter advanced is greater than 1/10 of a second, the runInPlace.execute() method advances the sprite's painter and resets the time for the last advance.

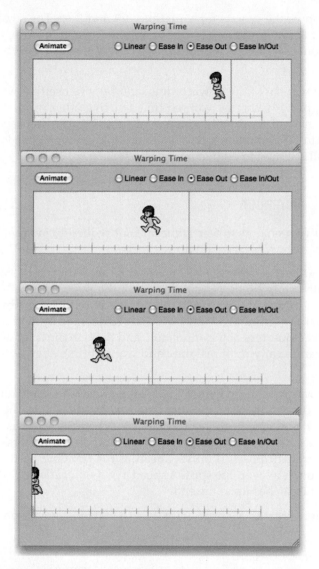

Figure 7.23 Warping movement and animation

```
runInPlace = {
   execute: function() {
      var elapsed = animationTimer.getElapsedTime();

      if (lastAdvance === 0) {  // Skip first time
         lastAdvance = elapsed;
      }
      else if (lastAdvance !== 0 &&
               elapsed - lastAdvance > PAGEFLIP_INTERVAL) {
         sprite.painter.advance();
         lastAdvance = elapsed;
      }
   }
},
```

The moveRightToLeft.execute() method moves the sprite by multiplying the sprite's velocity by the elapsed time since the last time the method moved the sprite.

```
moveRightToLeft = {
   lastMove: 0,
      reset: function () {
         this.lastMove = 0;
      },

      execute: function(sprite, context, time) {
      var elapsed = animationTimer.getElapsedTime(),
         advanceElapsed = elapsed - this.lastMove;

      if (this.lastMove === 0) { // Skip first time
         this.lastMove = elapsed;
      }
      else {
         sprite.left -= (advanceElapsed / 1000) * sprite.velocityX;
         this.lastMove = elapsed;
      }
   }
},
```

If the animation timer's getElapsedTime() method returns the actual elapsed time for the animation, then both the sprite's motion and the rate at which it animates through its cells will be linear. In fact, that's the case when the application first starts, when the linear algorithm is initially selected. However, when you click one of the radio buttons, the application changes the animation timer's time-warp function, for example:

```
easeInRadioButton.onchange = function (e) {
    animationTimer.timeWarp = AnimationTimer.makeEaseIn(1);
};
```

The sprite's motion and the rate at which it cycles through its animation cells, are ultimately controlled by that animation timer's time-warp function.

The application shown in Figure 7.23 is listed in Examples 7.9 and 7.10. Notice that the application uses a sprite sheet painter, which is discussed in Section 6.2.3, "Sprite," on p. 406, to paint the sprite's individual animation cells.

---

**Example 7.9** Warping motion and animation rate: HTML

---

```
<!DOCTYPE html>
<html>
    <head>
        <title>Warping Time</title>

        <style>
            body {
                background: #cdcdcd;
            }

            .controls {
                position: absolute;
                left: 150px;
                top: 10px;
                font: 12px Arial;
            }

            #canvas {
                position: absolute;
                left: 0px;
                top: 20px;
                margin: 20px;
                border: thin inset rgba(100,150,230,0.8);
                background: #efefef;
            }

            #animateButton {
                margin-left: 15px;
                margin-bottom: 10px;
            }
        </style>
    </head>
```

```html
<body>
   <input id='animateButton' type='button' value='Animate'/>

   <canvas id='canvas' width='420' height='100'>
      Canvas not supported
   </canvas>

   <div id='motionControls' class='controls'>
      <div id='motionRadios'>
         <input type='radio' name='motion'
                id='linearRadio' checked/>Linear

         <input type='radio' name='motion'
                id='easeInRadio'/>Ease In

         <input type='radio' name='motion'
                id='easeOutRadio'/>Ease Out

         <input type='radio' name='motion'
                id='easeInOutRadio'/>Ease In/Out
      </div>
   </div>

   <script src='stopwatch.js'></script>
   <script src='animationTimer.js'></script>
   <script src='requestNextAnimationFrame.js'></script>
   <script src='sprites.js'></script>
   <script src='example.js'></script>
</body>
</html>
```

---

**Example 7.10** Warping motion and animation rate: JavaScript

---

```javascript
var canvas = document.getElementById('canvas'),
    context = canvas.getContext('2d'),

    linearRadio = document.getElementById('linearRadio'),
    easeInRadio = document.getElementById('easeInRadio'),
    easeOutRadio = document.getElementById('easeOutRadio'),
    easeInOutRadio = document.getElementById('easeInOutRadio'),

    animateButton = document.getElementById('animateButton'),
    spritesheet = new Image(),
```

---

*(Continues)*

Example 7.10   *(Continued)*

```
runnerCells = [
  { left: 0,   top: 0, width: 47, height: 64 },
  { left: 55,  top: 0, width: 44, height: 64 },
  { left: 107, top: 0, width: 39, height: 64 },
  { left: 152, top: 0, width: 46, height: 64 },
  { left: 208, top: 0, width: 49, height: 64 },
  { left: 265, top: 0, width: 46, height: 64 },
  { left: 320, top: 0, width: 42, height: 64 },
  { left: 380, top: 0, width: 35, height: 64 },
  { left: 425, top: 0, width: 35, height: 64 },
],

interval,
lastAdvance = 0.0,

SPRITE_LEFT = canvas.width - runnerCells[0].width;
SPRITE_TOP = 10,

PAGEFLIP_INTERVAL = 100,
ANIMATION_DURATION = 3900,

animationTimer = new AnimationTimer(ANIMATION_DURATION,
                     AnimationTimer.makeLinear(1)),

LEFT = 1.5,
RIGHT = canvas.width - runnerCells[0].width,
BASELINE = canvas.height - 9.5,
TICK_HEIGHT = 8.5,
WIDTH = RIGHT-LEFT,

runInPlace = {
   execute: function() {
      var elapsed = animationTimer.getElapsedTime();

      if (lastAdvance === 0) {  // Skip first time
         lastAdvance = elapsed;
      }
      else if (lastAdvance !== 0 &&
              elapsed - lastAdvance > PAGEFLIP_INTERVAL) {
         sprite.painter.advance();
         lastAdvance = elapsed;
      }
   }
},
```

```
    moveRightToLeft = {
        lastMove: 0,
            reset: function () {
                this.lastMove = 0;
            },

            execute: function(sprite, context, time) {
            var elapsed = animationTimer.getElapsedTime(),
                advanceElapsed = elapsed - this.lastMove;

            if (this.lastMove === 0) { // Skip first time
                this.lastMove = elapsed;
            }
            else {
                sprite.left -= (advanceElapsed / 1000) * sprite.velocityX;
                this.lastMove = elapsed;
            }
        }
    },

    sprite = new Sprite('runner',
                        new SpriteSheetPainter(runnerCells),
                        [ moveRightToLeft, runInPlace ]);

// Functions.......................................................

function endAnimation() {
    animateButton.value = 'Animate';
    animateButton.style.display = 'inline';
    animationTimer.stop();

    lastAdvance = 0;
    sprite.painter.cellIndex = 0;
    sprite.left = SPRITE_LEFT;
    animationTimer.reset();
    moveRightToLeft.reset();
}

function startAnimation() {
    animationTimer.start();
    animateButton.style.display = 'none';
    window.requestNextAnimationFrame(animate);
}
```

*(Continues)*

Example 7.10 *(Continued)*

```javascript
function drawAxis() {
    context.lineWidth = 0.5;
    context.strokeStyle = 'cornflowerblue';

    context.moveTo(LEFT, BASELINE);
    context.lineTo(RIGHT, BASELINE);
    context.stroke();

    for (var i=0; i <= WIDTH; i+=WIDTH/20) {
        context.beginPath();
        context.moveTo(LEFT + i, BASELINE-TICK_HEIGHT/2);
        context.lineTo(LEFT + i, BASELINE+TICK_HEIGHT/2);
        context.stroke();
    }

    for (i=0; i < WIDTH; i+=WIDTH/4) {
        context.beginPath();
        context.moveTo(LEFT + i, BASELINE-TICK_HEIGHT);
        context.lineTo(LEFT + i, BASELINE+TICK_HEIGHT);
        context.stroke();
    }

    context.beginPath();
    context.moveTo(RIGHT, BASELINE-TICK_HEIGHT);
    context.lineTo(RIGHT, BASELINE+TICK_HEIGHT);
    context.stroke();
}

function drawTimeline() {
    var realElapsed = animationTimer.getRealElapsedTime(),
        realPercent = realElapsed / ANIMATION_DURATION;

    context.lineWidth = 0.5;
    context.strokeStyle = 'rgba(0,0,255,0.5)';

    context.beginPath();

    context.moveTo(WIDTH - realPercent*(WIDTH), 0);
    context.lineTo(WIDTH - realPercent*(WIDTH), canvas.height);
    context.stroke();
}
```

```
// Event handlers...............................................

animateButton.onclick = function (e) {
   if (animateButton.value === 'Animate') startAnimation();
   else                                   endAnimation();
};

linearRadio.onclick = function (e) {
   animationTimer.timeWarp = AnimationTimer.makeLinear(1);
};

easeInRadio.onclick = function (e) {
   animationTimer.timeWarp = AnimationTimer.makeEaseIn(1);
};

easeOutRadio.onclick = function (e) {
   animationTimer.timeWarp = AnimationTimer.makeFaseOut(1);
};

easeInOutRadio.onclick = function (e) {
   animationTimer.timeWarp = AnimationTimer.makeEaseInOut();
};

// Animation....................................................

function animate(time) {
   if (animationTimer.isRunning()) {
      elapsed = animationTimer.getElapsedTime();

      context.clearRect(0, 0, canvas.width, canvas.height);
      sprite.update(context, time);
      sprite.paint(context);

      drawTimeline();
      drawAxis();

      if (animationTimer.isOver()) {
         endAnimation();
      }
      window.requestNextAnimationFrame(animate);
   }
}
```

*(Continues)*

---

**Example 7.10**  *(Continued)*

---

```
// Initialization................................................

spritesheet.src = 'running-sprite-sheet.png';
sprite.left = SPRITE_LEFT;
sprite.top = SPRITE_TOP;
sprite.velocityX = 100; // pixels/second

drawAxis();

spritesheet.onload = function () {
   sprite.paint(context);
};
```

---

## 7.6  Conclusion

In this chapter we discussed fundamental physics that you can use in animations and games, beginning with modeling gravity. You saw how to model falling objects, things flying through the air, and nonlinear motion, such as pendulums.

Most movement is nonlinear, from cars that accelerate away from stoplights, to bouncing balls, so we explored warping time to create effects such as ease in and ease out. Because we warped time, we can warp its derivatives, such as motion and animation rate, as depicted by the last example in this chapter, which modifies not only the rate at which a sprite moves but also the rate at which the sprite animates through its animation cells.

In the next chapter we explore some more physics in the form of collision detection.

# CHAPTER 8

# Collision Detection

Collision detection, in one form or another, is a staple of many animations and nearly all games. In this chapter you will see how to implement collision detection, from simple strategies involving bounding areas and intersecting rays, to detecting collisions between arbitrary polygons, circles, images, and sprites.

Most of this chapter deals with implementing the separating axis theorem (SAT), which is a highly accurate and widely used method for detecting collisions between polygons, both in two and three dimensions. You will see how to implement the SAT with Canvas, and how to extend it for circles, images, and sprites.

This chapter concludes with a look at a byproduct of the SAT, the minimum translation vector (MTV), that coincides with the shortest distance you must move a colliding object so that it's no longer colliding. You can use that vector to decouple colliding objects, make objects stick to each other, and make objects bounce off each other.

## 8.1  Bounding Areas

Two-dimensional collision detection makes extensive use of bounding areas (bounding volumes for 3D), so we begin our discussion of collision detection by looking at a couple of examples that use bounding areas.

### 8.1.1 Rectangular Bounding Areas

Rectangles are often used as bounding areas and are more commonly known as bounding boxes; the application shown in Figure 8.1 illustrates their use. You can control the horizontal movement of the ball that's initially on the top ledge with the arrows; if you push the ball far enough to the left, it will fall off the ledge and land on the bottom ledge, provided that the ball and bottom ledge collide.

Figure 8.1   Rectangular bounding areas

The application determines whether the ball will hit the bottom ledge with the method listed below:

```
ballWillHitLedge: function (ledge) {
   var ballRight = ball.left + ball.width,
       ledgeRight = ledge.left + ledge.width,
       ballBottom = ball.top + ball.height,
       nextBallBottomEstimate = ballBottom + ball.velocityY / fps;

   return ballRight > ledge.left &&
          ball.left < ledgeRight &&
          ballBottom < ledge.top &&
          nextBallBottomEstimate > ledge.top;
}
```

The ballWillHitLedge() method calculates the bottom edge of the ball. Then, based on the ball's velocity and the current frame rate of the animation, the method estimates where the bottom of the ball will be for the next animation frame.

The ballWillHitLedge() method returns true if the ball is currently above the ledge, and the method estimates that it will fall below the ledge the next animation frame.

Besides using bounding boxes for collision detection, the application shown in Figure 8.1 implements *a priori* collision detection, meaning that it detects collisions before they happen. You can also implement collision detection *a posteriori*, which means you detect collisions after they happen. The next section illustrates how to implement a posteriori collision detection.

---

**NOTE: Your a priori estimate may be off**

In the preceding example, the application's estimate of where the ball will be in the next animation frame is fallible because the estimate is based on the current frame rate; if the frame rate suddenly changes, the estimate will be off.

If the ball is directly above the ledge and the application estimates that it will not collide with the ledge in the next animation frame, but it does, then the application will miss the collision.

The inaccuracy in the estimate is one of the drawbacks to a priori collision detection.

---

## 8.1.2 Circular Bounding Areas

Sometimes circular bounding areas are a better fit than rectangular bounding areas, as illustrated in Figure 8.2, which shows a ball falling into a bucket. If the ball collides with the circular bounding area inside the bucket, the application knows that the ball landed in the bucket.

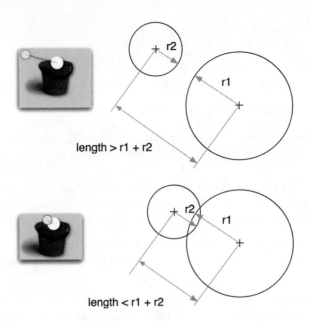

length > r1 + r2

length < r1 + r2

Figure 8.2  Collision between circles: The distance between centers is less than the combined radii

Figure 8.2 also illustrates how easy it is to check for collisions with circular bounding areas. If the distance between the centers of the two circles is less than the combined radii of those circles, then the circles have collided. The simplicity of that calculation makes circular bounding areas attractive.

Figure 8.3 shows the application that detects collisions between the ball and bucket shown in Figure 8.2.

The application determines whether the ball has landed in the bucket with the following method:

```
isBallInBucket: function() {
   var ballCenter = { x: ball.left + BALL_RADIUS,
                      y: ball.top  + BALL_RADIUS
   },

   distance = Math.sqrt(
      Math.pow(bucketHitCenter.x - ballCenter.x, 2) +
      Math.pow(bucketHitCenter.y - ballCenter.y, 2));

   return distance < BALL_RADIUS + bucketHitRadius;
}
```

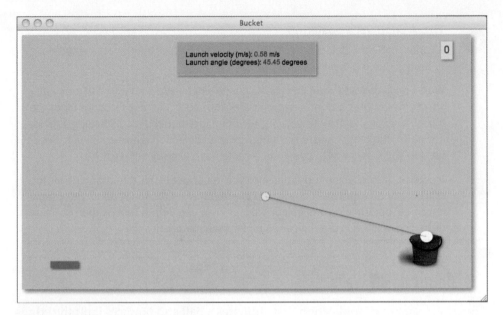

Figure 8.3 Circular bounding areas

In the preceding method, the bucketHitCenter object contains the coordinates for the center of the circular bounding area, and the method uses the Pythagorean theorem to calculate the distance between the center of the ball and the center of the circular bounding area, with Equation 8.1.

$$c = \sqrt{a^2 + b^2}$$

Equation 8.1  Distance between two points

The application shown in Figure 8.3 implements a posteriori collision detection, meaning it detects collisions after they have occurred.

Like the application in Figure 8.1, the collision detection implemented by the application shown in Figure 8.2 is not perfect. If the ball is moving fast enough, it can blow by the circular bounding area in one animation frame, and therefore the application will not detect the collision. The easiest way to solve that problem is to limit the velocity of small objects in your animations. Additionally, there are also more accurate collision detection methods which we explore later in this chapter.

**TIP: A priori vs. a posteriori**

A priori collision detection detects collisions before they occur, whereas a posteriori detects them after they occur.

With a priori collision detection you calculate where an object will be in the future, which means that a priori collision detection must take into account all of the things such as the object's velocity, etc., that are required for calculating that location. On the other hand, a posteriori collision detection requires no such calculation—you just check to see if the objects have already collided.

However, with a posteriori detection, you must deal with the aftermath of the collision. In general, dealing with the aftermath of a collision is about as complicated as determining an object's position in the future, so neither collision detection method is dramatically simpler than the other.

## 8.2 Bouncing Off Walls

Figure 8.4 shows an application that animates a ball and bounces it off the edges of a canvas.

If you're using bounding boxes for collision detection, it's a simple matter to bounce off the edges of the canvas by manipulating an object's position and velocity, as shown in Example 8.1.

**Example 8.1** Bouncing off walls

```
handleEdgeCollisions: function() {
   var bbox = getBoundingBox(ball),
       right = bbox.left + bbox.width,
       bottom = bbox.top + bbox.height;

   if (right > canvas.width || bbox.left < 0) {
      velocityX = -velocityX;

      if (right > canvas.width) {
         ball.left -= right-canvas.width;
      }

      if (bbox.left < 0) {
         ball.left -= bbox.left;
      }
   }
```

```
    if (bottom > canvas.height || bbox.top < 0) {
        velocityY = -velocityY;

        if (bottom > canvas.height) {
            ball.top -= bottom-canvas.height;
        }
        if (bbox.top < 0) {
            ball.top -= bbox.top;
        }
    }
};
```

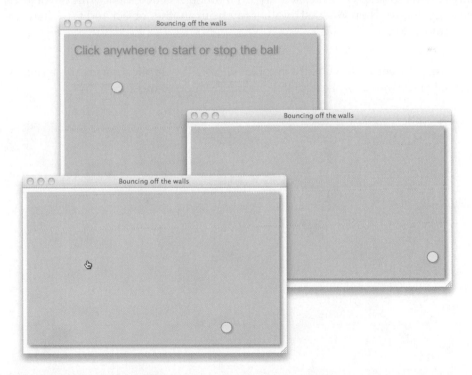

Figure 8.4 Bouncing off walls

Example 8.1 obtains the ball's bounding box and checks to see if the ball has moved out of the canvas bounds. If it has, the method reverses the ball's velocity in either the horizontal or vertical directions, and updates the ball's position so that it once again lies within the canvas boundaries.

Now that you have a good handle on using bounding areas to implement collision detection, let's look at a more rigorous approach: ray casting.

## 8.3 Ray Casting

As an alternative to bounding areas, you can use ray casting, which is more precise than bounding areas, to detect collisions. The application shown in Figure 8.5 uses ray casting to determine if the ball falls into the bucket. The application consists of a simple launch pad on the left and the bucket on the right. When the application starts, the ball rests on the launch pad. When a user clicks the mouse, the application launches the ball in the direction of the mouse cursor, with a velocity proportional to the distance from the cursor to the launch pad.

Ray casting is simple: You cast a ray from an object coincident with the object's velocity vector. Then you cast another ray from another object and see where the two rays intersect.

The application shown in Figure 8.5 creates a ray, labeled ray #1 in Figure 8.5, that's coincident with the ball's velocity vector. The application creates a second ray, labeled ray #2, and calculates the intersection of those two rays.

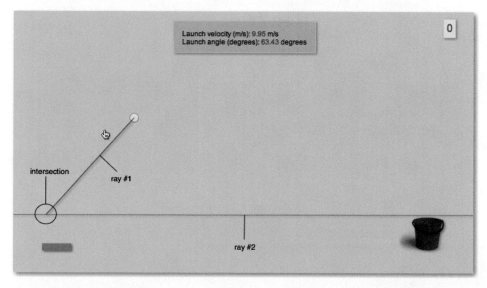

Figure 8.5  Ray casting

As the ball flies through the air, the application continuously erases and redraws ray #1, from the ball to where it intersects ray #2. You can see the effect in Figure 8.6.

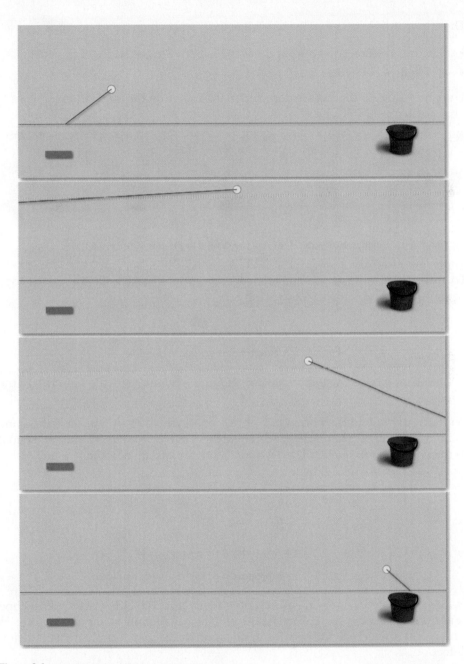

Figure 8.6 Constantly updating the ball's ray

The application knows that the ball fell in the bucket when two conditions are met:

- The intersection of ray #1 and ray #2 is between the edges of the bucket.
- The ball is below ray #2.

The preceding conditions are depicted in the image on the far right in Figure 8.7.

Figure 8.7  Ray casting closeups: The picture on the right is a score

To implement ray casting collision detection, let's start with the point-slope equation of a line, shown in Equation 8.2.

$$y = mx + b$$

Equation 8.2  Point-slope equation of a line

In Equation 8.2, $b$ is the $y$-intercept, meaning the place where the line crosses the Y axis.

We're trying to find the *intersection* of two lines, which by definition is the same point on both lines. Therefore, we can take the equation for ray #1 and set it equal to the equation for ray #2. Then we can solve for x (remember that $x_1$ and $x_2$ are equal), as Equation 8.3 illustrates.

$$mx_1 + b_1 = mx_2 + b_2$$
$$mx_1 - mx_2 = b_2 - b_1$$
$$x(m_1 - m_2) = b_2 - bx_1$$
$$x = (b_2 - b_1) / (m_1 - m_2)$$

Equation 8.3  The intersection of two lines (derivation)

Once you have solved for $x$, you can plug that value into either ray's point-slope equation, and solve for $y$. The result of that calculation is shown in code in Example 8.2, which shows how the application in Figure 8.5 implements collision detection.

Example 8.2 An object that implements collision detection with ray casting

```
catchBall = {
   intersectionPoint: { x: 0, y: 0 },

   isBallInBucket: function() {   // A posteriori
      if (lastBallPosition.left === ball.left ||
         lastBallPosition.top === ball.top) {
         return;
      }
      // (x1, y1) = Last ball position
      // (x2, y2) = Current ball position
      // (x3, y3) = Bucket left
      // (x4, y4) = Bucket right

      var x1 = lastBallPosition.left,
         y1 = lastBallPosition.top,
         x2 = ball.left,
         y2 = ball.top,
         x3 = BUCKET_LEFT + BUCKET_WIDTH/4,
         y3 = BUCKET_TOP,
         x4 = BUCKET_LEFT + BUCKET_WIDTH,
         y4 = y3,

         // m1 = slope of (x1, y1) to (x2, y2)

         m1 = (ball.top - lastBallPosition.top) /
            (ball.left - lastBallPosition.left),

         // m2 = slope of (x3, y3) to (x4, y4)

         m2 = (y4 - y3) / (x4 - x3), // Zero, but calculate
                                     // anyway for illustration
         // b1 = y-intercept for (x1, y1) to (x2, y2)

         b1 = y1 - m1*x1,

         // b2 = y-intercept for (x3, y3) to (x4, y4)

         b2 = y3 - m2*x3;

      this.intersectionPoint.x = (b2 - b1) / (m1 - m2);
      this.intersectionPoint.y = m1*this.intersectionPoint.x + b1;

      return this.intersectionPoint.x > x3 &&
            this.intersectionPoint.x < x4 &&
            ball.top + ball.height > y3 &&
            ball.left + ball.width < x4;
   }
};
```

**CAUTION: Horizontal and vertical lines**

The `isBallInBucket()` method disregards purely horizontal and purely vertical ball movement. That's because the slope of a ball moving horizontally is zero, and the slope of the ball moving vertically is infinite, neither of which is conducive to the calculations the method makes.

If you use the client-slope equation of a line, be aware that you will need special handling for horizontal and vertical lines.

## 8.3.1 Fine-tuning

Ray casting is more accurate than bounding areas. No matter how fast the ball is moving in Figure 8.5, the application will still detect collisions. However, like all collision detection, ray casting is not perfect, as Figure 8.8 illustrates.

Figure 8.8 An edge case

In Figure 8.8, the intersection between the ball's ray and the bucket's ray lies between the edges of the bucket (just barely), and the ball is below the top of the bucket; however, the ball is not in the bucket.

To account for that edge case, we can modify the return statement in Example 8.2, like this:

```
return intersectionPoint.x > x3 &&
       intersectionPoint.x < x4 &&
       ball.top + ball.height > y3 &&
       ball.left + ball.width < x4;
```

Now that we've looked at some simple techniques for collision detection, let's see how to detect collisions between polygons, circles, images, and sprites with the separating axis theorem and the minimum translation vector.

## 8.4 The Separating Axis Theorem (SAT) and Minimum Translation Vector (MTV)

So far in this chapter you've seen how to implement simple collision detection with bounding areas such as rectangles and circles. You've also seen how to detect collisions by casting rays. Although those techniques suffice for many use cases and are relatively easy to implement, they are not well suited for detecting collisions between arbitrarily shaped polygons.

The rest of this chapter shows you how to implement a much more precise collision detection algorithm based on the separating axis theorem (SAT). The SAT detects collisions between polygons, but you'll see how to use it with circles, images, and sprites, too.

You will also see how to use the SAT to calculate a minimum translation vector (MTV) that lets you react to collisions.

---

 **NOTE: Convex polygons only**

The SAT only works for convex polygons, meaning polygons whose interior angles are all less than 180 degrees. Vertices of convex polygons point outward from the center of the polygon. Examples are rectangles, triangles, squares, etc. Any shape with an interior angle of more than 180 degrees has a *dent*, like Pac-Man, and is concave. You cannot detect collisions between concave polygons with the SAT.

---

### 8.4.1 Detecting Collisions with the SAT

Figure 8.9 shows two polygons in the Canvas coordinate system. The polygons on the right are colliding.

Conceptually, the SAT is easy to understand. To detect collisions, the SAT performs the mathematical equivalent of shining a light on the two polygons in question and examining the shadows they cast on the walls behind them, as illustrated in Figures 8.10 and 8.11.

Mathematically, shadows are known as projections, and walls are axes. Figure 8.12 shows the polygons from Figures 8.10 and 8.11, the X and Y axes, and the projections along those axes.

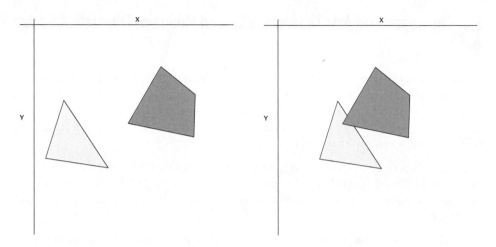

Figure 8.9  Two polygons, collision on the right

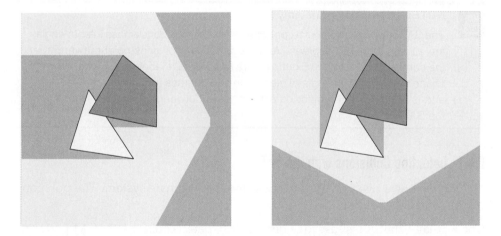

Figure 8.10  Shine a light on the polygons and look for separation in the shadows

Separation between projections on *any* axis means no collision. In Figure 8.12 you can see the separation on the X axis for the polygons on the left that are not colliding, whereas there is no separation along either axis for the polygons on the right that are colliding. *Separation means no collision; collision means no separation.*

Figure 8.12 may lead you to believe that testing along the X and Y axes is sufficient to detect collisions; however, as Figure 8.13 reveals, that is not the case.

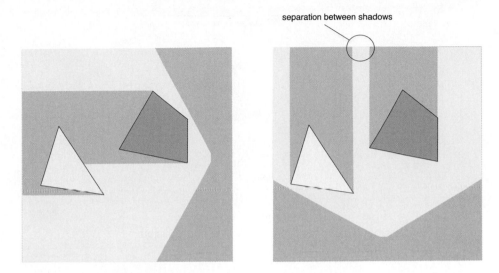

Figure 8.11  Any separation between shadows means no collision

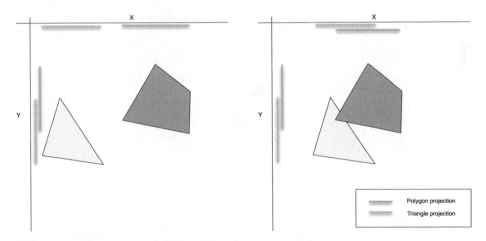

Figure 8.12  Projections on the X and Y axes

In Figure 8.13 the polygons are not colliding, however there is no separation along either the X or Y axes, so it's not sufficient to test for separation between projections only along the X and Y axes—you must shine the light from other directions as well.

Figure 8.14 shows all of the axes that you must test with the SAT.

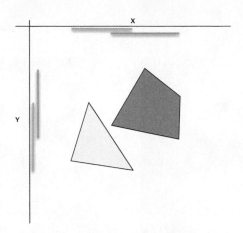

**Figure 8.13** No separation along the X and Y axes, but no collision

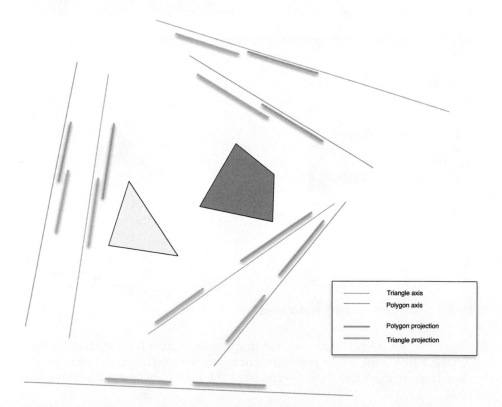

**Figure 8.14** The SAT tests all polygon axes until it finds separation on any axis

To detect collisions with the SAT, you must test all axes of both polygons as illustrated in Figure 8.14, until you find separation between projections along any axis.

The number of axes for a given polygon is the same as the number of polygon sides, so for example, in Figure 8.14, you must test *up to* seven axes for the three-sided triangle and the four sided-polygon.

Depending upon the number of sides for each polygon, you could potentially test many axes, which could be expensive from a performance perspective. However, because separation between projections along any axis indicates no collision, you can quit testing axes when you find separation between projections along any axis.

Figure 8.15 shows all of the axes, and their respective projections, when the two polygons collide.

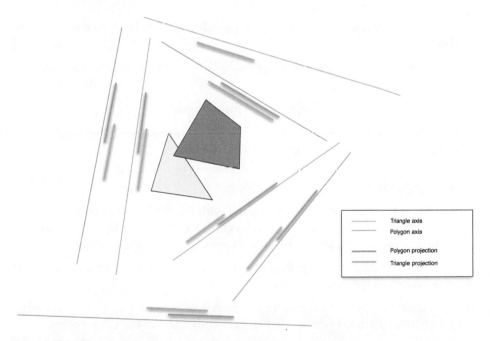

| | |
|---|---|
| ‑‑‑‑‑‑‑‑‑ | Triangle axis |
| ‑‑‑‑‑‑‑‑‑ | Polygon axis |
| ‑‑‑‑‑‑‑‑‑ | Polygon projection |
| ‑‑‑‑‑‑‑‑‑ | Triangle projection |

Figure 8.15  No separation on any axis for collisions

At a high level, for any two polygons, here's some pseudocode that implements the SAT:

```
// Returns true if the polygon1 and polygon2 have collided

function polygonsCollide(polygon1, polygon2) {
   var axes, projection1, projection2;

   axes = polygon1.getAxes();
   axes.push(polygon2.getAxes()); // axes is an axis array

   for (each axis in axes) {
      projection1 = polygon1.project(axis);
      projection2 = polygon2.project(axis);

      if ( ! projection1.overlaps(projection2))
         return false; // Separation means no collision
   }
   return true; // No separation on any axis means collision
}
```

Before we can implement the preceding pseudocode, we have to answer some questions:

• How do you get a polygon's axes?
• How do you project a polygon onto an axis?
• How do you detect overlap between projections?

In the sections that follow, we answer those questions and show you how to implement the separating axis theorem with Canvas.

### 8.4.1.1 Projection Axes

To detect collisions between two polygons with the SAT, you need to get all of the axes for each polygon given a polygon face. Figure 8.16 shows how to create the corresponding projection axis of an arbitrary polygon edge.

In Figure 8.16, an edge of the polygon is defined by a vector from p1 to p2. That vector is known as the edge vector.

The corresponding projection axis for collision detection with the SAT is the edge normal vector, which is normal (that is, perpendicular) to the edge vector.

Figure 8.16 shows the projection axis below and to the right of the polygon. It doesn't matter, however, where the axis is located in space because the axis is infinitely long and the polygon projection will always span the same segment of the axis regardless of the axis' location in space. It's only the direction of the axis that's significant.

Here's some code that creates an axis (which is a vector), given the points p1 and p2:

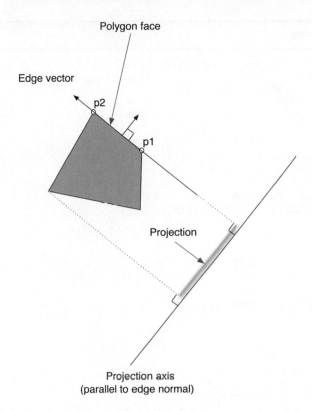

Figure 8.16 Projecting along a single axis corresponding to an edge of the polygon

```
// Getting an axis to project onto. That axis
// is normal to the edge from p1 to p2

var v1 = new Vector(p1.x, p1.y);
    v2 = new Vector(p2.x, p2.y);
    axis = v1.edge(v2).normal();
```

A Vector object with the preceding methods is implemented in Example 8.3.

Vectors have a magnitude that's calculated with the Pythagorean theorem, which states that the square of a right triangle's hypotenuse is equal to the sum of the squares of the other two sides of the triangle.

You can add or subtract vectors, and you can multiply them together. Vector multiplication is more commonly referred to as the dot product because a dot is often used to signify multiplication. You can also get the edge between two vectors by subtracting one from the other.

**Example 8.3** Vectors

```
// Constructor......................................................

var Vector = function(x, y) {
    this.x = x;
    this.y = y;
};

// Prototype........................................................

Vector.prototype = {
    getMagnitude: function () {
        return Math.sqrt(Math.pow(this.x, 2) +
                         Math.pow(this.y, 2));
    },

    add: function (vector) {
        var v = new Vector();
        v.x = this.x + vector.x;
        v.y = this.y + vector.y;
        return v;
    },

    subtract: function (vector) {
        var v = new Vector();
        v.x = this.x - vector.x;
        v.y = this.y - vector.y;
        return v;
    },

    dotProduct: function (vector) {
        return this.x * vector.x +
               this.y * vector.y;
    },

    edge: function (vector) {
        return this.subtract(vector);
    },

    perpendicular: function () {
        var v = new Vector();
        v.x = this.y;
        v.y = 0-this.x;
        return v;
    },
```

```
normalize: function () {
    var v = new Vector(0, 0),
        m = this.getMagnitude();

    if (m != 0) {
        v.x = this.x / m;
        v.y = this.y / m;
    }
    return v;
},

normal: function () {
    var p = this.perpendicular();
    return p.normalize();
}
};
```

Finally, you can get a perpendicular vector with perpendicular() or a perpendicular vector that's been normalized with normal(). Normalization is the process of stripping a vector of its magnitude—the magnitude of a normalized vector is 1, and for that reason, normalized vectors are known as unit vectors.

Unit vectors, because they have a magnitude of 1, indicate direction only; for example, the axis variable in the preceding code listing refers to a unit vector that indicates axis direction.

At this point, given two consecutive points on a polygon, we can create a vector that represents a projection axis for the polygon face defined by those two points. All that remains is to create projection axes for every face of each of the two polygons, project each polygon onto each axis, and check for separation between projections. If we find separation, there was no collision; otherwise, we know that a collision occurred. To do all of that, we need projections.

### 8.4.1.2 Projections

Projections, as you can see from Example 8.4, are simple: They just maintain minimum and maximum values along an axis. Projections can tell you whether they overlap with another projection, and that's all they can do.

Now that we are armed with vectors and projections and know how to create a projection axis, given a polygon face, we are ready to explore implementing collision detection with the SAT for shapes and polygons.

---

**Example 8.4** Projections

```
var Projection = function (min, max) {
    this.min = min;
    this.max = max;
};

Projection.prototype = {
  overlaps: function (projection) {
    return this.max > projection.min && projection.max > this.min;
  }
};
```

---

### 8.4.1.3 Shapes and Polygons

Ultimately, our goal in this chapter is to implement collision detection by using the SAT for polygons, circles, images, and sprites. To do that, we begin by implementing a Shape object that has the following methods:

- `boolean collidesWith(anotherShape)`
- `Vector[] getAxes()`
- `boolean separationOnAxes(axes, anotherShape)`
- `Projection project(axis)`

Here's how you use the `collidesWith()` method:

```
if (shape1.collidesWith(shape2)) {
    ...
}
```

In the preceding code, `collidesWith()` returns `true` if `shape1` collides with `shape2`.

Figure 8.17 depicts the axes and associated projections for a single shape. Recall that each axis is parallel to a vector that's perpendicular to a corresponding polygon edge, as illustrated in Figure 8.16.

The `Shape.getAxes()` method returns an array of vectors representing the axes, and `Shape.project(axis)` returns a projection that represents the shape's projection onto a specific axis.

Example 8.5 shows the implementation of the four Shape methods listed above.

---

Example 8.5  Shape collision detection methods

---

```
Shape.prototype = {
   ...
   // This shape collides with otherShape if there is no separation
   // along either of the shape's axes.

   collidesWith: function (otherShape) {
      var axes = this.getAxes().concat(otherShape.getAxes());
      return !this.separationOnAxes(axes, otherShape);
   },

   // Is there separation between this shape and
   // otherShape along any of the specified axes?

   separationOnAxes: function (axes, otherShape) {
      for (var i=0; i < axes.length; ++i) {

         axis = axes[i];
         projection1 = otherShape.project(axis);
         projection2 = this.project(axis);

         if (! projection1.overlaps(projection2)) {
            return true;
         }
      }
      return false;
   },

   // Get this shape's axes, to be used for collision detection by SAT

   getAxes: function () {
      throw 'getAxes() not implemented';
   },
   ...

   // Project this shape onto the specified axis

   project: function (axis) {
      throw 'project(axis) not implemented';
   }
};
```

---

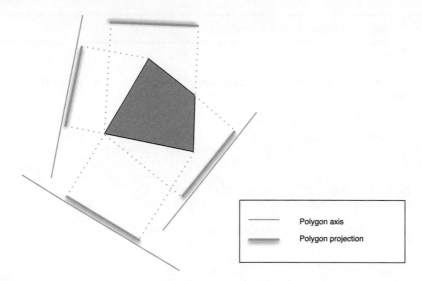

Figure 8.17 Shape.getAxes() returns a polygon's axes, and Shape.project() projects a polygon face onto an axis

The collidesWith() method calls getAxes() for each shape, and then passes those axes to separationOnAxes(), which projects both shapes onto each axis with the project() method. separationOnAxis() returns true as soon as it finds separation between projections on any single axis; otherwise, if it finds no separation, separationOnAxes() returns false.

The getAxes() and project() methods are implemented differently for polygons and circles, so it's up to the Polygon and Circle objects to implement those methods. Here's how Polygon implements them:

```
// Polygons have an array of points

var Polygon = function () {
   this.points = [];
   ...
};
...

// Polygons are shapes

Polygon.prototype = new Shape();
...
```

```
// Projects each point in the polygon onto the
// specified axis and then returns a projection
// with the minimum and maximum of those projected points.

Polygon.prototype.project = function (axis) {
   var scalars = [],
       v = new Vector();

   this.points.forEach( function (point) {
      v.x = point.x;
      v.y = point.y;
      scalars.push(v.dotProduct(axis));
   });

   return new Projection(Math.min.apply(Math, scalars),
                         Math.max.apply(Math, scalars));
};

// Returns all of the polygon's axes needed for
// collision detection testing with SAT

Polygon.prototype.getAxes = function () {
   var v1 = new Vector(),
       v2 = new Vector(),
       axes = [];

   for (var i=0; i < this.points.length-1; i++) {
      v1.x = this.points[i].x;
      v1.y = this.points[i].y;

      v2.x = this.points[i+1].x;
      v2.y = this.points[i+1].y;

      axes.push(v1.edge(v2).normal());
   }

   return axes;
};
```

Polygons are Shapes with meaningful implementations of project() and getAxes(). That means polygons are collision detection enabled.

The Circle implementations of project() and getAxes() are discussed in Section 8.4.1.5, "Circles," on p. 516.

The Shape and Polygon objects are listed in their entirety in Examples 8.6 and 8.7.

---

**Example 8.6** Shapes

```javascript
// Constructor....................................................

var Shape = function () {
   this.x = undefined;
   this.y = undefined;
   this.strokeStyle = 'rgba(255, 253, 208, 0.9)';
   this.fillStyle = 'rgba(147, 197, 114, 0.8)';
};

// Prototype......................................................

Shape.prototype = {
   // Collision detection methods..................................

   collidesWith: function (shape) {
      var axes = this.getAxes().concat(shape.getAxes());
      return !this.separationOnAxes(axes, shape);
   },

   separationOnAxes: function (axes, shape) {
      for (var i=0; i < axes.length; ++i) {
         axis = axes[i];
         projection1 = shape.project(axis);
         projection2 = this.project(axis);

         if (! projection1.overlaps(projection2)) {
            return true; // Don't have to test remaining axes
         }
      }
      return false;
   },

   project: function (axis) {
      throw 'project(axis) not implemented';
   },

   getAxes: function () {
      throw 'getAxes() not implemented';
   },

   move: function (dx, dy) {
      throw 'move(dx, dy) not implemented';
   },
```

```
// Drawing methods..............................................

createPath: function (context) {
   throw 'createPath(context) not implemented';
},

fill: function (context) {
   context.save();
   context.fillStyle = this.fillStyle;
   this.createPath(context);
   context.fill();
   context.restore();
},

stroke: function (context) {
   context.save();
   context.strokeStyle = this.strokeStyle;
   this.createPath(context);
   context.stroke();
   context.restore();
},

isPointInPath: function (context, x, y) {
   this.createPath(context);
   return context.isPointInPath(x, y);
},
};
```

**Example 8.7** Polygons (and points)

```
// Constructor.....................................................

var Point = function (x, y) {
   this.x = x;
   this.y = y;
};

var Polygon = function () {
   this.points = [];
   this.strokeStyle = 'blue';
   this.fillStyle = 'white';
};
```

*(Continues)*

**Example 8.7** *(Continued)*

```
// Prototype......................................................

Polygon.prototype = new Shape();

Polygon.prototype.getAxes = function () {
    var v1 = new Vector(),
        v2 = new Vector(),
        axes = [];

    for (var i=0; i < this.points.length-1; i++) {
        v1.x = this.points[i].x;
        v1.y = this.points[i].y;

        v2.x = this.points[i+1].x;
        v2.y = this.points[i+1].y;

        axes.push(v1.edge(v2).normal());
    }

    v1.x = this.points[this.points.length-1].x;
    v1.y = this.points[this.points.length-1].y;

    v2.x = this.points[0].x;
    v2.y = this.points[0].y;

    axes.push(v1.edge(v2).normal());

    return axes;
};

Polygon.prototype.project = function (axis) {
    var scalars = [],
        v = new Vector();

    this.points.forEach( function (point) {
        v.x = point.x;
        v.y = point.y;
        scalars.push(v.dotProduct(axis));
    });

    return new Projection(Math.min.apply(Math, scalars),
                          Math.max.apply(Math, scalars));
};

Polygon.prototype.addPoint = function (x, y) {
    this.points.push(new Point(x,y));
};
```

```
Polygon.prototype.createPath = function (context) {
   if (this.points.length === 0)
      return;

   context.beginPath();
   context.moveTo(this.points[0].x,
                  this.points[0].y);

   for (var i=0; i < this.points.length; ++i) {
      context.lineTo(this.points[i].x,
                     this.points[i].y);
   }

   context.closePath();
};

Polygon.prototype.move = function (dx, dy) {
   for (var i=0, point; i < this.points.length; ++i) {
      point = this.points[i];
      point.x += dx;
      point.y += dy;
   }
};
```

**NOTE: Polygon paths are implicitly closed**

Notice that the Polygon.createPath() method listed in Example 8.7 closes the path by invoking the Canvas context's closePath() method.

Polygons close their paths for two reasons. First, so you don't have to remember to close the path yourself by adding an extra point that coincides with the polygon's first point. Second, closing a path by adding an extra point to a polygon that coincides with the polygon's first point is not a good idea in the first place, because it will cause problems rendering the line join between the first and last (identical) points.

### 8.4.1.4 Collisions between Polygons

Now that we have all the necessary ingredients to detect collisions with the SAT, let's look at an application, shown in Figure 8.18, that detects collisions between polygons.

The application creates three draggable polygons. If you drag one polygon over or under another polygon, the application displays the word *collision* in the upper-left corner of the canvas with the color of the stationary polygon in the collision.

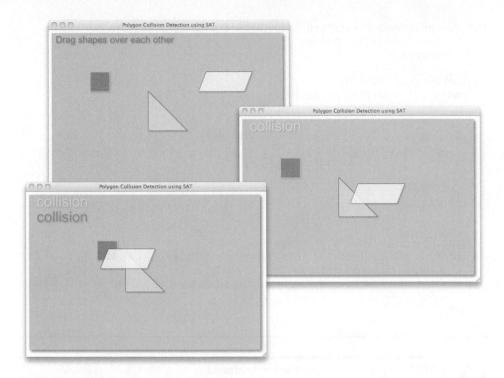

Figure 8.18 Collisions between polygons

Here's how the application performs collision detection:

```
function detectCollisions() {
   var textY = 30,
       numShapes = shapes.length,
       shape,
       i;
   if (shapeBeingDragged) {
      for(i = 0; i < numShapes; ++i) {
         shape = shapes[i];

         if (shape !== shapeBeingDragged) {
            if (shapeBeingDragged.collidesWith(shape)) {
               context.fillStyle = shape.fillStyle;
               context.fillText('collision', 20, textY);
               textY += 40;
            }
         }
      }
   }
}
```

If you drag a shape, the application sets a shapeBeingDragged variable to that shape, so when it's time to detect collisions, the detectCollisions() method listed above checks to see if that variable has been set. If it has, the method knows that you are dragging a shape.

If the shapeBeingDragged variable is set, the detectCollisions() method iterates over all the shapes, checking to see if the shape you are dragging has collided with another shape.

The complete JavaScript for the application is listed in Example 8.8.

---

**Example 8.8** Colliding polygons: JavaScript

---

```javascript
var canvas = document.getElementById('canvas'),
    context = canvas.getContext('2d'),
    shapes = [],
    polygonPoints = [
      // The paths described by these point arrays
      // are open. They are explicitly closed by
      // Polygon.createPath()

      [ new Point(250, 150), new Point(250, 250),
        new Point(350, 250) ],

      [ new Point(100, 100), new Point(100, 150),
        new Point(150, 150), new Point(150, 100) ],

      [ new Point(400, 100), new Point(380, 150),
        new Point(500, 150), new Point(520, 100) ]
    ],

    polygonStrokeStyles = [ 'blue', 'yellow', 'red'],
    polygonFillStyles   = [ 'rgba(255,255,0,0.7)',
                            'rgba(100,140,230,0.6)',
                            'rgba(255,255,255,0.8)' ],

    mousedown = { x: 0, y: 0 },
    lastdrag = { x: 0, y: 0 },
    shapeBeingDragged = undefined;

// Functions.........................................................

function windowToCanvas(x, y) {
    var bbox = canvas.getBoundingClientRect();
    return { x: x - bbox.left * (canvas.width  / bbox.width),
             y: y - bbox.top  * (canvas.height / bbox.height)
           };
}
```

---

*(Continues)*

**Example 8.8** *(Continued)*

```javascript
function drawShapes() {
   shapes.forEach( function (shape) {
      shape.stroke(context);
      shape.fill(context);
   });
}

function detectCollisions() {
   var textY = 30,
       numShapes = shapes.length,
       shape,
       i;

   if (shapeBeingDragged) {
      for(i = 0; i < numShapes; ++i) {
         shape = shapes[i];

         if (shape !== shapeBeingDragged) {
            if (shapeBeingDragged.collidesWith(shape)) {
               context.fillStyle = shape.fillStyle;
               context.fillText('collision', 20, textY);
               textY += 40;
            }
         }
      }
   }
}

// Event handlers.................................................

canvas.onmousedown = function (e) {
   var location = windowToCanvas(e.clientX, e.clientY);

   shapes.forEach( function (shape) {
      if (shape.isPointInPath(context, location.x, location.y)) {
         shapeBeingDragged = shape;
         mousedown.x = location.x;
         mousedown.y = location.y;
         lastdrag.x = location.x;
         lastdrag.y = location.y;
      }
   });
};

canvas.onmousemove = function (e) {
   var location,
       dragVector;
```

```javascript
      if (shapeBeingDragged !== undefined) {
         location = windowToCanvas(e.clientX, e.clientYe);
         dragVector = { x: location.x - lastdrag.x,
                        y: location.y - lastdrag.y
                      };

         shapeBeingDragged.move(dragVector.x, dragVector.y);

         lastdrag.x = location.x;
         lastdrag.y = location.y;

         context.clearRect(0, 0, canvas.width, canvas.height);
         drawShapes();
         detectCollisions();
      }
   };

   canvas.onmouseup = function (e) {
      shapeBeingDragged = undefined;
   };

   // Initialization.................................................

   for (var i=0; i < polygonPoints.length; ++i) {
      var polygon = new Polygon(),
          points = polygonPoints[i];

      polygon.strokeStyle = polygonStrokeStyles[i];
      polygon.fillStyle = polygonFillStyles[i];

      points.forEach( function (point) {
         polygon.addPoint(point.x, point.y);
      });

      shapes.push(polygon);
   }

   context.shadowColor = 'rgba(100,140,255,0.5)';
   context.shadowBlur = 4;
   context.shadowOffsetX = 2;
   context.shadowOffsetY = 2;
   context.font = '38px Arial';

   drawShapes();

   context.save();
   context.fillStyle = 'cornflowerblue';
   context.font = '24px Arial';
   context.fillText('Drag shapes over each other', 10, 25);
   context.restore();
```

Now that you've seen how to use the SAT to detect collisions between polygons, let's extend that algorithm to include circles.

### 8.4.1.5 Circles

As you've seen, to detect collisions between polygons, the SAT projects each polygon onto a set of axes and looks for separation between projections. The axes correspond to the polygon faces.

Circles present a problem for the SAT because a circle has an infinite number of faces, so testing them all is impossible. However, as it turns out, you only need to test one axis for circles. That axis is defined by a line from the center of circle to the polygon point that's closest to the circle, as shown in Figure 8.19.

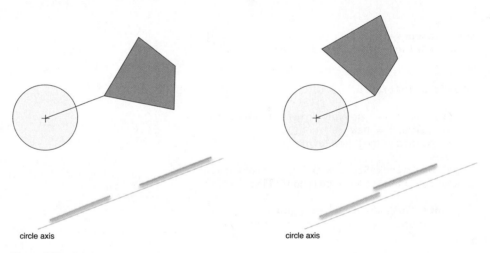

circle axis                                    circle axis

Figure 8.19  Collisions between polygons and circles

The circle and polygon on the right in Figure 8.19 are not colliding—however, there is no separation between their projections on the circle axis. That means that it's not enough to test only the circle axis; in fact, you must test not only the circle axis but the polygon axes also. If you test all required axes for the circle and polygon on the right in Figure 8.19, you will find separation, indicating no collision, as illustrated in Figure 8.20.

Example 8.9 lists a `Circle` object. The first thing to notice is that circles return `undefined` from their `getAxes()` method. That's because circles, by themselves, do not have an axis for collision detection. The circle axis for collision detection illustrated in Figure 8.19 can only be determined from the circle and the polygon.

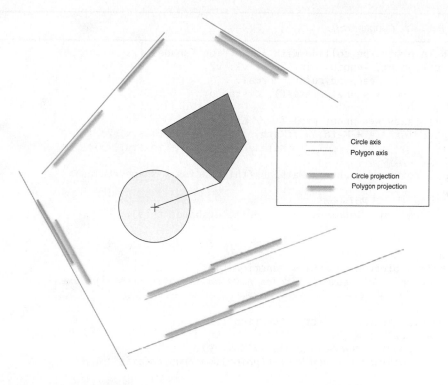

**Figure 8.20** Testing all axes for a circle and polygon reveals separation when there's no collision

---

**Example 8.9** Circles

```
// Constructor......................................................

var Circle = function (x, y, radius) {
   this.x = x;
   this.y = y;
   this.radius = radius;
   this.strokeStyle = 'rgba(255, 253, 208, 0.9)';
   this.fillStyle = 'rgba(147, 197, 114, 0.8)';
}

// Prototype.........................................................

Circle.prototype = new Shape();
```

---

*(Continues)*

**Example 8.9** *(Continued)*

```javascript
Circle.prototype.collidesWith = function (shape) {
    var point, length, min=10000, v1, v2,
        edge, perpendicular, normal,
        axes = shape.getAxes(), distance;

    if (axes === undefined) { // Circle
        distance = Math.sqrt(Math.pow(shape.x - this.x, 2) +
                             Math.pow(shape.y - this.y, 2));

        return distance < Math.abs(this.radius + shape.radius);
    }
    else { // Polygon
        return polygonCollidesWithCircle(shape, this);
    }
};

Circle.prototype.getAxes = function () {
    return undefined; // Circles have an infinite number of axes
};

Circle.prototype.project = function (axis) {
    var scalars = [],
        point = new Point(this.x, this.y);
        dotProduct = new Vector(point).dotProduct(axis);

    scalars.push(dotProduct);
    scalars.push(dotProduct + this.radius);
    scalars.push(dotProduct - this.radius);

    return new Projection(Math.min.apply(Math, scalars),
                          Math.max.apply(Math, scalars));
};

Circle.prototype.move = function (dx, dy) {
    this.x += dx;
    this.y += dy;
};
Circle.prototype.createPath = function (context) {
    context.beginPath();
    context.arc(this.x, this.y, this.radius, 0, Math.PI*2, false);
};
```

Circles also reimplement their collidesWith() method. That method checks to see if the collision axes associated with the shape passed to the method are undefined; if so, that object is a circle, and Circle.collidesWith() uses the circle-to-circle collision detection discussed in Section 8.1.2, "Circular Bounding Areas," on p. 485.

If the shape that you pass to `Circle.collidesWith()` has collision axes, then the object is a polygon, and `Circle.collidesWith()` invokes a method named `polygonCollidesWithCircle()`. That method is listed in Example 8.10.

---

**Example 8.10** Collisions between polygons and circles

---

```javascript
function getPolygonPointClosestToCircle(polygon, circle) {
   var min = 10000,
       length,
       testPoint,
       closestPoint;

   for (var i=0; i < polygon.points.length; ++i) {
      testPoint = polygon.points[i];
      length = Math.sqrt(Math.pow(testPoint.x - circle.x, 2),
                         Math.pow(testPoint.y - circle.y, 2));
      if (length < min) {
         min = length;
         closestPoint = testPoint;
      }
   }

   return closestPoint;
};

function polygonCollidesWithCircle (polygon, circle) {
   var min=10000, v1, v2,
       edge, perpendicular, normal,
       axes = polygon.getAxes(),
       closestPoint = getPolygonPointClosestToCircle(polygon, circle);

   v1 = new Vector(new Point(circle.x, circle.y));
   v2 = new Vector(new Point(closestPoint.x, closestPoint.y));

   axes.push(v1.subtract(v2).normalize());

   return !polygon.separationOnAxes(axes, circle);
};
```

---

In Example 8.10, `polygonCollidesWithCircle()` returns `true` if the polygon and circle that you pass to the method have collided. That method creates the circle axis from the circle center to the closest polygon point, and tests that axis, along with the polygon's axes, for separation between projections.

Although we now have circles that know how to collide with polygons, the inverse is not true: Polygons do not know how to collide with circles. We can fix that by refactoring the `Polygon.collidesWith()` method, as shown in Example 8.11.

---

**Example 8.11** `Polygon.collidesWith()` refactored

```
Polygon.prototype.collidesWith = function (shape) {
   var axes = shape.getAxes();

   if (axes === undefined) {
      return polygonCollidesWithCircle(this, shape);
   }
   else {
      axes.concat(this.getAxes());
      return !this.separationOnAxes(axes, shape);
   }
};
...
```

---

Figure 8.21 shows an application that uses the SAT to detect collisions between polygons and circles.

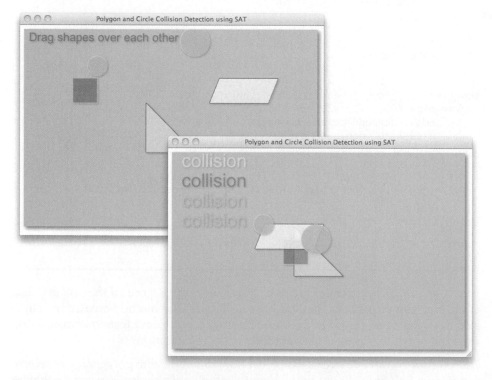

Figure 8.21  Collisions between polygons and circles

The code for the application shown in Figure 8.21 is identical to the application shown in Figure 8.18 on p. 512 and listed in Example 8.8 on p. 513 that detects collisions between polygons, except that the application in Figure 8.21 creates two circles and pushes them onto the array of shapes maintained by the application.

```
...
circle1 = new Circle(150, 75, 20);
circle2 = new Circle(350, 25, 30);
...
shapes.push(circle1);
shapes.push(circle2);
...
```

Now that you've seen how to use the SAT to detect collisions between polygons and circles, let's see how to use the SAT to detect collisions with images and sprites.

### 8.4.1.6 Images and Sprites

It's important to be able to detect collisions between arbitrary shapes such as polygons and circles, but it's also important to detect collisions for images and sprites.

Figure 8.22 shows an application that displays polygons, along with an image (the tennis ball) and a sprite (the golf ball). All of the objects are draggable, and

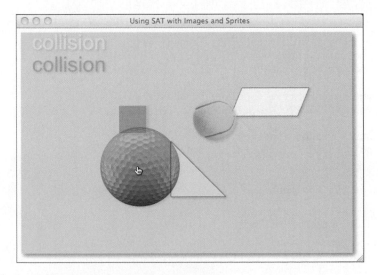

Figure 8.22 Using the SAT with images and sprites

the application detects collisions between the object you are dragging and the other objects in the application.

The application creates three polygons, an ImageShape, and a SpriteShape, and pushes all five of them onto an array of shapes, like this:

```
var canvas = document.getElementById('canvas'),
    context = canvas.getContext('2d'),
    shapes = [],

    ballSprite = new Sprite('ball',
                               new ImagePainter('tennis-ball.png')),

    polygonPoints = [
      [ new Point(250, 150), new Point(250, 250),
        new Point(350, 250), new Point(250, 150) ],

      [ new Point(100, 100), new Point(100, 150),
        new Point(150, 150), new Point(150, 100),
        new Point(100, 100) ],

      [ new Point(400, 100), new Point(380, 150),
        new Point(500, 150), new Point(520, 100),
        new Point(400, 100) ]
    ],

    polygonStrokeStyles = [ 'blue', 'yellow', 'red'],
    polygonFillStyles   = [ 'rgba(255,255,0,0.7)',
                            'rgba(100,140,230,0.6)',
                            'rgba(255,255,255,0.8)' ];

for (var i=0; i < polygonPoints.length; ++i) {
  var polygon = new Polygon(),
      points = polygonPoints[i];

  polygon.strokeStyle = polygonStrokeStyles[i];
  polygon.fillStyle = polygonFillStyles[i];

  points.forEach( function (point) {
    polygon.addPoint(point.x, point.y);
  });

  shapes.push(polygon);
}
...

shapes.push(new ImageShape('golfball.png', 50, 50));
shapes.push(new SpriteShape(ballSprite, 100, 100));
...
```

The application's function to detect collisions is unchanged from Example 8.8 on p. 513, and is listed again here for convenience:

```
function detectCollisions() {
   var textY = 30,
       numShapes = shapes.length,
       shape,
       i;

   if (shapeBeingDragged) {
      for(i = 0; i < numShapes; ++i) {
         shape = shapes[i];

         if (shape !== shapeBeingDragged) {
            if (shapeBeingDragged.collidesWith(shape)) {
               context.fillStyle = shape.fillStyle;
               context.fillText('collision', 20, textY);
               textY += 40;
            }
         }
      }
   }
}
```

The ImageShape and SpriteShape objects are listed in Examples 8.12 and 8.13, respectively.

---

Example 8.12 Image shapes

---

```
// Constructor......................................................

var ImageShape = function(imageSource, x, y, w, h) {
   var self = this;

   this.image = new Image();
   this.imageLoaded = false;
   this.points = [ new Point(x,y) ];
   this.x = x;
   this.y = y;

   this.image.src = imageSource;

   this.image.addEventListener('load', function (e) {
      self.setPolygonPoints();
      self.imageLoaded = true;
   }, false);
}
```

---

*(Continues)*

---

**Example 8.12** *(Continued)*

---

```
// Prototype......................................................

ImageShape.prototype = new Polygon();

ImageShape.prototype.fill = function (context) { }; // Nothing to do

ImageShape.prototype.setPolygonPoints = function() {
   this.points.push(new Point(this.x + this.image.width, this.y));
   this.points.push(new Point(this.x + this.image.width,
                              this.y + this.image.height));
   this.points.push(new Point(this.x, this.y + this.image.height));
};

ImageShape.prototype.drawImage = function (context) {
   context.drawImage(this.image, this.points[0].x, this.points[0].y);
};

ImageShape.prototype.stroke = function (context) {
   var self = this;

   if (this.imageLoaded) {
     context.drawImage(this.image,
                       this.points[0].x, this.points[0].y);
   }
   else {
     this.image.addEventListener('load', function (e) {
        self.drawImage(context);
     }, false);
   }
};
```

---

Both ImageShape and SpriteShape are polygons that represent bounding boxes around an image or sprite, respectively. Given an image source or a sprite, you can create the corresponding ImageShape or SpriteShape and detect collisions between those shapes.

**Example 8.13** Sprite shapes

```javascript
// Constructor.......................................................

var SpriteShape = function (sprite, x, y) {
   this.sprite = sprite;
   this.x = x;
   this.y = y;
   sprite.left = x;
   sprite.top = y;
   this.setPolygonPoints();
};

// Prototype.........................................................

SpriteShape.prototype = new Polygon();

SpriteShape.prototype.move = function (dx, dy) {
   var point, x;
   for(var i=0; i < this.points.length; ++i) {
      point = this.points[i];
      point.x += dx;
      point.y += dy;
   }
   this.sprite.left = this.points[0].x;
   this.sprite.top = this.points[0].y;
};

SpriteShape.prototype.fill = function (context) { };

SpriteShape.prototype.setPolygonPoints = function() {
   this.points.push(new Point(this.x, this.y));
   this.points.push(new Point(this.x + this.sprite.width, this.y));
   this.points.push(new Point(this.x + this.sprite.width,
                             this.y + this.sprite.height));
   this.points.push(new Point(this.x, this.y + this.sprite.height));
};

SpriteShape.prototype.stroke = function (context) {
   this.sprite.paint(context);
};
```

## 8.4.2 Reacting to Collisions with the Minimum Translation Vector

Now that you can detect collisions among polygons, circles, images, and sprites, you need to react to those collisions.

Typically, if each participant survives the collision, reacting to a collision involves decoupling the colliding objects. Once decoupled, the formerly colliding objects may bounce away from each other, stick to each other, or implement any behavior that you desire. But the first step is typically decoupling the colliding objects, and for that, we need the MTV.

### 8.4.2.1 The MTV

The MTV represents the shortest distance you can move a colliding object so that it is no longer colliding. Figure 8.23 illustrates the MTV for two colliding polygons.

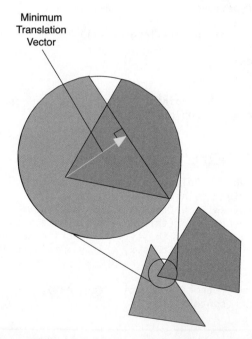

Figure 8.23 The minimum translation vector (MTV) for two colliding polygons

Example 8.14 shows a simple implementation of the MTV in JavaScript.

---

Example 8.14  Minimum translation vector

---

```
var MinimumTranslationVector = function (axis, overlap) {
    this.axis = axis;        // axis is a vector
    this.overlap = overlap;  // overlap is a scalar (single value)
};
```

---

The `MinimumTranslationVector` consists of an axis, which is a unit vector indicating direction, and a value representing the overlap along that axis.

You can calculate the MTV as you are testing for separation on the SAT axes. Recall the `Shape.separationOnAxes()` method from Example 8.5 on p. 505, that iterated over axes, projected polygons onto those axes, and looked for separation between projections, like this:

```
Shape.prototype = {
    ...
    separationOnAxes: function (axes, shape) {
        for (var i=0; i < axes.length; ++i) {
            axis = axes[i];
            projection1 = shape.project(axis);
            projection2 = this.project(axis);

            if (! projection1.overlaps(projection2)) {
                return true;
            }
        }
        return false;
    }
    ...
}
```

The `separationOnAxes()` method returns a boolean indicating whether there was any separation between projections on any of the specified axes.

Example 8.15 shows an alternative implementation of `separationOnAxes()` that calculates the minimum translation vector. That method, which is renamed to `minimumTranslationVector`, returns a `MinimumTranslationVector` object instead of a boolean value.

Like `separationOnAxes()`, the `minimumTranslationVector()` method projects the polygons onto each axis and checks for overlap. The difference is that `minimumTranslationVector()` keeps tabs on the axis with the smallest overlap.

**Example 8.15** `Shape.minimumTranslationVector(axes, shape)`

```
Shape.prototype = {
    ...
    minimumTranslationVector: function (axes, shape) {
        var minimumOverlap = 100000,
            overlap,
            axisWithSmallestOverlap;

        for (var i=0; i < axes.length; ++i) {
            axis = axes[i];
            projection1 = shape.project(axis);
            projection2 = this.project(axis);
            overlap = projection1.overlap(projection2);

            if (overlap === 0) {
                return { axis: undefined,   // No collision
                         overlap: 0
                       };
            }
            else {
                if (overlap < minimumOverlap) {
                    minimumOverlap = overlap;
                    axisWithSmallestOverlap = axis;
                }
            }
        }
        return { axis: axisWithSmallestOverlap, // Collision
                 overlap: minimumOverlap
               };
    }
    ...
}
```

If there is separation on any axis, there is no collision, and therefore no minimum translation vector. So, `minimumTranslationVector()` returns a `MinimumTranslationVector` object with an undefined axis and an overlap of zero. Otherwise, `minimumTranslationVector()` returns a `MinimumTranslationVector` object representing the axis with the smallest overlap.

Using `Shape.minimumTranslationVector()`, the methods listed in Example 8.16 can not only determine whether a collision occurred but can also obtain a reference to the MTV.

---

Example 8.16 Detecting collisions and determining the MTV

---

```javascript
// Collision between two polygons

function polygonCollidesWithPolygon (p1, p2) {
   var mtv1 = p1.minimumTranslationVector(p1.getAxes(), p2),
       mtv2 = p1.minimumTranslationVector(p2.getAxes(), p2);

   if (mtv1.overlap === 0 && mtv2.overlap === 0)
      return { axis: undefined, overlap: 0 };
   else
      return mtv1.overlap < mtv2.overlap ? mtv1 : mtv2;
}

// Collision between two circles

function circleCollidesWithCircle (c1, c2) {
   var distance = Math.sqrt( Math.pow(c2.x - c1.x, 2) +
                             Math.pow(c2.y - c1.y, 2)),
       overlap = Math.abs(c1.radius + c2.radius) - distance;

   return overlap < 0 ?
      new MinimumTranslationVector(undefined, 0) :
      new MinimumTranslationVector(undefined, overlap);
}

// Collision between a polygon and a circle

function polygonCollidesWithCircle (polygon, circle) {
   var axes = polygon.getAxes(),
       closestPoint = getPolygonPointClosestToCircle(polygon, circle);

   axes.push(getCircleAxis(circle, polygon, closestPoint));

   return polygon.minimumTranslationVector(axes, circle);
}
```

---

Example 8.17 shows refactored versions of the collidesWith() method for circles and polygons. The refactored methods use the minimumTranslationVector() function listed in Example 8.15.

Now that you know how to detect collisions and calculate a minimum translation vector, let's see how to put that vector to good use. If you have two shapes that have collided, you can decouple the shapes, given the MTV, as illustrated in Example 8.18.

**Example 8.17** collidesWith() refactored

```
// Circles.........................................................

Circle.prototype.collidesWith = function (shape) {
    if (shape.radius === undefined) {
        return polygonCollidesWithCircle(shape, this);
    }
    else {
        return circleCollidesWithCircle(this, shape);
    }
};


// Polygons.......................................................

Polygon.prototype.collidesWith = function (shape) {
    if (shape.radius !== undefined) {
        return polygonCollidesWithCircle(this, shape);
    }
    else {
        return polygonCollidesWithPolygon(this, shape);
    }
};
```

The separate() method listed in Example 8.18 works with polygons and circles. Circles have an MTV with an undefined axis, as discussed in Section 8.4.1.5, "Circles," on p. 516. If that's the case, the separate() method creates an axis along the velocity unit vector.

Because position is based on velocity, using the velocity unit vector will move the circle away from the collision. The MTV for that axis may not be the *minimum* translation vector; however, it's a good approximation, and it's still a translation vector, which will get us out of collision even if we have to move a little bit further than necessary.

Separating objects that have collided is the most fundamental thing you can do with the MTV. Let's take a look at two other use cases, sticking objects together and bouncing them off one another.

Example 8.18 Separating two colliding shapes

```
// Move the shape that's moving (shapeMoving) out of collision

function separate(shapeMoving, mtv) {
    var dx,
        dy,
        velocityMagnitude,
        point;

    if (mtv.axis === undefined) {   // circle
        point = new Point();
        velocityMagnitude = Math.sqrt(Math.pow(velocity.x, 2) +
                                      Math.pow(velocity.y, 2));

        point.x = velocity.x / velocityMagnitude;
        point.y = velocity.y / velocityMagnitude;

        mtv.axis = new Vector(point);
    }

    dy = mtv.axis.y * mtv.overlap;
    dx = mtv.axis.x * mtv.overlap

    if ((dx < 0 && velocity.x < 0) ||   // Don't move in same direction
        (dx > 0 && velocity.x > 0)) {
        dx = -dx;
    }

    if ((dy < 0 && velocity.y < 0) ||   // Don't move in same direction
        (dy > 0 && velocity.y > 0)) {
        dy = -dy;
    }

    shapeMoving.move(dx, dy);
}
```

### 8.4.2.2 Sticking

Figure 8.24 shows an application that contains circles and polygons. If you click a shape, the application animates it, bouncing it off the sides of the canvas until it collides with another shape.

When a collision occurs, the application stops the moving shape, and one half second later, moves the two colliding objects out of collision. Because the previously moving shape is no longer moving, the shapes appear to stick together, as illustrated in the bottom picture in Figure 8.24.

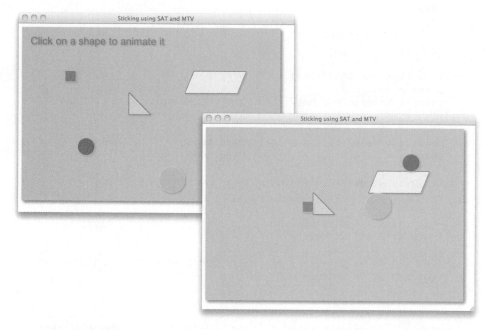

Figure 8.24  Sticking with MTV

The JavaScript for the application shown in Figure 8.24 is listed in Example 8.19. The application uses the window.requestNextAnimationFrame() discussed in Section 5.1.3, "A Portable Animation Loop," on p. 348 to perform the animation, and it uses the shapes discussed in this chapter.

When the detectCollisions() function in Example 8.19 detects a collision, it invokes stick(), passing the MTV returned from the shape's collidesWith() method.

The stick() function checks to see if the mtv.axis is undefined. If it is, then the moving object is a circle, and the stick() function sets the MTV's axis to coincide with the circle's velocity.

Subsequently, the stick() function calculates the necessary displacement in the X and Y direction and moves the moving object out of collision 500 ms later.

**Example 8.19** Sticking shapes with MTV

```javascript
var canvas = document.getElementById('canvas'),
    context = canvas.getContext('2d'),
    shapes = [],
    polygonPoints = [
      [ new Point(250, 150), new Point(250, 200),
        new Point(300, 200) ],

      [ new Point(100, 100), new Point(100, 125),
        new Point(125, 125), new Point(125, 100) ],

      [ new Point(400, 100), new Point(380, 150),
        new Point(500, 150), new Point(520, 100) ],
    ],

    polygonStrokeStyles = [ 'blue', 'yellow', 'red'],
    polygonFillStyles   = [ 'rgba(255,255,0,0.7)',
                            'rgba(100,140,230,0.6)',
                            'rgba(255,255,255,0.8)' ],
    shapeMoving = undefined,
    c1 = new Circle(150, 275, 20),
    c2 = new Circle(350, 350, 30),

    lastTime = undefined,
    velocity = { x: 350, y: 190 },
    lastVelocity = { x: 350, y: 190 },
    STICK_DELAY = 500,
    stuck = false;
    showInstructions = true;

// Functions.......................................................

function windowToCanvas(e) {
   var x = e.x || e.clientX,
       y = e.y || e.clientY,
       bbox = canvas.getBoundingClientRect();

   return { x: x - bbox.left * (canvas.width  / bbox.width),
            y: y - bbox.top  * (canvas.height / bbox.height)
          };
};

function drawShapes() {
   shapes.forEach( function (shape) {
      shape.stroke(context);
      shape.fill(context);
   });
}
```

*(Continues)*

Example 8.19 *(Continued)*

```javascript
function stick(mtv) {
    var dx,
        dy,
        velocityMagnitude,
        point;

    if (mtv.axis === undefined) { // The moving object is a circle.
        point = new Point();
        velocityMagnitude = Math.sqrt(Math.pow(velocity.x, 2) +
                                      Math.pow(velocity.y, 2));

        // Point the MTV axis in the direction of the circle's velocity.

        point.x = velocity.x / velocityMagnitude;
        point.y = velocity.y / velocityMagnitude;

        mtv.axis = new Vector(point);
    }

    // Calculate delta X and delta Y. The mtv.axis is a unit vector
    // indicating direction, and the overlap is the magnitude of
    // the translation vector.

    dx = mtv.axis.x * mtv.overlap;
    dy = mtv.axis.y * mtv.overlap;

    // If deltas and velocity are in the same direction,
    // turn deltas around.

    if ((dx < 0 && velocity.x < 0) || (dx > 0 && velocity.x > 0))
        dx = -dx;

    if ((dy < 0 && velocity.y < 0) || (dy > 0 && velocity.y > 0))
        dy = -dy;

    // In STICK_DELAY (500) ms, move the moving shape out of collision

    setTimeout(function () {
        shapeMoving.move(dx, dy);
    }, STICK_DELAY);

    // Reset pertinent variables
```

```
        lastVelocity.x = velocity.x;
        lastVelocity.y = velocity.y;
        velocity.x = velocity.y = 0;

        // Don't stick again before STICK_DELAY expires
        stuck = true;
}

function collisionDetected(mtv) {
    return mtv.axis != undefined || mtv.overlap !== 0;
}

function detectCollisions() {
    var textY = 30, bbox, mtv;

    if (shapeMoving) {
        shapes.forEach( function (shape) {
            if (shape !== shapeMoving) {
                mtv = shapeMoving.collidesWith(shape);

                if (collisionDetected(mtv)) {
                    if (!stuck)
                        stick(mtv);
                }
            }
        });

        bbox = shapeMoving.boundingBox();
        if (bbox.left + bbox.width > canvas.width || bbox.left < 0) {
            velocity.x = -velocity.x;
        }
        if (bbox.top + bbox.height > canvas.height || bbox.top < 0) {
            velocity.y = -velocity.y;
        }
    }
};

// Event handlers.........................................

canvas.onmousedown = function (e) {
    var location = windowToCanvas(e);

    if (showInstructions)
        showInstructions = false;

    velocity.x = lastVelocity.x;
    velocity.y = lastVelocity.y;
```

*(Continues)*

**Example 8.19** *(Continued)*

```javascript
   shapeMoving = undefined;
   stuck = false;

   shapes.forEach( function (shape) {
      if (shape.isPointInPath(context, location.x, location.y)) {
         shapeMoving = shape;
      }
   });
};

// Animation.......................................................

function animate(time) {
   var elapsedTime, deltaX;

   if (lastTime === 0) {
      if (time !== undefined)
         lastTime = time;

      window.requestNextAnimationFrame(animate);
      return;
   }

   context.clearRect(0, 0, canvas.width, canvas.height);

   if (shapeMoving !== undefined) {
      elapsedTime = parseFloat(time - lastTime) / 1000;
      shapeMoving.move(velocity.x * elapsedTime,
                       velocity.y * elapsedTime);
   }

   detectCollisions();
   drawShapes();
   lastTime = time;

   if (showInstructions) {
      context.fillStyle = 'cornflowerblue';
      context.font = '24px Arial';
      context.fillText('Click on a shape to animate it', 20, 40);
   }
   window.requestNextAnimationFrame(animate);
};

// Initialization..................................................
```

```
for (var i=0; i < polygonPoints.length; ++i) {
    var polygon = new Polygon(),
        points = polygonPoints[i];

    polygon.strokeStyle = polygonStrokeStyles[i];
    polygon.fillStyle = polygonFillStyles[i];

    points.forEach( function (point) {
        polygon.addPoint(point.x, point.y);
    });

    shapes.push(polygon);
}

c1.fillStyle = 'rgba(200, 50, 50, 0.5)';

shapes.push(c1);
shapes.push(c2);

context.shadowColor = 'rgba(100,140,255,0.5)';
context.shadowBlur = 4;
context.shadowOffsetX = 2;
context.shadowOffsetY = 2;
context.font = '38px Arial';

window.requestNextAnimationFrame(animate);
```

### 8.4.2.3  Bouncing

Figure 8.25 shows an application containing several shapes. If you click a shape, it will animate, bouncing off the sides of the canvas and the other shapes.

To bounce one shape off another, you need to reflect the incoming velocity about the edge normal vector of the edge you are colliding with, as illustrated in Figure 8.26.

To bounce one shape off the edge of another, you can use Equation 8.4, which reflects a vector about an axis. In this case, the vector is the incoming velocity vector, and the axis is the edge normal vector or the edge with which you are colliding.

$$\theta_{\text{outgoing}} = 2 \times (V \cdot L) \ / \ (L \cdot L) \times L - V$$

Equation 8.4  Reflection of one vector (*V*) about another (*L*)

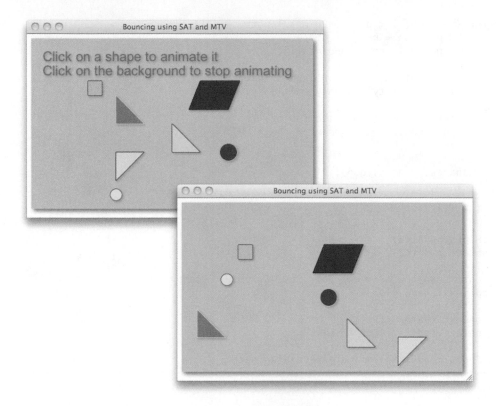

**Figure 8.25** Bouncing with MTV

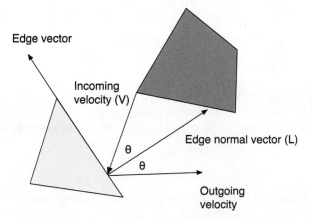

**Figure 8.26** Bouncing vectors

The application shown in Figure 8.25 has much in common with the application shown in Section 8.4.2.2, "Sticking," on p. 531. So, Example 8.20 lists only the code for the application that's pertinent to bouncing one shape off another. The bounce() method implements Equation 8.4.

---

**Example 8.20** Bouncing with MTV

---

```
function detectCollisions() {
   if (shapeMoving) {
      handleShapeCollisions();
      handleEdgeCollisions();
   }
};

function handleShapeCollisions() {
   var mtv;

   shapes.forEach( function (shape) {
      if (shape !== shapeMoving) {
         mtv = shapeMoving.collidesWith(shape);
         if (collisionDetected(mtv)) {
            bounce(mtv, shapeMoving, shape);
         }
      }
   });
}

function collisionDetected(mtv) {
   return mtv.axis != undefined || mtv.overlap !== 0;
}

function separate(mtv) {
   var dx, dy, velocityMagnitude, point;

   if (mtv.axis === undefined) {
      point = new Point();
      velocityMagnitude = Math.sqrt(Math.pow(velocity.x, 2) +
                                    Math.pow(velocity.y, 2));

      point.x = velocity.x / velocityMagnitude;
      point.y = velocity.y / velocityMagnitude;

      mtv.axis = new Vector(point);
   }

   dy = mtv.axis.y * mtv.overlap;
   dx = mtv.axis.x * mtv.overlap
```

---

*(Continues)*

Example 8.20    *(Continued)*

```
    if ((dx < 0 && velocity.x < 0) ||
        (dx > 0 && velocity.x > 0)) {
      dx = -dx;
    }

    if ((dy < 0 && velocity.y < 0) ||
        (dy > 0 && velocity.y > 0)) {
      dy = -dy;
    }

    shapeMoving.move(dx, dy);
}

function checkMTVAxisDirection(mtv, collider, collidee) {
    var centroid1, centroid2, centroidVector, centroidUnitVector;

    if (mtv.axis === undefined)
      return;

    centroid1 = new Vector(collider.centroid()),
    centroid2 = new Vector(collidee.centroid()),
    centroidVector = centroid2.subtract(centroid1),
    centroidUnitVector = (new Vector(centroidVector)).normalize();

    if (centroidUnitVector.dotProduct(mtv.axis) > 0) {
      mtv.axis.x = -mtv.axis.x;
      mtv.axis.y = -mtv.axis.y;
    }
};

function bounce(mtv, collider, collidee) {
    var dotProductRatio, vdotl, ldotl, point,
        velocityVector = new Vector(new Point(velocity.x, velocity.y)),
        velocityUnitVector = velocityVector.normalize(),
        velocityVectorMagnitude = velocityVector.getMagnitude(),
        perpendicular;

    if (shapeMoving) {
      checkMTVAxisDirection(mtv, collider, collidee)

      point = new Point();

      if (mtv.axis !== undefined) {
        perpendicular = mtv.axis.perpendicular();
      }
      else {
        perpendicular = new Vector(new Point(-velocityUnitVector.y,
                                             velocityUnitVector.x));
      }
```

```
    vdot1 = velocityUnitVector.dotProduct(perpendicular);
    ldot1 = perpendicular.dotProduct(perpendicular);
    dotProductRatio = vdot1 / ldot1;

    point.x = 2 * dotProductRatio * perpendicular.x -
            velocityUnitVector.x;

    point.y = 2 * dotProductRatio * perpendicular.y -
            velocityUnitVector.y;

    separate(mtv);

    velocity.x = point.x * velocityVectorMagnitude;
    velocity.y = point.y * velocityVectorMagnitude;
  }
}
```

## 8.5 Conclusion

Collision detection is a deep topic. Indeed, entire books are dedicated to the subject. In this chapter, you have seen simple strategies for collision detection that are easy to implement, including bounding boxes, bounding circles, and intersecting rays.

However, most of this chapter is dedicated to implementing the separating axis theorem (SAT), and the related minimum translation vector (MTV), which is an industrial-strength collision detection implementation that should suffice for nearly all of your collision detection needs.

In the next chapter, we use much of what we have covered in this chapter along with material from the preceding chapters to implement Canvas-based games.

# Game Development

Game development is the most fun you can have with a computer, but that doesn't mean it's easy. You need to have a fundamental understanding of mathematics, including algebra, trigonometry, and vectors, and you have to come to grips with some pretty complicated topics, such as implementing animations and collision detection. In the end, however, there's nothing quite as satisfying for software developers as being able to make the vision they originally had for a game come to life on screen.

Fortunately, we've been through all of that—mathematics, implementing animations, collision detection, etc.—in previous chapters in this book. After all that hard work, it's time to have some fun implementing games.

This chapter is divided into three sections:

- A game engine
- The ungame
- Pinball

The first section discusses a simple game engine (approximately 450 lines of JavaScript) that provides the fundamental tools you need to implement games, such as support for time-based motion, pausing the game, high scores, etc. The game engine is listed in its entirety in Example 9.9 on p. 561.

The second section discusses the ungame, the simplest of games that nonetheless embodies most of the fundamental things that you need to implement, not including the actual game itself. You can think of the ungame as a sort of Hello World for games.

Finally, this chapter discusses an industrial-strength pinball game that uses the game engine and many of the techniques from previous chapters.

## 9.1 A Game Engine

The game engine discussed in this chapter has the following features:

- Implements an animation loop: `start()`
- Draws sprites: `addSprite()`, `getSprite()`
- Supports time-based motion: `pixelsPerFrame()`
- Invokes callbacks: `startAnimate()`, `paintUnderSprites()`, `paintOverSprites()`, `endAnimate()`
- Pauses the game: `togglePaused()`
- Processes keystrokes: `addKeyListener()`
- Plays multitrack sound: `canPlaySound()`, `playSound()`
- Tracks frame rate: `fps`
- Tracks game time: `gameTime`
- Maintains high scores: `setHighScore()`, `getHighScores()`, `clearHighScores()`

The preceding list of functionality shows the corresponding properties and methods in the `GameEngine` object. For example, you can add sprites to the game engine with the `addSprite()` method, and you can obtain a reference to a sprite with the `getSprite()` method.

Fundamentally, the game engine uses `window.requestAnimationFrame()` (via the `window.requestNextAnimationFrame()` method discussed in Section 5.1.3, "A Portable Animation Loop," on p. 348) to implement a game loop. The game engine provides callbacks into that game loop so that you can interject functionality: when an animation frame starts, just before and after the game engine paints sprites, and when the animation ends.

The game engine has one simple method, `pixelsPerFrame()`, which returns the number of pixels an object should move for the current animation frame, given that object's velocity in pixels per second.

You can also access the current frame rate and the game time, which is the amount of time the game has been running minus the amount of time game has been paused. You pause and unpause the game with a `togglePaused()` method.

The game engine also provides fundamental support for high scores, key processing, and sound.

Example 9.1 shows the general procedure for implementing a game with the game engine: You create a game and some sprites, add sprites to the game, implement appropriate animation callbacks, and start the game.

---

**Example 9.1** Implementing a game with the game engine

---

```javascript
// Create the game
var game = new Game('nameOfYourGame', 'canvasElementId'),

    // Create some sprites, and add them to the
    // game with game.addSprite()

    s1 = new Sprite(...),
    s2 = new Sprite(...); // s2 will be drawn on top of s1

game.addSprite(s1);
game.addSprite(s2);

// Implement animation callbacks

game.paintUnderSprites = function () {
   drawBackground(); // Implement this
   // Paint under sprites...
};

game.paintOverSprites = function () {
   // Paint over sprites...
};

game.startAnimate = function () {
   // Things to do at the beginning of the animation frame
};

game.endAnimate = function () {
   // Things to do at the end of the animation frame
};

// Start the game
game.start();
```

---

When you create a Game object, you specify the game's name and the identifier of the canvas element in which the game will reside. The game engine uses the game's name to store high scores in local storage.

The following sections take a closer look at the game engine features.

## 9.1.1 The Game Loop

Here are the steps for the game loop:

1. If the game is paused, skip the following steps and invoke the game loop again in 100 ms.

2.  Update the frame rate.

3.  Set the game time.

4.  Clear the screen.

5.  Invoke animation start callback.

6.  Paint under sprites.

7.  Update sprites.

8.  Paint sprites.

9.  Paint over sprites.

10. Invoke animation end callback.

11. Request the next animation frame.

You can pause and unpause a game with the game engine's `togglePaused()` method. Initially, games are not paused, so the first call to `togglePaused()` will pause the game, and the next call will unpause the game.

If the game is paused, the game loop does nothing other than reschedule another call to the game loop in 100 ms. That time span is considerably longer than 16 ms, which equates to 60 frames per second and is the frame rate for many video games. That means that the game engine reduces CPU usage when a game is paused.

Many things, such as motion, depend on a game's frame rate, so if the game is not paused, the first thing the game loop does is update the frame rate and game time. The game loop then clears the screen in preparation for the next animation frame.

After clearing the screen, the game engine invokes the game's `startAnimate()` and `paintUnderSprites()` callbacks. The former takes care of housekeeping at the start of every animation frame; for instance, many games will invoke collision detection in their `startAnimate()` method. The `paintUnderSprites()` method typically paints the background and perhaps other parts of the game's world.

After giving the game an opportunity to paint underneath sprites, the game loop paints all of the game's visible sprites, and subsequently gives the game a chance to paint over the sprites by invoking the game's `paintOverSprites()` method.

Finally, the game loop invokes the game's `endAnimation()` method and requests the next animation frame with the polyfill method discussed in Section 5.1.3, "A Portable Animation Loop," on p. 348: `window.requestNextAnimationFrame()`.

The code that implements the preceding steps is listed in Example 9.2.

**Example 9.2** The game loop

```javascript
var Game = function (gameName, canvasId) {
   var canvas = document.getElementById(canvasId),
       self = this; // Used by key event handlers below

   // General

   this.context = canvas.getContext('2d');
   this.sprites = [];
   ...

   // Time

   this.startTime = 0;
   this.lastTime = 0;
   this.gameTime = 0;
   this.fps = 0;
   this.STARTING_FPS = 60;

   this.paused = false;
   this.startedPauseAt = 0;
   this.PAUSE_TIMEOUT = 100;
   ...

   return this;
};

// Game methods.....................................................

Game.prototype = {
   ...

   // Game loop.....................................................

   start: function () {
      var self = this;                 // The this variable is the game
      this.startTime = getTimeNow(); // Record game's startTime

      Starts the animation

      window.requestNextAnimationFrame(
         function (time) {
            // The this variable in this function is the window.

            self.animate.call(self, time); // self is the game
         });
   },
```

*(Continues)*

---

Example 9.2 *(Continued)*

---

```
// Drives the game's animation. This method is called by the
// browser when it's time for the next animation frame.

animate: function (time) {
   var self = this;

   if (this.paused) {
      // In PAUSE_TIMEOUT (100) ms, call this method again to see
      // if the game is still paused. There's no need to check
      // more frequently.

      setTimeout( function () {
         self.animate.call(self, time);
      }, this.PAUSE_TIMEOUT);
   }

   else {                        // Game is not paused
      this.tick(time);           // Update fps, game time
      this.clearScreen();        // Prepare for next frame

      this.startAnimate(time);   // Override as you wish
      this.paintUnderSprites();  // Override as you wish

      this.updateSprites(time);  // Invoke sprite behaviors
      this.paintSprites(time);   // Paint sprites in the canvas

      this.paintOverSprites();   // Override as you wish
      this.endAnimate();         // Override as you wish

      // Call this method again when it's time for
      // the next animation frame

      window.requestNextAnimationFrame(
         function (time) {
            self.animate.call(self, time);
         });
   }
},

// Update the frame rate, game time, and the last time the
// application drew an animation frame.

tick: function (time) {
   this.updateFrameRate(time);
   this.gameTime = (getTimeNow()) - this.startTime;
   this.lastTime = time;
},
```

```
// Update the frame rate, based on the amount of time it took
// for the last animation frame only.

updateFrameRate: function (time) {
   if (this.lastTime === 0) this.fps = this.STARTING_FPS;
   else                     this.fps = 1000 / (time - this.lastTime);
},

// Clear the entire canvas.

clearScreen: function () {
   this.context.clearRect(0, 0,
      this.context.canvas.width, this.context.canvas.height);
},

// Update all sprites. The sprite update() method invokes all
// of a sprite's behaviors.

updateSprites: function (time) {
   for(var i=0; i < this.sprites.length; ++i) {
      var sprite = this.sprites[i];
      sprite.update(this.context, time);
   };
},

// Paint all visible sprites.

paintSprites: function (time) {
   for(var i=0; i < this.sprites.length; ++i) {
      var sprite = this.sprites[i];
      if (sprite.visible)
         sprite.paint(this.context);
   };
},
...

// Override the following methods as desired. animate() calls
// the methods in the order they are listed.

startAnimate:       function (time) { },
paintUnderSprites:  function ()     { },
paintOverSprites:   function ()     { },
endAnimate:         function ()     { }
};
```

You create and start a game like this:

```
var game = new Game('gameName', 'canvasId');
...
game.start();
```

When you call the game engine's start() method, the this variable in the start() method is the game, which you would expect.

However, the this variable in the function that you pass to request-NextAnimationFrame() is the *window* object, not the game. If you try to invoke the game engine's animate() method in the function you pass to

Table 9.1 Game engine methods pertaining to the game loop

| Method | Description |
| --- | --- |
| start() | Starts the game by setting the game start time and requesting the first animation frame. |
| animate(time) | Implements the game loop. |
| tick(time) | Updates frame rate and game time, at the start of every animation frame. |
| updateFrameRate(time) | Updates the game's current frame rate. |
| clearScreen() | Uses context.clearRect() to clear the screen. |
| updateSprites(time) | Updates all sprites. |
| paintSprites(time) | Paints all visible sprites. |
| startAnimate() | The game engine calls this method at the start of the animation frame. This method does nothing by default: *left for games to implement.* |
| paintUnderSprites(time) | The game engine calls this method before sprites are drawn. This method does nothing by default: *left for games to implement.* |
| paintOverSprites(time) | The game engine calls this method after sprites are drawn. This method does nothing by default: *left for games to implement.* |
| endAnimate() | The game engine calls this method after it paints the current animation frame. This method does nothing by default: *left for games to implement.* |

requestNextAnimationFrame() with the this variable—this.animate(time)—you will be trying to invoke the presumably nonexistent animate() method on the window object.

The game engine's start() method uses JavaScript's built-in call() method to ensure that the this variable in the function that start() passes to requestNextAnimationFrame() refers to the game and not the window object. When you call start(), the this variable is the game, so the start() method stores that variable in a variable named self. The start() method subsequently uses that self variable when it invokes call().

The game engine's animate() method implements the 11 steps outlined at the beginning of this section. Then animate() invokes requestNextAnimationFrame(), using the technique used by start() to ensure that the this variable in the animate() is the game and not the window object.

The methods implemented by the game engine that constitute the game loop are listed in Table 9.1.

### 9.1.1.1 Pause

The game engine maintains a paused property that you can check to see whether the game is currently paused. If it is, the game engine does not execute the game loop, so nothing happens while the game engine's paused property is set.

Example 9.3 shows how the game engine pauses and unpauses a game.

When the ungame is paused, its animate() method calls setTimeout() to schedule another call to animate() in approximately 100 ms. To occasionally check whether the game is still paused, this use of setTimeout() is appropriate and simpler than using requestNextAnimationFrame().

When togglePaused() pauses a game, it records the time, which it uses when you subsequently unpause the game.

When togglePaused() restarts a paused game, it subtracts the amount of time the game was paused from the game's start time. That means the game picks up exactly where it left off, instead of making a (potentially huge) leap forward in time. Notice that the game engine's startTime may not actually represent the time that the game started; instead, the game engine uses the startTime property to adjust game time after a pause. If, for some reason, you need to know the exact time when your game started, you'll have to keep track of that yourself.

**Example 9.3** Toggling paused state

```javascript
var Game = function (gameName, canvasId) {
   var canvas = document.getElementById(canvasId),
      self = this; // Used by key event handlers below
   ...
   this.startTime = 0;
   this.lastTime = 0;

   this.paused = false;
   this.startedPauseAt = 0;
   this.PAUSE_TIMEOUT = 100;
   ...
   return this;
};

// Game methods.....................................................

Game.prototype = {

   start: function () {
      this.startTime = getTimeNow(); // Record game's startTime
      ...
      window.requestNextAnimationFrame(
         function (time) {
            self.animate.call(self, time); // self is the game
         });
   },

   animate: function (time) {
      var self = this;

      if (this.paused) {
         // After PAUSE_TIMEOUT (100) ms, call this method again
         // to see if the game is still paused. There's no need to
         // check more frequently.

         setTimeout( function () {
            self.animate.call(self, time); // self is the game
         }, this.PAUSE_TIMEOUT); // PAUSE_TIMEOUT is 100 ms
      }
      else { // Game is not paused
         // Paint the next animation frame
         ...
         window.requestNextAnimationFrame(
            function (time) {
               self.animate.call(self, time);
            });
      }
   },
```

```
togglePaused: function () {
    var now = getTimeNow();

    this.paused = !this.paused;

    if (this.paused) {
        this.startedPauseAt = now;
    }
    else { // Not paused
        // Adjust start time, so game starts where it left off when
        // the user paused it.

        this.startTime = this.startTime + now - this.startedPauseAt;
        this.lastTime = now;
    }
  },
};
```

Now that you've seen how the game engine controls time to pause and unpause a game, let's see how it uses time to tell you how far to move an object for the current animation frame.

### 9.1.1.2 Time-Based Motion

Section 5.6, "Time-Based Motion," on p. 367 discussed the benefits and the implementation of time-based motion. The game engine implements time-based motion with a simple but crucial method: pixelsPerFrame(), as listed in Example 9.4.

**Example 9.4** Game engine support for time-based motion

```
pixelsPerFrame: function (time, velocity) {
    // This method returns the amount of pixels an object should move
    // for the current animation frame, given the current time and
    // the object's velocity. Velocity is measured in pixels/second.
    //
    // Note: (pixels/second) * (second/frame) = pixels/second:

    return velocity / game.fps;
},
```

You pass pixelsPerFrame() the current time and a velocity, specified in pixels per second, and the method returns the number of pixels you should move an object for the current frame to maintain that velocity.

You will typically use pixelsPerFrame() in your startAnimate() or endAnimate() callbacks or in a sprite's update() method.

## 9.1.2 Loading Images

Many games are image intensive, and most of those games load images when the game starts. Image loading takes time, so it's best to display feedback to the user as the game loads images.

The game engine supports loading multiple images and keeps track of how many images have been loaded at any given time. Example 9.5 shows the pertinent code from the game engine that loads images. Games use the following three methods to load images and track image-loading progress:

- `queueImage(imageUrl)`: Places an image in the image loading queue.
- `loadImages()`: You call this method repeatedly, until it returns 100 (percent of images processed).
- `getImage(imageUrl)`: Returns an image. You should only call this method after `loadImages()` returns 100 percent.

You call `queueImage()` for each image that you want to load, and then you subsequently call `loadImages()` repeatedly until it returns 100. You can use the values returned by `loadImages()` to update the game's user interface to reflect loading progress, like this:

```
var game = new Game('gameName', 'canvasId');
...

game.queueImage('images/image1.png');
game.queueImage('images/image2.png');
...

interval = setInterval( function (e) {
   loadingPercentComplete = game.loadImages();

   if (loadingPercentComplete === 100) {
      clearInterval(interval);

      // Done loading images, update user interface accordingly
   }
   progressbar.draw(loadingPercentComplete);
}, 16);
```

Realize that some images may fail to load. You can check to see whether all images loaded by looking at the `imagesFailedToLoad` property, which represents the number of images that failed to load. However, regardless of whether some images fail to load, `loadImages()` returns 100 (percent) when it's done processing all the images.

---

Example 9.5 Loading images

---

```
var getTimeNow = function () {
    return +new Date();
};

var Game = function (gameName, canvasId) {
    var canvas = document.getElementById(canvasId),
    ...

    // Image loading

    this.imageLoadingProgressCallback;
    this.images = {};
    this.imageUrls = [];
    this.imagesLoaded = 0;
    this.imagesFailedToLoad = 0;
    this.imagesIndex = 0;
    ...

    return this;
};

// Game methods.......................................................

Game.prototype = {
    // Given a URL, return the associated image

    getImage: function (imageUrl) {
        return this.images[imageUrl];
    },

    // This method is called by loadImage() when
    // an image loads successfully.

    imageLoadedCallback: function (e) {
        this.imagesLoaded++;
    },

    // This method is called by loadImage() when
    // an image does not load successfully.

    imageLoadErrorCallback: function (e) {
        this.imagesFailedToLoad++;
    },

    // Loads a particular image
```

---

*(Continues)*

---

**Example 9.5** *(Continued)*

---

```
loadImage: function (imageUrl) {
    var image = new Image(),
        self = this;

    image.src = imageUrl;

    image.addEventListener('load',
        function (e) {
            self.imageLoadedCallback(e);
        });

    image.addEventListener('error',
        function (e) {
            self.imageLoadErrorCallback(e);
        });

    this.images[imageUrl] = image;
},

// You call this method repeatedly to load images that have been
// queued (by calling queueImage()). This method returns the
// percent of the game's images that have been processed. When
// the method returns 100, all images are loaded, and you can
// quit calling this method.

loadImages: function () {

    // If there are images left to load

    if (this.imagesIndex < this.imageUrls.length) {
        this.loadImage(this.imageUrls[this.imagesIndex]);
        this.imagesIndex++;
    }

    // Return the percent complete

    return (this.imagesLoaded + this.imagesFailedToLoad) /
            this.imageUrls.length * 100;
},

// Call this method to add an image to the queue. The image
// will be loaded by loadImages().

queueImage: function (imageUrl) {
    this.imageUrls.push(imageUrl);
},
...
};
```

---

Every time you call the game engine's queueImage() method, the game engine adds the image URL to an array. Every time you subsequently call loadImages(), that method loads the next image in the array and returns the percent of images that have been processed.

Notice that loadImage() uses the same technique as the game engine's start() and animate() methods to ensure that the this variables in the image load and image error callbacks refer to the game and not the window object.

### 9.1.3 Multitrack Sound

Games typically play several sounds at once; for example, a game may play music at the same time it produces sound effects, so the game engine implements support for multitrack sound, as shown in Example 9.6.

You can use the canPlay...() methods to determine whether the browser can play a particular sound format. You then use the playSound() method to play a sound.

The Game constructor function creates ten Audio elements and adds them to an array. When you call playSound(), the game engine uses the first available audio track to play the specified sound.

The playSound() method takes an element identifier that must correspond to an audio element. Given that element, the method plays its sound on the first available sound channel.

---

**Example 9.6  Sound support**

---

```
var Game = function (gameName, canvasId) {
   ...

   this.soundOn = true;
   this.soundChannels = [];
   this.audio = new Audio();
   this.NUM_SOUND_CHANNELS = 10;

   for (var i=0; i < this.NUM_SOUND_CHANNELS; ++i) {
      var audio = new Audio();
      this.soundChannels.push(audio);
   }

   ...

   return this;
};
```

---

*(Continues)*

---

Example 9.6  *(Continued)*

---

```
Game.prototype = {

    canPlayOggVorbis: function () {
        return "" != this.audio.canPlayType('audio/ogg; codecs="vorbis"');
    },

    canPlayMp4: function () {
        return "" != this.audio.canPlayType('audio/mp4');
    },

    getAvailableSoundChannel: function () {
        var audio;

        for (var i=0; i < this.NUM_SOUND_CHANNELS; ++i) {
            audio = this.soundChannels[i];
            if (audio.played && audio.played.length > 0) {
                if (audio.ended)
                    return audio;
            }
            else {
                if (!audio.ended)
                    return audio;
            }
        }
        return undefined; // All tracks in use
    },

    playSound: function (id) {
        var track = this.getAvailableSoundChannel(),
            element = document.getElementById(id);

        if (track && element) {
            track.src = element.src === '' ?
                        element.currentSrc : element.src;
            track.load();
            track.play();
        }
    },
};
```

## 9.1.4  Keyboard Events

Many games require interaction with the keyboard, so the game engine supports
key listeners, as shown in Example 9.7.

You use addKeyListener() to add key listeners to your game. The object that you
pass to that method must have properties named key and listener that represent

**Example 9.7** Key listeners and throttling events

```javascript
var Game = function (gameName, canvasId) {
   var canvas = document.getElementById(canvasId);
   ...
   this.keyListeners = [];
   ...
};

Game.prototype = {

   // Key listeners................................................

   addKeyListener: function (keyAndListener) {
      game.keyListeners.push(keyAndListener);
   },

   findKeyListener: function (key) {
      var listener = undefined;

      game.keyListeners.forEach(function (keyAndListener) {
         var currentKey = keyAndListener.key;
         if (currentKey === key) {
            listener = keyAndListener.listener;
         }
      });
      return listener;
   },

   keyPressed: function (e) {
      var listener = undefined,
          key = undefined;

      switch (e.keyCode) {
         // Add more keys as needed
         case 32: key = 'space';          break;
         case 83: key = 's';              break;
         case 80: key = 'p';              break;
         case 37: key = 'left arrow';     break;
         case 39: key = 'right arrow';    break;
         case 38: key = 'up arrow';       break;
         case 40: key = 'down arrow';     break;
      }

      listener = game.findKeyListener(key);
      if (listener) { // Listener is a function
         listener();  // Invoke the listener function
      }
   },
};
```

the key you want to listen to, and a function you want the game engine to invoke when that key is pressed, respectively.

By default, the game engine supports the keys you see listed in Example 9.7 (space, s, etc.). You can easily add support for other keys, see http://bit.ly/ tvU2NS for a list of JavaScript key codes.

### 9.1.5 High Scores

The game engine uses JavaScript Object Notation (JSON) and local storage to maintain an array of high scores, as shown in Example 9.8.

---

**Example 9.8** Game engine support for high scores

---

```javascript
var Game = function (gameName, canvasId) {
   var canvas = document.getElementById(canvasId);
   ...
   this.HIGH_SCORES_SUFFIX = '_highscores';
   ...
};

Game.prototype = {

   // High scores...............................................

   getHighScores: function () {
      var key = game.gameName + game.HIGH_SCORES_SUFFIX,
         highScoresString = localStorage[key];

      if (highScoresString == undefined) {
         localStorage[key] = JSON.stringify([]);
      }
      return JSON.parse(localStorage[key]);
   },

   setHighScore: function (highScore) {
      var key = game.gameName + game.HIGH_SCORES_SUFFIX,
         highScoresString = localStorage[key];

      highScores.unshift(highScore);
      localStorage[key] = JSON.stringify(highScores);
   },

   clearHighScores: function () {
      localStorage[game.gameName + game.HIGH_SCORES_SUFFIX] =
         JSON.stringify([]);
   },
};
```

The getHighScores() method appends _highscores to the game's name. It then uses the resulting string as a key to access the game's high scores in local storage.

The setHighScore() method retrieves high scores from local storage, adds a high score to the beginning of that list, and puts the resulting list back in local storage.

Finally, the clearHighScores() method sets the list of high scores in local storage to an empty array.

The methods listed in Example 9.8 are summarized in Table 9.2.

**Table 9.2** Game engine high score methods

| Method | Description |
|---|---|
| setHighScore(highScore) | Adds the high score to the game's list of high scores in local storage. |
| getHighScores() | Returns the game's list of high scores from local storage. |
| clearHighScores() | Clears the game's high scores in local storage. |

## 9.1.6 The Game Engine Listing

The game engine is listed in Example 9.9.

**Example 9.9** Game engine (gameEngine.js)

```
var getTimeNow = function () {
    return +new Date();
};

// Game.................................................

// This game engine implements a game loop that draws sprites.
//
// The game engine also has support for:
//
// Time-based motion (game.pixelsPerFrame())
// Pause (game.togglePaused())
// High scores (game.[get][clear]HighScores(), game.setHighScore())
// Sound (game.canPlaySound(), game.playSound())
// Accessing frame rate (game.fps)
// Accessing game time (game.gameTime)
// Key processing (game.addKeyListener())
//
```

*(Continues)*

Example 9.9 *(Continued)*

```javascript
// The game engine's animate() method invokes the following methods,
// in the order listed:
//
//     game.startAnimate()
//     game.paintUnderSprites()
//     game.paintOverSprites()
//     game.endAnimate()
//
// Those four methods are implemented by the game engine to do nothing.
// You override those methods to make the game come alive.

var Game = function (gameName, canvasId) {
   var canvas = document.getElementById(canvasId),
       self = this; // Used by key event handlers below

   // General

   this.context = canvas.getContext('2d');
   this.gameName = gameName;
   this.sprites = [];
   this.keyListeners = [];

   // High scores

   this.HIGH_SCORES_SUFFIX = '_highscores';

   // Image loading

   this.imageLoadingProgressCallback;
   this.images = {};
   this.imageUrls = [];
   this.imagesLoaded = 0;
   this.imagesFailedToLoad = 0;
   this.imagesIndex = 0;

   // Time

   this.startTime = 0;
   this.lastTime = 0;
   this.gameTime = 0;
   this.fps = 0;
   this.STARTING_FPS = 60;

   this.paused = false;
   this.startedPauseAt = 0;
   this.PAUSE_TIMEOUT = 100;
```

```
   // Sound

   this.soundOn = true;
   this.soundChannels = [];
   this.audio = new Audio();
   this.NUM_SOUND_CHANNELS = 10;

   for (var i=0; i < this.NUM_SOUND_CHANNELS; ++i) {
      var audio = new Audio();
      this.soundChannels.push(audio);
   }

   // The this object in the following event handlers is the
   // DOM window, which is why the functions call
   // self.keyPressed() instead of this.keyPressed(e).

   window.onkeypress = function (e) { self.keyPressed(e)  };
   window.onkeydown  = function (e) { self.keyPressed(e); };

   return this;
};

// Game methods......................................................

Game.prototype = {
   // Given a URL, return the associated image

   getImage: function (imageUrl) {
      return this.images[imageUrl];
   },

   // This method is called by loadImage() when
   // an image loads successfully.

   imageLoadedCallback: function (e) {
      this.imagesLoaded++;
   },

   // This method is called by loadImage() when
   // an image does not load successfully.

   imageLoadErrorCallback: function (e) {
      this.imagesFailedToLoad++;
   },

   // Loads a particular image
```

(Continues)

---

**Example 9.9** *(Continued)*

---

```
loadImage: function (imageUrl) {
    var image = new Image(),
        self = this;

    image.src = imageUrl;

    image.addEventListener('load',
        function (e) {
            self.imageLoadedCallback(e);
        });

    image.addEventListener('error',
        function (e) {
            self.imageLoadErrorCallback(e);
        });

    this.images[imageUrl] = image;
},

// You call this method repeatedly to load images that have been
// queued (by calling queueImage()). This method returns the
// percent of the game's images that have been processed. When
// the method returns 100, all images are loaded, and you can
// quit calling this method.

loadImages: function () {

    // If there are images left to load

    if (this.imagesIndex < this.imageUrls.length) {
        this.loadImage(this.imageUrls[this.imagesIndex]);
        this.imagesIndex++;
    }

    // Return the percent complete

    return (this.imagesLoaded + this.imagesFailedToLoad) /
            this.imageUrls.length * 100;
},

// Call this method to add an image to the queue. The image
// will be loaded by loadImages().

queueImage: function (imageUrl) {
    this.imageUrls.push(imageUrl);
},
```

```
// Game loop.................................................

// Starts the animation by calling window.requestNextAnimationFrame().
//
// window.requestNextAnimationFrame() is a polyfill method
// implemented in requestNextAnimationFrame.js. You pass
// requestNextAnimationFrame() a reference to a function
// that the browser calls when it's time to draw the next
// animation frame.
//
// When it's time to draw the next animation frame, the
// browser invokes the function that you pass to
// requestNextAnimationFrame(). Because that function is
// invoked by the browser (the window object, to be more exact),
// the this variable in that function will be the window object.
// We want the this variable to be the game instead, so we use
// JavaScript's built-in call() function to call the function,
// with the game specified as the this variable.

start: function () {
    var self = this;                 // The this variable is the game
    this.startTime = getTimeNow();   // Record game's startTime

    window.requestNextAnimationFrame(
        function (time) {
            // The this variable in this function is the window,
            // not the game, which is why we do not simply
            // do this: animate.call(time).

            self.animate.call(self, time); // self is the game
        });
},

// Drives the game's animation. This method is called by the
// browser when it's time for the next animation frame.
//
// If the game is paused, animate() reschedules another call to
// animate() in PAUSE_TIMEOUT (100) ms.
//
// If the game is not paused, animate() paints the next animation
// frame and reschedules another call to animate() when it's time
// to draw the next animation frame.
//
// The implementations of this.startAnimate(),
// this.paintUnderSprites(), this.paintOverSprites(), and
// this.endAnimate() do nothing. You override those methods to
// create the animation frame.
```

(Continues)

Example 9.9 *(Continued)*

```
animate: function (time) {
    var self = this;

    if (this.paused) {
        // In PAUSE_TIMEOUT (100) ms, call this method again to see
        // if the game is still paused. There's no need to check
        // more frequently.

        setTimeout( function () {
            self.animate.call(self, time);
        }, this.PAUSE_TIMEOUT);
    }
    else {                      // Game is not paused
        this.tick(time);        // Update fps, game time
        this.clearScreen();     // Prepare for the next frame

        this.startAnimate(time);   // Override as you wish
        this.paintUnderSprites();  // Override as you wish

        this.updateSprites(time);  // Invoke sprite behaviors
        this.paintSprites(time);   // Paint sprites in the canvas

        this.paintOverSprites();   // Override as you wish
        this.endAnimate();         // Override as you wish

        // Keep the animation going.

        window.requestNextAnimationFrame(
            function (time) {
                self.animate.call(self, time);
            });
    }
},

// Update the frame rate, game time, and the last time the
// application drew an animation frame.

tick: function (time) {
    this.updateFrameRate(time);
    this.gameTime = (getTimeNow()) - this.startTime;
    this.lastTime = time;
},

// Update the frame rate, based on the amount of time it took
// for the last animation frame only.
```

```
updateFrameRate: function (time) {
   if (this.lastTime === 0) this.fps = this.STARTING_FPS;
   else                     this.fps = 1000 / (time - this.lastTime);
},

// Clear the entire canvas.

clearScreen: function () {
   this.context.clearRect(0, 0,
      this.context.canvas.width, this.context.canvas.height);
},

// Update all sprites. The sprite update() method invokes all
// of a sprite's behaviors.

updateSprites: function (time) {
   for(var i=0; i < this.sprites.length; ++i) {
      var sprite = this.sprites[i];
      sprite.update(this.context, time);
   };
},

// Paint all visible sprites.

paintSprites: function (time) {
   for(var i=0; i < this.sprites.length; ++i) {
      var sprite = this.sprites[i];
      if (sprite.visible)
         sprite.paint(this.context);
   };
},

// Toggle the paused state of the game. If, after
// toggling, the paused state is unpaused, the
// application subtracts the time spent during
// the pause from the game's start time. That
// means the game picks up where it left off,
// without a potentially large jump in time.

togglePaused: function () {
   var now = getTimeNow();

   this.paused = !this.paused;

   if (this.paused) {
      this.startedPauseAt = now;
   }
```

---

Example 9.9 *(Continued)*

---

```
    else { // Not paused
        // Adjust start time, so game starts where it left off when
        // the user paused it.

        this.startTime = this.startTime + now - this.startedPauseAt;
        this.lastTime = now;
    }
},

// Given a velocity of some object, calculate the number of pixels
// to move that object for the current frame.

pixelsPerFrame: function (time, velocity) {
    // Sprites move a certain amount of pixels per frame
    // (pixels/frame). This methods returns the amount of
    // pixels a sprite should move for a given frame. Sprite
    // velocity is measured in pixels/second,
    // so: (pixels/second) * (second/frame) = pixels/frame:

    return velocity / this.fps;  // pixels/frame
},

// High scores...............................................

// Returns an array of high scores from local storage.

getHighScores: function () {
    var key = this.gameName + this.HIGH_SCORES_SUFFIX,
        highScoresString = localStorage[key];

    if (highScoresString == undefined) {
        localStorage[key] = JSON.stringify([]);
    }
    return JSON.parse(localStorage[key]);
},

// Sets the high score in local storage.

setHighScore: function (highScore) {
    var key = this.gameName + this.HIGH_SCORES_SUFFIX,
        highScoresString = localStorage[key];

    highScores.unshift(highScore);
    localStorage[key] = JSON.stringify(highScores);
},
```

```
// Removes the high scores from local storage.

clearHighScores: function () {
   localStorage[this.gameName + this.HIGH_SCORES_SUFFIX] =
   JSON.stringify([]);
},

// Key listeners................................................

// Add a (key, listener) pair to the keyListeners array.

addKeyListener: function (keyAndListener) {
   this.keyListeners.push(keyAndListener);
},

// Given a key, return the associated listener.

findKeyListener: function (key) {
   var listener = undefined;

   for(var i=0; i < this.keyListeners.length; ++i) {
      var keyAndListener = this.keyListeners[i],
          currentKey = keyAndListener.key;
      if (currentKey === key) {
         listener = keyAndListener.listener;
      }
   };
   return listener;
},

// This method is the callback for key down and key press events.

keyPressed: function (e) {
   var listener = undefined,
       key = undefined;

   switch (e.keyCode) {
      // Add more keys as needed

      case 32: key = 'space';        break;
      case 68: key = 'd';            break;
      case 75: key = 'k';            break;
      case 83: key = 's';            break;
      case 80: key = 'p';            break;
      case 37: key = 'left arrow';   break;
      case 39: key = 'right arrow';  break;
      case 38: key = 'up arrow';     break;
      case 40: key = 'down arrow';   break;
   }
```

*(Continues)*

**Example 9.9** *(Continued)*

```
      listener = this.findKeyListener(key);
      if (listener) { // Listener is a function
         listener();  // Invoke the listener function
      }
   },

   // Sound.....................................................

   // Returns true if the browser can play sounds in ogg file format.

   canPlayOggVorbis: function () {
      return "" != this.audio.canPlayType('audio/ogg; codecs="vorbis"');
   },

   // Returns true if the browser can play sounds in mp3 file format.

   canPlayMp3: function () {
      return "" != this.audio.canPlayType('audio/mpeg');
   },

   // Returns the first sound available channel.

   getAvailableSoundChannel: function () {
      var audio;

      for (var i=0; i < this.NUM_SOUND_CHANNELS; ++i) {
         audio = this.soundChannels[i];
         if (audio.played && audio.played.length > 0) {
            if (audio.ended)
               return audio;
         }
         else {
            if (!audio.ended)
               return audio;
         }
      }
      return undefined; // All channels in use
   },

   // Given an identifier, play the associated sound.
```

```
playSound: function (id) {
   var channel = this.getAvailableSoundChannel(),
       element = document.getElementById(id);

   if (channel && element) {
      channel.src = element.src === '' ?
                     element.currentSrc : element.src;
      channel.load();
      channel.play();
   }
},

// Sprites......................................................

// Add a sprite to the game. The game engine will update the sprite
// and paint it (if it's visible) in the animate() method.

addSprite: function (sprite) {
   this.sprites.push(sprite);
},

// It's probably a good idea not to access sprites directly,
// because it's better to write generalized code that deals with
// all sprites, so this method should be used sparingly.

getSprite: function (name) {
   for(i in this.sprites) {
      if (this.sprites[i].name === name)
         return this.sprites[i];
   }
   return null;
},

// The following methods, which do nothing, are called by animate()
// in the order they are listed. Override them as you wish.

startAnimate:      function (time) { },
paintUnderSprites: function ()     { },
paintOverSprites:  function ()     { },
endAnimate:        function ()     { }
};
```

Now that you've seen how the game engine is implemented, let's put it to use.

## 9.2 The Ungame

This section illustrates the use of the game engine discussed at the beginning of this chapter with the implementation of an ungame, shown in Figure 9.1.

Figure 9.1 Playing the ungame

Like the undead, who are not really dead, the ungame is not really a game. Its purpose is not to entertain you, but to show you how to use the game engine to implement your own games.

Playing the ungame consists of gazing at the scrolling background and clicking the Lose a life button. The ungame begins with three lives, which are depicted in the heads-up display in the game's upper-right corner.

The ungame embodies many of the characteristics that you find in most games, including

- A loading screen
- Asset management
- Sound
- A scrolling background with parallax
- Lives indicator
- High scores
- Key processing
- Pause and auto-pause
- Game-over sequence

Let's start by looking at the ungame's HTML.

## 9.2.1 The Ungame's HTML

The ungame's HTML is listed in Example 9.10. That HTML defines the following DIVs:

- `loadingToast`
- `scoreToast`
- `pausedToast`
- `gameOverToast`
- `highScoreToast`
- `loseLifeToast`

A toast is something you present to a user, that, in more mundane terms, could be described as a dialog box. The ungame has six of them, all listed above. When the game starts, only the `loadingToast` is displayed; all the other toasts are hidden by the ungame's CSS (not listed in the book for brevity's sake), which sets the toasts' `display` attribute to none.

The ungame has two canvases, one for the game's background and scrolling clouds and another for the lives indicator in the game's upper-right corner. The ungame also has two audio elements that the browser loads upfront. Those sounds are used by the ungame's JavaScript.

**Example 9.10** The ungame: HTML

```
<!DOCTYPE html>
<html>
   <head>
      <title>Ungame</title>
      <link rel="stylesheet" type="text/css" href="ungame.css"/>
   </head>

   <body>
      <!-- Game canvas......................................... -->

      <canvas id="gameCanvas" width="550" height="750">
         Canvas not supported
      </canvas>

      <!-- Loading Toast....................................... -->

      <div id='loadingToast' class='toast'>
         <span id='loadingToastTitle' class='title'>The Ungame</span>

         <span id='loadingToastBlurb' class='blurb'>
            <p>This game is an ungame, sort of like the undead:
               The undead are not really dead, and this is not really
               a game; however, it implements essential functionality
               pertient to most games.</p>

            <p>The ungame comes with:</p>

            <ul>
               <li>This loading screen</li>
               <li>Asset management</li>
               <li>Music and Sounds</li>
               <li>A scrolling background with parallax</li>
               <li>Lives indicator (upper right corner)</li>
               <li>Score indicator (appears when the ungame starts)</li>
               <li>High score functionality</li>
               <li>Key processing (including throttling)</li>
               <li>Pause (press 'p' key once the ungame starts)</li>
               <li>Auto-Pause (when the window loses focus)</li>
            </ul>

            <p>The ungame is implemented with a
               simple game engine (~200 lines of JavaScript).</p>
         </span>
```

```html
    <span id='loadButtonSpan'>
        <input type='button' id='loadButton' value='Load Game...'
               autofocus='true'/>
        <span id='loadingMessage'>Loading...</span>
    </span>

    <div id='progressDiv'></div>
</div>

<!-- Scores............................................... -->

<div id='scoreToast' class='toast'></div>

<!-- Lives............................................... -->

<canvas id='livesCanvas' width='90' height='40'>
    Canvas not supported
</canvas>

<!-- Paused............................................... -->

<div id='pausedToast' class='toast'>
    <p class='title' style='margin-left: 45px;'>Paused</p>
    <p>Click anywhere to start</p>
</div>

<!-- Game Over............................................... -->

<div id='gameOverToast' class='toast'>
    <p class='title'>Game Over</p><br/>
    <p><input id='clearHighScoresCheckbox' type='checkbox'/>
        clear high scores</p>
    <input id='newGameButton' type='button' value='new game'
           autofocus='true'/>
</div>

<!-- High scores............................................... -->

<p id='highScoreParagraph'></p>

<div id='highScoreToast' width='400' style='display: none'>
    <p class='title'>High score!</p>

    <p>What's your name?</p>

    <input id='nameInput' type='text' autofocus='true'>
    <input id='addMyScoreButton' type='button' value='add my score'
           disabled='true'>
```

*(Continues)*

---

Example 9.10   *(Continued)*

---

```html
        <input id='newGameFromHighScoresButton' type='button'
            value='new game'>

        <p class='title' id='previousHighScoresTitle' display='none'>
          Previous High Scores
        </p>

        <!-- The following ordered list is populated
                    by JavaScript in ungame.js -->
        <ol id='highScoreList'></ol>
    </div>

    <!-- Lose Life.............................................. -->

    <div id='loseLifeToast' class='toast'>
        <input id='loseLifeButton' type='button' value='Lose a life'
            autofocus='true'/>
    </div>

    <!-- Sounds................................................. -->

    <audio id='pop' preload='auto'>
        <source src='sounds/pop.ogg' type='audio/ogg'>
        <source src='sounds/pop.mp3' type='audio/mp3'>
    </audio>

    <audio id='whoosh' preload='auto'>
        <source src='sounds/whoosh.ogg' type='audio/ogg'>
        <source src='sounds/whoosh.mp3' type='audio/mp3'>
    </audio>

  <script src = 'requestNextAnimationFrame.js'></script>
  <script src = 'progressbar.js'></script>
  <script src = 'gameEngine.js'></script>
  <script src = 'ungame.js'></script>
  </body>
</html>
```

---

Next, let's look at the ungame's game loop.

## 9.2.2  The Ungame's Game Loop

The ungame creates a Game instance and reimplements paintUnderSprites() and paintOverSprites(). The ungame doesn't have any sprites, but the game engine invokes paintUnderSprites() and paintOverSprites() anyway, as shown in Example 9.11.

---

Example 9.11  Painting over and under sprites

---

```
var game = new Game('ungame', 'gameCanvas'),
    ...

game.paintOverSprites = function () {
    paintNearCloud(game.context, 120, 20);
    paintNearCloud(game.context, game.context.canvas.width+120, 20);
};

game.paintUnderSprites = function () {

    // Background erased by game engine's clearScreen()

    if (!gameOver && livesLeft === 0) {
        over();
    }
    else {
        paintSun(game.context);
        paintFarCloud(game.context, 20, 20);
        paintFarCloud(game.context, game.context.canvas.width+20, 20);

        if (!gameOver) {
            updateScore();
        }

        updateLivesDisplay();
    }
};
...

game.start();
```

---

The paintUnderSprites() method paints the sun and far (larger) cloud, and updates the score and lives display if the game is not over. paintOverSprites() paints the near (smaller) cloud. Both methods paint their cloud twice at fixed locations. As Example 9.12 illustrates, the ungame translates the context to make it appear as though the clouds are moving from left to right.

The scrollBackground() function, which the ungame calls for every animation frame, translates the context by a small amount. When the translate offset becomes greater than the width of the canvas, scrollBackground() resets the offset so it appears as though the background is continuously scrolling.

---

**Example 9.12** Background scrolling

---

```
var game = new Game('ungame', 'gameCanvas'),
    ...

// Scrolling the background.......................................

translateDelta = 0.025,
translateOffset = 0,

scrollBackground = function () {
   translateOffset = (translateOffset + translateDelta) %
                     game.canvas.width;
   game.context.translate(-translateOffset, 0);
},

// Paint Methods...................................................

paintClouds = function (context) {
   paintFarCloud(game.context, 0, 20);
   paintNearCloud(game.context, game.context.canvas.width + 120, 20);
},

paintSun = function (context) {
   ...
},

paintFarCloud = function (context, x, y) {
   context.save();
   scrollBackground();

   // Paint far cloud with quadratic curves...

   context.restore();
},

paintNearCloud = function (context, x, y) {
   context.save();
   scrollBackground();
   scrollBackground();

   // Paint near cloud with quadratic curves...

   context.restore();
},
```

---

**NOTE: The ungame and parallax**

The ungame's `scrollBackground()` function is invoked once by `paintFar-Cloud()` and twice by `paintNearCloud()`. As a result, the near cloud moves twice as fast as the far cloud, creating a mild parallax effect. See Section 5.8, "Parallax," on p. 377 for a discussion of a more pronounced parallax effect.

## 9.2.3 Loading the Ungame

When the ungame starts, it displays the loading screen shown in the upper-left corner of Figure 9.2. The loading screen contains a short description of the ungame, and a button that loads the game. When the user clicks the button, the ungame replaces the button with a progress bar, and the ungame loads its resources.

The `onclick` handler for the Load Game button is listed in Example 9.13.

The ungame doesn't use any images—it draws the sun and clouds directly—however, for illustration, it loads 12 images and displays the progress bar as they are loading. You can read more about loading images in Section 9.1.2, "Loading Images," on p. 554 and about progress bars in Section 10.2, "Progress Bars," on p. 625.

When the game engine is finished loading images, the `onclick` handler, listed in Example 9.13, uses `window.setTimeout()` to progressively make elements of the loading screen disappear. First, the progress bar disappears, followed by the text, and finally the loading toast itself.

**Example 9.13** Loading

```
loadButton.onclick = function (e) {
   var interval,
      loadingPercentComplete = 0;

   e.preventDefault();

   progressDiv.style.display = 'block';
   loadButton.style.display = 'none';

   loadingMessage.style.display = 'block';
   progressDiv.appendChild(progressbar.domElement);

   // The following images are not used. The ungame loads
   // to illustrate loading images at the beginning of a game.

   game.queueImage('images/image1.png');
```

*(Continues)*

**Example 9.13**  *(Continued)*

```
game.queueImage('images/image2.png');
game.queueImage('images/image3.png');
game.queueImage('images/image4.png');
game.queueImage('images/image5.png');
game.queueImage('images/image6.png');
game.queueImage('images/image7.png');
game.queueImage('images/image8.png');
game.queueImage('images/image9.png');
game.queueImage('images/image10.png');
game.queueImage('images/image11.png');
game.queueImage('images/image12.png');

interval = setInterval( function (e) {
    loadingPercentComplete = game.loadImages();

    if (loadingPercentComplete === 100) {
        clearInterval(interval);
        setTimeout( function (e) {
            loadingMessage.style.display = 'none';
            progressDiv.style.display = 'none';

            setTimeout( function (e) {
                loadingToastBlurb.style.display = 'none';
                loadingToastTitle.style.display = 'none';

                setTimeout( function (e) {
                    loadingToast.style.display = 'none';
                    loseLifeToast.style.display = 'block';
                    game.playSound('sounds/pop');

                    setTimeout( function (e) {
                        loading = false;
                        score = 10;
                        scoreToast.innerText = '10';
                        scoreToast.style.display = 'inline';
                        game.playSound('pop');
                    }, 1000);
                }, 500);
            }, 500);
        }, 500);
    }
    progressbar.draw(loadingPercentComplete);
}, 16);
};

// Start game.......................................................

game.start();
```

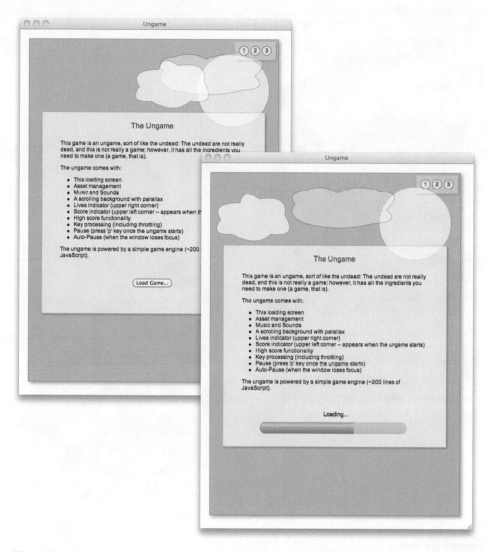

Figure 9.2 Loading

## 9.2.4 Pausing

In Section 9.1.1.1, "Pause," on p. 551 you saw how the game engine pauses and unpauses the game. As Figure 9.3 illustrates, when you pause the ungame, it displays a toast.

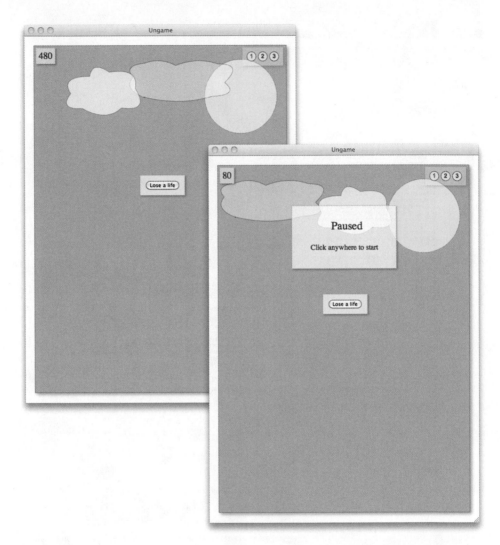

Figure 9.3  Pausing

Example 9.14 shows the ungame's togglePaused() method, which in turn invokes the game engine's method of the same name and displays the paused toast if the game is paused. You can unpause the game by clicking the toast. You can also press the P key to pause and unpause the game; see Section 9.2.5, "Key Listeners," on p. 584 for more information.

---

Example 9.14 Pausing

---

```
var game = new Game('ungame', 'gameCanvas'),
...

pausedToast = document.getElementById('pausedToast'),
...

// Paused........................................................

togglePaused = function () {
   game.togglePaused();
   pausedToast.style.display = game.paused ? 'inline' : 'none';
},

pausedToast.onclick = function (e) {
   pausedToast.style.display = 'none';
   togglePaused();
},
```

---

### 9.2.4.1 Auto-Pause

From Section 5.1.3, "A Portable Animation Loop," on p. 348 you know that you should use window.requestAnimationFrame() to drive your animations, in short, because the browser knows better than you do when to draw the next animation frame.

Additionally, window.requestAnimationFrame() typically clamps your animation's frame rate pretty severely if you open a new browser tab or move to another window. Browsers implement that clamping to save resources, both CPU cycles and battery life.

However, clamping the frame rate for your animations can have another unwanted consequence: Slow frame rates can wreak havoc for collision detection algorithms, and therefore it's best if you can avoid the browser's clamping behavior when the user opens a new tab or navigates to another window.

You can't change the browser's clamping behavior, but you can change your game's behavior so that your game automatically pauses when the window loses focus. When the window regains focus, you can automatically unpause the game or provide a means for the user to do so.

Example 9.15 shows how the ungame implements auto-pause.

---

**Example 9.15** Auto-pause

---

```
var game = new Game('ungame', 'gameCanvas'),
...
window.onblur = function windowOnBlur() {
   if (!gameOver && !game.paused) {
      togglePaused();
   }
},

window.onfocus = function windowOnFocus() {
   if (game.paused) {
      togglePaused();
   }
},
```

---

## 9.2.5 Key Listeners

In Section 9.1.4, "Keyboard Events," on p. 558, you saw how the game engine implements support for key listeners. The ungame uses that support to implement a key listener for the P key, as shown in Example 9.16.

---

**Example 9.16** Key Listeners

---

```
var game = new Game('ungame', 'gameCanvas'),
   ...
// Key listeners...............................................

game.addKeyListener(
   {
      key: 'p',
      listener: function () {
         game.togglePaused();
      }
   }
);
...
```

---

The ungame toggles the paused state of the game when you press the P key.

Now that you've seen how the ungame uses the game engine during the game, let's look at how it uses the game engine when the game is over.

### 9.2.6 Game Over and High Scores

Nearly all games implement high scores in the same manner. If you have the highest score when the game ends, the game displays the current high scores and gives you a chance to record yours.

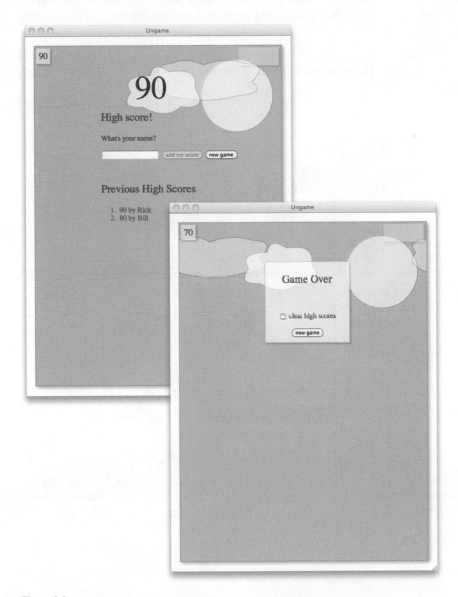

Figure 9.4  Ungame high scores

The ungame follows suit, as you can see from the screenshot in the upper-left corner of Figure 9.4, which shows how the ungame implements a high score heads-up display.

The bottom screenshot in Figure 9.4 shows the Game Over toast that the ungame displays when the game ends and you have not achieved the high score. Unlike most games, the ungame lets you clear the current high score list when you start a new game.

Figure 9.5 shows the names of the pertinent HTML elements for the high score heads-up display. Those names are used by the code in Example 9.17, which illustrates how the ungame implements high scores.

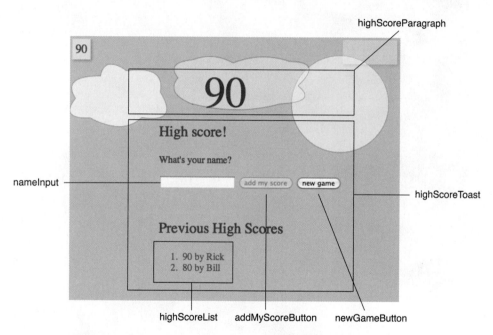

Figure 9.5 Heads-up display

Notice that the code in Example 9.17 is all about the user interface. The underlying grunt work of maintaining high scores in local storage is implemented by the game engine, as discussed in Section 9.1.5, "High Scores," on p. 560.

**Example 9.17** High scores

```javascript
var game = new Game('ungame', 'gameCanvas'),
    ...
    score = 0,
    lastScore = 0,
    lastScoreUpdate = undefined,

    // High score...............................................

    HIGH_SCORES_DISPLAYED = 10,

    highScoreToast = document.getElementById('highScoreToast'),
    highScoreParagraph = document.getElementById('highScoreParagraph'),
    highScoreList = document.getElementById('highScoreList'),
    nameInput = document.getElementById('nameInput'),
    addMyScoreButton = document.getElementById('addMyScoreButton'),
    newGameButton = document.getElementById('newGameButton'),

    previousHighScoresTitle =
        document.getElementById('previousHighScoresTitle'),

    newGameFromHighScoresButton =
        document.getElementById('newGameFromHighScoresButton'),

    clearHighScoresCheckbox =
        document.getElementById('clearHighScoresCheckbox'),

    // Game over...............................................

    gameOverToast = document.getElementById('gameOverToast'),
    gameOver = false,

    // Game over...............................................

    over = function () {
       var highScore;
       highScores = game.getHighScores();

       if (highScores.length == 0 || score > highScores[0].score) {
          showHighScores();
       }
       else {
          gameOverToast.style.display = 'inline';
       }
       gameOver = true;
       lastScore = score;
       score = 0;
    };
```

*(Continues)*

**Example 9.17** *(Continued)*

```javascript
// High scores..................................................

// Change game display to show high scores when
// player bests the high score.

showHighScores = function () {
   highScoreParagraph.style.display = 'inline';
   highScoreParagraph.innerText = score;
   highScoreToast.style.display = 'inline';
   updateHighScoreList();
};

// The game shows the list of high scores in
// an ordered list. This method creates that
// list element and populates it with the
// current high scores.

updateHighScoreList = function () {
   var el,
       highScores = game.getHighScores(),
       length = highScores.length,
       highScore,
       listParent = highScoreList.parentNode;

   listParent.removeChild(highScoreList);
   highScoreList = document.createElement('ol');
   highScoreList.id = 'highScoreList'; // So CSS takes effect
   listParent.appendChild(highScoreList);

   if (length > 0) {
      previousHighScoresTitle.style.display = 'block';

      length = length > 10 ? 10 : length;

      for (var i=0; i < length; ++i) {

         highScore = highScores[i];
         el = document.createElement('li');
         el.innerText = highScore.score +
                     ' by ' + highScore.name;
         highScoreList.appendChild(el);
      }
   }
   else {
      previousHighScoresTitle.style.display = 'none';
   }
}
```

Now that you've seen how to implement a simple but capable game engine and how to put that game engine to use for a minimal game, let's take a look at a more industrial-strength game.

## 9.3  A Pinball Game

We end this chapter with a pinball game, shown in **Figure 9.6**, that uses the game engine discussed at the beginning of this chapter.

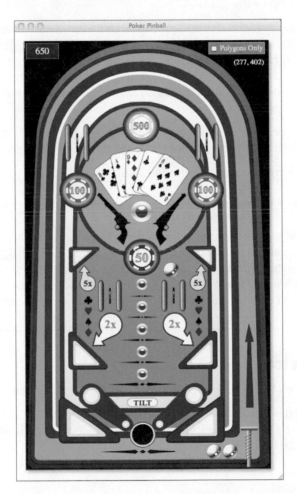

Figure 9.6  Poker pinball

Pinball games are challenging to implement because developers must

- Model gravity and friction for realistic ball motion
- Implement flipper motion, which is nonlinear
- Detect collisions, sometimes at high speed, between the ball and other objects
- Detect collisions between the ball and flippers, both of which may be moving at the same time
- Detect, and react properly to, collisions between the ball and the concave dome at the top of the game

The preceding list, which is formidable enough by itself, does not include any of the usual aspects of a game, such as loading resources, handling keystrokes, or implementing high scores. Fortunately, we have the ungame, discussed in Section 9.2, "The Ungame," on p. 572 and upon which the pinball game is based, that handles all those mundane details for us so we can get down to the business of implementing pinball.

Besides standing on the shoulders of the ungame and the underlying game engine, the pinball game uses a good deal of what we covered in Chapters 4–8.

Let's start by taking a look at the pinball game's game loop.

---

 **NOTE: The pinball game's source**

The pinball game's implementation is rather lengthy, at just under 1500 lines of code. Because it would span approximately 30 pages, the full listing of the pinball game is omitted from this book. The sections that follow discuss crucial aspects of the game's implementation and show the corresponding code only for those aspects. You can download the pinball game in its entirety, along with all the other examples from this book, at corehtml5canvas.com.

---

## 9.3.1 The Game Loop

Example 9.18 lists the pertinent code for the pinball game's game loop.

Recall from the discussion of the game engine in Section 9.1, "A Game Engine," on p. 544 that the game engine implements a game loop, with four callbacks that give you a chance to interject functionality into the loop:

- `startAnimate()`
- `paintUnderSprites()`
- `paintOverSprites()`
- `endAnimate()`

---

**Example 9.18** The pinball game loop

---

```javascript
var game = new Game('pinball', 'gameCanvas'),
    ... // Declarations omitted for brevity

game.startAnimate = function () {
   var collisionOccurred;

   if (loading || game.paused || launching)
      return;

   if (!gameOver && livesLeft === 0) {
      over();
      return;
   }

   if (ballOutOfPlay) {
      ballOutOfPlay = false;
      prepareForLaunch();
      brieflyShowTryAgainImage(2000);
      livesLeft--;
      return;
   }

   adjustRightFlipperCollisionPolygon();
   adjustLeftFlipperCollisionPolygon();

   collisionOccurred = detectCollisions();

   if (!collisionOccurred && applyGravityAndFriction) {
      applyFrictionAndGravity(); // Modifies ball velocity
   }
};

game.paintUnderSprites = function () {
   if (loading)
      return;

   updateLeftFlipper();
   updateRightFlipper();

   if (showPolygonsOnly) {
      drawCollisionShapes();
   }
   else {
      if (!showingHighScores) {
         game.context.drawImage(backgroundImage,0,0);

         drawLitBumper();
```

---

*(Continues)*

Example 9.18 *(Continued)*

```
        if (showTryAgain) {
            brieflyShowTryAgainImage(2000); // Show image for 2 seconds
        }

        paintLeftFlipper();
        paintRightFlipper();

        for (var i=0; i < livesLeft-1; ++i) {
            drawExtraBall(i);
        }
    }
  }
};
```

The preceding methods are listed in the order that they are invoked by the game engine. The pinball game implements two of those methods: startAnimate() and paintUnderSprites().

The startAnimate() method, which the game engine invokes when it starts a new animation frame, does nothing if the game is over, loading, paused, or launching the ball. Otherwise, the method checks to see if the ball is out of play and reacts accordingly.

Subsequently, startAnimate() adjusts each flipper's collision polygon (when flippers are in motion) and invokes the detectCollisions() method, which detects, and reacts to, collisions. Finally, the method applies friction and gravity if no collisions occurred and gravity and friction are currently being applied (gravity and friction are turned off while the ball is being launched). See Section 9.3.3, "Gravity and Friction," on p. 594 and Section 9.3.6, "Collision Detection," on p. 601 for more information about how the pinball game implements friction and gravity, and detects collisions, respectively.

The pinball game's paintUnderSprites() method paints the background and extra balls, and, when the ball has collided with a bumper, the method lights up the bumper.

The paintUnderSprites() method also updates and paints both flippers. The updateLeftFlipper() and updateRightFlipper() methods adjust the flipper's angle when the flippers are in motion.

Finally, notice that the startAnimate() method invokes a method named brieflyShowTryAgainImage() if the corresponding showTryAgain property is true. The brieflyShowTryAgainImage() method shows the Try Again image when the ball goes out of play, as illustrated in Figure 9.7.

Figure 9.7  Try again

## 9.3.2  The Ball

The pinball game only has two sprites: the ball and the actuator used to launch the ball. The ball's implementation is listed in Example 9.19.

---

Example 9.19  The ball

---

```
var game = new Game('pinball', 'gameCanvas'),
    ... // Declarations omitted for brevity

   lastBallPosition = new Point(),

   ballMover = {
      execute: function (sprite, context, time) {
         if (!game.paused && !loading) {
            lastBallPosition.x = sprite.left;
            lastBallPosition.y = sprite.top;

            if ( !launching && sprite.left < ACTUATOR_LEFT &&
                 (sprite.top > FLIPPER_BOTTOM || sprite.top < 0)) {
               ballOutOfPlay = true;
            }
            sprite.left += game.pixelsPerFrame(time, sprite.velocityX);
            sprite.top += game.pixelsPerFrame(time, sprite.velocityY);
         }
      },
   },

   ballSprite = new Sprite('ball',
                      new ImagePainter('images/ball.png'),
                      [ ballMover ]),
   ...
```

---

The ball sprite is created with an image painter, which is responsible for painting the image corresponding to the URL that you pass to its constructor. See Chapter 6 for more information about sprites and image painters.

The most interesting aspect of the ball is its behavior, which is implemented by the `ballMover` object. The `ballMover`'s `execute()` method records the current ball position and then moves the ball. The game uses the `lastBallPosition` to create a displacement vector for collision detection.

Notice that `ballMover.execute()` uses the game engine's `pixelsPerFrame()` method to calculate the number of pixels to move the ball in the X and Y directions. If the ball is out of play, the ball mover sets the game's `ballOutOfPlay` property to `true`, and the game subsequently places the ball on the launcher the next time `startAnimate()` is called by the game engine.

Also notice that the ball mover does not take gravity or friction into account when it moves the ball. That's left up to the `applyFrictionAndGravity()` method, which we look at next.

## 9.3.3  Gravity and Friction

Recall from Section 9.3.1, "The Game Loop," on p. 590 that the pinball game's `startAnimate()` method, which is invoked by the game engine at the start of every animation frame, applies gravity and friction by invoking the `applyFrictionAndGravity()` method, like this:

```
if (!collisionOccurred && applyGravityAndFriction) {
   applyFrictionAndGravity(parseFloat(time - game.lastTime));
}
```

The `startAnimate()` method passes the elapsed time, in milliseconds, for the last animation frame, to `applyFrictionAndGravity()`, which is listed in Example 9.20.

---

Example 9.20  Gravity and friction

---

```
applyFrictionAndGravity = function (time) {
   var lastElapsedTime = time / 1000,
      gravityVelocityIncrease = GRAVITY * seconds * 0.5;

   if (Math.abs(ballSprite.velocityX) > MIN_BALL_VELOCITY) {
      ballSprite.velocityX *= Math.pow(0.2, lastElapsedTime);
   }

   ballSprite.velocityY += gravityVelocityIncrease *
      parseFloat(game.context.canvas.height / GAME_HEIGHT_IN_METERS);
},
```

---

Given the time, in milliseconds, that it took for the last animation frame to execute, applyFrictionAndGravity() calculates the effects of friction and gravity.

To account for friction, applyFrictionAndGravity() reduces the ball's velocity at a rate of 50% per second. That rate was determined empirically, to approximate the feel of a ball rolling on a table.

To account for gravity, applyFrictionAndGravity() increases the ball's vertical velocity. That increase in velocity is calculated by multiplying the force of gravity (9.8 m/s/s) by the elapsed time of the last animation frame (in seconds), multiplied by 0.1. Multiplying by 0.1 applies only one-tenth of the gravity force because the slope of a pinball machine is much closer to horizontal than vertical, so gravity's role is greatly diminished.

Ball motion for the pinball game is relatively easy to implement. Flipper motion, however, is another story. Let's take a look at that next.

## 9.3.4  Flipper Motion

A pinball game's flippers move in a nonlinear fashion. When a flipper rises, it starts out quickly, but its velocity erodes as it rises; after all, in a real pinball game, the flippers cannot be moving at full velocity and instantaneously come to a halt when they reach their apex. Likewise, as flippers fall, they gain velocity as gravity constantly pulls down on them.

You may recognize those two forms of nonlinear motion as *ease out* for rising flippers and *ease in* for falling flippers. Those two forms of motion were discussed in Section 7.2, "Warping Time," on p. 450. In that chapter, we implemented ease-in and ease-out motion with a simple animation timer to which you can attach a time-warp function. Consequently, if you use the timer to control movement (which you should—see Section 5.6, "Time-Based Motion," on p. 367), using an animation timer that warps time results in nonlinear movement.

Example 9.21 shows how the pinball game uses animation timers to control the movement of the left flipper. The application creates two timers: one for raising the flipper and one for lowering it. The former's duration is 25 ms, whereas the latter's duration is 175 ms. That means that the flipper rises quickly and falls slowly in comparison.

Notice the lines of code in Example 9.21 that set the flipper angle. The application uses the timers to access the elapsed time that the flipper has been rising or falling, thereby resulting in ease-out or ease-in motion, respectively.

Example 9.21 also refers to constants for the left flipper's pivot and the pivot's offset, which are depicted in Figure 9.8.

**Example 9.21** Flipper motion

```
var game = new Game('pinball', 'gameCanvas'),
    ... // Some declarations omitted for brevity

    FLIPPER_RISE_DURATION = 25,    // Milliseconds
    FLIPPER_FALL_DURATION = 175,   // Milliseconds
    MAX_FLIPPER_ANGLE = Math.PI/4, // 45 degrees
    ...

    leftFlipperRiseTimer =
        new AnimationTimer(FLIPPER_RISE_DURATION,
                           AnimationTimer.makeEaseOut(3)),
    leftFlipperFallTimer =
        new AnimationTimer(FLIPPER_FALL_DURATION,
                           AnimationTimer.makeEaseIn(3)),

    leftFlipperAngle = 0,
    ...

function updateLeftFlipper() {
    if (leftFlipperRiseTimer.isRunning()) {    // Flipper is rising
        if (leftFlipperRiseTimer.isOver()) {   // Finished rising
            leftFlipperRiseTimer.stop();        // Stop rise timer
            leftFlipperAngle = MAX_FLIPPER_ANGLE; // Set flipper angle
            leftFlipperFallTimer.start();       // Start falling
        }
        else {                                 // Flipper is still rising
            leftFlipperAngle =
                MAX_FLIPPER_ANGLE/FLIPPER_RISE_DURATION *
                leftFlipperRiseTimer.getElapsedTime();
        }
    }
    else if (leftFlipperFallTimer.isRunning()) { // Flipper is falling
        if (leftFlipperFallTimer.isOver()) {    // Finished falling
            leftFlipperFallTimer.stop();         // Stop fall timer
            leftFlipperAngle = 0;                // Set flipper angle
        }
        else {                                  // Flipper is still falling
            leftFlipperAngle = MAX_FLIPPER_ANGLE -
                MAX_FLIPPER_ANGLE/FLIPPER_FALL_DURATION *
                leftFlipperFallTimer.getElapsedTime();
        }
    }
};
```

```
function paintLeftFlipper() {
   if (leftFlipperRiseTimer.isRunning() ||
       leftFlipperFallTimer.isRunning()) {
      game.context.save();
      game.context.translate(LEFT_FLIPPER_PIVOT_X,
                             LEFT_FLIPPER_PIVOT_Y);

      game.context.rotate(-leftFlipperAngle);

      game.context.drawImage(game.getImage('images/leftFlipper.png'),
                             -LEFT_FLIPPER_PIVOT_OFFSET_X,
                             -LEFT_FLIPPER_PIVOT_OFFSET_Y);
      game.context.restore();
   }
   else {
      game.context.drawImage(game.getImage('images/leftFlipper.png'),
         LEFT_FLIPPER_PIVOT_X - LEFT_FLIPPER_PIVOT_OFFSET_X,
         LEFT_FLIPPER_PIVOT_Y - LEFT_FLIPPER_PIVOT_OFFSET_Y);
   }
};
```

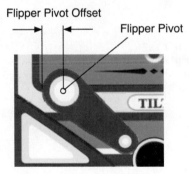

**Figure 9.8** Flipper pivots and offsets

## 9.3.5  Handling Keyboard Events

The pinball game handles keyboard events as follows.

- K activates right flipper and plays flipper sound.
- D activates left flipper and plays flipper sound.
- P toggles the game's paused state.
- ↑ moves the actuator up.
- ↓ moves the actuator down.

- Space launches the ball.

With the help of the game engine, the pinball game implements key listeners as illustrated in Example 9.22.

Example 9.22 Key listeners

```
var game = new Game('pinball', 'gameCanvas'),
    ...

lastKeyListenerTime = 0,  // For throttling

game.addKeyListener(
    {
        key: 'p',
        listener: function () {
            togglePaused();
        }
    }
);

game.addKeyListener(
    {
        key: 'k',
        listener: function () {
            if ( !launching && !gameOver) {
                rightFlipperAngle = 0;
                rightFlipperRiseTimer.start();
                game.playSound('flipper');
            }
        }
    }
);

game.addKeyListener(
    {
        key: 'd',
        listener: function () {
            if ( !launching && !gameOver) {
                leftFlipperAngle = 0;
                leftFlipperRiseTimer.start();
                game.playSound('flipper');
            }
        }
    }
);
```

```
game.addKeyListener(
    {
        key: 'up arrow',
        listener: function () {
            var now;

            if (!launching || launchStep === 1)
                return;

            now = +new Date();

            if (now - lastKeyListenerTime > 80) { // Throttle
                lastKeyListenerTime = now;

                launchStep--;

                ballSprite.top = BALL_LAUNCH_TOP + (launchStep-1) * 9;

                actuatorSprite.painter.image =
                    launchImages[launchStep-1];

                adjustActuatorPlatformShape();
            }
        }
    }
);

game.addKeyListener(
    {
        key: 'down arrow',
        listener: function () {
            var now;

            if (!launching || launchStep === LAUNCH_STEPS)
                return;

            now = +new Date();

            if (now - lastKeyListenerTime > 80) { // Throttle
                lastKeyListenerTime = now;
                launchStep++;
                actuatorSprite.painter.image = launchImages[launchStep-1];
                ballSprite.top = BALL_LAUNCH_TOP + (launchStep-1) * 9;
                adjustActuatorPlatformShape();
            }
        }
    }
);
```

*(Continues)*

---

Example 9.22  *(Continued)*

---

```
game.addKeyListener(
    {
        key: 'space',
        listener: function () {
            if (!launching && ballSprite.left === BALL_LAUNCH_LEFT &&
                ballSprite.velocityY === 0) {
                launching = true;
                ballSprite.velocityY = 0;
                applyGravityAndFriction = false;
                launchStep = 1;
            }
            if (launching) {
                ballSprite.velocityY = -300 * launchStep;
                launching = false;
                launchStep = 1;

                setTimeout( function (e) {
                    actuatorSprite.painter.image = launchImages[0];
                    adjustActuatorPlatformShape();
                }, 50);

                setTimeout( function (e) {
                    applyGravityAndFriction = true;
                    adjustRightBoundaryAfterLaunch();
                }, 2000);
            }
        }
    }
);
```

---

The P key toggles the paused state of the game by invoking the pinball game's togglePaused() method. That method, in turn, invokes the game engine's method of the same name and displays a paused toast, as shown in Figure 9.9.

The D and K keys, which activate the left and right flippers respectively, set the flipper angle to zero, start the flipper's rise timer, and play the flipper sound (thunk).

The ↑ and ↓ keys move the ball up and down, respectively, on the actuator. The pinball game throttles those events, so the game handles them only once every 80 ms. That throttling controls the rate of ascent and descent for the actuator when players hold down the ↑ or ↓ keys.

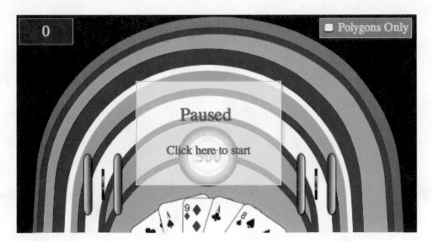

Figure 9.9  Pausing the pinball game

Finally, when a player presses the Space key, the pinball game launches the ball from the actuator. That key handler turns gravity and friction off for 50 ms following the launch so that the ball rolls smoothly along the edge of the dome. Two seconds after the launch, the key handler turns gravity and friction back on.

## 9.3.6  Collision Detection

The pinball game implements a posteriori (i.e., after the fact) collision detection primarily with the separating axis theorem (SAT), as discussed in Section 8.4, "The Separating Axis Theorem (SAT) and Minimum Translation Vector (MTV)," on p. 495. The SAT is great for slow-moving polygons that are relatively large, but it's not optimal for small, fast moving objects. Because of that deficiency, the pinball game augments the SAT collision detection with ray casting to detect collisions between the ball and moving flippers.

First, let's look at how the pinball game uses the SAT to detect collisions between the ball and everything except moving flippers.

### 9.3.6.1  SAT Collision Detection

Because the pinball game uses the separating axis theorem for collision detection, it creates polygons for the objects with which the ball can collide, as shown in Figure 9.10.

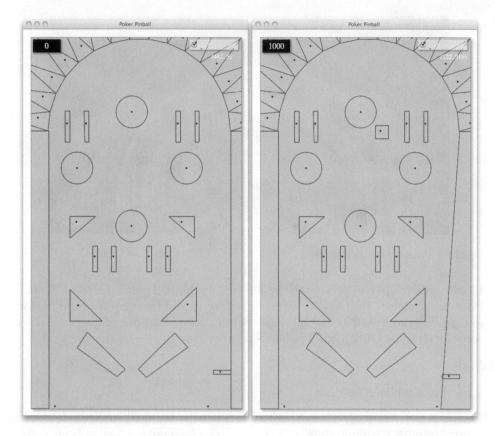

Figure 9.10 Pinball collision polygons: before launching the ball (*left*) and after the ball has been launched (*right*)

The pinball game provides a Polygons Only checkbox in the upper-right corner. When that checkbox is checked, the pinball game draws only collision detection polygons and the heads-up display.

When displaying collision detection polygons only, the pinball game is fully functional. Although showing collision detection polygons is not very interesting for the game's players, it's useful for developers because it lets them see exactly how collisions take place.

When the Polygons Only checkbox is checked, the pinball game draws collision shapes with the following method:

```
function drawCollisionShapes() {
   var centroid;

   shapes.forEach( function (shape) {
      shape.stroke(game.context);
      game.context.beginPath();
      centroid = shape.centroid();
      game.context.arc(centroid.x, centroid.y, 1.5, 0,
                   Math.PI*2, false);
      game.context.stroke();
   });
}
```

The preceding method invokes the shape's `stroke()` method, which draws the polygon. Then the method draws a tiny (1.5 pixel radius) circle to represent the approximate location of the shape's centroid.

To detect collisions, the pinball game first creates a circle or polygon for each object with which the ball can collide, like this:

```
var game = new Game('pinball', 'gameCanvas'),
    ...
    // Collision Detection.......................................

    shapes = [],
    ...

    fiveHundredBumper = new Circle(256, 187, 40),
    oneHundredBumperRight = new Circle(395, 328, 40),
    oneHundredBumperLeft = new Circle(116, 328, 40),
    fiftyBumper = new Circle(255, 474, 40),

    leftBoundary = new Polygon(),
    rightBoundary = new Polygon(),
    ...

leftBoundary.points.push(new Point(45, 235));
leftBoundary.points.push(new Point(45, game.context.canvas.height));
leftBoundary.points.push(new Point(-450, game.context.canvas.height));
leftBoundary.points.push(new Point(-450, 235));
leftBoundary.points.push(new Point(45, 235));

rightBoundary.points.push(new Point(508, 235));
rightBoundary.points.push(new Point(508, game.context.canvas.height));
rightBoundary.points.push(new Point(508*2, game.context.canvas.height));
rightBoundary.points.push(new Point(508*2, 235))
rightBoundary.points.push(new Point(508, 235));
...
shapes.push(leftBoundary);
shapes.push(rightBoundary);
...
```

For polygons, the application adds points representing each of the polygon's vertices. Then the application pushes each shape onto an array of shapes.

From Section 9.3.1, "The Game Loop," on p. 590, recall the pinball game's `startAnimate()` method, which looks like this:

```
game.startAnimate = function () {
   var collisionOccurred;

   ...

   adjustRightFlipperCollisionPolygon();
   adjustLeftFlipperCollisionPolygon();

   collisionOccurred = detectCollisions();

   if (!collisionOccurred && applyGravityAndFriction) {
      applyFrictionAndGravity(); // Modifies ball velocity
   }
};
```

At the start of each animation frame, the pinball game's `startAnimate()` method adjusts the collision detection polygons for each flipper (in case they are moving) and invokes the game's `detectCollisions()` method, listed in Example 9.23, which detects and reacts to collisions.

For every shape except the ball itself, the `detectCollisions()` method passes the shape and the ball's displacement vector to the ball shape's `collidesWith()` method, which uses the SAT to determine whether a collision occurred.

The ball shape's `collidesWith()` method returns a `MinimumTranslationVector` instance, which, as discussed in Section 8.4.2, "Reacting to Collisions with the Minimum Translation Vector," on p. 526, represents the minimum displacement required to move the ball out of collision. The pinball game's `detectCollisions()` method passes that vector to the game's `bounce()` method, which bounces the ball off the shape with which it collided.

The SAT, which is implemented by the ball shape's `collidesWith()` method, easily detects collisions between the ball and the flippers, provided the flippers are not in motion. However, because the ball may be moving rapidly (at a maximum of 400 pixels per second), and the flippers have a significant angular velocity when they're moving, the SAT may miss collisions between the ball and moving flippers. Therefore, the game's `detectCollisions()` method invokes a `detectFlipperCollision()` method for each flipper that uses ray casting to detect collisions between the ball and the flipper. See Example 9.26 on p. 612 for more information about the `detectFlipperCollision()` method.

**Example 9.23** Detecting collisions with the SAT

```
function collisionDetected(mtv) {
   return mtv.axis !== undefined && mtv.overlap !== 0;
};

function detectCollisions() {
   var mtv, shape, displacement, position, lastPosition;

   if (!launching && !loading && !game.paused) {
      ballShape.x = ballSprite.left;
      ballShape.y = ballSprite.top;
      ballShape.points = [];
      ballShape.setPolygonPoints();

      position = new Vector(new Point(ballSprite.left,
                                     ballSprite.top));

      lastPosition = new Vector(new Point(lastBallPosition.x,
                                          lastBallPosition.y));

      displacement = position.subtract(lastPosition);

      for (var i=0; i < shapes.length; ++i) {
         shape = shapes[i];

         if (shape !== ballShape) {
            mtv = ballShape.collidesWith(shape, displacement);
            if (collisionDetected(mtv)) {
               updateScore(shape);

               setTimeout ( function (e) {
                  bumperLit = undefined;
               }, 100);

               if (shape === twoXBumperLeft         ||
                   shape === twoXBumperRight         ||
                   shape === fiveXBumperRight        ||
                   shape === fiveXBumperLeft         ||
                   shape === fiftyBumper             ||
                   shape === oneHundredBumperLeft    ||
                   shape === oneHundredBumperRight   ||
                   shape === fiveHundredBumper) {
                  game.playSound('bumper');
                  bounce(mtv, shape, 4.5);
                  bumperLit = shape;
                  return true;
               }
```

*(Continues)*

---

**Example 9.23**  *(Continued)*

---

```
                    else if (shape === rightFlipperShape) {
                        if (rightFlipperAngle === 0) {
                            bounce(mtv, shape, 1 + rightFlipperAngle);
                            return true;
                        }
                    }
                    else if (shape === leftFlipperShape) {
                        if (leftFlipperAngle === 0) {
                            bounce(mtv, shape, 1 + leftFlipperAngle);
                            return true;
                        }
                    }
                    else if (shape === actuatorPlatformShape) {
                        bounce(mtv, shape, 0.2);
                        return true;
                    }
                    else {
                        bounce(mtv, shape, 0.96);
                        return true;
                    }
                }
            }
        }

        detectFlipperCollision(LEFT_FLIPPER);
        detectFlipperCollision(RIGHT_FLIPPER);

        return flipperCollisionDetected;
    }
    return false;
}
```

---

Our immediate concern, however, is the bounce() method, which bounces the ball off the shape with which it has collided. That method, along with its support methods, is listed in Example 9.24.

Given the ball's velocity, the bounce() method creates a velocity unit vector that it ultimately reflects around another vector that's perpendicular to the MTV. However, there are two such perpendicular vectors, so the game must determine which of those vectors to use.

---

Example 9.24  Bouncing the ball

---

```
function clampBallVelocity() {
    if (ballSprite.velocityX > MAX_BALL_VELOCITY)
        ballSprite.velocityX = MAX_BALL_VELOCITY;
    else if (ballSprite.velocityX < -MAX_BALL_VELOCITY)
        ballSprite.velocityX = -MAX_BALL_VELOCITY;

    if(ballSprite.velocityY > MAX_BALL_VELOCITY)
        ballSprite.velocityY = MAX_BALL_VELOCITY;
    else if (ballSprite.velocityY < -MAX_BALL_VELOCITY)
        ballSprite.velocityY = -MAX_BALL_VELOCITY;
};

function separate(mtv) {
    var dx, dy, velocityMagnitude, point, theta=0,
        velocityVector = new Vector(new Point(ballSprite.velocityX,
                                              ballSprite.velocityY)),
        velocityUnitVector = velocityVector.normalize();

    if (mtv.axis.x === 0) {
        theta = Math.PI/2;
    }
    else {
        theta = Math.atan(mtv.axis.y / mtv.axis.x);
    }

    dy = mtv.overlap * Math.sin(theta);
    dx = mtv.overlap * Math.cos(theta);

    if (mtv.axis.x < 0 && dx > 0 || mtv.axis.x > 0 && dx < 0) dx = -dx;
    if (mtv.axis.y < 0 && dy > 0 || mtv.axis.y > 0 && dy < 0) dy = -dy;

    ballSprite.left += dx;
    ballSprite.top  += dy;
}

function checkMTVAxisDirection(mtv, shape) {
    var flipOrNot,
        centroid1 = new Vector(ballShape.centroid()),
        centroid2 = new Vector(shape.centroid()),
        centroidVector = centroid2.subtract(centroid1),
        centroidUnitVector = (new Vector(centroidVector)).normalize();

    if (centroidUnitVector.dotProduct(mtv.axis) > 0) {
        mtv.axis.x = -mtv.axis.x;
        mtv.axis.y = -mtv.axis.y;
    }
}
```

---

*(Continues)*

---

Example 9.24 *(Continued)*

```
function bounce(mtv, shape, bounceCoefficient) {
    var velocityVector = new Vector(new Point(ballSprite.velocityX,
                                              ballSprite.velocityY)),
        velocityUnitVector = velocityVector.normalize(),
        velocityVectorMagnitude = velocityVector.getMagnitude(),
        reflectAxis, point;

    checkMTVAxisDirection(mtv, shape);

    if (!loading && !game.paused) {
        if (mtv.axis !== undefined) {
            reflectAxis = mtv.axis.perpendicular();
        }

        separate(mtv);

        point = velocityUnitVector.reflect(reflectAxis);

        if (shape === leftFlipperShape || shape === rightFlipperShape) {
            if (velocityVectorMagnitude < MIN_BALL_VELOCITY_OFF_FLIPPERS)
                velocityVectorMagnitude = MIN_BALL_VELOCITY_OFF_FLIPPERS;
        }

        ballSprite.velocityX = point.x * velocityVectorMagnitude *
                                bounceCoefficient;

        ballSprite.velocityY = point.y * velocityVectorMagnitude *
                                bounceCoefficient;

        clampBallVelocity();
    }
}
```

---

Determining the vector around which to reflect the ball's velocity is the responsibility of checkMTVAxisDirection(), which uses the dot product of the MTV axis and a vector from the ball's centroid to the centroid of the shape with which the ball collided. If the dot product between those two vectors is greater than zero, then the angle between the two vectors is acute, meaning the two vectors are pointing in roughly the same direction.

We want the ball to bounce *away* from the center of the centroid of the shape with which the ball collided, so if the dot product is greater than zero, we turn the MTV axis around so the ball will bounce away from the shape that it collided with.

After deciding on an axis about which to reflect the ball's velocity, the bounce() method invokes the separate() method, which uses the MTV to separate the ball from the shape with which it collided.

Next, the bounce() method sets the ball's velocity for bouncing. However, the method makes two adjustments to the ball's velocity. First, if the ball has collided with one of the flippers and is moving very slowly, the method sets the velocity vector to a minimum value. That ensures that the ball will bounce lively off the flippers, even when it is nearly at rest on top of a flipper. Finally, the method clamps the ball's velocity to a maximum value; otherwise, the ball could end up moving so fast that you can hardly see it, and collision detection may fail.

### 9.3.6.2 The Dome

As Figure 9.11 illustrates, the pinball game implements collision detection with the concave dome at the top of the game with triangles. The pinball game detects collisions between the ball and those triangles.

The pinball game creates the dome triangles like this:

```
var DOME_SIDES = 15,
    DOME_X = 275,
    DOME_Y = 235,
    DOME_RADIUS = 232,
    domePolygons = createDomePolygons(DOME_X, DOME_Y,
                                      DOME_RADIUS, DOME_SIDES);

domePolygons.forEach( function (polygon) {
   shapes.push(polygon);
});
```

The createDomePolygons() method, listed in Example 9.25, creates the triangles, and the game subsequently pushes each of those triangles on its array of collision detection shapes.

Example 9.25 is straightforward: It loops over the 15 triangles, creates a polygon for each triangle, and calculates each triangle's vertices. It pushes the triangles onto an array and returns that array.

One interesting aspect of the code is the midPointRadius, which the method uses to calculate the triangle vertex farthest from the dome's surface. That value has to be large enough to push the centroids of each triangle away from the surface of the dome. If you were to use a smaller value—say, radius*1.05 instead of radius*1.5—the triangles would look like those in Figure 9.12.

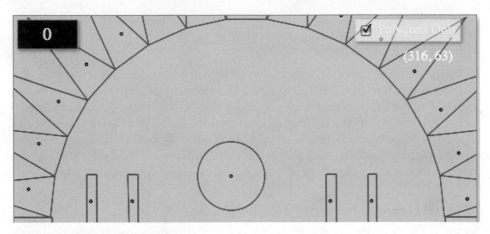

Figure 9.11  The pinball dome consists of triangles

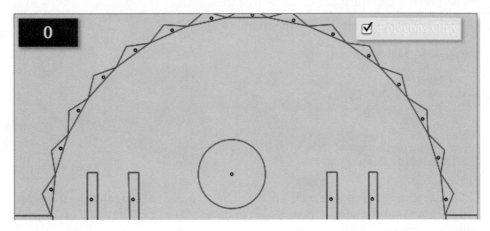

Figure 9.12  Dome triangles that are too small for accurate collision detection

Because the pinball game implements collision detection a posteriori, meaning it detects collisions after they have already occurred, it's possible for the centroid of the ball to move past the centroid of the triangle before the game detects the collision. If that happens, the centroid vector used to calculate how the ball bounces off triangles will point in the wrong direction, which means the ball's velocity will also point in the wrong direction—toward the triangle instead of away from it—and the ball will stick to the surface of the dome. To guarantee that the ball doesn't stick to the dome, you must push those triangle centroids farther away from the surface of the dome by using taller triangles, as illustrated in Figure 9.11.

Example 9.25  Creating dome polygons

```javascript
function createDomePolygons(centerX, centerY, radius, sides) {
   var polygon,
       polygons = [],
       startTheta = 0,
       endTheta,
       midPointTheta,
       thetaDelta = Math.PI/sides,
       midPointRadius = radius*1.5;

   for (var i=0; i < sides; ++i) {
      polygon = new Polygon();

      endTheta = startTheta + thetaDelta;
      midPointTheta = startTheta + (endTheta - startTheta)/2;

      polygon.points.push(
        new Point(centerX + radius * Math.cos(startTheta),
                  centerY - radius * Math.sin(startTheta)));

      polygon.points.push(
        new Point(centerX + midPointRadius * Math.cos(midPointTheta),
                  centerY - midPointRadius * Math.sin(midPointTheta)));

      polygon.points.push(
        new Point(centerX + radius * Math.cos(endTheta),
                  centerY - radius * Math.sin(endTheta)));

      polygon.points.push(
        new Point(centerX + radius * Math.cos(startTheta),
                  centerY - radius * Math.sin(startTheta)));

      polygons.push(polygon);

      startTheta += thetaDelta;
   }
   return polygons;
}
```

### 9.3.6.3  Flipper Collision Detection

The pinball game uses the SAT to detect collisions between the ball and stationary flippers. However, when the flippers are rising and the ball is moving at high speed, the SAT will miss collisions between the ball and the rising flipper.

Because the SAT is not optimal for small objects moving at high speed, the pinball game augments SAT collision detection with ray casting, which was introduced in Section 8.3, "Ray Casting," on p. 490. Example 9.26 shows the implementation of the pinball game's detectFlipperCollision() method, which is invoked by detectCollisions() when no collisions between the ball and stationary objects were detected.

**Example 9.26** Flipper collision detection

```
function detectFlipperCollision(flipper) {
   var v1, v2, l1, l2, surface, ip, bbox = {}, riseTimer;

   bbox.top    = 725;
   bbox.bottom = 850;

   if (flipper === LEFT_FLIPPER) {
      v1 = new Vector(leftFlipperBaselineShape.points[0].rotate(
                      LEFT_FLIPPER_ROTATION_POINT,
                      leftFlipperAngle));

      v2 = new Vector(leftFlipperBaselineShape.points[1].rotate(
                      LEFT_FLIPPER_ROTATION_POINT,
                      leftFlipperAngle));

      bbox.left  = 170;
      bbox.right = 265;
      riseTimer = leftFlipperRiseTimer;
   }
   else if (flipper === RIGHT_FLIPPER) {
      v1 = new Vector(rightFlipperBaselineShape.points[0].rotate(
                      RIGHT_FLIPPER_ROTATION_POINT,
                      rightFlipperAngle));

      v2 = new Vector(rightFlipperBaselineShape.points[1].rotate(
                      RIGHT_FLIPPER_ROTATION_POINT,
                      rightFlipperAngle));

      bbox.left  = 245;
      bbox.right = 400;
      riseTimer = rightFlipperRiseTimer;
   }
```

```
if ( ! flipperCollisionDetected && riseTimer.isRunning() &&
      ballSprite.top + ballSprite.height > bbox.top &&
      ballSprite.left < bbox.right) {

   surface = v2.subtract(v1);
   l1 = new Line(new Point(ballSprite.left, ballSprite.top),
                lastBallPosition),
   l2 = new Line(new Point(v2.x, v2.y), new Point(v1.x, v1.y)),
   ip = l1.intersectionPoint(l2);

   if (ip.x > bbox.left && ip.x < bbox.right) {
      reflectVelocityAroundVector(surface.perpendicular());

      ballSprite.velocityX = ballSprite.velocityX * 3.5;
      ballSprite.velocityY = ballSprite.velocityY * 3.5;

      if (ballSprite.velocityY > 0)
         ballSprite.velocityY = -ballSprite.velocityY;

      if (flipper === LEFT_FLIPPER && ballSprite.velocityX < 0)
         ballSprite.velocityX = -ballSprite.velocityX;
      else if (flipper === RIGHT_FLIPPER &&
               ballSprite.velocityX > 0)
         ballSprite.velocityX = -ballSprite.velocityX;
   }
}
}
```

The detectFlipperCollision() method creates two vectors: one in the direction from the origin to the first point on the surface of the flipper, and another from the origin to the second point on the surface of the flipper. The method subsequently subtracts the first vector from the second to obtain a vector along the flipper's edge.

The method also creates two lines, one from the ball's last position to the ball's current position, and another along the edge of the flipper. Then it checks to see where those two lines intersect.

Finally, if the ball is sufficiently close to the flipper and the intersection of the two lines is between the left and right edges of the flipper, a collision has occurred, and the method adjusts the ball's velocity accordingly.

## 9.4 Conclusion

After some significant preparation in the previous chapters, this chapter showed you how to implement games with HTML5 Canvas.

We began by discussing the implementation of a simple game engine, about 450 lines of JavaScript, that, despite its small size, implements most of the fundamentals you need to create a game, including a game loop and support for things such as time-based motion, pausing the game, keeping track of high scores, playing sounds, and implementing key listeners.

With a simple but capable game engine, we then turned our attention to the ungame, a Hello World for games that shows you how to implement many aspects of a game, without much of an actual game itself.

Finally, we discussed creating an industrial-strength pinball game. That game tackled some advanced aspects of game design, such as implementing angular motion, modeling gravity and friction, and using the SAT and ray casting for collision detection.

# CHAPTER 10

# Custom Controls

Throughout this book you've seen how to implement Canvas-based applications with one or more canvas elements combined with standard HTML controls, such as text inputs and buttons. Standard HTML controls are sufficient for many Canvas-based applications; however, some applications require custom controls, typically because either the controls are not available as standard HTML controls or the control is not supported by all browsers. Another reason to implement your own controls is when you require the same look-and-feel across HTML5-capable browsers.

In this chapter we discuss four controls, implemented from scratch:

- Rounded rectangle
- Progress bar
- Slider
- Image panner

The controls implemented in this chapter do the following:

- Reside in a global object named COREHTML5
- Draw into a canvas with a draw() method
- Put the canvas into a DIV and expose that DIV to the developer through the domElement property
- Implement an appendTo(element) method that appends the control's DOM element to an HTML element and then resizes the DOM element and its canvas to fit the enclosing element

In general, it's a good idea to keep newly created JavaScript objects out of the global namespace. In accordance with that goal, the controls implemented in this chapter all exist in a single object named COREHTML5. To instantiate an object you must go through that COREHTML5 object; for example, you create a rounded rectangle, which we discuss in Section 10.1, "Rounded Rectangles," on p. 617, like this:

```
roundedRectangle = new COREHTML5.RoundedRectangle(
                    'rgba(0,0,0,0.2)', 'darkgoldenrod', 90, 25);
```

The COREHTML5 object is known as a namespace. Namespaces reduce the possibility that someone else will implement a global object with the same name as one of your objects, thus overriding your object. It's quite likely that someone else may implement a Slider object, for example, but it's highly unlikely that someone else would implement a COREHTML5.Slider object.

Because the controls discussed in this chapter are Canvas-based, they all create a canvas element and subsequently draw the control into that canvas. You draw a control with its draw() method, which takes an optional context argument. That argument must be a Canvas context. If you specify the context argument, the control's draw() method draws the control into that context. If you do not specify a context, the draw() method draws into its own context.

To use the controls implemented in this chapter, you create an instance of the control and append the control's DOM element to an HTML element in your DOM tree. You can do that with the control's appendTo(element) method. Controls also expose their DOM element through the domElement property. That means that you can programmatically control the DOM element's style, like this:

```
roundedRectangle.domElement.style.position = 'absolute';
roundedRectangle.domElement.style.top = '50px';
roundedRectangle.domElement.style.left = '50px';
```

Or you could create a CSS class and programmatically assign that class to the control's DOM element:

```
roundedRectangle.domElement.className = 'customRectangle';
```

The preceding characteristics of the controls in this chapter are implemented with the methods listed in Table 10.1. All the controls in this chapter implement those methods.

**Table 10.1** Custom control methods

| Method | Description |
| --- | --- |
| appendTo(element) | Appends the control's DOM element to the element passed to the method and resizes both the control's DOM element and canvas to fit the enclosing DOM element. |
| createDOMElement() | Creates the control's DOM element. |
| createCanvas() | Creates the control's canvas element. |
| draw(context) | Draws the control. The context is optional; if you specify it, the control draws into that context, otherwise it draws into its own context. |
| erase() | Erases the control's canvas. |
| resize(width, height) | Resizes the control's canvas. |

**NOTE: Exposing a DIV**

The controls in this chapter create a canvas and a DIV, append the canvas to the DIV, and expose the DIV to developers with a domElement property. Developers can append that DIV to another element anywhere in the DOM tree.

Controls also implement an appendTo() method that appends the DIV to an element and resizes both the DIV and the canvas to fit the enclosing element.

# 10.1 Rounded Rectangles

Rounded rectangles, illustrated by the application in Figure 10.1, are the simplest of the four controls discussed in this chapter and are used by two other controls: progress bar and slider.

The application shown in Figure 10.1 contains a single rounded rectangle and two sliders that control the width and height of the rectangle. As you move the sliders, the rectangle continuously changes its size to match the sliders.

The HTML for the application, which is listed in Example 10.1, creates the two sliders and a DIV named roundedRectangleDiv.

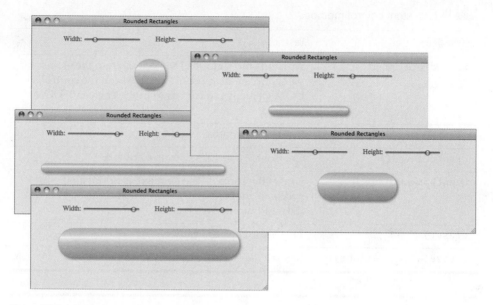

Figure 10.1  Rounded rectangles

Example 10.1  The rounded rectangle application: HTML

```html
<!DOCTYPE html>
  <head>
    <title>Rounded Rectangles</title>

    <style>
      body {
        background: bisque;
      }

      #roundedRectangleDiv {
        position: absolute;
        left: 50px;
        top: 70px;
        width: 450px;
        height: 80px;
      }

      .range {
        vertical-align: -5px;
      }
```

```
            #controls {
                color: blue;
                margin-top: 20px;
                margin-left: 65px;
            }

            #widthRangeDiv {
                margin-right: 30px;
                display: inline;
            }
        </style>
    </head>

    <body>
        <div id='controls'>
            <div id='widthRangeDiv'>
                Width:  <input id='widthRange' class='range' type='range'
                                minimum='5' maximum='100'/>
            </div>

            Height: <input id='heightRange' class='range' type='range'
                            minimum='5' maximum='100'/>
        </div>

        <div id='roundedRectangleDiv'></div>

        <script src='roundedRectangle.js'></script>
        <script src='example.js'></script>
    </body>
</html>
```

The application's JavaScript, which is listed in Example 10.2, creates a rounded rectangle and appends the rectangle's DIV to the roundedRectangleDiv with the rounded rectangle's appendTo() method. The application also adds a change event handler to the sliders that resizes and redraws the rectangle when the user changes a slider's value.

The application creates the rounded rectangle with all four arguments to the COREHTML5.RoundedRectangle constructor, which is listed in Example 10.3. The first two arguments represent the stroke and fill styles that the control uses when it draws the rounded rectangle. The last two arguments represent the size of the rounded rectangle relative to the size of the DOM element in which it resides. The values can range between 0 and 1.0 or between 0 and 100 and represent the percent of the rectangle's enclosing DOM element, in the horizontal and vertical directions, taken up by the rounded rectangle. The application in Figure 10.1 sets those arguments to match the initial values for the corresponding sliders. The application's original configuration is shown in Figure 10.2.

---

**Example 10.2** The rounded rectangle application: JavaScript

---

```javascript
var widthRange = document.getElementById('widthRange'),
    heightRange = document.getElementById('heightRange'),
    roundedRectangle = new COREHTML5.RoundedRectangle(
                            'rgba(0,0,0,0.2)', 'darkgoldenrod',
                            widthRange.value, heightRange.value);

// Event handlers.....................................................

function resize() {
    roundedRectangle.horizontalSizePercent = widthRange.value/100;
    roundedRectangle.verticalSizePercent   = heightRange.value/100;

    roundedRectangle.resize(roundedRectangle.domElement.offsetWidth,
                            roundedRectangle.domElement.offsetHeight);

    roundedRectangle.erase();
    roundedRectangle.draw();
}

// Initialization....................................................

widthRange.onchange  = resize;
heightRange.onchange = resize;

roundedRectangle.appendTo(
    document.getElementById('roundedRectangleDiv'));

roundedRectangle.draw();
```

---

**Example 10.3** The rounded rectangle object

---

```javascript
var COREHTML5 = COREHTML5 || {};

// Constructor.......................................................

COREHTML5.RoundedRectangle = function(strokeStyle, fillStyle,
                                      horizontalSizePercent,
                                      verticalSizePercent) {
    this.strokeStyle = strokeStyle ? strokeStyle : 'gray';
    this.fillStyle   = fillStyle   ? fillStyle   : 'skyblue';

    horizontalSizePercent = horizontalSizePercent || 100;
    verticalSizePercent   = verticalSizePercent   || 100;

    this.SHADOW_COLOR = 'rgba(100,100,100,0.8)';
    this.SHADOW_OFFSET_X = 3;
    this.SHADOW_OFFSET_Y = 3;
    this.SHADOW_BLUR = 3;
```

```
   this.setSizePercents(horizontalSizePercent, verticalSizePercent);
   this.createCanvas();
   this.createDOMElement();

   return this;
}

// Prototype.......................................................

COREHTML5.RoundedRectangle.prototype = {

   // General functions ..........................................

   createCanvas: function () {
      var canvas = document.createElement('canvas');
      this.context = canvas.getContext('2d');
      return canvas;
   },

   createDOMElement: function () {
      this.domElement = document.createElement('div');
      this.domElement.appendChild(this.context.canvas);
   },

   appendTo: function (element) {
      element.appendChild(this.domElement);
      this.domElement.style.width = element.offsetWidth + 'px';
      this.domElement.style.height = element.offsetHeight + 'px';
      this.resize(element.offsetWidth, element.offsetHeight);
   },

   resize: function (width, height) {
      this.HORIZONTAL_MARGIN = (width - width *
                               this.horizontalSizePercent)/2;
      this.VERTICAL_MARGIN   = (height - height *
                               this.verticalSizePercent)/2;

      this.cornerRadius = (this.context.canvas.height/2 -
                          2*this.VERTICAL_MARGIN)/2;

      this.top    = this.VERTICAL_MARGIN;
      this.left   = this.HORIZONTAL_MARGIN;
      this.right  = this.left + width  - 2*this.HORIZONTAL_MARGIN;
      this.bottom = this.top  + height - 2*this.VERTICAL_MARGIN;

      this.context.canvas.width = width;
      this.context.canvas.height = height;
   },
```

*(Continues)*

**Example 10.3** *(Continued)*

```
setSizePercents: function (h, v) {
    // horizontalSizePercent and verticalSizePercent
    // represent the size of the rounded rectangle in terms
    // of horizontal and vertical percents of the rectangle's
    // enclosing DOM element.

    this.horizontalSizePercent = h > 1 ? h/100 : h;
    this.verticalSizePercent   = v > 1 ? v/100 : v;
},

// Drawing functions..........................................

fill: function () {
    var radius = (this.bottom - this.top) / 2;

    this.context.save();
    this.context.shadowColor   = this.SHADOW_COLOR;
    this.context.shadowOffsetX = this.SHADOW_OFFSET_X;
    this.context.shadowOffsetY = this.SHADOW_OFFSET_Y;
    this.context.shadowBlur = 6;

    this.context.beginPath();

    this.context.moveTo(this.left + radius, this.top);

    this.context.arcTo(this.right, this.top,
                       this.right, this.bottom, radius);

    this.context.arcTo(this.right, this.bottom,
                       this.left, this.bottom, radius);

    this.context.arcTo(this.left, this.bottom,
                       this.left, this.top, radius);

    this.context.arcTo(this.left, this.top,
                       this.right, this.top, radius);

    this.context.closePath();

    this.context.fillStyle = this.fillStyle;
    this.context.fill();
    this.context.shadowColor = undefined;
},
```

```
overlayGradient: function () {
   var gradient =
      this.context.createLinearGradient(this.left, this.top,
                                        this.left, this.bottom);

   gradient.addColorStop(0,     'rgba(255,255,255,0.4)');
   gradient.addColorStop(0.2,   'rgba(255,255,255,0.6)');
   gradient.addColorStop(0.25,  'rgba(255,255,255,0.7)');
   gradient.addColorStop(0.3,   'rgba(255,255,255,0.9)');
   gradient.addColorStop(0.40,  'rgba(255,255,255,0.7)');
   gradient.addColorStop(0.45,  'rgba(255,255,255,0.6)');
   gradient.addColorStop(0.60,  'rgba(255,255,255,0.4)');
   gradient.addColorStop(1,     'rgba(255,255,255,0.1)');

   this.context.fillStyle = gradient;
   this.context.fill();

   this.context.lineWidth = 0.4;
   this.context.strokeStyle = this.strokeStyle;
   this.context.stroke();

   this.context.restore();
},

draw: function (context) {
   var originalContext;

   if (context) {
      originalContext = this.context;
      this.context = context;
   }

   this.fill();
   this.overlayGradient();

   if (context) {
      this.context = originalContext;
   }
},

erase: function() {
   // Erase the entire canvas

   this.context.clearRect(0, 0, this.context.canvas.width,
                          this.context.canvas.height);
   }
};
```

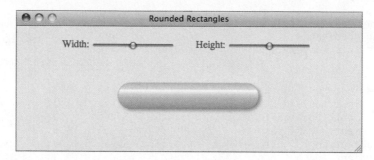

Figure 10.2  The application's original configuration

Notice the first line of Example 10.3: `var COREHTML5 = COREHTML5 || {};`. That line of code creates a global `COREHTML5` object if the object does not already exist. Subsequently, Example 10.3 adds a `RoundedRectangle` function and a corresponding prototype object to the global `COREHTML5` object.

The `COREHTML5.RoundedRectangle` methods are divided into two sections: The first section contains general functions, such as `appendTo()` and `resize()`, that manipulate the control's canvas and `DIV`. The second section draws the rounded rectangle. As you read through the listing, pay particular attention to the `appendTo()` and `draw()` methods.

The `appendTo()` method appends the rounded rectangle's DOM element to the specified HTML element; for example, the application shown in Figure 10.1 appends a rounded rectangle to a `DIV` named `roundedRectangleDiv`, as illustrated in Figure 10.3.

roundedRectangleDiv     roundedRectangle.domElement     roundedRectangle.context.canvas

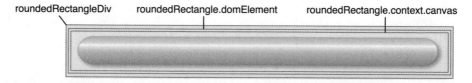

Figure 10.3  Appending a rounded rectangle to a `DIV`. Note: All three elements are the same size

Subsequently, the `appendTo()` method sets the size of the rounded rectangle's DOM element to match the size of the parent DOM element and calls `resize()`, which resizes the control's canvas to also match the size of the DOM element. For example, if you append a rounded rectangle to a `DIV` element that is 500 pixels wide and 400 pixels high then the rounded rectangle's `appendTo()` method resizes the rectangle's DOM element and its canvas to 500 pixels by 400 pixels—provided that the rectangle takes up all of the surrounding element's space. Recall that the amount of space the rectangle takes up can be specified with the last two arguments to the COREHTML5.RoundedRectangle constructor.

When you draw a rounded rectangle you can pass the draw() method a Canvas context so that the rounded rectangle will draw into that context. That feature is useful for drawing controls into offscreen canvases; in fact, Section 10.2, "Progress Bars," on p. 625 shows such a strategy implemented by the progress bar control.

If you do not pass a Canvas context to a rounded rectangle's draw() method, as is the case for the application shown in Figure 10.1 on p. 618, then the rounded rectangle draws into its own canvas.

Rounded rectangles are drawn in two steps. First, the draw() method fills the rounded rectangle with a solid shape, as shown in the top screenshot in Figure 10.4. Next, the draw() method overlays a white gradient on top of the solid fill, resulting in the illusion of curvature and overhead lighting, as illustrated in the bottom screenshot.

Figure 10.4 Translucent overlays

**TIP: Adapt the rounded rectangle control**

The rounded rectangle control discussed in this section serves two useful purposes. First, it serves to encapsulate functionality that is used by other controls; for example, both the progress bar and slider controls discussed in this chapter use rounded rectangles.

Second, you can use the rounded rectangle control to implement your own unrelated controls by retaining much of the general functionality in COREHTML5.RoundedRectangle, such as the appendTo() and resize() methods, and reimplementing the drawing code. In fact, that's exactly how the remaining controls in this chapter were implemented.

## 10.2 Progress Bars

The preceding section illustrated implementing Canvas-based controls with a simple rounded rectangle. In this section we explore *composite* controls—meaning

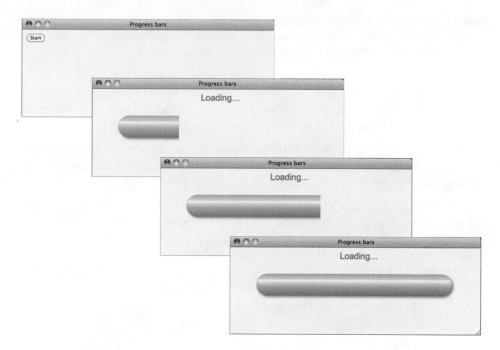

Figure 10.5  A progress bar progressing

controls that contain other controls—with a progress bar that uses a rounded rectangle. Figure 10.5 shows a progress bar in action.

The HTML for the application shown in Figure 10.5 is listed in Example 10.4.

The HTML creates the Start button and the loading span. The span is initially invisible, as shown in the top screenshot in Figure 10.5. The HTML also adds a DIV named progressbarDiv to the page.

The HTML loads the JavaScript for the COREHTML5.Progressbar and COREHTML5.RoundedRectangle controls. Because progress bars contain a rounded rectangle, the JavaScript file for the latter is necessary for the former. The HTML also loads the JavaScript for an animation polyfill method named requestNextAnimationFrame(), which is discussed in Section 5.1.3, "A Portable Animation Loop," on p. 348. That polyfill method drives the progress bar animation.

Example 10.5 lists the application's JavaScript.

The application creates a progress bar with a nearly translucent black stroke style and a teal fill style. The progress bar takes up 90 percent of its enclosing DOM

---

**Example 10.4** The progress bar application: HTML

```html
<!DOCTYPE html>
  <head>
    <title>Progress bars</title>

    <style>
       body {
          background: linen;
       }

       #loadingSpan {
          font: 20px Arial;
          font-align: center;
          position: absolute;
          left: 250px;
          color: teal;
          text-shadow: 1px 1px rgba(0,0,0,0.1);
       }

       #progressbarDiv {
          position: absolute;
          left: 35px;
          top: 50px;
          width: 500px;
          height: 70px;
       }
    </style>
  </head>

  <body>
    <input type='button' id='startButton' value='Start'/>
    <span id='loadingSpan' style='display: none'>Loading...</span>

    <div id='progressbarDiv'></div>

    <script src='roundedRectangle.js'></script>
    <script src='progressbar.js'></script>
    <script src='requestNextAnimationFrame.js'></script>
    <script src='example.js'></script>
  </body>
</html>
```

---

element's width and 70 percent of the element's height. The application then appends the progress bar to the progressbarDiv.

The application also implements an onclick event handler that animates the progress bar when a user clicks the Start button.

The COREHTML5.Progressbar object is listed in Example 10.6.

---

**Example 10.5** The progress bar application: JavaScript

---

```javascript
var startButton = document.getElementById('startButton'),
    loadingSpan = document.getElementById('loadingSpan'),
    progressbar = new COREHTML5.Progressbar('rgba(0,0,0,0.2)',
                                            'teal', 90, 70),

    percentComplete = 0;

// Event handlers................................................

startButton.onclick = function (e) {
    loadingSpan.style.display = 'inline';
    startButton.style.display = 'none';

    percentComplete += 1.0;

    if (percentComplete > 100) {
        percentComplete = 0;
        loadingSpan.style.display = 'none';
        startButton.style.display = 'inline';
    }
    else {
        progressbar.erase();
        progressbar.draw(percentComplete);
        requestNextAnimationFrame(startButton.onclick);
    }
};

// Initialization................................................

progressbar.appendTo(document.getElementById('progressbarDiv'));
```

---

Progress bars create four things:

- An instance of COREHTML5.RoundedRectangle
- An onscreen canvas
- An offscreen canvas
- A DOM element (a DIV)

The progress bar's appendTo() method draws the rounded rectangle into the offscreen canvas. Subsequently, the progress bar's draw() method copies the appropriate part of that offscreen canvas—based on the progress bar's percentComplete property—to the onscreen canvas.

So far in this chapter, you've seen how to implement simple controls and how to implement controls that use other controls. Next, we will look at a more complicated control that handles events.

Example 10.6 Progress bar objects

```
var COREHTML5 = COREHTML5 || {};

// Constructor...............................................

COREHTML5.Progressbar = function(strokeStyle, fillStyle,
                                 horizontalSizePercent,
                                 verticalSizePercent) {
   this.trough = new COREHTML5.RoundedRectangle(strokeStyle,
                                                fillStyle,
                                                horizontalSizePercent,
                                                verticalSizePercent);
   this.SHADOW_COLOR = 'rgba(255,255,255,0.5)';
   this.SHADOW_BLUR = 3;
   this.SHADOW_OFFSET_X = 2;
   this.SHADOW_OFFSET_Y = 2;

   this.percentComplete = 0;
   this.createCanvases();
   this.createDOMElement();

   return this;
}

// Prototype.................................................

   COREHTML5.Progressbar.prototype = {
      createDOMElement: function () {
         this.domElement = document.createElement('div');
         this.domElement.appendChild(this.context.canvas);
      },

      createCanvases: function () {
         this.context = document.createElement('canvas').
                   getContext('2d');

         this.offscreen = document.createElement('canvas').
                   getContext('2d');
      },

      appendTo: function (element) {
         element.appendChild(this.domElement);

         this.domElement.style.width  = element.offsetWidth  + 'px';
         this.domElement.style.height = element.offsetHeight + 'px';

         this.resize(); // Erases everything in the canvases
```

*(Continues)*

Example 10.6 *(Continued)*

```
      this.trough.resize(element.offsetWidth, element.offsetHeight);
      this.trough.draw(this.offscreen);
   },

   setCanvasSize: function () {
      var domElementParent = this.domElement.parentNode;

      this.context.canvas.width = domElementParent.offsetWidth;
      this.context.canvas.height = domElementParent.offsetHeight;
   },

   resize: function () {
      var domElementParent = this.domElement.parentNode,
      w = domElementParent.offsetWidth,
      h = domElementParent.offsetHeight;

      this.setCanvasSize();

      this.context.canvas.width = w;
      this.context.canvas.height = h;

      this.offscreen.canvas.width = w;
      this.offscreen.canvas.height = h;
   },

   draw: function (percentComplete) {
      if (percentComplete > 0) {

         // Copy the appropriate region of the foreground canvas
         // to the same region of the onscreen canvas

         this.context.drawImage(
            this.offscreen.canvas, 0, 0,
            this.offscreen.canvas.width*(percentComplete/100),
            this.offscreen.canvas.height,
            0, 0,
            this.offscreen.canvas.width*(percentComplete/100),
            this.offscreen.canvas.height);
      }
   },

   erase: function() {
      this.context.clearRect(0, 0,
                             this.context.canvas.width,
                             this.context.canvas.height);
   },
};
```

## 10.3 Sliders

Many controls fire events to registered listeners, so it's important that you know how to implement event handling in your Canvas-based controls. In this section we incorporate event handling into a slider, which is shown in Figure 10.6.

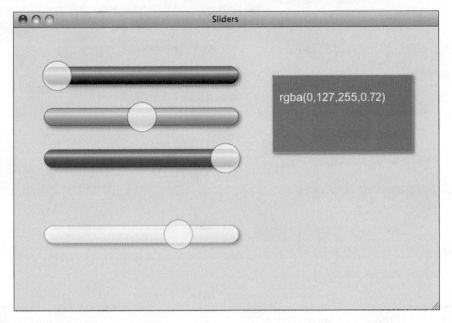

Figure 10.6 Using sliders

The application shown in Figure 10.6 is a simple color picker with three sliders for the color's red, green, and blue components, and a fourth slider for the color's opacity. As a user changes a slider's value by dragging the knob, the application not only modifies the color of the color patch on the right but also adjusts the color of the slider's rounded rectangle. Figure 10.7 shows how the application adjusts slider colors for various values.

The HTML for the application shown in Figure 10.6 is listed in Example 10.7.

The HTML creates a DIV for each slider and a canvas for the color patch. The application's JavaScript creates four sliders and appends each of them to the appropriate DIV. Figure 10.8 shows the element structure for the blue slider.

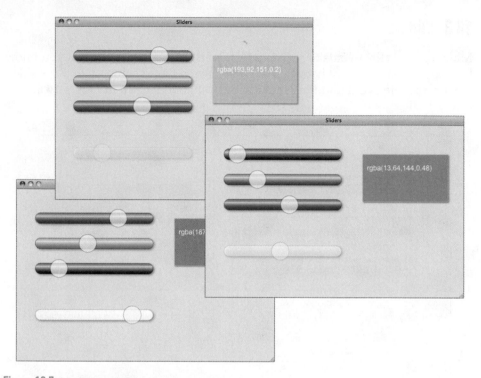

Figure 10.7 Various colors

---

Example 10.7 The sliders application: HTML

---

```html
<!DOCTYPE html>
  <head>
    <title>Sliders</title>

    <style>
      body {
        background: #dddddd;
      }

      #colorPatchCanvas {
        position: absolute;
        top: 75px;
        left: 410px;
        -webkit-box-shadow: rgba(0,0,0,0.5) 2px 2px 4px;
        -moz-box-shadow: rgba(0,0,0,0.5) 2px 2px 4px;
        box-shadow: rgba(0,0,0,0.5) 2px 2px 4px;
        border: thin solid rgba(0,0,0,0.2);
      }
```

```
      .slider {
          width: 324px;
          height: 50px;
      }

      #redSliderDiv {
          position: absolute;
          left: 40px;
          top: 50px;
      }

      #greenSliderDiv {
          position: absolute;
          left: 40px;
          top: 115px;
      }

      #blueSliderDiv {
          position: absolute;
          left: 40px;
          top: 180px;
      }

      #alphaSliderDiv {
          position: absolute;
          left: 40px;
          top: 300px;
      }
    </style>
  </head>

  <body>
    <div id='redSliderDiv'    class='slider'></div>
    <div id='greenSliderDiv'  class='slider'></div>
    <div id='blueSliderDiv'   class='slider'></div>
    <div id='alphaSliderDiv'  class='slider'></div>

    <canvas id='colorPatchCanvas' width='220' height='120'>
      Canvas not supported
    </canvas>

    <script src='roundedRectangle.js'></script>
    <script src='slider.js'></script>
    <script src='example.js'></script>
  </body>
</html>
```

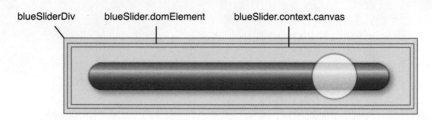

**Figure 10.8** Sliders: An HTML5 Canvas in a DIV (blueSlider.domElement) in a DIV (blueSliderDiv)

The application's JavaScript is listed in Example 10.8.

**Example 10.8** The sliders application: JavaScript

```
var colorPatchContext = document.getElementById('colorPatchCanvas').
                          getContext('2d'),

    redSlider   = new COREHTML5.Slider('rgb(0,0,0)',
                                       'rgba(255,0,0,0.8)', 0),

    blueSlider  = new COREHTML5.Slider('rgb(0,0,0)',
                                       'rgba(0,0,255,0.8)', 1.0),

    greenSlider = new COREHTML5.Slider('rgb(0,0,0)',
                                       'rgba(0,255,0,0.8)', 0.25),

    alphaSlider = new COREHTML5.Slider('rgb(0,0,0)',
                                       'rgba(255,255,255,0.8)', 0.5);

redSlider.appendTo('redSliderDiv');
blueSlider.appendTo('blueSliderDiv');
greenSlider.appendTo('greenSliderDiv');
alphaSlider.appendTo('alphaSliderDiv');

// Functions.....................................................

function updateColor() {
   var alpha = new Number((alphaSlider.knobPercent).toFixed(2));
   var color = 'rgba('
               + parseInt(redSlider.knobPercent * 255) + ','
               + parseInt(greenSlider.knobPercent * 255) + ','
               + parseInt(blueSlider.knobPercent * 255) + ','
               + alpha + ')';

   colorPatchContext.fillStyle = color;
```

```
    colorPatchContext.clearRect(0, 0, colorPatchContext.canvas.width,
                                colorPatchContext.canvas.height);

    colorPatchContext.fillRect(0, 0, colorPatchContext.canvas.width,
                               colorPatchContext.canvas.height);

    colorPatchContext.font = '18px Arial';
    colorPatchContext.fillStyle = 'white';
    colorPatchContext.fillText(color, 10, 40);

    alpha = (alpha + 0.2 > 1.0) ? 1.0 : alpha + 0.2;
    alphaSlider.opacity = alpha;
}

// Event handlers...................................................

redSlider.addChangeListener( function() {
    updateColor();
    redSlider.fillStyle = 'rgb(' +
        (redSlider.knobPercent * 255).toFixed(0) + ', 0, 0)';
});

greenSlider.addChangeListener( function() {
    updateColor();
    greenSlider.fillStyle = 'rgb(0, ' +
        (greenSlider.knobPercent * 255).toFixed(0) + ', 0)';
});

blueSlider.addChangeListener( function () {
    updateColor();
    blueSlider.fillStyle = 'rgb(0, 0, ' +
        (blueSlider.knobPercent * 255).toFixed(0) + ')';
});

alphaSlider.addChangeListener( function() {
    updateColor();
    alphaSlider.fillStyle = 'rgba(255, 255, 255, ' +
        (alphaSlider.knobPercent * 255).toFixed(0) + ')';

    alphaSlider.opacity = alphaSlider.knobPercent;
});

// Initialization...................................................

redSlider.fillStyle   = 'rgb(' +
    (redSlider.knobPercent * 255).toFixed(0) + ', 0, 0)';
```

*(Continues)*

---

**Example 10.8** *(Continued)*

---

```
greenSlider.fillStyle = 'rgb(0, ' +
   (greenSlider.knobPercent * 255).toFixed(0) + ', 0)';

blueSlider.fillStyle  = 'rgb(0, 0, ' +
   (blueSlider.knobPercent * 255).toFixed(0)  + ')';

alphaSlider.fillStyle = 'rgba(255, 255, 255, ' +
   (alphaSlider.knobPercent * 255).toFixed(0) + ')';

alphaSlider.opacity = alphaSlider.knobPercent;

alphaSlider.draw();
redSlider.draw();
greenSlider.draw();
blueSlider.draw();
```

---

The application creates four sliders and adds a change event listener to each. Whenever a slider's value changes, the slider invokes all change listeners that have registered with the addChangeListener() method. All four of the application's event handlers update the color of the color patch and their slider.

The COREHTML5.Slider object is listed in Example 10.9. As you read through the code, focus on the event handlers and the support for change events; that support distinguishes sliders from progress bars and rounded rectangles.

---

**Example 10.9** Slider objects

---

```
var COREHTML5 = COREHTML5 || {};

// Constructor.....................................................

COREHTML5.Slider = function(strokeStyle, fillStyle,
                            knobPercent, hpercent, vpercent) {
   this.trough = new COREHTML5.RoundedRectangle(strokeStyle, fillStyle,
                        hpercent || 95,  // Horizontal size percent
                        vpercent || 55); // Vertical size percent

   this.knobPercent = knobPercent || 0;
   this.strokeStyle = strokeStyle ? strokeStyle : 'gray';
   this.fillStyle = fillStyle ? fillStyle : 'skyblue';

   this.SHADOW_COLOR = 'rgba(100,100,100,0.8)';
   this.SHADOW_OFFSET_X = 3;
   this.SHADOW_OFFSET_Y = 3;
```

```
      this.HORIZONTAL_MARGIN = 2 * this.SHADOW_OFFSET_X;
      this.VERTICAL_MARGIN   = 2 * this.SHADOW_OFFSET_Y;

      this.KNOB_SHADOW_COLOR    = 'yellow';
      this.KNOB_SHADOW_OFFSET_X = 1;
      this.KNOB_SHADOW_OFFSET_Y = 1;
      this.KNOB_SHADOW_BLUR     = 0;

      this.KNOB_FILL_STYLE   = 'rgba(255,255,255,0.45)';
      this.KNOB_STROKE_STYLE = 'rgba(0,0,150,0.45)';

      this.context = document.createElement('canvas').getContext('2d');
      this.changeEventListeners = [];

      this.createDOMElement();
      this.addMouseHandlers();

      return this;
}

// Prototype.......................................................

COREHTML5.Slider.prototype = {

   // General functions to override..................................

   createDOMElement: function () {
      this.domElement = document.createElement('div');
      this.domElement.appendChild(this.context.canvas);
   },

   appendTo: function (elementName) {
      document.getElementById(elementName).
         appendChild(this.domElement);

      this.setCanvasSize();
      this.resize();
   },

   setCanvasSize: function () {
      var domElementParent = this.domElement.parentNode;

      this.context.canvas.width = domElementParent.offsetWidth;
      this.context.canvas.height = domElementParent.offsetHeight;
   },
```

*(Continues)*

Example 10.9 *(Continued)*

```
resize: function() {
   this.cornerRadius = (this.context.canvas.height/2 -
                           2*this.VERTICAL_MARGIN)/2;

   this.top    = this.HORIZONTAL_MARGIN;
   this.left   = this.VERTICAL_MARGIN;

   this.right  = this.left + this.context.canvas.width -
                   2*this.HORIZONTAL_MARGIN;

   this.bottom = this.top + this.context.canvas.height -
                   2*this.VERTICAL_MARGIN;

   this.trough.resize(this.context.canvas.width,
                   this.context.canvas.height);

   this.knobRadius = this.context.canvas.height/2 -
                   this.context.lineWidth*2;
},

// Event handlers..............................................

addMouseHandlers: function() {
   var slider = this; // Let DIV's event handlers access this object

   this.domElement.onmouseover = function(e) {
      slider.context.canvas.style.cursor = 'crosshair';
   };

   this.domElement.onmousedown = function(e) {
      var mouse = slider.windowToCanvas(e.clientX, e.clientY);

      e.preventDefault();

      if (slider.mouseInTrough(mouse) ||
          slider.mouseInKnob(mouse)) {

         slider.knobPercent = slider.knobPositionToPercent(mouse.x);
         slider.fireChangeEvent(e);
         slider.erase();
         slider.draw();
         slider.dragging = true;

      }
   };
```

```
    window.addEventListener('mousemove', function(e) {
        var mouse = null,
            percent = null;

        e.preventDefault();

        if (slider.dragging) {
            mouse = slider.windowToCanvas(e.clientX, e.clientY);
            percent = slider.knobPositionToPercent(mouse.x);

            if (percent >= 0 && percent <= 1.0) {
                slider.fireChangeEvent(e);
                slider.erase();
                slider.draw(percent);
            }
        }
    }, false);

    window.addEventListener('mouseup', function(e) {
        var mouse = null;

        e.preventDefault();

        if (slider.dragging) {
            slider.fireChangeEvent(e);
            slider.dragging = false;
        }
    }, false);
},

// Change events................................................

fireChangeEvent: function(e) {
    for (var i=0; i < this.changeEventListeners.length; ++i) {
        this.changeEventListeners[i](e);
    }
},

addChangeListener: function (listenerFunction) {
    this.changeEventListeners.push(listenerFunction);
},
```

*(Continues)*

---

**Example 10.9**　*(Continued)*

---

```
// Utility functions..........................................

mouseInKnob: function(mouse) {
   var position = this.knobPercentToPosition(this.knobPercent);
   this.context.beginPath();
   this.context.arc(position, this.context.canvas.height/2,
                    this.knobRadius, 0, Math.PI*2);

   return this.context.isPointInPath(mouse.x, mouse.y);
},

mouseInTrough: function(mouse) {
   this.context.beginPath();
   this.context.rect(this.left, 0,
      this.right - this.left, this.bottom);

   return this.context.isPointInPath(mouse.x, mouse.y);
},

windowToCanvas: function(x, y) {
   var bbox = this.context.canvas.getBoundingClientRect();

   return {
      x: x - bbox.left * (this.context.canvas.width  / bbox.width),
      y: y - bbox.top  * (this.context.canvas.height / bbox.height)
   };
},

knobPositionToPercent: function(position) {
   var troughWidth = this.right - this.left - 2*this.knobRadius;
   return (position - this.left - this.knobRadius)/ troughWidth;
},

knobPercentToPosition: function(percent) {
   if (percent > 1) percent = 1;
   if (percent < 0) percent = 0;
   var troughWidth = this.right - this.left - 2*this.knobRadius;
   return percent * troughWidth + this.left + this.knobRadius;
},

// Drawing functions..........................................
```

```
fillKnob: function (position) {
   this.context.save();

   this.context.shadowColor   = this.KNOB_SHADOW_COLOR;
   this.context.shadowOffsetX = this.KNOB_SHADOW_OFFSET_X;
   this.context.shadowOffsetY = this.KNOB_SHADOW_OFFSET_Y;
   this.context.shadowBlur    = this.KNOB_SHADOW_BLUR;

   this.context.beginPath();

   this.context.arc(position,
                 this.top + ((this.bottom - this.top) / 2),
                 this.knobRadius, 0, Math.PI*2, false);

   this.context.clip();

   this.context.fillStyle = this.KNOB_FILL_STYLE;
   this.context.fill();
   this.context.restore();
},

strokeKnob: function () {
   this.context.save();
   this.context.lineWidth = 1;
   this.context.strokeStyle = this.KNOB_STROKE_STYLE;
   this.context.stroke();
   this.context.restore();
},

drawKnob: function (percent) {
   if (percent < 0) percent = 0;
   if (percent > 1) percent = 1;

   this.knobPercent = percent;
   this.fillKnob(this.knobPercentToPosition(percent));
   this.strokeKnob();
},

drawTrough: function () {
   this.context.save();
   this.trough.fillStyle = this.fillStyle;
   this.trough.strokeStyle = this.strokeStyle;
   this.trough.draw(this.context);
   this.context.restore();
},
```

*(Continues)*

---

Example 10.9  *(Continued)*

---

```
draw: function (percent) {
   this.context.globalAlpha = this.opacity;

   if (percent === undefined) {
      percent = this.knobPercent;
   }

   this.drawTrough();
   this.drawKnob(percent);
},

erase: function() {
   this.context.clearRect(
      this.left - this.knobRadius, 0 - this.knobRadius,
      this.context.canvas.width  + 4*this.knobRadius,
      this.context.canvas.height + 3*this.knobRadius);
   }
};
```

---

Like progress bars, sliders create and use an instance of COREHTML5.
RoundedRectangle.

When a slider detects a mouse down event, it converts the window coordinates
stored in the event object to canvas coordinates and checks whether the cursor is
in the slider trough or knob; if it is, the event handler adjusts the knob's position
to coincide with the X coordinate of the mouse event. The event handler then
fires a change event, redraws the slider, and sets a flag to indicate that the user
has begun to drag the slider's knob.

As the user subsequently drags the mouse, the slider's mouse move event handler
continuously fires change events and redraws the slider. When the slider detects
a mouse up event, it fires a final change event and sets the dragging property to
false.

The COREHTML5.Slider constructor creates an empty array named
changeEventListeners. Sliders manipulate that array in two methods:
addChangeListener() and fireChangeEvent(), which add a change listener
function to a slider and invoke all the slider's change listeners, respectively.

One other interesting thing about sliders is the lighting effect they implement, as
illustrated in Figure 10.9: The slider's knob looks like a light that illuminates the
trough below. The slider creates the lighting effect by filling the knob with
semitransparent white and applying a yellow shadow. See the fillKnob() method
in Example 10.9.

Figure 10.9  Shadows as light

## 10.4  An Image Panner

By now you have a good understanding of how to implement Canvas-based controls. We conclude this chapter with an example of an image panner—shown in Figure 10.10—that uses what you have learned in this chapter, along with

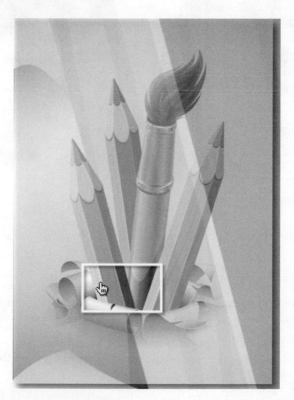

Figure 10.10  An image panner control

much of what you have learned elsewhere in this book, such as drawing, shadows, and image manipulation.

The image panner control displays a scaled-down version of a much larger image and furnishes a draggable viewport, as illustrated in Figure 10.10. As a user drags the viewport, the image panner displays the portion of the image within the viewport in an associated canvas, as illustrated by the application in Figure 10.11.

Figure 10.11  Panning an image

When you create an image panner, you specify the associated canvas and image, like this:

```
var pan = new COREHTML5.Pan(context.canvas, image);
```

The user drags the viewport to view different portions of the image, as shown in Figure 10.12.

The sliders at the top of the application let you adjust the size and opacity of the image panner, as shown in Figure 10.13, but they are not part of the image panner

Figure 10.12 Dragging the image panner's viewport

control. The image panner, in fact, is unaware of the sliders; it is the application that links them.

Example 10.10 lists the HTML for the application shown in Figure 10.11.

The HTML in Example 10.10 creates DIVs for the sliders at the top of the application and a canvas element where the application displays the image. The HTML subsequently includes the JavaScript for rounded rectangles, sliders, and the image panner control. Finally, the HTML includes the JavaScript for the application, which is listed in Example 10.11.

The HTML also creates two span elements for the slider displays. The application's JavaScript sets the values for those elements.

Finally, notice that the CSS in the HTML file declares a class named pan; however, if you study the HTML, you'll see that none of the elements declare a class with that name. It's the application's JavaScript that assigns the pan class to the image panner control.

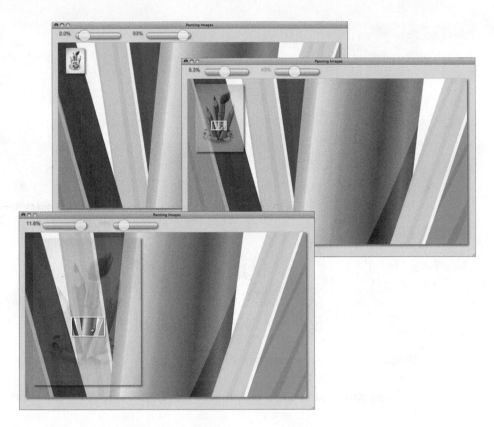

Figure 10.13 Controlling the size and opacity of the inset canvas

Example 10.10 Panning images: HTML

```
<!DOCTYPE html>
<html>
    <head>
        <title>Panning Images</title>

        <style>
            body {
                background: rgba(100,145,250,0.3);
            }
```

```
#canvas {
    position: absolute;
    left: 0px;
    top: 50px;
    margin-left: 20px;
    margin-right: 0;
    margin-bottom: 20px;
    padding: 0;
    -webkit-box-shadow: rgba(60,60,70,0.7) 5px 5px 7px;
    -moz-box-shadow: rgba(60,60,70,0.7) 5px 5px 7px;
    box-shadow: rgba(60,60,70,0.7) 5px 5px 7px;
    border: 1px solid rgba(100,140,130,0.5);
    cursor: crosshair;
}

.pan {
    position: absolute;
    left: 50px;
    top: 70px;
    -webkit-box-shadow: rgba(60,60,70,0.7) 5px 5px 7px;
    -moz-box-shadow: rgba(60,60,70,0.7) 5px 5px 7px;
    box-shadow: rgba(60,60,70,0.7) 5px 5px 7px;
    cursor: pointer;
}

#sizeSliderDiv {
    position: absolute;
    left: 20px;
    top: -5px;
    margin-left: 10px;
    display: inline;
    width: 175px;
    height: 45px;
}

#alphaSliderDiv {
    position: absolute;
    left: 270px;
    top: -5px;
    margin-left: 10px;
    display: inline;
    width: 175px;
    height: 45px;
}
```

*(Continues)*

Example 10.10 *(Continued)*

```
        #controls {
            position: absolute;
            left: 10px;
            margin-left: 35px;
            margin-bottom: 25px;
        }

        #alphaSpan {
            position: absolute;
            left: 240px;
            vertical-align: center;
            color: rgb(80,100,190);
            font: 18px Arial;
            text-shadow: 2px 2px 4px rgba(100,140,250,0.8);
        }

        #sizeSpan {
            position: absolute;
            left: -20px;
            vertical-align: center;
            color: rgb(80,100,190);
            font: 18px Arial;
            text-shadow: 2px 2px 4px rgba(100,140,250,0.8);
        }
    </style>
</head>

<body id='body'>

    <div id='controls'>
        <span id='sizeSpan'>0</span>
        <div id='alphaSliderDiv'></div>

        <span id='alphaSpan'>0</span>
        <div id='sizeSliderDiv'></div>
    </div>

    <canvas id='canvas' width='1000' height='600'>
        Canvas not supported
    </canvas>

    <script src='roundedRectangle.js'></script>
    <script src='slider.js'></script>
    <script src='pan.js'></script>
    <script src='example.js'></script>
</body>
</html>
```

Example 10.11 Panning Images: JavaScript

```javascript
var context = document.getElementById('canvas').getContext('2d'),
    image = new Image(),

    alphaSpan = document.getElementById('alphaSpan'),
    sizeSpan  = document.getElementById('sizeSpan'),

    sizeSlider  = new COREHTML5.Slider('blue', 'cornflowerblue',
                                 0.85, // Knob percent
                                 90,   // Take up % of width
                                 50),  // Take up % of height

    alphaSlider = new COREHTML5.Slider('blue', 'cornflowerblue',
                                 0.50, // Knob percent
                                 90,   // Take up % of width
                                 50),  // Take up % of height

    pan = new COREHTML5.Pan(context.canvas, image),
    e = pan.domElement,

    ALPHA_MAX = 1.0,
    SIZE_MAX = 12;

// Event handlers.....................................................

sizeSlider.addChangeListener(function (e) {
    var size = (parseFloat(sizeSlider.knobPercent) * 12);
    size = size < 2 ? 2 : size;
    sizeSpan.innerHTML = size.toFixed(1) + '%';

    pan.imageContext.setTransform(1,0,0,1,0,0); // Identity matrix
    pan.viewportPercent = size;

    pan.erase();
    pan.initialize();
    pan.draw();
});

alphaSlider.addChangeListener(function (e) {
    alphaSpan.innerHTML =
        parseFloat(alphaSlider.knobPercent * 100).toFixed(0) + '%';
    alphaSpan.style.opacity = parseFloat(alphaSlider.knobPercent);
    pan.panCanvasAlpha = alphaSlider.knobPercent;
    pan.erase();
    pan.draw();
});
```

*(Continues)*

---

**Example 10.11** *(Continued)*

---

```
// Initialization..............................................

image.src = 'pencilsAndBrush.jpg';
document.getElementById('body').appendChild(e);
e.className = 'pan';

alphaSlider.appendTo('alphaSliderDiv');
sizeSlider.appendTo('sizeSliderDiv');

pan.viewportPercent = sizeSlider.knobPercent * SIZE_MAX;
pan.panCanvasAlpha  = alphaSlider.knobPercent * ALPHA_MAX;

sizeSpan.innerHTML = pan.viewportPercent.toFixed(0) + '%';
alphaSpan.innerHTML = (pan.panCanvasAlpha * 100).toFixed(0)  + '%';

alphaSlider.draw();
sizeSlider.draw();
```

---

The application's JavaScript creates two sliders. Both sliders have a blue stroke style and a cornflowerblue fill style, and both of their troughs take up 90% of the width of the slider's surrounding element and 50% of its height. The application initially positions the size slider at 85% (of the difference between the slider's minimum and maximum values) and the alpha slider at 50%.

The application adds change listeners to each slider. The change listener for the size slider changes the size of the image panner corresponding to the slider's value. That listener also sets the inner HTML for the size span element to reflect the slider's value. Finally, the listener erases, initializes, and redraws the image.

The change listener for the alpha slider changes the opacity of the image panner's canvas and sets the alpha span's inner HTML to coincide with the slider's value.

The COREHTML5.Pan object is listed in Example 10.12.

---

**Example 10.12** The pan control

---

```
var COREHTML5 = COREHTML5 || { };

// Constructor.................................................

COREHTML5.Pan = function(imageCanvas, image,
                         viewportPercent, panCanvasAlpha) {
   var self = this;

   // Store arguments in member variables
```

```javascript
      this.imageCanvas = imageCanvas;
      this.image = image;
      this.viewportPercent = viewportPercent || 10;
      this.panCanvasAlpha = panCanvasAlpha || 0.5;

      // Get a reference to the image canvas's context
      // and create the pan canvas and the DOM element.
      // Put the pan canvas in the DOM element.

      this.imageContext = imageCanvas.getContext('2d');
      this.panCanvas = document.createElement('canvas');
      this.panContext = this.panCanvas.getContext('2d');

      this.domElement = document.createElement('div');
      this.domElement.appendChild(this.panCanvas);

      // If the image is not loaded, initialize when the image loads;
      // otherwise, initialize now.

      if (image.width == 0 || image.height == 0) { // Image not loaded
         image.onload = function(e) {
            self.initialize();
         };
      }
      else {
         this.initialize();
      }
      return this;
   };

// Prototype.....................................................

COREHTML5.Pan.prototype = {
   initialize: function () {
      var width = this.image.width  * (this.viewportPercent/100),
          height = this.image.height * (this.viewportPercent/100);

      this.addEventHandlers();
      this.setupViewport   (width, height);
      this.setupDOMElement(width, height);
      this.setupPanCanvas  (width, height);
      this.draw();
   },

   setupPanCanvas: function (w, h)  {
      this.panCanvas.width = w;
      this.panCanvas.height = h;
   },
```

*(Continues)*

---

Example 10.12   *(Continued)*

---

```
setupDOMElement: function (w, h)  {
   this.domElement.style.width = w + 'px';
   this.domElement.style.height = h + 'px';
   this.domElement.className = 'pan';
},

setupViewport: function (w, h) {
   this.viewportLocation = { x: 0, y: 0 };
   this.viewportSize = { width: 50, height: 50 };
   this.viewportLastLocation =  { x: 0, y: 0 };

   this.viewportSize.width  = this.imageCanvas.width *
                              this.viewportPercent/100;

   this.viewportSize.height = this.imageCanvas.height *
                              this.viewportPercent/100;
},

moveViewport: function(mouse, offset) {
   this.viewportLocation.x = mouse.x - offset.x;
   this.viewportLocation.y = mouse.y - offset.y;

   var delta = {
      x: this.viewportLastLocation.x - this.viewportLocation.x,
      y: this.viewportLastLocation.y - this.viewportLocation.y
   };

   this.imageContext.translate(
      delta.x * (this.image.width / this.panCanvas.width),
      delta.y * (this.image.height / this.panCanvas.height));

   this.viewportLastLocation.x = this.viewportLocation.x;
   this.viewportLastLocation.y = this.viewportLocation.y;
},

isPointInViewport: function (x, y) {
   this.panContext.beginPath();
   this.panContext.rect(this.viewportLocation.x,
                        this.viewportLocation.y,
                        this.viewportSize.width,
                        this.viewportSize.height);

   return this.panContext.isPointInPath(x, y);
},
```

```
addEventHandlers: function() {
   var pan = this;

   pan.domElement.onmousedown = function(e) {
      var mouse = pan.windowToCanvas(e.clientX, e.clientY),
          offset = null;

      e.preventDefault();

      if (pan.isPointInViewport(mouse.x, mouse.y)) {
         offset = { x: mouse.x - pan.viewportLocation.x,
                    y: mouse.y - pan.viewportLocation.y };

         pan.panCanvas.onmousemove = function(e) {
            pan.erase();

            pan.moveViewport(
               pan.windowToCanvas(e.clientX, e.clientY), offset);

            pan.draw();
         };

         pan.panCanvas.onmouseup = function(e) {
            pan.panCanvas.onmousemove = undefined;
            pan.panCanvas.onmouseup = undefined;
         };
      }
   };
},

erase: function() {
   this.panContext.clearRect(0, 0,
                             this.panContext.canvas.width,
                             this.panContext.canvas.height);
},

drawPanCanvas: function(alpha) {
   this.panContext.save();
   this.panContext.globalAlpha = alpha;
   this.panContext.drawImage(this.image,
                             0, 0,
                             this.image.width,
                             this.image.height,
                             0, 0,
                             this.panCanvas.width,
                             this.panCanvas.height);
   this.panContext.restore();
},
```

(Continues)

---

Example 10.12  *(Continued)*

---

```
drawImageCanvas: function() {
    this.imageContext.drawImage(this.image,
                                0, 0,
                                this.image.width,
                                this.image.height);
},

drawViewport: function () {
    this.panContext.shadowColor = 'rgba(0,0,0,0.4)';
    this.panContext.shadowOffsetX = 2;
    this.panContext.shadowOffsetY = 2;
    this.panContext.shadowBlur = 3;

    this.panContext.lineWidth = 3;
    this.panContext.strokeStyle = 'white';
    this.panContext.strokeRect(this.viewportLocation.x,
                               this.viewportLocation.y,
                               this.viewportSize.width,
                               this.viewportSize.height);
},

clipToViewport: function() {
    this.panContext.beginPath();
    this.panContext.rect(this.viewportLocation.x,
                         this.viewportLocation.y,
                         this.viewportSize.width,
                         this.viewportSize.height);
    this.panContext.clip();
},

draw: function() {
    this.drawImageCanvas();
    this.drawPanCanvas(this.panCanvasAlpha);

    this.panContext.save();
    this.clipToViewport();
    this.drawPanCanvas(1.0);
    this.panContext.restore();

    this.drawViewport();
},
```

```
windowToCanvas: function(x, y) {
    var bbox = this.panCanvas.getBoundingClientRect();

    return {
        x: x - bbox.left * (this.panCanvas.width  / bbox.width),
        y: y - bbox.top  * (this.panCanvas.height / bbox.height)
    };
  },
};
```

## 10.5 Conclusion

Although standard HTML controls suffice for many applications, there are many good reasons to implement your own Canvas-based controls; for example, you may need a control that's not covered by the HTML standard, or you may require a consistent look-and-feel across browsers.

In this chapter you have seen how to implement Canvas-based controls. You saw how to implement controls that create a canvas element, wrap that element in a DIV, and expose that DIV to developers. Because developers have access to that DIV, they can attach it to any element in the DOM tree.

You also saw how to implement composite controls, meaning controls that use other controls, such as the progress bar and slider. Finally, you saw how to incorporate event handling into controls and how to fire events to registered event listeners.

In the next chapter, we will look at implementing Canvas-based mobile web applications.

CHAPTER 11

# Mobile

In the 1990s, Java gained immense popularity because developers could write one application that ran on multiple operating systems. In the early 2000s, HTML5 is doing the same on the mobile front, letting developers implement a single application that runs on the desktop and multiple mobile operating systems.

In this chapter you will see how to get Canvas-based applications running on mobile devices; specifically, you will see how to configure the magnifying glass and paint applications discussed earlier in this book to run, indistinguishably from native applications, on the iPad.

The application shown in Figure 11.1 is the magnifying glass application discussed in Section 4.10, "A Magnifying Glass," on p. 321, running on both Mac OS X and iOS5 on the iPad. Visually, the application is identical on both operating systems, except for the title bar. The application supports both mouse and touch events, so the same code runs on either operating system.

This chapter illustrates how to make Canvas-based applications run on mobile devices by showing you how to do the following:

- Use the viewport metatag to optimally set the size of your application for particular devices and orientations: "The viewport Metatag," on p. 661
- Use CSS media queries for a different look on mobile devices: "Media Queries," on p. 666
- React to device orientation changes with media query listeners in JavaScript: "Reacting to Media Changes with JavaScript," on p. 668
- Handle touch events: "Touch Events," on p. 671
- Disable inertial scrolling: "Supporting Both Touch and Mouse Events," on p. 674

Figure 11.1 An application that runs on the desktop (*top*) and on an iPad (*bottom*)

- Prevent user zooming and DIV flashing: "The Mobile Viewport," on p. 659 and "Supporting Both Touch and Mouse Events," on p. 674
- Implement pinch and zoom: "Pinch and Zoom," on p. 675
- Implement a Canvas-based keyboard control for tablet computers: "A Virtual Keyboard," on p. 682

You will also see how to make Canvas-based applications indistinguishable from native applications on iOS5 by

- Creating application icons and startup images: "Application Icons and Startup Images," on p. 678
- Using media queries to select startup images and application icons: "Media Queries for iOS5 Application Icons and Startup Images," on p. 679

- Making your HTML5 application run fullscreen without any browser chrome: "Fullscreen with No Browser Chrome," on p. 680
- Setting the status bar's background color: "Application Status Bar," on p. 681

**NOTE: HTML5 vs. native applications**

As this book went to press there was much debate about whether HTML5 or native applications would win out on mobile devices. As this chapter shows, you can implement HTML5 applications that run on the iPad and that are indistinguishable from native applications.

Such implementations are only one aspect of the debate. Another aspect is access to native functionality such as gyroscopes and GPS positioning. HTML5 specifications are constantly being updated to include such functionality; moreover, you can always use a framework such as PhoneGap to access that functionality.

In any event, using HTML5 instead of implementing native applications can significantly reduce your software development costs if you plan to support multiple mobile devices and operating systems.

**NOTE: Canvas performance on mobile devices**

As most of this book was being written, Canvas performance on mobile devices was dismal. Whereas Canvas-based animations run smoothly on the desktop, the same animations on most mobile devices were choppy. However, as this book was nearing completion, iOS5 came out with hardware acceleration for Canvas, which entirely changed the game on the world's most popular mobile devices. That hardware acceleration dramatically improved performance, making it possible to implement smooth animations and video games.

## 11.1 The Mobile Viewport

As Figure 11.2 illustrates, mobile web browsers typically display webpages on screens smaller than those of their desktop counterparts. At the same resolution, mobile devices display a fraction of the webpage.

Most mobile browsers, however, do not initially display webpages as illustrated in Figure 11.2. If they did, nearly everyone would immediately zoom out to see the entire width of the page, as shown in Figure 11.3, so most mobile browsers automatically zoom out for you when they initially display a page.

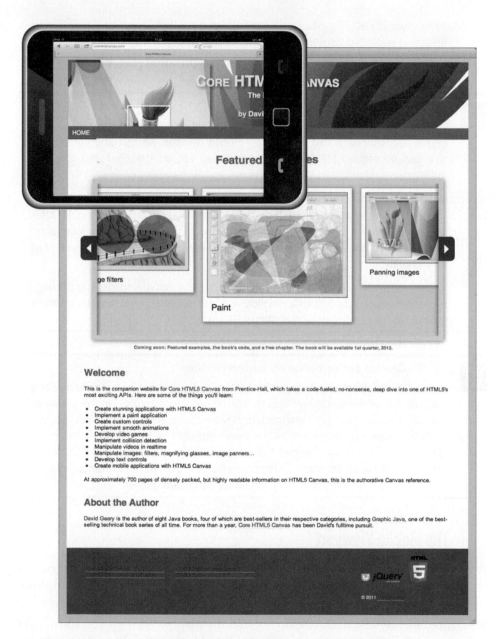

Figure 11.2  Mobile browsers have a smaller viewport than desktop browsers

Figure 11.3  How most mobile browsers initially display webpages by default

It's important to understand how mobile web browsers, including those that run on tablet computers like the iPad, initially scale webpages to fit the display.

Mobile web browsers initially draw webpages into an offscreen viewport, known as the *layout viewport*, to ensure that the page's CSS machinations produce a page that is proportionately similar to the page as it appears in a desktop browser. In fact, you can think of the webpage in Figure 11.2 as the layout viewport. The screen of the mobile device is referred to as the *visible* viewport.

The layout viewport is a fixed size for specific devices; for example, the iPad uses a layout viewport whose width is 980 pixels, and the width of the layout viewport on Android is 800 pixels, but in any event the width is similar to a typical window width on the desktop.

After initially drawing the webpage into the offscreen layout viewport, mobile web browsers copy the contents of the layout viewport to the *visible viewport* on the device, *scaling the layout viewport* along the way.

## 11.1.1 The `viewport` Metatag

The size of a mobile device's *visible* viewport is fixed whereas the size of the *layout* viewport is infinitely adjustable. With the `viewport` metatag, you can adjust not only the size of the browser's layout viewport, but other viewport properties, such as whether the user can scale the viewport, and the minimum and maximum scales.

**Figure 11.4** shows an application running on an iPad. The application contains a single DIV, 500 pixels wide by 50 pixels high. The top screenshot shows the application as it appears by default, without using the viewport metatag. The middle screenshot shows the viewport width set to 500 pixels, like this:

```
<meta name='viewport' content='width=500'/>
```

The bottom screenshot shows the application with a viewport width of 100 pixels.

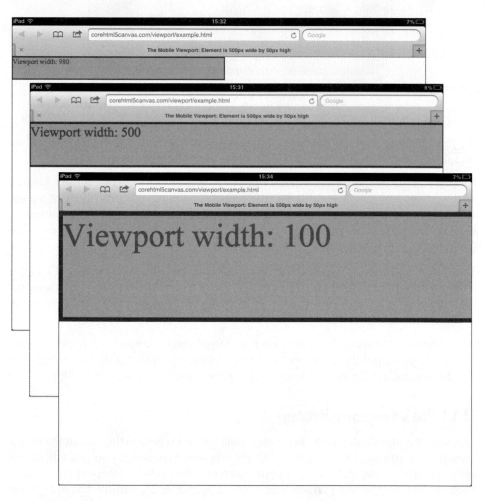

Figure 11.4  The mobile viewport

In the top screenshot in Figure 11.4, the iPad draws the webpage into the default layout viewport with a width of 980 pixels and scales the layout viewport to fit the visible viewport. The iPad's width is 1040 pixels in landscape mode, which is nearly the size of the layout viewport (980 pixels), so the two viewports are at approximately the same scale. Because the visible and layout viewports are nearly the same size, the 500-pixel-wide DIV element, which is about one half the width of the layout viewport, takes up approximately one half of the width of the iPad's display in landscape mode. None of those things are true for the other two screenshots, however.

As the viewport's width becomes smaller, the application zooms in on the DIV as it scales from successively smaller layout viewports to the fixed-size visible viewport. When the viewport width is 500, it's the same as the width of the DIV, so the DIV fits snugly on the screen in the horizontal direction. When the layout viewport width is 100 pixels, the browser crams the 500-pixel-wide DIV into 100 pixels, and then scales those 100 pixels to 1040, which magnifies the DIV considerably.

When you set the viewport's width, the browser determines the scale in the vertical direction by maintaining the ratio between the DIV's width and height. Although it's much more common to set the width of the viewport, you can also set its height; if you do, the browser will automatically set the scale in the horizontal direction, once again maintaining the width/height ratio.

The HTML for the application shown in Figure 11.4 is listed in Example 11.1.

The application uses the viewport metatag to set the viewport's width to 500 pixels. That value, along with the text displayed in the DIV, were modified for each of the three screenshots in Figure 11.4.

Here are some uses of the viewport metatag:

```
<meta name="viewport" content="width=480"/>
<meta name="viewport" content="width=device-width,
                       initial-scale=1.0, user-scalable=yes"/>
<meta name="viewport"
      content="width=device-width, initial-scale=1.0,
           maximum-scale=1.0, user-scalable=no"/>
```

The first use of the viewport metatag above sets the viewport's width to 480 pixels. You may want to hardcode the viewport's width to a numerical value when you have a narrow site that's displayed on a wider device. For example, if you have a site that's designed for iPhones whose width is 480 pixels, and that site is displayed on an iPhone with retina display, you probably want your application to fill the width of the device, like in the middle screenshot in Figure 11.4,—by specifying a viewport width of 480—instead of only filling part of the width, as in the top screenshot.

---

**Example 11.1** Using the `viewport` metatag

```
<!DOCTYPE html>
<html>
    <head>
        <title>
            The Mobile Viewport: Element is 500px wide by 50px high
        </title>

        <meta name='viewport' content='width=500'/>

        <style>

            body {
                margin: 0px;
                padding: 0px;
            }

            #box {
                background: goldenrod;
                border: 2px solid navy;
                color: blue;
                width: 500px;
                height: 50px;
            }
        </style>
    </head>

    <body>
        <div id='box'>Viewport width: 500</div>
    </body>
</html>
```

---

The second use of the `viewport` metatag sets the layout viewport's width to `device-width`, which equates to the width of the physical device, meaning the width is the same whether a device is in portrait or landscape mode. For web applications that were originally intended to run in desktop browsers—and are therefore typically as wide or wider than most mobile displays—it's a good idea to set the viewport width to `device-width`. The second use also sets the initial scale to `1.0` and lets the user scale the application.

The third use of the `viewport` metatag also sets the width and initial scale to `device-width` and `1.0`, respectively. Additionally, the maximum scale is set to `1.0`, and user scaling is disallowed.

The properties that you can specify in the `content` attribute of the `viewport` metatag are listed in Table 11.1.

**Table 11.1** `viewport` metatag content attributes

| Content Properties | Valid Values |
| --- | --- |
| `width` | Non-negative numbers between 1 and 10000 representing pixels. You can also specify `device-width`, which represents the physical width of the device. Unknown keywords and values resolve to 1px. |
| `height` | Non-negative numbers, between 1 and 10000, and `device-height`. You can specify `device-height`, which represents the physical height of the device. As with the `width` property, unknown keywords and values resolve to 1px. |
| `initial-scale,`<br>`minimum-scale,`<br>`maximum-scale` | Non-negative numbers between 0.1 and 10. You can also specify:<br><br>• `device-width` or `device-height`, which resolve to 10<br>• yes and no, which resolve to 1 and 0.1, respectively |
| `user-scalable` | yes and no: yes typically means the user can pinch and zoom your application to adjust the scale; no disallows that adjustment. |
| `target-densityDpi` | Numbers between 70 and 400 represent dpi (dots per inch). You can also specify:<br><br>• `device-width` or `device-height`, which resolve to 10<br>• yes and no, which resolve to 1 and 0.1, respectively<br><br>Although most browsers accept `target-densitydpi` for this property, the specification capitalizes the second d. |

Now that you have a good understanding of viewports on mobile devices and how they affect the layout of your application, let's see how to select CSS, startup icons, and splash screens for different devices.

 **TIP: Set the viewport's width to `device-width` instead of a numerical value**

For web applications that were originally implemented for the desktop, it's a good idea to set the viewport's width to `device-width` instead of a numerical value. That way, the offscreen layout viewport's width will be the same as the device width.

**TIP: Don't blow up on the iPad**

If you set a viewport's `initial-scale` to 1.0, the browser fits webpages horizontally, which is what you want most of the time. However, mobile Safari takes the term *initial scale* literally, and only sets the scale when you initially load the page. If you rotate the device from portrait to landscape mode, mobile Safari will scale the page as it maintains the width of the page. In that case you may want to set `maximum-scale` to 1.0 to make sure your webpage doesn't blow up when the user rotates from portrait to landscape.

## 11.2  Media Queries

Media queries, which are new for CSS3, let you select resources such as CSS and images according to the type of device upon which your application runs. You can also create media query listeners that the browser invokes when media parameters such as device orientation change.

### 11.2.1  Media Queries and CSS

In your CSS stylesheets you can declare sections for different types of devices with `@media` by detecting *media features* such as orientation or screen width, as illustrated in Example 11.2.

**Example 11.2** Selectively applying CSS with media queries

```
<!DOCTYPE html>
<html>
   <head>
      ...
      <style>
         ...

         @media all and (min-device-width: 481px) and
            (max-device-width: 1024px) and
            (orientation:portrait) {
            #controls {
               ...
            }
            ...
         }
```

```
@media all and (min-device-width: 481px)
    and (max-device-width: 1024px)
    and (orientation:landscape) {
    #controls {
        ...
    }
    ...
}
    ...
</style>
</head>

<body>
    ...
</body>
</html>
```

The CSS in Example 11.2 uses the `min-device-width`, `max-device-width`, and `orientation` media features to distinguish portrait and landscape modes on the iPad. Table 11.2 lists all the media features.

**Table 11.2** Media features

| Media Feature | Accepts min-/max- Prefixes | Description |
| --- | --- | --- |
| width | yes | The viewport width. |
| height | yes | The viewport height. |
| device-width | yes | The screen width. |
| device-height | yes | The screen height. |
| orientation | no | Either portrait or landscape. |
| aspect-ratio | yes | The width/height ratio. |
| device-aspect-ratio | yes | The device-width/device-height ratio. |
| color | yes | The number of bits per color component. |
| color-index | yes | The number of entries in the color lookup table. |

*(Continues)*

**Table 11.2**  *(Continued)*

| Media Feature | Accepts min–/max– Prefixes | Description |
| --- | --- | --- |
| `monochrome` | yes | The number of bits per pixel in a monochrome frame buffer. |
| `resolution` | yes | The pixel density of the device. |
| `scan` | no | The scanning process for TV devices. |
| `grid` | no | Valid values are 1, signifying a grid-based device, such as a tty terminal, and 0 for non-grid devices, such as a computer monitor. |

**CAUTION: Don't change canvas size with media queries and CSS**

There may be times when you use media queries to set the size of the canvas depending upon device media features. If you do that, recall from Section 1.1.1, "Canvas Element Size vs. Drawing Surface Size," on p. 5 that changing the size of the canvas with CSS only changes that element size and not the size of the canvas's drawing surface.

If you need to change the size of the canvas for different devices, you should implement a media query list listener that changes the canvas size in JavaScript.

## 11.2.2  Reacting to Media Changes with JavaScript

Sometimes you need to handle media feature changes dynamically at runtime; for example, you may need to change the size of one or more canvases when a media feature, such as orientation, changes. In that case, it's not enough to simply specify conditional CSS for different orientations because you must programmatically change the size of the canvas in addition to changing its size with CSS to ensure that the drawing surface matches the size of the canvas element. See Section 1.1.1, "Canvas Element Size vs. Drawing Surface Size," on p. 5 for more details about changing canvas size at runtime.

The magnifying glass application, shown in portrait mode in Figure 11.5, resizes the application's canvas when a user changes the device orientation.

Figure 11.5 Detecting orientation changes on the iPad

Example 11.3 shows how the application reacts to orientation changes. First, the code checks to see if the `window.matchMedia()` method exists; if so, the application invokes that method to create a media query list with a single media query pertaining to the device's orientation.

The application subsequently implements a media query list listener that the browser notifies when the orientation changes. When that happens, the application's media query list listener resizes both the application's canvas and the magnifying glass lens.

**Example 11.3** Media query listeners

```
if (window.matchMedia && screen.width < 1024) {
    var m = window.matchMedia("(orientation:portrait)"),
        lw = 0,
        lh = 0,
        lr = 0;

    function listener (mql) {
        var cr = canvas.getBoundingClientRect();

        if (mql.matches) {  // Portrait
            // Save landscape size to reset later
            lw = canvas.width;
            lh = canvas.height;
            lr = magnifyingGlassRadius;

            // Resize for portrait
            canvas.width = screen.width - 2*cr.left;
            canvas.height = canvas.width*canvasRatio;

            magnifyingGlassRadius *=
                (canvas.width + canvas.height) / (lw + lh);
        }
        else if (lw !== 0 && lh !== 0) { // Landscape
            // Reset landscape size
            canvas.width = lw;
            canvas.height = lh;

            magnifyingGlassRadius = lr;
        }

        // Setting canvas width and height resets and
        // erases the canvas, making a redraw necessary

        draw();
    }

    m.addListener(listener);
}
```

## 11.3 Touch Events

The most obvious difference between mobile and desktop web applications is the predominant use of touches—typically a finger or stylus—for the former and a mouse for the latter. Touch events and mouse events are similar, except for two major differences:

- There's only one mouse cursor, but there can be multiple touch points.
- The mouse can hover, but touch points cannot.

Handling touch events is, in many respects, analogous to handling mouse events; for example, you can add a touch start listener to a canvas by assigning a function to its ontouchstart property, like this:

```
canvas.ontouchstart = function (e) {
    alert('touch start');
};
```

You can also add a touch start listener with the addEventListener() method:

```
canvas.addEventListener('touchstart', function (e) {
    alert('touch start');
});
```

Table 11.3 lists the touch event types.

**Table 11.3** Touch events

| Event | Can Cancel | Bubbles | Description | Default Action |
|-------|-----------|---------|-------------|----------------|
| touchstart | Yes | Yes | The user placed a touch point on the touch surface. | Undefined |
| touchmove | Yes | Yes | The user moved a touch point along the touch surface. | Undefined |
| touchend | Yes | Yes | A touch point has left the touch area. | Varies: mousemove, mousedown, mouseup, click |
| touchcancel | No | Yes | A touch point has been disrupted, or there are more touch points than the device can handle. | None |

## 11.3.1 Touch Event Objects

The browser passes touch event listeners an event object that has the attributes listed in Table 11.4.

**Table 11.4** Touch event object attributes

| Attribute | Type | Description |
|---|---|---|
| touches | TouchList | The touches that are currently touching the surface. |
| changedTouches | TouchList | The touches that changed since the last touch event. For touchstart events, the touches that have changed are the ones that became active. For touchmove events, it's the touches that have moved, and for touchend and touchcancel events, it's the touches that were removed from the surface. |
| targetTouches | TouchList | The touches that are currently touching the surface and reside in the element in which they began. Until a touch is dragged out of the element in which it began, this list is the same as the touches list. |
| altKey, ctrlKey, metaKey, shiftKey | boolean | true if the associated key (Alt, Ctrl, Meta, or Shift) was held down during the touch event. Since many mobile devices do not have physical keyboards, these attributes are of dubious value. |

Most of the time you will only be concerned with the touches and changedTouches attributes. Both of those attributes represent touch lists, which are lists of touch objects. Let's take a look at those lists next.

## 11.3.2 Touch Lists

Touch lists have two properties:

- length
- Touch identifiedTouch(identifier)

Given a touch list, you can find out how many touches are in the list, with the length property, like this:

```
canvas.ontouchstart = function (e) {
    alert(e.touches.length + ' touches on the device');
};
```

You can access each touch in the list by treating the touch list like an array:

```
canvas.ontouchstart = function (e) {
    for(var i=0; i < e.touches.length; ++i) {
        alert('Touch at: ' + e.touches[i].pageX + ',' +
                            e.touches[i].pageY);
    }
};
```

Each touch has a unique identifier, and the `identifiedTouch()` method returns the touch with the specified identifier, if it exists in the list. That method can be useful when you need to know whether the same touch has contributed to multiple touch events.

## 11.3.3 Touch Objects

Ultimately, touch event listeners need to examine the touch objects themselves. Table 11.5 lists touch object attributes.

**Table 11.5** Touch object attributes

| Attribute | Type | Description |
|-----------|------|-------------|
| clientX | long | The X coordinate, relative to the viewport, excluding scrolling. |
| clientY | long | The Y coordinate, relative to the viewport, excluding scrolling. |
| identifier | long | A unique identifier for a given touch. Touches retain their identity across events. |
| pageX | long | The X coordinate, relative to the viewport, including scrolling. |
| pageY | long | The Y coordinate, relative to the viewport, including scrolling. |
| screenX | long | The X coordinate, relative to the screen. |
| screenY | long | The Y coordinate, relative to the screen. |
| target | EventTarget | The element in which a touch started. If you drag a touch out of its initial element, the `target` property still refers to the initial element. |

## 11.3.4 Supporting Both Touch and Mouse Events

Although touch and mouse events are similar, you must handle them separately. If you are implementing an application that runs in both desktop and mobile browsers, you may wish to equate touch and mouse events and encapsulate event handling in methods that do not need to know whether the event was a mouse or touch event. That strategy is illustrated in Example 11.4.

**Example 11.4** A template for supporting touch and mouse events

```
// Touch event handlers.....................................

canvas.ontouchstart = function (e) {
   e.preventDefault(e); // Optional
   mouseDownOrTouchStart(windowToCanvas(e.pageX, e.pageY));
};

canvas.ontouchmove = function (e) {
   e.preventDefault(e); // Optional
   mouseMoveOrTouchMove(windowToCanvas(e.pageX, e.pageX));
};

canvas.ontouchend = function (e) {
   e.preventDefault(e); // Optional
   mouseUpOrTouchEnd(windowToCanvas(e.pageX, e.pageX));
};

// Mouse event handlers.....................................

canvas.onmousedown = function (e) {
   e.preventDefault(e); // Optional
   mouseDownOrTouchStart(windowToCanvas(e.clientX, e.clientY));
};

canvas.onmousemove = function (e) {
   e.preventDefault(e); // Optional
   mouseMoveOrTouchMove(windowToCanvas(e.clientX, e.clientY));
};

canvas.onmouseup = function (e) {
   e.preventDefault(e); // Optional
   mouseUpOrTouchEnd(windowToCanvas(e.clientX, e.clientY));
};

// General functions.......................................
```

```
function mouseDownOrTouchStart(location) {
   // IMPLEMENT
};

function mouseMoveOrTouchMove(location) {
   // IMPLEMENT
};

function mouseUpOrTouchEnd(location) {
   // IMPLEMENT
};
```

This JavaScript implements short touch and mouse event handler functions that delegate to touch- and mouse-agnostic functions. The event handlers also invoke the event's preventDefault() method, which prevents the browser from interfering with the user's touch gestures and mouse events.

Notice the event handlers use the windowToCanvas() method discussed in Section 1.6.1.1, "Translating Mouse Coordinates to Canvas Coordinates," on p. 26 to determine the touch locations. For touch events, the application passes the touch's pageX and pageY attributes, which account for scrolling offsets, to that function.

 **TIP: Prevent scrolling, among other things**
You can inhibit default browser actions—*such as scrolling*—by calling the event's preventDefault() method. That method can prevent all sorts of unwanted browser interaction, such as zooming, accidental selections, and DIV flashing.

## 11.3.5 Pinch and Zoom

The HTML5 API for handling touch events gives you all the tools you need to implement portable pinch and zoom. The excerpt from the magnifying glass application in Example 11.5 shows how the magnifying glass lets users pinch and zoom to adjust the magnifying glass's magnification scale.

For touch start and touch move events, if there are two touches currently touching the device and one or more of them has changed, the user is pinching. If the user is pinching, the magnifying glass application's touch start event handler calculates the distance and the ratio of the current magnification scale divided by the distance.

Consequently, the touch move event handler also calculates the distance between the two touches and sets the magnification scale based on the previously calculated ratio.

**Example 11.5** Implementing pinch and zoom

```javascript
var magnificationScale = scaleOutput.innerHTML,
    pinchRatio,
    ...

function isPinching (e) {
    var changed = e.changedTouches.length,
        touching = e.touches.length;

    return changed === 1 || changed === 2 && touching === 2;
}

function isDragging (e) {
    var changed = e.changedTouches.length,
        touching = e.touches.length;

    return changed === 1 && touching === 1;
}

canvas.ontouchstart = function (e) {
    var changed = e.changedTouches.length,
        touching = e.touches.length,
        distance;

    e.preventDefault(e);

    if (isDragging(e)) {
        mouseDownOrTouchStart(windowToCanvas(e.pageX, e.pageY));
    }
    else if (isPinching(e)) {
        var touch1 = e.touches.item(0),
            touch2 = e.touches.item(1),
            point1 = windowToCanvas(touch1.pageX, touch1.pageY),
            point2 = windowToCanvas(touch2.pageX, touch2.pageY);

        distance = Math.sqrt(Math.pow(point2.x - point1.x, 2) +
                             Math.pow(point2.x - point1.x, 2));
        pinchRatio = magnificationScale / distance;
    }
};

canvas.ontouchmove = function (e) {
    var changed = e.changedTouches.length,
        touching = e.touches.length,
        distance, touch1, touch2;

    e.preventDefault(e);
```

```
   if (isDragging(e)) {
      mouseMoveOrTouchMove(windowToCanvas(e.pageX, e.pageY));
   }
   else if (isPinching(e)) {
      var touch1 = e.touches.item(0),
          touch2 = e.touches.item(1),
          point1 = windowToCanvas(touch1.pageX, touch1.pageY),
          point2 = windowToCanvas(touch2.pageX, touch2.pageY),
          scale;

      distance = Math.sqrt(Math.pow(point2.x - point1.x, 2) +
                           Math.pow(point2.x - point1.x, 2));

      scale = pinchRatio * distance;

      if (scale > 1 && scale < 3) {
         magnificationScale =
            parseFloat(pinchRatio * distance).toFixed(2);

         draw();
      }
   }
};

canvas.ontouchend = function (e) {
   e.preventDefault(e);
   mouseUpOrTouchEnd(windowToCanvas(e.pageX, e.pageY));
};
```

## 11.4 iOS5

Apple has invested heavily in native application infrastructure for iOS5, but they are also committed to ensuring that HTML5 applications can run—indistinguishably from native applications—on iOS5 devices. In this section we look at how you can make your HTML5 applications look like native iOS5 applications.

 **NOTE: iOS5 and Android**

Apple's iOS5 supports home screen icons, startup splash screens, and fullscreen mode, for HTML5 applications. When this book went to press Android also supported home screen icons, but did not yet support startup splash screens in fullscreen mode.

### 11.4.1 Application Icons and Startup Images

iOS5 lets you easily specify an icon and a splash screen for your HTML5 applications, like this:

```
<link rel='apple-touch-startup-image'
      href='startup-iPad-landscape.png'/>

<link rel='apple-touch-icon-precomposed' sizes='72x72'
      href='icon-ipad.png'/>
```

That's all there is to specifying icons and splash screens on iOS5. You can see the icons for the magnifying glass and paint applications in Figure 11.6, and the magnifying glass application's splash screen in Figure 11.7.

Figure 11.6  Application icons on iOS5

---

 **NOTE: iOS5 icons must be sized correctly**

If you use the `apple-touch-icon-precomposed` link to set your application's home screen icon, and the icon does not appear, you may need to resize your image. See http://bit.ly/yNkfHy for more information about icon sizes for iOS5.

---

Figure 11.7  A startup image on iOS5

## 11.4.2  Media Queries for iOS5 Application Icons and Startup Images

You can combine media queries and iOS5's support for icons and splash screens
to select those features for different devices, as shown in Example 11.6.

---

Example 11.6  iOS5 application icons and startup images

---

```
<!-- 320x460 for iPhone 3GS -->

<link rel='apple-touch-startup-image'
    media='(max-device-width: 480px)
        and not (-webkit-min-device-pixel-ratio: 2)'
    href='startup-iphone.png' />

<!-- 640x920 for retina display -->

<link rel='apple-touch-startup-image'
    media='(max-device-width: 480px)
        and (-webkit-min-device-pixel-ratio: 2)'
    href='startup-iphone4.png' />
```

*(Continues)*

**Example 11.6** *(Continued)*

```
<!-- iPad Portrait 768x1004 -->

<link rel='apple-touch-startup-image'
      media='(min-device-width: 768px) and (orientation: portrait)'
      href='startup-iPad-portrait.png' />

<!-- iPad Landscape 1024x748 -->

<link rel='apple-touch-startup-image'
      media='(min-device-width: 768px) and (orientation: landscape)'
      href='startup-iPad-landscape.png' />

<link rel='apple-touch-icon-precomposed' sizes='72x72'
      href='icon-ipad.png' />
```

### 11.4.3 Fullscreen with No Browser Chrome

As Figure 11.8 illustrates, you can add icons for URLs to your home screen on the iPad.

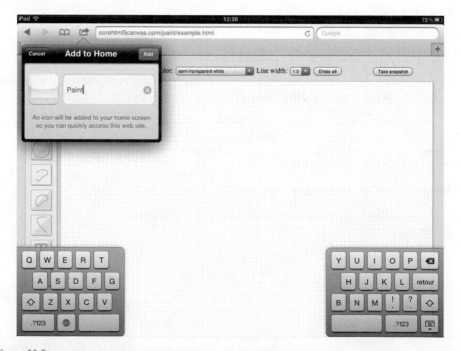

Figure 11.8 Adding the paint application to the home screen

If you add the following metatag to your web application, the application will run in fullscreen mode when the user starts it from the home screen.

```
<meta name='apple-mobile-web-app-capable' content='yes'/>
```

Figure 11.9 shows the paint application running in fullscreen mode.

Figure 11.9  The paint application—fullscreen—on the iPad

## 11.4.4 Application Status Bar

iOS5 also lets you control the look of the status bar, as shown in Figure 11.10.

To set the look of the status bar, use the following metatag:

```
<meta name='apple-mobile-web-app-status-bar-style'
      content='black-translucent'/>
```

You can use the following three values for the `content` attribute:

- `default`
- `black`
- `black-translucent`

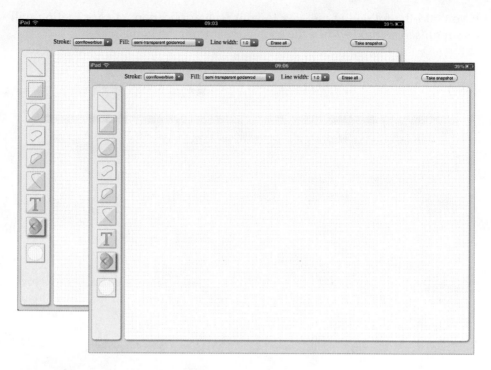

Figure 11.10   Black vs. black-translucent status bars

The default and black modes are the same, and are depicted in the top screenshot in Figure 11.10. black-translucent is a partially transparent version of the black status bar.

If you look closely at the screenshots in Figure 11.10, you will see that the controls are closer to the top of the screen when the status bar is black-translucent. When the status bar is opaque, meaning either black or default, iOS5 positions the top of the webpage at the bottom of the status bar. When the status bar is translucent, iOS5 positions the top of the webpage at the top of the status bar.

## 11.5   A Virtual Keyboard

The iPad comes with a built-in virtual keyboard, but it only displays its keyboard when a user taps in a text field. Short of going native, there is no way to show the keyboard and capture keystrokes on the iPad if your application lets users enter text without tapping in a text field. In fact, the paint application discussed in this chapter and throughout this book is just such an application. After you activate the text icon, you can click anywhere in the drawing canvas, and a cursor will appear. Subsequently you can type—provided that you have a keyboard—and the paint application draws the text, as depicted in Figure 11.11.

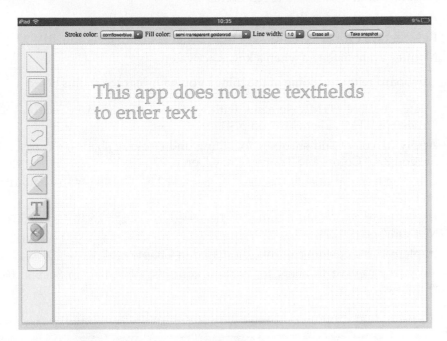

Figure 11.11 Entering text in the paint application

Because iOS5 only shows the keyboard when a user physically taps into a text field—programmatically giving a text field focus does not show the keyboard—most developers are stuck if they are developing an application that has an alternate text input strategy. However, for developers familiar with Canvas, it's possible to implement your own keyboard and show it yourself. The next section illustrates how to do that.

## 11.5.1 A Canvas–Based Keyboard Implementation

In this section we implement a Canvas-based keyboard, shown in Figure 11.12, that will work on any device. You can

- Show and hide the keyboard
- Make the keyboard translucent
- Attach the keyboard to any DIV
- Wire the keyboard to the underlying application

The keyboard automatically

- Supports both mouse and touch events
- Activates keys and makes them flash when you touch them
- Resizes the keyboard and its keys to fit the keyboard's enclosing DIV
- Notifies event listeners when a key is activated

The keyboard reiterates some of the things you have learned in this book:

- Using invisible HTML elements with a canvas, discussed in Section 1.8.1, "Invisible HTML Elements," on p. 41
- Applying colors and shadows for filling and stroking shapes, discussed in Section 2.4, "Colors and Transparency," on p. 72
- Creating linear gradients, discussed in Section 2.5, "Gradients and Patterns," on p. 76
- Implementing rounded rectangles, discussed in Section 2.9.3, "The arcTo() Method," on p. 127
- Implementing custom controls, discussed in Chapter 10
- Supporting event listeners for custom controls, discussed in Section 10.3, "Sliders," on p. 631

Figure 11.12 A keyboard with opaque keys on the iPad

- Handling both mouse and touch events, discussed in Section 11.3.4, "Supporting Both Touch and Mouse Events," on p. 674

You can also make the keyboard translucent, which, in turn, makes all of the keys translucent, as illustrated in Figure 11.13.

Figure 11.13  A keyboard with translucent keys on the iPad

The paint application makes the keyboard opaque when the text cursor is in the top half of the drawing canvas; otherwise, the application makes the keyboard translucent so the user can see the text as they type.

Like the custom controls discussed in Chapter 10, you attach the keyboard to a DOM element, typically a DIV. When you make that attachment, the keyboard resizes to fit its enclosing DOM element, as illustrated in Figure 11.14.

Before we take a look at the keyboard's implementation, let's see how the paint application uses the keyboard. Example 11.7 shows an excerpt from the paint application's HTML. That HTML includes an invisible DIV whose id is keyboard. The keyboard DIV is initially invisible by virtue of its CSS, which sets its height to zero pixels.

---

Example 11.7  An excerpt from the paint application's HTML

```html
<!DOCTYPE html>
<html>
  <head>
    ...
    <style>
      ...

      #keyboard {
        position: absolute;
        left: 25px;
        top: 0px;
        width: 1000px;
        height: 0px;

        background: rgba(129,129,138,0.4);

        -webkit-box-shadow: rgba(0,0,0,0.2) 3px 3px 4px;
        -moz-box-shadow: rgba(0,0,0,0.2) 3px 3px 4px;
        box-shadow: rgba(0,0,0,0.2) 3px 3px 4px;
      }

    </style>
  </head>

  <body>
    ...

    <canvas id='iconCanvas' width='75' height='685'>
      Canvas not supported
    </canvas>

    <canvas id='drawingCanvas' width='915' height='685'>
      Canvas not supported
    </canvas>

    <div id='keyboard'></div>
    ...

    <script src='keyboard.js'></script>
    <script src='example.js'></script>
  </body>
</html>
```

---

The paint application's JavaScript shows and hides the keyboard as appropriate. Example 11.8 lists that JavaScript.

Figure 11.14 The keyboard resizes to fit its enclosing HTML element

---

Example 11.8 Using the keyboard in the drawing application

---

```
var keyboard = new COREHTML5.Keyboard();
...

// Keyboard.....................................................

function showKeyboard() {
    var keyboardElement = document.getElementById('keyboard');

    keyboardElement.style.height = '370px';
    keyboardElement.style.top = '375px';
    keyboardElement.style.border = 'thin inset rgba(0,0,0,0.5)';
    keyboardElement.style.borderRadius = '20px';

    keyboard.resize(1000, 368);
    keyboard.translucent = mousedown.y > drawingCanvas.height/2;
    keyboard.draw();
}
```

---

*(Continues)*

---

Example 11.8  *(Continued)*

---

```
function hideKeyboard() {
    var keyboardElement = document.getElementById('keyboard');

    keyboardElement.style.height = '0px';
    keyboardElement.style.top = '760px';
    keyboardElement.style.border = '';
    keyboardElement.style.borderRadius = '';

    keyboard.resize(1000, 0);
}
...

// Text..........................................................

function startDrawingText() {
    drawingText = true;
    currentText = '';
    drawTextCursor();
    showKeyboard();
}
...

// Event handling functions.....................................

function mouseDownOrTouchStartInControlCanvas(loc) {
    if (drawingText) {
        drawingText = false;
        eraseTextCursor();
        hideKeyboard();
    }
    ...
};
...

// Initialization...............................................

keyboard.appendTo('keyboard');
...
```

---

When the paint application starts, it creates a new keyboard and appends the keyboard to the keyboard element.

The paint application implements two methods—showKeyboard() and hideKeyboard()—to show and hide the keyboard, respectively. Those methods obtain a reference to the keyboard DIV and resize the DIV's height to make it visible or invisible, respectively.

The paint application shows the keyboard when the user starts drawing text and hides the keyboard when the user subsequently taps an icon.

---

 **NOTE: The keyboard implemented here is incomplete**

In the interests of brevity, the keyboard implemented in this chapter is not very full-featured; for example, the keyboard does not have numeric keys, nor any provision for them.

The keyboard illustrates how to implement a keyboard control and integrate it into an HTML5 application running on a tablet computer, such as the iPad. Feel free to extend the keyboard's functionality and use it in your own applications.

---

The keyboard is implemented with two JavaScript objects: Key and Keyboard. Both of those objects exist in a global JavaScript object named COREHTML5 to reduce the possibility of name collisions, as discussed in Chapter 10.

Now that you've seen how to use the keyboard, let's see how it's implemented. We start by looking at the implementation of the keys.

## 11.5.1.1 The Keys

Keys are simple objects with—as you can see from the Key constructor listed in Example 11.9—three properties. Keys have text that they display, and keys can be selected and translucent.

---

Example 11.9  Key constructor

---

```
COREHTML5.Key = function (text) {
    this.text = text;
    this.selected = false;
    this.translucent = false;
}
```

---

The Key object's methods are implemented in its prototype, which is listed in Example 11.10.

Keys draw a rounded rectangle filled with a gradient, and they draw text centered in that rectangle. That drawing is done by the draw() method, which also creates the key gradient and sets context properties for the rectangle and the text. You can erase a key, redraw a key, make a key opaque or translucent, and select a key, which makes the key's gradient darker than the other keys.

**Example 11.10** Key methods

```
COREHTML5.Key.prototype = {
   createPath: function (context) {
      context.beginPath();

      if (this.width > 0)
         context.moveTo(this.left + this.cornerRadius, this.top);
      else
         context.moveTo(this.left - this.cornerRadius, this.top);

      context.arcTo(this.left + this.width, this.top,
                    this.left + this.width,
                    this.top + this.height,
                    this.cornerRadius);

      context.arcTo(this.left + this.width,
                    this.top + this.height,
                    this.left, this.top + this.height,
                    this.cornerRadius);

      context.arcTo(this.left, this.top + this.height,
                    this.left, this.top,
                    this.cornerRadius);

      if (this.width > 0) {
         context.arcTo(this.left, this.top,
                       this.left + this.cornerRadius, this.top,
                       this.cornerRadius);
      }
      else {
         context.arcTo(this.left, this.top,
                       this.left - this.cornerRadius, this.top,
                       this.cornerRadius);
      }
   },
```

```
createKeyGradient: function (context) {
   var keyGradient = context.createLinearGradient(
                        this.left, this.top,
                        this.left, this.top + this.height);
   if (this.selected) {
      keyGradient.addColorStop(0,   'rgb(208,208,210)');
      keyGradient.addColorStop(1.0, 'rgb(162,162,166)');
   }
   else if (this.translucent) {
      keyGradient.
         addColorStop(0,   'rgba(298,298,300,0.20)');
      keyGradient.
         addColorStop(1.0, 'rgba(255,255,255,0.20)');
   }
   else {
      keyGradient.addColorStop(0,   'rgb(238,238,240)');
      keyGradient.addColorStop(1.0, 'rgb(192,192,196)');
   }

   return keyGradient;
},

setKeyProperties: function (context, keyGradient) {
   context.shadowColor = 'rgba(0,0,0,0.8)';
   context.shadowOffsetX = 1;
   context.shadowOffsetY = 1;
   context.shadowBlur = 1;

   context.lineWidth = 0.5;

   context.strokeStyle = 'rgba(0,0,0,0.7)';
   context.fillStyle = keyGradient;
},

setTextProperties: function (context) {
   context.shadowColor = undefined;
   context.shadowOffsetX = 0;

   context.font = '100 ' + this.height/3 + 'px Helvetica';
   context.fillStyle = 'rgba(0,0,0,0.4)';
   context.textAlign = 'center';
   context.textBaseline = 'middle';
},
```

*(Continues)*

**Example 11.10** *(Continued)*

```
draw: function (context) {
    var keyGradient = this.createKeyGradient(context);

    context.save();

    this.createPath(context);

    this.setKeyProperties(context, keyGradient);
    context.stroke();
    context.fill();

    this.setTextProperties(context);
    context.fillText(this.text, this.left + this.width/2,
                                this.top + this.height/2);

    context.restore();
},

erase: function(context) {
    context.clearRect(this.left-2, this.top-2,
                      this.width+6, this.height+6);
},

redraw: function (context) {
    this.erase(context);
    this.draw(context);
},

toggleSelection: function (context) {
    this.selected = !this.selected;
},

isPointInKey: function (context, x, y) {
    this.createPath(context);
    return context.isPointInPath(x, y);
},

select: function () {
    this.selected = true;
},

deselect: function () {
    this.selected = false;
},
}
```

The Key object is used by the Keyboard object. Let's take a look at that next.

## 11.5.1.2 The Keyboard

The Keyboard object is a custom control, as defined in Chapter 10. Like the custom controls discussed in that chapter, you create keyboards and append them to an existing DOM element, typically a DIV.

The Keyboard constructor is listed in Example 11.11. That constructor creates a two-dimensional array with 4 rows and 11 columns, filled with Key objects. The constructor subsequently creates the keyboard's canvas and places that canvas into a DOM element.

---

Example 11.11 Keyboard constructor

```
// Constructor............................................

COREHTML5.Keyboard = function() {
   var keyboard = this;

   this.keys = [
      [ new COREHTML5.Key('Q'), new COREHTML5.Key('W'),
        new COREHTML5.Key('E'), new COREHTML5.Key('R'),
        new COREHTML5.Key('T'), new COREHTML5.Key('Y'),
        new COREHTML5.Key('U'), new COREHTML5.Key('I'),
        new COREHTML5.Key('O'), new COREHTML5.Key('P'),
        new COREHTML5.Key('<') ],

      [ new COREHTML5.Key('A'), new COREHTML5.Key('S'),
        new COREHTML5.Key('D'), new COREHTML5.Key('F'),
        new COREHTML5.Key('G'), new COREHTML5.Key('H'),
        new COREHTML5.Key('J'), new COREHTML5.Key('K'),
        new COREHTML5.Key('L'), new COREHTML5.Key('Enter') ],

      [ new COREHTML5.Key('^'), new COREHTML5.Key('Z'),
        new COREHTML5.Key('X'), new COREHTML5.Key('C'),
        new COREHTML5.Key('V'), new COREHTML5.Key('B'),
        new COREHTML5.Key('N'), new COREHTML5.Key('M'),
        new COREHTML5.Key(','), new COREHTML5.Key('.'),
        new COREHTML5.Key('^') ],

      [ new COREHTML5.Key(';'), new COREHTML5.Key(':'),
        new COREHTML5.Key(' '), new COREHTML5.Key('?'),
        new COREHTML5.Key('!') ]
   ];

   this.createCanvas();
   this.createDOMElement();

   this.translucent = false;
```

---

(Continues)

Example 11.11  *(Continued)*

```
this.shifted = false;
this.keyListenerFunctions = [];

this.context.canvas.onmousedown = function (e) {
    keyboard.mouseDownOrTouchStart(keyboard.context,
        keyboard.windowToCanvas(keyboard.context.canvas,
                                e.clientX, e.clientY));

    // Prevents inadvertent selections on desktop

    e.preventDefault();
};

this.context.canvas.ontouchstart = function (e) {
    keyboard.mouseDownOrTouchStart(keyboard.context,
        keyboard.windowToCanvas(keyboard.context.canvas,
                                e.touches[0].clientX,
                                e.touches[0].clientY));

    e.preventDefault(); // Prevents flashing on iPad
};

return this;
}
```

By default, keyboards are not translucent, meaning their keys are opaque. Also by default, keyboards are not shifted, meaning the user has not activated the Shift key. And every keyboard is created with an empty array of key listeners that the keyboard notifies when the user activates its keys.

Finally, the Keyboard constructor adds two event handlers to the keyboard's canvas, one for mouse down events and the other for touch start events. Those event handlers invoke a method that responds to both events.

Example 11.12 lists the Keyboard object's methods.

The keyboard's methods are split up into five logical groupings:

- General methods, which most custom controls implement
- Drawing methods, which draw the keyboard and its keys
- Key methods, which deal with keys, such as creating and activating keys
- Key listener methods, which support registering and firing events to listeners
- An event handler that handles both mouse and touch events

**Example 11.12**  Keyboard methods

```
// Prototype.......................................................

COREHTML5.Keyboard.prototype = {

   // General functions ..........................................

   windowToCanvas: function (canvas, x, y) {
      var bbox = canvas.getBoundingClientRect();
      return { x: x - bbox.left * (canvas.width  / bbox.width),
               y: y - bbox.top  * (canvas.height / bbox.height)
            };
   },

   createCanvas: function () {
      var canvas = document.createElement('canvas');
      this.context = canvas.getContext('2d');
   },

   createDOMElement: function () {
      this.domElement = document.createElement('div');
      this.domElement.appendChild(this.context.canvas);
   },

   appendTo: function (elementName) {
      var element = document.getElementById(elementName);

      element.appendChild(this.domElement);
      this.domElement.style.width = element.offsetWidth + 'px';
      this.domElement.style.height = element.offsetHeight + 'px';
      this.resize(element.offsetWidth, element.offsetHeight);
      this.createKeys();
   },

   resize: function (width, height) {
      this.domElement.style.width = width + 'px';
      this.domElement.style.height = height + 'px';

      this.context.canvas.width = width;
      this.context.canvas.height = height;
   },

   // Drawing functions.........................................
```

*(Continues)*

Example 11.12  *(Continued)*

```javascript
drawRoundedRect: function (context, cornerX, cornerY,
                           width, height, cornerRadius) {
   if (width > 0)
      this.context.moveTo(cornerX + cornerRadius, cornerY);
   else
      this.context.moveTo(cornerX - cornerRadius, cornerY);

   context.arcTo(cornerX + width, cornerY,
                 cornerX + width, cornerY + height,
                 cornerRadius);

   context.arcTo(cornerX + width, cornerY + height,
                 cornerX, cornerY + height,
                 cornerRadius);

   context.arcTo(cornerX, cornerY + height,
                 cornerX, cornerY,
                 cornerRadius);

   if (width > 0) {
      context.arcTo(cornerX, cornerY,
                    cornerX + cornerRadius, cornerY,
                    cornerRadius);
   }
   else {
      context.arcTo(cornerX, cornerY,
                    cornerX - cornerRadius, cornerY,
                    cornerRadius);
   }

   context.stroke();
   context.fill();
},

drawKeys: function () {
   for (var row=0; row < this.keys.length; ++row) {
      for (var col=0; col < this.keys[row].length; ++col) {
         key = this.keys[row][col];

         key.translucent = this.translucent;
         key.draw(this.context);
      }
   }
},
```

```
draw: function (context) {
    var originalContext, key;

    if (context) {
        originalContext = this.context;
        this.context = context;
    }

    this.context.save();
    this.drawKeys();

    if (context) {
        this.context = originalContext;
    }

    this.context.restore();
},

erase: function() {
    // Erase the entire canvas
    this.context.clearRect(0, 0, this.context.canvas.width,
                           this.context.canvas.height);
},

// Keys.......................................................

adjustKeyPosition: function (key, keyTop, keyMargin,
                             keyWidth, spacebarPadding) {
    var key = this.keys[row][col],
        keyMargin = this.domElement.clientWidth /
                    (this.KEY_COLUMNS*8),

        keyWidth = ((this.domElement.clientWidth - 2*keyMargin) /
                    this.KEY_COLUMNS) - keyMargin,

        keyLeft = keyMargin + col * keyWidth + col * keyMargin;

    if (row === 1) keyLeft += keyWidth/2;
    if (row === 3) keyLeft += keyWidth/3;

    key.left = keyLeft + spacebarPadding;
    key.top = keyTop;
},
```

*(Continues)*

Example 11.12    *(Continued)*

```
adjustKeySize: function (key, keyMargin, keyWidth, keyHeight) {
    if (key.text === 'Enter')   key.width = keyWidth * 1.5;
    else if (key.text === ' ')  key.width = keyWidth * 7;
    else                        key.width = keyWidth;

    key.height = keyHeight;
    key.cornerRadius = 5;
},

createKeys: function() {
    var key,
        keyMargin,
        keyWidth,
        keyHeight,
        spacebarPadding = 0;

    for (row=0; row < this.keys.length; ++row) {
        for (col=0; col < this.keys[row].length; ++col) {
            key = this.keys[row][col];

            keyMargin = this.domElement.clientWidth /
                        (this.KEY_COLUMNS*8);

            keyWidth = ((this.domElement.clientWidth - 2*keyMargin) /
                        this.KEY_COLUMNS) - keyMargin;

            keyHeight = ((this.KEYBOARD_HEIGHT - 2*keyMargin) /
                        this.KEY_ROWS) - keyMargin;

            keyTop = keyMargin + row * keyHeight + row * keyMargin;

            this.adjustKeyPosition(key, keyTop, keyMargin,
                                   keyWidth, spacebarPadding);

            this.adjustKeySize(key, keyMargin, keyWidth, keyHeight);

            if (this.keys[row][col].text === ' ') {
                spacebarPadding = keyWidth*6; // Pad from now on
            }
        }
    }
},
```

```
getKeyForLocation: function (context, loc) {
    var key;

    for (var row=0; row < this.keys.length; ++row) {
        for (var col=0; col < this.keys[row].length; ++col) {
            key = this.keys[row][col];

            if (key.isPointInKey(context, loc.x, loc.y)) {
                return key;
            }
        }
    }
    return null;
},

shiftKeyPressed: function (context) {
    for (var row=0; row < this.keys.length; ++row) {
        for (var col=0; col < this.keys[row].length; ++col) {
            nextKey = this.keys[row][col];

            if (nextKey.text === '^') {
                nextKey.toggleSelection();
                nextKey.redraw(context);
                this.shifted = nextKey.selected;
            }
        }
    }
},

activateKey: function (key, context) {
    key.select();
    setTimeout( function (e) {
                    key.deselect();
                    key.redraw(context);
                }, 200);

    key.redraw(context);

    this.fireKeyEvent(key);
},

// Key listeners.................................................

addKeyListener: function (listenerFunction) {
    this.keyListenerFunctions.push(listenerFunction);
},
```

*(Continues)*

Example 11.12  *(Continued)*

```
fireKeyEvent: function (key) {
   for (var i=0; i < this.keyListenerFunctions.length; ++i) {
      this.keyListenerFunctions[i](
         this.shifted ? key.text : key.text.toLowerCase());
   }
},

// Event handlers..............................................

mouseDownOrTouchStart: function (context, loc) {
   var key = this.getKeyForLocation(context, loc);

   if (key) {
      if (key.text === '^') {
         this.shiftKeyPressed(context);
      }
      else {
         if (this.shifted) this.activateKey(key, context);
         else              this.activateKey(key, context);
      }
   }
}
};
```

The general methods create the keyboard's canvas and DOM element, and append that element to an existing element in the DOM tree. The keyboard appendTo() method invokes resize(), which resizes the keyboard's canvas and DOM elements to fit into the enclosing DOM element. For more information about those methods, see the implementation of the other custom controls in Chapter 10.

The Keyboard object's drawing methods are straightforward. The draw() method takes an optional Canvas context; if you pass that optional context, the keyboard will draw into that context instead of its own. Either way, that drawing consists of drawing the keyboard's keys.

The key methods encapsulate most of the Keyboard object's grunt work, such as creating the keys, returning a key given a location in the keyboard's canvas, and activating keys.

The key listener methods—addKeyListener() and fireKeyEvent()—let you register key listeners with the keyboard and fire key events, respectively.

Finally, the mouseDownOrTouchStart() method reacts to mouse down and touch start events, by activating the key that was pressed, if any.

## 11.6 Conclusion

In this chapter you saw how to make your Canvas-based applications run on mobile devices. We began by looking at the mobile viewport and the associated viewport metatag, which lets you configure the offscreen layout viewport used by multiple browsers. Then we looked at media queries, how you can use them to customize CSS that you use for particular devices, and how you can use media query list listeners in JavaScript to react to media feature changes, such as device orientation changes.

You also saw how to handle touch events and how to portably implement pinch and zoom using the touch events API.

Then we took a short detour to examine how to make your HTML5 applications indistinguishable from native applications on iOS5, including creating application icons and startup images and running your applications fullscreen, with no browser chrome.

Finally, we concluded by examining the implementation of a virtual keyboard, which called upon several of the techniques that you have learned earlier in this book.

# Index

**Numbers**

3d
Canvas context, 11
simulating with parallax, 377–378
3D Monster Maze game, 359

**A**

acceleration. *See* ease in
add() method (Vector), 501–502
addChangeListener() method (Slider), 636, 642
addCirclePath() function (cutouts example), 99–103
addColorStop() method (CanvasGradient), 77–79
addEventListener() method (window), 26, 32, 671
addKeyListener() method
of Game object, 544, 558–560, 598–601
of Keyboard object, 700
addLine() method (Paragraph), 239, 242
addOuterRectanglePath() function (cutouts example), 99–103
addRectanglePath() function (cutouts example), 99–103
addSprite() method (Game), 544
addTrianglePath() function (cutouts example), 99–103
Adobe Illustrator, 23
bézier curves in, 137
paths in, 89
advance() method (SpriteSheetPainter), 407
air resistance, 461
algebraic equations, 54, 175–176
Alt key, 32, 672
altKey browser attribute, 32, 672
Android
home screen icons on, 677
layout viewport on, 661
angles, 54–55

animate() function, 195, 332, 353–354, 360, 410
locking up browser with, 341
time parameter of, 348, 350
animate() method (Game), 550–551
animation frames
dropping, 368
ending, 544–546, 550
number of pixels to move objects for.
*See* time-based motion
starting, 544–546, 550
animation loop, 340–357, 416
implementing, 544
portable. *See*
requestNextAnimationFrame()
sprite-based, 424
animation timers, 389–390, 429
for warping time, 595
starting, 416
animations, 14, 306–312, 339–391
allocating memory during, 390–391
best practices for, 390 391
callback for, 421–423
completion percentage of, 454
Flash-based, 339
linear vs. nonlinear, 423
performance of, 18–22, 366, 390–391, 404
period of, 421
separating updating and drawing in, 390
time-based, 345
timed, 385–390
warping, 473–482
AnimationTimer object, 389–390, 450–456
getElapsedTime() method, 386, 389, 451, 454–455, 464, 475
isOver() method, 389–390
isRunning() method, 386
makeBounce() method, 457
makeEaseIn() method, 456–457
makeEaseInOut() method, 457

AnimationTimer object *(cont.)*
  makeEaseOut() method, 457
  makeElastic() method, 457
  makeLinear() method, 457
  reset() method, 386
Animator.js library, 394
anti-aliasing, 107
appendTo() method
  for custom controls, 616–617
  of Keyboard object, 700
  of Slider object, 619, 624–625, 628
Apple, 329–330
Apple's Cocoa graphics system, 23
  bézier curves in, 137
  paths in, 89
apple-mobile-web-app-status-bar-style
    metatag, 681
apple-touch-icon-precomposed link, 678
applications
  desktop vs. mobile, 657–659, 671
  fullscreen mode of, 677, 680–681
  home screen icon of, 677–680
  native, 677
  splash screen of, 677–680
  status bar of, 681–682
applyFrictionAndGravity() method
    (Pinball), 594–595
arc() method (Canvas context), 22–23,
    91–92, 95–103, 124–125, 130, 136, 361
  optional argument of, 127
arcs, 124–136
  direction of, 99–100, 124, 127
  drawing, 91–92
  for text placement, 223–225
arcTo() method (Canvas context), 127–130
ArrayBuffer object, 291
aspect-ratio media feature, 667
audio. *See* sound
auto-pause, 583–584
axes, 495–525
  direction of, 503

**B**
background, 360–364
  blitting from offscreen, 360–361,
    363–364, 367, 390
  canvas for, 574

clipping to damaged areas, 360–364, 390
color of, 3
erasing, 360–361, 364–367
painting, 546, 592
redrawing, 360–361
restoring, 71, 322
scrolling, 265, 370–377, 577–579
  scrollBackground() function,
    577–579
Backspace key, 232, 237–241, 245–251
backspace() method (Paragraph),
    239–241, 245–251
ballMover object, 593–594
  execute() method, 594
ballWillHitLedge() function (bounding
    areas example), 485
beginPath() method (Canvas context), 12,
    22–23, 91–94, 100, 103, 110, 125, 136,
    361
behaviors, 394–395, 411–417
  combining, 412–415
  execute() method, 394, 411–417, 431,
    459, 473, 475, 594
  timed, 416–417
Bespin text editor, 252
bézier curves, 137–143
  cubic, 141–143
  cursorInControlPoint() function, 162
  cursorInEndPoint() function, 162
  drawing, 158–159
  editing, 158–169
  for rounded corners, 138–139
  quadratic, 137–141
Bézier, Pierre, 137
bezierCurveTo() method (Canvas
    context), 141–143
bit-shifting, 317, 320
blinkCursor() function (blinking cursor
    example), 230–231, 243
blitting, 360–361, 363–364, 367, 390
blushing (in animations), 450
bomb exploding application, 417–423
bounce() function (pinball game), 539, 604,
    609
bouncing, 459, 469, 471–472, 537–541
  after collisions between objects, 606
  and velocity, 609

handleEdgeCollisions() function,
    488–489
off stationary objects, 62, 488–489
bounding areas, 483–488
    accuracy of, 494
    ballWillHitLedge() function, 485
    circular, 485–488
    rectangular, 484–485
bounding volumes, 483
brieflyShowTryAgainImage() method
    (Pinball), 592
browsers, 13, 15–16
    backfilling functionality into, 350
    clamping in, 342, 583
    composition operations in, 85, 186–187
    custom controls in, 615
    desktop, 660
    domains in, 313
    double buffering in, 366–367, 390–391
    executing JavaScript in, 299–301, 340
    fallback content for, 3
    FileSystem API support in, 326
    font string values in, 210
    garbage collecting in, 391
    ignoring content outside canvas in, 265
    image loading in, 256
    line height in, 208, 210
    locking up with animate(), 341
    maximum width of text in, 205
    mobile, 659–666
    no scrolling into view in, 169
    px units in, 4
    reacting to events in, 31, 111
    scaling canvas in, 6–8
    scrolling in, 675
    setting frame rate in, 343–348
    shadows in, 85
    sound formats in, 557–558
    SVG support in, 74
    touch events in, 672
    video formats in, 329–330
    WebKit-based, 16–17, 19, 85
    web-safe fonts in, 209
    window coordinates in, 26, 30–31, 46,
        111, 673
    window focus of, 583
    z-index of elements in, 39

bucket game, 485–487, 490–494
    isBallInBucket() method, 486–487,
        493–494

C
CAD (computer-aided design systems),
    150
call() method (Function), 551
cancelRequestAnimationFrame() method
    (window), 344–345
canPlay...() methods (Game), 557–558
canPlaySound() method (Game), 544
canvas element (HTML), 1–8
    background color of, 3
    dir attribute, 211
    drawing:
        into canvas, 253, 258, 266–270,
            314–317, 325–326
        into itself, 266, 270, 274, 316–317, 322,
            324–325
        outside boundaries of, 260–266,
            370–377
    erasing, 24
    getContext() method, 4, 8
    hardware acceleration for, 659
    inappropriate uses of, 266
    offscreen, 51–53, 266, 270–274, 302,
        325–326, 628
        and performance, 274
        blitting from, 360–361, 363–364, 367,
            390
        created programmatically, 52
        for double buffering, 365
        invisibility of, 52
    onscreen, 628
    opacity of, 646, 650
    playing video in, 331–333
    printing, 46–51
    saving, 51
    scaling, 270–272, 316–317, 324–325
    size of, 4–8, 28
        changing, 646, 650, 668–670
        default, 5–6, 67, 272
        in CSS, 5–7
    state of, 12
    using HTML elements in, 36–46
    width and height attributes, 7

Canvas context, 9–11
  arc() method, 22–23, 91–92, 95–103,
      124–125, 127, 130, 136, 361
  arcTo() method, 127–130
  beginPath() method, 12, 22–23, 91–94,
      100, 103, 110, 125, 136, 361
  bezierCurveTo() method, 141–143
  canvas attribute, 9
  clearRect() method, 22, 24, 70–71, 188
  clip() method, 87, 187–197, 302
  closePath() method, 91–92, 511
  createImageData() method, 254,
      285–286
  createLinearGradient() method, 76–79
  createPattern() method, 80–83
  createRadialGradient() method, 78–79
  drawImage() method, 253–258, 266, 270,
      276, 282, 312–315, 322–324, 328, 332,
      407
  extending, 10, 118–120, 129
  fill() method, 23, 77, 91–92, 94–95, 148,
      398
  fillRect() method, 88
  fillStyle attribute, 4, 9, 12, 72–75,
      91–92, 136
  fillText() method, 4, 9–10, 23, 88, 201,
      210–211, 215, 222, 237, 266
  font attribute, 9
  getImageData() method, 12, 34,
      228–230, 253, 274–301, 306, 309, 313,
      317, 321–322
  globalAlpha attribute, 9, 69, 75, 256, 282,
      306–312
  globalCompositeOperation attribute,
      9, 12, 181–187, 282
  lineCap attribute, 9, 121, 123
  lineJoin attribute, 9, 70–72, 122–123
  lineTo() method, 23–24, 99, 103–104,
      110, 144
  lineWidth attribute, 9, 11, 71–72, 91,
      103–104, 123
  measureText() method, 201, 216–217,
      227–228, 237
  miterLimit attribute, 10, 72, 122–124
  moveTo() method, 23–24, 99, 103–104,
      110, 118–119, 125, 144

pointInPath() method, 151
putImageData() method, 34, 229, 253,
    274–301, 314, 322
quadraticCurveTo() method, 138–141
rect() function, 91–94, 99–100, 361
restore() method, 11–12, 85, 136, 185,
    194, 197
rotate() method, 172–175, 225
roundedRect() extension function,
    128–129
save() method, 11–12, 85, 136, 185, 194,
    197, 361
scale() method, 172–175
scrollPathIntoView() method, 169–170
setClip() method, 324–325
setTransform() method, 174–181
shadowBlur attribute, 10, 83–85, 88
shadowColor attribute, 10, 83–85, 88
shadowOffsetX and shadowOffsetY
    attributes, 10, 83–88
stroke() method, 23–24, 91–94, 103, 110,
    148, 398, 603
strokeRect() method, 88, 170
strokeStyle attribute, 4, 10, 12, 72–75,
    91–92, 136
strokeText() method, 4, 9–10, 88,
    201–207, 210, 215, 237
textAlign attribute, 10, 136, 201–202,
    210–215, 220–221
textBaseline attribute, 10, 136, 201–202,
    210–215, 220–221
toBlob() method, 8, 51
toDataURL() method, 8, 46–51, 313
transform() method, 174–181
translate() method, 170–175, 225
Canvas specification. See HTML5 Canvas
    specification
CanvasGradient object, 77–79
  addColorStop() method, 77–79
CanvasPattern object, 81
CanvasRenderingContext2D object. See
    Canvas context
captureCanvasPixels() function (rubber
    bands example), 285
captureRubberbandPixels() function
    (rubber bands example), 276, 280–281

caret, 233, 239
cell phones
    performance of, 280
    touch events in, 67
changedTouches browser attribute, 672
checkboxes, 137
checkMTVAxisDirection() function
    (pinball game), 608
Chrome browser, 15
    composition operations in, 186–187
    cross-domain images in, 313
    documentation for, 17
    FileSystem API support in, 326
    looping backwards in, 320
    maximum width of text in, 205
    requestAnimationFrame() in, 344,
        346–348
    time bug in, 348, 350
    timelines in, 19
    video formats in, 329
circles, 124–136
    axes for, 516
    colliding with polygons, 516–521
    drawing, 92
    MTV for, 530
    rubberband, 126–127
circular text, 223–225
    drawCircularText() function, 224
clamping, 342
clearHighScores() method (Game), 544,
    560–561
clearInterval() method (window), 231
clearRect() method (Canvas context), 22,
    24, 70–71, 188
clearScreen() method (Game), 550
clientX and clientY browser attributes,
    30, 673
clip() method (Canvas context), 87,
    187–197, 302, 361
clipping region, 187–197
    and drawing images, 256, 302
    applying filters with, 302
    compositing shadows into, 69
    default size of, 71, 187
    draw() method, 362–363
    drawDiscBackground() function, 363

erasing with, 187–194
    for background areas, 360–364, 390
    setting, 322, 324
    telescoping with, 194–197
clobbering, 121
clock application, 22–25, 398–404
    drawCenter() function, 23
    drawCircle() function, 23
    drawClock() function, 24
    drawNumerals() function, 23
    making snapshots of, 46–51
    using offscreen canvases for, 51–53
closePath() method (Canvas context),
    91–92, 511
collidesWith() method (Shape), 504–508,
    518–520, 529–530, 532, 604
collision detection, 56, 483–541, 546, 592,
    601–614
    a posteriori, 485–488, 601, 610
    a priori, 485, 488
    and clamping, 583
    and velocity, 461
    between ball and:
        flippers, 604, 611–614
        triangles, 609–611
    detectCollisions() function, 512, 532
    displacement vector for, 594
    separation after, 488, 526–541, 609
    techniques:
        bounding areas, 483–485
        circular bounding areas, 485–488
        ray casting, 490–494
        SAT, 495–541
color media feature, 667
color picker application, 631–643
color wheel, 75
color-index media feature, 667
colors, 72–75
    changing at edges, 296
    CSS strings for, 74
    inverting, 293
    lookup table for, 667
    names for, 74
Command design pattern (sprites), 394,
    412
Commodore Amiga computer, 393

compositing, 181–187
  and shadows, 85
  controversy of, 186–187
  global vs. local, 187
  operations for, 69, 181–187, 256
console object, 16
  log() method, 16
  profile() function, 17
  profileEnd() function, 17
contenteditable attribute (HTML5), 252
contexts, 8–12
  2d. *See* Canvas context
  3d, 11
controls
  checkboxes, 137
  custom. *See* custom controls
  input element, 252, 615
  textarea element, 252
coordinate system
  canvas vs. window, 26, 30–31, 46, 111, 674–675
  origin of, 67, 170
  rotating, 171–173, 176
  scaling, 173–176
  transforming, 67–68, 170–181
  translating, 26–31, 171–175, 222
  windowToCanvas() function, 27–28, 111, 195, 674–675
copyCanvasPixels() function (rubber bands example), 285–286
COREHTML5 object, 615–616, 624, 689
cos() method (Math), 54, 445–446
cosine, 55–56, 445
createCanvas() method (RoundedRectangle), 617
createDOMElement() method (custom controls), 617
createDomePolygons() method (Pinball), 609–611
createImageData() method (Canvas context), 254, 285–286
createLinearGradient() method (Canvas context), 76–79
createPath() method (Shape), 148, 172, 511
createPattern() method (Canvas context), 80–83

createPolygonPath() function (polygon example), 147
createRadialGradient() method (Canvas context), 78–79
CRTs (cathode ray tubes), 75
CSS (Cascading Style Sheets)
  absolute positioning in, 39, 46, 50
  changing canvas size with, 668
  color strings in, 74, 77, 88
  font strings in, 207, 210
  pixels in, 279–283, 295–299
  selecting with media queries, 666–668
  shadows in, 390
  tweening in, 458
Ctrl key, 237, 672
ctrlKey browser attribute, 32, 672
cursor, 225–231
  blinkCursor() function, 230–231
  blinking, 230–231
  erasing, 228–230
  moving, 242–243
  positioning, 215–216, 232–237
cursorInControlPoint() function (bézier curves example), 162
cursorInEndPoint() function (bézier curves example), 162
custom controls, 40, 615–655, 693–700
  appending to HTML elements, 616–617
  composite, 626
  draw() method, 616
  erase() method, 617
  floating, 181
  for text, 225–252
  image panner, 643–655
  positioning with CSS, 36
  progress bars, 579, 625–630
  rounded rectangles, 617–625
  sliders, 631–643
  virtual keyboard, 682–700
Cut the Rope game, 427
cutouts, 95–103, 136
  addCirclePath() function, 99–103
  addOuterRectanglePath() function, 99–103
  addRectanglePath() function, 99–103
  addTrianglePath() function, 99–103

# D

dashed lines, 10, 117–121
  dashedLineTo() function, 118–120
  drawDashedLine() function, 118
de Casteljau, Paul, 137
debuggers, 16
  and double buffering, 366
deceleration. *See* ease out
degrees, 54–55
depth perception, 377
detectCollisions() function (collision
    detection), 512, 532, 592, 604
detectFlipperCollision() function
    (pinball game), 604, 611–614
device-aspect-ratio media feature, 667
device-height
  content attribute (viewport), 665
  media feature, 667
devices
  grid-based, 668
  mobile. *See* mobile devices
  orientation of, 666–670
    and layout viewport, 663–664
  pixels in, 279–283, 295–299, 668
device-width
  content attribute (viewport), 664–665
  media feature, 667, 679–680
dials
  annotating polygons with, 171
  drawDial() function, 131
  drawing, 130–136
  labeling, 221–223
didThrow() function (user gestures
    example), 384
dir attribute (canvas), 211
dirty rectangles, 280–283
display context attribute, 52
DIV element (HTML), 37–46
document object
  getElementById() method, 4, 13
DOM Level 3, 32
domElement browser property, 616–617
dot product, 60–62, 501, 608
dotProduct() method (Vector), 501–502
double buffering, 364–367, 390–391
Drag and Drop API, 326

drawArrow() function (mirroring example),
    139, 173
drawCenter() function (clock application),
    23
drawCircle() function (clock application),
    23
drawCircularText() function (circular
    text example), 224–225
drawClock() function (clock application),
    24
drawCollisionShapes() method (Game),
    603
drawConnectors() function (sunglasses
    example), 302
drawDashedLine() function (dashed lines
    example), 118
drawDial() function (dials example), 131
drawDiscBackground() function (clipping
    animations example), 363
drawGrid() function (grid drawing
    example), 105–107
drawImage() method (Canvas context), 31,
    45, 253–258, 266, 270, 312–315, 328
  and global settings, 282
  and origin-clean flag, 312
  five-argument version of, 257–258, 332
  nine-argument version of, 257–258, 276,
    322–324, 407
drawing, 22–25, 65–199
  immediate vs. retained, 34, 147
  outside canvas boundaries, 260–266,
    370–377
  scaling context during development for,
    173
  separated from updating, 390
  temporarily, 228
  using rubber bands for, 65
drawing surface
  saving/restoring, 12, 33–35, 115, 228
  size of, 5–8, 28
    default, 6–8
    in CSS, 5–7
drawLenses() function (sunglasses
    example), 302
drawMagnifyingGlass() function
    (magnifying glass example), 322–324

drawNumerals() function (clock application), 23
drawRubberbandShape() function (rubber bands example), 116, 126–127, 147–148
drawScaled() function (watermarks example), 272–274
drawText() function (text positioning example), 185, 212–214
drawWatermark() function (watermarks example), 266–270
drawWire() function (sunglasses example), 302
drifting clouds, 370–377
dropping frames, 368

**E**

ease in, 451, 456–458, 463–465, 595
ease in/out, 458, 468–469
ease out, 458, 465–467, 595
edge detection, 296
edge() method (Vector), 502
elapsed time, 386, 433, 452
elastic motion, 469, 471
electromagnetic force, 428
em square, 211, 214
embossing filter, 295–299
  emboss() function, 296–298
enablePrivilege() function (PrivilegeManager), 313
endAnimate() method (Game), 544–546, 550, 553, 590, 592
endless loops, 340
Enter key, 238, 241, 244–245
eraseMagnifyingGlass() function (magnifying glass example), 322
erasing
  entire background, 360–361, 364–367
  paragraphs, 244
  text, 228–230, 239, 245–251
  with clipping region, 187–194
Esc key, 32
event handlers, 26–33
  onchange, 202, 619, 636, 650
  onclick, 40, 353, 423, 627
  onkeydown, 31–32, 241
  onkeypress, 31–33, 237, 241
  onkeyup, 31–32

onload, 256
onmessage, 301–302
onmousedown, 26, 40, 46, 111–115, 151, 195, 241
onmousemove, 26–27, 46, 115, 151, 162, 171, 185, 194, 280, 322, 642
onmouseout, 26
onmouseover, 26
onmouseup, 26, 46, 642
preventDefault() function, 31, 46, 111, 675
execute() method (behavior), 394, 411–417, 431, 459, 473, 475, 594
explorercanvas, 15–16
explosionAnimator sprite animator, 423

**F**

fallback content, 3
falling, 427–431, 436
FileSystem API, 326–328
fill() method (Canvas context), 23, 77, 91–92, 94–95, 148, 398
fillColor context attribute, 226
filling, 88–103
  and shadows, 84
  text, 201–207
  with gradients/patterns, 75, 205–207
fillKnob() method (Slider), 642
fillRect() method (Canvas context), 88
fillStyle context attribute, 4, 9, 12, 72–75, 91–92, 136
fillText() method (Canvas context), 4, 9–10, 23, 88, 201, 210–211, 215, 222, 237, 266
  optional argument of, 204–205
filters, 293–295
  black-and-white, 293–295
  embossing, 295–299
  negative, 293–294
  sunglasses, 299–301
fireChangeEvent() method (Slider), 642
Firefox, 15
  clamping in, 342
  composition operations in, 186–187
  console and debugger for, 16
  cross-domain images in, 313
  frame rate bug in, 346, 350

looping backwards in, 320
maximum width of text in, 205
requestAnimationFrame() in, 344–346, 350
shadows in, 85
video formats in, 329–330
fireKeyEvent() method (Keyboard), 700
Flash, 328, 339
    tweening in, 458
flippers (pinball game), 595–597
Flyweight design pattern (sprites), 394, 404
font context attribute, 4, 9, 201, 207–210, 226
font-family context attribute, 208–209
fonts
    em square of, 211, 214
    height of, 228
    properties of, 207–210
    web-safe, 209
font-size context attribute, 208
font-style context attribute, 207–208
font-variant context attribute, 207–208
font-weight context attribute, 207–208
fps() method (Game), 544
frame rate, 544
    calculating, 358–359
    clamping, 583
    for tasks, 359–360
    setting, 343–348, 544
    updating, 546, 550
friction, 432, 461, 592, 594–595
fuseBurningAnimator sprite animator, 423

G
Game object, 544–572
    addKeyListener() method, 544, 558–560, 598–601
    addSprite() method, 544
    animate() method, 550–551
    canPlay...() methods, 557–558
    canPlaySound() method, 544
    clearHighScore() method, 544, 560–561
    clearScreen() method, 550
    drawCollisionShapes() method, 603
    endAnimate() method, 544–546, 550, 553, 590, 592

fps() method, 544
getHighScore() method, 544, 560–561
getImage() method, 554
getSprite() method, 544
loadImages() method, 554–557
paintOverSprites() and
    paintUnderSprites() methods, 544–546, 550, 576–577, 590–592
paintSprites() method, 550
pixelsPerFrame() method, 544, 553, 594
playSound() method, 544, 557–558
queueImage() method, 554–557
setHighScore() method, 544, 560–561
start() method, 544, 550–551
startAnimate() method, 544–546, 550, 553, 590–592, 594, 604
tick() method, 550
togglePaused() method, 544, 546, 551–553, 582, 600
updateFrameRate() method, 550
updateSprites() method, 550
game engine, 544–572
    adding sprites to, 544
    full listing of, 561–572
game loop, 544
Game Over toast, 585–589
game time, 544
    setting, 544, 546
    updating, 550
games, 543–614
    3D Monster Maze, 359
    auto-pause in, 583–584
    Bucket, 432–444, 485–487, 490–494
    Cut the Rope, 427
    heads-up display in, 433, 436–437, 585–589
    multiplayer, 62, 367
    naming, 545
    Pac-Man, 495
    pausing, 544–546, 551–553
    performance of, 18–22, 404
    Pinball, 589–614
    Replica Island, 394
    scoreboard in, 433, 436–437, 585–589
    Sonic the Hedgehog, 427
    starting, 550, 554
    Ungame, 572–589

Gaussian blur, 10, 88
getAxes() method (Shape), 504–511, 516
getBoundingClientRect() method
    (window), 27
getContext() method (Canvas), 4, 8
getElapsedTime() method
    (AnimationTimer), 386, 389, 451,
    454–455, 464, 475
getElementById() method (document), 4,
    13
getHeight() method
    of TextCursor object, 226
    of TextLine object, 233
getHighScores() method (Game), 544,
    560–561
getImage() method (Game), 554
getImageData() method (Canvas context),
    12, 34, 228–230, 253, 274–301, 306, 309,
    322
    and origin-clean flag, 313
    calling repeatedly, 317, 321.
    slowness of, 280
getMagnitude() method (Vector), 501–502
getPoints() method (Polygon), 148
getPolygonPointClosestToCircle()
    function (polygon example), 519
getPolygonPoints() function (polygon
    example), 147
getSprite() method (Game), 544
getWidth() method (TextLine), 216, 233
glass pane, 37–40
globalAlpha context attribute, 9, 69, 75,
    256
    and putImageData(), 282
    fading images with, 306–312
globalCompositeOperation context
    attribute, 9, 12, 181–187
    and putImageData(), 282
Google, 16, 328–329
Google Chrome Frame, 15–16
GPS positioning, 659
gradients, 76–79
    and performance, 391
    color stops in, 77–79
    for stroke or fill, 75, 205–207
    linear, 76–78, 205
    radial, 78–79

graph axes
    drawing, 107–110
    labeling, 217–220
gravity, 427–450, 592, 594–595
    and nonlinear systems, 445–450
    applied to vertical velocity, 433
    constant of, 428, 431
grid, 11
    drawGrid() function, 105–107
    drawing, 40, 105–107
grid media feature, 668
guidewires
    annotating polygons with, 171
    drawing, 433
    temporary drawing surface for, 33–35
    turning on/off, 162
gyroscopes, 659

H
H.264 video format, 329
handleEdgeCollisions() function
    (bouncing off walls example), 488–489
hardware acceleration, 659
heads-up display, 433, 436–437, 585–589
height
    content attribute (viewport), 665
    context attribute, 4–8
    media feature, 667
hideKeyboard() function (keyboard
    example), 689
high scores, 436–437, 545, 560–561, 585–589
HSL (hue/saturation/lightness), 74–75
hsl() color definition (CSS), 74
HSLA (hue/saturation/lightness/alpha),
    74
hsla() color definition (CSS), 74
HTML elements
    appending custom controls to, 616–617
    canvas. See canvas element
    DIV, 37–46
    img, 8, 46, 50
    input, 252, 615
    invisible, 41–46
    meta, 661–666, 681
    output, 266
    source, 329
    span, 279

standard controls in, 615
textarea, 252
using in canvas, 36–46
video, 329, 331–333
*HTML5 Canvas* specification, 14
　best practices of, 252
　constantly evolving, 121
　drawing unloaded images in, 256
　glyph rendering in, 237
　immediate-mode graphics of, 34, 147
　no explicit support for animation in, 339
　rectangles with zero width or height in,
　　276
　text width in, 217
　uses for canvas element in, 266
　vs. native applications, 659, 677
*HTML5 video and audio* specification, 14
HTMLCanvasElement object, 258
HTMLImageElement object, 258
HTMLVideoElement object, 258, 329

**I**

icons
　floating, 181
　selected, 83
identifiedTouch() method (TouchList),
　672
identifier browser attribute, 673
image data
　accessing, 274–283
　arrays of, 286–291, 295
　blank, 254
　looping over, 292, 317–320
　modifying, 283–285, 301–302
　partial rendering, 280–283
　updating, 276
image painters, 398, 404–406, 594
　image loading policy of, 406
image panner application, 643–655
ImageData object, 254, 280–283
　creating, 285–286
ImagePainter object
　draw() method, 406
images, 253–327
　animating, 306–312
　centering, 260–266
　clipping, 302–306

colliding, 521–525
cross-domain, 312–313
dragging from desktop, 326–328
drawing, 69, 253–258, 314–317
fading, 306–312
filtering, 293–295, 306–312
loading, 255–256, 406, 554–557, 579–581
　failed, 554
manipulating, 274–301
　and performance, 298–301
scaling, 258–265, 316–317
security risks of, 312–313
startup. *See* applications, splash screens
　of
zooming into, 41–46
img element (HTML), 8, 46, 50
initial-scale content attribute
　(viewport), 665–666
input element (HTML), 252, 615
insert() method
　of Paragraph object, 239, 241, 243–244
　of TextLine object, 233
Internet Explorer
　console and debugger for, 16
　HTML5 support in, 15
　maximum width of text in, 205
　older versions of, 15–16
　requestAnimationFrame() in, 344, 348
　video formats in, 329
　WebGL support in, 11
invisible ink, 92
iOS4, no WebGL support in, 11
iOS5, 677–682
　fullscreen mode on, 677, 680–681
　hardware acceleration for Canvas in,
　　659
　home screen icons on, 677–680
　splash screens on, 677–680
　status bars on, 681–682
　title bar on, 657
iPad
　device orientation on, 667–670
　home screen icons on, 680–681
　layout viewport on, 661–663, 666
　looping backwards on, 320
　title bar on, 657
　virtual keyboard on, 682–700

iPhone, 663
isBallInBucket() method (bucket game), 486–487, 493–494
isOver() method (AnimationTimer), 389–390
isPointInside() method (Paragraph), 238
isRunning() method (AnimationTimer), 386

**J**
JavaScript
  benchmarks in, 20–22
  call() method, 551
  changing canvas size with, 668–670
  executed on main thread, 299–301, 340
  key codes in, 560
  loops in:
    backward, 317, 320
    endless, 340
  opague objects in, 81
  self variable, 551
  self-executing functions in, 349
  this variable, 550–551
JPEG image format, 8
JSON (JavaScript Object Notation), 560
jsPerf, 19–22, 317–319

**K**
Key object, 689–692
key codes, 32
key events, 31–33, 237, 544, 558–560, 597–601
  firing, 700
  keydown, 31–32, 241
  keypress, 31–33, 237, 241
  keyup, 31–32
  throttling, 600
key listeners, 234–237, 584, 598–601
  adding, 558–560, 700
Keyboard object, 689, 693–700
  addKeyListener() method, 700
  appendTo() method, 700
  draw() method, 690, 700
  fireKeyEvent() method, 700
  mouseDownOrTouchStart() method, 700
  resize() method, 700
keyboard, virtual. *See* virtual keyboard

keyCode browser property, 32
Khronos Group, 11

**L**
length property (TouchList), 672–673
lighting effect, 642
lineCap context attribute, 9, 121, 123
line-height context attribute, 208, 210
lineJoin context attribute, 9, 70–72, 122–123
lines, 103–123
  dashed, 10, 117–121
  endpoints of, 9, 121
  joins of, 122–124
  width of, 9, 11, 104–105
lineTo() method (Canvas context), 23–24, 99, 103–104, 110, 144
lineWidth context attribute, 9, 11, 71–72, 91, 103–104, 123
loadImages() method (Game), 554–557
lob behavior, 433
local storage, 545, 560–561
local variables, 317–320
log() method (console), 16

**M**
Mac OS X, 657
magnifying glass application, 253–254, 321–328
  drag and drop in, 326–328
  drawMagnifyingGlass() function, 322–324
  eraseMagnifyingGlass() function, 322
  home screen icon of, 678
  orientation of, 668–670
  pinch and zoom in, 675–677
  splash screen of, 679
  throwing in, 383–385
  using offscreen canvas in, 270, 325–326
makeBounce() method (AnimationTimer), 457
makeEaseIn() method (AnimationTimer), 456–457
makeEaseInOut() method (AnimationTimer), 457
makeEaseOut() method (AnimationTimer), 457

makeElastic() method (AnimationTimer), 457

makeLinear() method (AnimationTimer), 457

matchMedia() method (window), 669

Math object
cos() function, 54, 445–446
sin() function, 54, 446
tan() function, 54

mathematics, 53–64
algebraic equations, 54, 175–176
angles, degrees, radians, 54–55
Pythagorean theorem, 57, 487
scalars, 60
trigonometry, 54–56, 145, 176, 221–223, 445, 468
vectors, 56–62

max-device-width. *See* device-width

maximum-scale content attribute (viewport), 665–666

measureText() method (Canvas context), 201, 216–217, 227–228, 237

media features, 667–668

media queries, 666–670
changing canvas size with, 668
for icons and splash screens, 679–680

@media CSS annotation, 666–668

meta element (HTML), 661–666, 681

Meta key, 237, 672

metaKey browser attribute, 32, 672

metaprogramming, 121

min-device-width. *See* device-width

minimum-scale content attribute (viewport), 665

minimumTranslationVector() method (Shape), 527–529

mirroring, 173
drawArrow() function, 139, 173

miterLimit context attribute, 10, 72, 122–124

mobile devices, 657–701
battery life of, 583
performance of, 18–22
pinch and zoom in, 675–677
scrolling into view in, 170
touch events in, 67

monitors, 668
refresh rate of, 367

monkey patching, 121

monochrome media feature, 668

motion
bouncing, 459, 469, 471–472
ease in, 451, 456–458, 463–465, 595
ease in/out, 458, 468–469
ease out, 458, 465–467, 595
elastic, 459, 469, 471
harmonic, 427
linear, 453, 458, 461–463
nonlinear, 427, 445, 458–473, 595–597
running in place, 411–417
time-based, 62–64, 350, 358–359, 367–370, 390–391, 416–417
warping, 458–473

mouse events, 26–31, 671
mousedown, 26, 40, 46, 111–115, 151, 195, 241, 642, 694
mousemove, 26–27, 46, 115, 151, 162, 171, 185, 194, 280, 322, 642
mouseout, 26
mouseover, 26
mouseup, 26, 46, 642
supporting together with touch events, 674–675, 684, 694
translating to canvas coordinates, 26, 30–31, 46, 111, 195, 674–675

mouseDownOrTouchStart() method (Keyboard), 700

move() method (Shape), 148, 150

moveCursor() method
of Paragraph object, 242–243
of TextCursor object, 228

moveCursorCloseTo() method (Paragraph), 238, 241, 243

moveTo() method (Canvas context), 23–24, 99, 103–104, 110, 125, 144
position last passed to, 118–119

Mozilla, 329

mozkitRequestAnimationFrame() method (window), 344–346, 350

MPEG-4 video format, 329

msCancelAnimationFrame() method (window), 344, 348

msRequestAnimationFrame() method (window), 344, 348
MTV (minimum translation vector), 526–541
    sticking with, 531–537

**N**
namespaces, 616, 689
native applications, 659
newline() method (Paragraph), 239–241, 244–245
Newtonian mechanics, 461
nextVideoFrame() function (video processing example), 333
Nokia, 329–330
nonlinear systems, 445–473
nonzero winding rule, 94–95
normal() method (Vector), 502–503
normalize() method (Vector), 502
nuclear force, 428

**O**
Ogg Theora video format, 329–330
onkeydown() method (window), 241
onkeypress() method (window), 237, 241
onmousedown() method (window), 241
ontouchstart browser property, 671
OpenGL ES 2.0 API, 11
Opera, 15
    arc() method in, 127
    composition operations in, 186–187
    console and debugger for, 16
    shadows in, 85
    video formats in, 329
orientation media feature, 667, 679–680
origin-clean flag (Canvas), 312–313
output element (HTML), 266

**P**
Pac-Man game, 495
pageX and pageY browser attributes, 673
paint application, 65–67
    eraser in, 86
    hideKeyboard() function, 689
    home screen icon of, 678
    icons in, 83, 179–181
    rubber bands in, 110–116
    showKeyboard() function, 689
    virtual keyboard for, 682–700
paint() method (Sprite), 394–398, 404
paintOverSprites() method (Game), 544–546, 550, 576–577, 590
paintSprites() method (Game), 550
paintUnderSprites() method (Game), 544–546, 550, 576–577, 590–592
Paragraph object, 238–252
    addLine() method, 239, 242
    backspace() method, 239–241, 245–251
    insert() method, 239, 241, 243–244
    isPointInside() method, 238
    moveCursor() method, 242–243
    moveCursorCloseTo() method, 238, 241, 243
    newline() method, 239–241, 244–245
paragraphs, 238–252
    creating, 242
    erasing, 244
    inserting text into, 243–244
parallax, 377–382, 579
    draw() method, 379
patent issues, 329–330
paths, 88–103
    arc, 89
    circular, 23
    closed, 89, 91–92, 511
    current, 93, 256
    direction of, 92, 99–100
    drawing, 91
    filling, 84, 94–95
    manipulating, 150–170
    open, 89, 91–92
    rectangular, 89
    resetting, 12
    scrolling into view, 169–170
    self-intersecting, 94–95
    stroking, 10, 84
    subpaths of, 92–94
patterns, 79–83
    creating, 81
    for stroke or fill, 75, 205–207
    repeating, 80–83
Paused toast, 600

pendulums, 427
  nonlinear motion of, 445–450
  weight of, 445
percentComplete browser property, 628
performance, 18–22, 313–321, 390–391
  and double buffering, 366
  and getImageData(), 280
  and gradients, 391
  and image manipulations, 298–301
  and number of objects, 404
  and offscreen canvases, 274
  and shadows, 88, 390–391
  bottlenecks of, 20–22
  for drawing canvas into itself vs. from
    offscreen canvas, 326
  monitoring, 390–391
perpendicular() method (Vector),
  502–503
physics, 427–482
pinball game, 589–614
  bounce() function, 609
  collision detection for, 601–614
  detectCollisions() function, 592, 604
  flipper motion in, 595–597
  game loop of, 590–593
  key events for, 597–601
  pausing, 600
  separate() function, 609
  *See also* game engine
Pinball object
  applyFrictionAndGravity() method,
    594–595
  bounce() function, 604
  brieflyShowTryAgainImage() method,
    592
  checkMTVAxisDirection() function, 608
  createDomePolygons() method, 609–611
  detectFlipperCollision() function,
    604, 611–614
  updateLeftFlipper() method, 592
  updateRightFlipper() method, 592
pinch and zoom, 675–677
pixels
  boundaries of, 104–105
  capturing, 280–283
  clearing, 71

CSS vs. device, 279–283, 295–299
density of, 668
edge detection for, 296
looping over, 317, 320
manipulating, 253, 274–301
modifying transparency of, 283–285
scaling, 325
to move, per animation frame. *See*
  time-based motion
pixelsPerFrame() method (Game), 544,
  553, 594
playSound() method (Game), 544, 557–558
pointInPath() method (Canvas context),
  151
polyfill method. *See*
  requestNextAnimationFrame()
Polygon object, 147–150
  arrays of, 151–157
  createPath() method, 511
  getPoints() method, 148
  move() method, 150
polygons, 144–150
  closed paths for, 511
  colliding, 601–609
    polygonCollidesWithCircle()
      function, 519
    polygonsCollide() function, 500
    with circles, 516–521
    with polygons, 56, 495, 500, 504–516,
      526
  concave vs. convex, 495
  createPolygonPath() function, 147
  dragging, 34, 151–157
  drawing, 33–35, 144–147
  getPolygonPoints() function, 147
  manipulating, 147–150
  rotating, 151, 171–172
polymorphism, 350
Porter-Duff operators, 181
power curves, 464–465, 467
preventDefault() function (Event), 31,
  46, 111, 675
PrivilegeManager object
  enablePrivilege() function, 313
profile() function (console), 17
profileEnd() function (console), 17

profilers, 20–22, 390–391
  starting/stopping, 17
progress bars, 579, 625–630
Progressbar object
  draw() method, 628
projectile trajectories, 427, 432–444
  applying gravity to, 433
  vs. falling, 436
Projection object
  project() function, 504–511
  prototype() method, 504
projections, 495–525
  overlapping, 503–504, 527
  separation on, 527
putImageData() method (Canvas context),
      34, 229, 253, 274–301, 314, 322
  and global settings, 282
  seven-argument version of, 280–283
putSunglassesOn() function (sunglasses
      example), 301
px units, 4, 7–8
Pythagorean theorem, 57, 487, 501

Q
quadraticCurveTo() method (Canvas
      context), 138–141
queueImage() method (Game), 554–557

R
radians, 54–55
radioactive decay, 428
ray casting, 490–494, 601, 604, 611–614
  accuracy of, 494
  intersection of lines for, 492
rect() method (Canvas context), 91–94,
      99–100, 361
rectangles
  direction of, 99–100
  drawing, 91
  rounded, 71–72, 128, 138–139, 390,
      617–625
    appending to HTML elements, 624
    resizing, 624
  with square corners, 70
  with zero width or height, 276
Replica Island game, 394

requestAnimationFrame() method
      (window), 14, 342–345, 348, 360, 390,
      437, 544, 583
  browser-specific implementations of,
      344–348
requestNextAnimationFrame() method
      (window), 331–333, 349–357, 388, 404,
      421, 437, 532, 544, 546, 550–551, 626
reset() method (AnimationTimer), 386
resize() method
  for custom controls, 617
  of Keyboard object, 700
  of RoundedRectangle object, 624–625
resolution media feature, 668
restore() method (Canvas context),
      11–12, 85, 136, 185, 194, 197
restoreRubberbandPixels() function
      (rubber bands example), 280–281
RGB (red/green/blue), 74–75
rgb() color definition (CSS), 74
RGBA (red/green/blue/alpha), 74
rgba() color definition (CSS), 74
rotate() method (Canvas context),
      172–175, 225
rotating
  after translating, 225
  coordinate system, 171–173, 176
  polygons, 151, 171–172
  text, 177–179
roundedRect() function (rounded
      rectangles example), 128–129
RoundedRectangle object
  draw() method, 625
  resize() method, 624–625
rubber bands, 110–116
  bounding box of, 275
  captureCanvasPixels() function, 285
  captureRubberbandPixels() function,
      276, 280–281
  circular, 126–127
  copyCanvasPixels() function, 285–286
  drawRubberbandShape() function, 116,
      126–127, 147–148
  erasing, 115
  for interactive drawing, 65
  modifying transparency with, 283–285

restoreRubberbandPixels() function, 280–281

rubberbandEnd() function, 46, 276

rubberbandStart() function, 46

rubberbandStretch() function, 46, 276

selecting with, 274–283

temporary drawing surface for, 33

zooming with, 41–46

**S**

Safari, 15

composition operations in, 186–187

console and debugger for, 16

layout viewport on, 666

looping backwards in, 320

maximum width of text in, 205

timelines in, 19

video formats in, 329

SAT (separating axis theorem), 495–541, 601–609

for circles, 516–521

for images and sprites, 521–525

for polygons, 504–516

not for small fast objects, 611

pseudocode for, 499–500

using MTV for, 526–541

save() method (Canvas context), 11–12, 85, 136, 185, 194, 197, 361

scalars, 60

scale() method (Canvas context), 172–175

scaling

canvas, 270–272, 316–317

coordinate system, 173–176

during development, 173

images, 258–265

text, 177–179

video frames, 331

scan media feature, 668

screen

clearing, 544, 546, 550, 579

height of, 667

width of, 659, 666–667

screenX and screenY browser attributes, 673

scrollBackground() method (background scrolling example), 577–579

scrollPathIntoView() method (Canvas context), 169–170

security, 312–313

SECURITY_ERR exception, 313

self variable (JavaScript), 551

separate() function (separating colliding shapes example), 530–531, 609

separationOnAxes() method (Shape), 504–508, 527

setClip() method (Canvas context), 324–325

setHighScore() method (Game), 544, 560–561

setInterval() method (window), 14, 24, 306, 341–343, 390

setTimeout() method (window), 14, 341–343, 349–350, 390, 551, 579

clamping, 342

setTransform() method (Canvas context), 174–181

shadowBlur context attribute, 10, 83–85, 88

shadowColor context attribute, 10, 83–85, 88

undefined, 85

shadowOffsetX and shadowOffsetY context attributes, 10, 83–88

shadows, 83–88

and performance, 88, 390–391

applying to text, 202

color of, 10

enabling, 69, 185

partially transparent colors for, 85

settings for, 69, 256

spreading out, 10

turning on/off, 85

with negative offset, 85–87

Shape

collidesWith() method, 504–508, 518–520, 529–530, 532, 604

createPath() method, 148, 172

getAxes() method, 504–511, 516

minimumTranslationVector() method, 527–529

move() method, 148

separationOnAxes() method, 504–508, 527

shear, 179–181
Shift key, 672, 694
shiftKey browser attribute, 32, 672
showKeyboard() function (keyboard
    example), 689
sin() method (Math), 54, 446
Sinclair ZX81 computer, 359
sine, 55–56, 468
Slider object, 634, 636
    addChangeListener() method, 636, 642
    appendTo() method, 619, 624–625, 628
    fireChangeEvent() method, 642
sliders, 173, 325, 631–643
    fillKnob() method, 642
smart phones, 33
social network, 312
Sonic the Hedgehog game, 427
sound
    formats of, 557–558
    multitrack, 544, 557–558
source element (HTML), 329
span element (HTML), 279
springs, 427
Sprite object, 394–397
    paint() method, 394–398, 404
    properties of, 395
    update() method, 394, 411, 416–417,
        553
sprite sheets, 26–30
    painters for, 398, 406–410, 476
SpriteAnimator object, 419–423
    start() method, 419–421
sprites, 393–425, 431
    adding to game engine, 544
    animating, 417–423
    colliding, 521–525
    creating, 397, 594
    painters for, 394–395, 397–410, 419, 421
        advancing, 407, 410
        decoupling from, 394
    painting, 394, 424
        under/over, 544–546, 550, 576,
            577
    updating, 424, 544–546, 550
SpriteSheetPainter object
    advance() method, 407
src HTML attribute, 8, 46

start() method
    of Game object, 544, 550–551
    of SpriteAnimator object, 419–421
    of Stopwatch object, 385
startAnimate() method (Game), 544–546,
    550, 553, 590–592, 594, 604
stick() function (sticking with MTV
    example), 532–537
sticking, 531–537
Stopwatch object
    start() method, 385
    stop() method, 385
stopwatches, 385–388
Strategy design pattern (sprites), 394, 398
stroke and fill painters, 398–404
stroke() method (Canvas context), 23–24,
    91–94, 103, 110, 148, 398, 603
strokeRect() method (Canvas context),
    88
    simplifying by translating the origin,
        170
strokeStyle context attribute, 4, 10, 12,
    72–75, 91–92, 136
strokeText() method (Canvas context),
    4, 9–10, 88, 201–207, 210, 215, 237
    optional argument of, 204–205
stroking, 88–103
    and shadows, 84
    text, 201–207
    with gradients/patterns, 75, 205–207
subtract() method (Vector), 501–502
sunglasses application, 299–306
    drawConnectors() function, 302
    drawLenses() function, 302
    drawWire() function, 302
    putSunglassesOn() function, 301
SVG (Scalable Vector Graphics)
    color names in, 74
    list of objects in, 34
    paths in, 89
swing behavior, 445–446

T
tablet computers, 33
    performance of, 280
    touch events in, 67
tan() method (Math), 54

tangent, 55–56
target browser attribute, 673
target-densityDpi content attribute
    (viewport), 665
targetTouches browser attribute, 672
telescoping animation, 194–197
Texas Instruments 9918(A) video display
    processor, 393
text, 201–252
    applying shadows to, 202
    centering, 3–4, 214–215
    drawing around arc, 223–225
    editing, 232–237, 252
    erasing, 239, 245–251
    filling, 84, 201–207
    font properties of, 201, 207–210
    inserting, 239, 243–244
    maximum width of, 204–205
    measuring, 201, 215–216, 227–228
    new lines in, 244–245
    paragraphs of, 238–252
    positioning, 136, 201, 210–225
        drawText() function, 212–214
    rotating, 177–179
    scaling, 177–179, 205
    stroking, 84, 201–207
textAlign context attribute, 10, 136,
    201–202, 210–215, 220–221
textarea element (HTML), 252
textBaseline context attribute, 10, 136,
    201–202, 210–215, 220–221
TextCursor object, 225–231
    erase() method, 228–230
    getHeight() method, 226
    moveCursor() method, 228
TextLine object, 232–238, 242
    draw() method, 233
    erase() method, 233, 237, 244
    getHeight() method, 233
    getWidth() method, 216, 233
    insert() method, 233
TextMetrics object, 216–217
this variable (JavaScript), 550–551
tick() method (Game), 550
time
    elapsed, 386, 433, 452
    warping, 390, 427, 450–456, 595

time-based motion, 62–64, 350, 358–359,
    367–370, 390–391, 416–417, 544, 553,
    594
timelines, 19, 390–391
*Timing control for script-based animations*
    specification, 14, 344
toasts, 573
    Game Over, 585–589
    Paused, 600
    Try Again, 592
toBlob() method (Canvas context), 8, 51
toDataURL() method (Canvas context), 8,
    46–51
    and origin-clean flag, 313
togglePaused() method (Game), 544, 546,
    551–553, 582–583, 600
touch events, 33, 67, 671–677
    supporting together with mouse events,
        674–675, 684, 694
    touchcancel, 671–672
    touchend, 671–672
    touchmove, 671–672, 675
    touchstart, 671–672, 675, 694
touch objects, 673
touches browser attribute, 672
TouchList object, 672
    identifiedTouch() method, 672
    length property, 672
transform() method (Canvas context),
    174–181
translate() method (Canvas context),
    170–175, 225, 372
translating
    before rotating, 225
    coordinate system, 171–175
translucent overlays, 625
transparency, 9, 72–75
trigonometry, 54–56, 145, 445, 468
    for positioning circular text, 221–223
    for rotating, 176
Try Again toast, 592
tty terminals, 668
TypedArray object, 291

U
UA (User Agents), 13
Uint8ClampedArray object, 291

ungame, 572–589
  game loop of, 576–579
  loading, 579–581
  pausing, 581–584
  *See also* game engine
units of measure, 62–64, 431
update() method (Sprite), 350, 394, 411, 416–417, 553
updateFrameRate() method (Game), 550
updateLeftFlipper() method (Pinball), 592
updateRightFlipper() method (Pinball), 592
updateSprites() method (Game), 550
user gestures, 383–385
  didThrow() function, 384
user-scalable content attribute (viewport), 665

**V**
Vector object
  add() method, 501–502
  dotProduct() method, 501–502
  edge() method, 502
  getMagnitude() method, 501–502
  normal() method, 502–503
  normalize() method, 502
  perpendicular() method, 502–503
  subtract() method, 501–502
vectors, 56–62
  adding, 59–60
  direction of, 58–59
  displacement, 594, 604
  dot product of, 60–62, 501, 608
  edge, 57, 60, 500
  edge normal, 500
  magnitude of, 57, 501–503
  multiplicating, 501
  normalized. *See* vectors, unit
  perpendicular, 503
  reflecting, 537–541
  subtracting, 59–60, 501
  unit, 58–59, 503, 530, 606
velocity
  and air resistance, 461
  and collisions, 461, 530
  and current frame rate, 62
  and friction, 461, 595
  clamping, 609
  constant vs. nonlinear, 463–469
  for bouncing, 537–541, 609
  initial, 436
  limiting, for small objects, 487
  vertical, 428–432, 595
    applying gravity to, 433
video element (HTML), 328–329
  invisible, 331–333
videos, 328–337
  formats of, 329–330
  frames of, 328–337
    drawing into canvas, 253, 258, 328
    scaling, 331
  playing in canvas, 331–333
  processing, 333–337
    nextVideoFrame() function, 333
viewport metatag, 661–666
  device-height attribute, 665
  device-width attribute, 664–665
  height attribute, 665
  initial-scale attribute, 665–666
  maximum-scale attribute, 665–666
  minimum-scale attribute, 665
  target-densityDpi attribute, 665
  user-scalable attribute, 665
  width attribute, 665
viewports
  draggable, 644
  height of, 667
  layout, 661
    set to device-width, 664
  mobile, 659–666
  scaling, 661–666
  visible, 661
  width of, 667
    hardcoded, 663
virtual keyboard, 682–700
  hideKeyboard() function, 689
  resizing, 684–685, 700
  showKeyboard() function, 689
  translucent, 685, 694
  visibility of, 689
VP8 video format, 329

## W

W3C (World Wide Web Consortium), 14
warping
  animation, 473–482
  motion, 458–473
  time, 390, 427, 450–456, 595
    with functions, 454–458
watermarks, 266–274
  drawScaled() function, 272–274
  drawWatermark() function, 266–270
web browsers. *See* browsers
web workers, 299–301
WebGL 3d context, 11
webkitCancelAnimationFrame() method
  (window), 344, 347
webkitRequestAnimationFrame() method
  (window), 344, 346–348, 350
WebM video format, 329
WHATWG (Web Hypertext Application
  Technology Working Group), 14, 252
while loop (JavaScript), 340
width
  content attribute (viewport), 665
  context attribute, 4–7
  media feature, 667
window object
  cancelRequestAnimationFrame()
    method, 344–345
  clearInterval() method, 231
  getBoundingClientRect() method, 27
  matchMedia() method, 669
  mozkitRequestAnimationFrame()
    method, 344–346, 350
  msCancelAnimationFrame() method,
    344, 348
  msRequestAnimationFrame() method,
    344, 348
  onkeydown() method, 241
  onkeypress() method, 237, 241
  onmousedown() method, 241
  requestAnimationFrame() method, 14,
    342–348, 360, 390, 437, 544, 583
  requestNextAnimationFrame() method,
    331–333, 349–357, 388, 404, 421, 437,
    532, 544, 546, 550–551, 626

setInterval() method, 14, 24, 306,
  341–343, 390
setTimeout() method, 14, 341–343,
  349–350, 390, 551, 579
webkitCancelAnimationFrame()
  method, 344, 347
webkitRequestAnimationFrame()
  method, 344, 346–348, 350
windowToCanvas() function (translating
  coordinates example), 27–28, 111, 195,
  674–675
Worker object
  onmessage() method, 301–302

## X

x browser attribute, 30

## Y

y browser attribute, 30
YouTube, 328

## Z

z-index property (CSS), 39
zooming in, with rubber bands, 41–46

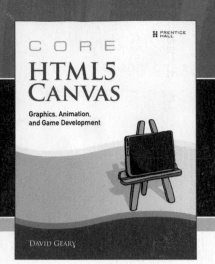

# Safari Books Online

## FREE Online Edition

Your purchase of *Core HTML5 Canvas* includes access to a free online edition for 45 days through the **Safari Books Online** subscription service. Nearly every Prentice Hall book is available online through **Safari Books Online**, along with thousands of books and videos from publishers such as Addison-Wesley Professional, Cisco Press, Exam Cram, IBM Press, O'Reilly Media, Que, Sams, and VMware Press.

**Safari Books Online** is a digital library providing searchable, on-demand access to thousands of technology, digital media, and professional development books and videos from leading publishers. With one monthly or yearly subscription price, you get unlimited access to learning tools and information on topics including mobile app and software development, tips and tricks on using your favorite gadgets, networking, project management, graphic design, and much more.

## Activate your FREE Online Edition at informit.com/safarifree

**STEP 1:** Enter the coupon code: ADLXNGA.

**STEP 2:** New Safari users, complete the brief registration form. Safari subscribers, just log in.

If you have difficulty registering on Safari or accessing the online edition, please e-mail customer-service@safaribooksonline.com